American Medical Association
Physicians dedicated to the health of America

Clinical Practice Guidelines Directory

2000 Edition

idelines

easurement

alysis

owledge

Clinical Practice Guidelines Directory, 2000 Edition

Additional copies of this book may be ordered from the
American Medical Association.
For order information, call toll free 800 621-8335.
Mention product number OP270300.
ISBN 1-57947-008-4

BP12:99-99:1.2M:5/00

Table of Contents

Foreword

Dear Colleague:

As part of ongoing efforts to enhance the quality and appropriate utilization of health care services, the American Medical Association (AMA), in conjunction with numerous medical specialty and state medical societies, the federal government, and others, continues to promote the development and implementation of scientifically sound, clinically relevant clinical practice guidelines. Clinical practice guidelines are strategies for patient management, developed to assist patients, physicians, and other health care professionals in clinical decision-making.

Properly developed clinical practice guidelines provide a promising mechanism to rationalize clinical practice and improve the value of health care services. The AMA continues to work through the Practice Parameters Partnership[*] and Practice Parameters Forum[‡] to refine the process by which clinical practice guidelines are developed and evaluated and, thereby, enhance their clinical utility.

While it is generally recognized that the clinical recommendations in properly developed practice guidelines may serve as a useful resource, they may not be appropriate for an individual patient. Clinical practice guidelines are an aid to, not a substitute for, professional judgment in addressing individual patient needs.

The AMA strongly promotes the development of clinical practice guidelines by or in conjunction with physician organizations that have the necessary expertise for the development of scientifically sound, clinically relevant guidelines. The *Clinical Practice Guidelines Directory, 2000 Edition,* lists approximately 2,000 clinical practice guidelines developed by almost 90 physician organizations and other groups. The 2000 *Directory* contains information about the Clinical Practice Guideline Recognition Program as well as *Attributes to Guide the Development and Evaluation of Clinical Practice Guidelines,* on which the criteria for the Recognition Program are based. Through the Practice Parameters Partnership and Practice Parameters Forum, the AMA continues to work with numerous physician organizations and other groups to ensure that the *Directory* remains a current, comprehensive, and practical resource on clinical practice guidelines.

The ability of organized medicine to maintain its leadership position with regard to the development and implementation of clinical practice guidelines relies heavily on the cooperation of physician organizations. I would like to express my gratitude for the tremendous level of cooperation demonstrated by physician organizations and others in efforts to enhance the development and appropriate implementation of clinical practice guidelines. Special thanks are extended to the many organizations and to the thousands of physicians and other professionals who have participated in the development, dissemination, and implementation of clinical practice guidelines. Clearly, critical to the success of this effort is the broad array of activities, by countless physicians and other health care professionals, to use clinical practice guidelines in caring for patients. I would also like to thank the staff of the AMA Department of Clinical Quality Improvement, Margaret C. Toepp, PhD, and Naomi Kuznets, PhD, for their tremendous efforts in compiling this *Directory*.

E. Ratcliffe Anderson, Jr., MD
Executive Vice President, CEO
American Medical Association

* Members of the Practice Parameters Partnership: Agency for Health Care Policy and Research, American Academy of Family Physicians, American Academy of Ophthalmology, American Academy of Orthopaedic Surgeons, American Academy of Pediatrics, American College of Cardiology, American College of Obstetricians and Gynecologists, American College of Physicians, American College of Radiology, American College of Surgeons, American Hospital Association, American Medical Association, American Psychiatric Association, American Society of Anesthesiologists, American Society of Internal Medicine, American Urological Association, College of American Pathologists, Health Care Financing Administration, and Joint Commission on Accreditation of Healthcare Organizations.

† Members of the Practice Parameters Forum include over 80 physician organizations, including specialty societies, state, county, and metropolitan physician organizations, as well as other groups.

Introduction

The American Medical Association (AMA) strongly supports the use of clinical practice guidelines as a method to improve the quality of medical care and ensure the appropriate utilization of health care resources. Clinical practice guidelines are strategies for patient management, developed to assist patients, physicians, and other health care professionals in clinical decision-making. Clinical practice guidelines provide an effective mechanism to disseminate the results of outcomes research, technology assessments, and benefit/risk analyses.

Development of the *Clinical Practice Guidelines Directory*

Since 1989, the AMA has maintained a clinical practice guidelines database from which the annual *Clinical Practice Guidelines Directory* (formerly *Directory of Clinical Practice Guidelines, Directory of Practice Parameters*) is published. The AMA established the clinical practice guidelines database by surveying physician and other organizations to determine the extent of clinical practice guideline activity. Survey respondents were asked to identify those products that they considered to be clinical practice guidelines. In 1990, the AMA, in cooperation with the Practice Parameters Partnership and Practice Parameters Forum (now the Practice Guidelines Partnership and Clinical Quality Improvement Forum, respectively), established a system to track the development, completion, publication, and withdrawal of clinical practice guidelines. Information from the tracking system is published in the annual *Directory*. Contributors are regularly asked to review and comment on the information that they provide to the clinical practice guidelines database in order to ensure its accuracy and completeness.

Since its establishment, the number of clinical practice guidelines listed in the AMA's clinical practice guidelines directories has increased significantly;[1,2,3,4,5,6,7,8,9,10] the 2000 *Clinical Practice Guidelines Directory*

---

[1] *Listing of Practice Parameters, Guidelines, and Technology Assessments.* Chicago: American Medical Association, November 1989.

[2] *Directory of Practice Parameters.* Chicago: American Medical Association, October 1990.

[3] *Directory of Practice Parameters - 1992 Edition.* Chicago: American Medical Association, 1991.

[4] *Directory of Practice Parameters - 1993 Edition.* Chicago: American Medical Association, 1992.

[5] *Directory of Practice Parameters - 1994 Edition.* Chicago: American Medical Association, 1993.

[6] *Directory of Practice Parameters - 1995 Edition.* Chicago: American Medical Association, 1995.

[7] *Directory of Practice Parameters - 1996 Edition.* Chicago: American Medical Association, 1996.

identifies approximately 2,000 clinical practice guidelines. To reflect current activities and emerging issues, the 2000 *Directory* provides updated information about the AMA's Clinical Practice Guideline Recognition Program, as well as the frequently requested publication *Attributes to Guide the Development and Evaluation of Practice Parameters/Guidelines*. For the first time, the *Directory* also includes information on each guideline's Internet availability (location, availability of full text, and cost [if any]). The AMA plans to continue to publish the *Clinical Practice Guidelines Directory* on an annual basis and welcomes suggestions and corrections to this publication.

How to Use the *Clinical Practice Guidelines Directory*

Section I of the *Clinical Practice Guidelines Directory* lists clinical practice guidelines by subject and specifies:

1. Title of the clinical practice guideline;
2. Source of information, including the name of the book or journal in which the clinical practice guideline was published, publication date, journal volume number, and page numbers;
3. Length of the clinical practice guideline and the number of references in its bibliography;
4. Name of the sponsoring organization(s) responsible for producing the clinical practice guideline;
5. Cost information to obtain the clinical practice guideline;
6. Ordering information;
7. Internet availability (address, availability of full text, and cost [if any]); and
8. Key terms.

All of the clinical practice guidelines in Section I were considered current by their sponsoring organizations at the time of the *Directory's* compilation in August 1999.

Section II lists clinical practice guidelines by sponsoring organization. This section is particularly useful for the review of clinical practice guidelines developed in a particular field of medicine or by a particular organization.

Section III lists clinical practice guidelines by title and provides an additional method of searching for specific clinical practice guidelines.

Clinical practice guidelines that are currently in development are listed in Section IV. This section is designed to assist guideline developers in the coordination of development efforts. Listings in this section can also provide a starting point for readers who are looking for guidelines on topics that have not been addressed in guidelines previously.

Section V lists recently replaced clinical practice guidelines. Sponsoring organizations have indicated that these clinical practice guidelines are obsolete and should no longer be used. Because these guidelines have been replaced by new guidelines, readers will also find a reference to related new guidelines (Section I).

---

[8] *Directory of Clinical Practice Guidelines - 1997 Edition.* Chicago: American Medical Association, 1997.

[9] *Directory of Clinical Practice Guidelines - 1998 Edition.* Chicago: American Medical Association, 1997.

[10] *Clinical Practice Guidelines Directory - 1999 Edition.* Chicago: American Medical Association, 1998.

Section VI lists recently withdrawn clinical practice guidelines. Sponsoring organizations have indicated that these clinical practice guidelines are obsolete, should no longer be used, and have not been replaced with new guidelines.

Section VII lists the names, addresses, telephone numbers, and Internet addresses (where available) of the sponsoring organizations.

The Appendix includes updated information on and an application for the Clinical Practice Guideline Recognition Program (CPGRP). The *Attributes to Guide the Development and Evaluation of Practice Parameters/Guidelines,* on which the criteria for the CPGRP are based, is also included.

Obtaining Clinical Practice Guidelines

In many instances, clinical practice guidelines are published in professional journals that are available in most medical libraries. The *Directory* listings include information on the cost and how readers may order clinical practice guidelines by contacting (via telephone and/or mail) the sponsoring organization(s). Frequently physician organizations will provide a complimentary single copy of a clinical practice guideline. However, if ordering multiple clinical practice guidelines or if asking for multiple copies of one clinical practice guideline, you should expect to pay for photocopying, shipping, and handling. Some organizations offer clinical practice guidelines to their members at a discount. Member and nonmember prices for clinical practice guidelines refer to your membership status in the sponsoring organization. Readers will also find information about electronic guideline availability and cost (as applicable) in the *new* "Internet availability" section of guideline listings. Please note that cost information presented in this book is subject to change without notice.

Acknowledgments

The 2000 *Clinical Practice Guidelines Directory* is compiled and produced by the AMA Division of Clinical Quality Improvement. This publication is produced in cooperation with the Practice Guidelines Partnership and Clinical Quality Improvement Forum. The AMA has used its best efforts in collecting information for the *Clinical Practice Guidelines Directory;* however, the AMA does not represent or warrant that the information in the *Clinical Practice Guidelines Directory* is complete or accurate, and the AMA expressly disclaims any liability to any person for any loss or damage caused by errors or omissions in the *Clinical Practice Guidelines Directory.*

In addition to the efforts of the many physician organizations and others involved in developing clinical practice guidelines, special thanks are due to Shirley Rice Bono, Manyan Mickles, Marsha Mildred, and Jean Roberts for their contributions to ensuring that the document is a current and comprehensive resource on clinical practice guidelines. Thanks also to Selby Toporek for her services in the production of the book, and to Patrick Dati for his outstanding efforts in coordinating the distribution of this book.

Margaret C. Toepp, PhD
Director
Division of Clinical Quality Improvement

Naomi Kuznets, PhD
Senior Policy Associate
Division of Clinical Quality Improvement

List of Abbreviations

Am Coll Surg Bulletin
American College of Surgeons Bulletin

Am Fam Phys
American Family Physician

Am J Card
American Journal of Cardiology

Am J Clin Pathol
American Journal of Clinical Pathology

Am J Gastroenterol
American Journal of Gastroenterology

Am J Kidney Dis
American Journal of Kidney Diseases

Am J Prev Med
American Journal of Preventive Medicine

Am J Psych
American Journal of Psychiatry

Am J Respir Crit Care Med
American Journal of Respiratory Critical Care Medicine

Am Rev Resp Dis
American Review of Respiratory Disease

Ann Allergy Asthma Immun
Annals of Allergy, Asthma, and Immunology

Ann Emerg Med
Annals of Emergency Medicine

Ann Intern Med
Annals of Internal Medicine

Arch Intern Med
Archives of Internal Medicine

Arch Path Lab Med
Archives of Pathology & Laboratory Medicine

Arch P M & R
Archives of Physical Medicine and Rehabilitation

Arch Surg
Archives of Surgery

Arthritis Rheum
Arthritis and Rheumatism

ATS News
American Thoracic Society News

Clin Inf Dis
Clinical Infectious Diseases

Critical Care Med
Critical Care Medicine

Digest Dis Sci
Digestive Diseases and Sciences

Dis Colon Rectum
Diseases of the Colon and Rectum

Gastrointest Endosc
Gastrointestinal Endoscopy

Immun Allergy Practice
Immunology Allergy Practice

Infect Control Hosp Epidemiol
Infection Control & Hospital Epidemiology

J Allergy Clin Immun
Journal of Allergy and Clinical Immunology

J Am Acad Child Adol Psych
Journal of the American Academy of Child and Adolescent Psychiatry

J Am Acad Derm
Journal of the American Academy of Dermatology

J Am Coll Cardiol
Journal of the American College of Cardiology

J Am Ger Soc
Journal of the American Geriatrics Society

JAMA
Journal of the American Medical Association

J Bone Mineral Research
Journal of Bone and Mineral Research

J Clinical Oncol
Journal of Clinical Oncology

J Infect Dis
Journal of Infectious Diseases

J Nuclear Med
Journal of Nuclear Medicine

J Occupation Med
Journal of Occupational Medicine

J Oral & Maxillofacial Surg
Journal of Oral and Maxillofacial Surgeons

J Vasc Surg
Journal of Vascular Surgery

JVIR
Journal of Vascular and Interventional Radiology

Morbid Mortal Weekly Report
Morbidity and Mortality Weekly Report

Neurol
Neurology

Pediatr
Pediatrics

Section I
Clinical Practice
Guidelines by
Subject

Abdomen, Acute/Diagnosis
Abdominal Pain/Diagnosis

Nontraumatic Acute Abdominal Pain. *Ann Emerg Med.* 1994;23:906-922. 17pp. 34refs. Sponsored by the American College of Emergency Physicians. Cost: ACEP members free copy, fee nonmembers. To order call ACEP 1 800 798-1822 x6. Key terms: nontraumatic abdominal pain; postpubescent; Emergency Department.

Abdomen/Ultrasonography

Ultrasonic Imaging of the Abdomen: Report of the Ultrasonography Task Force. *JAMA.* 1991;265:1726-1731. 6pp. 56refs. Sponsored by the American Medical Association, Council on Scientific Affairs. Cost: free. To order call Nancy Nolan, AMA, 312 464-5046.

Abdominal Injuries
Emergency Treatment
Pregnancy Complications

Obstetric Aspects of Trauma Management. *ACOG Educational Bulletin.* 1998;251. 7pp. 37refs. Sponsored by the American College of Obstetricians and Gynecologists. Cost: free copy. Set of Bulletins $70 + s/h ACOG members, $125 + s/h nonmembers. One-year subscription $55 member, $65 nonmember. To order single copy, call ACOG Resource Center 202 863-2518; to order set or subscription, call ACOG Distribution Center, 1 800 762-2264. Available on the Internet to members only at acog.org. Key terms: accidents; seat belts; pregnancy complications.

Abdominal Muscles/Surgery
Surgery, Plastic

Abdominoplasty. 1996. 6pp. Sponsored by the American Society of Plastic and Reconstructive Surgeons. Cost: $25 members, $55 nonmembers (full set of guidelines), + s/h. To order call 1 800 766-4955.

Abnormalities/Etiology
Contraceptives, Oral/Adverse Effects

Contraceptives and Congenital Anomalies. *ACOG Committee Opinion.* 1993;124. 2pp. 3refs. Sponsored by the American College of Obstetricians and Gynecologists. Cost: free copy. Set of Opinions $55 + s/h ACOG members, $75 + s/h nonmembers. One-year subscription $55 member, $65 nonmember. To order single copy, call ACOG Resource Center 202 863-2518; to order set or subscription, call ACOG Distribution Center, 1 800 762-2264. Available on the Internet to members only at acog.org. Key terms: contraceptives: oral.

Abortion, Habitual

Recurrent Pregnancy Loss. 1993. 7pp. 53refs. Sponsored by the American Society for Reproductive Medicine. Cost: $1. To order call ASRM Publication Department 205 978-5000.

Abortion, Habitual

Early Pregnancy Loss. *ACOG Technical Bulletin.* 1995;212. 8pp. 45refs. Sponsored by the American College of Obstetricians and Gynecologists. Cost: free copy. Set of Bulletins $70 + s/h ACOG members, $125 + s/h nonmembers. One-year subscription $55 member, $65 nonmember. To order single copy, call ACOG Resource Center 202 863-2518; to order set or subscription, call ACOG Distribution Center, 1 800 762-2264. Available on the Internet to members only at acog.org. Key terms: abortion; placenta previa; antiphospholipid syndrome.

Abortion, Induced

Abortion, Induced. *ACOG Statement of Policy.* 1993. 1pp. Sponsored by the American College of Obstetricians and Gynecologists. Cost: free copy. To order single copy, call ACOG Resource Center 202 863-2518; to order set or subscription, call ACOG Distribution Center, 1 800 762-2264. Available on the Internet to members only at acog.org. Key terms: ethics: medical.

Abortion, Induced

Methods of Midtrimester Abortion. *ACOG Technical Bulletin.* 1987;109. 4pp. 8refs. Sponsored by the American College of Obstetricians and Gynecologists. Cost: free copy. Set of Bulletins $70 + s/h ACOG members, $125 + s/h nonmembers. One-year subscription $55 member, $65 nonmember. To order single copy, call ACOG Resource Center 202 863-2518; to order set or subscription, call ACOG Distribution Center, 1 800 762-2264. Available on the Internet to members only at acog.org. Key terms: abortion: induced; pregnancy: first trimester; pregnancy: second trimester.

Abscess/Therapy
Drainage/Methods

Quality Improvement Guidelines for Adult Percutaneous Abscess and Fluid Drainage. *JVIR.* 1994;6:68-70. 3pp. 18refs. Sponsored by the Society of Cardiovascular and Interventional Radiology. Cost: free copy. To order call SCVIR 703 691-1805.

Absorptiometry, Photon

ACR Standard for the Performance of Dual Energy X-ray Absorptiometry (DXA). 1998. 7pp. 43refs. Sponsored by the American College of Radiology. Cost: $25 ACR nonmembers. To order call ACR Dept of Quality Assurance 703 716-7592. Available free on the Internet at acr.org. Key terms: bone density; absorptiometry; osteoporosis.

Accident Prevention
Accidents, Home/Prevention and Control

Counseling to Prevent Household and Recreational Injuries. *Guide to Clinical Preventive Services, 2nd Ed.* 1996. Sponsored by the US Preventive Services Task Force. To order call Williams & Wilkins 1 800 638-0672.

Accidental Falls
Risk Factors

Falls and Fall Risk. 1998. 12pp. 23refs. Sponsored by the American Medical Directors Association. Cost: $8. To order call 1 800 876-2632 or 410 740-9743.

Accidents, Traffic/Prevention and Control
Accident Prevention

Counseling to Prevent Motor Vehicle Injuries. *Guide to Clinical Preventive Services, 2nd Ed.* 1996. Sponsored by the US Preventive Services Task Force. To order call Williams & Wilkins 1 800 638-0672.

Acid-Base Equilibrium
Fetal Blood/Chemistry

Utility of Umbilical Cord Blood Acid-Base Assessment. *ACOG Committee Opinion.* 1994;138. 2pp. 12refs. Sponsored by the American College of Obstetricians and Gynecologists. Cost: free copy. Set of Opinions $55 + s/h ACOG members, $75 + s/h nonmembers. One-year subscription $55 member, $65 nonmember. To order single copy, call ACOG Resource Center 202 863-2518; to order set or subscription, call ACOG Distribution Center, 1 800 762-2264. Available on the Internet to members only at acog.org. Key terms: pH; fetal distress; fetal maturity.

Acid-Base Equilibrium
Umbilical Arteries/Chemistry

Umbilical Artery Blood Acid-Base Analysis. *ACOG Technical Bulletin.* 1995;216. 6pp. 22refs. Sponsored by the American College of Obstetricians and Gynecologists. Cost: free copy. Set of Bulletins $70 + s/h ACOG members, $125 + s/h nonmembers. One-year subscription $55 member, $65 nonmember. To order single copy, call ACOG Resource Center 202 863-2518; to order set or subscription, call ACOG Distribution Center, 1 800 762-2264. Available on the Internet to members only at acog.org. Key terms: fetal blood; fetal distress; pH.

Acid Rain/Adverse Effects
Environmental Health

The Report on the ATS Workshop on the Health Effects of Atmospheric Acids and Their Precursors. *Amer Rev Resp Dis.* 1991;144:2. Sponsored by the American Thoracic Society. Cost: $6. To order send check payable to American Thoracic Society, 1740 Broadway, New York, NY 10019-4374; for credit card orders, call 212 315-8863.

Acne Vulgaris/Therapy

Guidelines of Care for Acne Vulgaris (including Guidelines for Prescribing Isotretinoin in the Tx of Female Acne Patients of Childbearing Potential). *J Am Acad Derm.* 1990;22:676-680. 5pp. 19refs. Sponsored by the American Academy of Dermatology. Cost: free copy. To order call Alice Bell 847 330-0230 x333. Available on the Internet at aad.org. Key terms: acne vulgaris; diagnosis; therapy.

Acquired Immunodeficiency Syndrome
Specimen Handling/Standards

1988 Agent Summary Statement for Human Immunodeficiency Virus and Report on Laboratory-Acquired Infection with Human Immunodeficiency Virus. *Morbid Mortal Weekly Report.* 1988;37(S-4). 1pp. Sponsored by the Centers for Disease Control and Prevention. Cost: $1. To order call US Govt Printing Office 202 783-3238.

Acquired Immunodeficiency Syndrome/Complications
Nervous System Diseases/Etiology

Guidelines for Prevention of Transmissions of HIV Type I in Neurologic Practice. *Neurol.* 1989;39:119-122. 4pp. 49refs. Sponsored by the American Academy of Neurology. Cost: individual statements are free. To order call AAN Member Service Center 1 800 879-1960. Available on the Internet at aan.com.

Acquired Immunodeficiency Syndrome/Complications Opportunistic Infections/Pathology

Mycobacteriosis and Acquired Immunodeficiency Syndrome. *Amer Rev Resp Dis*. 1987;136:2. Sponsored by the American Thoracic Society. Cost: $4. To order send check payable to American Thoracic Society, 1740 Broadway, New York, NY 10019-4374; for credit card orders, call 212 315-8863.

Acquired Immunodeficiency Syndrome/Complications Pneumonia, Pneumocystis carinii/ Prevention and Control

Guidelines for Prophylaxis Against Pneumocystis carinii Pneumonia for Persons Infected with Human Immunodeficiency Virus. *Morbid Mortal Weekly Report*. 1989;38(S-5). 10pp. 19refs. Sponsored by the Centers for Disease Control and Prevention. Cost: $1. To order call US Govt Printing Office 202 783-3238.

Acquired Immunodeficiency Syndrome/Complications Syphilis/Diagnosis

Recommendations for Diagnosing and Treating Syphilis in HIV-Infected Patients. *Morbid Mortal Weekly Report*. 1988;37:600-608. 9pp. Sponsored by the Centers for Disease Control and Prevention. Cost: $1. To order call US Govt Printing Office 202 783-3238.

Acquired Immunodeficiency Syndrome/Epidemiology HIV Infections/Epidemiology

1993 Revised Classification System for HIV Infection and Expanded Surveillance Case Definition for AIDS Among Adolescents and Adults. *Morbid Mortal Weekly Report*. 1992;41(no. RR-17). Sponsored by the Centers for Disease Control and Prevention. Cost: $1. To order call US Govt Printing Office 202 783-3238.

Acquired Immunodeficiency Syndrome/Immunology Bone Transplantation

Transmission of HIV Through Bone Transplantation: Case Report and Public Health Recommendation. *Morbid Mortal Weekly Report*. 1988;37:597-599. 3pp. Sponsored by the Centers for Disease Control and Prevention. Cost: $1. To order call US Govt Printing Office 202 783-3238.

Acquired Immunodeficiency Syndrome/Immunology Measles Vaccine/Administration and Dosage

Immunization of Children Infected with Human Immunodeficiency Virus-Supplement. *Morbid Mortal Weekly Report*. 1988;37:181-183. 3pp. Sponsored by the Centers for Disease Control and Prevention. Cost: $1. To order call US Govt Printing Office 202 783-3238.

Acquired Immunodeficiency Syndrome/Prevention and Control Antibodies, Viral/Analysis

Public Health Service Guidelines for Counseling and Antibody Testing to Prevent HIV Infection and AIDS. *Morbid Mortal Weekly Report*. 1987;36:509-515. 7pp. Sponsored by the Centers for Disease Control and Prevention. Cost: $1. To order call US Govt Printing Office 202 783-3238.

Acquired Immunodeficiency Syndrome/Prevention and Control Occupational Diseases/Prevention and Control

Recommendations for Prevention of HIV Transmission in Health-Care Settings. *Morbid Mortal Weekly Report*. 1987;36(suppl):2s. 1pp. Sponsored by the Centers for Disease Control and Prevention. Cost: $1. To order call US Govt Printing Office 202 783-3238.

Acquired Immunodeficiency Syndrome/Prevention and Control Zidovudine/Therapeutic Use

Public Health Service Statement on Management of Occupational Exposure to HIV, Including Considerations Regarding Zidovudine Postexposure Use. *Morbid Mortal Weekly Report*. 1990;39(no. RR-1):1-14. 14pp. 30refs. Sponsored by the Centers for Disease Control and Prevention. Cost: $1. To order call US Govt Printing Office 202 783-3238.

Acquired Immunodeficiency Syndrome/ Transmission Health Occupations

Guidelines for Prevention of Transmission of Human Immunodeficiency Virus and Hepatitis B Virus to Health-Care and Public-Safety Workers. *Morbid Mortal Weekly Report*. 1989;38(S-6):1-37. 37pp. 37refs. Sponsored by the Centers for Disease Control and Prevention. Cost: $1. To order call US Govt Printing Office 202 783-3238.

Acupuncture

Acupuncture. *NIH Consensus Development Conference Statement*. 1997;15(5):1[Conf. No. 107]. 34pp. 65refs. Sponsored by the National Institutes of Health. Cost: free copy. To order call 1 888 644-2667. Available on the Internet at consensus.nih.gov.

ADD (see Attention Deficit Disorder with Hyperactivity)

Adenocarcinoma
Endometrial Neoplasms

Carcinoma of the Endometrium. *ACOG Technical Bulletin*. 1991;162. 6pp. 30refs. Sponsored by the American College of Obstetricians and Gynecologists. Cost: free copy. Set of Bulletins $70 + s/h ACOG members, $125 + s/h nonmembers. One-year subscription $55 member, $65 nonmember. To order single copy, call ACOG Resource Center 202 863-2518; to order set or subscription, call ACOG Distribution Center, 1 800 762-2264. Available on the Internet to members only at acog.org. Key terms: endometrial neoplasms.

Adenoidectomy

Adenoidectomy. *Clinical Indicators Compendium*. 1999. 2pp. 20refs. Sponsored by the American Academy of Otolaryngology-Head and Neck Surgery. Cost: $10 AAO-HNS members, $15 nonmembers. To order write to AAO-HNS, 1 Prince St, Alexandria, VA 22314.

Adenoidectomy
Tonsillectomy

Tonsillectomy, Adenoidectomy, Adenotonsillectomy. *Clinical Indicators Compendium*. 1999. 1pp. 20refs. Sponsored by the American Academy of Otolaryngology-Head and Neck Surgery. Cost: $10 AAO-HNS members, $15 nonmembers. To order write to AAO-HNS, 1 Prince St, Alexandria, VA 22314. Key terms: adenoid; tonsils; tonsillitis; hypertrophy; abscess.

Adipose Tissue/Transplantation
Skin/Surgery

Soft Tissue Augmentation Fat Transplantation. *J Am Acad Derm*. 1996;34:690-694. 5pp. 16refs. Sponsored by the American Academy of Dermatology. Cost: free copy. To order call Alice Bell 847 330-0230 x333. Available on the Internet at aad.org. Key terms: adipose tissue; lipectomy; transplantation; surgery.

Adnexitis/Drug Therapy
Antibiotics/Therapeutic Use

Antibiotics and Gynecologic Infections. *ACOG Educational Bulletin*. 1997;237. 8pp. 20refs. Sponsored by the American College of Obstetricians and Gynecologists. Cost: free copy. Set of Bulletins $70 + s/h ACOG members, $125 + s/h nonmembers. One-year subscription $55 member, $65 nonmember. To order single copy, call ACOG Resource Center 202 863-2518; to order set or subscription, call ACOG Distribution Center, 1 800 762-2264. Available on the Internet to members only at acog.org. Key terms: antibiotics.

Adnexitis/Prevention and Control

Pelvic Inflammatory Disease: Guidelines for Prevention and Management. *Morbid Mortal Weekly Report*. 1991;40(no. RR-5):1-25. 25pp. 62refs. Sponsored by the Centers for Disease Control and Prevention. Cost: $1. To order call US Govt Printing Office 202 783-3238.

Adolescent Health Services/Organization and Administration
Preventive Health Services/Organization and Administration

Guidelines for Adolescent Preventive Services. 1992. Sponsored by the American Medical Association, Division of Health Science. Cost: free copy—multiple copies $1 each. To order call Mary Kizer, AMA 312 464-5570.

Adolescent Psychiatry
Psychiatric Status Rating Scales

Practice Parameters for the Psychiatric Assessment of Children and Adolescents. *J Am Acad Child Adol Psych*. 1995;35(10):1386-1402. 17pp. 84refs. Sponsored by the American Academy of Child and Adolescent Psychiatry. Cost: $10 AACAP members/ $20 others. To order call Communications Department 202 966-7300. Key terms: psychiatric assessment; psychiatric diagnoses; child and adolescent psychiatry; practice parameters; guidelines.

Adoption
Ethics, Medical

Obstetrician-Gynecologists' Ethical Responsibilities, Concerns, and Risks Pertaining to Adoption. *ACOG Committee Opinion*. 1997;194. 4pp. 6refs. Sponsored by the American College of Obstetricians and Gynecologists. Cost: free copy. Set of Opinions $55 + s/h ACOG members, $75 + s/h nonmembers. One-year subscription $55 member, $65 nonmember. To order single copy, call ACOG Resource Center 202 863-2518; to order set or subscription, call ACOG Distribution Center, 1 800 762-2264. Available on the Internet to members only at acog.org. Key terms: adoption; ethics; medical; physician's role; ob/gyn.

Adrenal Cortex Hormones/
Therapeutic Use
Fetal Organ Maturity/Drug Effects

Effect of Corticosteroids for Fetal Maturation on Perinatal Outcomes. *NIH Consensus Development Conference Statement*. 1994;12(2):1-24[Conf. No. 95]. 25pp. Sponsored by the National Institutes of Health. Cost: free copy. To order call 1 888 644-2667. Available on the Internet at consensus.nih.gov.

Adrenergic Beta-Agonists/
Adverse Effects

Adverse Effects and Complications of Treatment With Beta-Adrenergic Agonist Drugs. *J Allergy Clin Immun*. 1985;75:443-449, Position Statement No. 11. 7pp. 68refs. Sponsored by the American Academy of Allergy, Asthma, and Immunology. Cost: free copy. To order call 414 272-6071.

Adrenergic Beta-Antagonists/
Adverse Effects
Desensitization, Immunologic/
Adverse Effects

Beta-Adrenergic Blockers, Immunotherapy and Skin Testing. *J Allergy Clin Immun*. 1989;84:129-130, Position Statement No. 17. 2pp. 2refs. Sponsored by the American Academy of Allergy, Asthma, and Immunology. Cost: free copy. To order call 414 272-6071.

Adrenergic Beta-Agonists/Pharmacology
Asthma/Drug Therapy

Safety and Appropriate Use of Salmeterol in the Treatment of Asthma. *J Allergy Clin Immun*. 1996;98:475-480, Position Statement No. 29. 6pp. 29refs. Sponsored by the American Academy of Allergy, Asthma, and Immunology. Cost: free copy. To order call 414 272-6071. Available on the Internet at aaaai.org/professional/physicianreference/positionstatements/default.stm.

Affective Disorders, Psychotic/
Prevention and Control
Antidepressive Agents, Tricyclic/
Therapeutic Use

Mood Disorders: Pharmacologic Prevention of Recurrences. *NIH Consensus Development Conference Statement*. 1984;5(4):1-23[Conf. No. 44]. 24pp. Sponsored by the National Institutes of Health. Cost: free copy. To order call 1 888 644-2667. Available on the Internet at consensus.nih.gov.

Aging/Physiology
Infertility, Female/Etiology
Maternal Age

Age Related Infertility. 1995. 6pp. 46refs. Sponsored by the American Society for Reproductive Medicine. Cost: $1. To order call ASRM Publication Department 205 978-5000.

Agranulocytosis/Complications
Neutropenia/Complications

Guidelines for the Use of Antimicrobial Agents in Neutropenic Patients with Unexplained Fever. *Clin Inf Dis*. 1997;25:551. 23pp. 195refs. Sponsored by the Infectious Diseases Society of America. To obtain request from medical library or download via the Internet. Available on the Internet at idsociety.org/practice.

AIDS (see also Acquired Immunodeficiency Syndrome)

AIDS
Serodiagnosis/Standards

Recommendations for HIV Testing Services for Inpatients and Outpatients in Acute-Care Settings; and Technical Guidance on HIV Counseling. *Morbid Mortal Weekly Report*. 1993;42(no. RR-2). Sponsored by the Centers for Disease Control and Prevention. Cost: $1. To order call US Govt Printing Office 202 783-3238.

AIDS-Related Opportunistic Infections/Diagnosis
Brain Neoplasms/Diagnosis

Evaluation and Management of Intracranial Mass Lesions in AIDS. *Neurol.* 1998;50:21-26. 6pp. 52refs. Sponsored by the American Academy of Neurology. Cost: individual statements are free. To order call AAN Member Service Center 1 800 879-1960. Available on the Internet at aan.com.

AIDS-Related Opportunistic Infections/Diagnosis
Esophageal Diseases/Complications

Diagnosis and Treatment of Esophageal Diseases Associated with HIV Infection. *Am J Gastroenterol.* 1996;91:2265-2269. 5pp. 76refs. Sponsored by the American College of Gastroenterology. Cost: free copy. To order call ACG 703 820-7400.

AIDS-Related Opportunistic Infections/Pathology
Mycoses/Pathology

Fungal Infections in HIV-Infected Persons. *Am J Respir Crit Care Med.* 1995;152:2. Sponsored by the American Thoracic Society. Cost: $4. To order send check payable to American Thoracic Society, 1740 Broadway, New York, NY 10019-4374; for credit card orders, call 212 315-8863.

AIDS-Related Opportunistic Infections/Prevention and Control

1997 USPHS/IDSA Guidelines for the Prevention of Opportunistic Infections in Persons Infected with Human Immunodeficiency Virus. *Morbid Mortal Weekly Report.* 1997;46(no. RR-12). Sponsored by the Centers for Disease Control and Prevention. Cost: $1. To order call US Govt Printing Office 202 783-3238.

AIDS-Related Opportunistic Infections/Prevention and Control
Antitubercular Agents/Prevention and Control

Appendix—Recommended Treatment Options for Persons with Human Immunodeficiency Virus-Related Tuberculosis Infection and Disease. 1998;47(no. RR-20). Sponsored by the Centers for Disease Control and Prevention. To order call US Govt Printing Office 202 783-3238.

AIDS-Related Opportunistic Infections/Prevention and Control
HIV Infections/Immunology

USPHS/IDSA Guidelines for the Prevention of Opportunistic Infections in Persons Infected with Human Immunodeficiency Virus: A Summary. *Morbid Mortal Weekly Report.* 1995;44(no. RR-8). Sponsored by the Centers for Disease Control and Prevention. Cost: $1. To order call US Govt Printing Office 202 783-3238.

AIDS-Related Opportunistic Infections/Prevention and Control
Skin Tests

Anergy Skin Testing and Preventive Therapy for HIV-Infected Persons: Revised Recommendations. *Morbid Mortal Weekly Report.* 1997;46(no. RR-15). Sponsored by the Centers for Disease Control and Prevention. Cost: $1. To order call US Govt Printing Office 202 783-3238.

AIDS-Related Opportunistic Infections/Prevention and Control
Tuberculosis/Prevention and Control

Prevention and Treatment of Tuberculosis Among Patients Infected with Human Immunodeficiency Virus: Principles of Therapy and Revised Recommendations. *Morbid Mortal Weekly Report.* 1998;47(no. RR-20) 7pp. 9refs. Sponsored by the Centers for Disease Control and Prevention. Cost: $1. To order call US Govt Printing Office 202 783-3238. Available on the Internet at cdc.gov/epo/mmwr/review/ind98_rr.html.

Air Pollutants/Adverse Effects
Environmental Exposure/Adverse Effects

Clinical Ecology. 1992. Sponsored by the American Medical Association, Council on Scientific Affairs. Cost: free. To order call Nancy Nolan, AMA, 312 464-5046.

Air Pollutants/Adverse Effects
Environmental Exposure/Adverse Effects

Clinical Ecology. *J Allergy Clin Immun.* 1986;78:269-277, Position Statement No. 14. 2pp. 9refs. Sponsored by the American Academy of Allergy, Asthma, and Immunology. Cost: free copy. To order call 414 272-6071. Available on the Internet at aaaai.org/professional/physicianreference/positionstatements/default.stm.

Air Pollution/Adverse Effects
Environmental Health

Guidelines as to What Constitutes an Adverse Respiratory Health Effect, with Special Reference to Epidemiologic Studies of Air Pollution. *Amer Rev Resp Dis*. 1985;131:4. Sponsored by the American Thoracic Society. Cost: $4. To order send check payable to American Thoracic Society, 1740 Broadway, New York, NY 10019-4374; for credit card orders, call 212 315-8863.

Air Pollution/Prevention and Control
Lung Disease/Etiology

Environmental Controls and Lung Disease. *Amer Rev Resp Dis*. 1990;142:4. Sponsored by the American Thoracic Society. Cost: $6. To order send check payable to American Thoracic Society, 1740 Broadway, New York, NY 10019-4374; for credit card orders, call 212 315-8863.

Albuminuria/Diagnosis
Diabetes Mellitus/Complications

Screening of Microalbuminuria in Patients with Diabetes. *Am J Kidney Dis*. 1995;25:107-112. 18pp. 7refs. Sponsored by the National Kidney Foundation. To order call NKF 212 889-2210.

Alcoholism

Alcohol Use Disorders in Older Adults, Pocket Guide. 1997. Sponsored by the American Geriatrics Society. Cost: free. To order call AGS 212 308-1414.

Alcoholism/Diagnosis

Screening for Problem Drinking. *Guide to Clinical Preventive Services, 2nd Ed*. 1996. Sponsored by the US Preventive Services Task Force. To order call Williams & Wilkins 1 800 638-0672.

Alcoholism/Prevention and Control

Alcoholism in the Elderly: Diagnosis, Treatment, and Prevention. 1995. 17pp. Sponsored by the American Medical Association, Division of Health Science. Cost: $2.50 each. To order call Georgianne Cooper, AMA 312 464-5066.

Alcoholism/Therapy

Guidelines for Clinical Assessment and Management of Alcoholism in the Elderly. *Practice-Related Report of the AMA Council on Scientific Affairs*. 1993. Sponsored by the American Medical Association, Council on Scientific Affairs. Cost: free. To order call Nancy Nolan, AMA, 312 464-5046.

Allergens
Skin Tests/Standards

Allergen Standardization. *J Allergy Clin Immun*. 1980;66:431, Position Statement No. 6. 1pp. Sponsored by the American Academy of Allergy, Asthma, and Immunology. Cost: free copy. To order call 414 272-6071.

Allergens/Administration and Dosage
Immunotherapy/Adverse Effects

Personnel and Equipment to Treat Systemic Reactions Caused by Immunotherapy with Allergenic Extracts. *J Allergy Clin Immun*. 1985;77:271, Position Statement No. 12. 3pp. Sponsored by the American Academy of Allergy, Asthma, and Immunology. Cost: free copy. To order call 414 272-6071.

Allergens/Adverse Effects
Asthma/Prevention and Control

Environmental Allergen Avoidance in Allergic Asthma. *J Allergy Clin Immun*. 1999;103:203-205, Position Statement No. 36. 3pp. 45refs. Sponsored by the American Academy of Allergy, Asthma, and Immunology. Cost: free copy. To order call 414 272-6071. Available on the Internet at aaaai.org/ professional/physicianreference/positionstatements/ default.stm.

Allergens/Analysis
Skin Tests

Allergen Skin Testing. *J Allergy Clin Immun*. 1993;92:636-637, Position Statement No. 24. 2pp. 12refs. Sponsored by the American Academy of Allergy, Asthma, and Immunology. Cost: free copy. To order call 414 272-6071.

Allergens/Diagnostic Use
Immunotherapy/Adverse Effects

Use of Anhydrous Theophylline in the Management of Asthma. 1990. Position Statement No. 20. Sponsored by the American Academy of Allergy, Asthma, and Immunology. Cost: free copy. To order call 414 272-6071.

Allergens/Diagnostic Use
Immunotherapy/Adverse Effects

The Waiting Period After Allergen Skin Testing and Immunotherapy. *J Allergy Clin Immun*. 1990;85:526, Position Statement No. 19. 1pp. 22refs. Sponsored by the American Academy of Allergy, Asthma, and Immunology. Cost: free copy. To order call 414 272-6071.

Allergens/Therapeutic Use
Antibodies/Analysis

Use of In Vitro Tests for IgE Antibody in the Specific Diagnosis of IgE Mediated Disorders and the Formulation of Allergen Immunotherapy. *J Allergy Clin Immun*. 1992;90:263-267, Position Statement No. 21. 5pp. 27refs. Sponsored by the American Academy of Allergy, Asthma, and Immunology. Cost: free copy. To order call 414 272-6071.

Allergy (see also Hypersensitivity)

Allergy and Immunology

Role of Allergists in Hospitals. 1982. Position Statement No. 9. 1pp. Sponsored by the American Academy of Allergy, Asthma, and Immunology. Cost: free copy. To order call 414 272-6071.

Allergy and Immunology
Resuscitation/Instrumentation

Statement on Resuscitative Equipment. *J Allergy Clin Immun*. 1981;67:1, Position Statement No. 7. 1pp. Sponsored by the American Academy of Allergy, Asthma, and Immunology. Cost: free copy. To order call 414 272-6071.

Allergy and Immunology/Education

The Future of the Subspecialty of Allergy and Immunology. *J Allergy Clin Immun*. 1997;100:441-443, Position Statement No. 32. 3pp. 11refs. Sponsored by the American Academy of Allergy, Asthma, and Immunology. Cost: free copy. To order call 414 272-6071. Available on the Internet at aaaai.org/professional/physicianreference/positionstatements/default.stm.

Allergy and Immunology/Manpower
Healthcare Reform

Training Program Directors Committee Position Statement on Health Care Reform. *J Allergy Clin Immun*. 1996;98:719-720, Position Statement No. 30. 2pp. 16refs. Sponsored by the American Academy of Allergy, Asthma, and Immunology. Cost: free copy. To order call 414 272-6071. Available on the Internet at aaaai.org/professional/physicianreference/positionstatements/default.stm.

Allergy and Immunology/Trends
Physician's Role

Role of the Allergist/Immunologist as a Subspecialist. *J Allergy Clin Immun*. 1997;100:288-289, Position Statement No. 31. 2pp. 6refs. Sponsored by the American Academy of Allergy, Asthma, and Immunology. Cost: free copy. To order call 414 272-6071. Available on the Internet at aaaai.org/professional/physicianreference/positionstatements/default.stm.

Allied Health Personnel
Electrodiagnosis

Responsibilities of an Electrodiagnostic Technologist. *Muscle Nerve*. 1999;(suppl)8:S17-S18. 2pp. Sponsored by the American Association of Electrodiagnostic Medicine. Cost: free. To order write AAEM, 421 First Avenue SW, #300E, Rochester, MN 55902. Available on the Internet at aaem.net/pdffiles/reponsibilities_of_edx_techs.pdf. Key terms: electrodiagnostic medicine; technologist; electomyography; nerve conduction studies.

Alopecia Areata

Guidelines of Care for Alopecia Areata. *J Am Acad Derm*. 1992;26:247-250. 4pp. 34refs. Sponsored by the American Academy of Dermatology. Cost: free copy. To order call Alice Bell 847 330-0230 x333. Available on the Internet at aad.org. Key terms: alopecia areata; differential diagnosis; therapy.

Alopecia/Therapy
Enzyme Inhibitors/Therapeutic Use

Androgenetic Alopecia. *J Am Acad Derm*. 1996;35:464-469. 4pp. 22refs. Sponsored by the American Academy of Dermatology. Cost: free copy. To order call Alice Bell 847 330-0230 x333. Available on the Internet at aad.org. Key terms: alopecia; diagnosis; pathology; therapy.

Alpha 1-Antitrypsin/Deficiency

Guidelines for the Approach to the Patient with Severe Hereditary Alpha-1-Antitrypsin Deficiency. *Amer Rev Resp Dis*. 1989;140:5. Sponsored by the American Thoracic Society. Cost: $4. To order send check payable to American Thoracic Society, 1740 Broadway, New York, NY 10019-4374; for credit card orders, call 212 315-8863.

Alpha-Fetoproteins/Analysis
Abnormalities/Prevention and Control

Maternal Serum Screening. *ACOG Educational Bulletin*. 1996;228. 10pp. 34refs. Sponsored by the American College of Obstetricians and Gynecologists. Cost: free copy. Set of Bulletins $70 + s/h ACOG members, $125 + s/h nonmembers. One-year subscription $55 member, $65 nonmember. To order single copy, call ACOG Resource Center 202 863-2518; to order set or subscription, call ACOG Distribution Center, 1 800 762-2264. Available on the Internet to members only at acog.org. Key terms: prenatal care; AFP; Down Syndrome; prenatal diagnosis.

Alpha-Fetoproteins/Blood
Down's Syndrome/Diagnosis

Maternal Serum Alpha-Fetoprotein Testing for Down's Syndrome. *JAMA*. 1988;260:1779-1782. 4pp. Sponsored by the American Medical Association, Diagnostic and Therapeutic Technology Assessment Program. Cost: free copy. DATTA subscription available. To order call AMA Department of Technology Assessment 312 464-4531.

Alprostadil/Therapeutic Use
Impotence/Therapy

Vasoactive Intracavernous Pharmacotherapy for Impotence: Intracavernous Injection of Prostaglandin E1. *JAMA*. 1991;265:3321-3323. 3pp. 22refs. Sponsored by the American Medical Association, Diagnostic and Therapeutic Technology Assessment Program. Cost: free copy. DATTA subscription available. To order call AMA Department of Technology Assessment 312 464-4531.

Alzheimer's Disease

Alzheimer's Disease. *AHCPR*. 1996;Publication No. 97-0702. 143pp. 178refs. Sponsored by the Federal Agency for Health Care Policy and Research. To order call AHCPR Clearinghouse 1 800 358-9295.

Alzheimer's Disease/Therapy
Dementia/Therapy

Practice Guideline for the Treatment of Patients with Alzheimer's Disease and Other Dementias of Late Life. *Am J Psych*. 1997;154(suppl):5. 39pp. 243refs. Sponsored by the American Psychiatric Association. Cost: $22.50. To order call 1 800 368-5777 order #SPCT2310. Key terms: Alzheimer's.

Amblyopia

Amblyopia Preferred Practice Pattern. 1997. 28pp. 85refs. Sponsored by the American Academy of Ophthalmology. Cost: $11 members, $16 nonmembers. AAO members first copy free upon publication. To order call AAO Order Dept 415 561-8540. Key terms: eye; amblyopia; pediatric.

Ambulatory Care Facilities/Classification
Dermatology

Guidelines of Care for Office Surgical Facilities, Part II. *J Am Acad Derm*. 1995;33:265-270. 6pp. 27refs. Sponsored by the American Academy of Dermatology. Cost: free copy. To order call Alice Bell 847 330-0230 x333. Available on the Internet at aad.org. Key terms: ambulatory care facilities; classification; ambulatory surgery; standards.

Ambulatory Care/Standards
Endoscopy, Gastrointestinal/Standards

Guidelines for Office Endoscopic Services. *Surgical Endoscopy*. 1998;12. 2pp. 2refs. Sponsored by the Society of American Gastrointestinal and Endoscopic Surgeons. Cost: free. To order call 310 314-2404. Available on the Internet at sages.org. Key terms: surgery; endoscopy; office.

Ambulatory Surgical
Procedures/Standards
Skin Diseases/Surgery

Guidelines of Care for Office Surgical Facilities, Part I. *J Am Acad Derm*. 1992;26:763-765. 3pp. 31refs. Sponsored by the American Academy of Dermatology. Cost: free copy. To order call Alice Bell 847 330-0230 x333. Available on the Internet at aad.org. Key terms: ambulatory care facilities; skin diseases; ambulatory surgery; standards.

Amenorrhea

Amenorrhea. *ACOG Technical Bulletin*. 1989;128. 7pp. 13refs. Sponsored by the American College of Obstetricians and Gynecologists. Cost: free copy. Set of Bulletins $70 + s/h ACOG members, $125 + s/h nonmembers. One-year subscription $55 member, $65 nonmember. To order single copy, call ACOG Resource Center 202 863-2518; to order set or subscription, call ACOG Distribution Center, 1 800 762-2264. Available on the Internet to members only at acog.org.

Amenorrhea/Diagnosis
Amenorrhea/Drug Therapy

Current Evaluation and Treatment of Amenorrhea. 1994. 10pp. 46refs. Sponsored by the American Society for Reproductive Medicine. Cost: $1. To order call ASRM Publication Department 205 978-5000.

Amniocentesis
Chorionic Villi Sampling

Chorionic Villus Sampling and Amniocentesis: Recommendations for Prenatal Counseling. *Morbid Mortal Weekly Report.* 1995;44(no. RR-9). Sponsored by the Centers for Disease Control and Prevention. Cost: $1. To order call US Govt Printing Office 202 783-3238.

Amyotrophic Lateral Sclerosis/ Drug Therapy
Thiazoles/Therapeutic Use
Excitatory Amino Acid Antagonists/ Therapeutic Use

Practice Advisory on the Treatment of Amyotrophic Lateral Sclerosis with Riluzole. *Neurol.* 1997;49:657-659. 3pp. 3refs. Sponsored by the American Academy of Neurology. Cost: individual statements are free. To order call AAN Member Service Center 1 800 879-1960. Available on the Internet at aan.com.

Amyotrophic Lateral Sclerosis/Therapy

Practice Parameter: The Care of the Patient with Amyotrophic Lateral Sclerosis (an evidence-based review). *Neurol.* 1999;52:1311-1323. 13pp. 112refs. Sponsored by the American Academy of Neurology. Cost: individual statements are free. To order call AAN Member Service Center 1 800 879-1960. Available on the Internet at aan.com.

Analgesia
Critical Care

Practice Parameters for Intraveneous Analgesia and Sedation for Patients in the Intensive Care Unit: An Executive Summary. *Critical Care Med.* 1995;23:1596-1600. 5pp. 13refs. Sponsored by the Society of Critical Care Medicine. Cost: $5 for a single guideline. To order call SCCM 714 282-6000 or access Book Store on the SCCM website. Available free on the Internet at sccm.org. Key terms: analgesia; sedation; intensive care unit; morphine sulfate; fentanyl.

Analgesia, Obstetrical
Anesthesia, Obstetrical

Obstetric Analgesia and Anesthesia. *ACOG Technical Bulletin.* 1996;225. 11pp. 31refs. Sponsored by the American College of Obstetricians and Gynecologists. Cost: free copy. Set of Bulletins $70 + s/h ACOG members, $125 + s/h nonmembers. One-year subscription $55 member, $65 nonmember. To order single copy, call ACOG Resource Center 202 863-2518; to order set or subscription, call ACOG Distribution Center, 1 800 762-2264. Available on the Internet to members only at acog.org. Key terms: epidural.

Analgesia/Standards
Pain, Postoperative/Drug Therapy

Practice Guidelines for Acute Pain in the Perioperative Setting. *Anesthesiology.* 1994;82:1071-1081. 11pp. 464refs. Sponsored by the American Society of Anesthesiologists. Cost: free copy. To order call ASA 847 825-5586. Available on the Internet at asahq.org. Key terms: acute pain; perioperative pain; acute pain management.

Analgesia/Standards
Pain, Postoperative/Drug Therapy

Practice Guidelines for Sedation and Analgesia by Non-Anesthesiologists. *Anesthesiology.* 1996;84:459-471. 13pp. 269refs. Sponsored by the American Society of Anesthesiologists. Cost: free copy. To order call ASA 847 825-5586. Available on the Internet at asahq.org. Key terms: analgesia; sedation; conscious sedation.

Anaphylaxis/Diagnosis

The Diagnosis and Management of Anaphylaxis. *J Allergy Clin Immun.* 1998;101:S465-S528. 63pp. Sponsored by the American Academy of Allergy, Asthma, and Immunology, American College of Allergy, Asthma, and Immunology, Joint Council of Allergy, Asthma, and Immunology. Cost: free copy. To order call 847 934-1918. Available on the Internet at jcaai.org.

Anaphylaxis/Drug Therapy
Epinephrine/Therapeutic

Use of Epinephrine in the Treatment of Anaphylaxis. *J Allergy Clin Immun.* 1994;94:666-668, Position Statement No. 26. 3pp. 13refs. Sponsored by the American Academy of Allergy, Asthma, and Immunology. Cost: free copy. To order call 414 272-6071.

Anaphylaxis/Prevention and Control
Child Day Care Center

Anaphylaxis in Schools and Other Child-Care Settings. *J Allergy Clin Immun*. 1998;101:173-176, Position Statement No. 34. 4pp. 10refs. Sponsored by the American Academy of Allergy, Asthma, and Immunology. Cost: free copy. To order call 414 272-6071. Available on the Internet at aaaai.org/professional/physicianreference/positionstatements/default.stm.

Androgens/Adverse Effects

Evaluation and Treatment of Androgen Excess. 1995. 7pp. 15refs. Sponsored by the American Society for Reproductive Medicine. Cost: $1. To order call ASRM Publication Department 205 978-5000.

Anemia, Hypochromic/Diagnosis

CDC Criteria for Anemia in Children and Childbearing-Aged Women. *Morbid Mortal Weekly Report*. 1989;38:400-404. 5pp. Sponsored by the Centers for Disease Control and Prevention. Cost: $1. To order call US Govt Printing Office 202 783-3238.

Anemia, Sickle Cell/Diagnosis
Anemia, Sickle Cell/Therapy

Sickle Cell Disease: Screening, Diagnosis, Management, and Counseling in Newborns and Infants. *AHCPR*. 1993;Publication No. 93-0562. 97pp. 140refs. Sponsored by the Federal Agency for Health Care Policy and Research. To order call AHCPR Clearinghouse 1 800 358-9295.

Anemia, Sickle Cell/Epidemiology
Hemoglobinopathies/Epidemiology

Newborn Screening for Sickle Cell Disease and Other Hemoglobinopathies. *NIH Consensus Development Conference Statement*. 1987;6(9):1-22[Conf. No. 61]. 22pp. Sponsored by the National Institutes of Health. Cost: free copy. To order call 1 888 644-2667. Available on the Internet at consensus.nih.gov.

Anemia/Therapy
Blood, Component Transfusion/
Standards

Indications for Red Blood Transfusion. *Ann Intern Med*. 1992;116:403-406. 4pp. Sponsored by the American College of Physicians. To order call ACP Clinical Efficacy Assessment Project 1 800 523-1546.

Anesthesia

Guidelines for the Pediatric Perioperative Anesthesia Environment. *Pediatr*. 1999;103(2):512-515. 4pp. 36refs. Sponsored by the American Academy of Pediatrics. Cost: $1.95. Discounted set of policies available. To order call 1 800 433-9016.

Anesthesia
Intubation, Intratracheal/Methods

Practice Guidelines for Management of the Difficult Airway. *Anesthesiology*. 1993;78:597-602. 6pp. 233refs. Sponsored by the American Society of Anesthesiologists. Cost: free copy. To order call ASA 847 825-5586. Available on the Internet at asahq.org. Key terms: difficult airway; difficult intubation; tracheal intubation; difficult ventilation.

Anesthesia
Preoperative Care/Methods

Evaluation and Preparation of Pediatric Patients Undergoing Anesthesia. *Pediatr*. 1996;98(3):502-508. 7pp. 54refs. Sponsored by the American Academy of Pediatrics. Cost: $1.95. Discounted set of policies available. To order call 1 800 433-9016.

Anesthesia, Conduction
Anesthesia, Local

Guidelines of Care for Local and Regional Anesthesia in Cutaneous Surgery. *J Am Acad Derm*. 1995;33:504-509. 6pp. 23refs. Sponsored by the American Academy of Dermatology. Cost: free copy. To order call Alice Bell 847 330-0230 x333. Available on the Internet at aad.org. Key terms: epinephrine; administration and dosage; local anesthesia.

Anesthesia, Dental
Ambulatory Surgical Procedures

Anesthesia in Outpatient Facilities. *J Oral & Maxillofacial Surg*. 1995. Sponsored by the American Association of Oral and Maxillofacial Surgeons. To order call AAOMS Publications 1 800 366-6725.

Anesthesia, Dental
Anesthesia, General

Anesthesia and Sedation in the Dental Office. *NIH Consensus Development Conference Statement*. 1985;5(10):1-18[Conf. No. 50]. 19pp. Sponsored by the National Institutes of Health. Cost: free copy. To order call 1 888 644-2667. Available on the Internet at consensus.nih.gov.

Anesthesia, Obstetrical
Delivery

Anesthesia for Emergency Deliveries. *ACOG Committee Opinion*. 1992;104. 1pp. Sponsored by the American College of Obstetricians and Gynecologists. Cost: free copy. Set of Opinions $55 + s/h ACOG members, $75 + s/h nonmembers. One-year subscription $55 member, $65 nonmember. To order single copy, call ACOG Resource Center 202 863-2518; to order set or subscription, call ACOG Distribution Center, 1 800 762-2264. Available on the Internet to members only at acog.org. Key terms: anesthesia: obstetric; cesarean section; time factors.

Anesthesia, Obstetrical/Standards

Practice Guidelines for Obstetrical Anesthesia. *Anesthesiology*. 1999;90:600-611. 12pp. 528refs. Sponsored by the American Society of Anesthesiologists. Cost: free copy. To order call ASA 847 825-5586. Available on the Internet at asahq.org. Key terms: anesthesia; cesarean section; analgesia; labor and delivery.

Anesthesia Recovery Period

Standards for Postanesthesia Care. *ASA Standards, Guidelines and Statements*. 1998;3-4. 2pp. 1ref. Sponsored by the American Society of Anesthesiologists. Cost: free copy. To order call ASA 847 825-5586. Available on the Internet at asahq.org. Key terms: postanesthesia care; postanesthesia management; postanesthesia care unit.

Anesthesiology/Standards
Fasting
Pneumonia, Aspiration/Prevention and Control

Practice Guidelines for Preoperative Fasting and the Use of Pharmacologic Agents to Reduce the Risk of Pulmonary Aspiration. *Anesthesiology*. 1999;90:896-905. 10pp. 232refs. Sponsored by the American Society of Anesthesiologists. Cost: free copy. To order call ASA 847 825-5586. Available on the Internet at asahq.org. Key terms: NPO status; preoperative preparation; pulmonary aspiration prophylaxis.

Aneurysm, Ruptured/Therapy
Cerebral Aneurysm/Therapy

Guidelines for the Management of Aneurysmal Subarachnoid Hemorrhage. *Circulation*. 1994;90:2592-2605. 14pp. 208refs. Sponsored by the American Heart Association. Cost: free copy. To order call 1 800 242-8721 (US only) or write to: American Heart Association, Public Inquiries, 7272 Greenville Ave, Dallas TX 75231-4596.

Angina, Unstable/Diagnosis
Angina, Unstable/Drug Therapy

Unstable Angina: Diagnosis and Management. *AHCPR*. 1994;Publication No. 94-0602. 154pp. 146refs. Sponsored by the Federal Agency for Health Care Policy and Research. To order call AHCPR Clearinghouse 1 800 358-9295.

Angiography

Standard for Diagnostic Arteriography in Adults. 1997. 12pp. 34refs. Sponsored by the American College of Radiology. Cost: $25 (ACR nonmembers). To order call ACR Dept of Quality Assurance 703 716-7592. Available free on the Internet at acr.org. Key terms: arteriography; angiography; aortography; threshold; contrast.

Angiography
Viscera/Blood Supply

Credentialing Criteria: Peripheral and Visceral Arteriography. *JVIR*. 1989;2:59-65. 7pp. Sponsored by the Society of Cardiovascular and Interventional Radiology. Cost: free copy. To order call SCVIR 703 691-1805.

Angiography/Standards
Laboratories, Hospital/Standards

Optimal Resources for the Examination and Endovascular Treatment of Peripheral and Visceral Vascular Systems. *Circulation*. 1994;89(3):1481-1493. 12pp. 65refs. Sponsored by the American Heart Association. Cost: free copy. To order call 1 800 242-8721 (US only) or write to: American Heart Association, Public Inquiries, 7272 Greenville Ave, Dallas TX 75231-4596.

Angioplasty, Balloon
Aortic Diseases/Therapy

Guidelines for Peripheral Percutaneous Transluminal Angioplasty of the Abdominal Aorta and Lower Extremity Vessels. *Circulation*. 1994;89:511-531. 21pp. 207refs. Sponsored by the American Heart Association. Cost: free copy. To order call 1 800 242-8721 (US only) or write to: American Heart Association, Public Inquiries, 7272 Greenville Ave, Dallas TX 75231-4596.

Angioplasty, Balloon
Stents

Carotid Stenting and Angioplasty. *Circulation*. 1998;97:121-123. 3pp. 18refs. Sponsored by the American Heart Association. Cost: free copy. To order call 1 800 242-8721 (US only) or write to: American Heart Association, Public Inquiries, 7272 Greenville Ave, Dallas TX 75231-4596.

Angioplasty, Balloon/Standards

Angioplasty Standard of Practice. *JVIR*. 1992;3:269-271. 3pp. 15refs. Sponsored by the Society of Cardiovascular and Interventional Radiology. Cost: free copy. To order call SCVIR 703 691-1805.

Angioplasty, Balloon/Standards

Credentialing Criteria: Peripheral, Renal and Visceral Percutaneous Transluminal Angioplasty. *JVIR*. 1991;2:59-65. 7pp. Sponsored by the Society of Cardiovascular and Interventional Radiology. Cost: free copy. To order call SCVIR 703 691-1805.

Angioplasty, Balloon/Standards
Peripheral Vascular Diseases/Therapy

Position Statement: Recommendations for Peripheral Transluminal Angioplasty: Training and Facilities. *J Am Coll Cardiol*. 1993;21:546-548. 3pp. Sponsored by the American College of Cardiology. Cost: free copy. To order call Educational Services Department 1 800 257-4740.

Angioplasty, Transluminal,
Percutaneous

Percutaneous Transluminal Angioplasty. *Ann Intern Med*. 1983;99:864-869. 6pp. Sponsored by the American College of Physicians. To order call ACP Clinical Efficacy Assessment Project 1 800 523-1546.

Angioplasty, Transluminal,
Percutaneous

Percutaneous Transluminal Coronary Angioplasty. 1991. JRA-01. 151pp. 232refs. Sponsored by the RAND, Academic Medical Center Consortium, American Medical Association. To order call RAND 310 393-0411, x7002. Key terms: percutaneous transluminal coronary angioplasty; appropriateness; treatment outcomes; utilization; complications.

Angioplasty, Transluminal,
Percutaneous, Coronary
Coronary Disease/Therapy

Guidelines for Percutaneous Transluminal Angioplasty. *JVIR*. 1990;3:5-15. 11pp. 93refs. Sponsored by the Society of Cardiovascular and Interventional Radiology. Cost: free copy. To order call SCVIR 703 691-1805. Key terms: arteries; transluminal angioplasty.

Angioplasty/Standards
Peripheral Vascular Diseases/Therapy

Reporting Standards for Clinical Evaluation of New Peripheral Arterial Revascularization Devices. *JVIR*. 1997;8:137-149. 23pp. 77refs. Sponsored by the Society of Cardiovascular and Interventional Radiology. Cost: free copy. To order call SCVIR 703 691-1805. Key terms: arteries: extremities; arteries: stenosis or obstruction; arteries: transluminal angioplasty; interventional procedures; radiology and radiologists.

Animal Testing Alternatives
Research

Alternatives to Animal Use in Biomedical Research. *Practice-Related Report of the AMA Council on Scientific Affairs*. 1990. 5pp. 5refs. Sponsored by the American Medical Association, Council on Scientific Affairs. Cost: free. To order call Nancy Nolan, AMA, 312 464-5046.

Ankle Injuries

Clinical Guideline on Ankle Injury. 1996. 12pp. 34refs. Sponsored by the American Academy of Orthopaedic Surgeons, North American Spine Society. Cost: $10 AAOS member, $20 nonmember. To order call 1 800 626-6276. Available on the Internet free at guidelines.gov. Key terms: ankle injury; inversion sprain; eversion sprain; muscle injury; tendon injury.

Anorexia Nervosa
Bulimia

Eating Disorders. *Treatments of Psychiatric Disorders, Second Edition, Volume II.* 1995;Section 10. 151pp. 384refs. Sponsored by the American Psychiatric Association. Cost: $250 for 2-volume set. To order call 1 800 368-5777 order #SPCT8700. Key terms: TPD; disorders; treatment.

Anovulation/Drug Therapy
Ovulation Induction

Managing the Anovulatory State: Medical Induction of Ovulation. *ACOG Technical Bulletin.* 1994;197. 8pp. 20refs. Sponsored by the American College of Obstetricians and Gynecologists. Cost: free copy. Set of Bulletins $70 + s/h ACOG members, $125 + s/h nonmembers. One-year subscription $55 member, $65 nonmember. To order single copy, call ACOG Resource Center 202 863-2518; to order set or subscription, call ACOG Distribution Center, 1 800 762-2264. Available on the Internet to members only at acog.org. Key terms: clomiphene citrate.

Anovulation/Etiology
Hyperandrogenism/Complications

Hyperandrogenic Anovulation. *ACOG Technical Bulletin.* 1995;202. 7pp. 26refs. Sponsored by the American College of Obstetricians and Gynecologists. Cost: free copy. Set of Bulletins $70 + s/h ACOG members, $125 + s/h nonmembers. One-year subscription $55 member, $65 nonmember. To order single copy, call ACOG Resource Center 202 863-2518; to order set or subscription, call ACOG Distribution Center, 1 800 762-2264. Available on the Internet to members only at acog.org.

Anterior Eye Segment/Surgery
Eye Diseases/Surgery
Laser Surgery/Instrumentation

Nd: YAG Photodisruptors Ophthalmic Procedure Assessment. *Ophthalmology.* 1993;100:1736-1742. 7pp. 89refs. Sponsored by the American Academy of Ophthalmology. Cost: $11 members, $16 nonmembers. AAO members first copy free upon publication. To order call AAO Order Dept 415 561-8540. Key terms: eye; laser surgery; YAG laser.

Anti-HIV Agents

Appendix—Characteristics of Available Antiretroviral Drugs. *Morbid Mortal Weekly Report.* 1998;47(no. RR-4). Sponsored by the Centers for Disease Control and Prevention. To order call US Govt Printing Office 202 783-3238. Available on the Internet at cdc.gov/epo/mmwr/preview/ind98_rr.html.

Anti-HIV Agents/Therapeutic Use
Disease Transmission, Vertical/
Prevention and Control

Public Health Service Task Force Recommendations for the Use of Antiretroviral Drugs in Pregnant Women Infected with HIV-1 for Maternal Health and for Reducing Perinatal HIV-1 Transmission in the United States. *Morbid Mortal Weekly Report.* 1998;47(no. RR-02). Sponsored by the Centers for Disease Control and Prevention. Cost: $1. To order call US Govt Printing Office 202 783-3238.

Anti-HIV Agents/Therapeutic Use
HIV/Drug Effects

Report of the NIH Panel to Define Principles of Therapy of HIV Infection and Guidelines for the Use of Antiretroviral Agents in HIV-Infected Adults and Adolescents. *Morbid Mortal Weekly Report.* 1998;47(no. RR-05). Sponsored by the Centers for Disease Control and Prevention. Cost: $1. To order call US Govt Printing Office 202 783-3238.

Anti-HIV Agents/Therapeutic Use
HIV Infections/Drug Therapy

Guidelines for the Use of Antiretroviral Agents in Pediatric HIV Infection. *Morbid Mortal Weekly Report.* 1998;47(no. RR-04). Sponsored by the Centers for Disease Control and Prevention. Cost: $1. To order call US Govt Printing Office 202 783-3238.

Anti-HIV Agents/Therapeutic Use
HIV Infections/Prevention and Control

Management of Possible Sexual, Injecting-Drug-Use, or Other Nonoccupational Exposure to HIV, Including Considerations Related to Antiretroviral Therapy Public Health Service Statement. 1998. 47(no. RR-17). Sponsored by the Centers for Disease Control and Prevention. To order call US Govt Printing Office 202 783-3238. Available on the Internet at cdc.gov/mmwr/mmwr_rr.html.

Anti-Infective Agents/Administration and Dosage
Community Medicine/Economics

Practice Guidelines for Community-Based Parenteral Anti-Infective Therapy. *Clin Inf Dis.* 1997;25:787. 15pp. 101refs. Sponsored by the Infectious Diseases Society of America. To obtain request from medical library or download via the Internet. Available on the Internet at idsociety.org/practice.

Anti-Inflammatory Agents, Non-Steroidal/Adverse Effects
Peptic Ulcer/Chemically Induced
Peptic Ulcer/Therapy

A Guideline for the Treatment and Prevention of NSAID-Induced Ulcers. *Am J Gastroenterol.* 1998;93:2037-2046. 10pp. 121refs. Sponsored by the American College of Gastroenterology. Cost: free copy. To order call ACG 703 820-7400.

Anti-Ulcer Agents/Therapeutic Use
Helicobacter Infections

Medical Treatment of Peptic Ulcer Disease Practice Guidelines. *JAMA.* 1996;275:622-629. 8pp. 99refs. Sponsored by the American College of Gastroenterology. Cost: free copy. To order call ACG 703 820-7400.

Antibiotic Prophylaxis
Carrier State/Prevention and Control

Prevention of Perinatal Group B Streptococcal Disease: A Public Health Perspective. *Morbid Mortal Weekly Report.* 1996;45(no. RR-7). Sponsored by the Centers for Disease Control and Prevention. Cost: $1. To order call US Govt Printing Office 202 783-3238.

Antibiotics/Administration and Dosage
Fibromyalgia/Drug Therapy

Empiric Parenteral Antibiotic Treatment of Patients with Fibromyalgia and a Positive Serologic Result for Lyme Disease. *Ann Intern Med.* 1993;119. 7pp. 37refs. Sponsored by the American College of Rheumatology, Infectious Diseases Society of America. To order call 404 633-3777.

Antibiotics/Standards

Antibiotic Therapy. *AAOMS Surgical Update.* 1994. Sponsored by the American Association of Oral and Maxillofacial Surgeons. To order call AAOMS Publications 1 800 366-6725.

Antibiotics/Therapeutic Use
Colonoscopy
Endocarditis, Bacterial/Prevention and Control

Practice Parameters for Antibiotic Prophylaxis to Prevent Infective Endocarditis of Infected Prosthesis During Colon and Rectal Surgery. *Dis Colon Rectum.* 1992;35(3):277-285. 9pp. 59refs. Sponsored by the American Society of Colon and Rectal Surgeons. Cost: free. To order write ASCRS, 85 W Algonquin Rd, #550, Arlington Hts, IL 60005.

Antibiotics/Therapeutic Use
Premedication/Standards

Quality Standard for Antimicrobial Prophylaxis in Surgical Procedures. *Infect Control Hosp Epidemiol.* 1994;15:182-188. 7pp. 49refs. Sponsored by the Society for Healthcare Epidemiology of America. Cost: free. To order visit our website at medscape.com/shea. Available on the Internet at medscape.com/shea. Key terms: uniform and reliable administration of prophylactic antimicrobial; optimal timing of drug administration; optimal dose; reduction in rates of postoperative wound infection; repeated doses during surgical procedure.

Antibiotics, Glycopeptide/Pharmacology
Vancomycin/Pharmacology

Recommendations for Preventing the Spread of Vancomycin Resistance. *Morbid Mortal Weekly Report.* 1995;44(no. RR-12). Sponsored by the Centers for Disease Control and Prevention. Cost: $1. To order call US Govt Printing Office 202 783-3238.

Antibodies, Anti-Idiotypic/Immunology
Coombs' Test/Methods

Utilizing Monospecific Antihuman Globulin to Test Blood-Group Compatibility. *Am J Clin Pathol.* 1995;104:122-125. 3pp. 27refs. Sponsored by the American Society of Clinical Pathologists. Cost: free copy. To order call Felicia Nelson 312 738-1336 x1350. Key terms: antihuman globulin; antiglobulin testing; antibody detection; monospecific antihuman globulin; polyspecific antihuman globulin.

Antibodies, Monoclonal/Therapeutic Use
Bacteremia/Therapy

Antiendotoxin Monoclonal Antibodies for Gram-Negative Sepsis. *Clin Inf Dis.* 1992;14:973-976. 4pp. Sponsored by the Infectious Diseases Society of America. To order obtain request from medical library.

Anticoagulants

Oral Anticoagulation for Older Adults, Pocket Guide. 1997. Sponsored by the American Geriatrics Society. Cost: free. To order call AGS 212 308-1414.

Anticonvulsants
Head Injuries/Drug Therapy

Prophylactic Anticonvulsants. *Guidelines for the Management of Severe Head Injury.* 1996;160-166. 7pp. Sponsored by the American Association of Neurological Surgeons. Cost: $45. To order call AANS 847 692-9500.

Anticonvulsants/Adverse Effects
Epilepsy/Drug Therapy

Practice Parameter: Management Issues for Women with Epilepsy. *Neurol.* 1998;51:944-948. 5. Sponsored by the American Academy of Neurology. Cost: individual statements are free. To order call AAN Member Service Center 1 800 879-1960. Available on the Internet at aan.com.

Anticonvulsants/Standards

Generic Substitution for Antiepileptic Medication. *Neurol.* 1990;40:1641-1643. 3pp. 27refs. Sponsored by the American Academy of Neurology. Cost: individual statements are free. To order call AAN Member Service Center 1 800 879-1960. Available on the Internet at aan.com.

Anticonvulsants/Therapeutic Use
Epilepsy/Drug Therapy

Practice Advisory: The Use of Felbamate in the Treatment of Patients with Intractable Epilepsy. *Neurol.* 1999;52:1540-1545. 6pp. 39refs. Sponsored by the American Academy of Neurology. Cost: individual statements are free. To order call AAN Member Service Center 1 800 879-1960. Available on the Internet at aan.com.

Anticonvulsants/Therapeutic Use
Epilepsy/Drug Therapy

Practice Parameter: A Guideline for Discontinuing Antiepileptic Drugs in Seizure-Free Patients. *Neurol.* 1996;47:600-602. 3pp. 16refs. Sponsored by the American Academy of Neurology. Cost: individual statements are free. To order call AAN Member Service Center 1 800 879-1960. Available on the Internet at aan.com.

Anticonvulsants/Therapeutic Use
Seizures/Drug Therapy

Practice Parameter: Antiepileptic Drug Treatment of Posttraumatic Seizures. *Arch PM & R.* 1998;79:594-597. 4pp. 42refs. Sponsored by the American Academy of Physical Medicine and Rehabilitation. Cost: free. To order call 312 464-9700.

Antiemetics/Therapeutic Use

Use of Anti-Emetic Agents. *J Clin Oncol.* 1999;17. 281refs. Sponsored by the American Society of Clinical Oncology. Cost: free copy. To order call ASCO 703 299-0150 or e-mail: guidelines@asco.org. Available free on the Internet at asco.org.

Antigen-Antibody Complex/Analysis
Food Analysis

Measurement of Circulating IgG and IgE Food-Immune Complexes. *J Allergy Clin Immun.* 1988;81:758-760, Position Statement No. 15. 3pp. 27refs. Sponsored by the American Academy of Allergy, Asthma, and Immunology. Cost: free copy. To order call 414 272-6071.

Antimalarials/Administration and Dosage
Malaria/Drug Therapy

Treatment with Quinidine Gluconate of Persons with Severe Plasmodium Falciparum Infection: Discontinuation of Parenteral Quinine from CDC Drug Service. *Morbid Mortal Weekly Report.* 1991;40(no. RR-4):21-23. 3pp. 16refs. Sponsored by the Centers for Disease Control and Prevention. Cost: $1. To order call US Govt Printing Office 202 783-3238.

Antineoplastic Agents
Antiemetics/Therapeutic Use
Nausea/Chemically Induced

Oral Health Care Series: Patients Receiving Cancer Chemotherapy. 1996. 10pp. 15refs. Sponsored by the American Dental Association. Cost: $8 ADA members, $12 nonmembers. To order call ADA Dept of Salable Materials 1 800 947-4776.

Antineoplastic Agents/Antagonists and Inhibitors
Radiation Protective Agents

The Use of Chemotherapy and Radiotherapy Protectants. *J Clin Oncol.* 1999;17. 113refs. Sponsored by the American Society of Clinical Oncology. Cost: free copy. To order call ASCO 703 299-0150 or e-mail: guidelines@asco.org. Available free on the Internet at asco.org.

Antiphospholipid Syndrome

Antiphospholipid Syndrome. *ACOG Educational Bulletin.* 1998;244. 10pp. 78refs. Sponsored by the American College of Obstetricians and Gynecologists. Cost: free copy. Set of Bulletins $70 + s/h ACOG members, $125 + s/h nonmembers. One-year subscription $55 member, $65 nonmember. To order single copy, call ACOG Resource Center 202 863-2518; to order set or subscription, call ACOG Distribution Center, 1 800 762-2264. Available on the Internet to members only at acog.org. Key terms: abortion; habitual; antiphospholipid syndrome.

Antitubercular Agents/Therapeutic Use
Health Priorities

National Action Plan to Combat Multidrug-Resistant Tuberculosis. *Morbid Mortal Weekly Report.* 1992;41(no. RR-11):1-49. 50pp. Sponsored by the Centers for Disease Control and Prevention. Cost: $1. To order call US Govt Printing Office 202 783-3238.

Antitubercular Agents/Therapeutic Use
Tuberculosis/Drug Therapy

Initial Therapy for Tuberculosis in the Era of Multidrug Resistance. *Morbid Mortal Weekly Report.* 1993;42(no. RR-7). Sponsored by the Centers for Disease Control and Prevention. Cost: $1. To order call US Govt Printing Office 202 783-3238.

Antitubercular Agents/Therapeutic Use
Tuberculosis/Drug Therapy

Treatment of Tuberculosis and Tuberculosis Infection in Adults and Children. *Am J Respir Crit Care Med.* 1994;149:5. Sponsored by the American Thoracic Society. Cost: $6. To order send check payable to American Thoracic Society, 1740 Broadway, New York, NY 10019-4374; for credit card orders, call 212 315-8863.

Anus Diseases/Diagnosis
Rectal Diseases/Diagnosis

Anorectal Testing Techniques. *Gastroenterology.* 1999;116:735-760. 25pp. 239refs. Sponsored by the American Gastroenterological Association. Cost: $10. To order call AGA 301 654-2055. Key terms: anorectal; fecal incontinence; constipation; IBS.

Anus Neoplasms/Therapy

Anal Cancer (6 variants). 1998. 14pp. 29refs. Sponsored by the American College of Radiology. Cost: Vols. 1 & 2 $25 each (ACR members); $75/set (ACR nonmembers). To order call ACR Appropriateness Criteria 703 716-7583 x7596. Available free on the Internet at acr.org/f-appcrit.html. Key terms: anal cancer; brachytherapy; chemotherapy; radiotherapy.

Anxiety Disorders
Dissociative Disorders

Anxiety Disorders, Dissociative Disorders, and Adjustment Disorders. *Treatments of Psychiatric Disorders, Second Edition, Volume II.* 1995;Section 7. 298pp. 1024refs. Sponsored by the American Psychiatric Association. Cost: $250 for 2-volume set. To order call 1 800 368-5777 order #SPCT8700. Key terms: TPD; disorders; treatment.

Anxiety Disorders
Serotonin Uptake Inhibitors/
Therapeutic Use

Practice Parameters for the Assessment and Treatment of Children and Adolescents with Anxiety Disorders. *J Am Acad Child Adol Psych.* 1997;36(10 suppl): 695-845. 15pp. 161refs. Sponsored by the American Academy of Child and Adolescent Psychiatry. Cost: $10 AACAP members/$20 others. To order call Communications Department 202 966-7300. Key terms: anxiety disorders; anxiolytics; antidepressants; practice parameters; guidelines.

Aortic Aneurysm, Abdominal/Diagnosis
Aortic Rupture/Prevention and Control

Screening for Abdominal Aortic Aneurysm. *Guide to Clinical Preventive Services, 2nd Ed.* 1996. Sponsored by the US Preventive Services Task Force. To order call Williams & Wilkins 1 800 638-0672.

Aortic Aneurysm, Abdominal/Surgery

Abdominal Aortic Aneurysm Surgery. 1992. JRA-04. 103pp. 97refs. Sponsored by RAND, Academic Medical Center Consortium. To order call RAND 310 393-0411 x7002. Key terms: abdominal aortic aneurysm surgery; utilization; complications.

Aortic Aneurysm/Diagnosis
Aortic Rupture/Surgery

Recommended Indications for Operative Treatment of Abdominal Aortic Aneurysms. *J Vasc Surg.* 1992;15:1046-1056. 11pp. Sponsored by the Society for Vascular Surgery/North American Chapter, ICVS. Cost: free. To order call 978 526-8330.

Apgar Score
Fetal Anoxia/Diagnosis

Use and Abuse of the Apgar Score. *ACOG Committee Opinion.* 1996;174. 3pp. 11refs. Sponsored by the American College of Obstetricians and Gynecologists. Cost: free copy. Set of Opinions $55 + s/h ACOG members, $75 + s/h nonmembers. One-year subscription $55 member, $65 nonmember. To order single copy, call ACOG Resource Center 202 863-2518; to order set or subscription, call ACOG Distribution Center, 1 800 762-2264. Available on the Internet to members only at acog.org.

Apnea/Prevention and Control
Home Nursing

Infantile Apnea and Home Monitoring. *NIH Consensus Development Conference Statement.* 1986;6(6):1-10[Conf. No. 58]. 11pp. Sponsored by the National Institutes of Health. Cost: free copy. To order call 1 888 644-2667. Available on the Internet at consensus.nih.gov.

Apolipoproteins B/Blood
Apolipoproteins E/Blood

Use of Plasma Concentrations of Apolipoproteins. *Diagnostic and Therapeutic Technology Assessment (DATTA).* 1995;11pp. 94refs. Sponsored by the American Medical Association, Diagnostic and Therapeutic Technology Assessment Program. Cost: free copy. DATTA subscription available. To order call AMA Department of Technology Assessment 312 464-4531.

Appendectomy
Cecal Diseases/Surgery

Incidental Appendectomy. *ACOG Committee Opinion.* 1995;164. 2pp. 7refs. Sponsored by the American College of Obstetricians and Gynecologists. Cost: free copy. Set of Opinions $55 + s/h ACOG members, $75 + s/h nonmembers. One-year subscription $55 member, $65 nonmember. To order single copy, call ACOG Resource Center 202 863-2518; to order set or subscription, call ACOG Distribution Center, 1 800 762-2264. Available on the Internet to members only at acog.org. Key terms: surgery; gynecological surgery; incidental.

Appendectomy/Methods
Surgical Procedures, Laparoscopic

SAGES Position Statement—Laparoscopic Appendectomy. *SAGES Guideline.* 1992. 1pp. Sponsored by the Society of American Gastrointestinal and Endoscopic Surgeons. Cost: free. To order call 310 314-2404. Available on the Internet at sages.org. Key terms: surgery; laparoscopic; appendectomy.

Appetite Depressants/Therapeutic Use

Anorectic Usage Guidelines. 1998. 8pp. 18refs. Sponsored by the American Society of Bariatric Physicians. Cost: free. To order call the American Society of Bariatric Physicians 303 770-2526 x10. Key terms: obesity; appetite suppressants; overweight; fat.

Arrhythmia/Diagnosis
Hospitalization

Position Statement: In-Hospital Cardiac Monitoring of Adults for Detection of Arrhythmia. 1991. Sponsored by the American College of Cardiology. Cost: free copy. To order call Educational Services Department 1 800 257-4740.

Arrhythmia/Physiopathology
Heart Rate

Position Statement: Heart Rate Variability for Risk Stratification of Life-Threatening Arrhythmias. *J Am Coll Cardiol.* 1993;22:948-950. 3pp. 17refs. Sponsored by the American College of Cardiology. Cost: free copy. To order call Educational Services Department 1 800 257-4740.

Arrhythmia/Prevention and Control
Catheter Ablation/Instrumentation

Clinical Investigation of Antiarrhythmic Devices. *Circulation.* 1995;91:2097-2109. 13pp. 115refs. Sponsored by the American Heart Association. Cost: free copy. To order call 1 800 242-8721 (US only) or write to: American Heart Association, Public Inquiries, 7272 Greenville Ave, Dallas TX 75231-4596.

Arrhythmia/Therapy
Pacemaker, Artificial

ACC/AHA Guidelines for Implantation of Cardiac Pacemakers and Antiarrhythmia Devices. *J Am Coll Cardiol.* 1991;18:1-13. 13pp. 115refs. Sponsored by the American College of Cardiology, American Heart Association. Cost: free copy. To order call Educational Services Department 1 800 257-4740.

Arrhythmia/Therapy
Pacemaker, Artificial

Guidelines for Implantation of Cardiac Pacemakers and Antiarrhythmia Devices. *Circulation.* 1998;97:1325-1335. 11pp. 333refs. Sponsored by the American Heart Association, American College of Cardiology. Cost: free copy. To order write the Office of Scientific Affairs, AHA, 7272 Greenville Ave, Dallas, TX 75231.

Arteriovenous Shunt, Surgical
Hemodialysis

NKF-DOQI Clinical Practice Guidelines for Vascular Access. 1997. 168pp. 207refs. Sponsored by the National Kidney Foundation. Cost: $13. To order call NKF 1 800 622-9010. Key terms: hemodialysis adequacy; peritoneal dialysis adequacy; vascular access; anemia management; executive summaries.

Arthritis, Rheumatoid/Drug Therapy
Drug Monitoring

Guidelines for Monitoring Drug Therapy in Rheumatoid Arthritis. *Arthritis Rheum.* 1996;39(5):723-731. 9pp. 68refs. Sponsored by the American College of Rheumatology. To order call 404 633-3777. Available free on the Internet at rheumatology.org. Key terms: arthritis; chronic; joint; musculoskeletal; pain.

Arthritis, Rheumatoid/Drug Therapy
Liver Diseases/Chemically Induced
Methotrexate/Adverse Effects

Methotrexate for Rheumatoid Arthritis: Suggested Guidelines for Monitoring Liver Toxicity. *Arthritis Rheum.* 1994;37:316-328. 13pp. 63refs. Sponsored by the American College of Rheumatology. To order call 404 633-3777. Available free on the Internet at rheumatology.org. Key terms: methotrexate; liver; rheumatoid; monitoring; toxicity.

Arthritis, Rheumatoid/Therapy

Guidelines for the Management of Rheumatoid Arthritis. *Arthritis Rheum.* 1996;39(5):713-722. 10pp. 66refs. Sponsored by the American College of Rheumatology. To order call 404 633-3777. Available free on the Internet at rheumatology.org. Key terms: arthritis; chronic; joint; musculoskeletal; pain.

Arthroscopy

Suggested Guidelines for the Practice of Arthroscopic Surgery. 1990. Sponsored by the Arthroscopy Association of North America. Cost: free copy. To order call AANA 847 292-2262.

Asbestos/Adverse Effects
Lung Diseases

Diagnosis of Non-Malignant Disease Related to Asbestos. *Amer Rev Resp Dis.* 1986;134:2. Sponsored by the American Thoracic Society. Cost: $4. To order send check payable to American Thoracic Society, 1740 Broadway, New York, NY 10019-4374; for credit card orders, call 212 315-8863.

Asphyxia Neonatorum/Classification
Fetal Distress/Classification

Inappropriate Use of the Terms Fetal Distress and Birth Asphyxia. *ACOG Committee Opinion.* 1998;197. 2pp. 2refs. Sponsored by the American College of Obstetricians and Gynecologists. Cost: free copy. Set of Opinions $55 + s/h ACOG members, $75 + s/h nonmembers. One-year subscription $55 member, $65 nonmember. To order single copy, call ACOG Resource Center 202 863-2518; to order set or subscription, call ACOG Distribution Center, 1 800 762-2264. Available on the Internet to members only at acog.org. Key terms: asphyxia neonatorum; fetal anoxia; fetal distress; nomenclature.

Aspirin/Administration and Dosage
Pre-Eclampsia/Prevention and Control

Aspirin Prophylaxis in Pregnancy. *Guide to Clinical Preventive Services, 2nd Ed.* 1996. Sponsored by the US Preventive Services Task Force. To order call Williams & Wilkins 1 800 638-0672.

Aspirin/Therapeutic Use
Cardiovascular Diseases/Drug Therapy

Aspirin as a Therapeutic Agent in Cardiovascular Disease. *Circulation.* 1997;96:2751-2753. 3pp. 20refs. Sponsored by the American Heart Association. Cost: free copy. To order call 1 800 242-8721 (US only) or write to: American Heart Association, Public Inquiries, 7272 Greenville Ave, Dallas TX 75231-4596.

Asthma
Inflammation

Progress at the Interface of Inflammation and Asthma: Report of the ALA/ATS. *Am J Respir Crit Care Med.* 1995;152:1. Sponsored by the American Thoracic Society. Cost: $4. To order send check payable to American Thoracic Society, 1740 Broadway, New York, NY 10019-4374; for credit card orders, call 212 315-8863.

Asthma
Patient Education
Patient Compliance

Advice for the Patient. *USP DI.* 2000;Volume II. 1865pp. Sponsored by US Pharmacopeia/Micromedex, Inc. Cost: $75 per year subscription. To order call 1 800 877-6209. Key terms: patient drug information; patient education; compliance.

Asthma/Diagnosis
Asthma/Therapy

Guidelines for the Diagnosis and Management of Asthma. *NIH Publication No. 97-4051.* 1997. 146pp. Sponsored by the National Heart, Lung, and Blood Institute. Cost: $7. To order contact the NHLBI Information Center, PO Box 30105, Bethesda, MD 20824-0105, 301 251-1222.

Asthma/Diagnosis
Asthma/Therapy
Algorithms

Algorithm for the Diagnosis and Management of Asthma. *Ann Allergy Asthma Immun.* 1998;81:415-420. 5pp. Sponsored by the American Academy of Allergy, Asthma, and Immunology; American College of Allergy, Asthma, and Immunology; Joint Council of Allergy, Asthma, and Immunology. Cost: free copy. To order call 847 934-1918.

Asthma/Diagnosis
Disability Evaluation

Guidelines for the Evaluation of Impairment/Disability in Patients with Asthma. *Amer Rev Resp Dis.* 1993;147:4. Sponsored by the American Thoracic Society. Cost: $6. To order send check payable to American Thoracic Society, 1740 Broadway, New York, NY 10019-4374; for credit card orders, call 212 315-8863.

Asthma/Diagnosis
Occupational Diseases/Diagnosis

Assessment of Asthma in the Workplace. *Chest.* 1995;108:1084-1117. 34pp. 159refs. Sponsored by the American College of Chest Physicians. Cost: $5. To order call ACCP 1 800 343-2227 or 1 847 498-1400 (credit card orders). Key terms: occupational disease; asthma.

Asthma/Drug Therapy
Beta-Adrenergic Agonists/
Administration and Dosage

Inhaled Beta-Adrenergic Agonists in Asthma. *J Allergy Clin Immun.* 1993;91:1234-1237, Position Statement No. 22. 4pp. 57refs. Sponsored by the American Academy of Allergy, Asthma, and Immunology. Cost: free copy. To order call 414 272-6071.

Asthma/Drug Therapy
School Health Services

Use of Inhaled Medications in School by Students with Asthma. *J Allergy Clin Immun.* 1989;84:400, Position Statement No. 18. 1pp. Sponsored by the American Academy of Allergy, Asthma, and Immunology. Cost: free copy. To order call 414 272-6071.

Asthma/Therapy
Histamine H1 Antagonists

Use of Antihistamines in Patients with Asthma. *J Allergy Clin Immun.* 1988;82:481-482, Position Statement No. 16. 2pp. 23refs. Sponsored by the American Academy of Allergy, Asthma, and Immunology. Cost: free copy. To order call 414 272-6071.

Asthma/Therapy
Pregnancy Complications/Therapy

Working Group Report on Management of Asthma During Pregnancy. *PB 96-141593.* 1993. 84pp. Sponsored by the National Heart, Lung, and Blood Institute. Cost: $21.50. To order contact the NHLBI Information Center, PO Box 30105, Bethesda, MD 20824-0105, 301 251-1222.

Atherosclerosis/Prevention and Control
Preventive Medicine

Position Statement: Preventive Cardiology and Atherosclerotic Disease. *J Am Coll Cardiol.* 1994;24:838. 1pp. Sponsored by the American College of Cardiology. Cost: free copy. To order call Educational Services Department 1 800 257-4740.

Athletic Injuries/Therapy
Brain Concussion/Therapy

Practice Parameter: The Management of Concussion in Sports. *Neurol.* 1997;48:581-585. 5pp. 12refs. Sponsored by the American Academy of Neurology. Cost: individual statements are free. To order call AAN Member Service Center 1 800 879-1960. Available on the Internet at aan.com.

Attention Deficit Disorder with Hyperactivity/Diagnosis
Attention Deficit Disorder with Hyperactivity/Therapy

Diagnosis and Treatment of Attention Deficit Hyperactivity Disorder (ADHD). *NIH Consensus Development Conference Statement.* 1998;16(2):1[Conf. No. 110]. 27pp. 112refs. Sponsored by the National Institutes of Health. Cost: free copy. To order call 1 888 644-2667. Available on the Internet at consensus.nih.gov.

Attention Deficit Disorder with Hyperactivity/Diagnosis
Central Nervous System Stimulants/Therapeutic Use

Practice Parameters for the Assessment and Treatment of Children and Adolescents with Attention Deficit Hyperactivity Disorder. *J Am Acad Child Adol Psych.* 1997;36(10 suppl): 855-1215. 36pp. 398refs. Sponsored by the American Academy of Child and Adolescent Psychiatry. Cost: $10 AACAP members/ $20 others. To order call Communications Department 202 966-7300. Key terms: attention-deficit/hyperactivity disorder; psychopharmacology; methylphenidate; dextroamphetamine.

Attention Deficit Disorder with Hyperactivity/Drug Therapy
Food, Formulated

Defined Diets and Childhood Hyperactivity. *NIH Consensus Development Conference Statement.* 1982;4(3):1-11[Conf. No. 32]. 12pp. Sponsored by the National Institutes of Health. Cost: free copy. To order call 1 888 644-2667. Available on the Internet at consensus.nih.gov.

Autoimmune Diseases/Therapy
Purpura, Thrombocytopenic, Idiopathic/Therapy

Idiopathic Thrombocytopenic Purpura. *Blood.* 1996;88(1). 40pp. 295refs. Sponsored by the American Society of Hematology. Cost: free. To order call ASH 202 857-1118. Available on the Internet at hematology.org. Key terms: ITP; platelet count; thrombocytopenia; complete blood count; reticulocyte count.

Autoimmune Diseases/Therapy
Thrombocytopenia/Therapy

Protein A Columns for Immune Thrombocytopenia. *AHCPR Health Technology Assessment.* 1990;No. 7 (AHCPR Publication No. 91-0008). 8pp. 56refs. Sponsored by the Federal Agency for Health Care Policy and Research. To order call AHCPR Clearinghouse 1 800 358-9295.

Autonomic Nervous System/ Physiopathology
Neurologic Examination

Assessment: Clinical Autonomic Testing. *Neurol.* 1996;46:873-880. 8pp. 101refs. Sponsored by the American Academy of Neurology. Cost: individual statements are free. To order call AAN Member Service Center 1 800 879-1960. Available on the Internet at aan.com.

Autopsy

Autopsy. *JAMA.* 1987;258:364-369. 6pp. Sponsored by the American Medical Association, Council on Scientific Affairs. Cost: free. To order call Nancy Nolan, AMA, 312 464-5046.

Autopsy
Confidentiality
HIV Seropositivity

Confidentiality of HIV Status on Autopsy Reports. *Arch Path Lab Med.* 1992;116:1120-1123. 4pp. Sponsored by the American Medical Association, Council on Ethical and Judicial Affairs. Cost: free copy.

Autopsy/Methods
Pathology, Surgical/Methods

Practice Guidelines for Autopsy Pathology: Perinatal and Pediatric Autopsy. *Arch Path Lab Med.* 1997;121:368-376. 9pp. 54refs. Sponsored by the College of American Pathologists. Cost: reprints: free. To order call CAP 1 800 323-4040 x7378. Key terms: autopsy; pathology; fetal death; neonatal death.

Autopsy/Standards
Central Nervous System/Pathology

Autopsy Procedures for Brain, Spinal Cord and Neuromuscular System. *Arch Path Lab Med.* 1995;119:777-783. 7pp. 26refs. Sponsored by the College of American Pathologists. Cost: reprints: free. To order call CAP 1 800 323-4040 x7378. Key terms: autopsy; pathology; CNS.

Autopsy/Standards
Pathology, Clinical/Methods

Practice Guidelines for Autopsy Pathology: Autopsy Performance (Reaffirmed, 1996). *Arch Path Lab Med.* 1994;118:19-25. 7pp. 27refs. Sponsored by the College of American Pathologists. Cost: reprints: free. To order call CAP 1 800 323-4040 x7378. Key terms: autopsy; pathology.

Autopsy/Standards
Pathology, Clinical/Methods

Practice Guidelines for Autopsy Pathology: Autopsy Reporting. *Arch Path Lab Med.* 1995;119:123-130. 8pp. 30refs. Sponsored by the College of American Pathologists. Cost: reprints: free. To order call CAP 1 800 323-4040 x7378. Key terms: autopsy; pathology.

Aversive Therapy

Aversion Therapy. *JAMA.* 1987;258:2562-2566. 5pp. Sponsored by the American Medical Association, Council on Scientific Affairs. Cost: free. To order call Nancy Nolan, AMA, 312 464-5046.

Back Pain/Diagnosis
Magnetic Resonance Imaging

Practice Parameters: MRI in the Evaluation of Low Back Syndrome. *Neurol.* 1994;44:767-770. 4pp. 1ref. Sponsored by the American Academy of Neurology. Cost: individual statements are free. To order call AAN Member Service Center 1 800 879-1960. Available on the Internet at aan.com.

Bacteremia/Drug Therapy

Quality Standard for the Treatment of Bacteremia. *Infect Control Hosp Epidemiol.* 1994;15:189-192. 1pp. 19refs. Sponsored by the Society for Healthcare Epidemiology of America. Cost: free. To order visit our website at medscape.com/shea. Available on the Internet at medscape.com/shea. Key terms: appropriate dosing; most cost-effective selection; proper antibiotic levels in serum; least toxicity; narrowest spectrum.

Bacteremia/Drug Therapy
Microbial Sensitivity Tests/Standards

Quality Standard for the Treatment of Bacteremia. *Clin Inf Dis.* 1994;18:428-430. 3pp. 19refs. Sponsored by the Infectious Diseases Society of America. To obtain request from medical library.

Bacterial Infections/Radionuclide Imaging

ACR Standard for the Performance of Scintigraphy for Infections and Inflammations. 1999. 6pp. 11refs. Sponsored by the American College of Radiology. Cost: $25 (ACR nonmembers). To order call ACR Dept of Quality Assurance 703 716-7592. Available free on the Internet at acr.org. Key terms: nuclear medicine; infection; inflammatory scintigraphy.

Bacterial Vaccines
Pneumonia, Pneumococcal/Prevention and Control

Pneumococcal Polysaccharide Vaccine. *Morbid Mortal Weekly Report*. 1989;38:64-76. 13pp. Sponsored by the Centers for Disease Control and Prevention. Cost: $1. To order call US Govt Printing Office 202 783-3238.

Bacterial Typing Techniques
Seroepidemiologic Studies

How to Select and Interpret Molecular Strain Typing Methods for Epi Studies of Bacterial Infections: A Review for Healthcare Epidemiologists. *Infect Control Hosp Epidemiol*. 1997;18:426-439. 14pp. 75refs. Sponsored by the Society for Healthcare Epidemiology of America. Cost: free. To order visit our website at medscape.com/shea. Available on the Internet at medscape.com/shea. Key terms: strain typing; molecular technology; pulsed-field gel electrophoresis.

Bacterial Vaccines

Pneumococcal Vaccine. *Ann Intern Med*. 1986;104:118-120. 3pp. Sponsored by the American College of Physicians. To order call ACP Clinical Efficacy Assessment Project 1 800 523-1546.

Bacterial Vaccines/Adverse Effects
Vaccination/Adverse Effects

Update: Vaccine Side Effects, Adverse Reactions, Contraindications, and Precautions. *Morbid Mortal Weekly Report*. 1996;45(no. RR-12). Sponsored by the Centers for Disease Control and Prevention. Cost: $1. To order call US Govt Printing Office 202 783-3238.

Bacteriological Techniques
Blood/Microbiology

Blood Cultures. *Ann Intern Med*. 1987;106:246-253. 8pp. Sponsored by the American College of Physicians. To order call ACP Clinical Efficacy Assessment Project 1 800 523-1546.

Bacteriuria/Diagnosis

Screening for Asymptomatic Bacteriuria. *Guide to Clinical Preventive Services, 2nd Ed*. 1996. Sponsored by the US Preventive Services Task Force. To order call Williams & Wilkins 1 800 638-0672.

Baldness (see Alopecia)

Balloon Dilation
Prostatic Hyperplasia/Therapy

Endoscopic Balloon Dilation of the Prostate. *JAMA*. 1992;267:1123-1126. 4pp. 18refs. Sponsored by the American Medical Association, Diagnostic and Therapeutic Technology Assessment Program. Cost: free copy. DATTA subscription available. To order call AMA Department of Technology Assessment 312 464-4531.

Balloon Dilation/Methods
Esophageal Stenosis/Therapy

Esophageal Dilation. *Gastrointest Endosc*. 1991;37:122-124. 3pp. 18refs. Sponsored by the American Society for Gastrointestinal Endoscopy. Cost: free. To order call ASGE 978 526-8330.

Barium Sulfate/Diagnostic Use
Enema/Standards

ACR Standard for the Performance of Adult Barium Enema Examinations. 1999. 3pp. 7refs. Sponsored by the American College of Radiology. Cost: $25 (ACR nonmembers). To order call ACR Dept of Quality Assurance. Available free on the Internet at acr.org. Key terms: lower GI; enema barium; colon.

Bibliography

Clinical Practice Guidelines Bibliography. 1996. Sponsored by the American Geriatrics Society. Cost: free. To order call AGS 212 308-1414.

Bicycling
Head Injuries/Prevention and Control
Head Protective Devices

Injury-Control Recommendations: Bicycle Helmets. *Morbid Mortal Weekly Report*. 1995;44(no. RR-1). Sponsored by the Centers for Disease Control and Prevention. Cost: $1. To order call US Govt Printing Office 202 783-3238.

Biliary Tract/Radionuclide Imaging
Radiopharmaceuticals/Diagnostic Use

ACR Standard for the Performance of Hepatobiliary Scintigraphy. 1999. 4pp. 9refs. Sponsored by the American College of Radiology. Cost: $25 (ACR nonmembers). To order call ACR Dept of Quality Assurance 703 716-7592. Available free on the Internet at acr.org. Key terms: liver disease; nuclear medicine; hepatobiliary.

Biliary Tract Diseases/Diagnosis
Pancreatic Diseases/Diagnosis

Role of Endoscopy in Diseases of the Biliary Tract and Pancreas: Guidelines for Clinical Application. *Gastrointest Endosc.* 1989;34:598-9. 2pp. 23refs. Sponsored by the American Society for Gastrointestinal Endoscopy. Cost: free. To order call ASGE 978 526-8330.

Biliary Tract Diseases/
Radionuclide Imaging
Liver Diseases/Radionuclide Imaging

Procedure Guideline for Hepatobiliary Scintigraphy. *J Nuclear Med.* 1997;38:1654-1657. 4pp. 35refs. Sponsored by the Society of Nuclear Medicine. Cost: free. To order call Bill Uffelman 703 708-9000. Available on the Internet at snm.org. Key terms: routine diagnostic tests; radionuclide imaging; hepatobiliary scintigraphy; biliary tract diseases; gallbladder.

Biliary Tract Diseases/Therapy
Endoscopy, Digestive System

Endoscopic Therapy of Biliary Tract and Pancreatic Diseases. *Gastrointest Endosc.* 1991;37:117-119. 3pp. 29refs. Sponsored by the American Society for Gastrointestinal Endoscopy. Cost: free. To order call ASGE 978 526-8330.

Biliary Tract Surgical Procedures
Cholecystectomy, Laparoscopic

Guidelines for the Clinical Application of Laparoscopic Biliary Tract Surgery. 1994. 8. 4pp. 10refs. Sponsored by the Society of American Gastrointestinal and Endoscopic Surgeons. Cost: free. To order call 310 314-2404. Available on the Internet at sages.org. Key terms: surgery; laparoscopy; biliary.

Biocompatible Materials
Skin/Surgery

Soft Tissue Augmentation (3): Gelatin Matrix Implant. *J Am Acad Derm.* 1996;34:695-697. 3pp. 5refs. Sponsored by the American Academy of Dermatology. Cost: free copy. To order call Alice Bell 847 330-0230 x333. Available on the Internet at aad.org. Key terms: artificial implants; gelatin; chemistry; 6-aminocaproic acid.

Biofeedback (Psychology)
Gastrointestinal Diseases/Therapy

Biofeedback for Gastrointestinal Disorders. *Ann Intern Med.* 1985;103:291-293. 3pp. Sponsored by the American College of Physicians. To order call ACP Clinical Efficacy Assessment Project 1 800 523-1546.

Biofeedback (Psychology)
Headache/Therapy

Biofeedback for Headaches. *Ann Intern Med.* 1985;102:128-131. 4pp. Sponsored by the American College of Physicians. To order call ACP Clinical Efficacy Assessment Project 1 800 523-1546.

Biofeedback (Psychology)
Hypertension/Therapy

Biofeedback for Hypertension. *Ann Intern Med.* 1985;102:709-715. 7pp. Sponsored by the American College of Physicians. To order call ACP Clinical Efficacy Assessment Project 1 800 523-1546.

Biofeedback (Psychology)
Neuromuscular Diseases/Rehabilitation

Biofeedback for Neuromuscular Disorders. *Ann Intern Med.* 1985;102:854-858. 5pp. Sponsored by the American College of Physicians. To order call ACP Clinical Efficacy Assessment Project 1 800 523-1546.

Biopsy, Needle/Methods

ACR Standard for the Performance of Imaging-Guided Percutaneous Needle Biopsy in Adults. 1999. 5pp. 10refs. Sponsored by the American College of Radiology. Cost: $25 (ACR nonmembers). To order call ACR Dept of Quality Assurance 703 716-7592. Available free on the Internet at acr.org. Key terms: transthoracic; needle biopsy; abscess; lesion.

Biopsy, Needle/Methods
Breast Neoplasms/Diagnosis

Image-Guided Breast Biopsy. *Diagnostic and Therapeutic Technology Assessment (DATTA).* 1996. 11pp. 32refs. Sponsored by the American Medical Association, Diagnostic and Therapeutic Technology Assessment Program. Cost: free copy. DATTA subscription available. To order call AMA Department of Technology Assessment 312 464-4531.

Biopsy, Needle/Methods
Lung/Pathology

Guidelines for Percutaneous Transthoracic Needle Biopsy. *Amer Rev Resp Dis.* 1989;140:1. Sponsored by the American Thoracic Society. Cost: $4. To order send check payable to American Thoracic Society, 1740 Broadway, New York, NY 10019-4374; for credit card orders, call 212 315-8863.

Biopsy, Needle/Methods
Pleura/Pathology

Guidelines for Thoracentesis and Needle Biopsy of the Pleura. *Amer Rev Resp Dis.* 1989;140:1. Sponsored by the American Thoracic Society. Cost: $4. To order send check payable to American Thoracic Society, 1740 Broadway, New York, NY 10019-4374; for credit card orders, call 212 315-8863.

Biopsy, Needle/Standards
Nephrology/Standards

Clinical Competence in Percutaneous Renal Biopsy. *Ann Intern Med.* 1988;108:301-303. 3pp. Sponsored by the American College of Physicians. To order call ACP Clinical Efficacy Assessment Project 1 800 523-1546.

Biopsy/Standards
Endoscopy, Gastrointestinal/Standards

Tissue Sampling and Analysis. *Gastrointest Endosc.* 1991;37:663-665. 6pp. 30refs. Sponsored by the American Society for Gastrointestinal Endoscopy. Cost: free. To order call ASGE 978 526-8330.

Bipolar Disorder

Practice Parameters for the Assessment and Treatment of Children and Adolescents with Bipolar Disorder. *J Am Acad Child Adol Psych.* 1997;36(1):138-157. 19pp. 120refs. Sponsored by the American Academy of Child and Adolescent Psychiatry. Cost: $10 AACAP members/$20 others. To order call Communications Department 202 966-7300. Key terms: bipolar disorder; children; adolescents; early onset; practice parameters.

Bipolar Disorder/Therapy

Practice Guideline for the Treatment of Patients with Bipolar Disorder. *Am J Psych.* 1994;152(suppl):12. 36pp. 258refs. Sponsored by the American Psychiatric Association. Cost: $22.50. To order call 1 800 368-5777 order #SPCT2302. Key terms: bipolar.

Bird Diseases/Prevention and Control
Chlamydia psittaci

Appendix B—Treatment Options for Pet Birds with Avian Chlamydiosis. *Morbid Mortal Weekly Report.* 1998;47(no. RR-10). Sponsored by the Centers for Disease Control and Prevention. To order call US Govt Printing Office. Available on the Internet at cdc.gov/epo/mmwr/preview/ind98_rr.html.

Bird Diseases/Prevention and Control
Chlamydia psittaci

Compendium of Measures to Control Chlamydia psittaci Infection Among Humans (Psittacosis) and Pet Birds (Avian Chlamydiosis). *Morbid Mortal Weekly Report.* 1998;47(no. RR-10). Sponsored by the Centers for Disease Control and Prevention. To order call US Govt Printing Office. Available on the Internet at cdc.gov/epo/mmwr/preview/ind98_rr.html.

Bird Diseases/Prevention and Control
Ornithosis/Prevention and Control

Compendium of Psittacosis (Chlamydiosis) Control, 1997. *Morbid Mortal Weekly Report.* 1997;46(no. RR-13). Sponsored by the Centers for Disease Control and Prevention. Cost: $1. To order call US Govt Printing Office 202 783-3238.

Bladder/Radiography
Urethra/Radiography

ACR Standard for the Performance of Voiding Cystourethrography in Children. 1999. 7pp. 12refs. Sponsored by the American College of Radiology. Cost: $25 (ACR nonmembers). To order call ACR Dept of Quality Assurance 703 716-7592. Available free on the Internet at acr.org. Key terms: radiology; pediatric voiding cystourethrography.

Bladder Neoplasms/Therapy
BCG Vaccine/Therapeutic Use

Reassessment of BCG Immunotherapy in Bladder Cancer. *JAMA.* 1988;259:2153-2155. 3pp. Sponsored by the American Medical Association, Diagnostic and Therapeutic Technology Assessment Program. Cost: free copy. DATTA subscription available. To order call AMA Department of Technology Assessment 312 464-4531.

Bladder/Radionuclide Imaging

ACR Standard for the Performance of Radionuclide Cystography. 1996. 5pp. 13refs. Sponsored by the American College of Radiology. Cost: $25 (ACR nonmembers). To order call ACR Dept of Quality Assurance 703 716-7592. Available free on the Internet at acr.org. Key terms: nuclear medicine; cystography.

Bladder/Radionuclide Imaging

Procedure Guideline for Radionuclide Cystography in Children. *J Nuclear Med.* 1997;38:1650-1654. 5pp. 6refs. Sponsored by the Society of Nuclear Medicine. Cost: free. To order call Bill Uffelman 703 708-9000. Available on the Internet at snm.org. Key terms: routine diagnostic tests; radionuclide imaging; pediatric; bladder; vesicoureteral reflux.

Bleeding Time
Preoperative Care

CAP/ASCP Position Paper: The Preoperative Bleeding Time Test Lacks Clinical Benefit. *Arch Surg.* 1998;133:134-139. 6pp. 80refs. Sponsored by the American Society of Clinical Pathologists. Cost: reprints: free. To order call Felicia Nelson 312 738-1336 x1350. Key terms: bleeding time; preoperative tests/screen; bleeding disorder.

Blepharitis

Blepharitis Preferred Practice Pattern. *Ophthalmology.* 1998. 16pp. 27refs. Sponsored by the American Academy of Ophthalmology. Cost: $11 members, $16 nonmembers. AAO members first copy free upon publication. To order call AAO Order Dept 415 561-8540. Key terms: eye; blepharitis; external eye disease; treatment.

Blepharoplasty
Eyelids/Surgery

Functional Indications for Upper and Lower Eyelid Blepharoplasty Ophthalmic Procedure Assessment. *Ophthalmology.* 1995;102:693-695. 3pp. 27refs. Sponsored by the American Academy of Ophthalmology. Cost: $11 members, $16 nonmembers. AAO members first copy free upon publication. To order call AAO Order Dept 415 561-8540. Key terms: eye; eye surgery; plastic surgery; eyelid surgery.

Blepharoplasty
Insurance, Health

Position Paper: Recommended Criteria for Insurance Coverage of Blepharoplasty. 1992. 2pp. Sponsored by the American Society of Plastic and Reconstructive Surgeons. To order call ASPRS 847 228-9900.

Blepharoplasty
Laser Surgery

Laser Blepharoplasty and Skin Resurfacing Ophthalmic Procedure Assessment. *Ophthalmology.* 1998;105:2154-2159. 6pp. 34refs. Sponsored by the American Academy of Ophthalmology. Cost: $11 members, $16 nonmembers. AAO members first copy free upon publication. To order call AAO Order Dept 415 561-8540. Key terms: eye; eye surgery; eye laser surgery; plastic surgery; cosmetic surgery.

Blood Banks/Standards
Blood Donors

US Public Health Service Guidelines for Testing and Counseling Blood and Plasma Donors for Human Immunodeficiency Virus Type 1 Antigen. *Morbid Mortal Weekly Report.* 1996;45(no. RR-2). Sponsored by the Centers for Disease Control and Prevention. Cost: $1. To order call US Govt Printing Office 202 783-3238.

Blood Cell Count
Leukocyte Count

Complete Blood Count and Leukocyte Differential Count: An Approach to Their Rational Application. *Ann Intern Med.* 1987;106:65-74. 10pp. Sponsored by the American College of Physicians. To order call ACP Clinical Efficacy Assessment Project 1 800 523-1546.

Blood Cells/Radiation Effects
Blood Component Transfusion/
Standards

Use of Irradiated Blood Components. *Am J Clin Pathol.* 1996;106:6-11. 5pp. 55refs. Sponsored by the American Society of Clinical Pathologists. Cost: free copy. To order call Felicia Nelson 312 738-1336 x1350. Key terms: transfusion-associated graft-versus-host disease; blood irradiation; platelet irradiation; directed donations; family donors.

Blood Chemical Analysis
Mass Screening/Methods

Biochemical Profiles: Applications in Ambulatory Screening and Preadmission Testing of Adults. *Ann Intern Med*. 1987;106:403-413. 11pp. Sponsored by the American College of Physicians. To order call ACP Clinical Efficacy Assessment Project 1 800 523-1546.

Blood Component Transfusion

Blood Component Therapy. *ACOG Technical Bulletin*. 1994;199. 6pp. 14refs. Sponsored by the American College of Obstetricians and Gynecologists. Cost: free copy. Set of Bulletins $70 + s/h ACOG members, $125 + s/h nonmembers. One-year subscription $55 member, $65 nonmember. To order single copy, call ACOG Resource Center 202 863-2518; to order set or subscription, call ACOG Distribution Center, 1 800 762-2264. Available on the Internet to members only at acog.org. Key terms: blood donations; autologous.

Blood Component Transfusion

Modern Component Usage in Transfusion Therapy, 1992. *Practice-Related Report of the AMA Council on Scientific Affairs*. 1992. Sponsored by the American Medical Association, Council on Scientific Affairs. Cost: free. To order call Nancy Nolan, AMA, 312 464-5046.

Blood Component Transfusion
Intraoperative Care

Perioperative Red Cell Transfusion. *NIH Consensus Development Conference Statement*. 1988;7(4):1-19[Conf. No. 70]. 20pp. Sponsored by the National Institutes of Health. Cost: free copy. To order call 1 888 644-2667. Available on the Internet at consensus.nih.gov.

Blood Component
Transfusion/Standards
Blood Preservation/Standards

Practice Parameter for the Use of Fresh-Frozen Plasma, Cryoprecipitate, and Platelets. *JAMA*. 1994;271:777-781. 5pp. 27refs. Sponsored by the College of American Pathologists. Cost: reprints: free. To order call CAP 1 800 323-4040 x7378. Key terms: transfusion medicine; blood component therapy; platelets; cryoprecipitate; FFP.

Blood Donors
Hepatitis B/Diagnosis

Public Health Service Inter-Agency Guidelines for Screening Donors of Blood, Plasma, Organs, Tissues, and Semen for Evidence of Hepatitis B and Hepatitis C. *Morbid Mortal Weekly Report*. 1991;40(no. RR-4):1-7. 7pp. 76refs. Sponsored by the Centers for Disease Control and Prevention. Cost: $1. To order call US Govt Printing Office 202 783-3238.

Blood Gas Analysis

Indications for Arterial Blood Gas Analysis. *Ann Intern Med*. 1986;105:390-398. 9pp. Sponsored by the American College of Physicians. To order call ACP Clinical Efficacy Assessment Project 1 800 523-1546.

Blood Glucose
Diabetes Mellitus, Insulin-Dependent

The Benefits and Risks of Controlling Blood Glucose Levels in Patients with Type 2 Diabetes Mellitus. 1999. Sponsored by the American Academy of Family Physicians. Available on the Internet at aafp.org/clinical/. Key terms: complications; management; glycemic control; family practice.

Blood Platelets
Blood Transfusion

Platelet Transfusion Therapy. *NIH Consensus Development Conference Statement*. 1986;6(7):1-6[Conf. No .59]. 7pp. Sponsored by the National Institutes of Health. Cost: free copy. To order call 1 888 644-2667. Available on the Internet at consensus.nih.gov.

Blood Platelets
Skin Ulcer/Drug Therapy

Procuren: A Platelet-Derived Wound Healing Formula. *AHCPR Health Technology Review*. 1992;No. 2 (AHCPR Publication No. 92-0065). 3pp. 7refs. Sponsored by the Federal Agency for Health Care Policy and Research. To order call AHCPR Clearinghouse 1 800 358-9295.

Blood Pressure Determination/ Instrumentation

Improving Clinical and Consumer Use of Blood Pressure Measuring Devices. *NIH Consensus Development Conference Statement*. 1979;2(4):23-27[Conf. No. 14]. 4pp. Sponsored by the National Institutes of Health. Cost: free copy. To order call 1 888 644-2667. Available on the Internet at consensus.nih.gov.

Blood Pressure Determination/Methods
Blood Pressure Monitors

Human Blood Pressure Determination by Sphygmomanometry. *Circulation*. 1993;88:2460-2470. 11pp. 43refs. Sponsored by the American Heart Association. Cost: free copy. To order call 1 800 242-8721 (US only) or write to: American Heart Association, Public Inquiries, 7272 Greenville Ave, Dallas TX 75231-4596.

Blood Pressure Monitoring, Ambulatory
Electrocardiography,
Ambulatory/Standards

Automated Ambulatory Blood Pressure Monitoring. 1993. Sponsored by the American College of Physicians. To order call ACP Clinical Efficacy Assessment Project 1 800 523-1546.

Blood Pressure Monitors/Standards

Position Statement: Ambulatory Blood Pressure Monitoring. *J Am Coll Cardiol*. 1994. Sponsored by the American College of Cardiology. Cost: free copy. To order call Educational Services Department 1 800 257-4740.

Blood Sedimentation

Erythrocyte Sedimentation Rate: Guidelines for Rational Use. *Ann Intern Med*. 1986;104:515-523. 9pp. Sponsored by the American College of Physicians. To order call ACP Clinical Efficacy Assessment Project 1 800 523-1546.

Blood Transfusion
Communicable Diseases/Diagnosis

Infectious Disease Testing for Blood Transfusions. *NIH Consensus Development Conference Statement*. 1995;13(1):1-27[Conf. No. 99]. 27pp. Sponsored by the National Institutes of Health. Cost: free copy. To order call 1 888 644-2667. Available on the Internet at consensus.nih.gov.

Blood Transfusion
Plasma

Fresh Frozen Plasma: Indications and Risks. *NIH Consensus Development Conference Statement*. 1984;5(5):1-12[Conf. No. 45]. 13pp. Sponsored by the National Institutes of Health. Cost: free copy. To order call 1 888 644-2667. Available on the Internet at consensus.nih.gov.

Blood Transfusion, Autologous
Transplantation, Autologous

Transfusion Alert: Use of Autologous Blood. *NIH Publication No. 94-3038*. 1994;20pp. 81rcfs. Sponsored by the National Heart, Lung, and Blood Institute. Cost: $3. To order contact the NHLBI Information Center, PO Box 30105, Bethesda, MD 20824-0105, 301 251-1222.

Blood Vessel Prosthesis
Prosthesis Design

Guidelines for the Development and Use of Transluminally Placed Endovascular Prosthetic Grafts in the Arterial System. *JVIR*. 1995;6(3):477-492. 16pp. 37refs. Sponsored by the Society of Cardiovascular and Interventional Radiology. Cost: free copy. To order call SCVIR 703 691-1805. Key terms: arteries; grafts; prostheses.

Blood Vessels/Ultrasonography

Ultrasonic Imaging of the Vascular System. *Practice-Related Report of the AMA Council on Scientific Affairs*. 1990. 21pp. 73refs. Sponsored by the American Medical Association, Council on Scientific Affairs. Cost: free. To order call Nancy Nolan, AMA, 312 464-5046.

Bloodborne Pathogens
HIV Infections/Prevention and Control

SCVIR HIV/Bloodborne Pathogens Guidelines. *JVIR*. 1997;8:667-676. 10pp. 60refs. Sponsored by the Society of Cardiovascular and Interventional Radiology. Cost: free copy. To order call SCVIR 703 691-1805. Key terms: hepatitis; human immunodeficiency virus; radiology and radiologists.

Blunt Trauma (see Wounds, Nonpenetrating)

Body Composition
Electric Impedance

Bioelectrical Impedance Analysis in Body Composition Measurement. *NIH Technology Assessment Conference Statement*. 1994. 35pp. Sponsored by the National Institutes of Health. Cost: free copy. To order call 1 888 644-2667. Available on the Internet at consensus.nih.gov.

Body Height
Growth Substances/Therapeutic Use

Growth Hormone for Short Stature. *Diagnostic and Therapeutic Technology Assessment (DATTA)*. 1996. 16pp. 101refs. Sponsored by the American Medical Association, Diagnostic and Therapeutic Technology Assessment Program. Cost: free copy. DATTA subscription available. To order call AMA Department of Technology Assessment 312 464-4531.

Bone and Bones/Radiography

ACR Standard for Skeletal Surveys in Children. 1997. 4pp. 11refs. Sponsored by the American College of Radiology. Cost: $25 (ACR nonmembers). To order call ACR Dept of Quality Assurance 703 716-7592. Available free on the Internet at acr.org. Key terms: pediatric; suspected abuse; bone; skeletal survey.

Bone and Bones/Radionuclide Imaging

Procedure Guideline for Bone Scintigraphy. *J Nuclear Med.* 1996;37:1903-1906. 4pp. 6refs. Sponsored by the Society of Nuclear Medicine. Cost: free. To order call Bill Uffelman 703 708-9000. Available on the Internet at snm.org. Key terms: bone scintigraphy; routine diagnostic tests; radionuclide imaging; neoplasm metastasis; skeleton.

Bone Density

Clinical Indications for Bone Mass Measurements. *J Bone Mineral Research.* 1989;suppl 2. 28pp. 200refs. Sponsored by the National Osteoporosis Foundation. Cost: free copy. To order fax Fulfillment Department, NOF, 202 223-2237.

Bone Density
Absorptiometry, Photon

Bone Densitometry: Patients Receiving Prolonged Steroid Therapy. *AHCPR Health Technology Assessment.* 1996;No. 9 (AHCPR Publication No. 96-0058). 31pp. 198refs. Sponsored by the Federal Agency for Health Care Policy and Research. To order call AHCPR Clearinghouse 1 800 358-9295.

Bone Density
Densitometry, X-ray/Standards

Measurement of Bone Density with Dual Energy X-ray Absorptiometry (DEXA). *JAMA.* 1992;267:286-294. 9pp. 70refs. Sponsored by the American Medical Association, Diagnostic and Therapeutic Technology Assessment Program. Cost: free copy. DATTA subscription available. To order call AMA Department of Technology Assessment 312 464-4531.

Bone Diseases/Radionuclide Imaging

ACR Standard for the Performance of Skeletal Scintigraphy (Revised). 1998. 4pp. 7refs. Sponsored by the American College of Radiology. Cost: $25 (ACR nonmembers). To order call ACR Dept of Quality Assurance 703 716-7592. Available free on the Internet at acr.org. Key terms: bone; nuclear medicine; skeletal scintigraphy.

Bone Marrow Transplantation

Reassessment of Autologous Bone Marrow Transplantation. *JAMA.* 1990;263:881-887. 7pp. 57refs. Sponsored by the American Medical Association, Diagnostic and Therapeutic Technology Assessment Program. Cost: free copy. DATTA subscription available. To order call AMA Department of Technology Assessment 312 464-4531.

Bone Marrow Transplantation
Leukemia, Myeloid, Chronic/Surgery

Allogeneic Bone Marrow Transplantation for Chronic Myelogenous Leukemia. *JAMA.* 1990;264:3208-3211. 4pp. 37refs. Sponsored by the American Medical Association, Diagnostic and Therapeutic Technology Assessment Program. Cost: free copy. DATTA subscription available. To order call AMA Department of Technology Assessment 312 464-4531.

Bone Neoplasms/Secondary

Bone Metastases (25 variants). *Int J Radiat Oncol Biol Phys.* 1999;43(1):125-168. 31pp. 22refs. Sponsored by the American College of Radiology. Cost: Vols. 1 & 2 $25 each (ACR members); $75/set (ACR nonmembers). To order call ACR Appropriateness Criteria™ 703 716-7583 x7596. Available free on the Internet at acr.org/f-appcrit.html. Key terms: bone; metastases; palliation; radiotherapy.

Bone Screws
Spinal Fusion/Methods

Pedicle Screw Fixation System for Spinal Instability. *Diagnostic and Therapeutic Technology Assessment (DATTA).* 1997. 7pp. 16refs. Sponsored by the American Medical Association, Diagnostic and Therapeutic Technology Assessment Program. Cost: free copy. DATTA subscription available. To order call AMA Department of Technology Assessment 312 464-4531.

Botulinum Toxins/Therapeutic Use

Clinical Use of Botulinum Toxin. *NIH Consensus Development Conference Statement*. 1990;8(8):1-20[Conf. No. 83]. 21pp. Sponsored by the National Institutes of Health. Cost: free copy. To order call 1 888 644-2667. Available on the Internet at consensus.nih.gov.

Botulinum Toxins/Therapeutic Use
Nervous System Diseases/Drug Therapy

Assessment: The Clinical Usefulness of Botulinum Toxin-A in Treating Neurological Disorders. *Neurol*. 1990;40:1332-1336. 5pp. 62refs. Sponsored by the American Academy of Neurology. Cost: individual statements are free. To order call AAN Member Service Center 1 800 879-1960. Available on the Internet at aan.com.

Botulinum Toxins/Therapeutic Use
Nervous System Diseases/Drug Therapy

Training Guidelines for the Use of Botulinum Toxin for the Treatment of Neurologic Disorders. *Neurol*. 1994;44:2401-2403. 3pp. 26refs. Sponsored by the American Academy of Neurology. Cost: individual statements are free. To order call AAN Member Service Center 1 800 879-1960. Available on the Internet at aan.com.

Brachial Plexus/Injuries
Microsurgery

Microsurgical Reconstruction for Brachial Plexus Injury. *Diagnostic and Therapeutic Technology Assessment (DATTA)*. 1986. Sponsored by the American Medical Association, Diagnostic and Therapeutic Technology Assessment Program. Cost: free copy. DATTA subscription available. To order call AMA Department of Technology Assessment 312 464-4531.

Brachytherapy
Physics

ACR Standard for Brachytherapy Physics: Manually Loaded Sources. 1995. 8pp. 11refs. Sponsored by the American College of Radiology. Cost: $25 (ACR nonmembers). To order call ACR Dept of Quality Assurance 703 716-7592. Available free on the Internet at acr.org. Key terms: radiation oncology; physics; brachytherapy.

Brachytherapy
Radiation Dosage

ACR Standard for the Performance of High-Dose-Rate Brachytherapy. 1996. 6pp. 1ref. Sponsored by the American College of Radiology. Cost: $25 (ACR nonmembers). To order call ACR Dept of Quality Assurance 703 716-7592. Available free on the Internet at acr.org. Key terms: radiation oncology; brachytherapy.

Brachytherapy
Radiation Dosage

ACR Standard for the Performance of Low-Dose-Rate Brachytherapy. 1996. 6pp. 1ref. Sponsored by the American College of Radiology. Cost: $25 (ACR nonmembers). To order call ACR Dept of Quality Assurance 703 716-7592. Available free on the Internet at acr.org. Key terms: radiation oncology; brachytherapy.

Brain/Physiology
Electroencephalogy/Methods

Assessment of Digital EEG, Quantitive EEG, and EEG Brain Mapping. *Neurol*. 1997;49:277-292. 16pp. 352refs. Sponsored by the American Academy of Neurology, American Clinical Neurophysiology Society. Cost: individual statements are free. To order call AAN Member Service Center 1 800 879-1960. Available on the Internet at aan.com.

Brain/Radionuclide Imaging

ACR Standard for the Performance of Cerebral Scintigraphy. 1999. 4pp. 8refs. Sponsored by the American College of Radiology. Cost: $25 (ACR nonmembers). To order call ACR Dept of Quality Assurance 703 716-7592. Available free on the Internet at acr.org. Key terms: brain death; cerebral; scintigraphy.

Brain/Radionuclide Imaging
Nuclear Medicine

Procedure Guideline for Brain Perfusion Single Photon Emission Computed Tomography (SPECT) Using Tc99m Radiopharmaceuticals. *J Nuclear Med*. 1998;39:923-926. 4pp. 10refs. Sponsored by the Society of Nuclear Medicine. Cost: free. To order call Bill Uffelman 703 708-9000. Available on the Internet at snm.org. Key terms: brain SPECT perfusion scintigraphy; single-photon emission-computed tomography; cerebrovascular circulation; diagnostic tests; radionuclide imaging.

Subject

Brain/Radionuclide Imaging Tomography, Emission-Computed, Single-Photon

Assessment of Brain SPECT. *Neurol.* 1996;46:278-285. 8pp. 97refs. Sponsored by the American Academy of Neurology. Cost: individual statements are free. To order call AAN Member Service Center 1 800 879-1960. Available on the Internet at aan.com.

Brain Abscess/Surgery
Craniotomy
Brain Neoplasms/Surgery

Craniotomy for Tumor of Brain or Associated Structures, or Brain Abscess. 1993. Sponsored by the American Association of Neurological Surgeons. To order call AANS 847 692-9500.

Brain Chemistry
Tomography, Emission-Computed

Positron Emission Tomography—A New Approach to Brain Chemistry. *JAMA.* 1988;260:2704-2710. 7pp. Sponsored by the American Medical Association, Council on Scientific Affairs. Cost: free. To order call Nancy Nolan, AMA, 312 464-5046.

Brain Death/Diagnosis

Practice Parameter: Determining Brain Death in Adults. *Neurol.* 1995;45:1012-1014. 3pp. Sponsored by the American Academy of Neurology. Cost: individual statements are free. To order call AAN Member Service Center 1 800 879-1960. Available on the Internet at aan.com.

Brain Injuries/Physiopathology
Intracranial Pressure
Cerebral Ischemia/Physiopathology

Cerebral Perfusion Pressure Monitoring. *Guidelines for the Management of Severe Head Injury.* 1996;95-104. 10pp. Sponsored by the American Association of Neurological Surgeons. Cost: $45. To order call AANS 847 692-9500.

Brain Injuries/Rehabilitation

Rehabilitation of Persons with Traumatic Brain Injury. *NIH Consensus Development Conference Statement.* 1998;16(1):1[Conf. No. 109]. 30pp. 66refs. Sponsored by the National Institutes of Health. Cost: free copy. To order call 1 888 644-2667. Available on the Internet at consensus.nih.gov.

Brain Injuries/Therapy
Nutritional Support

Nutritional Support. *Guidelines for the Management of Severe Head Injury.* 1996;144-159. 16pp. Sponsored by the American Association of Neurological Surgeons. Cost: $45. To order call AANS 847 692-9500.

Breast/Abnormalities
Mammaplasty

Female Breast Hypoplasia/Breast Augmentation. 1996. 4pp. Sponsored by the American Society of Plastic and Reconstructive Surgeons. Cost: $25 members, $55 nonmembers (full set of guidelines), + s/h. To order call 1 800 766-4955.

Breast/Pathology
Frozen Sections

Breast Frozen Section Biopsies. *Am J Clin Pathol.* 1995;103:6-7. 2pp. 9refs. Sponsored by the American Society of Clinical Pathologists. Cost: free copy. To order call Felicia Nelson 312 738-1336 x1350. Key terms: breast; breast biopsy; carcinoma of breast; frozen section; intraoperative consultation.

Breast/Pathology
Mammaplasty

Female Breast Hypertrophy/Breast Reduction. 1993. 7pp. Sponsored by the American Society of Plastic and Reconstructive Surgeons. Cost: $25 members, $55 nonmembers (full set of guidelines), + s/h. To order call 1 800 766-4955.

Breast Diseases

Nonmalignant Conditions of the Breast. *ACOG Technical Bulletin.* 1991;156. 6pp. 18refs. Sponsored by the American College of Obstetricians and Gynecologists. Cost: free copy. Set of Bulletins $70 + s/h ACOG members, $125 + s/h nonmembers. One-year subscription $55 member, $65 nonmember. To order single copy, call ACOG Resource Center 202 863-2518; to order set or subscription, call ACOG Distribution Center, 1 800 762-2264. Available on the Internet to members only at acog.org. Key terms: breast disease.

Breast Diseases/Diagnosis

Role of the Obstetrician-Gynecologist in the Diagnosis and Treatment of Breast Disease. *ACOG Committee Opinion*. 1997;186. 2pp. 7refs. Sponsored by the American College of Obstetricians and Gynecologists. Cost: free copy. Set of Opinions $55 + s/h ACOG members, $75 + s/h nonmembers. One-year subscription $55 member, $65 nonmember. To order single copy, call ACOG Resource Center 202 863-2518; to order set or subscription, call ACOG Distribution Center, 1 800 762-2264. Available on the Internet to members only at acog.org. Key terms: breast disease; physician's role; gynecology; biopsy.

Breast Diseases/Ultrasonography

ACR Standard for the Performance of Breast Ultrasound Examination. 1998. 6pp. 12refs. Sponsored by the American College of Radiology. Cost: $25 (ACR nonmembers). To order call ACR Dept of Quality Assurance 703 716-7592. Available free on the Internet at acr.org. Key terms: breast evaluation; surgery; ultrasound-guided.

Breast Feeding
Hepatitis C/Transmission

Breastfeeding and the Risk of Hepatitis C Virus Transmission. *ACOG Committee Opinion*. 1999;220. 1pp. 1refs. Sponsored by the American College of Obstetricians and Gynecologists. Cost: free copy. Set of Bulletins $70 + s/h ACOG members, $125 + s/h nonmembers. One-year subscription $55 member, $65 nonmember. To order single copy, call ACOG Resource Center 202 863-2518; to order set or subscription, call ACOG Distribution Center, 1 800 762-2264. Available on the Internet to members only at acog.org. Key terms: Hepatitis C; breast feeding.

Breast Feeding
Organizational Policy
Pediatrics

Breastfeeding and the Use of Human Milk. *Pediatr.* 1997;100(6):1035-1039. 5pp. 111refs. Sponsored by the American Academy of Pediatrics. Cost: $1.95. Discounted set of policies available. To order call 1 800 433-9016.

Breast Implants
Re-Operation

Position Paper: Recommended Criteria for Insurance Coverage of Re-Operation on Women with Breast Implants. 1992. 2pp. Sponsored by the American Society of Plastic and Reconstructive Surgeons. To order call ASPRS 847 228-9900.

Breast Implants/Adverse Effects
Nervous System Diseases/Etiology
Silicones

Silicone Breast Implants and Neurologic Disorders. *Neurol.* 1997;48:1504-1507. 4pp. 16refs. Sponsored by the American Academy of Neurology. Cost: individual statements are free. To order call AAN Member Service Center 1 800 879-1960. Available on the Internet at aan.com.

Breast Neoplasms

Locally Advanced Breast Cancer (5 variants). 1996. 19pp. 111refs. Sponsored by the American College of Radiology. Cost: Vols. 1 & 2 $25 each (ACR members); $75/set (ACR nonmembers). To order call ACR Appropriateness Criteria™ 703 716-7583 x7596. Available free on the Internet at acr.org/f-appcrit.html. Key terms: breast neoplasms; locally advanced; radiotherapy; outcomes.

Breast Neoplasms

Standards for Diagnosis and Management of Invasive Breast Carcinoma (Revised). *CA.* 1997;48(2):83-107. 21pp. 92refs. Sponsored by the American College of Radiology, American College of Surgeons, College of American Pathologists, Society of Surgical Oncology. Cost: $25 (ACR nonmembers). To order call ACR Dept of Quality Assurance 703 716-7592. Available free on the Internet at acr.org. Key terms: breast cancer; conserving surgery; radiation therapy.

Breast Neoplasms
Health Personnel

Screening for Breast Cancer for Health Professionals. 1996. 18pp. Sponsored by the National Cancer Institute. To order call 1 800 4CA-NCER. Also available on the Internet, at http://cancernet.nci.nih.gov.

Breast Neoplasms/Diagnosis
Breast Neoplasms/Surgery

Conservative Surgery and Radiation in the Treatment of Stage I and II Carcinoma of the Breast (9 variants). 1996. 18pp. 22refs. Sponsored by the American College of Radiology. Cost: Vols. 1 & 2 $25 each (ACR members); $75/set (ACR nonmembers). To order call ACR Appropriateness Criteria™ 703 716-7583 x7596. Available free on the Internet at acr.org/f-appcrit.html. Key terms: breast neoplasm; radiotherapy; breast-conserving therapy.

Breast Neoplasms/Diagnosis
Breast Neoplasms/Therapy

Carcinoma of the Breast. *ACOG Technical Bulletin.* 1991;158. 7pp. 25refs. Sponsored by the American College of Obstetricians and Gynecologists. Cost: free copy. Set of Bulletins $70 + s/h ACOG members, $125 + s/h nonmembers. One-year subscription $55 member, $65 nonmember. To order single copy, call ACOG Resource Center 202 863-2518; to order set or subscription, call ACOG Distribution Center, 1 800 762-2264. Available on the Internet to members only at acog.org. Key terms: breast neoplasms.

Breast Neoplasms/Diagnosis
Breast Neoplasms/Therapy
Medical Oncology/Standards

1998 Update of Recommended Breast Cancer Surveillance Guidelines. *J Clin Oncol.* 1999;17:1080-1082. 3pp. 5refs. Sponsored by the American Society of Clinical Oncology. Cost: free copy. To order call ASCO 703 299-0150 or e-mail: guidelines@asco.org. Available free on the Internet at asco.org.

Breast Neoplasms/Diagnosis
Medical Oncology

Recommended Breast Cancer Surveillance Guidelines. *J Clin Oncol.* 1997;15:2149-2156. 8pp. 38refs. Sponsored by the American Society of Clinical Oncology. Cost: free copy. To order call ASCO 703 299-0150 or e-mail: guidelines@asco.org. Available free on the Internet at asco.org.

Breast Neoplasms/Diagnosis
Ovarian Neoplasms/Diagnosis

Breast-Ovarian Cancer Screening. *ACOG Committee Opinion.* 1996;176. 2pp. Sponsored by the American College of Obstetricians and Gynecologists. Cost: free copy. Set of Opinions $55 + s/h ACOG members, $75 + s/h nonmembers. One-year subscription $55 member, $65 nonmember. To order single copy, call ACOG Resource Center 202 863-2518; to order set or subscription, call ACOG Distribution Center, 1 800 762-2264. Available on the Internet to members only at acog.org. Key terms: BRCAI+2; genetic screening; genetic counseling; breast neoplasms; ovarian neoplasms.

Breast Neoplasms/Drug Therapy
Antineoplastic Agents, Combined/
Therapeutic Use

Systemic Therapy for Breast Cancer. *Practice-Related Report of the AMA Council on Scientific Affairs.* 1991. Sponsored by the American Medical Association, Council on Scientific Affairs. Cost: free. To order call Nancy Nolan, AMA, 312 464-5046.

Breast Neoplasms/
Prevention and Control
Mammography

Mammography Screening in Asymptomatic Women Forty Years and Older. *JAMA.* 1989;261:2535-2542. 8pp. Sponsored by the American Medical Association, Council on Scientific Affairs. Cost: free. To order call Nancy Nolan, AMA, 312 464-5046.

Breast Neoplasms/
Prevention and Control
Mammography

Practice Policy Statement: Screening Mammography for Breast Cancer. *Am J Prev Med.* 1996;12(5):340-341. 2pp. 14refs. Sponsored by the American College of Preventive Medicine. To order reprint address request to ACPM, 1660 L St NW, #206, Washington, DC 20036.

Breast Neoplasms/
Prevention and Control
Mammography/Standards

Breast Cancer Screening for Women Ages 40-49. *NIH Consensus Development Conference Statement.* 1997;15(1):1-35[Conf. No.103]. 35pp. 74refs. Sponsored by the National Institutes of Health. Cost: free copy. To order call 1 888 644-2667. Available on the Internet at consensus.nih.gov.

Breast Neoplasms/
Prevention and Control
Mass Screening

Screening for Breast Cancer. *Ann Intern Med.* 1989;111:389-399. 11pp. 30refs. Sponsored by the American College of Physicians. To order call ACP Clinical Efficacy Assessment Project 1 800 523-1546.

Breast Neoplasms/ Prevention and Control
Mastectomy

Position Paper: Recommended Criteria for Insurance Coverage of Prophylactic Mastectomy. 1992. 2pp. Sponsored by the American Society of Plastic and Reconstructive Surgeons. To order call ASPRS 847 228-9900.

Breast Neoplasms/Radiography

American Cancer Society Guidelines for the Early Detection of Breast Cancer: Update 1997. *CA-A Cancer J for Clinicians*. 1997;47:150-153. 4pp. 15refs. Sponsored by the American Cancer Society. To order contact local American Cancer Society office. Key terms: breast cancer; screening; cancer detection; mammography; breast exam.

Breast Neoplasms/Radionuclide Imaging Technetium Tc99mSestamibi/ Diagnostic Use

Procedure Guideline for Breast Scintigraphy. *J Nucl Med*. 1999;40:1233-1235. 3pp. 9refs. Sponsored by the Society of Nuclear Medicine. Cost: free. To order call Bill Uffelman 703 708-9000. Available on the Internet at snm.org.

Breast Neoplasms/Radiotherapy

Postmastectomy Radiotherapy (15 variants). 1996. 27pp. 76refs. Sponsored by the American College of Radiology. Cost: Vols. 1 & 2 $25 each (ACR members); $75/set (ACR nonmembers). To order call ACR Appropriateness Criteria™ 703 716-7583 x7596. Available free on the Internet at acr.org/f-appcrit.html. Key terms: breast neoplasms; postmastectomy; radiotherapy.

Breast Neoplasms/Surgery
Medical Oncology/Methods

Breast Cancer Surgical Practice Guidelines. *Oncology*. 1997;11(6):877. 7pp. 17refs. Sponsored by the Society of Surgical Oncology. Cost: call 516 424-8900 x316. To order write Oncology, PRR, Inc, 17 Prospect St, Huntington NY 11743. Key terms: breast.

Breast Neoplasms/Therapy

Early Stage Breast Cancer. *NIH Consensus Development Conference Statement*. 1990;8(6):1-19[Conf. No. 81]. 19pp. Sponsored by the National Institutes of Health. Cost: free copy. To order call 1 888 644-2667. Available on the Internet at consensus.nih.gov.

Breast Neoplasms/Therapy
Glioma/Therapy
Hyperthermia, Induced

Hyperthermia as Adjuvant Treatment for Recurrent Breast Cancer and Primary Malignant Glioma. *Diagnostic and Therapeutic Technology Assessment (DATTA)*. 1994. 15pp. 42refs. Sponsored by the American Medical Association, Diagnostic and Therapeutic Technology Assessment Program. Cost: free copy. DATTA subscription available. To order call AMA Department of Technology Assessment 312 464-4531.

Breath Tests
Carbon Radioisotopes/Diagnostic Use

Procedure Guideline for C-14 Urea Breath Test. *J Nuclear Med*. 1998;39:2012-2014. 3pp. 4refs. Sponsored by the Society of Nuclear Medicine. Cost: free. To order call Bill Uffelman 703 708-9000. Available on the Internet at snm.org. Key terms: peptic ulcer; Helicobacter pylori; C-14 urea breath test; routine diagnostics tests; radionuclide imaging.

Breech Presentation
Delivery

Management of Breech Presentation. *ACOG Technical Bulletin*. 1986;95. 4pp. 10refs. Sponsored by the American College of Obstetricians and Gynecologists. Cost: free copy. Set of Bulletins $70 + s/h ACOG members, $125 + s/h nonmembers. One-year subscription $55 member, $65 nonmember. To order single copy, call ACOG Resource Center 202 863-2518; to order set or subscription, call ACOG Distribution Center, 1 800 762-2264. Available on the Internet to members only at acog.org.

Bromocriptine/Therapeutic Use

Use of Bromocriptine. 1991. 4pp. 21refs. Sponsored by the American Society for Reproductive Medicine. Cost: $1. To order call ASRM Publication Department 205 978-5000.

Bronchoalveolar Lavage Fluid
Lung Diseases/Diagnosis

Clinical Role of Bronchoalveolar Lavage. *Amer Rev Resp Dis*. 1990;142:2. Sponsored by the American Thoracic Society. Cost: $4. To order send check payable to American Thoracic Society, 1740 Broadway, New York, NY 10019-4374; for credit card orders, call 212 315-8863.

Bronchoscopy

Flexible Endoscopy of the Pediatric Airway. *Amer Rev Resp Dis.* 1992;145:1. Sponsored by the American Thoracic Society. Cost: $4. To order send check payable to American Thoracic Society, 1740 Broadway, New York, NY 10019-4374; for credit card orders, call 212 315-8863.

Bulimia
Anorexia Nervosa

Eating Disorders: Anorexia Nervosa and Bulimia: Position Paper. *Ann Intern Med.* 1986;105:790-794. 5pp. Sponsored by the American College of Physicians. To order call ACP Clinical Efficacy Assessment Project 1 800 523-1546.

Bunyaviridae Infections/Prevention and Control
Hantavirus

Hantavirus Infection—Southwestern United States: Interim Recommendations for Risk Reduction. *Morbid Mortal Weekly Report.* 1993;42(no. RR-11). Sponsored by the Centers for Disease Control and Prevention. Cost: $1. To order call US Govt Printing Office 202 783-3238.

Bunyaviridae Infections/Prevention and Control
Laboratory Infection/Prevention and Control

Laboratory Management of Agents Associated with Hantavirus Pulmonary Syndrome: Interim Biosafety Guidelines. *Morbid Mortal Weekly Report.* 1994;43(no. RR-7). Sponsored by the Centers for Disease Control and Prevention. Cost: $1. To order call US Govt Printing Office 202 783-3238.

Cachexia/Therapy
HIV Infections

Guidelines for the Management of Malnutrition and Cachexia, Chronic Diarrhea, and Hepatobiliary Disease in Patients with HIV Infection. *Gastroenterology.* 1996;111:1722-1752. 32pp. 312refs. Sponsored by the American Gastroenterological Association. Cost: $3. To order call AGA 301 654-2055. Key terms: malnutrition; cachexia; diarrhea; hepatobiliary; HIV.

Calcium/Administration and Dosage Osteoporosis/Prevention and Control

Optimal Calcium Intake. *NIH Consensus Development Conference Statement.* 1994;12(4):1-31[Conf. No. 97]. 32pp. Sponsored by the National Institutes of Health. Cost: free copy. To order call 1 888 644-2667. Available on the Internet at consensus.nih.gov.

Canavan Disease/Diagnosis
Fetal Diseases/Diagnosis
Prenatal Diagnosis

Screening for Canavan Disease. *ACOG Committee Opinion.* 1998;212. 2pp. 6refs. Sponsored by the American College of Obstetricians and Gynecologists. Cost: free copy. Set of Bulletins $70 + s/h ACOG members, $125 + s/h nonmembers. One-year subscription $55 member, $65 nonmember. To order single copy, call ACOG Resource Center 202 863-2518; to order set or subscription, call ACOG Distribution Center, 1 800 762-2264. Available on the Internet to members only at acog.org. Key terms: Canavan Disease; genetic screening; genetic counseling; prenatal diagnosis.

Cancer (see Neoplasms; see Carcinoma)

Candidiasis, Chronic Mucocutaneous/ Drug Therapy

Superficial Mycotic Infections of the Skin: Mucocutaneous Candidiasis. *J Am Acad Derm.* 1996;34:110-115. 6pp. 17refs. Sponsored by the American Academy of Dermatology. Cost: free copy. To order call Alice Bell 847 330-0230 x333. Available on the Internet at aad.org. Key terms: chronic mucocutaneous candidiasis; diagnosis; drug therapy.

Candidiasis/Immunology
Hypersensitivity/Microbiology

Candidiasis Hypersensitivity Syndrome. *J Allergy Clin Immun.* 1986;78:269-277, Position Statement No. 14. 8pp. 4refs. Sponsored by the American Academy of Allergy, Asthma, and Immunology. Cost: free copy. Available on the Internet at aaaai.org/professional/ physicianreference/positionstatements/default.stm. To order call 414 272-6071.

Carcinoembryonic Antigen/Analysis
Neoplasms/Diagnosis

Carcinoembryonic Antigen. *Ann Intern Med.* 1986;104:66-73. 8pp. Sponsored by the American College of Physicians. To order call ACP Clinical Efficacy Assessment Project 1 800 523-1546.

Carcinoma In Situ
Carcinoma, Infiltrating Duct
Breast Neoplasms

Standards for Management of Ductal Carcinoma In Situ (DCIS) (Revised). *CA*. 1997;48(2):108-128. 21pp. Sponsored by the American College of Radiology, American College of Surgeons, College of American Pathologists, Society of Surgical Oncology. Cost: $25 (ACR nonmembers). To order call ACR Dept of Quality Assurance 703 716-7592. Available free on the Internet at acr.org. Key terms: breast cancer; DCIS; conserving surgery.

Carcinoma, Basal Cell/Therapy
Skin Neoplasms/Therapy

Guidelines of Care for Basal Cell Carcinoma. *J Am Acad Derm*. 1992;26:117-120. 4pp. 36refs. Sponsored by the American Academy of Dermatology. Cost: free copy. To order call Alice Bell 847 330-0230 x333. Available on the Internet at aad.org. Key terms: basal cell carcinoma; diagnosis; therapy; skin neoplasms.

Carcinoma, Infiltrating Duct
Carcinoma in Situ

Ductal Carcinoma in Situ and Microinvasive Disease (10 variants). *International Journal of Radiology Oncology Biology Physics*. 1999;43(1):125-168. 18pp. 33refs. Sponsored by the American College of Radiology. Cost: Vols. 1 & 2 $25 each (ACR members); $75/set (ACR nonmembers). To order call ACR Appropriateness Criteria™ 703 716-7583 x7596. Available free on the Internet at acr.org/f-appcrit.html. Key terms: breast neoplasms; pagets disease mammary.

Carcinoma, Squamous Cell/Therapy
Skin Neoplasms/Therapy

Guidelines of Care for Cutaneous Squamous Cell Carcinoma. *J Am Acad Derm*. 1993;28:628-631. 4pp. 23refs. Sponsored by the American Academy of Dermatology. Cost: free copy. To order call Alice Bell 847 330-0230 x333. Available on the Internet at aad.org. Key terms: squamous carcinoma; skin neoplasms; diagnosis; surgery; therapy.

Carcinoma, Non-Small-Cell Lung

Clinical Practice Guidelines for the Treatment of Unresectable Non-Small-Cell Lung Cancer. *J Clin Oncol*. 1997;15:2996-3018. 23pp. 159refs. Sponsored by the American Society of Clinical Oncology. Cost: free copy. To order call ASCO 703 299-0150 or e-mail: guidelines@asco.org. Available free on the Internet at asco.org.

Carcinoma, Non-Small-Cell Lung
Follow-Up Studies

Follow-Up of Non-Small-Cell Lung Carinoma (5 variants). 1996. 12pp. 33refs. Sponsored by the American College of Radiology. Cost: Vols. 1 & 2 $25 each (ACR members); $75/set (ACR nonmembers). To order call ACR Appropriateness Criteria™ 703 716-7583 x7596. Available free on the Internet at acr.org/f-appcrit.html. Key terms: lung cancer; follow-up.

Carcinoma, Non-Small-Cell
Lung/Radiotherapy

Postoperative Radiotherapy in Non-Small-Cell Lung Cancer (18 variants). 1996. 24pp. 21refs. Sponsored by the American College of Radiology. Cost: Vols. 1 & 2 $25 each (ACR members); $75/set (ACR nonmembers). To order call ACR Appropriateness Criteria™ 703 716-7583 x7596. Available free on the Internet at acr.org/f-appcrit.html. Key terms: lung cancer; postoperative; radiotherapy.

Carcinoma, Non-Small-Cell
Lung/Surgery

Neoadjuvant Therapy for Marginally Resectable (Clinical N2) Non-Small-Cell Lung Carcinoma (1 variant). 1996. 11pp. 62refs. Sponsored by the American College of Radiology. Cost: Vols. 1 & 2 $25 each (ACR members); $75/set (ACR nonmembers). To order call ACR Appropriateness Criteria™ 703 716-7583 x7596. Available free on the Internet at acr.org/f-appcrit.html. Key terms: lung cancer; neoadjuvant therapy; resectable.

Carcinoma, Non-Small-Cell
Lung/Therapy

Non-Aggressive, Non-Surgical Treatment of Inoperable Non-Small-Cell Lung Cancer. 1996. 18pp. 52refs. Sponsored by the American College of Radiology. Cost: Vols. 1 & 2 $25 each (ACR members); $75/set (ACR nonmembers). To order call ACR Appropriateness Criteria™ 703 716-7583 x7596. Available free on the Internet at acr.org/f-appcrit.html. Key terms: lung cancer; inoperable; nonsurgical treatment.

Carcinoma, Non-Small-Cell Lung/Therapy

Non-Small-Cell Lung Carcinoma, Non-Surgical Aggressive Therapy (8 variants). *International Journal of Radiation Oncology Biology Physics.* 1999;43(1):125-168. 13pp. 17refs. Sponsored by the American College of Radiology. Cost: Vols. 1 & 2 $25 each (ACR members); $75/set (ACR nonmembers). To order call ACR Appropriateness Criteria™ 703 716-7583 x7596. Available free on the Internet at acr.org/f-appcrit.html. Key terms: lung cancer; non-surgical therapy.

Cardiac Output Cardiography, Impedance

Measuring Cardiac Output by Electrical Bioimpedance. *AHCPR Health Technology Assessment.* 1991;No. 6 (AHCPR Publication No. 92-0073). 13pp. 132refs. Sponsored by the Federal Agency for Health Care Policy and Research. To order call AHCPR Clearinghouse 1 800 358-9295.

Cardiac Surgical Procedures Patient Admission

Position Statement: Same Day Surgical Admission. *J Am Coll Cardiol.* 1993;22:946-947. 2pp. 1ref. Sponsored by the American College of Cardiology. Cost: free copy. To order call Educational Services Department 1 800 257-4740.

Cardiology Ethics, Medical

Ethics in Cardiovascular Medicine. *J Am Coll Cardiol.* 1990. Sponsored by the American College of Cardiology. Cost: free copy. To order call Educational Services Department 1 800 257-4740.

Cardiology Heart Transplantation

Cardiac Transplantation: Recipient Selection, Donor Procurement, and Medical Follow-Up. *Circulation.* 1992;86:1061-1079. 19pp. 177refs. Sponsored by the American Heart Association. Cost: free copy. To order write the Office of Scientific Affairs, AHA, 7272 Greenville Ave, Dallas, TX 75231.

Cardiology Mucocutaneous Lymph Node Syndrome/Therapy

Guidelines for Long-Term Management of Patients with Kawasaki Disease. *Circulation.* 1994;89:916-922. 7pp. 17refs. Sponsored by the American Heart Association. Cost: free copy. To order call 1 800 242-8721 (US only) or write to: American Heart Association, Public Inquiries, 7272 Greenville Ave, Dallas TX 75231-4596.

Cardiology/Education

ACC Core Cardiology Training Symposium (COCATS) Guidelines for Training in Adult Cardiovascular Medicine. *J Am Coll Cardiol.* 1995;24:1-34. 35pp. Sponsored by the American College of Cardiology. Cost: free copy. To order call Educational Services Department 1 800 257-4740.

Cardiology/Manpower

Trends in the Practice of Cardiology: Implications for Manpower. *J Am Coll Cardiol.* 1988. Sponsored by the American College of Cardiology. Cost: free copy. To order call Educational Services Department 1 800 257-4740.

Cardiology/Standards Exercise Test/Standards

Guidelines for Exercise Testing. *Circulation.* 1997;96:345-354. 10pp. 343refs. Sponsored by the American Heart Association, American College of Cardiology. Cost: free copy. To order write the Office of Scientific Affairs, AHA, 7272 Greenville Ave, Dallas, TX 75231.

Cardiovascular Diseases

Cardiovascular Disease in the Elderly. *J Am Coll Cardiol.* 1987. Sponsored by the American College of Cardiology. Cost: free copy. To order call Educational Services Department 1 800 257-4740.

Cardiovascular Diseases/Diagnosis Electrocardiography

ACC/AHA Guidelines for Electrocardiography. *J Am Coll Cardiol.* 1992;19:473-481. 9pp. 34refs. Sponsored by the American College of Cardiology, American Heart Association. Cost: free copy. To order call Educational Services Department 1 800 257-4740.

Cardiovascular Diseases/Diagnosis
Electrocardiography

Guidelines for Electrocardiography. *Circulation.* 1992;85:1221-1228. 8pp. 34refs. Sponsored by the American Heart Association. Cost: free copy. To order call 1 800 242-8721 (US only) or write to: American Heart Association, Public Inquiries, 7272 Greenville Ave, Dallas TX 75231-4596.

Cardiovascular Diseases/Diagnosis
Heart Diseases/Diagnosis

Noninvasive Diagnostic Instrumentation for Assessment of Cardiovascular Disease in the Young. *J Am Coll Cardiol.* 1985. Sponsored by the American College of Cardiology. Cost: free copy. To order call Educational Services Department 1 800 257-4740.

Cardiovascular Diseases/Diagnosis
Magnetic Resonance Imaging

Magnetic Resonance Imaging of the Cardiovascular System. *JAMA.* 1988;259:253-259. 7pp. Sponsored by the American Medical Association, Council on Scientific Affairs. Cost: free. To order call Nancy Nolan, AMA, 312 464-5046.

Cardiovascular Diseases/Diagnosis
Sports

Cardiovascular Abnormalities in the Athlete: Recommendations Regarding Eligibility for Competition. *J Am Coll Cardiol.* 1994. Sponsored by the American College of Cardiology. Cost: free copy. To order call Educational Services Department 1 800 257-4740.

Cardiovascular Diseases/Epidemiology
Women's Health

Cardiovascular Disease in Women. *Circulation.* 1997;96:2468-2482. 14pp. 204refs. Sponsored by the American Heart Association. Cost: free copy. To order call 1 800 242-8721 (US only) or write to: American Heart Association, Public Inquiries, 7272 Greenville Ave, Dallas TX 75231-4596.

Cardiovascular Diseases/
Physiopathology
Surgical Procedures, Operative

Perioperative Cardiovascular Evaluation for Non-Cardiac Surgery. *Circulation.* 1996;93:1278-1317. 40pp. 229refs. Sponsored by the American Heart Association, American College of Cardiology. Cost: free copy. To order call Educational Services Department 1 800 257-4740.

Cardiovascular Diseases/
Prevention and Control
Exercise

Physical Activity and Cardiovascular Health. *NIH Consensus Development Conference Statement.* 1995;13(3):1-33[Conf. No. 101]. 34pp. Sponsored by the National Institutes of Health. Cost: free copy. To order call 1 888 644-2667. Available on the Internet at consensus.nih.gov.

Cardiovascular Diseases/
Prevention and Control
Postoperative Complication/
Prevention and Control

ACC/AHA Guidelines for Perioperative Cardiovascular Evaluation of Noncardiac Surgery. *J Am Coll Cardiol.* 1996;27(4):910-948. 38pp. 229refs. Sponsored by the American College of Cardiology, American Heart Association. Cost: free copy. To order call Educational Services Department 1 800 257-4740.

Cardiovascular Diseases/Radiography
Contrast Media

Position Statement: Use of Nonionic or Low Osmolar Contrast Agents in Cardiovascular Procedures. *J Am Coll Cardiol.* 1993;21:269-273. 5pp. 42refs. Sponsored by the American College of Cardiology. Cost: free copy. To order call Educational Services Department 1 800 257-4740.

Cardiovascular Diseases/Rehabilitation
Program Development

Cardiac Rehabilitation Programs. *Circulation.* 1994;90(30):1602-1610. 8pp. 144refs. Sponsored by the American Heart Association. Cost: free copy. To order call 1 800 242-8721 (US only) or write to: American Heart Association, Public Inquiries, 7272 Greenville Ave, Dallas TX 75231-4596.

Cardiovascular Diseases/Rehabilitation
Program Development

Cardiac Rehabilitation Programs. *AHCPR Health Technology Assessment.* 1991;No. 3 (AHCPR Publication No. 92-0015). 10pp. 40refs. Sponsored by the Federal Agency for Health Care Policy and Research. To order call AHCPR Clearinghouse 1 800 358-9295.

Cardiovascular Diseases/Therapy
Dental Care for Chronically Ill/Methods

Oral Health Care Series: Patients with Cardiovascular Disease. 1996. 19pp. 15refs. Sponsored by the American Dental Association. Cost: $8 ADA members, $12 nonmembers. To order call ADA Dept of Salable Materials 1 800 947-4776.

Cardiovascular Diseases/Therapy
Health Services Accessibility

Position Statement: Access to Cardiovascular Care. 1992. 3pp. Sponsored by the American College of Cardiology. Cost: free copy. To order call Educational Services Department 1 800 257-4740.

Care Management
Managed Care Programs

Care Management, Position Statement. 1998. Sponsored by the American Geriatrics Society.

Carotid Arteries/Surgery
Endarterectomy

Interim Assessment: Carotid Endarterectomy. *Neurol.* 1990;40:682-683. 2pp. 11refs. Sponsored by the American Academy of Neurology. Cost: individual statements are free. To order call AAN Member Service Center 1 800 879-1960. Available on the Internet at aan.com.

Carotid Artery Diseases/Diagnosis

Diagnostic Evaluation of Carotid Arteries. *Ann Intern Med.* 1988;109:835-837. 3pp. Sponsored by the American College of Physicians. To order call ACP Clinical Efficacy Assessment Project 1 800 523-1546.

Carotid Artery Diseases/Surgery
Endarterectomy, Carotid

Guidelines for Carotid Endarterectomy. *Circulation.* 1995;91:566-579. 14pp. 175refs. Sponsored by the American Heart Association. Cost: free copy. To order call 1 800 242-8721 (US only) or write to: American Heart Association, Public Inquiries, 7272 Greenville Ave, Dallas TX 75231-4596.

Carotid Artery Diseases/ Ultrasonography

ACR Standard for the Performance of an Ultrasound Examination of the Extracranial Cerebrovascular System (Revised). 1998. 5pp. 7refs. Sponsored by the American College of Radiology. Cost: $25 (ACR nonmembers). To order call ACR Dept of Quality Assurance 703 716-7592. Available free on the Internet at acr.org. Key terms: cerebrovascular; ultrasound; extracranial.

Carotid Body/Surgery

Carotid Body Resection. *J Allergy Clin Immun.* 1986;78:269-277, Position Statement No. 14. 2pp. 15refs. Sponsored by the American Academy of Allergy, Asthma, and Immunology. Cost: free copy. To order call 414 272-6071.

Carotid Stenosis/Diagnosis

Screening for Asymptomatic Carotid Artery Stenosis. *Guide to Clinical Preventive Services, 2nd Ed.* 1996. Sponsored by the US Preventive Services Task Force. To order call Williams & Wilkins 1 800 638-0672.

Carpal Tunnel Syndrome/Diagnosis
Carpal Tunnel Syndrome/Therapy

Practice Parameters: Carpal Tunnel Syndrome. *Neurol.* 1993;43:2406-2409. 4pp. 1ref. Sponsored by the American Academy of Neurology. Cost: individual statements are free. To order call AAN Member Service Center 1 800 879-1960. Available on the Internet at aan.com.

Carpal Tunnel Syndrome/Diagnosis
Electrodiagnosis

Practice Parameter for Electrodiagnostic Studies in Carpal Tunnel Syndrome. *Muscle Nerve.* 1999;8(suppl):S141-S167. 27pp. 165refs. Sponsored by the American Association of Electrodiagnostic Medicine. Cost: $10 members, $20 nonmembers. To order write AAEM, 421 First Avenue SW, #300E, Rochester, MN 55902. Key terms: carpal tunnel syndrome; electromyography; literature review; nerve conduction study; reference values.

Carpal Tunnel Syndrome/Diagnosis
Electrodiagnosis

Practice Parameter for Electrodiagnostic Studies in Carpal Tunnel Syndrome. *Neurol.* 1993;43:2404-2405. 2pp. Sponsored by the American Academy of Neurology. Cost: individual statements are free. To order call AAN Member Service Center 1 800 879-1960. Available on the Internet at aan.com.

Carpal Tunnel Syndrome/Surgery

Carpal Tunnel Release. 1993. Sponsored by the American Association of Neurological Surgeons. To order call AANS 847 692-9500.

Carpal Tunnel Syndrome/Surgery
Surgical Procedures, Endoscopic

Carpal Tunnel Syndrome. *Practice-Related Report of the AMA Council on Scientific Affairs.* 1991. Sponsored by the American Medical Association, Council on Scientific Affairs. Cost: free. To order call Nancy Nolan, AMA, 312 464-5046.

Carpal Tunnel Syndrome/Surgery
Surgical Procedures, Endoscopic

Endoscopic Release of the Carpal Ligament. *Diagnostic and Therapeutic Technology Assessment (DATTA).* 1992;11pp. 26refs. Sponsored by the American Medical Association, Diagnostic and Therapeutic Technology Assessment Program. Cost: free copy. DATTA subscription available. To order call AMA Department of Technology Assessment 312 464-4531.

CAT Scan (See Tomography, X-ray Computed)

Cataract
Cataract Extraction

Cataract in the Adult Eye. 1996. 24pp. 73refs. Sponsored by the American Academy of Ophthalmology. Cost: $11 members, $16 nonmembers. AAO members first copy free upon publication. To order call AAO Order Dept 415 561-8540. Key terms: eye; eye surgery; cataract.

Cataract/Therapy
Cataract Extraction

Cataract in Adults: Management of Functional Impairment. *AHCPR.* 1993;Publication No. 93-0542. 226pp. 324refs. Sponsored by the Federal Agency for Health Care Policy and Research. To order call AHCPR Clearinghouse 1 800 358-9295.

Cataract Extraction

Cataract Surgery. 1993. JRA-06. 292pp. 296refs. Sponsored by RAND. To order call RAND 310 393-0411 x7002. Key terms: cataract surgery; appropriateness; treatment outcomes; utilization; complications.

Catheter Ablation
Heart Diseases/Surgery

Guidelines for Clinical Intracardiac Electrophysiologic and Catheter Ablation Procedures. *Circulation.* 1995;92(3):673-691. 19pp. 182refs. Sponsored by the American Heart Association, American College of Cardiology. Cost: free copy. To order call 1 800 242-8721 (US only) or write to: American Heart Association, Public Inquiries, 7272 Greenville Ave, Dallas TX 75231-4596.

Catheter Ablation
Heart Diseases/Surgery

ACC/AHA Guidelines for Clinical Intracardiac Electrophysiologic and Catheter Ablation Procedures (Revision of 1989 Guidelines). *J Am Coll Cardiol.* 1995;26(2):555-573. 19pp. 182refs. Sponsored by the American College of Cardiology, American Heart Association. Cost: free copy. To order call Educational Services Department 1 800 257-4740.

Catheter Ablation
Tachycardia, Atrioventricular Nodal Reentry/Diagnosis

Radiofrequency Catheter Ablation of Aberrant Conducting Pathways of the Heart. *JAMA.* 1992;268:2091-2098. 4pp. 59refs. Sponsored by the American Medical Association, Diagnostic and Therapeutic Technology Assessment Program. Cost: free copy. DATTA subscription available. To order call AMA Department of Technology Assessment 312 464-4531.

Catheterization, Central Venous

Quality Improvement Guidelines for Central Venous Access. *JVIR.* 1997;8:475-479. 5pp. 59refs. Sponsored by the Society of Cardiovascular and Interventional Radiology. Cost: free copy. To order call SCVIR 703 691-1805. Key terms: catheters and catheterization; central venous access; interventional radiology.

Catheterization, Swan-Ganz

Practice Guidelines for Pulmonary Artery Catheterization Monitoring. *Anesthesiology.* 1993;78:380-394. 15pp. 89refs. Sponsored by the American Society of Anesthesiologists. Cost: free copy. To order call ASA 847 825-5586. Available on the Internet at asahq.org. Key terms: analgesia.

Cd4 Lymphocyte Count
HIV Infections/Immunology
Immunophenotyping/Standards

1997 Revised Guidelines for Performing CD4+ T-Cell Determinations in Persons Infected with Human Immunodeficiency Virus (HIV). *Morbid Mortal Weekly Report.* 1997;46(no. RR-2). Sponsored by the Centers for Disease Control and Prevention. Cost: $1. To order call US Govt Printing Office 202 783-3238.

Celiac Sprue (see Celiac Disease)

Central Nervous System
Diseases/Diagnosis
Magnetic Resonance Imaging

Magnetic Resonance Imaging of the Central Nervous System. *JAMA.* 1988;259:1211-1222. 12pp. Sponsored by the American Medical Association, Council on Scientific Affairs. Cost: free. To order call Nancy Nolan, AMA, 312 464-5046.

Central Nervous System Stimulants/
Therapeutic Use
Narcolepsy/Drug Therapy

Practice Parameters for the Use of Stimulants in the Treatment of Narcolepsy. *Sleep.* 1994;17(4):348-351. 4pp. 3refs. Sponsored by the American Academy of Sleep Medicine. Cost: $30 + s/h for a complete set of current AASM Guidelines. To order call AASM 507 287-6006. Key terms: cataplexy-narcolepsy; therapy-narcolepsy; drug therapy-pharmacology-sleep; REM.

Cerebral Angiography
Spinal Cord Injuries/Diagnosis
Subarachnoid Hemorrhage/Diagnosis

Angiography, Cerebral or Cervical. 1993. Sponsored by the American Association of Neurological Surgeons. To order call AANS 847 692-9500.

Cerebral Arteries/Physiopathology
Cerebrovascular Circulation

Assessment: Transcranial Doppler. *Neurol.* 1990;40:680-681. 2pp. 8refs. Sponsored by the American Academy of Neurology. Cost: individual statements are free. To order call AAN Member Service Center 1 800 879-1960. Available on the Internet at aan.com.

Cerebral Ischemia/Drug Therapy
CerebroVascular Disorders/
Drug Therapy

Practice Advisory: Thrombolytic Therapy for Acute Ischemic Stroke (rt-PA)—Summary Statement. *Neurol.* 1996;47:835-839. 5pp. 6refs. Sponsored by the American Academy of Neurology. Cost: individual statements are free. To order call AAN Member Service Center 1 800 879-1960. Available on the Internet at aan.com.

Cerebral Ischemia/
Prevention and Control
Cerebrovascular Disorders/
Prevention and Control

Extracranial-Intracranial Bypass to Reduce the Risk of Ischemic Stroke. *AHCPR Health Technology Assessment.* 1990;No. 6 (AHCPR Publication No. 91-3473). 9pp. 44refs. Sponsored by the Federal Agency for Health Care Policy and Research. To order call AHCPR Clearinghouse 1 800 358-9295.

Cerebral Ischemia/Therapy
Cerebrovascular Disorders/Therapy

Guidelines for the Management of Patients with Acute Ischemic Stroke. *Circulation.* 1994;90:1588-1601. 14pp. 179refs. Sponsored by the American Heart Association. Cost: free copy. To order call 1 800 242-8721 (US only) or write to: American Heart Association, Public Inquiries, 7272 Greenville Ave, Dallas TX 75231-4596.

Cerebral Ischemia, Transient/Therapy

Guidelines for the Management of Transient Ischemic Attacks. *Circulation.* 1994;89:1320-1335. 16pp. 184refs. Sponsored by the American Heart Association. Cost: free copy. To order call 1 800 242-8721 (US only) or write to: American Heart Association, Public Inquiries, 7272 Greenville Ave, Dallas TX 75231-4596.

Cerebral Palsy/Etiology

Fetal and Neonatal Neurologic Injury. *ACOG Technical Bulletin.* 1992;163. 5pp. 28refs. Sponsored by the American College of Obstetricians and Gynecologists. Cost: free copy. Set of Bulletins $70 + s/h ACOG members, $125 + s/h nonmembers. One-year subscription $55 member, $65 nonmember. To order single copy, call ACOG Resource Center 202 863-2518; to order set or subscription, call ACOG Distribution Center, 1 800 762-2264. Available on the Internet to members only at acog.org. Key terms: birth injuries; cerebral palsy.

Cerebral Palsy/Surgery
Spinal Nerve Roots/Surgery

Dorsal Rhizotomy. *JAMA*. 1990;264:2569-2574. 4pp. 26refs. Sponsored by the American Medical Association, Diagnostic and Therapeutic Technology Assessment Program. Cost: free copy. DATTA subscription available. To order call AMA Department of Technology Assessment 312 464-4531.

Cerebrospinal Fluid
Spinal Puncture

Diagnostic Spinal Tap. *Ann Intern Med*. 1986;104:880-885. 6pp. Sponsored by the American College of Physicians. To order call ACP Clinical Efficacy Assessment Project 1 800 523-1546.

Cerebrospinal Fluid Shunts
Cerebral Ventricles

Cerebrospinal Fluid Shunting Procedure. 1993. Sponsored by the American Association of Neurological Surgeons. To order call AANS 847 692-9500.

Cerebrovascular Disorders/
Classification
Disability Evaluation

The American Heart Association Stroke Outcome Classification Executive Summary. *Circulation*. 1998;97:2474-2478. 5pp. 25refs. Sponsored by the American Heart Association. Cost: free copy. To order call 1 800 242-8721 (US only) or write to: American Heart Association, Public Inquiries, 7272 Greenville Ave, Dallas TX 75231-4596.

Cerebrovascular Disorders/
Classification
Outcome Assessment
(Health Care)/Classification

The American Heart Association Stroke Outcome Classification. *Stroke*. 1998;29:1274-1280. 7pp. 45refs. Sponsored by the American Heart Association. Cost: free copy. To order call 1 800 242-8721 (US only) or write to: American Heart Association, Public Inquiries, 7272 Greenville Ave, Dallas TX 75231-4596.

Cerebrovascular Disorders/
Prevention and Control

Medical Treatment for Stroke Prevention. *Ann Intern Med*. 1994;121:41-53. 13pp. 77refs. Sponsored by the American College of Physicians. To order call ACP Customer Service 215 351-2600.

Cerebrovascular Disorders/
Prevention and Control
Atrial Fibrillation

Stroke Prevention in Patients with Nonvalvular Atrial Fibrillation. *Neurol*. 1998;51:671-673. 3pp. 16refs. Sponsored by the American Academy of Neurology. Cost: individual statements are free. To order call AAN Member Service Center 1 800 879-1960. Available on the Internet at aan.com.

Cerebrovascular Disorders/
Rehabilitation

Post-Stroke Rehabilitation. *AHCPR*. 1995;Publication No. 95-0662. 248pp. 483refs. Sponsored by the Federal Agency for Health Care Policy and Research. To order call AHCPR Clearinghouse 1 800 358-9295.

Certification

Position Statement: Physician Recertification. 1990. 1pp. Sponsored by the American College of Cardiology. Cost: free copy. To order call Educational Services Department 1 800 257-4740.

Certification

Recertification. *ACOG Committee Opinion*. 1992;110. 1pp. Sponsored by the American College of Obstetricians and Gynecologists. Cost: free copy. Set of Opinions $55 + s/h ACOG members, $75 + s/h nonmembers. One year subscription $55 member, $65 nonmember. To order single copy, call ACOG Resource Center 202 863-2518; to order set or subscription, call ACOG Distribution Center, 1 800 762-2264. Available on the Internet to members only at acog.org.

Cervical Vertebrae/Radiography

ACR Standard for the Performance of Radiography of the Cervical Spine in Children and Adults. 1999. 6pp. 20refs. Sponsored by the American College of Radiology. Cost: $25 (ACR nonmembers). To order call ACR Dept of Quality Assurance 703 716-7592. Available free on the Internet at acr.org. Key terms: cervical; spine; radiography; neck; imaging.

Cervical Vertebrae/Surgery
Spinal Diseases/Surgery

Cervical Spine Surgery. 1993. Sponsored by the American Association of Neurological Surgeons. To order call AANS 847 692-9500.

Cervix Neoplasms

Screening for Cervical Cancer. *Guide to Clinical Preventive Services, 2nd Ed.* 1996. Sponsored by the US Preventive Services Task Force. To order call Williams & Wilkins 1 800 638-0672.

Cervix Neoplasms
Health Policy

Practice Policy Statement: Cervical Cancer Screening. *Am J Prev Med.* 1996;12(5):342-344. 3pp. 22refs. Sponsored by the American College of Preventive Medicine. To order reprint address request to ACPM, 1660 L St NW, #206, Washington, DC 20036.

Cervix Neoplasms
Mass Screening

Screening for Cervical Carcinoma in Elderly Women. 1993. Sponsored by the American Geriatrics Society. Cost: free. To order call AGS 212 308-1414.

Cervix Neoplasms/Diagnosis

Cervical Cancer. *NIH Consensus Development Conference Statement.* 1996;14(1):1-38[Conf. No. 102]. 38pp. 81refs. Sponsored by the National Institutes of Health. Cost: free copy. To order call 1 888 644-2667. Available on the Internet at consensus.nih.gov.

Cervix Neoplasms/Diagnosis

Diagnosis and Management of Invasive Cervical Carcinomas. *ACOG Technical Bulletin.* 1989;138. 6pp. 29refs. Sponsored by the American College of Obstetricians and Gynecologists. Cost: free copy. Set of Bulletins $70 + s/h ACOG members, $125 + s/h nonmembers. One-year subscription $55 member, $65 nonmember. To order single copy, call ACOG Resource Center 202 863-2518; to order set or subscription, call ACOG Distribution Center, 1 800 762-2264. Available on the Internet to members only at acog.org. Key terms: cervix neoplasm.

Cervix Neoplasms/Diagnosis
Mass Screening/Methods
Vaginal Smears/Methods

New Pap Test Screening Techniques. *ACOG Committee Opinion.* 1998;206. 3pp. 4refs. Sponsored by the American College of Obstetricians and Gynecologists. Cost: free copy. Set of Opinions $55 + s/h ACOG members, $75 + s/h nonmembers. One year subscription $55 member, $65 nonmember. To order single copy, call ACOG Resource Center 202 863-2518; to order set or subscription, call ACOG Distribution Center, 1 800 762-2264. Available on the Internet to members only at acog.org. Key terms: vaginal smears; technology assessment; diagnosis; computer assisted; diagnostic errors.

Cervix Neoplasms/Epidemiology
Mass Screening

Screening for Cervical Cancer. *Ann Intern Med.* 1990;113:214 226. 13pp. 69refs. Sponsored by the American College of Physicians. To order call ACP Clinical Efficacy Assessment Project 1 800 523-1546.

Cervix Neoplasms/Microbiology
Papillomavirus, Human/Isolation
and Purification

Human Papillomavirus DNA Testing in the Management of Cervical Neoplasia. *JAMA.* 1993. Sponsored by the American Medical Association, Diagnostic and Therapeutic Technology Assessment Program. Cost: free copy. DATTA subscription available. To order call AMA Department of Technology Assessment 312 464-4531.

Cervix Uteri/Pathology
Vaginal Smears

Absence of Endocervical Cells on a Pap Test. *ACOG Committee Opinion.* 1995;153. 1pp. 1ref. Sponsored by the American College of Obstetricians and Gynecologists. Cost: free copy. Set of Opinions $55 + s/h ACOG members, $75 + s/h nonmembers. One-year subscription $55 member, $65 nonmember. To order single copy, call ACOG Resource Center 202 863-2518; to order set or subscription, call ACOG Distribution Center, 1 800 762-2264. Available on the Internet to members only at acog.org. Key terms: vaginal smears; diagnostic errors.

Cesarean Section
Disease Transmission, Vertical
HIV Infections/Prevention and Control

Scheduled Cesarean Delivery and the Prevention of Vertical Transmission of HIV Infection. *ACOG Committee Opinion*. 1999;219. 3pp. 11refs. Sponsored by the American College of Obstetricians and Gynecologists. Cost: free copy. Set of Bulletins $70 + s/h ACOG members, $125 + s/h nonmembers. One-year subscription $55 member, $65 nonmember. To order single copy, call ACOG Resource Center 202 863-2518; to order set or subscription, call ACOG Distribution Center, 1 800 762-2264. Available on the Internet to members only at acog.org. Key terms: cesarean section; HIV Infection/pc; pregnancy complications; infectious/pc; vertical transmission/pc.

Cesarean Section
Sterilization, Tubal

Tubal Ligation with Cesarean Delivery. *ACOG Committee Opinion*. 1998;205. 1pp. Sponsored by the American College of Obstetricians and Gynecologists. Cost: free copy. Set of Opinions $55 + s/h ACOG members, $75 + s/h nonmembers. One-year subscription $55 member, $65 nonmember. To order single copy, call ACOG Resource Center 202 863-2518; to order set or subscription, call ACOG Distribution Center, 1 800 762-2264. Available on the Internet to members only at acog.org. Key terms: cesarean section; sterilization; tubal; reimbursement; time factors.

Cesarean Section, Repeat
Trial of Labor

Trial of Labor versus Elective Repeat Cesarean Section for the Woman with a Previous Cesarean Section. 1995. 75pp. 386refs. Sponsored by the American Academy of Family Physicians. Cost: free + s/h. To order call AAFP Order Department 1 800 944-0000, order #981. Available on the Internet at aafp.org/clinical/. Key terms: maternity care; family practice.

Chelating Agents/Therapeutic Use
Arteriosclerosis/Therapy

Chelation Therapy (with EDTA) for Atherosclerosis. *JAMA*. 1983;250:672. 1pp. Sponsored by the American Medical Association, Diagnostic and Therapeutic Technology Assessment Program. Cost: free copy. DATTA subscription available. To order call AMA Department of Technology Assessment 312 464-4531.

Chelation Therapy

Position Statement: Chelation Therapy (Reapproved). 1997. Sponsored by the American College of Cardiology. Cost: free copy. To order call Educational Services Department 1 800 257-4740.

Chemexfoliation

Guidelines of Care for Chemical Peeling. *J Am Acad Derm*. 1995;33:497-503. 7pp. 20refs. Sponsored by the American Academy of Dermatology. Cost: free copy. To order call Alice Bell 847 330-0230 x333. Available on the Internet at aad.org. Key terms: chemexfoliation; adverse effects; methods.

Chemical Peel (see Chemexfoliation)

Chemical Warfare Agents/
Adverse Effects
Hazardous Waste/Adverse Effects

Recommendations for Protecting Human Health Against Potential Adverse Effects of Long-Term Exposure to Low Doses of Chemical Warfare Agents. *Morbid Mortal Weekly Report*. 1988;37:72-79. 8pp. Sponsored by the Centers for Disease Control and Prevention. Cost: $1. To order call US Govt Printing Office 202 783-3238.

Chemiluminescence
Thyrotropin/Blood

Immunochemiluminometric Assays (ICMA) of Thyroid-Stimulating Hormone (TSH) for the Diagnosis of Thyroid Disorders and for Monitoring Response to Therapy. *Diagnostic and Therapeutic Technology Assessment (DATTA)*. 1994. 20pp. 63refs. Sponsored by the American Medical Association, Diagnostic and Therapeutic Technology Assessment Program. Cost: free copy. DATTA subscription available. To order call AMA Department of Technology Assessment 312 464-4531.

Chemotherapy (see Antineoplastic Agents)

Chest Pain/Diagnosis
Triage

Position Statement: Early Triage of Patients with Chest Discomfort, Approaches to. 1990. Sponsored by the American College of Cardiology. Cost: free copy. To order call Educational Services Department 1 800 257-4740.

Chest Pain/Etiology
Emergency Medicine/Standards

Clinical Policy for the Initial Approach to Adults Presenting with a Chief Complaint of Chest Pain, with No History of Trauma. *Ann Emerg Med.* 1995;25:274-299. 26pp. 123refs. Sponsored by the American College of Emergency Physicians. Cost: ACEP members free copy, fee nonmembers. To order call ACEP 1 800 798-1822 x6. Key terms: chest pain; adults; Emergency Department.

Chickenpox/Prevention and Control
Chickenpox Vaccine

Prevention of Varicella: Updated Recommendations of the Advisory Committee on Immunization Practices (ACIP). *Morbid Mortal Weekly Report.* 1999;48(no. RR-6). Sponsored by the Centers for Disease Control and Prevention. Cost: $1. To order call US Govt Printing Office 202 783-3238. Available on the Internet at cdc.gov/mmwr/mmwr_rr.html.

Child Abuse

Child Physical Abuse and Neglect. 1992. 26pp. Sponsored by the American Medical Association, Division of Health Science. Cost: AMA members $2.25 nonmembers $3. To order call AMA 312 464-5066.

Child Abuse/Diagnosis
Forensic Medicine

Practice Parameters for the Forensic Evaluation of Children and Adolescents Who May Have Been Physically or Sexually Abused. *J Am Acad Child Adol Psych.* 1997;36(3):423-442. 19pp. 183refs. Sponsored by the American Academy of Child and Adolescent Psychiatry. Cost: $10 AACAP members/$20 others. To order call Communications Department 202 966-7300. Key terms: child abuse; sexual abuse; forensic; evaluation; practice parameters.

Child Abuse, Sexual

Child Sexual Abuse. 1992. 26pp. Sponsored by the American Medical Association, Division of Health Science. Cost: AMA members $2.25 nonmembers $3. To order call AMA 312 464-5066.

Child Behavior
Punishment

Guidance for Effective Discipline. *Pediatr.* 1998;101:723. 6pp. 32refs. Sponsored by the American Academy of Pediatrics. Cost: $1.95. Discounted set of policies available. To order call 1 800 433-9016.

Child Custody/Legislation and Jurisprudence
Expert Testimony/Legislation and Jurisprudence

Practice Parameters for Child Custody Evaluation. *J Am Acad Child Adol Psych.* 1997;36(10 suppl): 575-685. 11pp. 58refs. Sponsored by the American Academy of Child and Adolescent Psychiatry. Cost: $10 AACAP members/$20 others. To order call Communications Department 202 966-7300. Key terms: child custody; forensic psychiatry; joint custody; court; parenting.

Child Psychiatry
Psychiatric Status Rating Scales

Practice Parameters for the Psychiatric Assessment of Infants and Toddlers. *J Am Acad Child Adol Psych.* 1997;36(10 suppl): 215-365. 15pp. 75refs. Sponsored by the American Academy of Child and Adolescent Psychiatry. Cost: $10 AACAP members/$20 others. To order call Communications Department 202 966-7300. Key terms: infant psychiatry; infant; toddler; interdisciplinary assessment; mental status examination.

Chlamydia Infections/Diagnosis

Screening for Chlamydial Infection. *Guide to Clinical Preventive Services, 2nd Ed.* 1996. Sponsored by the US Preventive Services Task Force. To order call Williams & Wilkins 1 800 638-0672.

Chlamydia Infections/ Prevention and Control
Sexually Transmitted Diseases/ Prevention and Control

Chlamydia Trachomatis Infections: Policy Guidelines for Prevention and Control. *Morbid Mortal Weekly Report.* 1985;34(suppl):3s. 1pp. Sponsored by the Centers for Disease Control and Prevention. Cost: $1. To order call US Govt Printing Office 202 783-3238.

Chlamydia psittaci
Bird Diseases/Diagnosis

Appendix A—Methods for Diagnosing Avian Chlamydiosis. *Morbid Mortal Weekly Report.* 1998;47(no. RR-10). Sponsored by the Centers for Disease Control and Prevention. To order call US Govt Printing Office. Available on the Internet at cdc.gov/epo/mmwr/preview/ind98_rr.html.

Chlamydia Trachomatis
Chlamydia Infections/
Prevention and Control

Recommendations for Prevention and Management of Chlamydia trachomatis Infections, 1993. *Morbid Mortal Weekly Report.* 1993;42(no. RR-12). Sponsored by the Centers for Disease Control and Prevention. Cost: $1. To order call US Govt Printing Office 202 783-3238.

Choice Behavior
Fetal Diseases/Psychology
Maternal Welfare

Patient Choice and the Maternal-Fetal Relationship. *ACOG Committee Opinion.* 1999;214. 3pp. 6refs. Sponsored by the American College of Obstetricians and Gynecologists. Cost: free copy. Set of Opinions $55 + s/h ACOG members, $75 + s/h nonmembers. One-year subscription $55 member, $65 nonmember. To order single copy, call ACOG Resource Center 202 863-2518; to order set or subscription, call ACOG Distribution Center, 1 800 762-2264. Available on the Internet to members only at acog.org. Key terms: maternal fetal conflict; decision making; informed consent; informed refusal; pregnancy complications.

Cholangiography/Standards
Bile Ducts, Intrahepatic/Surgery

Quality Improvement Guidelines for Percutaneous Transhepatic Cholangiography and Biliary Drainage. *JVIR.* 1997;8:677-681. 5pp. 31refs. Sponsored by the Society of Cardiovascular and Interventional Radiology. Cost: free copy. To order call SCVIR 703 691-1805. Key terms: bile duct radiography; cholangiography; quality assurance; bile ducts; drainage.

Cholangiopancreatography,
Endosopic, Retrograde

Guidelines for Training in Diagnostic and Therapeutic Endoscopic Retrograde Cholangiopancreatography (ERCP). *Surgical Endoscopy.* 1993;17. 2pp. Sponsored by the Society of American Gastrointestinal and Endoscopic Surgeons. Cost: free. To order call 310 314-2404. Available on the Internet at sages.org. Key terms: surgery; ERCP; training; endoscopy.

Cholecystectomy, Laparoscopic
Cholelithiasis/Therapy

Gallstones and Laparoscopic Cholecystectomy. *NIH Consensus Development Conference Statement.* 1992;10(3):1-20[Conf. No. 90]. 21pp. Sponsored by the National Institutes of Health. Cost: free copy. To order call 1 888 644-2667. Available on the Internet at consensus.nih.gov.

Cholecystectomy, Laparoscopic
Cholelithiasis/Therapy

Statement on Laparoscopic Cholecystectomy. *Am Coll Surg Bulletin.* 1990;75(6):23. 1pp. Sponsored by the American College of Surgeons. Cost: free copy. To order call ACS Socioeconomic Affairs Dept 312 664-4050.

Cholecystectomy/Methods
Laparoscopy

Laparoscopic Cholecystectomy. *JAMA.* 1991;265:1585-1587. 3pp. 5refs. Sponsored by the American Medical Association, Diagnostic and Therapeutic Technology Assessment Program. Cost: free copy. DATTA subscription available. To order call AMA Department of Technology Assessment 312 464-4531.

Cholecystitis/Diagnosis
Diagnostic Imaging

How to Study the Gallbladder. *Ann Intern Med.* 1988;109:752-754. 3pp. Sponsored by the American College of Physicians. To order call ACP Clinical Efficacy Assessment Project 1 800 523-1546.

Cholelithiasis/Therapy

Management of Gallstones. 1993. Sponsored by the American College of Physicians. To order call ACP Clinical Efficacy Assessment Project 1 800 523-1546.

Cholesterol/Blood
Coronary Disease/
Prevention and Control

Cholesterol Screening (Update). *Ann Intern Med.* 1996;124. Sponsored by the American College of Physicians. To order call ACP Customer Service 215 351-2600.

Cholesterol/Blood
Coronary Disease/
Prevention and Control

Lowering Blood Cholesterol to Prevent Heart Disease. *NIH Consensus Development Conference Statement.* 1984;5(7):1-11[Conf. No. 47]. 12pp. Sponsored by the National Institutes of Health. Cost: free copy. To order call 1 888 644-2667. Available on the Internet at consensus.nih.gov.

Cholesterol/Blood
Coronary Disease/
Prevention and Control

NCEP Report of the Expert Panel on Blood Cholesterol Levels in Children and Adolescents. *NIH Publication No. 91-2732; No. 91-2731.* 1991. 119pp. 10refs. Sponsored by the National Heart, Lung, and Blood Institute. Cost: $5. To order contact the NHLBI Information Center, PO Box 30105, Bethesda, MD 20824-0105, 301 251-1222.

Cholesterol/Blood
Triglycerides/Blood
Lipoproteins, HDL Cholesterol/Blood

Cholesterol in Childhood. *Pediatr.* 1998;101(1):141-147. 7pp. 52refs. Sponsored by the American Academy of Pediatrics. Cost: $1.95. Discounted set of policies available. To order call 1 800 433-9016.

Chorionic Villi Sampling

Chorionic Villus Sampling. *ACOG Committee Opinion.* 1995;160. 3pp. 12refs. Sponsored by the American College of Obstetricians and Gynecologists. Cost: free copy. Set of Opinions $55 + s/h ACOG members, $75 + s/h nonmembers. One-year subscription $55 member, $65 nonmember. To order single copy, call ACOG Resource Center 202 863-2518; to order set or subscription, call ACOG Distribution Center, 1 800 762-2264. Available on the Internet to members only at acog.org.

Chorionic Villi Sampling
Fetal Diseases/Diagnosis

Chorionic Villus Sampling: A Reassessment. *JAMA.* 1990;263:305-306. 2pp. 13refs. Sponsored by the American Medical Association, Diagnostic and Therapeutic Technology Assessment Program. Cost: free copy. DATTA subscription available. To order call AMA Department of Technology Assessment 312 464-4531.

Cineangiography
Coronary Angiography

Position Statement: Cardiac Angiography Without Cine Film: Creating a "Tower of Babel" in the Cardiac Catheterization Laboratory. *J Am Coll Cardiol.* 1994;24:834-837. 4pp. Sponsored by the American College of Cardiology. Cost: free copy. To order call Educational Services Department 1 800 257-4740.

Circumcision

Circumcision Policy Statement (formerly, Report of the Task Force on Circumcision). *Pediatr.* 1999;103(3):686-693. 7pp. 119refs. Sponsored by the American Academy of Pediatrics. Cost: $1.95. Discounted set of policies available. To order call 1 800 433-9016.

Circumcision
Infant, Newborn

Neonatal Circumcision. Sponsored by the American Academy of Family Physicians. Available on the Internet at aafp.org/clinical/.

Circumcision, Female

Female Genital Mutilation. *ACOG Committee Opinion.* 1995;151. 1pp. Sponsored by the American College of Obstetricians and Gynecologists. Cost: free copy. Set of Opinions $55 + s/h ACOG members, $75 + s/h nonmembers. One-year subscription $55 member, $65 nonmember. To order single copy, call ACOG Resource Center 202 863-2518; to order set or subscription, call ACOG Distribution Center, 1 800 762-2264. Available on the Internet to members only at acog.org. Key terms: ethics: medical.

Circumcision, Female
Medicine, Traditional
Ethics, Medical

Female Genital Mutilation. *Pediatr.* 1998;102(1):153-156. 4pp. 24refs. Sponsored by the American Academy of Pediatrics. Cost: $1.95. Discounted set of policies available. To order call 1 800 433-9016.

Cleft Lip/Surgery
Cleft Palate/Surgery

Cleft Lip and Cleft Palate. *Clinical Practice Guidelines: Plastic and Maxillofacial Surgery.* 1995. 47pp. 45refs. Sponsored by the American Society of Maxillofacial Surgeons. Cost: Maxillofacial Surgery Guidelines $25 for entire set (not sold separately). Binder $10 (price includes shipping). To order call 1 800 766-4955.

Cleft Lip/Surgery
Insurance, Health
Cleft Palate/Surgery

Position Paper: Recommended Criteria for Insurance Coverage of Cleft Lip and Palate Surgery. 1992. 2pp. Sponsored by the American Society of Plastic and Reconstructive Surgeons. To order call ASPRS 847 228-9900.

Cleft Lip/Surgery
Maxilla/Surgery
Oral Surgical Procedures

Orthognathic, Cleft, Craniofacial Surgery and Adjunctive Procedures. *J Oral & Maxillofacial Surg.* 1995. Sponsored by the American Association of Oral and Maxillofacial Surgeons. To order call AAOMS Publications 1 800 366-6725.

Clinical Competence
Electrocardiography, Ambulatory/
Standards

Clinical Competence in Ambulatory Electrocardiography. *Circulation.* 1993;88:337-341. 5pp. Sponsored by the American Heart Association, American College of Cardiology. Cost: free copy. To order write the Office of Scientific Affairs, AHA, 7272 Greenville Ave, Dallas, TX 75231.

Clinical Competence/Standards
Angioplasty, Transluminal,
Percutaneous, Coronary/Standards

Position Statement: Recommendations for Development and Maintenance of Competence in Coronary Interventional Procedures. *J Am Coll Cardiol.* 1993;22:629-631. 3pp. 5refs. Sponsored by the American College of Cardiology. Cost: free copy. To order call Educational Services Department 1 800 257-4740.

Clinical Competence/Standards
Critical Care

Guidelines for Advanced Training for Physicians in Critical Care. *Critical Care Med.* 1997;25:1601-1607. 7pp. 8refs. Sponsored by the Society of Critical Care Medicine. Cost: Complete Set $60 + s/h SCCM members, $80 + s/h nonmembers; $5 for a single guideline. To order call SCCM 714 282-6000 or access Book Store on the SCCM website. Available free on the Internet at sccm.org. Key terms: critical care; medical education; training programs; intensive care unit.

Clinical Competence/Standards
Electric Countershock/Standards

Clinical Competence in Elective Direct Current (DC) Cardioversion. *J Am Coll Cardiol.* 1993;22:36-39. 4pp. 10refs. Sponsored by the American College of Cardiology, American College of Physicians, American Heart Association. Cost: free copy. To order call Educational Services Department 1 800 257-4740.

Clinical Competence/Standards
Electrocardiography,
Ambulatory/Standards

Clinical Competence in Ambulatory Electrocardiography. *J Am Coll Cardiol.* 1993;22:331-335. 5pp. 26refs. Sponsored by the American College of Cardiology, American College of Physicians, American Heart Association. Cost: free copy. To order call Educational Services Department 1 800 257-4740.

Clinical Competence/Standards
Electrophysiology/Standards

Clinical Competence in Electrophysiologic Studies. *J Am Coll Cardiol.* 1994;23:1258-1261. 4pp. 34refs. Sponsored by the American College of Cardiology, American College of Physicians, American Heart Association. Cost: free copy. To order call Educational Services Department 1 800 257-4740.

Clinical Competence/Standards
Hemodynamics

Clinical Competence in Hemodynamic Monitoring. *J Am Coll Cardiol.* 1990;15:1460-1464. 5pp. 8refs. Sponsored by the American College of Physicians, American College of Cardiology, American Heart Association. Cost: free copy. To order call ACC Griffith Resource Library 301 897-5400.

Clinical Competence/Standards
Pacemaker, Artificial

Clinical Competence in Insertion of a Temporary Transvenous Ventricular Pacemaker. *J Am Coll Cardiol.* 1994;23:1254-1257. 4pp. 24refs. Sponsored by the American College of Cardiology, American College of Physicians, American Heart Association. Cost: free copy. To order call Educational Services Department 1 800 257-4740.

Clinical Nursing Research
Respiratory Tract Diseases/Nursing

Research Priorities in Respiratory Nursing. *Amer Rev Resp Dis.* 1990;142:6. Sponsored by the American Thoracic Society. Cost: $4. To order send check payable to American Thoracic Society, 1740 Broadway, New York, NY 10019-4374; for credit card orders, call 212 315-8863.

Clinical Protocols
Fever/Therapy

Pediatric Fever. *Ann Emerg Med.* 1993;22:628-637. 10pp. 40refs. Sponsored by the American College of Emergency Physicians. Cost: ACEP members free copy, fee nonmembers. To order call ACEP 1 800 798-1822 x6. Key terms: fever under two years; Emergency Department.

Clinical Trials

Position Statement: Clinical Trials. 1990. 1pp. Sponsored by the American College of Cardiology. Cost: free copy. To order call Educational Services Department 1 800 257-4740.

Clomiphene/Therapeutic Use
Ovulation Induction

Induction of Ovulation with Clomiphene Citrate. 1991. 6pp. 28refs. Sponsored by the American Society for Reproductive Medicine. Cost: $1. To order call ASRM Publication Department 205 978-5000.

Clostridium Difficile
Diarrhea/Microbiology
Enterocolitis Pseudomembranous/
Diagnosis

Guidelines for the Diagnosis and Management of Clostridium-Difficile-Associated Diarrhea and Colitis. *Am J Gastroenterol.* 1997;92:739-750. 12pp. 63refs. Sponsored by the American College of Gastroenterology. Cost: free copy. To order call ACG 703 820-7400.

Clostridium Infections
Diarrhea/Microbiology

Clostridium difficile—Associated Diarrhea and Colitis. *Infect Control Hosp Epidemiol.* 1995;16:459-477. 19pp. 195refs. Sponsored by the Society for Healthcare Epidemiology of America. Cost: free. To order visit our website at medscape.com/shea. Available on the Internet at medscape.com/shea. Key terms: definition of CDAD; diagnostic techniques; specimen collection and transport; detection of C difficile toxins; new methodologies.

Cocaine-Related Disorders/Therapy
Substance-Related Disorders/Therapy

Practice Guideline for Treatment of Patients with Substance Use Disorders: Alcohol, Cocaine, Opioids. *Am J Psych.* 1995;152(suppl):11. 55pp. 481refs. Sponsored by the American Psychiatric Association. Cost: $22.50. To order call 1 800 368-5777 order #SPCT2303. Key terms: substance use; alcohol; cocaine; opioids.

Cochlear Implantation
Ambulatory Surgical Procedures

Cochlear Implantation in Outpatient Settings. *AHCPR Health Technology Review.* 1992;No. 3 (AHCPR Publication No. 92-0065). 3pp. 5refs. Sponsored by the Federal Agency for Health Care Policy and Research. To order call AHCPR Clearinghouse 1 800 358-9295.

Cochlear Implants

Cochlear Implants in Adults and Children. *NIH Consensus Development Conference Statement.* 1995;13(2):1-31[Conf. No. 100]. 32pp. Sponsored by the National Institutes of Health. Cost: free copy. To order call 1 888 644-2667. Available on the Internet at consensus.nih.gov.

Cognition Disorders/Etiology
Mental Processes

Clinical Policy for the Initial Approach to Patients Presenting with Altered Mental Status. *Ann Emerg Med.* 1999;33:251-281. 31pp. 49refs. Sponsored by the American College of Emergency Physicians. Cost: ACEP members free copy, fee nonmembers. To order call ACEP 1 800 798-1822 x6. Key terms: nontraumatic; Emergency Department; acute change in alertness or awareness.

Colitis, Ulcerative/Diagnosis

Ulcerative Colitis. *Am J Gastroenterol.* 1997;92:204-211. 8pp. Sponsored by the American College of Gastroenterology. To order call 601 984-4540.

Colitis, Ulcerative/Diagnosis
Colonoscopy

Role of Colonoscopy in the Management of Patients with Inflammatory Bowel Disease: Guidelines for Clinical Application. *Gastrointest Endosc.* 1988;34(suppl):10s-11s. 2pp. 17refs. Sponsored by the American Society for Gastrointestinal Endoscopy. Cost: free. To order call ASGE 978 526-8330.

Collagen
Skin/Surgery

Soft Tissue Augmentation Collagen Implant. *J Am Acad Derm*. 1996;34:698-702. 5pp. 14refs. Sponsored by the American Academy of Dermatology. Cost: free copy. To order call Alice Bell 847 330-0230 x333. Available on the Internet at aad.org. Key terms: artificial implants; collagen; surgery.

Collateral Ligaments/Injuries
Thumb

Ulnar Collateral Ligament Injury of the Thumb. *Clinical Policies*. 1996. 4pp. 7refs. Sponsored by the American Academy of Orthopaedic Surgeons, North American Spine Society. Cost: $50 (set of 15) for nonmembers. To order call 1 800 626-6276. Key terms: ligament injury; thumb sprain/tear; American Academy of Orthopaedic Surgeons.

Colonic Diseases, Functional/Diagnosis
Colonic Diseases, Functional/Therapy

Irritable Bowel Syndrome. *Gastroenterology*. 1997;112:2118-2137. 20pp. 190refs. Sponsored by the American Gastroenterological Association. Cost: $6. To order call AGA 301 654-2055. Key terms: bowel; irritable; IBS; intestine; gastrointestinal.

Colonic Neoplasms/Therapy
Rectal Neoplasms/Therapy

Adjuvant Therapy for Patients with Colon and Rectum Cancer. *NIH Consensus Development Conference Statement*. 1990;8(4):1-25[Conf. No. 79]. 25pp. Sponsored by the National Institutes of Health. Cost: free copy. To order call 1 888 644-2667. Available on the Internet at consensus.nih.gov.

Colonic Polyps/Diagnosis
Colonoscopy

Role of Colonoscopy in the Management of Patients with Colonic Polyps: Guidelines for Clinical Application. *Gastrointest Endosc*. 1988;34(suppl):6s-7s. 2pp. 16refs. Sponsored by the American Society for Gastrointestinal Endoscopy. Cost: free. To order call ASGE 978 526-8330.

Colonic Polyps/Diagnosis
Colorectal Neoplasms/Diagnosis
Population Surveillance/Methods

American Cancer Society Guidelines for Screening and Surveillance for Early Detection of Colorectal Polyps and Cancer: Update 1997. *CA-A Cancer J for Clinicians*. 1997;47:154-160. 7pp. 20refs. Sponsored by the American Cancer Society. To order contact local American Cancer Society office. Key terms: colorectal cancer; screening; cancer detection; sigmoidoscopy; blood testing.

Colonic Polyps/Diagnosis, Therapy

Management of Polyps of the Colon. *Ann Intern Med*. 1993;119:836-843. 8pp. Sponsored by the American College of Gastroenterology. To order call 601 984-4540.

Colonic Polyps/Therapy

Polyp Guideline: Diagnosis, Treatment and Surveillance for Patients with Nonfamilial Colorectal Polyps. *Ann Intern Med*. 1993;119:836-843. 8pp. 90refs. Sponsored by the American College of Gastroenterology. Cost: free copy. To order call ACG 703 820-7400.

Colonoscopy
Gastrointestinal Hemorrhage

Role of Endoscopy in the Patient with Lower Gastrointestinal Bleeding: Guidelines for Clinical Application. *Gastrointest Endosc*. 1988;34(suppl):23s-25s. 3pp. 16refs. Sponsored by the American Society for Gastrointestinal Endoscopy. Cost: free. To order call ASGE 978 526-8330.

Colony-Stimulating Factors/
Therapeutic Use
Neoplasms/Therapy

1997 Update of Recommendations for the Use of Hematopoietic Colony-Stimulating Factors. *J Clin Oncol*. 1997;15:3288. 1pp. 2refs. Sponsored by the American Society of Clinical Oncology. Cost: free copy. To order call ASCO 703 299-0150 or e-mail: guidelines@asco.org. Available free on the Internet at asco.org.

Colorectal Neoplasms/Diagnosis

Detection and Surveillance of Colorectal Cancer. *JAMA*. 1989;261:580-585. 6pp. 65refs. Sponsored by the American Gastroenterological Association. Cost: free. To order call AGA 301 654-2055.

Colorectal Neoplasms/Diagnosis

Practice Parameters for the Detection of Colorectal Neoplasms. *Dis Colon Rectum*. 1991;35(4):389-394. 6pp. 43refs. Sponsored by the American Society of Colon and Rectal Surgeons. Cost: free. To order write ASCRS, 85 W Algonquin Rd, #550, Arlington Hts, IL 60005.

Colorectal Neoplasms/Diagnosis

Screening for Colorectal Cancer. *Guide to Clinical Preventive Services, 2nd Ed*. 1996. Sponsored by the US Preventive Services Task Force. To order call Williams & Wilkins 1 800 638-0672.

Colorectal Neoplasms/Diagnosis
Mass Screening/Methods

Screening for Colorectal Cancer. *Ann Intern Med*. 1990;113:373-384. 12pp. 39refs. Sponsored by the American College of Physicians. To order call ACP Clinical Efficacy Assessment Project 1 800 523-1546.

Colorectal Neoplasms/
Prevention and Control
Mass Screening/Methods

Colorectal Cancer Screening. *Gastroenterology*. 1997;112:594-642. 49pp. 220refs. Sponsored by the American Gastroenterological Association. Cost: $10. To order call AGA 301 654-2055. Key terms: cancer; screening; colorectal; surveillance.

Colorectal Neoplasms/
Prevention and Control
Occult Blood

Suggested Technique for Fecal Occult Blood Testing and Interpretation in Colorectal Cancer Screening. *Ann Intern Med*. 1997;126:808-810. 3pp. Sponsored by the American College of Physicians. To order call ACP Clinical Efficacy Assessment Project 1 800 523-1546.

Colorectal Neoplasms/Surgery

Colorectal Cancer Surgical Practice Guidelines. *Oncology*. 1997;11(6):1051. 7pp. 9refs. Sponsored by the Society of Surgical Oncology. Cost: call 516 424-8900 x316. To order write Oncology, PRR, Inc, 17 Prospect St, Huntington NY 11743. Key terms: colorectal.

Colorectal Surgery
Rectal Neoplasms/Surgery

Practice Parameters for Treatment of Rectal Carcinoma. *Dis Colon Rectum*. 1993;36:989-1006. 18pp. 63refs. Sponsored by the American Society of Colon and Rectal Surgeons. Cost: free. To order write ASCRS, 85 W Algonquin Rd, #550, Arlington Hts, IL 60005.

Colposcopy
Cervix Uteri/Pathology
Curriculum

Colposcopy Training and Practice. *ACOG Committee Opinion*. 1994;133. 2pp. 6refs. Sponsored by the American College of Obstetricians and Gynecologists. Cost: free copy. Set of Opinions $55 + s/h ACOG members, $75 + s/h nonmembers. One-year subscription $55 member, $65 nonmember. To order single copy, call ACOG Resource Center 202 863-2518; to order set or subscription, call ACOG Distribution Center, 1 800 762-2264. Available on the Internet to members only at acog.org. Key terms: education: medical.

Commerce
Ethics, Medical

Commercial Ventures in Medicine; Concerns about the Patenting of Procedures 1993. *ACOG Committee Opinion*. 1993;129. 1pp. Sponsored by the American College of Obstetricians and Gynecologists. Cost: free copy. Set of Opinions $55 + s/h ACOG members, $75 + s/h nonmembers. One-year subscription $55 member, $65 nonmember. To order single copy, call ACOG Resource Center 202 863-2518; to order set or subscription, call ACOG Distribution Center, 1 800 762-2264. Available on the Internet to members only at acog.org. Key terms: ethics: medical; commerce; patents; conflict of interest.

Common Cold/Drug Therapy

Common Cold. *USP DI*. 1997; Volume I. Sponsored by US Pharmacopeia/Micromedex, Inc. Cost: $125 per year subscription. To order call 1 800 877-6733. Key terms: common cold; pharmacologic management.

Communicable Disease Control
Immunization/Standards

Quality Standards for Immunization. *Clin Inf Dis*. 1997;25:782. 5pp. 15refs. Sponsored by the Infectious Diseases Society of America. To obtain request from medical library or download via the Internet. Available on the Internet at idsociety.org/practice.

Communicable Disease Control International Cooperation

Recommendations of the International Task Force for Disease Eradication. *Morbid Mortal Weekly Report.* 1993;42(no. RR-16). Sponsored by the Centers for Disease Control and Prevention. Cost: $1. To order call US Govt Printing Office 202 783-3238.

Communicable Disease Control/ Legislation and Jurisprudence Physician's Role

Mandatory Reporting of Infectious Diseases by Clinicians and Mandatory Reporting of Occupational Diseases by Clinicians. *Morbid Mortal Weekly Report.* 1990;39(no. RR-9):1-28. 28pp. 24refs. Sponsored by the Centers for Disease Control and Prevention. Cost: $1. To order call US Govt Printing Office 202 783-3238.

Communicable Disease Control/Standards Emigration and Immigration

Recommendations for Prevention and Control of Tuberculosis Among Foreign-Born Persons Report of the Working Group on Tuberculosis Among Foreign-Born Persons. 1998;47(no. RR-16). Sponsored by the Centers for Disease Control and Prevention. To order call US Govt Printing Office 202 783-3238. Available on the Internet at cdc.gov/mmwr/mmwr_rr.html.

Communicable Diseases/ Prevention and Control

Postexposure Prophylaxis for Selected Infectious Diseases. *Guide to Clinical Preventive Services, 2nd Ed.* 1996. Sponsored by the US Preventive Services Task Force. To order call Williams & Wilkins 1 800 638-0672.

Communicable Diseases Pharmacy Service, Hospital/Standards

Hospital Pharmacists and Infectious Disease Specialists. *Clin Inf Dis.* 1997;25:802. 1pp. 1refs. Sponsored by the Infectious Diseases Society of America. To order obtain request from medical library or download via the Internet. Available on the Internet at idsociety.org/practice.

Community-Acquired Infections Pneumonia

Community-Aquired Pneumonia in Adults: Guidelines for Management. *Clin Inf Dis.* 1998;26:811. 28pp. 145refs. Sponsored by the Infectious Diseases Society of America. To order obtain request from medical library or download via the Internet. Available on the Internet at idsociety.org/practice.

Comorbidity

Comorbidity. *Practice-Related Report of the AMA Council on Scientific Affairs.* 1991. 23pp. 81refs. Sponsored by the American Medical Association, Council on Scientific Affairs. Cost: free. To order call Nancy Nolan, AMA, 312 464-5046.

Computers Electrodiagnosis/Instrumentation Neurology/Instrumentation

Technology Review: Nervepace Digital Electroneurometer. *Muscle Nerve.* 1999;8(suppl):S243-S246. 4pp. 7refs. Sponsored by the American Association of Electrodiagnostic Medicine. Cost: $10 members, $20 nonmembers. To order write AAEM, 421 First Avenue SW, #300E, Rochester, MN 55902. Available on the Internet at aaem.net/pdffiles/tech_rvw_nervepace.pdf. Key terms: carpal tunnel; nerve conduction; electrodiagnosis; Nervepace Digital Electroneurometer.

Computers/Standards Respiratory Function

Computer Guidelines for Pulmonary Laboratories. *Amer Rev Resp Dis.* 1986;134:3. Sponsored by the American Thoracic Society. Cost: $4. To order send check payable to American Thoracic Society, 1740 Broadway, New York, NY 10019-4374; for credit card orders, call 212 315-8863.

Condoms/Supply and Distribution Sexually Transmitted Diseases/ Prevention and Control

Condom Availability for Adolescents. *ACOG Committee Opinion.* 1995;154. 4pp. 24refs. Sponsored by the American College of Obstetricians and Gynecologists. Cost: free copy. Set of Opinions $55 + s/h ACOG members, $75 + s/h nonmembers. One-year subscription $55 member, $65 nonmember. To order single copy, call ACOG Resource Center 202 863-2518; to order set or subscription, call ACOG Distribution Center, 1 800 762-2264. Available on the Internet to members only at acog.org. Key terms: health services for adolescents; access to school-based clinics.

Conduct Disorder/Diagnosis

Practice Parameters for the Assessment and Treatment of Children and Adolescents with Conduct Disorder. *J Am Acad Child Adol Psych*. 1997;36(10 suppl): 1225-1395. 17pp. 228refs. Sponsored by the American Academy of Child and Adolescent Psychiatry. Cost: $10 AACAP members/$20 others. To order call Communications Department 202 966-7300. Key terms: conduct disorder; adolescents; children; disruptive behavior disorders; delinquency.

Confidentiality

Confidential Care for Minors. *Reports of CEJA*. 1992;3:39-49. 11pp. Sponsored by the American Medical Association, Council on Ethical and Judicial Affairs. Cost: free copy. To order call AMA 312 464-5223.

Confidentiality
Adolescent Health Services

Confidentiality in Adolescent Health Care. *ACOG Educational Bulletin*. 1998;249. 5pp. 10refs. Sponsored by the American College of Obstetricians and Gynecologists. Cost: free copy. Set of Bulletins $70 + s/h ACOG members, $125 + s/h nonmembers. One-year subscription $55 member, $65 nonmember. To order single copy, call ACOG Resource Center 202 863-2518; to order set or subscription, call ACOG Distribution Center, 1 800 762-2264. Available on the Internet to members only at acog.org. Key terms: confidentiality; health services for adolescents; physician-patient relations.

Congresses

Conference Participation. 1977. Position Statement No. 3. 1pp. Sponsored by the American Academy of Allergy, Asthma, and Immunology. Cost: free copy. To order call 414 272-6071.

Conjunctivitis

Conjunctivitis Preferred Practice Pattern. 1998. 24pp. 33refs. Sponsored by the American Academy of Ophthalmology. Cost: $11 members, $16 nonmembers. AAO members first copy free upon publication. To order call AAO Order Dept 415 561-8540. Key terms: eye; conjunctivitis; external eye disease; treatment; pediatric.

Conscious Sedation/Methods
Emergency Treatment/Standards

Procedural Sedation and Analgesia in the Emergency Department. *Ann Emerg Med*. 1998;31:663-677. 15pp. 43refs. Sponsored by the American College of Emergency Physicians. Cost: ACEP members free copy, fee nonmembers. To order call ACEP 1 800 798-1822 x6. Key terms: conscious sedation; analgesia; sedation; Emergency Department.

Continuity of Patient Care
Physician-Patient Relations

Physician/Patient Responsibility for Follow-Up of Diagnosis and Treatment. *ACOG Committee Opinion*. 1997;193. 1pp. Sponsored by the American College of Obstetricians and Gynecologists. Cost: free copy. Set of Opinions $55 + s/h ACOG members, $75 + s/h nonmembers. One-year subscription $55 member, $65 nonmember. To order single copy, call ACOG Resource Center 202 863-2518; to order set or subscription, call ACOG Distribution Center, 1 800 762-2264. Available on the Internet to members only at acog.org. Key terms: follow-up; physician's role; patient compliance; communication.

Contraceptive Agents
Contraceptive Devices

Contraceptive Choices. 1994. 7pp. 8refs. Sponsored by the American Society for Reproductive Medicine. Cost: $1. To order call ASRM Publication Department 205 978-5000.

Contraceptives, Oral, Hormonal/
Adverse Effects
Contraceptive Agents, Female

Hormonal Contraception. *ACOG Technical Bulletin*. 1994;198. 12pp. 79refs. Sponsored by the American College of Obstetricians and Gynecologists. Cost: free copy. Set of Bulletins $70 + s/h ACOG members, $125 + s/h nonmembers. One-year subscription $55 member, $65 nonmember. To order single copy, call ACOG Resource Center 202 863-2518; to order set or subscription, call ACOG Distribution Center, 1 800 762-2264. Available on the Internet to members only at acog.org. Key terms: contraception: oral; Norplant; Depo-Provera.

Contraceptives, Oral/Adverse Effects
Safety/Standards

Safety of Oral Contraceptives for Teenagers. *ACOG Committee Opinion*. 1991;90. 4pp. 36refs. Sponsored by the American College of Obstetricians and Gynecologists. Cost: free copy. Set of Opinions $55 + s/h ACOG members, $75 + s/h nonmembers. One-year subscription $55 member, $65 nonmember. To order single copy, call ACOG Resource Center 202 863-2518; to order set or subscription, call ACOG Distribution Center, 1 800 762-2264. Available on the Internet to members only at acog.org. Key terms: contraceptives: oral; adolescent behavior; adverse effects.

Contraceptives, Postcoital

Emergency Contraception. *ACOG Practice Patterns*. 1997;3. 8pp. 34refs. Sponsored by the American College of Obstetricians and Gynecologists. Cost: free copy. Multiples of 25: $20 + s/h member, $30 + s/h nonmember. To order single copy, call ACOG Resource Center 202 863-2518; to order set or subscription, call ACOG Distribution Center, 1 800 762-2264. Available on the Internet to members only at acog.org. Key terms: contraception; postcoital.

Contrast Media
Barium Enema/Diagnostic Use

ACR Standard for the Performance of Pediatric Contrast Enema. 1997. 7pp. 26refs. Sponsored by the American College of Radiology. Cost: $25 (ACR nonmembers). To order call ACR Dept of Quality Assurance 703 716-7592. Available free on the Internet at acr.org. Key terms: intestinal; intussusception; meconium; radiology; Hirschsprung's.

Contrast Media
Gastrointestinal System/Radiography

ACR Standard for the Performance of Pediatric Contrast Examinations of the Upper Gastrointestinal Tract. 1997. 4pp. 11refs. Sponsored by the American College of Radiology. Cost: $25 (ACR nonmembers). To order call ACR Dept of Quality Assurance 703 716-7592. Available free on the Internet at acr.org. Key terms: pediatric; gastrointestinal; reflux; swallowing; abdominal.

Convulsions (see Seizures; see Epilepsy)

Convulsions
Febrile/Diagnosis

Neurodiagnostic Evaluation of a First, Simple Febrile Seizure in Children. *Pediatr*. 1996;97(5):769-772. 4pp. 15refs. Sponsored by the American Academy of Pediatrics. Cost: $1.95. Discounted set of policies available. To order call 1 800 433-9016.

COPD (see Lung Diseases, Obstructive)

Cornea/Surgery
Corneal Transplantation/Methods

Automated Lamellar Keratoplasty Preliminary Procedure Assessment. *Ophthalmology*. 1996;103:852-861. 10pp. 15refs. Sponsored by the American Academy of Ophthalmology. Cost: $11 members, $16 nonmembers. AAO members first copy free upon publication. To order call AAO Order Dept 415 561-8540. Key terms: eye; eye surgery; laser surgery; cornea; refractive surgery.

Cornea/Transplantation
Corneal Transplantation

Corneal Transplantation. *JAMA*. 1988;259:719-722. 4pp. Sponsored by the American Medical Association, Council on Scientific Affairs. Cost: free. To order call Nancy Nolan, AMA, 312 464 5046.

Corneal Opacity

Corneal Opacification Preferred Practice Pattern. *Ophthalmology*. 1995;106:1628-1638. 11pp. 79refs. Sponsored by the American Academy of Ophthalmology. Cost: $11 members, $16 nonmembers. AAO members first copy free upon publication. To order call AAO Order Dept 415 561-8540. Key terms: eye; cornea; corneal opacities.

Corneal Topography

Corneal Topography Opthalamic Procedure Assessment. *Ophthalmology*. 1999;106:1628-1638. 11pp. 79refs. Sponsored by the American Academy of Ophthalmology. Cost: $11 members, $16 nonmembers. AAO members first copy free upon publication. To order call AAO Order Dept 415 561-8540. Key terms: eye; cornea; corneal topography; video keratography.

Subject

Coronary Angiography

Coronary Angiography. 1992. JRA-03. 238pp. 340refs. Sponsored by RAND, Academic Medical Center Consortium, American Medical Association. To order call RAND 310 393-0411 x7002. Key terms: coronary angiography; appropriateness; treatment outcomes; utilization; complications.

Coronary Artery Bypass

Coronary Artery Bypass Graft. 1991. JRA-02. 268pp. 322refs. Sponsored by RAND, Academic Medical Center Consortium, American Medical Association. To order call RAND 310 393-0411 x7002. Key terms: coronary artery bypass graft; appropriateness; treatment outcomes; utilization; complications.

Coronary Artery Bypass Angioplasty, Transluminal, Percutaneous Coronary

Coronary Artery Bypass Graft Surgery and Percutaneous Transluminal Coronary Angioplasty. 1993. MR-128. 139pp. 8refs. Sponsored by RAND, Academic Medical Center Consortium. To order call RAND 310 393-0411 x7002. Key terms: coronary artery bypass graft; percutaneous transluminal coronary angioplasty; appropriateness; treatment outcomes; utilization.

Coronary Artery Bypass/Methods Coronary Disease/Surgery

Guidelines and Indications for Coronary Artery Bypass Graft Surgery. *Circulation*. 1991;83:1125-1173. 49pp. 135refs. Sponsored by the American Heart Association. Cost: free copy. To order call 1 800 242-8721 (US only) or write to: American Heart Association, Public Inquiries, 7272 Greenville Ave, Dallas TX 75231-4596.

Coronary Bypass Coronary Disease/Surgery

ACC/AHA Guidelines and Indications for Coronary Artery Bypass Graft Surgery. *J Am Coll Cardiol*. 1991;17:543-589. 47pp. 135refs. Sponsored by the American College of Cardiology, American Heart Association. Cost: free copy. To order call Educational Services Department 1 800 257-4740.

Coronary Disease/Diagnosis

Screening for Asymptomatic Coronary Artery Disease. *Guide to Clinical Preventive Services, 2nd Ed*. 1996. Sponsored by the US Preventive Services Task Force. To order call Williams & Wilkins 1 800 638-0672.

Coronary Disease/Diagnosis Electrokymography

Reassessment of Cardiokymography for the Diagnosis of Coronary Artery Disease. *JAMA*. 1987;257:2973-2974. 2pp. Sponsored by the American Medical Association, Diagnostic and Therapeutic Technology Assessment Program. Cost: free copy. DATTA subscription available. To order call AMA Department of Technology Assessment 312 464-4531.

Coronary Disease/Diagnosis Tomography, Emission-Computed, Single-Photon

Myocardial Perfusion Imaging Utilizing Single-Photon Emission-Computed Tomography (SPECT). *Diagnostic and Therapeutic Technology Assessment (DATTA)*. 1994. 22pp. 20refs. Sponsored by the American Medical Association, Diagnostic and Therapeutic Technology Assessment Program. Cost: free copy. DATTA subscription available. To order call AMA Department of Technology Assessment 312 464-4531.

Coronary Disease/Economics Employment Insurance, Health

Insurability and Employability of the Patient with Ischemic Heart Disease. *J Am Coll Cardiol*. 1989. Sponsored by the American College of Cardiology. Cost: free copy. To order call Educational Services Department 1 800 257-4740.

Coronary Disease/Epidemiology Triglycerides/Blood

Triglyceride, High Density Lipoprotein, and Coronary Heart Disease. *NIH Consensus Development Conference Statement*. 1992;10(2):1-28[Conf. No. 89]. 29pp. Sponsored by the National Institutes of Health. Cost: free copy. To order call 1 888 644-2667. Available on the Internet at consensus.nih.gov.

Coronary Disease/ Prevention and Control Cholesterol/Blood

Screening Low Risk, Asymptomatic Adults for Cardiac Risk Factors: Serum Cholesterol and Triglycerides. *Ann Intern Med*. 1989;110:622-639. 18pp. 107refs. Sponsored by the American College of Physicians. To order call ACP Clinical Efficacy Assessment Project 1 800 523-1546.

Coronary Disease/Radionuclide Imaging

ACR Standard for the Performance of Cardiac Scintigraphy. 1999. 12pp. 11refs. Sponsored by the American College of Radiology. Cost: $25 (ACR nonmembers). To order call ACR Dept of Quality Assurance 703 716-7592. Available on the Internet at acr.org. Key terms: nuclear medicine; cardiac; scintigraphy.

Coronary Disease/Radionuclide Imaging Heart/Radionuclide Imaging

ACC/AHA Guidelines for Clinical Use of Cardiac Radionuclide Imaging (Revision of 1986 Report). *J Am Coll Cardiol.* 1995;25:521-547. 26pp. 274refs. Sponsored by the American College of Cardiology, American Heart Association. Cost: free copy. To order call Educational Services Department 1 800 257-4740.

Coronary Disease/Radionuclide Imaging Heart Diseases/Radionuclide Imaging

Guideline for Clinical Use of Cardiac Radionuclide Imaging. *Circulation.* 1995;91:1278-1303. 26pp. 274refs. Sponsored by the American Heart Association. Cost: free copy. To order call 1 800 242-8721 (US only) or write to: American Heart Association, Public Inquiries, 7272 Greenville Ave, Dallas TX 75231-4596.

Coronary Disease/Radionuclide Imaging Tomography, Emission-Computed

Cardiac Positron Emission Tomography. *Circulation.* 1991;84:447-454. 8pp. 56refs. Sponsored by the American Heart Association. Cost: free copy. To order call 1 800 242-8721 (US only) or write to: American Heart Association, Public Inquiries, 7272 Greenville Ave, Dallas TX 75231-4596.

Coronary Disease/Radionuclide Imaging Tomography, Emission-Computed

Procedure Guideline for Myocardial Perfusion Imaging. *J Nuclear Med.* 1998;39:918-923. 6pp. 5refs. Sponsored by the Society of Nuclear Medicine. Cost: free. To order call Bill Uffelman 703 708-9000. Available on the Internet at snm.org. Key terms: routine diagnostic tests; radionuclide imaging; coronary disease; myocardial ischemia; myocardial infarction.

Coronary Disease/Rehabilitation Exercise Therapy

Cardiac Rehabilitation. *AHCPR.* 1995;Publication No. 69-0672. 202pp. 234refs. Sponsored by the Federal Agency for Health Care Policy and Research. To order call AHCPR Clearinghouse 1 800 358-9295.

Coronary Disease/Surgery Atherectomy, Coronary

Endovascular Atherectomy for Coronary Artery Disease: Directional Coronary Atherectomy. *Diagnostic and Therapeutic Technology Assessment (DATTA).* 1994;18pp. 27refs. Sponsored by the American Medical Association, Diagnostic and Therapeutic Technology Assessment Program. Cost: free copy. DATTA subscription available. To order call AMA Department of Technology Assessment 312 464-4531.

Coronary Disease/Therapy Angioplasty, Transluminal, Percutaneous, Coronary

ACC/AHA Guidelines for Percutaneous Transluminal Coronary Angioplasty (Revision of 1988 Guidelines). *J Am Coll Cardiol.* 1993;22:2033-2054. 21pp. 174refs. Sponsored by the American College of Cardiology, American Heart Association. Cost: free copy. To order call Educational Services Department 1 800 257-4740.

Coronary Disease/Therapy Angioplasty, Transluminal, Percutaneous, Coronary

Guidelines for Percutaneous Transluminal Coronary Angioplasty. *Circulation.* 1993;88:2987-3007. 21pp. 175refs. Sponsored by the American Heart Association. Cost: free copy. To order call 1 800 242-8721 (US only) or write to: American Heart Association, Public Inquiries, 7272 Greenville Ave, Dallas TX 75231-4596.

Coronary Diseases/Complications Primary Prevention/Methods

Preventing Heart Attack and Death in Patients with Coronary Disease. *Circulation.* 1995;92:2-4. 3pp. 17refs. Sponsored by the American Heart Association. Cost: free copy. To order call 1 800 242-8721 (US only) or write to: American Heart Association, Public Inquiries, 7272 Greenville Ave, Dallas TX 75231-4596.

Coronary Diseases/ Prevention and Control

Primary Prevention of Coronary Heart Disease: A Guidance from Framingham. *Circulation.* 1998;97:1876-1887. 12pp. 175refs. Sponsored by the American Heart Association. Cost: free copy. To order call 1 800 242-8721 (US only) or write to: American Heart Association, Public Inquiries, 7272 Greenville Ave, Dallas TX 75231-4596.

Cough

Managing Cough as a Defense Mechanism and as a Symptom. *Chest.* 1998;114(suppl):1335-1825. 49pp. 325refs. Sponsored by the American College of Chest Physicians. Cost: $14. To order call ACCP 1 800 343-2227 or 1 847 498-1400 (credit card orders). Key terms: cough; gastoesophageal reflux; asthma; postnasal drip syndrome.

Craniofacial Abnormalities/Surgery

Surgery of Craniofacial Anomalies. 1993. Sponsored by the American Association of Neurological Surgeons. To order call AANS 847 692-9500.

Craniosynostoses

Craniosynostosis (Including Syndromal Craniosynostosis, Brachycephaly, Plagiocephaly, Trigonocephaly, Scaphocephaly). *Clinical Practice Guidelines: Plastic and Maxillofacial Surgery.* 1995. 42pp. 109refs. Sponsored by the American Society of Maxillofacial Surgeons. Cost: Maxillofacial Surgery Guidelines $25 for entire set (not sold separately). Binder $10 (price includes shipping). To order call 1 800 766-4955.

Craniosynostoses/Surgery

Craniostenosis (Synostosis) Surgery. 1993. Sponsored by the American Association of Neurological Surgeons. To order call AANS 847 692-9500.

Craniotomy (see also Trephining)

Craniotomy Cerebral Aneurysm Arteriovenous Malformations

Craniotomy for Intracranial Aneurysm or AVM. 1993. Sponsored by the American Association of Neurological Surgeons. To order call AANS 847 692-9500.

Craniotomy Hypophysectomy Pituitary Neoplasms/Surgery

Craniotomy for Hypophysectomy or Pituitary Tumor. 1993. Sponsored by the American Association of Neurological Surgeons. To order call AANS 847 692-9500.

Credentialing Endoscopy, Gastrointestinal

Granting of Privileges for Gastrointestinal Endoscopy by Surgeons. *Surgical Endoscopy.* 1998;12. 4pp. 13refs. Sponsored by the Society of American Gastrointestinal and Endoscopic Surgeons. Cost: free. To order call 310 314-2404. Available on the Internet at sages.org. Key terms: surgery; privileging; credentialing; endoscopy; gastrointestinal.

Credentialing Medical Staff Privileges

Recommendations for Credentialing and Privileging. *J Am Acad Derm.* 1998;39:765-780. 18pp. 22refs. Sponsored by the American Academy of Dermatology. Cost: free copy. To order call Alice Bell 847 330-0230 x333. Available on the Internet at aad.org.

Credentialing Surgery, Ultrasonography/Standards

Granting of Ultrasonography Privileges for Surgeons. *Surgical Endoscopy.* 1996;12:186-188. 4pp. 2refs. Sponsored by the Society of American Gastrointestinal and Endoscopic Surgeons. Cost: free. To order call 310 314-2404. Available on the Internet at sages.org. Key terms: surgery; ultrasonography; privileging; credentialing.

Credentialing Surgical Procedures, Laparoscopic

Guidelines for Granting of Privileges for Laparoscopic and Thoracoscopic General Surgery. *Surgical Endoscopy.* 1998;12. 4pp. 11refs. Sponsored by the Society of American Gastrointestinal and Endoscopic Surgeons. Cost: free. To order call 310 314-2404. Available on the Internet at sages.org. Key terms: surgery; privileging; credentialing; laparoscopic; thoracoscopic.

Credentialing/Standards
Endoscopy

Hospital Credentialing Standards for Physicians who Perform Endoscopies. *Gastroenterology.* 1993;104:1563-1565. 3pp. 3refs. Sponsored by the American Gastroenterological Association. Cost: $3. To order call AGA 301 654-2055. Key terms: hospital credentialing; endoscopies; hospital privileges.

Cretinism/Diagnosis

Screening for Congenital Hypothyroidism. *Guide to Clinical Preventive Services, 2nd Ed.* 1996. Sponsored by the US Preventive Services Task Force. To order call Williams & Wilkins 1 800 638-0672.

Critical Care
Internship and Residency/Standards

Guidelines for Resident Training in Critical Care Medicine. *Critical Care Med.* 1995;23:1920-1923. 4pp. 2refs. Sponsored by the Society of Critical Care Medicine. Cost: Complete Set $60 + s/h SCCM members, $80 + s/h nonmembers; $5 for a single guideline. To order call SCCM 714 282-6000 or access Book Store on the SCCM website. Available free on the Internet at sccm.org. Key terms: critical care; medical education; training programs; intensive care unit.

Critical Care
Neuromuscular Blocking Agents/ Therapeutic Use

Practice Parameters for Sustained Neuromuscular Blockade in the Adult Critically Ill Patient: An Executive Summary. *Critical Care Med.* 1995;23:1601-1605. 5pp. 12refs. Sponsored by the Society of Critical Care Medicine. Cost: $5 for a single guideline. To order call SCCM 714 282-6000 or access Book Store on the SCCM website. Available free on the Internet at sccm.org. Key terms: neuromuscular blockade; paralysis; intensive care unit; critical illness; pancuronium.

Critical Care
Practice Guidelines

Guidelines for Granting Privileges for the Performance of Procedures in Critically Ill Patients. *Critical Care Med.* 1993;19:275-278. 4pp. Sponsored by the Society of Critical Care Medicine. Cost: Complete Set $60 + s/h SCCM members, $80 + s/h nonmembers; $5 for a single guideline. To order call SCCM 714 282-6000 or access Book Store on the SCCM website. Available free on the Internet at sccm.org.

Critical Care
Pulmonary Disease (Specialty)

Role of Pulmonary and Critical Care Medicine Physician in the American Health Care System. *Am J Respir Crit Care Med.* 1995;152:6. Sponsored by the American Thoracic Society. To order send check payable to American Thoracic Society, 1740 Broadway, New York, NY 10019-4374; for credit card orders, call 212 315-8863.

Critical Care
Specialties, Medical

Critical Care Medicine. *NIH Consensus Development Conference Statement.* 1983;4(6):1-26[Conf. No. 35]. 27pp. Sponsored by the National Institutes of Health. Cost: free copy. To order call 1 888 644-2667. Available on the Internet at consensus.nih.gov.

Critical Care/Standards
Clinical Laboratory Information Systems/Standards

Critical Values. *Am J Clin Pathol.* 1997;108:247-253. 7pp. 23refs. Sponsored by the American Society of Clinical Pathologists. Cost: free copy. To order call Felicia Nelson 312 738-1336 x1350. Key terms: panic values; alert values; critical limits; good laboratory practice; CLIA.

Critical Care/Standards
Intensive Care

Guidelines for the Definition of an Intensivist and the Practice of Critical Care Medicine. *Critical Care Med.* 1992;20:540-542. 3pp. Sponsored by the Society of Critical Care Medicine. Cost: Complete Set $60 + s/h SCCM members, $80 + s/h nonmembers; $5 for a single guideline. To order call SCCM 714 282-6000 or access Book Store on the SCCM website. Available free on the Internet at sccm.org. Key terms: critical care; patient care team; intensive care unit; mechanical ventilation; hemodynamics.

Critical Care/Standards
Patient Transfer/Standards

Guidelines for the Transfer of Critically Ill Patients. *Critical Care Med.* 1993;21:931-937. 7pp. 33refs. Sponsored by the Society of Critical Care Medicine. Cost: Complete Set $60 + s/h SCCM members, $80 + s/h nonmembers; $5 for a single guideline. To order call SCCM 714 282-6000 or access Book Store on the SCCM website. Available free on the Internet at sccm.org. Key terms: patient transfer; critical care; health planning guidelines; interdisciplinary health care team.

Critical Illness
Fever/Etiology

Practice Guidelines for Evaluating New Fever in Critically Ill Adult Patients. *Clin Inf Dis.* 1998;26:1042. 18pp. 106refs. Sponsored by the Infectious Diseases Society of America. To order obtain request from medical library or download via the Internet. Available on the Internet at idsociety.org/practice.

Crohn Disease/Diagnosis

Crohn's Disease. *Am J Gastroenterol.* 1997;92:559-566. 8pp. Sponsored by the American College of Gastroenterology. To order call 601 984-4540.

Cross Infection/Economics
Diagnosis-Related Groups

Description of Case-Mix Adjusters by Severity of Illness Working Group of the Society for Healthcare Epidemiologists of America (SHEA). *Infect Control Hosp Epidemiol.* 1988;9:309-316. 8pp. 43refs. Sponsored by the Society for Healthcare Epidemiology of America. Cost: free. To order visit our website at medscape.com/shea. Available on the Internet at medscape.com/shea. Key terms: diagnosis-related groups; acute physiologic and chronic health education; disease staging done by clinical staging or coded staging method; computerized severity index; patient management categories.

Cross Infection/Epidemiology
Outcome Assessment
(Health Care)/Standards

An Approach to the Evaluation of Quality Indicators of the Outcome of Care in Hospitalized Patients with a Focus on Nosocomial Infection Indicators. *Infect Control Hosp Epidemiol.* 1995;16:308-316. 9pp. 37refs. Sponsored by the Society for Healthcare Epidemiology of America. Cost: free. To order visit our website at medscape.com/shea. Available on the Internet at medscape.com/shea. Key terms: current status of utilization of quality indicators; important issues in evaluating quality indicators; use of outcome or process indicators; selection of quality indicators; definition of indicator.

Cross Infection/Prevention and Control
Endoscopy

Infection Control During Gastrointestinal Endoscopy: Guidelines for Clinical Application. *Gastrointest Endosc.* 1988;34(suppl):37s-40s. 4pp. 21refs. Sponsored by the American Society for Gastrointestinal Endoscopy. Cost: free. To order call ASGE 978 526-8330.

Cross Infection/Prevention and Control
Hospital Administration/Standards

Requirements for Infrastructure and Essential Activities of Infection Control and Epidemiology in Hospitals: A Consensus Panel Report. *Infect Control Hosp Epidemiol.* 1998;19:114-124. 11pp. 59refs. Sponsored by the Society for Healthcare Epidemiology of America. To order visit our website at mcdscape.com/shea. Available on the Internet at medscape.com/shea. Key terms: nosocomial infection prevention and control programs; infrastructure and essential activities for infection control and epidemiology programs; need for healthy and effective hospital-based infection control program.

Cross Infection/Prevention and Control
Pneumonia/Prevention and Control

Guidelines for Prevention of Nosocomial Pneumonia. *Morbid Mortal Weekly Report.* 1997;46(no. RR-1). Sponsored by the Centers for Disease Control and Prevention. Cost: $1. To order call US Govt Printing Office 202 783-3238.

Cryosurgery
Skin Diseases/Surgery

Cryosurgery. *J Am Acad Derm.* 1994;31:648-653. 6pp. 38refs. Sponsored by the American Academy of Dermatology. Cost: free copy. To order call Alice Bell 847 330-0230 x333. Available on the Internet at aad.org. Key terms: cryosurgery; instrumentation; methods.

CT Scan (see Tomography, X-ray Computed)

Cultural Diversity
Physician-Patient Relations

Cultural Competency in Health Care. *ACOG Committee Opinion.* 1998;201. 4pp. 11refs. Sponsored by the American College of Obstetricians and Gynecologists. Cost: free copy. Set of Bulletins $70 + s/h ACOG members, $125 + s/h nonmembers. One-year subscription $55 member, $65 nonmember. To order single copy, call ACOG Resource Center 202 863-2518; to order set or subscription, call ACOG Distribution Center, 1 800 762-2264. Available on the Internet to members only at acog.org. Key terms: cross-cultural comparison; physician-patient relations.

Communicable Diseases/Diagnosis
Diarrhea/Diagnosis

Guidelines on Acute Infectious Diarrhea in Adults. *Am J Gastroenterol.* 1997;92:1962-1975. 14pp. 104refs. Sponsored by the American College of Gastroenterology. Cost: one free copy. To order call ACG 703 820-7400.

Curriculum
Internship and Residency
Surgical Procedures, Laparoscopic

Advanced Laparoscopy into Surgical Residency Training. 1997;24. 4pp. 1ref. Sponsored by the Society of American Gastrointestinal and Endoscopic Surgeons. Cost: free. To order call 310 314-2404. Available on the Internet at sages.org. Key terms: surgery; residency; training; laparoscopy.

Cystic Fibrosis/Genetics
Genetic Screening

Genetic Testing for Cystic Fibrosis. *NIH Consensus Development Conference Statement.* 1997;15(4):1-37[Conf. No.106]. 37pp. 64refs. Sponsored by the National Institutes of Health. Cost: free copy. To order call 1 888 644-2667. Available on the Internet at consensus.nih.gov.

Cystic Fibrosis/Genetics
Heterozygote Detection

Current Status of Cystic Fibrosis Carrier Screening. *ACOG Committee Opinion.* 1991;101. 2pp. 10refs. Sponsored by the American College of Obstetricians and Gynecologists. Cost: free copy. Set of Opinions $55 + s/h ACOG members, $75 + s/h nonmembers. One-year subscription $55 member, $65 nonmember. To order single copy, call ACOG Resource Center 202 863-2518; to order set or subscription, call ACOG Distribution Center, 1 800 762-2264. Available on the Internet to members only at acog.org. Key terms: genetic screening.

Cystic Fibrosis/Prevention and Control
Mass Screening/Standards

Newborn Screening for Cystic Fibrosis: A Paradigm for Public Health Genetics Policy Development. *Morbid Mortal Weekly Report.* 1997;46(no. RR-16). Sponsored by the Centers for Disease Control and Prevention. Cost: $1. To order call US Govt Printing Office 202 783-3238.

Cytomegalovirus/
Prevention and Control
Blood Transfusion/Methods

Prevention of Transfusion-Associated CMV Infection. *Am J Clin Pathol.* 1996;106:163-169. 6pp. 67refs. Sponsored by the American Society of Clinical Pathologists. Cost: free copy. To order call Felicia Nelson 312 738-1336 x1350. Key terms: cytomegalovirus infection; transfusion-related infection; blood filtration; screen blood components.

Cytotoxicity, Immunologic

Cytotoxicity Testing (Bryan's Testing). *J Allergy Clin Immun.* 1981;67:333-338, Position Statement No. 8—Controversial Techniques. 2pp. 15refs. Sponsored by the American Academy of Allergy, Asthma, and Immunology. Cost: free copy. To order call 414 272-6071.

Death
Family
Students, Medical

Informing Families of a Patient's Death: Guidelines for the Involvement of Medical Students. *Reports of CEJA.* 1989;1:106-108. 3pp. Sponsored by the American Medical Association, Council on Ethical and Judicial Affairs. Cost: free copy. To order call AMA 312 464-5223.

Death, Sudden
Heart Diseases

Sudden Cardiac Death. *J Am Coll Cardiol.* 1985. Sponsored by the American College of Cardiology. Cost: free copy. To order call Educational Services Department 1 800 257-4740.

Deception
Ethics, Medical

Deception. *ACOG Committee Opinion.* 1990;87. 2pp. Sponsored by the American College of Obstetricians and Gynecologists. Cost: free copy. Set of Opinions $55 + s/h ACOG members, $75 + s/h nonmembers. One-year subscription $55 member, $65 nonmember. To order single copy, call ACOG Resource Center 202 863-2518; to order set or subscription, call ACOG Distribution Center, 1 800 762-2264. Available on the Internet to members only at acog.org. Key terms: lying; ethics: medical.

Decision Making

Medical Treatment Decisions Concerning Elderly People, Position Statement. 1993. Sponsored by the American Geriatrics Society. Cost: free. To order call AGS 212 308-1414.

Decision Making
Advance Directives

Making Treatment Decisions for Incapacitated Elderly Patients without Advance Directives, Position Statement. 1998. Sponsored by the American Geriatrics Society. Cost: free. To order call AGS 212 308-1414.

Decision Making
Ethics

Ethical Decision-Making in Obstetrics and Gynecology. *ACOG Technical Bulletin*. 1989;136. 7pp. 9refs. Sponsored by the American College of Obstetricians and Gynecologists. Cost: free copy. Set of Bulletins $70 + s/h ACOG members, $125 + s/h nonmembers. One-year subscription $55 member, $65 nonmember. To order single copy, call ACOG Resource Center 202 863-2518; to order set or subscription, call ACOG Distribution Center, 1 800 762-2264. Available on the Internet to members only at acog.org. Key terms: ethics: medical; ob/gyn.

Decision Making
Health Services for the Aged

Geriatric Assessment Methods for Clinical Decision-Making. *NIH Consensus Development Conference Statement*. 1987;6(13):1-21[Conf. No. 65]. 22pp. Sponsored by the National Institutes of Health. Cost: free copy. To order call 1 888 644-2667. Available on the Internet at consensus.nih.gov.

Decision Making
Infant, Newborn
Intensive Care

Treatment Decisions for Seriously Ill Newborns. *Reports of CEJA*. 1992;3:66-75. 10pp. Sponsored by the American Medical Association, Council on Ethical and Judicial Affairs. Cost: free copy. To order call AMA 312 464-5223.

Decision Making
Patient Participation

End-of-Life Decision Making: Understanding the Goals of Care. *ACOG Committee Opinion*. 1995;156. 6pp. 25refs. Sponsored by the American College of Obstetricians and Gynecologists. Cost: free copy. Set of Opinions $55 + s/h ACOG members, $75 + s/h nonmembers. One-year subscription $55 member, $65 nonmember. To order single copy, call ACOG Resource Center 202 863-2518; to order set or subscription, call ACOG Distribution Center, 1 800 762-2264. Available on the Internet to members only at acog.org. Key terms: ethics: physician-patient interactions; communication.

Decubitus Ulcer

Pressure Sores. 1996. 6pp. Sponsored by the American Society of Plastic and Reconstructive Surgeons. Cost: $25 members, $55 nonmembers (full set of guidelines), + s/h. To order call 1 800 766-4955.

Decubitus Ulcer

Pressure Ulcers. 1996. 16pp. 18refs. Sponsored by the American Medical Directors Association. Cost: $8. To order call 1 800 876-2632 or 410 740-9743.

Decubitus Ulcer/Nursing Care
Practice Guidelines

Treatment of Pressure Ulcers. *AHCPR*. 1994;Publication No. 95-0652. 154pp. 335refs. Sponsored by the Federal Agency for Health Care Policy and Research. To order call AHCPR Clearinghouse 1 800 358-9295.

Decubitus Ulcer/Prevention and Control
Practice Guidelines

Pressure Ulcers in Adults: Prediction and Prevention. *AHCPR*. 1992;Publication No. 92-0047. 63pp. 129refs. Sponsored by the Federal Agency for Health Care Policy and Research. To order call AHCPR Clearinghouse 1 800 358-9295.

Defibrillators, Implantable
Patient Selection

Implantation of the Automatic Cardioverter-Defibrillator—Non-Inducibility of Ventricular Tachyarrhythmia as a Patient Selection Criteria. *AHCPR Health Technology Assessment*. 1990;No. 10 (AHCPR Publication No. 91-0041). 9pp. 70refs. Sponsored by the Federal Agency for Health Care Policy and Research. To order call AHCPR Clearinghouse 1 800 358-9295.

Deglutition Disorders
Oropharynx/Physiopathology

Management of Oropharyngeal Dysphagia. *Gastroenterology*. 1998;116:452-454. 2pp. Sponsored by the American Gastroenterological Association. Cost: $3. To order call AGA 301 654-2055. Key terms: dysphagia; oropharyngeal.

Deglutition Disorders/Etiology
Esophageal Diseases/Complications

Management of Patients with Dysphagia Caused by Benign Disorders of the Distal Esophagus. *Gastroenterology*. 1999. Sponsored by the American Gastroenterological Association. To order call AGA 301 654-2055.

Delirium
Dementia

Delirium, Dementia, Amnesia, and Other Cognitive Disorders. *Treatments of Psychiatric Disorders, Second Edition, Volume I*. 1995;Section 3. 219pp. 1007refs. Sponsored by the American Psychiatric Association. Cost: $250 for 2-volume set. To order call 1 800 368-5777 order #SPCT8700. Key terms: TPD; disorders; treatment.

Delirium/Therapy

Practice Guideline for the Treatment of Patients with Delirium. *Am J Psych*. 1999;156:5(suppl). 64pp, 135refs. Sponsored by the American Psychiatric Association. Cost: $22.50. To order call 1 800 368-5777 order #SPCT2313. Key terms: delirium; dementia; delusions.

Delivery/Economics
Health Care Costs/Standards

Financial Influences on Mode of Delivery. *ACOG Committee Opinion*. 1994;149. 1pp. Sponsored by the American College of Obstetricians and Gynecologists. Cost: free copy. Set of Opinions $55 + s/h ACOG members, $75 + s/h nonmembers. One-year subscription $55 member, $65 nonmember. To order single copy, call ACOG Resource Center 202 863-2518; to order set or subscription, call ACOG Distribution Center, 1 800 762-2264. Available on the Internet to members only at acog.org. Key terms: delivery reimbursement.

Delivery of Health Care
Allergy and Immunology

Remote Practice of Allergy. *J Allergy Clin Immun*. 1986;77:651-652, Position Statement No. 13. 1pp. Sponsored by the American Academy of Allergy, Asthma, and Immunology. Cost: free copy. To order call 414 272-6071.

Delivery of Health Care/Economics
Acquired Immunodeficiency
Syndrome/Economics

Financing Care of Patients with AIDS. *Ann Intern Med*. 1988;108:470-473. 4pp. Sponsored by the American College of Physicians. To order call ACP Clinical Efficacy Assessment Project 1 800 523-1546.

Delivery of Health Care/Economics
Quality of Health Care

Cost Containment in Medical Care. *ACOG Committee Opinion*. 1996;171. 2pp. Sponsored by the American College of Obstetricians and Gynecologists. Cost: free copy. Set of Opinions $55 + s/h ACOG members, $75 + s/h nonmembers. One-year subscription $55 member, $65 nonmember. To order single copy, call ACOG Resource Center 202 863-2518; to order set or subscription, call ACOG Distribution Center, 1 800 762-2264. Available on the Internet to members only at acog.org. Key terms: managed care.

Dementia

Dementia. 1998. 28pp. 35refs. Sponsored by the American Medical Directors Association. Cost: $8. To order call 1 800 876-2632 or 410 740-9743.

Dementia/Diagnosis

Practice Parameter: Diagnosis and Evaluation of Dementia. *Neurol*. 1994;44:2203-2206. 4pp. Sponsored by the American Academy of Neurology. Cost: individual statements are free. To order call AAN Member Service Center 1 800 879-1960. Available on the Internet at aan.com.

Dementia/Diagnosis

Screening for Dementia. *Guide to Clinical Preventive Services, 2nd Ed*. 1996. Sponsored by the US Preventive Services Task Force. To order call Williams & Wilkins 1 800 638-0672.

Dementia/Diagnosis
Diagnosis, Differential

Differential Diagnosis of Dementing Diseases. *NIH Consensus Development Conference Statement.* 1987;6(11):1-27[Conf. No. 63]. 28pp. Sponsored by the National Institutes of Health. Cost: free copy. To order call 1 888 644-2667. Available on the Internet at consensus.nih.gov.

Demyelinating Diseases/Diagnosis

Research Criteria for Diagnosis of Chronic Inflammatory Demyelinating Polyneuropathy (CIDP). *Neurol.* 1991;41:617-618. 2pp. Sponsored by the American Academy of Neurology. Cost: individual statements are free. To order call AAN Member Service Center 1 800 879-1960. Available on the Internet at aan.com.

Demyelinating Diseases/Therapy
Plasmapheresis

Apheresis in Chronic Inflammatory Demyelinating Polyneuropathy and in Renal Transplantation. *Ann Intern Med.* 1985;103:630-633. 4pp. Sponsored by the American College of Physicians. To order call ACP Clinical Efficacy Assessment Project 1 800 523-1546.

Dental Care for Chronically Ill/Methods
Diabetes Mellitus, Insulin-Dependent/Therapy
Diabetes Mellitus, Non-Insulin-Dependent/Therapy

Oral Health Care Series: Patients with Diabetes. 1994. 17pp. 45refs. Sponsored by the American Dental Association. Cost: $8 ADA members, $12 nonmembers. To order call ADA Dept of Salable Materials 1 800 947-4776.

Dental Care for Chronically Ill/Methods
Liver Diseases

Oral Health Care Series: Patients with Hepatic Disease. 1996. 13pp. 15refs. Sponsored by the American Dental Association. Cost: $8 ADA members, $12 nonmembers. To order call ADA Dept of Salable Materials 1 800 947-4776.

Dental Care For Chronically Ill/Methods
Substance-Related Disorders

Oral Health Care Series: Chemically Dependent Patients. 1993. 50pp. 71refs. Sponsored by the American Dental Association. Cost: $8 ADA members, $12 nonmembers. To order call ADA Dept of Salable Materials 1 800 947-4776.

Dental Care for Disabled
Health Services Needs and Demand

Oral Health Care Series: Patients with Physical and Mental Disorders. 1993. 77pp. 30refs. Sponsored by the American Dental Association. Cost: $8 ADA members, $12 nonmembers. To order call ADA Dept of Salable Materials 1 800 947-4746.

Dental Caries/Prevention and Control
Fluoridation

Public Health Service Report on Fluoride Benefits and Risks. *Morbid Mortal Weekly Report.* 1991;40(no. RR-7):1-8. 9pp. Sponsored by the Centers for Disease Control and Prevention. Cost: $1. To order call US Govt Printing Office 202 783-3238.

Dental Implantation

Dental Implants. *NIH Consensus Development Conference Statement.* 1988;7(3):1-22[Conf. No. 69]. 23pp. Sponsored by the National Institutes of Health. Cost: free copy. To order call 1 888 644-2667. Available on the Internet at consensus.nih.gov.

Dental Materials/Adverse Effects

Effects and Side Effects of Dental Restorative Materials. *NIH Consensus Development Conference Statement.* 1991;18pp. Sponsored by the National Institutes of Health. Cost: free copy. To order call 1 888 644-2667. Available on the Internet at consensus.nih.gov.

Dentistry/Standards
Infection Control/Standards

Recommended Infection-Control Practices for Dentistry. *Morbid Mortal Weekly Report.* 1993;42(no. RR-8). Sponsored by the Centers for Disease Control and Prevention. Cost: $1. To order call US Govt Printing Office 202 783-3238.

Dentistry/Standards
Mouth Diseases

Dental Practice Parameters. 1997. Sponsored by the American Dental Association. Cost: $39.95. To order call ADA Dept of Salable Materials 312 440-2500.

Depression

Depression. 1996. 16pp. 38refs. Sponsored by the American Medical Directors Association. Cost: $8. To order call 1 800 876-2632 or 410 740-9743.

Depression
Psychotropic Drugs

Pharmacotherapy Companion to the 1996 Depression Clinical Practice Guideline. 1998. 24pp. 27refs. Sponsored by the American Medical Directors Association. Cost: $8. To order call 1 800 876-2632 or 410 740-9743.

Depression/Diagnosis
Depression/Therapy

Diagnosis and Treatment of Depression in Late Life. *NIH Consensus Development Conference Statement.* 1991;9(3):1-27[Conf. No. 86]. 28pp. Sponsored by the National Institutes of Health. Cost: free copy. To order call 1 888 644-2667. Available on the Internet at consensus.nih.gov.

Depression/Therapy
Primary Health Care

Treatment of Depression by Primary Care Physicians: Psychotherapeutic Treatments for Depression. *Practice-Related Report of the AMA Council on Scientific Affairs.* 1991. 13pp. 23refs. Sponsored by the American Medical Association, Council on Scientific Affairs. Cost: free. To order call Nancy Nolan, AMA, 312 464-5046.

Depressive Disorder
Primary Health Care

Treatment of Depression by Primary Care Physicians: Pharmacological Approaches. *Practice-Related Report of the AMA Council on Scientific Affairs.* 1991. 37pp. 72refs. Sponsored by the American Medical Association, Council on Scientific Affairs. Cost: free. To order call Nancy Nolan, AMA, 312 464-5046.

Depressive Disorder
Women's Health

Depression in Women's Health. *ACOG Technical Bulletin.* 1993;182. 8pp. 31refs. Sponsored by the American College of Obstetricians and Gynecologists. Cost: free copy. Set of Bulletins $70 + s/h ACOG members, $125 + s/h nonmembers. One-year subscription $55 member, $65 nonmember. To order single copy, call ACOG Resource Center 202 863-2518; to order set or subscription, call ACOG Distribution Center, 1 800 762-2264. Available on the Internet to members only at acog.org.

Depressive Disorder/Diagnosis
Depressive Disorder/Therapy

Depression in Primary Care: Volume I: Detection and Diagnosis; Volume II: Treatment of Major Depression. *AHCPR.* 1993;Vol. I Publication No. 93-0550; Vol. II Publication No. 93-0551. Vol. I: 124pp; Vol. II: 175pp. Vol. I: 239refs; Vol. II: 216refs. Sponsored by the Federal Agency for Health Care Policy and Research. To order call AHCPR Clearinghouse 1 800 358-9295.

Depressive Disorder/Diagnosis
Primary Health Care

Recognition and Treatment of Depression in Medical Practice. *Practice-Related Report of the AMA Council on Scientific Affairs.* 1991. 35pp. 72refs. Sponsored by the American Medical Association, Council on Scientific Affairs. Cost: free. To order call Nancy Nolan, AMA, 312 464-5046.

Depressive Disorder Therapy

Practice Guideline for Major Depressive Disorder in Adults. *Am J Psych.* 1993;150(suppl):4. 26pp. 169refs. Sponsored by the American Psychiatric Association. Cost: $22.50. To order call 1 800 368-5777 order #SPCT2301. Key terms: depressive disorder.

Dermabrasion
Skin Diseases/Surgery

Dermabrasion. *J Am Acad Derm.* 1994;31:654-657. 4pp. 23refs. Sponsored by the American Academy of Dermatology. Cost: free copy. To order call Alice Bell 847 330-0230 x333. Available on the Internet at aad.org. Key terms: dermabrasion; adverse effects; methods; skin diseases; diagnosis.

Dermatitis, Atopic/Therapy

Disease Management of Atopic Dermatitis: A Practice Parameter. *Ann Allergy Asthma Immun.* 1997;70:197-211, Practice Parameter. 14pp. Sponsored by the American Academy of Allergy, Asthma, and Immunology; American College of Allergy, Asthma, and Immunology; Joint Council of Allergy, Asthma, and Immunology. Cost: free copy. To order call 847 934-1918 or e-mail sgjcaai@aol.com. Available on the Internet at jcaai.org.

Dermatitis, Atopic/Therapy

Guidelines of Care for Atopic Dermatitis. *J Am Acad Derm.* 1992;26:485-488. 4pp. 17refs. Sponsored by the American Academy of Dermatology. Cost: free copy. To order call Alice Bell 847 330-0230 x333. Available on the Internet at aad.org. Key terms: atopic dermatitis; diagnosis; therapy.

Dermatitis, Contact/Therapy

Contact Dermatitis. *J Am Acad Derm.* 1995;32:109-113. 5pp. 16refs. Sponsored by the American Academy of Dermatology. Cost: free copy. To order call Alice Bell 847 330-0230 x333. Available on the Internet at aad.org. Key terms: contact dermatitis; diagnosis; etiology; therapy.

Dermatologic Agents/Therapy
Glucocorticoids, Topical/Therapy

Topical Glucocorticosteroids. *J Am Acad Derm.* 1996;35:615-619. 5pp. 32refs. Sponsored by the American Academy of Dermatology. Cost: free copy. To order call Alice Bell 847 330-0230 x333. Available on the Internet at aad.org. Key terms: topical glucocorticoids; administration and dosage; therapeutic use.

Dermatomyositis/Therapy
Dermatomyositis/Diagnosis

Dermatomyositis. *J Am Acad Derm.* 1996;34:824-829. 6pp. Sponsored by the American Academy of Dermatology. Cost: free copy. To order call Alice Bell 847 330-0230 x333. Available on the Internet at aad.org. Key terms: dermatomyositis; classification; diagnosis; therapy.

Desensitization, Immunologic/Adverse Effects
Hypersensitivity, Immediate/Therapy

Guidelines to Minimize the Risk from Systemic Reactions Caused by Immunotherapy with Allergenic Extracts. *J Allergy Clin Immun.* 1994;93:811-812, Position Statement No. 25. 2pp. 6refs. Sponsored by the American Academy of Allergy, Asthma, and Immunology. Cost: free copy. To order call 414 272-6071.

Desensitization, Immunologic
Hypersensitivity/Therapy

Vivo Diagnostic Testing and Immunotherapy for Allergy: Part I. *JAMA.* 1987;258:1363-1368. 6pp. Sponsored by the American Medical Association, Council on Scientific Affairs. Cost: free. To order call Nancy Nolan, AMA, 312 464-5046.

Desensitization, Immunologic
Hypersensitivity/Therapy

Vivo Diagnostic Testing and Immunotherapy for Allergy: Part II. *JAMA.* 1987;258:1505-1509. 5pp. Sponsored by the American Medical Association, Council on Scientific Affairs. Cost: free. To order call Nancy Nolan, AMA, 312 464-5046.

Developmental Disabilities/Diagnosis

Screening Infants and Young Children for Developmental Disabilities. *Pediatr.* 1997;93(5):863-865. 3pp. 8refs. Sponsored by the American Academy of Pediatrics. Cost: $1.95. Discounted set of policies available. To order call 1 800 433-9016.

Dexamethasone/Diagnostic Use
Depressive Disorder/Diagnosis

Dexamethasone Suppression Test for the Detection, Diagnosis, and Management of Depression. *Ann Intern Med.* 1984;100:307-308. 2pp. Sponsored by the American College of Physicians. To order call ACP Clinical Efficacy Assessment Project 1 800 523-1546.

Diabetes, Gestational

Medical Management of Pregnancy Complicated by Diabetes, 2nd Edition. 1995. 126pp. Sponsored by the American Diabetes Association. Cost: $39.95. To order call 1 800 232-6733; online bookstore: merchant.diabetes.org. Available on the Internet at merchant.diabetes.org. Key terms: pregnancy; contraception and physiological; diabetes management.

Diabetes Mellitus
Exercise

The Health Professional's Guide to Diabetes and Exercise. 1995. 335pp. Sponsored by the American Diabetes Association. Cost: $49.95. To order call 1 800 232-6733; online bookstore: merchant. diabetes.org. Available on the Internet at merchant. diabetes.org. Key terms: exercise; diabetes; guidelines; complications; obesity.

Diabetes Mellitus/Blood
Hemoglobin A, Glycosylated/Analysis

Glycosylated Hemoglobin Assays in the Management and Diagnosis of Diabetes Mellitus. *Ann Intern Med.* 1984;101:710-713. 4pp. Sponsored by the American College of Physicians. To order call ACP Clinical Efficacy Assessment Project 1 800 523-1546.

Diabetes Mellitus/Complications
Diabetic Retinopathy/Therapy

Guidelines for Eye Care in Patients with Diabetes Mellitus. *Arch Intern Med.* 1989;149:769-770. 2pp. Sponsored by the Kentucky Diabetic Retinopathy Group. To obtain request from medical library. Key terms: retinopathy; diabetic retinopathy; eye; diabetes mellitus; vision.

Diabetes Mellitus/Complications
Hypertension/Drug Therapy

Working Report on Hypertension in Diabetes. *NIH Publication No. 94-3530.* 1994. 32pp. 116refs. Sponsored by the National Heart, Lung, and Blood Institute. Cost: $3. To order contact the NHLBI Information Center, PO Box 30105, Bethesda, MD 20824-0105, 301 251-1222.

Diabetes Mellitus/Diagnosis

Screening for Diabetes Mellitus. *Guide to Clinical Preventive Services, 2nd Ed.* 1996. Sponsored by the US Preventive Services Task Force. To order call Williams & Wilkins 1 800 638-0672.

Diabetes Mellitus/Drug Therapy

Management of Diabetes Mellitus. 1994. 32pp. 10refs. Sponsored by the American Association of Clinical Endocrinologists. To order call AACE 904 353-7878. Key terms: diabetes; glucose; insulin; blood sugar; self-management.

Diabetes Mellitus/Drug Therapy
Diabetes Mellitus/Complications

Intensive Diabetes Management, 2nd Edition. 1998. 169pp. Sponsored by the American Diabetes Association. Cost: $39.95. To order call 1 800 232-6733; onlinebookstore: merchant.diabetes. org. Available on the Internet at merchant. diabetes. org. Key terms: DCCT; dosage schedules; insulin action; diabetes.

Diabetes Mellitus/Epidemiology
Vital Statistics

Diabetes: 1996 Vital Statistics. 1995. 112pp. Sponsored by the American Diabetes Association. Cost: $18.50. To order call 1 800 232-6733; online bookstore: merchant.diabetes.org. Available on the Internet at merchant.diabetes.org. Key terms: incidence; prevalence; use of health care; mortality; diabetes.

Diabetes Mellitus/
Prevention and Control
Mass Screening

Screening for Diabetes Mellitus in Apparently Healthy, Asymptomatic Adults. *Ann Intern Med.* 1988;109:639-649. 11pp. 124refs. Sponsored by the American College of Physicians. To order call ACP Clinical Efficacy Assessment Project 1 800 523-1546.

Diabetes Mellitus/Therapy
Blood Glucose/Analysis

Selected Methods for the Management of Diabetes Mellitus. *Ann Intern Med.* 1983;99:272-274. 3pp. Sponsored by the American College of Physicians. To order call ACP Clinical Efficacy Assessment Project 1 800 523-1546.

Diabetes Mellitus/Therapy
Diabetes Mellitus/Complications

Therapy for Diabetes Mellitus and Related Disorders, 3rd Edition. 1998. 480pp. Sponsored by the American Diabetes Association. Cost: $49.95. To order call 1 800 232-6733; online bookstore: merchant.diabetes.org. Available on the Internet at merchant.diabetes.org. Key terms: diabetes management; medications; medical complications.

Diabetes Mellitus/Therapy
Quality Assurance, Health Care

Clinical Practice Recommendations. 1999. 114pp. Sponsored by the American Diabetes Association. Cost: $12.50. To order call 1 800 232-6733; online bookstore: merchant.diabetes.org. Available on the Internet at merchant.diabetes.org. Key terms: diabetes guidelines; position statements.

Diabetes Mellitus, Insulin-Dependent
Hyperglycemia/Prevention and Control

Medical Management of Insulin-Dependent (Type 1) Diabetes, 3rd Edition. 1998. 246pp. Sponsored by the American Diabetes Association. Cost: $39.95. To order call 1 800 232-6733; online bookstore: merchant. diabetes.org. Available on the Internet at merchant. diabetes.org. Key terms: diagnosis; classification; pathogenesis; management; diabetes.

Diabetes Mellitus,
Non-Insulin-Dependent

Medical Management of Non-Insulin-Dependent (Type 2) Diabetes, 4th Edition. 1998. 139pp. Sponsored by the American Diabetes Association. Cost: $39.95. To order call 1 800 232-6733; online bookstore: merchant.diabetes.org. Available on the Internet at merchant.diabetes.org. Key terms: diagnosis; complications; management; behavioral; diabetes.

Diabetes Mellitus, Non-Insulin-
Dependent/Diet Therapy
Exertion

Diet and Exercise in Non-Insulin-Dependent Diabetes Mellitus. *NIH Consensus Development Conference Statement.* 1986;6(8):1-21[Conf. No. 60]. 22pp. Sponsored by the National Institutes of Health. Cost: free copy. To order call 1 888 644-2667. Available on the Internet at consensus.nih.gov.

Diabetic Diet
Diabetes Mellitus, Insulin-Dependent/
Diet Therapy

Diabetes Medical Nutrition Therapy. 1997. 290pp. Sponsored by the American Diabetes Association. Cost: $24.95. To order call 1 800 232-6733; online bookstore: merchant.diabetes.org. Available on the Internet at merchant.diabetes.org. Key terms: nutrition assessment; goal setting; intervention; outcome evaluation.

Diabetic Retinopathy

Diabetic Retinopathy Preferred Practice Patterns. 1998. 36pp. 60refs. Sponsored by the American Academy of Ophthalmology. Cost: $11 members, $16 nonmembers. AAO members first copy free upon publication. To order call AAO Order Dept 415 561-8540. Key terms: eye; diabetes; diabetic retinopathy; prevention; treatment.

Diabetic Retinopathy/Surgery
Light Coagulation/Methods

Photocoagulation for Diabetic Retinopathy. *JAMA.* 1991;266:1263-1265. 3pp. 10refs. Sponsored by the National Eye Institute. Cost: free copy. To order write Dr Ferris, National Eye Institute, Bldg 31, Rm 6A52, 31 Center Dr MSC 2510, Bethesda, MD 20892-2510. Key terms: photocoagulation; laser; neovascularization; diabetic retinopathy; therapy.

Diagnosis

Diagnostic and Therapeutic Procedures. 1989. 75pp. Sponsored by the American Society for Gastrointestinal Endoscopy. Cost: $10. To order call ASGE 978 526-8330.

Diagnostic Imaging

ACR Standard on Communication—Diagnostic Radiology. 1999. 2pp. Sponsored by the American College of Radiology. Cost: $25 (ACR nonmembers). To order call ACR Dept of Quality Assurance 703 716-7592. Available free on the Internet at acr.org. Key terms: radiology; diagnostic; practice; reporting.

Diagnostic Imaging
Pregnancy

Guidelines for Diagnostic Imaging During Pregnancy. *ACOG Committee Opinion.* 1995;158. 4pp. 21refs. Sponsored by the American College of Obstetricians and Gynecologists. Cost: free copy. Set of Opinions $55 + s/h ACOG members, $75 + s/h nonmembers. One-year subscription $55 member, $65 nonmember. To order single copy, call ACOG Resource Center 202 863-2518; to order set or subscription, call ACOG Distribution Center, 1 800 762-2264. Available on the Internet to members only at acog.org. Key terms: prenatal diagnosis; ultrasound; MRI; x-rays.

Diagnostic Techniques, Ophthalmological/Diagnosis
Optic Nerve
Retina/Pathology

Optic Nerve Head and Retinal Fiber Analysis Ophthalmic Procedure Assessment. *Ophthalmology.* 1999;106:1414 1424. 11pp. 53refs. Sponsored by the American Academy of Ophthalmology. Cost: $11 members, $16 nonmembers. AAO members first copy free upon publication. To order call AAO Order Dept 415 561-8540. Key terms: eye; glaucoma; optic nerve; optic nerve head analysis; retinal nerve fiber layer.

Diagnostic Tests, Routine

Common Diagnostic Tests: Use and Interpretation, 2nd edition. 1990. 441pp. Sponsored by the American College of Physicians, Blue Cross/Blue Shield Association. Cost: $31 ACP members, $37 nonmembers. To order call ACP Clinical Efficacy Assessment Project 1 800 523-1546.

Diagnostic Tests, Routine

Common Screening Tests. 1991. 417pp. Sponsored by the American College of Physicians. Cost: $31 ACP members, $37 nonmembers. To order call ACP Clinical Efficacy Assessment Project 1 800 523-1546.

Diagnostic Tests, Routine
Laboratories, Hospital

Practice Parameter on Laboratory Panel Testing for Screening and Case Finding in Asymptomatic Adults. *Arch Path Lab Med.* 1996;120:929-943. 15pp. 118refs. Sponsored by the College of American Pathologists. Cost: reprints: free. To order call CAP 1 800 323-4040 x7378. Key terms: panel testing; screening; case finding; wellness.

Diagnostic Tests, Routine
Mass Chest X-ray

Utility of Routine Chest Radiographs. *Ann Intern Med.* 1986;104:663-670. 8pp. Sponsored by the American College of Physicians. To order call ACP Clinical Efficacy Assessment Project 1 800 523-1546.

Diagnostic Tests, Routine
Preoperative Care

Statement on Routine Preoperative Laboratory and Diagnostic Screening. *ASA Standards, Guidelines and Statements.* 1998;26. 1pp. Sponsored by the American Society of Anesthesiologists. Cost: free copy. To order call ASA 847 825-5586. Available on the Internet at asahq.org. Key terms: preanesthetic laboratory testing; preanesthetic diagnostic testing.

Diagnostic Tests, Routine
Preoperative Care

Utility of the Routine Electrocardiogram Before Surgery and on General Hospital Admission: Critical Review and New Guidelines. *Ann Intern Med.* 1986;105:552-557. 6pp. Sponsored by the American College of Physicians. To order call ACP Clinical Efficacy Assessment Project 1 800 523-1546.

Diagnostic Tests/Routine
Electrolytes/Blood

Serum Electrolytes, Serum Osmolality, Blood Urea Nitrogen, and Serum Creatinine. *Common Diagnostic Tests: Use and Interpretation.* 1987. 25pp. Sponsored by the American College of Physicians. To order call ACP Clinical Efficacy Assessment Project 1 800 523-1546.

Diarrhea
Travel

Travelers' Diarrhea. *NIH Consensus Development Conference Statement.* 1985;5(8):1-19[Conf. No. 48]. 20pp. Sponsored by the National Institutes of Health. Cost: free copy. To order call 1 888 644-2667. Available on the Internet at consensus.nih.gov.

Diarrhea/Therapy
Gastroenterology

Chronic Diarrhea. *Gastroenterology.* 1999;116:1461-1486. 25pp. 217refs. Sponsored by the American Gastroenterological Association. Cost: $10. To order call AGA 301 654-2055. Key terms: diarrhea; chronic.

Diet
Counseling

Counseling to Promote a Healthy Diet. *Guide to Clinical Preventive Services, 2nd Ed.* 1996. Sponsored by the US Preventive Services Task Force. To order call Williams & Wilkins 1 800 638-0672.

Diet Therapy
Diabetes Mellitus

American Diabetes Association Guide to Medical Nutrition Therapy for Diabetes. 1999. 400pp. Sponsored by the American Diabetes Association. Cost: $49.95. To order call 1 800 232-6733; online bookstore: merchant.diabetes.org. Available on the Internet at merchant.diabetes.org. Key terms: nutrition therapy; diabetes complications; lifestyle; special populations.

Dietary Fiber/Therapeutic Use
Health Status

Dietary Fiber and Health. *JAMA*. 1989;262:542-546. 5pp. Sponsored by the American Medical Association, Council on Scientific Affairs. Cost: free. To order call Nancy Nolan, AMA, 312 464-5046.

Dietary Supplements
Vitamin A
Pregnancy

Vitamin A Supplementation During Pregnancy. *ACOG Committee Opinion*. 1998;196. 2pp. 1ref. Sponsored by the American College of Obstetricians and Gynecologists. Cost: free copy. Set of Opinions $55 + s/h ACOG members, $75 + s/h nonmembers. One-year subscription $55 member, $65 nonmember. To order single copy, call ACOG Resource Center 202 863-2518; to order set or subscription, call ACOG Distribution Center, 1 800 762-2264. Available on the Internet to members only at acog.org. Key terms: vitamin A; prenatal care.

Diethylstilbestrol
Vaginal Neoplasms/Chemically Induced

Diethylstilbestrol 1993. *ACOG Committee Opinion*. 1993;131. 1pp. 5refs. Sponsored by the American College of Obstetricians and Gynecologists. Cost: free copy. Set of Opinions $55 + s/h ACOG members, $75 + s/h nonmembers. One-year subscription $55 member, $65 nonmember. To order single copy, call ACOG Resource Center 202 863-2518; to order set or subscription, call ACOG Distribution Center, 1 800 762-2264. Available on the Internet to members only at acog.org. Key terms: DES.

Dihydroergotamine/Therapeutic Use
Ergotamine/Therapeutic Use
Migraine/Drug Therapy

Practice Parameters: Appropriate Use of Ergotamine and Dihydroergotamine in the Treatment of Migraine and Status Migrainosus. *Neurol*. 1995;45:585-587. 3pp. Sponsored by the American Academy of Neurology. Cost: individual statements are free. To order call AAN Member Service Center 1 800 879-1960. Available on the Internet at aan.com.

Dinoprostone
Labor, Induced
Fetal Monitoring

Monitoring during Induction of Labor with Dinoprostone. *ACOG Committee Opinion*. 1998;209. 1pp. 3refs. Sponsored by the American College of Obstetricians and Gynecologists. Cost: free copy. Set of Bulletins $70 + s/h ACOG members, $125 + s/h nonmembers. One-year subscription $55 member, $65 nonmember. To order single copy, call ACOG Resource Center 202 863-2518; to order set or subscription, call ACOG Distribution Center, 1 800 762-2264. Available on the Internet to members only at acog.org. Key terms: induced labor; dinoprostone; cervidil fetal monitoring; uterine contractions.

Diphtheria-Tetanus-Pertussis Vaccine
Whooping Cough/
Prevention and Control

Pertussis Vaccination: Acellular Pertussis Vaccine for Reinforcing and Booster Use—Supplementary ACIP Statement. *Morbid Mortal Weekly Report*. 1992;41(no. RR-1):1-10. 11pp. Sponsored by the Centers for Disease Control and Prevention. Cost: $1. To order call US Govt Printing Office 202 783-3238.

Diphtheria-Tetanus-Pertussis Vaccine/
Administration and Dosage
Tetanus/Prevention and Control

Diphtheria, Tetanus, and Pertussis: Recommendations for Vaccine Use and Other Preventive Measures: Recommendations of the Immunization Practices Advisory Committee (ACIP). *Morbid Mortal Weekly Report*. 1991;40(no. RR-10):1-28. 28pp. 96refs. Sponsored by the Centers for Disease Control and Prevention. Cost: $1. To order call US Govt Printing Office 202 783-3238.

Diphtheria-Tetanus-Pertussis Vaccine/
Administration and Dosage
Whooping Cough/
Prevention and Control

Pertussis Vaccination: Use of Acellular Pertussis Vaccines Among Infants and Young Children. *Morbid Mortal Weekly Report*. 1997;46(no. RR-7). Sponsored by the Centers for Disease Control and Prevention. Cost: $1. To order call US Govt Printing Office 202 783-3238.

Diptheria-Tetanus-Pertussis Vaccine/ Adverse Effects

Assessment: DTP Vaccination. *Neurol.* 1992;42:471-472. 2pp. 14refs. Sponsored by the American Academy of Neurology. Cost: individual statements are free. To order call AAN Member Service Center 1 800 879-1960. Available on the Internet at aan.com.

Disability Evaluation
Practice Guidelines

Guides to the Evaluation of Permanent Impairment. 1993. Sponsored by the American Medical Association, Division of Health Science. To order call Linda Cocchiarella, MD 312 464-4010.

Disabled Persons
Health Services Accessibility

Access to Health Care for Women with Physical Disabilities. *ACOG Committee Opinion.* 1998;202. 5pp. 15refs. Sponsored by the American College of Obstetricians and Gynecologists. Cost: free copy. Set of Opinions $55 + s/h ACOG members, $75 + s/h nonmembers. One-year subscription $55 member, $65 nonmember. To order single copy, call ACOG Resource Center 202 863-2518; to order set or subscription, call ACOG Distribution Center, 1 800 762-2264. Available on the Internet to members only at acog.org. Key terms: health services accessibility; disabled; women's health services.

Disasters
Emergency Medicine

The Pediatrician's Role in Disaster Preparedness. *Pediatr.* 1997;99(1):103-133. 31pp. 16refs. Sponsored by the American Academy of Pediatrics. Cost: $1.95. Discounted set of policies available. To order call 1 800 433-9016.

Disease Notification

Case Definitions for Infectious Conditions Under Public Health Surveillance. *Morbid Mortal Weekly Report.* 1997;46(no. RR-10). Sponsored by the Centers for Disease Control and Prevention. Cost: $1. To order call US Govt Printing Office 202 783-3238.

Disease Outbreaks
Gastroenteritis/Diagnosis

Recommendations for Collection of Laboratory Specimens Associated with Outbreaks of Gastroenteritis. *Morbid Mortal Weekly Report.* 1990;39(no. RR-14):1-13. 13pp. 14refs. Sponsored by the Centers for Disease Control and Prevention. Cost: $1. To order call US Govt Printing Office 202 783-3238.

Disease Transmission
Hepatitis B/Transmission

Hepatitis Virus Infections in Obstetrician-Gynecologists. *ACOG Committee Opinion.* 1998;203. 2pp. 10refs. Sponsored by the American College of Obstetricians and Gynecologists. Cost: free copy. Set of Opinions $55 + s/h ACOG members, $75 + s/h nonmembers. One-year subscription $55 member, $65 nonmember. To order single copy, call ACOG Resource Center 202 863-2518; to order set or subscription, call ACOG Distribution Center, 1 800 762-2264. Available on the Internet to members only at acog.org. Key terms: hepatitis; ob-gyn; physician's role; disease transmission; physician to patient.

Disease Transmission, Vertical/ Prevention and Control
HIV Infections/Prevention and Control

Recommendations for Human Immunodeficiency Virus Counseling and Voluntary Testing for Pregnant Women. *Morbid Mortal Weekly Report.* 1995;44(no. RR-7). Sponsored by the Centers for Disease Control and Prevention. Cost: $1. To order call US Govt Printing Office 202 783-3238.

Disposable Equipment/Standards
Hemodialysis/Standards

National Kidney Foundation Report on Dialyzer Reuse. *Am J Kidney Dis.* 1988;11:1-6. 6pp. Sponsored by the National Kidney Foundation. To order call NKF 212 889-2210.

Diuretics/Diagnostic Use
Radioisotope Renography

Procedure Guideline for Diuretic Renography in Children. *J Nuclear Med.* 1997;38:1647-1650. 4pp. 7refs. Sponsored by the Society of Nuclear Medicine. Cost: free. To order call Bill Uffelman 703 708-9000. Available on the Internet at snm.org. Key terms: routine diagnostic tests; radionuclide imaging; pediatric; ureteral obstruction; hydronephrosis.

Subject

Diverticulitis, Colonic/Therapy

Practice Parameters for Sigmoid Diverticulitis. *Dis Colon Rectum*. 1995;38:125-132. 8pp. 69refs. Sponsored by the American Society of Colon and Rectal Surgeons. Cost: free. To order write ASCRS, 85 W Algonquin Rd, #550, Arlington Hts, IL 60005.

Documentation/Standards
Portasystemic Shunt,
Transjugular Intrahepatic

Reporting Standards on Transjugular Intrahepatic Portosystemic Shunts (TIPS). *JVIR*. 1997;8:289-297. 9pp. 74refs. Sponsored by the Society of Cardiovascular and Interventional Radiology. Cost: free copy. To order call SCVIR 703 691-1805.

Domestic Violence

Domestic Violence: A Directory of Protocols for Healthcare Providers. 1992. 27pp. Sponsored by the American Medical Association, Division of Health Science. Cost: AMA members $2.25 nonmembers $3. To order call AMA 312 464-5066.

Domestic Violence

Screening for Family Violence. *Guide to Clinical Preventive Services, 2nd Ed.* 1996. Sponsored by the US Preventive Services Task Force. To order call Williams & Wilkins 1 800 638-0672.

Domestic Violence
Mental Disorders

Diagnostic and Treatment Guidelines on Mental Health Effects of Family Violence. 1995. 34pp. Sponsored by the American Medical Association, Division of Health Science. Cost: AMA members $2.25 nonmembers $3. To order call AMA 312 464-5066.

Down Syndrome/
Prevention and Control
Prenatal Diagnosis/Methods

Screening for Down Syndrome. *Guide to Clinical Preventive Services, 2nd Ed.* 1996. Sponsored by the US Preventive Services Task Force. To order call Williams & Wilkins 1 800 638-0672.

Drug Approval
Pharmaceutical Preparations/Standards

Approved Drug Products and Legal Requirements. *USP DI*. 2000;Volume III. 1488pp. Sponsored by US Pharmacopeia/Micromedex, Inc. Cost: $125 per year subscription. To order call 800 877-6209. Key terms: therapeutic equivalence; orange book; usp requirements.

Drug Eruptions/Therapy
Skin Care

Cutaneous Adverse Drug Reactions. *J Am Acad Derm*. 1996;35:458-461. 4pp. 37refs. Sponsored by the American Academy of Dermatology. Cost: free copy. To order call Alice Bell 847 330-0230 x333. Available on the Internet at aad.org. Key terms: drug eruptions; etiology; therapy; adverse effects.

Drug Evaluation

Drug Evaluation and Surveillance, Position Statement. 1993. Sponsored by the American Geriatrics Society. Cost: free. To order call AGS 212 308-1414.

Drug Industry
Physicians
Ethics, Professional

Physicians and the Pharmaceutical Industry. *Amer Rev Resp Dis*. 1990;142:3. Sponsored by the American Thoracic Society. Cost: $4. To order send check payable to American Thoracic Society, 1740 Broadway, New York, NY 10019-4374; for credit card orders, call 212 315-8863.

Drug Information Services

Drug Information for the Health Care Professional. *USP DI*. 2000;Volume I. 3700pp. Sponsored by US Pharmacopeia/Micromedex, Inc. Cost: $135 per year subscription. To order call 1 800 877-6209. Key terms: drug information; pharmacologic management; off-label uses; rational prescribing.

Drug Resistance, Microbial
Hospitals

Guidelines for the Prevention of Antimicrobial Resistance in Hospitals (SHEA/ISDA Joint Statement). *Infect Control Hosp Epidemiol.* 1997;18:275. 17pp. 84refs. Sponsored by the Society for Healthcare Epidemiology of America. Cost: free. To order visit our website at medscape.com/shea. Available on the Internet at medscape.com/shea. Key terms: system for monitoring bacterial resistance/antibiotic usage; practice and monitor guidelines and policies to control the use of antibiotics and respond to data from the monitoring system.

Drug Resistance, Microbial
Hospitals

Society for Healthcare Epidemiology of America and Infectious Diseases Society of America Joint Committee on the Prevention of Antimicrobial Resistance: Guidelines for the Prevention of Antimicrobial Resistance in Hospitals. *Clin Inf Dis.* 1997;25:584. 16pp. 84refs. Sponsored by the Infectious Diseases Society of America. To obtain request from medical library or download via the Internet. Available on the Internet at idsociety.org/practice.

Drug Resistance, Microbial
Long-Term Care

Antimicrobial Use in Long Term Care Facilities and Antimicrobial Resistance in Long Term Care Facilities. *Infect Control Hosp Epidemiol.* 1996;17:119. 10pp. 56refs. Sponsored by the Society for Healthcare Epidemiology of America. Cost: free. To order visit our website at medscape.com/shea. Available on the Internet at medscape.com/shea. Key terms: problems in optimizing uses of antibiotics in LTCFs; antibiotics and comfort care; upper respiratory tract infection; lower respiratory tract infection; urinary tract infection.

Drug Screening
Ethics, Medical

Drug Screening in the Workplace: Ethical Guidelines. *J Occupation Med.* 1991;33:651-652. 2pp. Sponsored by the American College of Occupational and Environmental Medicine. Cost: free copy. To order call Marianne Dreger 847 228-6850 x18.

Drugs, Prescription

The Use of Drugs of Questionable Efficacy in the Elderly, Position Statement. 1993. Sponsored by the American Geriatrics Society. Cost: free. To order call AGS 212 308-1414.

Dry Eye Syndromes

Dry Eye Syndrome. 1998. 18pp. 29refs. Sponsored by the American Academy of Ophthalmology. Cost: $11 members, $16 nonmembers. AAO members first copy free upon publication. To order call AAO Order Dept 415 561-8540. Key terms: dry eye; treatment; prevention.

Dry Eye Syndromes/Surgery
Lacrimal Apparatus/Surgery

Punctal Occlusion for the Dry Eye Ophthalmic Procedure Assessment. *Ophthalmology.* 1997;104:1521-1524. 4pp. 16refs. Sponsored by the American Academy of Ophthalmology. Cost: $11 members, $16 nonmembers. AAO members first copy free upon publication. To order call AAO Order Dept 415 561-8540. Key terms: eye; dry eye; occlusion; punctal occlusion; tear duct.

Dupuytren's Contracture

Dupuytren's Contracture. 1993. 5pp. Sponsored by the American Society of Plastic and Reconstructive Surgeons. Cost: $25 members, $55 nonmembers (full set of guidelines), + s/h. To order call 1 800 766-4955.

Dyslexia

Dyslexia. *JAMA.* 1989;261:2236-2239. 4pp. Sponsored by the American Medical Association, Council on Scientific Affairs. Cost: free. To order call Nancy Nolan, AMA, 312 464-5046.

Dyspepsia/Diagnosis

Evaluation of Dyspepsia. *Gastroenterology.* 1998;114:579-595. 17pp. 165refs. Sponsored by the American Gastroenterological Association. Cost: $3. To order call AGA 301 654-2055. Key terms: dyspepsia; H. Pylori; NSAID.

Dyspepsia/Etiology
Esophagoscopy/Methods

Endoscopy in the Evaluation of Dyspepsia. *Ann Intern Med.* 1985;102:266-269. 4pp. Sponsored by the American College of Physicians. To order call ACP Clinical Efficacy Assessment Project 1 800 523-1546.

Dysphagia (see Deglutition Disorders)

Dystocia

Shoulder Dystocia. *ACOG Practice Patterns*. 1997;7. 8pp. 26refs. Sponsored by the American College of Obstetricians and Gynecologists. Cost: free copy. Multiples of 25: $20 + s/h member, $30 + s/h nonmember. To order single copy, call ACOG Resource Center 202 863 2518; to order set or subscription, call ACOG Distribution Center, 1 800 762-2264. Available on the Internet to members only at acog.org. Key terms: dystocia; shoulder; fetal macrosomia.

Dystocia/Therapy
Labor, Induced

Dystocia and the Augmentation of Labor. *ACOG Technical Bulletin*. 1995;218. 8pp. 40refs. Sponsored by the American College of Obstetricians and Gynecologists. Cost: free copy. Set of Bulletins $70 + s/h ACOG members, $125 + s/h nonmembers. One-year subscription $55 member, $65 nonmember. To order single copy, call ACOG Resource Center 202 863-2518; to order set or subscription, call ACOG Distribution Center, 1 800 762-2264. Available on the Internet to members only at acog.org. Key terms: labor: induced.

Ear, External/Abnormalities

Ear Deformity: Prominent Ears. 1994. Sponsored by the American Society of Plastic and Reconstructive Surgeons. Cost: $25 members, $55 nonmembers (full set of guidelines), + s/h. To order call 1 800 766-4955.

Ear Infection (see Otitis Media with Effusion)

Echocardiography
Heart Diseases/Ultrasonography

ACC/AHA Guidelines for the Clinical Application of Echocardiography (Revision). *Circulation*. 1997;95(6). 58pp. 514refs. Sponsored by the American College of Cardiology, American Heart Association. Cost: free copy. To order call Educational Services Department 1 800 257-4740.

Echocardiography
Heart Diseases/Ultrasonography

Guidelines for the Clinical Application of Echocardiography. *Circulation*. 1997;95:1686-1744. 59pp. 514refs. Sponsored by the American Heart Association, American College of Cardiology. Cost: free copy. To order write the Office of Scientific Affairs, AHA, 7272 Greenville Ave, Dallas, TX 75231.

Echocardiography, Doppler
Fetal Diseases/Diagnosis

Position Statement: Doppler Echocardiography in the Human Fetus. 1988. Sponsored by the American College of Cardiology. Cost: free copy. To order call Educational Services Department 1 800 257-4740.

Echocardiography, Transesophageal/ Standards
Monitoring, Intraoperative

Practice Guidelines for Perioperative Transesophageal Echocardiography. *Anesthesiology*. 1996;84:986-1006. 21pp. 21refs. Sponsored by the American Society of Anesthesiologists. Cost: free copy. To order call ASA 847 825-5586. Available on the Internet at asahq.org. Key terms: perioperative echocardiography; transesophageal echocardiography.

Education, Medical
Endoscopy/Standards

Standards of Practice of Gastrointestinal Endoscopy. *Gastrointest Endosc*. 1988;34(suppl):8s. 1pp. 1ref. Sponsored by the American Society for Gastrointestinal Endoscopy. Cost: free. To order call ASGE 978 526-8330.

Education, Medical
Geriatrics

Education in Geriatric Medicine, Position Statement. 1993. Sponsored by the American Geriatrics Society. Cost: free. To order call AGS 212 308-1414.

Education, Medical, Continuing/ Standards

ACR Standard for Continuing Medical Education (CME) (Revised). 1996. 2pp. Sponsored by the American College of Radiology. Cost: $25 (ACR nonmembers). To order call ACR Dept of Quality Assurance 703 716-7592. Available free on the Internet at acr.org. Key terms: continuing medical education (CME).

Education, Medical, Continuing/Standards Gastrointestinal System/Surgery

Framework for Post-Residency Surgical Education & Training. *SAGES Publication*. 1998;17. 8pp. 20refs. Sponsored by the Society of American Gastrointestinal and Endoscopic Surgeons. Cost: free. To order call 310 314-2404. Available on the Internet at sages.org. Key terms: surgery; postresidency; education; training.

Education, Medical, Continuing/Standards Lithotripsy/Standards

Guidelines for Training in Gallstone Lithotripsy. *Ann Intern Med*. 1991;114:977-79. 3pp. Sponsored by the American Gastroenterological Association. Cost: free. To order call AGA 301 654-2055.

Education, Medical, Graduate

Implementation of Geriatric Medicine Fellowship Guidelines: Suggestions for Program Directors. 1988. Sponsored by the American Geriatrics Society. Cost: free. To order call AGS 212 308-1414.

Education, Medical, Graduate

List of Available Gastroenterology Training Programs. *Gastroenterology*. 1996;111:537-563. 27pp. Sponsored by the American Gastroenterological Association. Cost: $3. To order call AGA 301 654-2055. Key terms: training; gastroenterology; liver disease; ACGME.

Education, Medical, Graduate Geriatrics

The Training of Geriatrics Fellows in Rehabilitation. 1997. Sponsored by the American Geriatrics Society. Cost: free. To order call AGS 212 308-1414.

Education, Medical, Graduate/Standards Vascular Diseases

Position Statement: Recommendations for Training in Vascular Medicine. *J Am Coll Cardiol*. 1993;22:626-628. 3pp. 1ref. Sponsored by the American College of Cardiology. Cost: free copy. To order call Educational Services Department 1 800 257-4740.

Elder Abuse

Elder Abuse and Neglect. *JAMA*. 1987;257:966-971. 6pp. Sponsored by the American Medical Association, Council on Scientific Affairs. Cost: free. To order call Nancy Nolan, AMA, 312 464-5046.

Electric Countershock Cardiovascular Diseases/Therapy

Low-Energy Biphasic Waveform Defibrillation. *Circulation*. 1998;97:1654-1667. 14pp. 59refs. Sponsored by the American Heart Association. Cost: free copy. To order call 1 800 242-8721 (US only) or write to: American Heart Association, Public Inquiries, 7272 Greenville Ave, Dallas TX 75231-4596.

Electric Countershock/Instrumentation Arrhythmia/Therapy

Position Statement: Indications for Implantation of the Automatic Implanted Cardioverter Defibrillator. 1990. 5pp. 21refs. Sponsored by the American College of Cardiology. Cost: free copy. To order call Educational Services Department 1 800 257-4740.

Electric Countershock/Methods

Position Statement: Early Defibrillation. 1991. Sponsored by the American College of Cardiology. Cost: free copy. To order call Educational Services Department 1 800 257-4740.

Electric Stimulation Therapy/Methods Sjogren's Syndrome/Therapy

Salivary Electrostimulation in Sjogren's Syndrome. *AHCPR Health Technology Review*. 1990;No. 8 (AHCPR Publication No. 91-0009). 7pp. 20refs. Sponsored by the Federal Agency for Health Care Policy and Research. To order call AHCPR Clearinghouse 1 800 358-9295.

Electrocardiography Coronary Disease/ Prevention and Control

Screening for Asymptomatic Coronary Artery Disease: The Resting Electrocardiogram. *Ann Intern Med*. 1989;111:489-502. 14pp. 56refs. Sponsored by the American College of Physicians. To order call ACP Clinical Efficacy Assessment Project 1 800 523-1546.

Electrocardiography, Ambulatory

Indications for Holter Monitoring. *Ann Intern Med.* 1990;113:77-79. 3pp. Sponsored by the American College of Physicians. To order call ACP Clinical Efficacy Assessment Project 1 800 523-1546.

Electrocardiography/Instrumentation
Intensive Care Units

Instrumentation and Practice Standards of Electrocardiographic Monitoring in Special Care Units. *Circulation.* 1989;79:464-471. 8pp. 18refs. Sponsored by the American Heart Association. Cost: free copy. To order call 1 800 242-8721 (US only) or write to: American Heart Association, Public Inquiries, 7272 Greenville Ave, Dallas TX 75231-4596.

Electrocardiography/Methods
Heart Diseases/Diagnosis

Expert Consensus Document: Signal-Averaged Electrocardiography. *J Am Coll Cardiol.* 1996;27:238-249. 12pp. 138refs. Sponsored by the American College of Cardiology. Cost: free copy. To order call Educational Services Department 1 800 257-4740.

Electrocardiography/Standards
Signal Processing, Computer-Assisted

Recommendations for Standardization and Specifications in Automated Electrocardiography: Bandwidth and Digital Signal Processing. *Circulation.* 1990;81:730-739. 10pp. 66refs. Sponsored by the American Heart Association. Cost: free copy. To order call 1 800 242-8721 (US only) or write to: American Heart Association, Public Inquiries, 7272 Greenville Ave, Dallas TX 75231-4596.

Electrocoagulation/Methods
Gastrointestinal Hemorrhage/Surgery

Endoscopic Electrocoagulation for Gastrointestinal Hemorrhage. *JAMA.* 1985;253:2733-2734. 2pp. Sponsored by the American Medical Association, Diagnostic and Therapeutic Technology Assessment Program. Cost: free copy. DATTA subscription available. To order call AMA Department of Technology Assessment 312 464-4531.

Electrocoagulation/Methods
Gastrointestinal Hemorrhage/Surgery

Endoscopic Thermal Coagulation for Gastrointestinal Hemorrhage. *JAMA.* 1985;253:2733. 1pp. Sponsored by the American Medical Association, Diagnostic and Therapeutic Technology Assessment Program. Cost: free copy. DATTA subscription available. To order call AMA Department of Technology Assessment 312 464-4531.

Electroconvulsive Therapy
Mental Disorders/Therapy

Electroconvulsive Therapy. *NIH Consensus Development Conference Statement.* 1985;5(11):1-23[Conf. No. 51]. 24pp. Sponsored by the National Institutes of Health. Cost: free copy. To order call 1 888 644-2667. Available on the Internet at consensus.nih.gov.

Electroconvulsive Therapy/Education
Electroconvulsive Therapy/Methods

Practice of ECT: Recommendations for Treatment, Training, and Privileging. 1990. 186pp. 320refs. Sponsored by the American Psychiatric Association. Cost: $31. To order call 1 800 368-5777 order #SPCT2229. Key terms: ECT.

Electrodiagnosis

The Scope of Electrodiagnostic Medicine. *Muscle Nerve.* 1999;(suppl)8:S5-S339. 35pp. Sponsored by the American Association of Electrodiagnostic Medicine. Cost: $10 members, $20 nonmembers. To order write AAEM, 421 First Avenue SW, #300E, Rochester, MN 55902. Key terms: EMG; qualifications; equipment; reports; laboratory organization.

Electrodiagnosis
Guidelines

Guidelines in Electrodiagnostic Medicine. *Muscle Nerve.* 1999;8(suppl):S1-S300. 300pp. Sponsored by the American Association of Electrodiagnostic Medicine. Cost: $75 members, $150 nonmembers. To order write AAEM, 421 First Avenue SW, #300E, Rochester, MN 55902. Key terms: electrodiagnostic; qualifications; risks; standards; electromyography.

Electrodiagnosis
Job Description

Job Descriptions for Electrodiagnostic Technologists. *Muscle Nerve*. 1999;8(suppl):S19-S23. 5pp. Sponsored by the American Association of Electrodiagnostic Medicine. Cost: free. To order write AAEM, 421 First Avenue SW, #300E, Rochester, MN 55902. Available on the Internet at aaem.net/pdffiles/job_descriptions_edx_techs.pdf. Key terms: job description; electrodiagnostic medicine; technologist.

Electrodiagnosis
Neurologic Examination/
Instrumentation

Technology Review: The Neurometer Current Perception Threshold (CPT). *Muscle Nerve*. 1999;8(suppl):S247-S259. 13pp. 56refs. Sponsored by the American Association of Electrodiagnostic Medicine. Cost: $10 members, $20 nonmembers. To order write AAEM, 421 First Avenue SW, #300E, Rochester, MN 55902. Available on the Internet at aaem.net/pdffiles/tech_rvw_neurometer_cpt.pdf. Key terms: neurometer; current perception threshold.

Electrodiagnosis
Outcome Assessment (Health Care)

Guidelines for Outcome Studies in Electrodiagnostic Medicine. *Muscle Nerve*. 1999;8(suppl):S277-S286. 10pp. 27refs. Sponsored by the American Association of Electrodiagnostic Medicine. Cost: $10 members, $20 nonmembers. To order write AAEM, 421 First Avenue SW, #300E, Rochester, MN 55902. Key terms: outcome studies; electrodiagnostic medicine; guidelines.

Electrodiagnosis
Referral and Consultation

The Electrodiagnostic Medicine Consultation. *Muscle Nerve*. 1999;8(suppl):S73-S108. 36pp. Sponsored by the American Association of Electrodiagnostic Medicine. Cost: $10 members, $20 nonmembers. To order write AAEM, 421 First Avenue SW, #300E, Rochester, MN 55902. Key terms: electrodiagnostic; nerve conduction; electromyography; sudomotor; myopathies.

Electrodiagnosis
Risk

Risks in Electrodiagnostic Medicine. *Muscle Nerve*. 1999;8(suppl):S53-S69. 17pp. 44refs. Sponsored by the American Association of Electrodiagnostic Medicine. Cost: $10 members, $20 nonmembers. To order write AAEM, 421 First Avenue SW, #300E, Rochester, MN 55902. Key terms: electrodiagnostic medicine; infection control; pacemakers; defibrillators; protective barriers.

Electrodiagnosis
Ulnar Nerve/Physiopathology

Practice Parameter: Electrodiagnostic Studies in Ulnar Neuropathy at the Elbow. *Neurol*. 1999;52:688-690. 3pp. Sponsored by the American Academy of Neurology. Cost: individual statements are free. To order call AAN Member Service Center 1 800 879-1960. Available on the Internet at aan.com.

Electrodiagnosis
Ulnar/Physiopathology

Practice Parameters for Electrodiagnostic Studies in Ulnar Neuropathy at the Elbow. *Muscle Nerve*. 1999;8(suppl):S171-S205. 36pp. 103refs. Sponsored by the American Association of Electrodiagnostic Medicine. Cost: $10 members, $20 nonmembers. To order write AAEM, 421 First Avenue SW, #300E, Rochester, MN 55902. Key terms: ulnar; neuropathy; elbow; electromyography

Electrodiagnosis/Standards
Ethics, Medical

Guidelines for Ethical Behavior Relating to Clinical Practice Issues in Electrodiagnostic Medicine. *Muscle Nerve*. 1999;8(suppl):S43-S49. 7pp. 1refs. Sponsored by the American Association of Electrodiagnostic Medicine. Cost: free copy. To order write AAEM, 421 First Avenue SW, #300E, Rochester, MN 55902. Available on the Internet at aaem.net/pdffiles/gl_ethical_behavior.pdf. Key terms: ethics; electrodiagnostic medicine; informed consent; research.

Electrodiagnostic

Recommended Policy for Electrodiagnostic Medicine. *Muscle Nerve*. 1999;8(suppl):S91-S105. 15pp. Sponsored by the American Association of Electrodiagnostic Medicine. Cost: free. To order write AAEM, 421 First Avenue SW, #300E, Rochester, MN 55902. Available on the Internet at aaem.net/pdffiles/recommended_policy.pdf. Key terms: nerve conduction; electromyography; H reflex; F wave; neuromuscular junction.

Electroencephalography
Epilepsy/Diagnosis

Assessment: Intensive EEG/Video Monitoring for Epilepsy. *Neurol.* 1989;39:1101-1102. 2pp. 3refs. Sponsored by the American Academy of Neurology. Cost: individual statements are free. To order call AAN Member Service Center 1 800 879-1960. Available on the Internet at aan.com.

Electroencephalography/Methods
Videotape Recording/Standards

Electroencephalographic (EEG) Video Monitoring. *AHCPR Health Technology Assessment.* 1990;No. 4 (AHCPR Publication No. 91-3471). 14pp. 46refs. Sponsored by the Federal Agency for Health Care Policy and Research. To order call AHCPR Clearinghouse 1 800 358-9295.

Electromyography
Gain/Physiology
Movement/Physiology

Technology Review: Dynamic Electromyography in Gait and Motion Analysis. *Muscle Nerve.* 1999;8(suppl):S233-S238. 6pp. 56refs. Sponsored by the American Association of Electrodiagnostic Medicine. Cost: $10 members, $20 nonmembers. To order write AAEM, 421 First Avenue SW, #300E, Rochester, MN 55902. Key terms: motion analysis; gait measurement; dynamic electromyography; surface electromyography.

Electromyography
Neuromuscular Diseases/Diagnosis

Technology Review: The Use of Surface EMG in the Diagnosis and Treatment of Nerve and Muscle Disorders. *Muscle Nerve.* 1999;8(suppl):S239-S242. 4pp. 21refs. Sponsored by the American Association of Electrodiagnostic Medicine. Cost: $10 members, $20 nonmembers. To order write AAEM, 421 First Avenue SW, #300E, Rochester, MN 55902. Available on the Internet at aaem.net/pdffiles/ tech_rvw_surface_emg.pdf. Key terms: electromyography; myopathy; radiculopathy; surface electromyography.

Electronystagmography
Nystagmus/Diagnosis

Assessment: Electronystagmography. *Neurol.* 1996;46:1763-1766. 4pp. 9refs. Sponsored by the American Academy of Neurology. Cost: individual statements are free. To order call AAN Member Service Center 1 800 879-1960. Available on the Internet at aan.com.

Electrophysiology/Education
Cardiology/Education
Cardiac Pacing, Artificial

Position Statement: Training in Adult Clinical Cardiac Electrophysiology. 1990. 4pp. Sponsored by the American College of Cardiology. Cost: free copy. To order call Educational Services Department 1 800 257-4740.

Electrosurgery
Vaginal Smears

Role of Loop Electrosurgical Excision Procedure in the Evaluation of Abnormal Pap Test Results. *ACOG Committee Opinion.* 1997;195. 2pp. 5refs. Sponsored by the American College of Obstetricians and Gynecologists. Cost: free copy. Set of Opinions $55 + s/h ACOG members, $75 + s/h nonmembers. One-year subscription $55 member, $65 nonmember. To order single copy, call ACOG Resource Center 202 863-2518; to order set or subscription, call ACOG Distribution Center, 1 800 762-2264. Available on the Internet to members only at acog.org. Key terms: electrocautery; cervix diseases; vaginal smears.

Embolization, Therapeutic/Standards

Quality Improvement Guidelines for Percutaneous Transcatheter Embolization. *JVIR.* 1997;8:889-895. 7pp. 89refs. Sponsored by the Society of Cardiovascular and Interventional Radiology. Cost: free copy. To order call SCVIR 703 691-1805.

Embryo
Research
Ethics

Preembryo Research: History, Scientific Background, and Ethical Considerations. *ACOG Committee Opinion.* 1994;136. 10pp. 32refs. Sponsored by the American College of Obstetricians and Gynecologists. Cost: free copy. Set of Opinions $55 + s/h ACOG members, $75 + s/h nonmembers. One-year subscription $55 member, $65 nonmember. To order single copy, call ACOG Resource Center 202 863-2518; to order set or subscription, call ACOG Distribution Center, 1 800 762-2264. Available on the Internet to members only at acog.org.

Embryology
Laboratories/Standards

Guidelines for Human Embryology and Human Andrology Laboratories. 1992. 16pp. 16refs. Sponsored by the American Society for Reproductive Medicine. Cost: $5. To order call ASRM Publication Department 205 978-5000.

Emergency Medical Services
Heart Diseases/Therapy

Emergency Cardiac Care. *Am J Card.* 1982. Sponsored by the American College of Cardiology. Cost: free copy. To order call Educational Services Department 1 800 257-4740.

Emergency Medical Services/Standards
Heart Arrest

Recommended Guidelines for Uniform Reporting of Data from Out-of-Hospital Cardiac Arrest: The Utstein Style. *Circulation.* 1991;84:960-975. 16pp. 90refs. Sponsored by the American Heart Association. Cost: free copy. To order call 1 800 242-8721 (US only) or write to: American Heart Association, Public Inquiries, 7272 Greenville Ave, Dallas TX 75231-4596.

Emergency Medicine
Seizures/Diagnosis

Clinical Policy for the Initial Approach to Patients Presenting with a Chief Complaint of Seizure Who Are Not in Status Epilepticus. *Ann Emerg Med.* 1997;29:706-724. 19pp. 91refs. Sponsored by the American College of Emergency Physicians. Cost: ACEP members free copy, fee nonmembers. To order call ACEP 1 800 798-1822 x6. Key terms: seizure in emergency department; nonstatus epilepticus.

Emergency Medicine/Methods
Hazardous Substances/Administration
and Dosage
Poisoning/Therapy

Acute Toxic Ingestion or Dermal or Inhalation Exposure. *Ann Emerg Med.* 1999;33:735-761. 29pp. 89refs. Sponsored by the American College of Emergency Physicians. Cost: ACEP members free copy, fee nonmembers. To order call ACEP 1 800 798-1822 x6. Key terms: acute toxic ingestion; dermal exposure; inhalation exposure; Emergency Department.

Emergency Treatment/Methods
Drug Therapy/Methods
Pediatrics/Methods

Drugs for Pediatric Emergencies. *Pediatr.* 1998;101(1):e13. 1pp. 4refs. Sponsored by the American Academy of Pediatrics. Cost: $1.95. Discounted set of policies available. To order call 1 800 433-9016.

Emergency Treatment/Standards
Wounds, Penetrating/Therapy

Penetrating Extremity Trauma. *Ann Emerg Med.* 1999;33:612-636. 25pp. 103refs. Sponsored by the American College of Emergency Physicians. Cost: ACEP members free copy, fee nonmembers. To order call ACEP 1 800 798-1822 x6. Key terms: penetrating extremity injuries; lacerations; gunshot wounds; mammalian bites.

Encephalitis, Japanese/
Prevention and Control
Travel

Inactivated Japanese Encephalitis Virus Vaccine. *Morbid Mortal Weekly Report.* 1993;42(no. RR-1). Sponsored by the Centers for Disease Control and Prevention. Cost: $1. To order call US Govt Printing Office 202 783-3238.

Endarterectomy
Carotid Artery Diseases/Surgery

Carotid Endarterectomy. *Ann Intern Med.* 1989;111:660-670. 11pp. 108refs. Sponsored by the American College of Physicians. To order call ACP Clinical Efficacy Assessment Project 1 800 523-1546.

Endarterectomy, Carotid

Carotid Endarterectomy (Revised). *AHCPR Health Technology Assessment.* 1990;No. 5R (AHCPR Publication No. 91-0029). 13pp. 130refs. Sponsored by the Federal Agency for Health Care Policy and Research. To order call AHCPR Clearinghouse 1 800 358-9295.

Endarterectomy, Carotid/Standards
Cerebrovascular Disorders/Surgery

Carotid Endarterectomy: Practice Guidelines Report of the Ad Hoc Committee. *J Vasc Surg.* 1992;15:469-479. 11pp. 93refs. Sponsored by the Society for Vascular Surgery/North American Chapter, ICVS. Cost: free. To order call 978 526-8330.

Endocarditis, Bacterial/Drug Therapy
Antibiotics/Therapeutic Use

Antimicrobial Treatment of Infective Endocarditis Due to Viridans Streptococci, Enterococci, and Staphylococci. *JAMA.* 1995;274:1706-1713. 8pp. 43refs. Sponsored by the American Heart Association. Cost: free copy. To order call 1 800 242-8721 (US only) or write to: American Heart Association, Public Inquiries, 7272 Greenville Ave, Dallas TX 75231-4596.

Endocarditis, Bacterial/ Prevention and Control

Prevention of Bacterial Endocarditis: Recommendations by the American Heart Association. *Circulation.* 1997;96:3102-3110. 9pp. 66refs. Sponsored by the American Heart Association. Cost: free copy. To order call 1 800 242-8721 (US only) or write to: American Heart Association, Public Inquiries, 7272 Greenville Ave, Dallas TX 75231-4596.

Endocardium/Physiology Heart Conduction System/Physiology

Diagnostic Endocardial Electrical Recording and Stimulation. *Ann Intern Med.* 1984;100:452-454. 3pp. Sponsored by the American College of Physicians. To order call ACP Clinical Efficacy Assessment Project 1 800 523-1546.

Endometrial Neoplasms Estrogen Replacement Therapy

Estrogen Replacement Therapy and Endometrial Cancer. *ACOG Committee Opinion.* 1993;126. 1pp. Sponsored by the American College of Obstetricians and Gynecologists. Cost: free copy. Set of Opinions $55 + s/h ACOG members, $75 + s/h nonmembers. One-year subscription $55 member, $65 nonmember. To order single copy, call ACOG Resource Center 202 863-2518; to order set or subscription, call ACOG Distribution Center, 1 800 762-2264. Available on the Internet to members only at acog.org.

Endometriosis

Endometriosis. *ACOG Technical Bulletin.* 1993;184. 6pp. 27refs. Sponsored by the American College of Obstetricians and Gynecologists. Cost: free copy. Set of Bulletins $70 + s/h ACOG members, $125 + s/h nonmembers. One-year subscription $55 member, $65 nonmember. To order single copy, call ACOG Resource Center 202 863-2518; to order set or subscription, call ACOG Distribution Center, 1 800 762-2264. Available on the Internet to members only at acog.org.

Endometriosis/Diagnosis

Evaluation and Treatment of Endometriosis. 1992. 3pp. 11refs. Sponsored by the American Society for Reproductive Medicine. Cost: $1. To order call ASRM Publication Department 205 978-5000.

Endometrium/Surgery Laser Surgery

Laser Ablation of the Endometrium. *Diagnostic and Therapeutic Technology Assessment (DATTA).* 1991. 10pp. 34refs. Sponsored by the American Medical Association, Diagnostic and Therapeutic Technology Assessment Program. Cost: free copy. DATTA subscription available. To order call AMA Department of Technology Assessment 312 464-4531.

Endoscopy Gastrointestinal Hemorrhage/Diagnosis

Role of Endoscopy in the Management of Upper Gastrointestinal Hemorrhage. *Gastrointest Endosc.* 1988;34(suppl):4s-5s. 2pp. 20refs. Sponsored by the American Society for Gastrointestinal Endoscopy. Cost: free. To order call ASGE 978 526-8330.

Endoscopy Hospital Units

Guidelines for Establishment of Gastrointestinal Endoscopy Areas. *Gastrointest Endosc.* 1988;34(suppl):3s. 1pp. 3refs. Sponsored by the American Society for Gastrointestinal Endoscopy. Cost: free. To order call ASGE 978 526-8330.

Endoscopy Nose Diseases/Diagnosis

Diagnostic Nasal Endoscopy. *Clinical Indicators Compendium.* 1999. 1pp. Sponsored by the American Academy of Otolaryngology-Head and Neck Surgery. Cost: $10 AAO-HNS members, $15 nonmembers. To order write to AAO-HNS, 1 Prince St, Alexandria, VA 22314. Key terms: endoscopy; nasal; diagnostic; sinus; nose.

Endoscopy, Gastrointestinal

Appropriate Use of Gastrointestinal Endoscopy. 1992. 11pp. Sponsored by the American Society for Gastrointestinal Endoscopy. Cost: $3. To order call ASGE 978 526-8330.

Endoscopy, Gastrointestinal Esophagus/Radiography

ACR Standard for the Performance of Adult Esophagrams & Upper Gastrointestinal Examinations. 1999. 8pp. 9refs. Sponsored by the American College of Radiology. Cost: $25 (ACR nonmembers). To order call ACR Dept of Quality Assurance 703 716-7592. Available on the Internet at acr.org. Key terms: radiology; upper gastrointestinal; esophagram; stomach; esophagus.

Endoscopy, Gastrointestinal
Foreign Bodies

Guideline for Management of Ingested Foreign Bodies. 1994. Sponsored by the American Society for Gastrointestinal Endoscopy. To order call ASGE 978 526-8330.

Endoscopy, Gastrointestinal
Gastrointestinal Hemorrhage

Role of Endoscopy in the Management of Acute Nonvariceal Upper Gastrointestinal Bleeding. *Gastrointest Endosc.* 1992. Sponsored by the American Society for Gastrointestinal Endoscopy. Cost: free. To order call ASGE 978 526-8330.

Endoscopy, Gastrointestinal
Medical Staff Privileges

Methods of Granting Hospital Privileges to Perform Gastrointestinal Endoscopy. *Gastrointest Endosc.* 1992;37. 2pp. Sponsored by the American Society for Gastrointestinal Endoscopy. Cost: free. To order call ASGE 978 526-8330.

Endoscopy, Gastrointestinal
Monitoring, Physiologic

Conscious Sedation and Monitoring of Patients Undergoing GI Endoscopic Procedures. 1994. Sponsored by the American Society for Gastrointestinal Endoscopy. To order call ASGE 978 526-8330.

Endoscopy, Gastrointestinal
Monitoring, Physiologic

Monitoring of Patients Undergoing Gastrointestinal Endoscopic Procedures. *Gastrointest Endosc.* 1991;37:120-121. 2pp. 9refs. Sponsored by the American Society for Gastrointestinal Endoscopy. Cost: free. To order call ASGE 978 526-8330.

Endoscopy, Gastrointestinal
Multiphasic Screening

The Role of Screening Tests Before Gastrointestinal Endoscopic Procedures. 1993. Sponsored by the American Society for Gastrointestinal Endoscopy. To order call ASGE 978 526-8330.

Endoscopy, Gastrointestinal
Peptic Ulcer Hemorrhage/Therapy

Therapeutic Endoscopy and Bleeding Ulcers. *NIH Consensus Development Conference Statement.* 1989;7(6):1-22[Conf. No. 72]. 23pp. Sponsored by the National Institutes of Health. Cost: free copy. To order call 1 888 644-2667. Available on the Internet at consensus.nih.gov.

Endoscopy, Gastrointestinal
Quality Assurance, Health Care

Quality Assurance of Gastrointestinal Endoscopy. 1988. 4pp. 4refs. Sponsored by the American Society for Gastrointestinal Endoscopy. Cost: $3. To order call ASGE 978 526-8330.

Endoscopy/Education
Gastroscopy/Education

Statement on Endoscopic Training. *Gastrointest Endosc.* 1988;34(suppl):12s-13s. 2pp. 2refs. Sponsored by the American Society for Gastrointestinal Endoscopy. Cost: free. To order call ASGE 978 526-8330.

Endoscopy/Education
Gastroscopy/Education

Statement on Role of Short Courses in Endoscopic Training. *Gastrointest Endosc.* 1988;34(suppl):14s-15s. 2pp. 5refs. Sponsored by the American Society for Gastrointestinal Endoscopy. Cost: free. To order call ASGE 978 526-8330.

Endoscopy, Gastrointestinal/Standards
Medical Staff Privileges/Standards

Proctoring and Hospital Endoscopy Privileges. *Gastrointest Endosc.* 1991;37:666-667. 5pp. 12refs. Sponsored by the American Society for Gastrointestinal Endoscopy. Cost: free. To order call ASGE 978 526-8330.

Endothelium, Corneal
Photography

Corneal Endothelial Photography Ophthalmic Procedure Assessment. *Ophthalmology.* 1997;104:1360-1365. 6pp. 41refs. Sponsored by the American Academy of Ophthalmology. Cost: $11 members, $16 nonmembers. AAO members first copy free upon publication. To order call AAO Order Dept 415 561-8540. Key terms: eye; cornea; corneal endothelial photography.

Enteral Nutrition

Guidelines for the Use of Enteral Nutrition. *Gastroenterology.* 1995;108:1280-1301. 22pp. 192refs. Sponsored by the American Gastroenterological Association. Cost: $3. To order call AGA 301 654-2055. Key terms: nutrition; enteral; tube feeding.

Enteral Nutrition
Gastrostomy/Methods

Role of Percutaneous Endoscopic Gastrostomy: Guidelines for Clinical Application. *Gastrointest Endosc.* 1988;34(suppl):35s-36s. 2pp. 18refs. Sponsored by the American Society for Gastrointestinal Endoscopy. Cost: free. To order call ASGE 978 526-8330.

Enzyme Tests
Myocardial Infarction/Diagnosis

Serum Enzyme Assays in the Diagnosis of Acute Myocardial Infarction: Recommendations Based on a Quantitative Analysis. *Ann Intern Med.* 1986;105:221-233. 13pp. Sponsored by the American College of Physicians. To order call ACP Clinical Efficacy Assessment Project 1 800 523-1546.

Epidemiologic Studies
Infection Control

Consensus Panel on Infrastructure and Essential Activities of Hospital Epidemiology and Infection Control Programs. *Infect Control Hosp Epidemiol.* 1998. Sponsored by the Society for Healthcare Epidemiology of America. To order visit our website at medscape.com/shea. Available on the Internet at medscape.com/shea.

Epikeratophakia

Epikeratoplasty Ophthalmic Procedure Assessment. *Ophthalmology.* 1996;103:983-990. 8pp. 62refs. Sponsored by the American Academy of Ophthalmology. Cost: $11 members, $16 nonmembers. AAO members first copy free upon publication. To order call AAO Order Dept 415 561-8540. Key terms: eye; eye surgery; epikeratoplasty; cornea.

Epilepsy, Tonic-Clonic
Automobile Driving

Driving Following an Unprovoked Generalized Single Tonic Clonic Seizure. 1992. 5pp. Sponsored by the American Academy of Neurology. Cost: individual statements are free. To order call AAN Member Service Center 1 800 879-1960. Available on the Internet at aan.com.

Epilepsy/Surgery

Surgery for Epilepsy. *NIH Consensus Development Conference Statement.* 1990;8(2):1-20[Conf. No. 77]. 20pp. Sponsored by the National Institutes of Health. Cost: free copy. To order call 1 888 644-2667. Available on the Internet at consensus.nih.gov.

Epilepsy/Therapy
Vagus Nerve/Physiology

Assessment of Vagus Nerve Stimulation for Epilepsy. *Neurol.* 1999;53. Sponsored by the American Academy of Neurology. Cost: individual statements are free. To order call AAN Member Service Center 1 800 879-1960. Available on the Internet at aan.com.

Epinephrine/Therapeutic Use

Epinephrine Injection. 1977. Position Statement No. 3. 1pp. Sponsored by the American Academy of Allergy, Asthma, and Immunology. Cost: free copy. To order call 414 272-6071.

Ergonovine/Diagnostic Use
Coronary Vasospasm/Diagnosis

Performance of Ergonovine Provocative Testing for Coronary Artery Spasm. *Ann Intern Med.* 1984;100:151-152. 2pp. Sponsored by the American College of Physicians. To order call ACP Clinical Efficacy Assessment Project 1 800 523-1546.

Erythrocyte Transfusion

Practice Parameter for the Use of Red Blood Cell Transfusions. *Arch Path Lab Med.* 1998;122:130-138. 9pp. 69refs. Sponsored by the College of American Pathologists. Cost: reprints: free. To order call CAP 1 800 323-4040 x7378. Key terms: transfusion medicine; blood component therapy; red blood cells.

Esophageal and Gastric Varices/Complications
Gastrointestinal Hemorrhage/Diagnosis
Hypertension, Portal/Diagnosis

Diagnosis and Treatment of Gastrointestinal Bleeding Secondary to Portal Hypertension. *Am J Gastroenterol.* 1997;92:1081-1091. 11pp. 150refs. Sponsored by the American College of Gastroenterology. Cost: free copy. To order call ACG 703 820-7400.

Esophageal and Gastric Varices/ Drug Therapy
Sclerotherapy

Role of Endoscopic Sclerotherapy in the Management of Variceal Bleeding: Guidelines for Clinical Application. *Gastrointest Endosc.* 1989;34:600-601. 2pp. 16refs. Sponsored by the American Society for Gastrointestinal Endoscopy. Cost: free. To order call ASGE 978 526-8330.

Esophageal and Gastric Varices/Therapy
Sclerosing Solutions/ Administration and Dosage

Endoscopic Sclerotherapy for Esophageal Varices. *Ann Intern Med.* 1984;100:608-610. 3pp. Sponsored by the American College of Physicians. To order call ACP Clinical Efficacy Assessment Project 1 800 523-1546.

Esophageal Diseases/Diagnosis

Clinical Esophageal pH Recording. *Gastroenterology.* 1996;110(6). 16pp. 108refs. Sponsored by the American Gastroenterological Association. Cost: $3. To order call AGA 301 654-2055. Key terms: esophageal; pH recording; esophageal acid.

Esophageal Neoplasms/Diagnosis
Esophageal Neoplasms/Therapy

Esophageal Cancer. *Am J Gastroenterol.* 1999;94:20-29. 10pp. 133refs. Sponsored by the American College of Gastroenterology. Cost: free copy. To order call ACG 703 820-7400. Available on the Internet at elsevier.com/locate/amjgastro.

Esophageal Neoplasms/Diagnosis
Esophagoscopy

Role of Endoscopy in the Surveillance of Premalignant Conditions of the Upper Gastrointestinal Tract: Guidelines for Clinical Application. *Gastrointest Endosc.* 1988;34(suppl):18s-20s. 3pp. 32refs. Sponsored by the American Society for Gastrointestinal Endoscopy. Cost: free. To order call ASGE 978 526-8330.

Esophageal Neoplasms/Surgery

Esophageal Cancer Surgical Practice Guidelines. *Oncology.* 1997;11(6):1059. 5pp. 15refs. Sponsored by the Society of Surgical Oncology. Cost: call 516 424-8900 x316. To order write Oncology, PRR, Inc, 17 Prospect St, Huntington NY 11743. Key terms: esophageal.

Esophagitis, Peptic/Diagnosis
Esophagoscopy

Role of Endoscopy in the Management of Esophagitis. *Gastrointest Endosc.* 1988;34(suppl):9s. 1pp. 8refs. Sponsored by the American Society for Gastrointestinal Endoscopy. Cost: free. To order call ASGE 978 526-8330.

Esophagus/Physiology
Manometry

Clinical Use of Esophageal Manometry. *Gastroenterology.* 1994;107:1865-1884. 20pp. 140refs. Sponsored by the American Gastroenterological Association. Cost: $3. To order call AGA 301 654-2055. Key terms: manometry; esophageal; esophageal sphincter.

Esotropia

Esotropia Preferred Practice Pattern. 1997. 24pp. 67refs. Sponsored by the American Academy of Ophthalmology. Cost: $11 members, $16 nonmembers. AAO members first copy free upon publication. To order call AAO Order Dept 415 561-8540. Key terms: eye; esotropia; pediatric.

Estrogen Replacement Therapy

Guidelines for Counseling Postmenopausal Women about Preventive Hormone Therapy. *Ann Intern Med.* 1992;117:1038-1041. 4pp. Sponsored by the American College of Physicians. To order call ACP Clinical Efficacy Assessment Project 1 800 523-1546.

Estrogen Replacement Therapy

Hormone Therapy to Prevent Disease and Prolong Life in Postmenopausal Women. *Ann Intern Med.* 1992;117:1016-1037. 21pp. Sponsored by the American College of Physicians. To order call ACP Clinical Efficacy Assessment Project 1 800 523-1546.

Estrogen Replacement Therapy/Methods Breast Neoplasms/Drug Therapy

Estrogen Replacement Therapy in Women with Previously Treated Breast Cancer. *ACOG Committee Opinion.* 1994;135. 4pp. 39refs. Sponsored by the American College of Obstetricians and Gynecologists. Cost: free copy. Set of Opinions $55 + s/h ACOG members, $75 + s/h nonmembers. One-year subscription $55 member, $65 nonmember. To order single copy, call ACOG Resource Center 202 863-2518; to order set or subscription, call ACOG Distribution Center, 1 800 762-2264. Available on the Internet to members only at acog.org.

Ethics
Health Care Reform/Standards

Ethical Issues in Health Care System Reform. *JAMA.* 1994;272:1056-1062. 7pp. 39refs. Sponsored by the American Medical Association, Council on Ethical and Judicial Affairs. Cost: free copy. To order call AMA 312 464-5223.

Ethics Committees/Legislation and Jurisprudence
Physicians/Legislation and Jurisprudence

Institutional Responsibility to Provide Legal Representation. *ACOG Committee Opinion.* 1998;204. 1pp. 2refs. Sponsored by the American College of Obstetricians and Gynecologists. Cost: free copy. Set of Opinions $55 + s/h ACOG members, $75 + s/h nonmembers. One-year subscription $55 member, $65 nonmember. To order single copy, call ACOG Resource Center 202 863-2518; to order set or subscription, call ACOG Distribution Center, 1 800 762-2264. Available on the Internet to members only at acog.org. Key terms: clinical competence; ethics; medical; department of obstetrics and gynecology; liability.

Ethics, Institutional

Endorsement of Institutional Ethics Committees. *ACOG Committee Opinion.* 1985;46. 3pp. 11refs. Sponsored by the American College of Obstetricians and Gynecologists. Cost: free copy. Set of Opinions $55 + s/h ACOG members, $75 + s/h nonmembers. One-year subscription $55 member, $65 nonmember. To order single copy, call ACOG Resource Center 202 863-2518; to order set or subscription, call ACOG Distribution Center, 1 800 762-2264. Available on the Internet to members only at acog.org.

Ethics, Medical
Acquired Immunodeficiency Syndrome

Ethical Issues in the Growing AIDS Crisis. *JAMA.* 1988;259:1360-1361. 2pp. Sponsored by the American Medical Association, Council on Ethical and Judicial Affairs. Cost: free copy. To order call AMA 312 464-5223.

Ethics, Medical
Diagnostic Tests, Routine

Ethical Guidance for Patient Testing. *ACOG Committee Opinion.* 1995;159. 3pp. Sponsored by the American College of Obstetricians and Gynecologists. Cost: free copy. Set of Opinions $55 + s/h ACOG members, $75 + s/h nonmembers. One-year subscription $55 member, $65 nonmember. To order single copy, call ACOG Resource Center 202 863-2518; to order set or subscription, call ACOG Distribution Center, 1 800 762-2264. Available on the Internet to members only at acog.org. Key terms: ethics; mass screening; prenatal diagnosis; informed consent.

Ethics, Medical
Expert Testimony/Standards

Ethical Issues Related to Expert Testimony by Obstetricians and Gynecologists. *ACOG Committee Opinion.* 1999;217. 2pp. 3refs. Sponsored by the American College of Obstetricians and Gynecologists. Cost: free copy. Set of Opinions $55 + s/h ACOG members, $75 + s/h nonmembers. One-year subscription $55 member, $65 nonmember. To order single copy, call ACOG Resource Center 202 863-2518; to order set or subscription, call ACOG Distribution Center, 1 800 762-2264. Available on the Internet to members only at acog.org. Key terms: expert testimony; medical ethics.

Ethics, Medical
Informed Consent

Sterilization of Women, Including Those with Mental Disabilities. *ACOG Committee Opinion.* 1999;216. 4pp. 3refs. Sponsored by the American College of Obstetricians and Gynecologists. Cost: free copy. Set of Opinions $55 + s/h ACOG members, $75 + s/h nonmembers. One-year subscription $55 member, $65 nonmember. To order single copy, call ACOG Resource Center 202 863-2518; to order set or subscription, call ACOG Distribution Center, 1 800 762-2264. Available on the Internet to members only at acog.org. Key terms: tubal sterilization; sexual sterilization; medical ethics; disabled; mentally handicapped.

Ethics, Medical
Life Support Care

Ethical and Moral Guidelines for the Initiation, Continuation, and Withdrawal of Intensive Care. *Chest.* 1990;97:949-958. 10pp. 30refs. Sponsored by the American College of Chest Physicians. Cost: $5. To order call ACCP 1 800 343-2227 or 1 847 498-1400 (credit card orders). Key terms: ethics; intensive care; medical decision making.

Ethics, Medical
Pregnancy Reduction, Multifetal

Nonselective Embryo Reduction: Ethical Guidance for the Obstetrician-Gynecologist. *ACOG Committee Opinion.* 1999;215. 4pp. 25refs. Sponsored by the American College of Obstetricians and Gynecologists. Cost: free copy. Set of Opinions $55 + s/h ACOG members, $75 + s/h nonmembers. One-year subscription $55 member, $65 nonmember. To order single copy, call ACOG Resource Center 202 863-2518; to order set or subscription, call ACOG Distribution Center, 1 800 762-2264. Available on the Internet to members only at acog.org. Key terms: therapeutic abortion; superfetation; medical ethics; decision making.

Ethics, Medical
Pregnancy Research/Standards

Ethical Considerations in Research Involving Pregnant Women. *ACOG Committee Opinion.* 1998;213. 4pp. 14refs. Sponsored by the American College of Obstetricians and Gynecologists. Cost: free copy. Set of Bulletins $70 + s/h ACOG members, $125 + s/h nonmembers. One-year subscription $55 member, $65 nonmember. To order single copy, call ACOG Resource Center 202 863-2518; to order set or subscription, call ACOG Distribution Center, 1 800 762-2264. Available on the Internet to members only at acog.org. Key terms: medical ethics; human experimentation research; informed consent; informed refusal; maternal-fetal conflict.

Ethics, Medical
Sexual Harassment/
Prevention and Control

Sexual Misconduct in the Practice of Obstetrics and Gynecology: Ethical Considerations. *ACOG Committee Opinion.* 1994;144. 4pp. 12refs. Sponsored by the American College of Obstetricians and Gynecologists. Cost: free copy. Set of Opinions $55 + s/h ACOG members, $75 + s/h nonmembers. One-year subscription $55 member, $65 nonmember. To order single copy, call ACOG Resource Center 202 863-2518; to order set or subscription, call ACOG Distribution Center, 1 800 762-2264. Available on the Internet to members only at acog.org.

Ethmoid Sinus/Surgery

Ethmoidectomy. *Clinical Indicators Compendium.* 1999. 1pp. 20refs. Sponsored by the American Academy of Otolaryngology-Head and Neck Surgery. Cost: $10 AAO-HNS members, $15 nonmembers. To order write to AAO-HNS, 1 Prince St, Alexandria, VA 22314. Key terms: ethmoid; sinusitis; endoscopy; polyps; neoplasm.

Euthanasia, Passive
Life Support Care

Withdrawing and Withholding Life-Sustaining Therapy. *Amer Rev Resp Dis.* 1991;144:3. Sponsored by the American Thoracic Society. Cost: $4. To order send check payable to American Thoracic Society, 1740 Broadway, New York, NY 10019-4374; for credit card orders, call 212 315-8863.

Evoked Potentials, Auditory
Brain Stem/Physiology

Auditory Brainstem Response. *Clinical Indicators Compendium*. 1999. 1pp. Sponsored by the American Academy of Otolaryngology-Head and Neck Surgery. Cost: $10 AAO-HNS members, $15 nonmembers. To order write to AAO-HNS, 1 Prince St, Alexandria, VA 22314. Key terms: ABR; hearing; auditory; nerve; brainstem.

Evoked Potentials, Somatosensory

Somatosensory Evoked Potentials: Clinical Uses. *Muscle Nerve*. 1999;8(suppl):S111-S118. 8pp. 103refs. Sponsored by the American Association of Electrodiagnostic Medicine. Cost: $5 members, $10 nonmembers. To order write AAEM, 421 First Avenue SW, #300E, Rochester, MN 55902. Key terms: evoked potentials; intraoperative monitoring; spinal cord; neuropathy; plexopathy.

Evoked Potentials, Somatosensory
Skin Physiology
Brain/Physiology

Assessment: Dermatomal Somatosensory Evoked Potentials. *Neurol*. 1997;49:1127-1130. 4pp. 20refs. Sponsored by the American Academy of Neurology. Cost: individual statements are free. To order call AAN Member Service Center 1 800 879-1960. Available on the Internet at aan.com.

Evoked Potentials,
Somatosensory/Physiology
Peripheral Nerves/Physiology

Guidelines for Somatosensory Evoked Potentials. *Muscle Nerve*. 1999;8(suppl):S121-S138. 17pp. 38refs. Sponsored by the American Association of Electrodiagnostic Medicine. Cost: $10 members, $20 nonmembers. To order write AAEM, 421 First Avenue SW, #300E, Rochester, MN 55902. Key terms: SEPs; evoked potentials; SSEPs.

Exercise
Counseling

Counseling to Promote Physical Activity. *Guide to Clinical Preventive Services, 2nd Ed*. 1996. Sponsored by the US Preventive Services Task Force. To order call Williams & Wilkins 1 800 638-0672.

Exercise
Women's Health

Women and Exercise. *ACOG Technical Bulletin*. 1992;173. 9pp. 28refs. Sponsored by the American College of Obstetricians and Gynecologists. Cost: free copy. Set of Bulletins $70 + s/h ACOG members, $125 + s/h nonmembers. One-year subscription $55 member, $65 nonmember. To order single copy, call ACOG Resource Center 202 863-2518; to order set or subscription, call ACOG Distribution Center, 1 800 762-2264. Available on the Internet to members only at acog.org. Key terms: women's health.

Exercise Test
Cardiology
Practice Guidelines

ACC/AHA Guidelines for Exercise Testing (Revision of 1986 Report). *J Am Coll Cardiol*. 1997. Sponsored by the American College of Cardiology, American Heart Association. Cost: free copy. To order call Educational Services Department 1 800 257-4740.

Exercise Test
Exercise Therapy

Exercise Standards. *Circulation*. 1995;91:580-615. 36pp. 140refs. Sponsored by the American Heart Association. Cost: free copy. To order call 1 800 242-8721 (US only) or write to: American Heart Association, Public Inquiries, 7272 Greenville Ave, Dallas TX 75231-4596.

Exercise Test
Thallium Radioisotopes/Diagnostic Use

Exercise Thallium-201 Myocardial Perfusion Scintigraphy in the Diagnosis of Coronary Artery Disease. *Ann Intern Med*. 1990;113:684-702. 19pp. 193refs. Sponsored by the American College of Physicians. To order call ACP Clinical Efficacy Assessment Project 1 800 523-1546.

Exercise/Physiology
Pregnancy
Puerperium

Exercise During Pregnancy and the Postpartum Period. *ACOG Technical Bulletin*. 1994;189. 5pp. 44refs. Sponsored by the American College of Obstetricians and Gynecologists. Cost: free copy. Set of Bulletins $70 + s/h ACOG members, $125 + s/h nonmembers. One-year subscription $55 member, $65 nonmember. To order single copy, call ACOG Resource Center 202 863-2518; to order set or subscription, call ACOG Distribution Center, 1 800 762-2264. Available on the Internet to members only at acog.org. Key terms: prenatal care; puerperium.

Eye Diseases/Diagnosis

Comprehensive Adult Eye Evaluation Preferred Practice Pattern. 1996. 12pp. 30refs. Sponsored by the American Academy of Ophthalmology. Cost: $11 members, $16 nonmembers. AAO members first copy free upon publication. To order call AAO Order Dept 415 561-8540. Key terms: eye; eye examination; adult eye examination.

Eye Diseases/Prevention and Control
Vision Disorders/Prevention and Control

Pediatric Eye Evaluations. 1996. 11pp. 10refs. Sponsored by the American Academy of Ophthalmology. Cost: $11 members, $16 nonmembers. AAO members first copy free upon publication. To order call AAO Order Dept 415 561-8540. Key terms: prevention; screening.

Eyeglasses/Standards

Ready-to-Wear Reading Glasses Ophthalmic Procedure Assessment. *Ophthalmology.* 1991;98:1469-1470. 2pp. 3refs. Sponsored by the American Academy of Ophthalmology. Cost: $11 members, $16 nonmembers. AAO members first copy free upon publication. To order call AAO Order Dept 415 561-8540. Key terms: eye; glasses.

Eyelids/Surgery
Blepharoplasty

Eyelid Surgery. 1994. Sponsored by the American Society of Plastic and Reconstructive Surgeons. Cost: $25 members, $55 nonmembers (full set of guidelines), + s/h. To order call 1 800 766-4955.

Facial Dermatoses/Microbiology
Tinea/Drug Therapy

Superficial Mycotic Infections of the Skin: Tinea capitis and Tinea barbae. *J Am Acad Derm.* 1996;34:290-294. 5pp. 21refs. Sponsored by the American Academy of Dermatology. Cost: free copy. To order call Alice Bell 847 330-0230 x333. Available on the Internet at aad.org. Key terms: facial dermatoses; hair follicle; antifungal agents; drug therapy.

Facility Regulation and Control
Nursing Homes

Regulation of Nursing Facilities, Position Statement. 1993. Sponsored by the American Geriatrics Society. Cost: free. To order call AGS 212 308-1414.

Fallopian Tube Diseases

Tubal Disease. 1993. 7pp. 24refs. Sponsored by the American Society for Reproductive Medicine. Cost: $1. To order call ASRM Publication Department 205 978-5000.

Family Practice/Education
Internship and Residency/Standards

Recommended Core Educational Guidelines for Family Practice Residents: Maternity and Gynecologic Care. *ACOG Statement of Policy.* 1998;73. 3pp. Sponsored by the American College of Obstetricians and Gynecologists. Cost: free copy. To order single copy, call ACOG Resource Center 202 863-2518; to order set or subscription, call ACOG Distribution Center, 1 800 762-2264. Available on the Internet to members only at acog.org. Key terms: curriculum; family practice; internship and residency; obstetrics; gynecology.

Family Practice/Standards
Gynecology/Standards
Obstetrics/Standards

Delineation of Obstetric-Gynecologic Primary Care Practice. *ACOG Committee Opinion.* 1999;218. 1pp. Sponsored by the American College of Obstetricians and Gynecologists. Cost: free copy. Set of Bulletins $70 + s/h ACOG members, $125 + s/h nonmembers. One-year subscription $55 member, $65 nonmember. To order single copy, call ACOG Resource Center 202 863-2518; to order set or subscription, call ACOG Distribution Center, 1 800 762-2264. Available on the Internet to members only at acog.org. Key terms: primary preventative care; obstetrics; gynecology; women's health services.

Febrile Seizure (see Convulsions, Febrile)

Femoral Neck Fractures

Femoral Neck Fracture (Adult). *Clinical Policies.* 1996. 6pp. 17refs. Sponsored by the American Academy of Orthopaedic Surgeons, North American Spine Society. Cost: $50 (set of 15) for nonmembers. To order call 1 800 626-6276. Key terms: femoral neck fracture; hip; leg; osteoporosis; American Academy of Orthopaedic Surgeons.

Fertilization
Prenatal Care

Preconceptional Care. *ACOG Technical Bulletin.* 1995;205. 6pp. 32refs. Sponsored by the American College of Obstetricians and Gynecologists. Cost: free copy. Set of Bulletins $70 + s/h ACOG members, $125 + s/h nonmembers. One-year subscription $55 member, $65 nonmember. To order single copy, call ACOG Resource Center 202 863-2518; to order set or subscription, call ACOG Distribution Center, 1 800 762-2264. Available on the Internet to members only at acog.org.

Fetal Blood
Hematopoietic Stem-Cell
Transplantation

Routine Storage of Umbilical Cord Blood for Potential Future Transplantation. *ACOG Committee Opinion.* 1997;183. 3pp. 8refs. Sponsored by the American College of Obstetricians and Gynecologists. Cost: free copy. Set of Opinions $55 + s/h ACOG members, $75 + s/h nonmembers. One-year subscription $55 member, $65 nonmember. To order single copy, call ACOG Resource Center 202 863-2518; to order set or subscription, call ACOG Distribution Center, 1 800 762-2264. Available on the Internet to members only at acog.org. Key terms: stem cells; technology assessment; fetal tissue transplantation.

Fetal Death/Diagnosis

Diagnosis and Management of Fetal Death. *ACOG Technical Bulletin.* 1993;176. 8pp. 23refs. Sponsored by the American College of Obstetricians and Gynecologists. Cost: free copy. Set of Bulletins $70 + s/h ACOG members, $125 + s/h nonmembers. One-year subscription $55 member, $65 nonmember. To order single copy, call ACOG Resource Center 202 863-2518; to order set or subscription, call ACOG Distribution Center, 1 800 762-2264. Available on the Internet to members only at acog.org.

Fetal Death/Genetics
Genetic Counseling

Genetic Evaluation of Stillbirths and Neonatal Deaths. *ACOG Committee Opinion.* 1996;178. 3pp. 17refs. Sponsored by the American College of Obstetricians and Gynecologists. Cost: free copy. Set of Opinions $55 + s/h ACOG members, $75 + s/h nonmembers. One-year subscription $55 member, $65 nonmember. To order single copy, call ACOG Resource Center 202 863-2518; to order set or subscription, call ACOG Distribution Center, 1 800 762-2264. Available on the Internet to members only at acog.org. Key terms: genetic screening; fetal death; infant mortality.

Fetal Diseases/Diagnosis
Fetal Movement
Heart Rate, Fetal

Antepartum Fetal Surveillance. *ACOG Technical Bulletin.* 1994;188. 5pp. 21refs. Sponsored by the American College of Obstetricians and Gynecologists. Cost: free copy. Set of Bulletins $70 + s/h ACOG members, $125 + s/h nonmembers. One-year subscription $55 member, $65 nonmember. To order single copy, call ACOG Resource Center 202 863-2518; to order set or subscription, call ACOG Distribution Center, 1 800 762-2264. Available on the Internet to members only at acog.org. Key terms: fetal monitoring; ultrasound: prenatal.

Fetal Diseases/Genetics
Paternal Age

Advanced Paternal Age: Risks to the Fetus. *ACOG Committee Opinion.* 1997;189. 2pp. 9refs. Sponsored by the American College of Obstetricians and Gynecologists. Cost: free copy. Set of Opinions $55 + s/h ACOG members, $75 + s/h nonmembers. One-year subscription $55 member, $65 nonmember. To order single copy, call ACOG Resource Center 202 863-2518; to order set or subscription, call ACOG Distribution Center, 1 800 762-2264. Available on the Internet to members only at acog.org. Key terms: fathers; age factors; pregnancy outcome; risk factors.

Fetal Diseases/Ultrasonography
Ultrasonography, Prenatal

Ultrasonic Evaluation of the Fetus. *Practice-Related Report of the AMA Council on Scientific Affairs.* 1990. 32pp. 107refs. Sponsored by the American Medical Association, Council on Scientific Affairs. Cost: free. To order call Nancy Nolan, AMA, 312 464-5046.

Fetal Growth Retardation/
Ultrasonography
Umbilical Arteries/Ultrasonography

Utility of Antepartum Umbilical Artery Doppler Velocimetry in Intrauterine Growth Restriction. *ACOG Committee Opinion.* 1997;188. 2pp. 10refs. Sponsored by the American College of Obstetricians and Gynecologists. Cost: free copy. Set of Opinions $55 + s/h ACOG members, $75 + s/h nonmembers. One-year subscription $55 member, $65 nonmember. To order single copy, call ACOG Resource Center 202 863-2518; to order set or subscription, call ACOG Distribution Center, 1 800 762-2264. Available on the Internet to members only at acog.org. Key terms: fetal monitoring; umbilical artery; laser-Doppler flowmetry; technology assessment; biomedical.

Fetal Macrosomia

Fetal Macrosomia. *ACOG Technical Bulletin.* 1991;159. 5pp. 27refs. Sponsored by the American College of Obstetricians and Gynecologists. Cost: free copy. Set of Bulletins $70 + s/h ACOG members, $125 + s/h nonmembers. One-year subscription $55 member, $65 nonmember. To order single copy, call ACOG Resource Center 202 863-2518; to order set or subscription, call ACOG Distribution Center, 1 800 762-2264. Available on the Internet to members only at acog.org.

Fetal Membranes, Premature Rupture

Premature Rupture of Membranes. *ACOG Practice Bulletin.* 1998;1. 10pp. 70refs. Sponsored by the American College of Obstetricians and Gynecologists. Cost: free copy. Multiples of 25: $20 + s/h member, $30 + s/h nonmember. To order single copy, call ACOG Resource Center 202 863-2518; to order set or subscription, call ACOG Distribution Center, 1 800 762-2264. Available on the Internet to members only at acog.org.

Fetal Membranes, Premature Rupture Glucocorticoids, Synthetic, Therapeutic Use Infants, Premature, Diseases/ Prevention and Control

Antenatal Corticosteroid Therapy for Fetal Maturation. *ACOG Committee Opinion.* 1998;210. 2pp. 12refs. Sponsored by the American College of Obstetricians and Gynecologists. Cost: free copy. Set of Opinions $55 + s/h ACOG members, $75 + s/h nonmembers. One-year subscription $55 member, $65 nonmember. To order single copy, call ACOG Resource Center 202 863-2518; to order set or subscription, call ACOG Distribution Center, 1 800 762-2264. Available on the Internet to members only at acog.org. Key terms: adrenal cortex hormones; fetal organ maturity; lung; premature labor.

Fetal Monitoring

Intrapartum Electronic Fetal Monitoring. *Guide to Clinical Preventive Services, 2nd Ed.* 1996. Sponsored by the US Preventive Services Task Force. To order call Williams & Wilkins 1 800 638-0672.

Fetal Monitoring
Heart Rate, Fetal

Fetal Heart Rate Patterns: Monitoring, Interpretation, and Management. *ACOG Technical Bulletin.* 1995;207. 10pp. 46refs. Sponsored by the American College of Obstetricians and Gynecologists. Cost: free copy. Set of Bulletins $70 + s/h ACOG members, $125 + s/h nonmembers. One-year subscription $55 member, $65 nonmember. To order single copy, call ACOG Resource Center 202 863-2518; to order set or subscription, call ACOG Distribution Center, 1 800 762-2264. Available on the Internet to members only at acog.org. Key terms: fetal distress.

Fetal Organ Maturity
Lung/Embryology

Assessment of Fetal Lung Maturity. *ACOG Educational Bulletin.* 1997;230. 8pp. 26refs. Sponsored by the American College of Obstetricians and Gynecologists. Cost: free copy. Set of Bulletins $70 + s/h ACOG members, $125 + s/h nonmembers. One-year subscription $55 member, $65 nonmember. To order single copy, call ACOG Resource Center 202 863-2518; to order set or subscription, call ACOG Distribution Center, 1 800 762-2264. Available on the Internet to members only at acog.org. Key terms: lung; fetal organ maturity; prenatal diagnosis.

Fetal Viability
Perinatal Care

Perinatal Care at the Threshold of Fetal Viability. *ACOG Committee Opinion.* 1995;163. 4pp. 14refs. Sponsored by the American College of Obstetricians and Gynecologists. Cost: free copy. Set of Opinions $55 + s/h ACOG members, $75 + s/h nonmembers. One-year subscription $55 member, $65 nonmember. To order single copy, call ACOG Resource Center 202 863-2518; to order set or subscription, call ACOG Distribution Center, 1 800 762-2264. Available on the Internet to members only at acog.org.

Fever/Diagnosis

Practice Parameters for Evaluating New Fever in Critically Ill Adult Patients. *Critical Care Med.* 1998;26:392-408. 17pp. 105refs. Sponsored by the Society of Critical Care Medicine. Cost: Complete Set $60 + s/h SCCM members, $80 + s/h nonmembers; $10 for a single guideline. To order call SCCM 714 282-6000 or access Book Store on the SCCM website. Available free on the Internet at sccm.org. Key terms: fever; intensive care unit; critical illness; blood cultures; catheter infection.

Fever/Drug Therapy
Serzone

Long-term Treatment of the Child with Simple Febrile Seizures. *Pediatr.* 1999;103:1307-1309. 3pp. 17refs. Sponsored by the American Academy of Pediatrics. To order call 1 800 433-9016.

Fibrinolytic Agents/Therapeutic Use
Thrombolytic Therapy

Fifth ACCP Consensus Conference on Antithrombotic Therapy. *Chest.* 1998;114(suppl):439s-769s. 330pp. 3435refs. Sponsored by the American College of Chest Physicians. Cost: $14. To order call ACCP 1 800 343-2227 or 1 847 498-1400 (credit card orders). Key terms: antithrombotic therapy; anticoagulation; pulmonary embolism; thrombosis.

Fibronectins/Analysis
Labor, Premature/Diagnosis

Fetal Fibronectin Preterm Labor Risk Test. *ACOG Committee Opinion.* 1997;187. 1pp. Sponsored by the American College of Obstetricians and Gynecologists. Cost: free copy. Set of Opinions $55 + s/h ACOG members, $75 + s/h nonmembers. One-year subscription $55 member, $65 nonmember. To order single copy, call ACOG Resource Center 202 863-2518; to order set or subscription, call ACOG Distribution Center, 1 800 762-2264. Available on the Internet to members only at acog.org. Key terms: fibronectins; labor; premature; technology assessment; biomedical.

Fissure in Anus/Therapy

Practice Parameters for Anal Fissure. *Dis Colon Rectum.* 1992;35(2):206-208. 3pp. 40refs. Sponsored by the American Society of Colon and Rectal Surgeons. Cost: free. To order write ASCRS, 85 W Algonquin Rd, #550, Arlington Hts, IL 60005.

Flatfoot

Pes Planus (Congenital, Acquired, Flexible and Rigid). *Clinical Policies.* 1996. 9pp. 17refs. Sponsored by the American Academy of Orthopaedic Surgeons, North American Spine Society. Cost: $50 (set of 15) for nonmembers. To order call 1 800 626-6276. Key terms: Pes planus; flatfoot; tarsal coalition; foot pain; American Academy of Orthopaedic Surgeons.

Fluoridation/Standards
Public Health

Fluoridation of Public Water Supplies. *Am Fam Phys.* 1996;53:2373-2377. 5pp. 45refs. Sponsored by the American Academy of Family Physicians. Cost: free copy. To order call AAFP 816 333-9700 x3114. Available on the Internet at aafp.org/clinical/.

Fluorides/Immunology
Fluoridation

Statement on the Question of Allergy to Fluoride as Used in the Fluoridation of Community Water Supplies. *J Allergy Clin Immun.* 1971;47:347, Position Statement No. 1. 1pp. 7refs. Sponsored by the American Academy of Allergy, Asthma, and Immunology. Cost: free copy. To order call 414 272-6071.

Fluoroscopy
Heart Catheterization

Use of Radiographic Devices by Cardiologists. *J Am Coll Cardiol.* 1995;25:1738-1739. 2pp. 13refs. Sponsored by the American College of Cardiology. Cost: free copy. To order call Educational Services Department 1 800 257-4740.

Folic Acid/Therapeutic Use
Neural Tube Defects/
Prevention and Control

Recommendations for the Use of Folic Acid to Reduce the Number of Cases of Spina Bifida and Other Neural Tube Defects. *Morbid Mortal Weekly Report.* 1992;41(no. RR-14). Sponsored by the Centers for Disease Control and Prevention. Cost: $1. To order call US Govt Printing Office 202 783-3238.

Food Hypersensitivity/Diagnosis

Provocative Testing (Sublingual). *J Allergy Clin Immun.* 1981;67:333-338, Position Statement No. 8—Controversial Techniques. 6pp. 13refs. Sponsored by the American Academy of Allergy, Asthma, and Immunology. Cost: free copy. To order call 414 272-6071.

Food Hypersensitivity/Diagnosis
Cytotoxicity Tests, Immunologic

Provocative and Neutralization Testing (Subcutaneous). *J Allergy Clin Immun.* 1981;67:333-338, Position Statement No. 8—Controversial Techniques. 2pp. 11refs. Sponsored by the American Academy of Allergy, Asthma, and Immunology. Cost: free copy. To order call 414 272-6071.

Forms and Records Control
Diabetes Mellitus

American Diabetes Association Guide to Diabetes Coding. 1999. 65pp. Sponsored by the American Diabetes Association. Cost: $55.95. To order call 1 800 232-6733; online bookstore: merchant.diabetes. org. Available on the Internet at merchant. diabetes. org. Key terms: evaluation; coding system; classification; reimbursement; procedures.

Fragile X-Syndrome/Diagnosis

Fragile X-Syndrome. *ACOG Committee Opinion.* 1995;161. 2pp. 4refs. Sponsored by the American College of Obstetricians and Gynecologists. Cost: free copy. Set of Opinions $55 + s/h ACOG members, $75 + s/h nonmembers. One-year subscription $55 member, $65 nonmember. To order single copy, call ACOG Resource Center 202 863-2518; to order set or subscription, call ACOG Distribution Center, 1 800 762-2264. Available on the Internet to members only at acog.org. Key terms: genetic screening.

Fundoplication/Methods
Surgical Procedures, Laparoscopic/Methods

Laparoscopic Nissen Fundoplication. *Diagnostic and Therapeutic Technology Assessment (DATTA).* 1997. 9pp. 43refs. Sponsored by the American Medical Association, Diagnostic and Therapeutic Technology Assessment Program. Cost: free copy. DATTA subscription available. To order call AMA Department of Technology Assessment 312 464-4531.

Fungi/Isolation and Purification
Lung Disease, Fungal/Diagnosis

Laboratory Diagnosis of Mycotic Infections and Specific Fungal Infections. *Amer Rev Resp Dis.* 1985;132:6. Sponsored by the American Thoracic Society. Cost: $4. To order send check payable to American Thoracic Society, 1740 Broadway, New York, NY 10019-4374; for credit card orders, call 212 315-8863.

Gallium Radioisotopes
Neoplasms/Radionuclide Imaging

Procedure Guideline for Gallium Scintigraphy in the Evaluation of Malignant Disease. *J Nuclear Med.* 1997;38:990-994. 5pp. 36refs. Sponsored by the Society of Nuclear Medicine. Cost: free. To order call Bill Uffelman 703 708-9000. Available on the Internet at snm.org. Key terms: gallium scintigraphy; neoplasm; routine diagnostic tests; radionuclide imaging; malignant disease.

Gallium Radioisotopes/Diagnostic Use
Inflammation/Radionuclide Imaging

Procedure Guideline for Gallium Scintigraphy in Inflammation. *J Nuclear Med.* 1997;38:994-997. 4pp. 14refs. Sponsored by the Society of Nuclear Medicine. Cost: free. To order call Bill Uffelman 703 708-9000. Available on the Internet at snm.org. Key terms: routine diagnostic tests; radionuclide imaging; gallium scintigraphy; inflammation; infection.

Gamete Intrafallopian Transfer

Gamete Intrafallopian Transfer (GIFT). *Diagnostic and Therapeutic Technology Assessment (DATTA).* 1991. 13pp. 37refs. Sponsored by the American Medical Association, Diagnostic and Therapeutic Technology Assessment Program. Cost: free copy. DATTA subscription available. To order call AMA Department of Technology Assessment 312 464-4531.

Gamma Cameras
Neoplasms/Radionuclide Imaging

ACR Standard for the Performance of Tumor Scintigraphy (with Gamma Cameras). 1996. 7pp. 18refs. Sponsored by the American College of Radiology. Cost: $25 (ACR nonmembers). To order call ACR Dept of Quality Assurance 703 716-7592. Available free on the Internet at acr.org. Key terms: nuclear medicine; tumor; scintigraphy.

Gastric Bypass
Gastroplasty

Gastric Restrictive Surgery. *JAMA.* 1989;261:1491-1494. 4pp. Sponsored by the American Medical Association, Diagnostic and Therapeutic Technology Assessment Program. Cost: free copy. DATTA subscription available. To order call AMA Department of Technology Assessment 312 464-4531.

Gastric Emptying
Gastrointestinal Motility

Procedure Guideline for Gastric Emptying and Motility. *J Nucl Med.* 1999;40:1236-1239. 4pp. 8refs. Sponsored by the Society of Nuclear Medicine. Cost: free. To order call Bill Uffelman 703 708-9000. Available on the Internet at snm.org.

Gastroenteritis/Therapy

Management of Acute Gastroenteritis in Young Children. *Pediatr.* 1996;97(3):424-436. 13pp. 93refs. Sponsored by the American Academy of Pediatrics. Cost: $1.95. Discounted set of policies available. To order call 1 800 433-9016.

Gastroenterology
Outcome Assessment (Healthcare)

A Primer on Outcomes Research for the Gastroenterologist: Report of the AGA Taskforce on Outcomes Research. *Gastroenterology.* 1995;109:302-306. 5pp. 30refs. Sponsored by the American Gastroenterological Association. Cost: $3. To order call AGA 301 654-2055. Key terms: outcomes; gastroenterology.

Gastroesophageal Reflux/Diagnosis
Gastroenterology

Updated Guidelines for the Guidelines for the Diagnosis and Treatment of Gastroesophageal Reflux Disease. *Am J Gastroenterol.* 1999;94:1434-1442. 9pp. 118refs. Sponsored by the American College of Gastroenterology. Cost: free copy. To order call ACG 703 820-7400. Available on the Internet at elsevier.com/locate/amjgastro.

Gastroesophageal Reflux/Diagnosis
Hydrogen-Ion Concentration

Continuous Ambulatory Esophageal pH Monitoring in the Evaluation of Patients with Gastroesophageal Reflux. *JAMA.* 1995;274(8):622-668. 7pp. 58refs. Sponsored by the American Medical Association, Diagnostic and Therapeutic Technology Assessment Program. Cost: free copy. DATTA subscription available. To order call AMA Department of Technology Assessment 312 464-4531.

Gastroesophageal Reflux/Surgery
Prostheses and Implants

Angelchik Antireflux Prosthesis Treatment of Gastroesophageal Reflux. *JAMA.* 1986;256:1358-1360. 3pp. Sponsored by the American Medical Association, Diagnostic and Therapeutic Technology Assessment Program. Cost: free copy. DATTA subscription available. To order call AMA Department of Technology Assessment 312 464-4531.

Gastroesophageal Reflux/Surgery
Surgical Procedures, Laparoscopic/Standards

Guidelines for Surgical Treatment of Gastroesophageal Reflux Disease (GERD). *Surgical Endoscopy.* 1998;12:186-188. 6pp. 38refs. Sponsored by the Society of American Gastrointestinal and Endoscopic Surgeons. Cost: free. To order call 310 314-2404. Available on the Internet at sages.org. Key terms: surgery; GERD; reflux.

Gastrointestinal Diseases/Diagnosis
Laparoscopy

Role of Laparoscopy in the Diagnosis and Management of Gastrointestinal Disease: Guidelines for Clinical Application. *Gastrointest Endosc.* 1988;34(suppl):30s-32s. 2pp. 14refs. Sponsored by the American Society for Gastrointestinal Endoscopy. Cost: free. To order call ASGE 978 526-8330.

Gastrointestinal Hemorrhage/Diagnosis

Management of the Adult Patient with Acute Lower GI Bleeding. *Am J Gastroenterol.* 1998;93:1202-1208. 7pp. 46refs. Sponsored by the American College of Gastroenterology. Cost: free copy. To order call ACG 703 820-7400.

Gastrointestinal Hemorrhage/
Radionuclide Imaging
Meckel's Diverticulum/
Radionuclide Imaging

Procedure Guideline for Gastrointestinal Bleeding and Meckel's Diverticulum Scintigraphy. *J Nucl Med.* 1999;40:1226-1232. 7pp. 27refs. Sponsored by the Society of Nuclear Medicine. Cost: free. To order call Bill Uffelman 703 708-9000. Available on the Internet at snm.org.

Gastrointestinal Hemorrhage/Therapy
Fibrinogen/Therapeutic Use

Endoscopic Topical Therapy for Gastrointestinal Hemorrhage. *JAMA.* 1985;253:2734-2735. 2pp. Sponsored by the American Medical Association, Diagnostic and Therapeutic Technology Assessment Program. Cost: free copy. DATTA subscription available. To order call AMA Department of Technology Assessment 312 464-4531.

Gastrointestinal System/
Radionuclide Imaging

ACR Standard for the Performance of Gastrointestinal Scintigraphy. 1996. 11pp. 32refs. Sponsored by the American College of Radiology. Cost: $25 (ACR nonmembers). To order call ACR Dept of Quality Assurance 703 716-7592. Available free on the Internet at acr.org. Key terms: nuclear medicine; gastrointestinal; scintigraphy.

Gastroscopy
Premedication

Preparation of Patients for Gastrointestinal Endoscopy: Guidelines for Clinical Application. *Gastrointest Endosc.* 1988;34(suppl):32s-34s. 3pp. 15refs. Sponsored by the American Society for Gastrointestinal Endoscopy. Cost: free. To order call ASGE 978 526-8330.

Gated Blood-Pool Imaging

Procedure Guideline for Gated Equilibrium Radionuclide Ventriculography. *J Nuclear Med.* 1997;38:1658-1661. 4pp. 22refs. Sponsored by the Society of Nuclear Medicine. Cost: free. To order call Bill Uffelman 703 708-9000. Available on the Internet at snm.org. Key terms: gated blood-pool imaging; myocardial contraction; routine diagnostic tests; radionuclide imaging; cardiovascular system.

Gated Blood-Pool Imaging/Standards
Magnetic Resonance Imaging

Surface/Specialty Coil Devices and Gating Techniques in Magnetic Resonance Imaging. *AHCPR Health Technology Assessment.* 1990;No. 3 (AHCPR Publication No. 90-3458). 23pp. 107refs. Sponsored by the Federal Agency for Health Care Policy and Research. To order call AHCPR Clearinghouse 1 800 358-9295.

Gaucher's Disease/Diagnosis
Gaucher's Disease/Therapy

Gaucher Disease: Current Issues in Diagnosis and Treatment. *NIH Technology Assessment Conference Statement.* 1995;26pp. Sponsored by the National Institutes of Health. Cost: free copy. To order call 1 888 644-2667. Available on the Internet at consensus.nih.gov.

Gender Identity/Therapy
Sexual and Gender Disorders/Therapy

Sexual and Gender Identity Disorders. *Treatments of Psychiatric Disorders, Second Edition, Volume II.* 1995;Section 9. 244pp. 742refs. Sponsored by the American Psychiatric Association. Cost: $250 for 2-volume set. To order call 1 800 368-5777 order #SPCT8700. Key terms: TPD; disorders; treatment.

Genetic Screening

Genetic Testing Alert. *Neurol.* 1996;47:1343-1344. 2pp. Sponsored by the American Academy of Neurology. Cost: individual statements are free. To order call AAN Member Service Center 1 800 879-1960. Available on the Internet at aan.com.

Genetic Screening/Standards
Tissue Donors

Genetic Screening of Gamete Donors. *ACOG Committee Opinion.* 1997;192. 3pp. 18refs. Sponsored by the American College of Obstetricians and Gynecologists. Cost: free copy. Set of Opinions $55 + s/h ACOG members, $75 + s/h nonmembers. One-year subscription $55 member, $65 nonmember. To order single copy, call ACOG Resource Center 202 863-2518; to order set or subscription, call ACOG Distribution Center, 1 800 762-2264. Available on the Internet to members only at acog.org. Key terms: genetic screening; artificial insemination; tissue donors; oocytes.

Genetic Techniques
Hereditary Diseases/Genetics

Genetic Technologies. *ACOG Technical Bulletin.* 1995;208. 10pp. 11refs. Sponsored by the American College of Obstetricians and Gynecologists. Cost: free copy. Set of Bulletins $70 + s/h ACOG members, $125 + s/h nonmembers. One-year subscription $55 member, $65 nonmember. To order single copy, call ACOG Resource Center 202 863-2518; to order set or subscription, call ACOG Distribution Center, 1 800 762-2264. Available on the Internet to members only at acog.org. Key terms: technology assessment; genetics; genetic screening.

Genital Diseases, Female/Diagnosis
Ultrasonography

ACR Standard for the Performance of the Ultrasound Examination of the Female Pelvis. 1999. 3pp. 7refs. Sponsored by the American College of Radiology. Cost: $25 (ACR nonmembers). To order call ACR Dept of Quality Assurance 703 716-7592. Key terms: ultrasound; pelvis; female.

Genital Diseases, Female/Diagnosis
Vaginal Diseases/Diagnosis

Pediatric Gynecologic Disorders. *ACOG Technical Bulletin*. 1995;201. 6pp. 9refs. Sponsored by the American College of Obstetricians and Gynecologists. Cost: free copy. Set of Bulletins $70 + s/h ACOG members, $125 + s/h nonmembers. One-year subscription $55 member, $65 nonmember. To order single copy, call ACOG Resource Center 202 863-2518; to order set or subscription, call ACOG Distribution Center, 1 800 762-2264. Available on the Internet to members only at acog.org. Key terms: pediatric gynecology.

Genital Diseases, Female/
Ultrasonography

Gynecologic Ultrasonography. *ACOG Technical Bulletin*. 1995;215. 10pp. 42refs. Sponsored by the American College of Obstetricians and Gynecologists. Cost: free copy. Set of Bulletins $70 + s/h ACOG members, $125 + s/h nonmembers. One-year subscription $55 member, $65 nonmember. To order single copy, call ACOG Resource Center 202 863-2518; to order set or subscription, call ACOG Distribution Center, 1 800 762-2264. Available on the Internet to members only at acog.org. Key terms: gynecologic diagnosis.

Genital Diseases/Female
Papillomavirus, Human

Genital Human Papillomavirus Infections. *ACOG Technical Bulletin*. 1994;193. 7pp. 34refs. Sponsored by the American College of Obstetricians and Gynecologists. Cost: free copy. Set of Bulletins $70 + s/h ACOG members, $125 + s/h nonmembers. One-year subscription $55 member, $65 nonmember. To order single copy, call ACOG Resource Center 202 863-2518; to order set or subscription, call ACOG Distribution Center, 1 800 762-2264. Available on the Internet to members only at acog.org. Key terms: cervix neoplasms; condylomata.

Genital Neoplasm, Female/
Prevention and Control
Counseling

Counseling to Prevent Gynecologic Cancers. *Guide to Clinical Preventive Services, 2nd Ed.* 1996. Sponsored by the US Preventive Services Task Force. To order call Williams & Wilkins 1 800 638-0672.

Geriatric Assessment

Comprehensive Geriatric Assessment for the Older Patient, Position Statement. 1993. Sponsored by the American Geriatrics Society. Cost: free. To order call AGS 212 308-1414.

Geriatrics
Education, Medical, Graduate

Guidelines for Fellowship Training Programs in Geriatric Medicine. 1997. Sponsored by the American Geriatrics Society. Cost: free. To order call AGS 212 308-1414.

Glaucoma, Angle-Closure

Primary Angle-Closure Glaucoma Preferred Practice Pattern. 1996. 14pp. 27refs. Sponsored by the American Academy of Ophthalmology. Cost: $11 members, $16 nonmembers. AAO members first copy free upon publication. To order call AAO Order Dept 415 561-8540. Key terms: eye; glaucoma; angle-closure glaucoma.

Glaucoma, Angle-Closure/Surgery
Iris/Surgery
Laser Surgery/Methods

Laser Peripheral Iridotomy for Pupillary-Block Glaucoma Ophthalmic Procedure Assessment. *Ophthalmology*. 1994;101:1749-1758. 10pp. 45refs. Sponsored by the American Academy of Ophthalmology. Cost: $11 members, $16 nonmembers. AAO members first copy free upon publication. To order call AAO Order Dept 415 561-8540. Key terms: eye; glaucoma; iridotomy; iridoplasty; pupillary-block glaucoma.

Glaucoma, Open-Angle

Primary Open-Angle Glaucoma. 1996. 28pp. 107refs. Sponsored by the American Academy of Ophthalmology. Cost: $11 members, $16 nonmembers. AAO members first copy free upon publication. To order call AAO Order Dept 415 561-8540. Key terms: glaucoma; screening; treatment; adult.

Glaucoma, Open-Angle/Diagnosis

Primary Open-Angle Glaucoma Suspect Preferred Practice Pattern. 1995. 11pp. 12refs. Sponsored by the American Academy of Ophthalmology. Cost: $11 members, $16 nonmembers. AAO members first copy free upon publication. To order call AAO Order Dept 415 561-8540. Key terms: eye; glaucoma; glaucoma suspect; open-angle glaucoma; screening.

Glaucoma/Diagnosis

Screening for Glaucoma. *Guide to Clinical Preventive Services, 2nd Ed.* 1996. Sponsored by the US Preventive Services Task Force. To order call Williams & Wilkins 1 800 638-0672.

Glucocorticoids/Adverse Effects Osteoporosis/Chemically Induced

Recommendations for the Prevention and Treatment of Glucocorticoid-Induced Osteoporosis. *Arthritis Rheum.* 1996;39(11):1791-1801. 11pp. 87refs. Sponsored by the American College of Rheumatology. To order call 404 633-3777. Available free on the Internet at rheumatology.org. Key terms: osteoporosis; bone; musculoskeletal; drugs; steroid.

Glucocorticoids/Therapeutic Use Infection/Drug Therapy

Guidelines for the Use of Systemic Glucocorticosteroids in the Management of Selected Infections. *J Infect Dis.* 1992;165:1-13. 14pp. Sponsored by the Infectious Diseases Society of America. To order obtain request from medical library.

Gonorrhea

Gonorrhea in Prepubertal Children. *Pediatr.* 1998;101:134. 2pp. 11refs. Sponsored by the American Academy of Pediatrics. Cost: $1.95. Discounted set of policies available. To order call 1 800 433-9016.

Gonorrhea/Diagnosis

Screening for Gonorrhea. *Guide to Clinical Preventive Services, 2nd Ed.* 1996. Sponsored by the US Preventive Services Task Force. To order call Williams & Wilkins 1 800 638-0672.

Growth Hormone (see Somatotropin)

Guidelines Insomnia/Diagnosis

Practice Parameters for the Use of Polysomnography in the Evaluation of Insomnia. *Sleep.* 1995;18(1):55-57. 3pp. 2refs. Sponsored by the American Academy of Sleep Medicine. Cost: $30 + s/h for a complete set of current AASM Guidelines. To order call AASM 507 287-6006. Key terms: insomnia; sleep disorders; sleep; polysomnography; monitoring.

Gynecologic Surgical Procedures/Standards Length of Stay

Length of Stay for Gynecologic Procedures. *ACOG Committee Opinion.* 1997;191. 1pp. Sponsored by the American College of Obstetricians and Gynecologists. Cost: free copy. Set of Opinions $55 + s/h ACOG members, $75 + s/h nonmembers. One-year subscription $55 member, $65 nonmember. To order single copy, call ACOG Resource Center 202 863-2518; to order set or subscription, call ACOG Distribution Center, 1 800 762-2264. Available on the Internet to members only at acog.org. Key terms: length of stay; surgery; gynecologic; hospitalization.

Gynecomastia

Gynecomastia. 1996. 6pp. Sponsored by the American Society of Plastic and Reconstructive Surgeons. Cost: $25 members, $55 nonmembers (full set of guidelines), + s/h. To order call 1 800 766-4955.

Haemophilus Infections/ Prevention and Control Bacterial Vaccines

Haemophilus b Conjugate Vaccines for Prevention of Haemophilus Influenza Type b Disease Among Infants and Children Two Months of Age and Older: Recommendations of the Immunization Practices Advisory Committee. *Morbid Mortal Weekly Report.* 1991;40(no. RR-1):1-7. 7pp. Sponsored by the Centers for Disease Control and Prevention. Cost: $1. To order call US Govt Printing Office 202 783-3238.

Haemophilus Vaccines/ Administration and Dosage Tetanus Toxoid/ Administration and Dosage

Recommendations for Use of Haemophilus b Conjugate Vaccines and a Combined Diphtheria, Tetanus, Pertussis, and Haemophilus b Vaccine. *Morbid Mortal Weekly Report.* 1993;42(no. RR-13):1-15. 15pp. 52refs. Sponsored by the Centers for Disease Control and Prevention. Cost: $1. To order call US Govt Printing Office 202 783-3238.

Hallux Valgus

Hallux Valgus. *Clinical Policies.* 1996. 7pp. 27refs. Sponsored by the American Academy of Orthopaedic Surgeons, North American Spine Society. Cost: $50 (set of 15) for nonmembers. To order call 1 800 626-6276. Key terms: Hallux valgus; foot pain; bunion; metatarsophalangeal joint; American Academy of Orthopaedic Surgeons.

Hamartoma/Therapy
Nevus/Therapy

Non-Melanocytic Nevi, Hamartomas and Potentially Malignant Lesions, Part II. *J Am Acad Derm.* 1995;32:104-108. 5pp. 37refs. Sponsored by the American Academy of Dermatology. Cost: free copy. To order call Alice Bell 847 330-0230 x333. Available on the Internet at aad.org. Key terms: hamartoma; precancerous conditions; diagnosis; therapy.

Head and Neck Neoplasms/Radiotherapy
Carcinoma, Squamous Cell/
Drug Therapy

Oral Health Care Series: Head and Neck Cancer Patients Receiving Radiation Therapy. 1996. 16pp. 18refs. Sponsored by the American Dental Association. Cost: $8 ADA members, $12 nonmembers. To order call ADA Dept of Salable Materials 1 800 947-4776.

Head Injuries
Hyperventilation

Hyperventilation. *Guidelines for the Management of Severe Head Injury.* 1996;105-114. 10pp. Sponsored by the American Association of Neurological Surgeons. Cost: $45. To order call AANS 847 692-9500.

Head Injuries, Closed

Minor Closed Head Trauma in Children. 1999. 52pp. Sponsored by the American Academy of Family Physicians. To order call 1 800 944-0000. Available on the Internet at aafp.org/clinical/.

Head Injuries, Closed/Diagnosis
Head Injuries, Closed/Drug Therapy

Evaluation and Management of Closed Head Injuries. *Neurosurgical Case Screening Guidelines.* 1989. 4pp. Sponsored by the American Association of Neurological Surgeons. Cost: $50 for set of guidelines. To order call AANS 847 692-9500.

Head Injuries/Drug Therapy
Barbiturates

Barbiturates. *Guidelines for the Management of Severe Head Injury.* 1996;127-133. 7pp. Sponsored by the American Association of Neurological Surgeons. Cost: $45. To order call AANS 847 692-9500.

Head Injuries/Drug Therapy
Glucocorticoids/Therapeutic Use

Steroids. *Guidelines for the Management of Severe Head Injury.* 1996;134-140. 7pp. Sponsored by the American Association of Neurological Surgeons. Cost: $45. To order call AANS 847 692-9500.

Head Injuries/Physiopathology
Hypotension

Resuscitation of Blood Pressure and Oxygenation. *Guidelines for the Management of Severe Head Injury.* 1996;31-41. 11pp. Sponsored by the American Association of Neurological Surgeons. Cost: $45. To order call AANS 847 692-9500.

Head Injuries/Surgery
Neurosurgery/Standards

Trauma Systems, Pre-Hospital Care, and the Neurosurgeon. *Guidelines for the Management of Severe Head Injury.* 1996;7-16. 10pp. Sponsored by the American Association of Neurological Surgeons. Cost: $45. To order call AANS 847 692-9500.

Head Injuries/Therapy
Critical Pathways

Critical Pathway for the Treatment of Established Intracranial Hypertension. *Guidelines for the Management of Severe Head Injury.* 1996;141-143. 3pp. Sponsored by the American Association of Neurological Surgeons. Cost: $45. To order call AANS 847 692-9500.

Head Injuries/Therapy
Intracranial Pressure

Intracranial Pressure Treatment Threshold. *Guidelines for the Management of Severe Head Injury.* 1996;71-76. 6pp. Sponsored by the American Association of Neurological Surgeons. Cost: $45. To order call AANS 847 692-9500.

Head Injuries/Therapy
Resuscitation

Brain-Specific Treatments in the Initial Resuscitation of the Head Injury Patient. *Guidelines for the Management of Severe Head Injury.* 1996;17-30. 14pp. Sponsored by the American Association of Neurological Surgeons. Cost: $45. To order call AANS 847 692-9500.

Head Protective Devices/Standards
Accidents, Traffic/Statistics and
Numerical Data

Helmets and Preventing Motorcycle and Bicycle-Related Injuries. *JAMA.* 1994;272:1535-1538. 4pp. 36refs. Sponsored by the American Medical Association, Council on Scientific Affairs. Cost: free. To order call Nancy Nolan, AMA, 312 464-5046.

Headache/Diagnosis
Emergency Medicine

Clinical Policy for the Initial Approach to Adolescents and Adults Presenting to the Emergency Department with a Chief Complaint of Headache. *Ann Emerg Med.* 1996;27:821-844. 24pp. 37refs. Sponsored by the American College of Emergency Physicians. Cost: ACEP members free copy, fee nonmembers. To order call ACEP 1 800 798-1822 x6. Key terms: headache; secondary headache syndromes; (in) Emergency Department.

Headache/Diagnosis
Magnetic Resonance Imaging

Practice Parameters: Utility of Neuroimaging in the Evaluation of Headache in Patients with Normal Neurologic Examinations. *Neurol.* 1994;44:1353-1354. 2pp. Sponsored by the American Academy of Neurology. Cost: individual statements are free. To order call AAN Member Service Center 1 800 879-1960. Available on the Internet at aan.com.

Headache/Physiopathology
Electroencephalography

Practice Parameter: Electroencephalogram in the Evaluation of Headache. *Neurol.* 1995;45:1411-1413. 3pp. Sponsored by the American Academy of Neurology. Cost: individual statements are free. To order call AAN Member Service Center 1 800 879-1960. Available on the Internet at aan.com.

Health Care Rationing

Rational Allocation of Medical Care. 1996. Sponsored by the American Geriatrics Society. Cost: free. To order call AGS 212 308-1414.

Health Manpower
Hepatitis B/Prevention and Control

Recommendations for Preventing Transmission of Human Immunodeficiency Virus and Hepatitis B Virus to Patients During Exposure-Prone Invasive Procedures. *Morbid Mortal Weekly Report.* 1991;40(no. RR-8):1-9. 9pp. 44refs. Sponsored by the Centers for Disease Control and Prevention. Cost: $1. To order call US Govt Printing Office 202 783-3238.

Health Manpower/Standards
Respiratory Function Tests

Pulmonary Function Laboratory Personnel Qualifications. *Amer Rev Resp Dis.* 1986;134:3. Sponsored by the American Thoracic Society. Cost: $4. To order send check payable to American Thoracic Society, 1740 Broadway, New York, NY 10019-4374; for credit card orders, call 212 315-8863.

Health Occupations
HIV Infections/Prevention and Control

The HIV-Infected Healthcare Worker. *Infect Control Hosp Epidemiol.* 1990;11:647-656. 10pp. 31refs. Sponsored by the Society for Healthcare Epidemiology of America. Cost: free. To order visit our website at medscape.com/shea. Available on the Internet at medscape.com/shea. Key terms: practice issues; disclosure issues; exposure management; testing issues.

Health Personnel
HIV Infections/Prevention and Control

Appendix—First-Line Drugs for HIV Postexposure Prophylaxis (PEP). 1998;47(no. RR-7). Sponsored by the Centers for Disease Control and Prevention. To order call US Govt Printing Office. Available on the Internet at cdc.gov/epo/mmwr/preview/ ind98_rr.html.

Health Personnel
HIV Infections/Prevention and Control

Public Health Service Guidelines for the Management of Health-Care Worker Exposure to HIV and Recommendations for Postexposure Prophylaxis. *Morbid Mortal Weekly Report.* 1998;47(no. RR-07). Sponsored by the Centers for Disease Control and Prevention. Cost: $1. To order call US Govt Printing Office 202 783-3238.

Health Personnel/Standards
Immunization/Standards

Immunization of Health-Care Workers. *Morbid Mortal Weekly Report*. 1997;46(no. RR-18). Sponsored by the Centers for Disease Control and Prevention. Cost: $1. To order call US Govt Printing Office 202 783-3238.

Health Personnel/Standards
Measles/Immunology

Quality Standard for Assurance of Measles Immunity Among Health Care Workers. *Clin Inf Dis*. 1994;18:431-436. 6pp. 36refs. Sponsored by the Infectious Diseases Society of America. To obtain request from medical library.

Health Promotion
Physical Fitness

Physical Activity and Public Health. *JAMA*. 1995;273:402-407. 6pp. 85refs. Sponsored by the Centers for Disease Control and Prevention, American College of Sports Medicine. To obtain request from medical library.

Health Services Needs and Demand
Cardiology/Manpower

25th Bethesda Conference Report: Future Personnel Needs for Cardiovascular Health Care. *J Am Coll Cardiol*. 1994;24:275-328. 53pp. Sponsored by the American College of Cardiology. Cost: free copy. To order call Educational Services Department 1 800 257-4740.

Health Services Needs and
Demands/Economics
Financing, Government

Public Financing of Catastrophic Care for the Older Patient, Position Statement. 1993. Sponsored by the American Geriatrics Society. Cost: free. To order call AGS 212 308-1414.

Hearing Disorders/Diagnosis

Screening for Hearing Impairment. *Guide to Clinical Preventive Services, 2nd Ed*. 1996. Sponsored by the US Preventive Services Task Force. To order call Williams & Wilkins 1 800 638-0672.

Hearing Disorders/
Prevention and Control
Mass Screening/Methods

Early Identification of Hearing Impairment in Infants and Young Children. *NIH Consensus Development Conference Statement*. 1993;11(1):1-24[Conf. No. 92]. 25pp. Sponsored by the National Institutes of Health. Cost: free copy. To order call 1 888 644-2667. Available on the Internet at consensus.nih.gov.

Hearing Loss, Noise-Induced

Noise and Hearing Loss. *NIH Consensus Development Conference Statement*. 1990;8(1):1-24[Conf. No. 76]. 25pp. Sponsored by the National Institutes of Health. Cost: free copy. To order call 1 888 644-2667. Available on the Internet at consensus.nih.gov.

Heart Catheterization
Heart Defects, Congenital/Therapy

Pediatric Therapeutic Cardiac Catheterization. *Circulation*. 1998;97:609-625. 15pp. 264refs. Sponsored by the American Heart Association. Cost: free copy. To order call 1 800 242-8721 (US only) or write to: American Heart Association, Public Inquiries, 7272 Greenville Ave, Dallas TX 75231-4596.

Heart Catheterization/Methods

Safety and Efficacy of Ambulatory Cardiac Catheterization in Hospital and Freestanding Setting. *Ann Intern Med*. 1985;103:294-298. 5pp. Sponsored by the American College of Physicians. To order call ACP Clinical Efficacy Assessment Project 1 800 523-1546.

Heart Catheterization/Standards
Cardiac Surgical Procedures/Standards

Position Statement: Interventional Catheterization Procedures and Cardiothoracic Surgical Consultation. 1992. Sponsored by the American College of Cardiology. Cost: free copy. To order call Educational Services Department 1 800 257-4740.

Heart Catheterization/Standards
Laboratories, Hospital/Standards

ACC/AHA Guidelines for Cardiac Catheterization and Cardiac Catheterization Laboratories. *J Am Coll Cardiol*. 1991;18:1149-82. 34pp. 68refs. Sponsored by the American College of Cardiology, American Heart Association. Cost: free copy. To order call Educational Services Department 1 800 257-4740.

Heart Catheterization/Standards
Laboratories, Hospital/Standards

Practice Guideline: Cardiac Catheterization and Cardiac Catheterization Laboratories. *Circulation*. 1991;84:2213-2247. 35pp. 68refs. Sponsored by the American Heart Association. Cost: free copy. To order call 1 800 242-8721 (US only) or write to: American Heart Association, Public Inquiries, 7272 Greenville Ave, Dallas TX 75231-4596.

Heart Defects, Congenital

Congenital Heart Disease After Childhood: An Expanding Patient Population. *J Am Coll Cardiol*. 1991;32pp. 84refs. Sponsored by the American College of Cardiology. Cost: free copy. To order call Educational Services Department 1 800 257-4740.

Heart Defects, Congenital/Diagnosis
Heart Defects, Congenital/Therapy

Guidelines for Evaluation and Management of Common Congenital Cardiac Problems in Infants, Children, and Adolescents. *Circulation*. 1994;90:2180-2188. 9pp. 31refs. Sponsored by the American Heart Association. Cost: free copy. To order write the Office of Scientific Affairs, AHA, 7272 Greenville Ave, Dallas, TX 75231.

Heart Defects, Congenital/Economics
Insurance, Health

Insurability of the Adolescent and Young Adult with Heart Disease. *Circulation*. 1992;86:703-710. 8pp. 15refs. Sponsored by the American Heart Association. Cost: free copy. To order call 1 800 242-8721 (US only) or write to: American Heart Association, Public Inquiries, 7272 Greenville Ave, Dallas TX 75231-4596.

Heart Diseases/Diagnosis

Noninvasive Technology in the Assessment of Ventricular Function. *Am J Card*. 1982. Sponsored by the American College of Cardiology. Cost: free copy. To order call Educational Services Department 1 800 257-4740.

Heart Diseases/Etiology
Obesity/Complications

Obesity and Heart Disease. *Circulation*. 1997;96:3248-3250. 3pp. 55refs. Sponsored by the American Heart Association. Cost: free copy. To order call 1 800 242-8721 (US only) or write to: American Heart Association, Public Inquiries, 7272 Greenville Ave, Dallas TX 75231-4596.

Heart Diseases/Rehabilitation

Cardiac Rehabilitation Services. *JAMA*. 1987;258:1959-1962. 4pp. Sponsored by the American Medical Association, Diagnostic and Therapeutic Technology Assessment Program. Cost: free copy. DATTA subscription available. To order call AMA Department of Technology Assessment 312 464-4531.

Heart Diseases/Surgery

Guidelines for Minimal Standards in Cardiac Surgery. *Am Coll Surg Bulletin*. 1991;76:27-29. 3pp. Sponsored by the American College of Surgeons. Cost: free copy. To order call ACS Socioeconomic Affairs Dept 312 664-4050.

Heart Diseases/Surgery
Heart Transplantation

Selection and Treatment of Candidates for Heart Transplantation. *Circulation*. 1995;92:3593-3612. 19pp. 139refs. Sponsored by the American Heart Association. Cost: free copy. To order call 1 800 242-8721 (US only) or write to: American Heart Association, Public Inquiries, 7272 Greenville Ave, Dallas TX 75231-4596.

Heart Failure, Congestive/Diagnosis
Heart Failure, Congestive/Therapy

Guidelines for the Evaluation and Management of Heart Failure. *Circulation*. 1995;92:2764-2784. 20pp. 112refs. Sponsored by the American Heart Association. Cost: free copy. To order call 1 800 242-8721 (US only) or write to: American Heart Association, Public Inquiries, 7272 Greenville Ave, Dallas TX 75231-4596.

Heart Failure, Congestive/Mortality

Heart Failure. 1996. 8pp. 15refs. Sponsored by the American Medical Directors Association. Cost: $8. To order call 1 800 876-2632 or 410 740-9743.

Heart Failure, Congestive/Therapy

ACC/AHA Guidelines for the Management of Heart Failure. *J Am Coll Cardiol*. 1995;26(5):1376-1398. 23pp. 112refs. Sponsored by the American College of Cardiology, American Heart Association. Cost: free copy. To order call Educational Services Department 1 800 257-4740.

Heart Failure, Congestive/Therapy
Ventricular Function

Heart Failure: Evaluation and Care of Patients with Left-Ventricular Systolic Dysfunction. *AHCPR.* 1994;Publication No. 94-0612. 122pp. 237refs. Sponsored by the Federal Agency for Health Care Policy and Research. To order call AHCPR Clearinghouse 1 800 358-9295.

Heart Function Tests/Methods
Myocardial Infarction/Physiopathology

Evaluation of Patients after Recent Acute Myocardial Infarction. *Ann Intern Med.* 1989;110:485-488. 4pp. 1ref. Sponsored by the American College of Physicians. To order call ACP Clinical Efficacy Assessment Project 1 800 523-1546.

Heart Transplantation
Organ Procurement/
Organization and Administration

24th Bethesda Conference Report: Cardiac Transplantation. *J Am Coll Cardiol.* 1993;22:1-64. 64pp. Sponsored by the American College of Cardiology. Cost: free copy. To order call Educational Services Department 1 800 257-4740.

Heart-Lung Transplantation
Patient Selection

Institutional and Patient Criteria for Heart-Lung Transplantation. *AHCPR Health Technology Assessment.* 1994;No. 1 (AHCPR Publication No. 94-0042). 19pp. 46refs. Sponsored by the Federal Agency for Health Care Policy and Research. To order call AHCPR Clearinghouse 1 800 358-9295.

Heart/Physiology
Sleep/Physiology

Indications and Standards for Cardiopulmonary Sleep Studies. *Amer Rev Resp Dis.* 1989;139:2. Sponsored by the American Thoracic Society. Cost: $6. To order send check payable to American Thoracic Society, 1740 Broadway, New York, NY 10019-4374; for credit card orders, call 212 315-8863.

Helicobacter Infections
Peptic Ulcer

Helicobacter pylori. *NIH Consensus Development Conference Statement.* 1994;12(1):1-23[Conf. No. 94]. 24pp. Sponsored by the National Institutes of Health. Cost: free copy. To order call 1 888 644-2667. Available on the Internet at consensus.nih.gov.

Helicobacter Infections/Therapy
Helicobacter pylori

Guidelines for the Management of Helicobacter Pylori Infection. *Am J Gastroenterol.* 1998;93:2330-2338. 8pp. 53refs. Sponsored by the American College of Gastroenterology. Cost: free copy. To order call ACG 703 820-7400.

Hemangioma/Etiology

Hemangiomas of Infancy. *J Am Acad Derm.* 1997;37:631-637. 7pp. 56refs. Sponsored by the American Academy of Dermatology. Cost: free copy. To order call Alice Bell 847 330-0230 x333. Available on the Internet at aad.org. Key terms: skin neoplasms; congenital; diagnosis; therapy; counseling.

Hematoma, Epidural/Surgery
Trephining
Hematoma, Subdural/Surgery

Surgical Procedures for Managing Extradural or Subdural Hematomas by Burr Hole or Twist Drill Evacuation. *Neurosurgical Case Screening Guidelines.* 1989;4pp. Sponsored by the American Association of Neurological Surgeons. Cost: $50 for set of guidelines. To order call AANS 847 692-9500.

Hematopoietic Stem-Cell
Transplantation

Autologous Peripheral Stem-Cell Transplantation. *AHCPR Health Technology Assessment.* 1995;No. 5 (AHCPR Publication No. 95-0074). 16pp. 196refs. Sponsored by the Federal Agency for Health Care Policy and Research. To order call AHCPR Clearinghouse 1 800 358-9295.

Hematopoietic Stem-Cell
Transplantation
Multiple Myeloma/Therapy

Hematopoietic Stem-Cell Transplantation in Multiple Myeloma. *AHCPR Health Technology Review.* 1995;No. 12 (AHCPR Publication No. 95-0072). 10pp. 73refs. Sponsored by the Federal Agency for Health Care Policy and Research. To order call AHCPR Clearinghouse 1 800 358-9295.

Subject

Hemochromatosis/Genetics
Hemochromatosis/Diagnosis

Practice Parameter for Hereditary Hemochromatosis. *Clinica Chimica Acta*. 1996;245:139-200. 61pp. 202refs. Sponsored by the College of American Pathologists. Cost: reprints: free. To order call CAP 1 800 323-4040 x7378. Key terms: hereditary hemochromatosis; iron overload; pathology.

Hemodialysis

Adequacy of Hemodialysis. *Clinical Policy*. 1993;1. 105pp. 154refs. Sponsored by the Renal Physicians Association. Cost: $21.95 + s/h. To order write to RPA, 4701 Randolph Rd, #102, Rockville, MD 20852, or call 301 468-3515. Key terms: ESRD; hemodialysis; urea kinetic modeling; dialysis prescription; dialysis adequacy.

Hemodialysis
Kidney Failure, Chronic/Diagnosis

Laboratory Tests in End-Stage Renal Disease Patients Undergoing Dialysis. *AHCPR Health Technology Assessment*. 1994;No. 2 (AHCPR Publication No. 94-0053). 12pp. 42refs. Sponsored by the Federal Agency for Health Care Policy and Research. To order call AHCPR Clearinghouse 1 800 358-9295.

Hemodialysis
Kidney Failure, Chronic/Therapy

Morbidity and Mortality of Dialysis. *NIH Consensus Development Conference Statement*. 1993;11(2):1-33[Conf. No. 93]. 34pp. Sponsored by the National Institutes of Health. Cost: free copy. To order call 1 888 644-2667. Available on the Internet at consensus.nih.gov.

Hemodialysis/Instrumentation
Arteriovenous Shunt, Surgical/
Adverse Effects

Quality Improvement Guidelines for Dialysis Access. 1997. Sponsored by the Society of Cardiovascular and Interventional Radiology. Cost: free copy. To order call SCVIR 703 691-1805.

Hemodialysis/Standards

NKF-DOQI Clinical Practice Guidelines for Hemodialysis Adequacy. 1997. 168pp. 185refs. Sponsored by the National Kidney Foundation. Cost: $13. To order call NKF 1 800 622-9010. Key terms: hemodialysis adequacy; peritoneal dialysis adequacy; vascular access; anemia management; executive summaries.

Hemodynamics/Physiology
Catheterization, Central Venous

Invasive Hemodynamic Monitoring in Obstetrics and Gynecology. *ACOG Technical Bulletin*. 1992;175. 6pp. 15refs. Sponsored by the American College of Obstetricians and Gynecologists. Cost: free copy. Set of Bulletins $70 + s/h ACOG members, $125 + s/h nonmembers. One-year subscription $55 member, $65 nonmember. To order single copy, call ACOG Resource Center 202 863-2518; to order set or subscription, call ACOG Distribution Center, 1 800 762-2264. Available on the Internet to members only at acog.org.

Hemoglobinopathies/Genetics
Genetic Screening/Methods

Genetic Screening for Hemoglobinopathies. *ACOG Committee Opinion*. 1996;168. 2pp. 4refs. Sponsored by the American College of Obstetricians and Gynecologists. Cost: free copy. Set of Opinions $55 + s/h ACOG members, $75 + s/h nonmembers. One-year subscription $55 member, $65 nonmember. To order single copy, call ACOG Resource Center 202 863-2518; to order set or subscription, call ACOG Distribution Center, 1 800 762-2264. Available on the Internet to members only at acog.org.

Hemoglobinopathies/
Prevention and Control

Screening for Hemoglobinopathies. *Guide to Clinical Preventive Services, 2nd Ed.* 1996. Sponsored by the US Preventive Services Task Force. To order call Williams & Wilkins 1 800 638-0672.

Hemorrhagic Fevers, Viral/Diagnosis

Management of Patients with Suspected Viral Hemorrhagic Fever. *Morbid Mortal Weekly Report*. 1988;37(S-3). 1pp. Sponsored by the Centers for Disease Control and Prevention. Cost: $1. To order call US Govt Printing Office 202 783-3238.

Hemorrhoids/Therapy

Practice Parameters for the Treatment of Hemorrhoids. *Dis Colon Rectum*. 1993;36:1118-1120. 3pp. Sponsored by the American Society of Colon and Rectal Surgeons. Cost: free. To order write ASCRS, 85 W Algonquin Rd, #550, Arlington Hts, IL 60005.

Heparin/Therapeutic Use
Thromboembolism/Drug Therapy

Guide to Anticoagulant Therapy. *Circulation.* 1994;89(3):1449-1480. 31pp. 102refs. Sponsored by the American Heart Association. Cost: free copy. To order call 1 800 242-8721 (US only) or write to: American Heart Association, Public Inquiries, 7272 Greenville Ave, Dallas TX 75231-4596.

Heparin, Low-Molecular-Weight/
Therapeutic Use
Pregnancy Complications,
Cardiovascular/Drug Therapy
Thromboembolism/Drug Therapy

Anticoagulation with Low-Molecular-Weight Heparin during Pregnancy. *ACOG Committee Opinion.* 1998;211. 2pp. 7refs. Sponsored by the American College of Obstetricians and Gynecologists. Cost: free copy. Set of Bulletins $70 + s/h ACOG members, $125 + s/h nonmembers. One-year subscription $55 member, $65 nonmember. To order single copy, call ACOG Resource Center 202 863-2518; to order set or subscription, call ACOG Distribution Center, 1 800 762-2264. Available on the Internet to members only at acog.org. Key terms: Heparin; low-molecular-weight; pregnancy complications; cardiovascular/ prevention and control; pulmonary embolism.

Hepatitis

Hepatitis Guidelines. 1994. Sponsored by the American Medical Association, Division of Health Science. Cost: $1.50. To order call Georgianne Cooper, AMA 312 464-5066.

Hepatitis A/Prevention and Control
Immunization, Passive/Standards

Prevention of Hepatitis A Through Active or Passive Immunization. *Morbid Mortal Weekly Report.* 1996;45(no. RR-15). Sponsored by the Centers for Disease Control and Prevention. Cost: $1. To order call US Govt Printing Office 202 783-3238.

Hepatitis A/Prevention and Control
Viral Hepatitis Vaccines/Therapeutic Use

Prevention of Hepatitis A Infections: Guidelines for Use of Hepatitis A Vaccine and Immune Globulin. *Pediatr.* 1996;98:1207. 9pp. 50refs. Sponsored by the American Academy of Pediatrics. Cost: $1.95. Discounted set of policies available. To order call 1 800 433-9016.

Hepatitis B Vaccines

Hepatitis B Immunization for Adolescents. *ACOG Committee Opinion.* 1997;184. 1pp. 2refs. Sponsored by the American College of Obstetricians and Gynecologists. Cost: free copy. Set of Opinions $55 + s/h ACOG members, $75 + s/h nonmembers. One-year subscription $55 member, $65 nonmember. To order single copy, call ACOG Resource Center 202 863-2518; to order set or subscription, call ACOG Distribution Center, 1 800 762 2264. Available on the Internet to members only at acog.org. Key terms: adolescent health services.

Hepatitis B/Immunology
Vaccination

Hepatitis B Virus: A Comprehensive Strategy for Eliminating Transmission in the United States Through Universal Childhood Vaccination. *Morbid Mortal Weekly Report.* 1991;40(no. RR-13):1-25. 26pp. Sponsored by the Centers for Disease Control and Prevention. Cost: $1. To order call US Govt Printing Office 202 783-3238.

Hepatitis B/Prevention and Control
Viral Vaccines

Hepatitis B Vaccine. *Ann Intern Med.* 1984;100:149-150. 2pp. Sponsored by the American College of Physicians. To order call ACP Clinical Efficacy Assessment Project 1 800 523-1546.

Hepatitis C

Hepatitis C Virus Infection. *Pediatr.* 1998;101:481. 5pp. 39refs. Sponsored by the American Academy of Pediatrics. Cost: $1.95. Discounted set of policies available. To order call 1 800 433-9016.

Hepatitis C/Therapy

Management of Hepatitis C. *NIH Consensus Development Conference Statement.* 1997;15(3):1-41[Conf. No.105]. 41pp. 82refs. Sponsored by the National Institutes of Health. Cost: free copy. To order call 1 888 644-2667. Available on the Internet at consensus.nih.gov.

Hepatitis C, Chronic/
Prevention and Control

Recommendations for Prevention and Control of Hepatitis C Virus (HCV) Infection and HCV-Related Chronic Disease. 1998. 47(no. RR-19). Sponsored by the Centers for Disease Control and Prevention. To order call US Govt Printing Office 202 783-3238. Available on the Internet at cdc.gov/mmwr/ mmwr_rr.html.

Hepatitis, Viral, Human/Diagnosis
Pregnancy Complications, Infectious/Therapy

Viral Hepatitis in Pregnancy. *ACOG Educational Bulletin*. 1998;248. 7pp. 24refs. Sponsored by the American College of Obstetricians and Gynecologists. Cost: free copy. Set of Bulletins $70 + s/h ACOG members, $125 + s/h nonmembers. One-year subscription $55 member, $65 nonmember. To order single copy, call ACOG Resource Center 202 863-2518; to order set or subscription, call ACOG Distribution Center, 1 800 762-2264. Available on the Internet to members only at acog.org. Key terms: hepatitis; pregnancy complications; infectious; vertical transmission.

Hepatitis, Viral, Human/ Prevention and Control

Protection Against Viral Hepatitis: Recommendations of the Immunization Practices Advisory Committee (ACIP). *Morbid Mortal Weekly Report*. 1990;39(no. RR-2):1-26. 26pp. 75refs. Sponsored by the Centers for Disease Control and Prevention. Cost: $1. To order call US Govt Printing Office 202 783-3238.

Hernia, Inguinal/Surgery Surgical Procedures, Laparoscopic

Laparoscopic Herniorrhaphy. *JAMA*. 1996;275(14):1075-82. 7pp. Sponsored by the American Medical Association, Diagnostic and Therapeutic Technology Assessment Program. Cost: free copy. DATTA subscription available. To order call AMA Department of Technology Assessment 312 464-4531.

Hip Dislocation, Congenital/Ultrasonography

ACR Standard for the Performance of the Ultrasound Examination for Detection of Developmental Dysplasia of the Hip. 1998. 3pp. 12refs. Sponsored by the American College of Radiology. Cost: $25 (ACR nonmembers). To order call ACR Dept of Quality Assurance 703 716-7592. Available free on the Internet at acr.org. Key terms: ultrasound; congenital disorders; dislocation; hip.

Hip Joint

Clinical Guideline on Hip Pain. 1996. 7pp. 4refs. Sponsored by the American Academy of Orthopaedic Surgeons, North American Spine Society. Cost: $10 AAOS member, $20 nonmember. To order call 1 800 626-6276. Available on the Internet free at guidelines.gov. Key terms: hip pain; osteoarthritis; inflammatory arthritis; avascular necrosis; developmental abnormalities (eg, developmental dysplasia of the hip).

Hip Prosthesis

Total Hip Replacement. *NIH Consensus Development Conference Statement*. 1994;12(5):1-31[Conf. No. 98]. 31pp. Sponsored by the National Institutes of Health. Cost: free copy. To order call 1 888 644-2667. Available on the Internet at consensus.nih.gov.

Hirsutism/Diagnosis
Hirsutism/Drug Therapy

Evaluation and Treatment of Hirsute Women. *ACOG Technical Bulletin*. 1995;203. 6pp. 17refs. Sponsored by the American College of Obstetricians and Gynecologists. Cost: free copy. Set of Bulletins $70 + s/h ACOG members, $125 + s/h nonmembers. One-year subscription $55 member, $65 nonmember. To order single copy, call ACOG Resource Center 202 863-2518; to order set or subscription, call ACOG Distribution Center, 1 800 762-2264. Available on the Internet to members only at acog.org. Key terms: hirsutism.

HIV Infections/Classification

1994 Revised Classification System for Human Immunodeficiency Virus Infection in Children Less Than 3 Years of Age. *Morbid Mortal Weekly Report*. 1994;43(no. RR-12). Sponsored by the Centers for Disease Control and Prevention. Cost: $1. To order call US Govt Printing Office 202 783-3238.

HIV Infections/Complications
Pentamidine/Administration and Dosage

Aerosolized Pentamidine for HIV Patients. *JAMA*. 1990;263:2510. 1pp. Sponsored by the American Medical Association, Diagnostic and Therapeutic Technology Assessment Program. Cost: free copy. DATTA subscription available. To order call AMA Department of Technology Assessment 312 464-4531.

HIV Infections/Complications Pneumonia, Pneumocystis carinii/ Prevention and Control

Recommendations for Prophylaxis Against Pneumocystis carinii Pneumonia for Adults and Adolescents Infected with Human Immunodeficiency Virus. *Morbid Mortal Weekly Report.* 1992;41(no. RR-4):1-11. 12pp. Sponsored by the Centers for Disease Control and Prevention. Cost: $1. To order call US Govt Printing Office 202 783-3238.

HIV Infections/Complications Skin Diseases/Complications

Dermatologic Conditions in Patients Infected with Human Immunodeficiency Virus (HIV). *J Am Acad Derm.* 1997;37:450-472. 24pp. 72refs. Sponsored by the American Academy of Dermatology. Cost: free copy. To order call Alice Bell 847 330-0230 x333. Available on the Internet at aad.org. Key terms: HIV; skin diseases.

HIV Infections/Diagnosis

Screening for Human Immunodeficiency Virus Infection. *Guide to Clinical Preventive Services, 2nd Ed.* 1996. Sponsored by the US Preventive Services Task Force. To order call Williams & Wilkins 1 800 638-0672.

HIV Infections/Diagnosis Counseling

HIV Blood Test Counseling: AMA Physician Guidelines, 2nd Edition. 1993. 7pp. 25refs. Sponsored by the American Medical Association, Division of Health Science. Cost: $2. To order call Georgianne Cooper, AMA 312 464-5066.

HIV Infections/Epidemiology Risk-Taking

Interventions to Prevent HIV Risk Behaviors. *NIH Consensus Development Conference Statement.* 1997;15(2):1-41[Conf. No. 104]. 41pp. 83refs. Sponsored by the National Institutes of Health. Cost: free copy. To order call 1 888 644-2667. Available on the Internet at consensus.nih.gov.

HIV Infections/Immunology

Surrogate Markers of Progressive HIV Disease. *JAMA.* 1992;267:2948-2952. 5pp. 55refs. Sponsored by the American Medical Association, Diagnostic and Therapeutic Technology Assessment Program. Cost: free copy. DATTA subscription available. To order call AMA Department of Technology Assessment 312 464-4531.

HIV Infections/Prevention and Control

Physician Guide to HIV Prevention. 1996. 16pp. Sponsored by the American Medical Association, Division of Health Science. Cost: $2. To order call Georgianne Cooper, AMA 312 464-5066.

HIV Infections/Prevention and Control HIV Infections/Congenital

Evaluation and Medical Treatment of the HIV-Exposed Infant. *Pediatr.* 1997;99:909. 9pp. 47refs. Sponsored by the American Academy of Pediatrics. Cost: $1.95. Discounted set of policies available. To order call 1 800 433-9016.

HIV Infections/Prevention and Control Organ Procurement/Standards

Guidelines for Preventing Transmission of Human Immunodeficiency Virus Through Transplantation of Human Tissue and Organs. *Morbid Mortal Weekly Report.* 1994;43(no. RR-8). 17pp. 32refs. Sponsored by the Centers for Disease Control and Prevention. Cost: $1. To order call US Govt Printing Office 202 783-3238.

HIV Infections/Prevention and Control Sexually Transmitted Diseases/ Prevention and Control

Counseling to Prevent Human Immunodeficiency Virus Infection and Other Sexually Transmitted Diseases. *Guide to Clinical Preventive Services, 2nd Ed.* 1996. Sponsored by the US Preventive Services Task Force. To order call Williams & Wilkins 1 800 638-0672.

HIV Infections/Prevention and Control Sexually Transmitted Diseases/ Prevention and Control

HIV Prevention Through Early Detection and Treatment of Other Sexually Transmitted Disease—United States. *Morbid Mortal Weekly Report.* 1998;47(no. RR-12). Sponsored by the Centers for Disease Control and Prevention. Cost: $1. To order call US Govt Printing Office 202 783-3238.

HIV Infections/Prevention and Control Zidovudine/Therapeutic Use

Recommendations of the US Public Health Service Task Force on the Use of Zidovudine to Reduce Perinatal Transmission of Human Immunodeficiency Virus. *Morbid Mortal Weekly Report.* 1994;43(no. RR-11). 20pp. 57refs. Sponsored by the Centers for Disease Control and Prevention. Cost: $1. To order call US Govt Printing Office 202 783-3238.

HIV Infections/Theory
Primary Health Care

Primary Care of Patients Infected with Human Immunodeficiency Virus. *Clin Inf Dis.* 1998;26:275. 2pp. 9refs. Sponsored by the Infectious Diseases Society of America. To obtain request from medical library or download via the Internet. Available on the Internet at idsociety.org/practice.

HIV Infections/Therapy
Ethics, Medical

Human Immunodeficiency Virus Infection: Physician's Responsibilities. *ACOG Committee Opinion.* 1993;130. 4pp. Sponsored by the American College of Obstetricians and Gynecologists. Cost: free copy. Set of Opinions $55 + s/h ACOG members, $75 + s/h nonmembers. One-year subscription $55 member, $65 nonmember. To order single copy, call ACOG Resource Center 202 863-2518; to order set or subscription, call ACOG Distribution Center, 1 800 762-2264. Available on the Internet to members only at acog.org. Key terms: physician-patient interactions; ethics: medical; physician's role.

HIV Seropositivity
Acquired Immunodeficiency Syndrome

AIDS and Infection with HIV. *Ann Intern Med.* 1988;108:460-469. 10pp. Sponsored by the American College of Physicians. To order call ACP Clinical Efficacy Assessment Project 1 800 523-1546.

HIV Seropositivity
Toxoplasmosis/Prevention and Control

Prophylactic Treatment of Opportunistic Infections in HIV-Positive Patients: Toxoplasma gondii Prophylaxis. *Diagnostic and Therapeutic Technology Assessment (DATTA).* 1991;8pp. 22refs. Sponsored by the American Medical Association, Diagnostic and Therapeutic Technology Assessment Program. Cost: free copy. DATTA subscription available. To order call AMA Department of Technology Assessment 312 464-4531.

Home Care Services
Delivery of Health Care

Guidelines for the Medical Management of the Home Care Patient. 1992. Sponsored by the American Medical Association, Division of Health Science. Cost: $3 single copy, $50 for packages of 25. To order call Georgianne Cooper, AMA 312 464-5563.

Home Care Services
Reimbursement Mechanisms

Home Care and Home Care Reimbursement, Position Statement. 1993. Sponsored by the American Geriatrics Society. Cost: free. To order call AGS 212 308-1414.

Home Care Services
Respiration, Artificial

Home Mechanical Ventilation of Pediatric Patients. *Amer Rev Resp Dis.* 1990;141:1. Sponsored by the American Thoracic Society. Cost: $4. To order send check payable to American Thoracic Society, 1740 Broadway, New York, NY 10019-4374; for credit card orders, call 212 315-8863.

Home Care Services/Economics
Parenting

The Role of Home Visitation Programs in Improving Health Outcomes for Children and Families. *Pediatr.* 1998;101:486. 4pp. 21refs. Sponsored by the American Academy of Pediatrics. Cost: $1.95. Discounted set of policies available. To order call 1 800 433-9016.

Homeless Persons
Tuberculosis/Prevention and Control

Prevention and Control of Tuberculosis Among Homeless Persons. *Morbid Mortal Weekly Report* 1992;41(no. RR-5):13-21. 9pp. Sponsored by the Centers for Disease Control and Prevention. Cost: $1. To order call US Govt Printing Office 202 783-3238.

Homes for the Elderly
Tuberculosis/Prevention and Control

Prevention and Control of Tuberculosis in Facilities Providing Long-Term Care to the Elderly: Recommendations of the Advisory Committee for the Elimination of Tuberculosis. *Morbid Mortal Weekly Report.* 1990;39(no. RR-10):7-20. 14pp. 17refs. Sponsored by the Centers for Disease Control and Prevention. Cost: $1. To order call US Govt Printing Office 202 783-3238.

Hormone Replacement Therapy

Hormone Replacement Therapy. *ACOG Educational Bulletin*. 1998;247. 10pp. 48refs. Sponsored by the American College of Obstetricians and Gynecologists. Cost: free copy. Set of Bulletins $70 + s/h ACOG members, $125 + s/h nonmembers. One-year subscription $55 member, $65 nonmember. To order single copy, call ACOG Resource Center 202 863-2518; to order set or subscription, call ACOG Distribution Center, 1 800 762-2264. Available on the Internet to members only at acog.org. Key terms: ERT.

Hormone Replacement Therapy

Postmenopausal Hormone Prophylaxis. *Guide to Clinical Preventive Services, 2nd Ed*. 1996. Sponsored by the US Preventive Services Task Force. To order call Williams & Wilkins 1 800 638-0672.

Hospital Design and Construction
Intensive Care Units

Guidelines for Intensive Care Unit Design. *Critical Care Med*. 1995;23:582-588. 7pp. 27refs. Sponsored by the Society of Critical Care Medicine. Cost: Complete Set $60 + s/h SCCM members, $80 + s/h nonmembers; $5 for a single guideline. To order call SCCM 714 282-6000 or access Book Store on the SCCM website. Available free on the Internet at sccm.org. Key terms: intensive care unit; facility design and construction; health facility planning; health care team; critical care.

Hospital Units
Patient Admission/Standards

Guidelines on Admission and Discharge for Adult Intermediate Care Units. *Critical Care Med*. 1998;26:607-610. 4pp. 21refs. Sponsored by the Society of Critical Care Medicine. Cost: Complete Set $60 + s/h SCCM members, $80 + s/h nonmembers; $5 for a single guideline. To order call SCCM 714 282-6000 or access Book Store on the SCCM website. Available free on the Internet at sccm.org. Key terms: critical care; intermediate care unit; monitoring; discharge policy; admission policy.

Hospitalization
Myocardial Infarction/Diagnosis

Guidelines for Risk Stratification after Myocardial Infarction. *Ann Intern Med*. 1997;126:556-560. 5pp. 11refs. Sponsored by the American College of Physicians. To order call ACP Clinical Efficacy Assessment Project 1 800 523-1546.

House Calls
Physician's Role

The Role of Physicians in House Calls in Geriatric Practice. 1998. Sponsored by the American Geriatrics Society. Cost: free. To order call AGS 212 308-1414.

HTLV-I Infections
HTLV-II Infections

Recommendations for Counseling Persons Infected with Human T-Lymphotrophic Virus, Types I and II. *Morbid Mortal Weekly Report*. 1993;42(no. RR-9). Sponsored by the Centers for Disease Control and Prevention. Cost: $1. To order call US Govt Printing Office 202 783-3238.

Humerus/Injuries
Fractures

Proximal Humeral Fracture. *Clinical Policies*. 1996. 9pp. 13refs. Sponsored by the American Academy of Orthopaedic Surgeons, North American Spine Society. Cost: $50 (set of 15) for nonmembers. To order call 1 800 626-6276. Key terms: proximal humeral fracture; shoulder pain; American Academy of Orthopaedic Surgeons.

Hymenoptera/Immunology
Hypersensitivity/Therapy

The Discontinuation of Hymenoptera Venon Immunotherapy. *J Allergy Clin Immun*. 1998;101:573-575, Position Statement No. 33. 3pp. 22refs. Sponsored by the American Academy of Allergy, Asthma, and Immunology. Cost: free copy. To order call 414 272-6071. Available on the Internet at aaaai.org/professional/physicianreference/positionstatements/default.stm.

Hypercholesterolemia/Diagnosis
Hyperlipidemia/Diagnosis

Screening for High Blood Cholesterol and Other Lipid Abnormalities. *Guide to Clinical Preventive Services, 2nd Ed*. 1996. Sponsored by the US Preventive Services Task Force. To order call Williams & Wilkins 1 800 638-0672.

Hypercholesterolemia/Drug Therapy Coronary Disease/ Prevention and Control

Second Report of the Expert Panel on Detection, Evaluation, and Treatment of High Blood Cholesterol in Adults. *NIH Publication No. 93-3095; No. 93-3096.* 1993. 180pp. 640refs. Sponsored by the National Heart, Lung, and Blood Institute. Cost: $5. To order contact the NHLBI Information Center, PO Box 30105, Bethesda, MD 20824-0105, 301 251-1222.

Hyperlipidemia/Prevention and Control Mass Screening

Screening Test for Dyslipidemia. *Am J Clin Pathol.* 1995;103:380-385. 6pp. 37refs. Sponsored by the American Society of Clinical Pathologists. Cost: free copy. To order call Felicia Nelson 312 738-1336 x1350. Key terms: Lipid; total cholesterol; high density lipoprotein; hyperlipidemia; hypercholesteremia.

Hyperparathyroidism/Therapy

Diagnosis and Management of Asymptomatic Primary Hyperparathyroidism. *NIH Consensus Development Conference Statement.* 1990;8(7):1-18[Conf. No. 82]. 19pp. Sponsored by the National Institutes of Health. Cost: free copy. To order call 1 888 644-2667. Available on the Internet at consensus.nih.gov.

Hypersensitivity

Participation in Meetings Advocating Unproven Techniques. *J Allergy Clin Immun.* 1980;66:431, Position Statement No. 6. 1pp. Sponsored by the American Academy of Allergy, Asthma, and Immunology. Cost: free copy. To order call 414 272-6071.

Hypersensitivity IgE/Immunology

The Clinical Utility and Appropriate Use of In Vitro Allergy Testing. *Immun Allergy Practice.* 1990;12:342-347. 6pp. 29refs. Sponsored by the American In Vitro Allergy/Immunology Society. Cost: free. To order write AIAIS PO Box 341461, Bethesda, MD 20827-1461.

Hypersensitivity Practice Guidelines

Practice Guidelines for Respiratory Allergy. 1996. 4pp. Sponsored by the American Academy of Otolaryngic Allergy. Cost: free copy. To order call AAOA 301 588-1800.

Hypersensitivity/Diagnosis

Allergy Diagnostic Testing. *Ann Allergy Asthma Immun.* 1995;75(suppl):543-625, Practice Parameter. 84pp. Sponsored by the American Academy of Allergy, Asthma, and Immunology; American College of Allergy, Asthma, and Immunology; Joint Council of Allergy, Asthma, and Immunology. Cost: free copy. To order call 847 934-1918 or e-mail sgjcaai@aol.com. Available on the Internet at jcaai.org.

Hypersensitivity/Diagnosis

Vitro Tests for Allergy. *JAMA.* 1987;258:1639-1644. 6pp. Sponsored by the American Medical Association, Council on Scientific Affairs. Cost: free. To order call Nancy Nolan, AMA, 312 464-5046.

Hypersensitivity/Diagnosis Asthma/Drug Therapy

Diagnosis and Treatment of Asthma. *J Allergy Clin Immun.* 1995;96(suppl):710-870, Practice Parameter. 81pp. Sponsored by the American Academy of Allergy, Asthma, and Immunology; American College of Allergy, Asthma, and Immunology; Joint Council of Allergy, Asthma, and Immunology. Cost: free copy. To order call 847 934-1918 or e-mail sgjcaai@aol.com. Available on the Internet at jcaai.org.

Hypersensitivity/Diagnosis Desensitization, Immunologic/Methods

Some Untested Diagnostic and Therapeutic Procedures in Clinical Allergy. *J Allergy Clin Immun.* 1975;56:168-169, Position Statement No. 2. 1pp. Sponsored by the American Academy of Allergy, Asthma, and Immunology. Cost: free copy. To order call 414 272-6071.

Hypersensitivity/Diagnosis IgG/Analysis

Measurement of Specific and Nonspecific IgG4 Levels as Diagnostic and Prognostic Tests for Clinical Allergy. *J Allergy Clin Immun.* 1995;95:652-654, Position Statement No. 28. 3pp. 26refs. Sponsored by the American Academy of Allergy, Asthma, and Immunology. Cost: free copy. To order call 414 272-6071.

Hypersensitivity/Diagnosis Immunologic Diseases/Diagnosis

Unproven Procedures for Diagnosis and Treatment of Allergic and Immunologic Diseases. *J Allergy Clin Immun.* 1986;78:269-277, Position Statement No. 14. 3pp. 16refs. Sponsored by the American Academy of Allergy, Asthma, and Immunology. Cost: free copy. To order call 414 272-6071.

Hypersensitivity/Therapy
Insect Bites and Stings/Immunology

Stinging Insect Hypersensitivity: A Practice Parameter. *J Allergy Clin Immun.* 1999;103:963-980. 17pp. Sponsored by the American Academy of Allergy, Asthma, and Immunology; American College of Allergy, Asthma, and Immunology; Joint Council of Allergy, Asthma, and Immunology. Cost: free copy. To order call 847 934-1918. Available on the Internet at jcaai.org.

Hypertension

Working Group Report on Hypertension in the Elderly. *Order No. 55-635.* 1994. 20pp. 49refs. Sponsored by the National Heart, Lung, and Blood Institute. Cost: $1.50. To order contact the NHLBI Information Center, PO Box 30105, Bethesda, MD 20824-0105, 301 251-1222.

Hypertension/Diagnosis
Hypertension/Therapy

Sixth Report of the Joint National Committee on Detection, Evaluation, and Treatment of High Blood Pressure (JNC VI). *NIH Publication No. 98-4080.* 1998. Sponsored by the National Heart, Lung, and Blood Institute. To order contact the NHLBI Information Center, PO Box 30105, Bethesda, MD 20824-0105, 301 251-1222.

Hypertension/Prevention and Control
Blood Pressure Determination/Methods

Management of Hypertension after Ambulatory Blood Pressure Monitoring. *Ann Intern Med.* 1992;118:833-837. 5pp. Sponsored by the American College of Physicians. To order call ACP Clinical Efficacy Assessment Project 1 800 523-1546.

Hypertension/Prevention and Control
Mass Screening

Screening for Hypertension. *Ann Intern Med.* 1990;112:192-202. 11pp. 46refs. Sponsored by the American College of Physicians. To order call ACP Clinical Efficacy Assessment Project 1 800 523-1546.

Hypertension/Prevention and Control
Primary Prevention

Working Group Report on Primary Prevention of Hypertension. *NIH Publication No. 93-2669.* 1993. 49pp. 327refs. Sponsored by the National Heart, Lung, and Blood Institute. Cost: $3. To order contact the NHLBI Information Center, PO Box 30105, Bethesda, MD 20824-0105, 301 251-1222.

Hypertension, Pulmonary

Primary Pulmonary Hypertension. *Chest.* 1993;104:236-250. 14pp. 89refs. Sponsored by the American College of Chest Physicians. Cost: $5. To order call ACCP 1 800 343-2227 or 1 847 498-1400 (credit card orders). Key terms: primary pulmonary hypertension.

Hypertension, Renovascular/
Radionuclide Imaging
Radioisotope Renography

Procedure Guideline for Diagnosis of Renovascular Hypertension. *J Nuclear Med.* 1998;39:1297-1302. 6pp. 52refs. Sponsored by the Society of Nuclear Medicine. Cost: free. To order call Bill Uffelman 703 708-9000. Available on the Internet at snm.org. Key terms: routine diagnostic tests; radionuclide imaging; renovascular hypertension; kidney function tests; procedure guideline.

Hyperthermia, Induced/Standards
Antineoplastic Agents, Combined/
Therapeutic Use

Hyperthermia Alone or Combined with Chemotherapy for the Treatment of Cancer. *AHCPR Health Technology Assessment.* 1991;No. 2 (AHCPR Publication No. 92-0014). 16pp. 76refs. Sponsored by the Federal Agency for Health Care Policy and Research. To order call AHCPR Clearinghouse 1 800 358-9295.

Hyperthyroidism/Therapy
Hypothyroidism/Therapy

Clinical Practice Guidelines for the Evaluation and Treatment of Hyperthyroidism and Hypothyroidism. 1995. 24pp. 22refs. Sponsored by the American Association of Clinical Endocrinologists. To order call AACE 904 353-7878. Key terms: hyperthyroidism; hypothyroidism; thyroid; hormone; goiter (Grave's disease.

Hypnotics and Sedatives
Radionuclide Imaging

Procedure Guideline for Pediatric Sedation in Nuclear Medicine. *J Nuclear Med.* 1997;38:1640-1643. 4pp. 14refs. Sponsored by the Society of Nuclear Medicine. Cost: free. To order call Bill Uffelman 703 708-9000. Available on the Internet at snm.org. Key terms: pediatrics; sedation; diagnostic imaging; practice guideline; life support.

Hypogonadism/Diagnosis
Hypogonadism/Drug Therapy

Clinical Practice Guidelines for the Evaluation and Treatment of Hypogonadism in Adult Male Patients. 1996. 28pp. 69refs. Sponsored by the American Association of Clinical Endocrinologists. To order call AACE 904 353-7878. Key terms: hypogonadism; testosterone; gonadotropins; sexual dysfunction; Kallmann's syndrome.

Hypothermia/Prevention and Control

Hypothermia Prevention. *Morbid Mortal Weekly Report.* 1988;37:780-782. 3pp. Sponsored by the Centers for Disease Control and Prevention. Cost: $1. To order call US Govt Printing Office 202 783-3238.

Hysterectomy

Hysterectomy. 1997;MR-592/3. 130pp. 326refs. Sponsored by RAND. To order call RAND 310 393-0411 x7002. Key terms: hysterectomy; appropriateness; treatment outcomes; utilization; complications.

Hysterectomy, Vaginal
Laparoscopy

Laparoscopically Assisted Vaginal Hysterectomy. *ACOG Committee Opinion.* 1994;146. 1pp. Sponsored by the American College of Obstetricians and Gynecologists. Cost: free copy. Set of Opinions $55 + s/h ACOG members, $75 + s/h nonmembers. One-year subscription $55 member, $65 nonmember. To order single copy, call ACOG Resource Center 202 863-2518; to order set or subscription, call ACOG Distribution Center, 1 800 762-2264. Available on the Internet to members only at acog.org. Key terms: laparoscopic surgery.

Hysteroscopy
Laser Surgery/Instrumentation

Hysteroscopy. *ACOG Technical Bulletin.* 1994;191. 5pp. 9refs. Sponsored by the American College of Obstetricians and Gynecologists. Cost: free copy. Set of Bulletins $70 + s/h ACOG members, $125 + s/h nonmembers. One-year subscription $55 member, $65 nonmember. To order single copy, call ACOG Resource Center 202 863-2518; to order set or subscription, call ACOG Distribution Center, 1 800 762-2264. Available on the Internet to members only at acog.org.

IgE/Metabolism
Anaphylaxis/Diagnosis

Skin Testing and Radioallergosorbent Testing (RAST) for Diagnosis of Specific Allergens Responsible for IgE Mediated Diseases. *J Allergy Clin Immun.* 1983;72:515-517, Position Statement No. 10. 3pp. 10refs. Sponsored by the American Academy of Allergy, Asthma, and Immunology. Cost: free copy. To order call 414 272-6071.

Immunization

Adult Immunizations. *Guide to Clinical Preventive Services, 2nd Ed.* 1996. Sponsored by the US Preventive Services Task Force. To order call Williams & Wilkins 1 800 638-0672.

Immunization

Childhood Immunizations. *Guide to Clinical Preventive Services, 2nd Ed.* 1996. Sponsored by the US Preventive Services Task Force. To order call Williams & Wilkins 1 800 638-0672.

Immunization

Guide for Adult Immunization, 2nd Edition. 1990. Sponsored by the American College of Physicians. Cost: $13 ACP members, $16 nonmembers. To order call ACP Clinical Efficacy Assessment Project 1 800 523-1546.

Immunization
Vaccines, Combined

Combination Vaccines for Childhood Immunization: Recommendations of the Advisory Committee on Immunization Practices (ACIP), the American Academy of Pediatrics (AAP), and the American Academy of Family Physicians (AAFP). *Pediatr.* 1999;48(no. RR-5). Sponsored by the Centers for Disease Control and Prevention. To order call US Govt Printing Office 202 783-3238. Available on the Internet at cdc.gov/mmwr/mmwr_rr.html.

Immunization
Yellow Fever/Prevention and Control

Yellow Fever Vaccine: Recommendations of the Immunization Practices Advisory Panel (ACIP). *Morbid Mortal Weekly Report.* 1990;39(no. RR-6):1-6. 6pp. 16refs. Sponsored by the Centers for Disease Control and Prevention. Cost: $1. To order call US Govt Printing Office 202 783-3238.

Immunization/Standards

General Recommendations on Immunization. *Morbid Mortal Weekly Report.* 1994;43(no. RR-1). 38pp. 86refs. Sponsored by the Centers for Disease Control and Prevention. Cost: $1. To order call US Govt Printing Office 202 783-3238.

Immunization Schedule
Preventive Medicine/Standards

Practice Policy Statement: Childhood Immunizations. *Am J Prev Med.* 1997;13(2):74-77. 4pp. 21refs. Sponsored by the American College of Preventive Medicine. To order reprint address request to ACPM, 1660 L St NW, #206, Washington, DC 20036.

Immunization Schedule
Vaccination/Standards

Recommended Childhood Immunization Schedule— United States, January–December 1999. *Pediatr.* 1999;103(1):182-185. 4pp. Sponsored by the American Academy of Pediatrics. Cost: $1.95. Discounted set of policies available. To order call 1 800 433-9016.

Immunization, Passive
Immunoglobulins/Administration and Dosage

Intravenous Immunoglobulin. *NIH Consensus Development Conference Statement.* 1990;8(5):1-23[Conf. No. 80]. 23pp. Sponsored by the National Institutes of Health. Cost: free copy. To order call 1 888 644-2667. Available on the Internet at consensus.nih.gov.

Immunizations, Passive/Standards
Immunocompromised Host

Uses of Vaccines and Immune Globulins in Persons with Altered Immunocompetence. *Morbid Mortal Weekly Report.* 1993;42(no. RR-4). Sponsored by the Centers for Disease Control and Prevention. Cost: $1. To order call US Govt Printing Office 202 783-3238.

Immunologic Deficiency Syndromes/Diagnosis
Immunologic Deficiency Syndromes/Therapy

Diagnosis and Management of Immunodeficiency. *Ann Allergy Asthma Immun.* 1996;76:282-294, Practice Parameter. 13pp. Sponsored by the American Academy of Allergy, Asthma, and Immunology; Amcrican College of Allergy, Asthma, and Immunology; Joint Council of Allergy, Asthma, and Immunology. Cost: free copy. To order call 847 934-1918 or e-mail sgjcaai@aol.com. Available on the Internet at jcaai.org.

Immunosuppression/Methods

Introduction to the Management of Immunosuppression. *JAMA.* 1987;257:1781-1785. 5pp. Sponsored by the American Medical Association, Council on Scientific Affairs. Cost: free. To order call Nancy Nolan, AMA, 312 464-5046.

Immunotherapy/Methods
Neoplasms/Therapy

Immuno-Augmentative Therapy for Cancer. *JAMA.* 1988;259:3477-3478. 2pp. Sponsored by the American Medical Association, Diagnostic and Therapeutic Technology Assessment Program. Cost: free copy. DATTA subscription available. To order call AMA Department of Technology Assessment 312 464-4531.

Immunotherapy/Standards
Allergens/Therapeutic Use

Allergen Immunotherapy. *J Allergy Clin Immun.* 1996;98:1001-1011, Practice Parameter. 11pp. Sponsored by the American Academy of Allergy, Asthma, and Immunology; American College of Allergy, Asthma, and Immunology; Joint Council of Allergy, Asthma, and Immunology. Cost: free copy. To order call 847 934-1918 or e-mail sgjcaai@aol.com. Available on the Internet at jcaai.org.

Impotence

Impotence. *NIH Consensus Development Conference Statement.* 1992;10(4):1-33[Conf. No. 91]. 34pp. Sponsored by the National Institutes of Health. Cost: free copy. To order call 1 888 644-2667. Available on the Internet at consensus.nih.gov.

Impotence/Drug Therapy
Papaverine/Therapeutic Use

Intracavernous Pharmacotherapy for Impotence: Papaverine and Phentolamine. *JAMA*. 1990;264:752-754. 3pp. 35refs. Sponsored by the American Medical Association, Diagnostic and Therapeutic Technology Assessment Program. Cost: free copy. DATTA subscription available. To order call AMA Department of Technology Assessment 312 464-4531.

Impotence/Surgery
Prostheses and Implants

Penile Implants for Erectile Impotence. *JAMA*. 1988;260:997-1000. 4pp. Sponsored by the American Medical Association, Diagnostic and Therapeutic Technology Assessment Program. Cost: free copy. DATTA subscription available. To order call AMA Department of Technology Assessment 312 464-4531.

Impotence/Therapy

Treatment of Organic Erectile Dysfunction. 1996. 80pp. 209refs. Sponsored by the American Urological Association. Cost: $49 members, $69 nonmembers. To order write Health Policy Dept, AUA, 1120 N Charles St, Baltimore, MD 21201. Key terms: impotence; penile erection; erectile dysfunction; guidelines.

Impulse Control Disorders/
Drug Therapy

Disorders of Impulse Control. *Treatments of Psychiatric Disorders, Second Edition, Volume II*. 1995;Section 13. 16pp. 100refs. Sponsored by the American Psychiatric Association. Cost: $250 for 2-volume set. To order call 1 800 368-5777 order #SPCT8700. Key terms: TPD; disorders; treatment.

Incontinence (see Urinary Incontinence)

Indium Radioisotopes/Diagnostic Use
Infection/Radionuclide Imaging

Procedure Guideline for In-111 Leukocyte Scintigraphy for Suspected Infection/Inflammation. *J Nuclear Med*. 1997;38:997-1001. 5pp. 16refs. Sponsored by the Society of Nuclear Medicine. Cost: free. To order call Bill Uffelman 703 708-9000. Available on the Internet at snm.org. Key terms: routine diagnostic tests; radionuclide imaging; indium leukocyte scintigraphy; inflammation; infection.

Indocyanine Green
Fluorescein Angiography

Indocyanine Green Angiography Ophthalmic Procedure Assessment. *Ophthalmology*. 1998;105:1564-1569. 6pp. 47refs. Sponsored by the American Academy of Ophthalmology. Cost: $11 members, $16 nonmembers. AAO members first copy free upon publication. To order call AAO Order Dept 415 561-8540. Key terms: eye; ICG; angiography; retina.

Infant Mortality
Statistics/Standards

Perinatal and Infant Mortality Statistics. *ACOG Committee Opinion*. 1995;167. 3pp. 3refs. Sponsored by the American College of Obstetricians and Gynecologists. Cost: free copy. Set of Opinions $55 + s/h ACOG members, $75 + s/h nonmembers. One-year subscription $55 member, $65 nonmember. To order single copy, call ACOG Resource Center 202 863-2518; to order set or subscription, call ACOG Distribution Center, 1 800 762-2264. Available on the Internet to members only at acog.org. Key terms: data collection.

Infant, Newborn
Length of Stay
Obstetrics/Standard

Hospital Stay for Healthy Term Newborns. *Pediatr*. 1998;96:788 790. 3pp. 27refs. Sponsored by the American Academy of Pediatrics. Cost: $1.95. Discounted set of policies available. To order call 1 800 433-9016.

Infant, Premature, Diseases/Nursing
Patient Discharge

Hospital Discharge of the High-Risk Neonate. *Pediatr*. 1998;102(2):411-417. 7pp. 102refs. Sponsored by the American Academy of Pediatrics. Cost: $1.95. Discounted set of policies available. To order call 1 800 433-9016.

Infection
Practice Guidelines

Practice Guidelines for Infectious Diseases: Rationale for Work in Progress. *Clin Inf Dis*. 1998;26:1037. 5pp. 33refs. Sponsored by the Infectious Diseases Society of America. To obtain request from medical library or download via the Internet. Available on the Internet at idsociety.org/practice.

Infection/Radionuclide Imaging
Leukocytes

Procedure Guideline for Tc-99m Hexametazime (HMPAO) Labeled Leukocyte Scintigraphy for Suspected Infection/Inflammation. *J Nuclear Med.* 1997;38:987-990. 4pp. 13refs. Sponsored by the Society of Nuclear Medicine. Cost: free. To order call Bill Uffelman 703 708-9000. Available on the Internet at snm.org. Key terms: technetium leukocyte scintigraphy; routine diagnostic tests; radionuclide imaging; inflammation; infection.

Infection/Therapy
Quality of Health Care/Standards

Purpose of Quality Standards for Infectious Diseases. *Clin Inf Dis.* 1994;18:421. 1pp. 2refs. Sponsored by the Infectious Diseases Society of America. To obtain request from medical library.

Infection Control
Tuberculosis, Multidrug-Resistant/
Prevention and Control

Institutional Infection Control Measures for Tuberculosis in the Era of Multiple Drug Resistance. *Chest.* 1995;108:1690-1710. 21pp. 143refs. Sponsored by the American College of Chest Physicians. Cost: $5. To order call ACCP 1 800 343-2227 or 1 847 498-1400 (credit card orders). Key terms: tuberculosis; infection; hospital infection control.

Infection Control/Methods
Personnel, Hospital

"Look Back" Notifications for HIV/HBV-Positive Healthcare Workers. *Infect Control Hosp Epidemiol.* 1992;13:482-484. 3pp. 12refs. Sponsored by the Society for Healthcare Epidemiology of America. Cost: free. To order visit our website at medscape.com/shea. Available on the Internet at medscape.com/shea. Key terms: specific nature of procedures and technical skills of the healthcare worker; potential for injury to the healthcare worker; assessment of the health status and competency of healthcare worker to perform the procedures.

Infection Control/Standards
Cross-Infection/Prevention and Control

Infection Prevention and Control in the Long-Term-Care Facility. *Infect Control Hosp Epidemiol.* 18:831-849. 19pp. 181refs. Sponsored by the Society for Healthcare Epidemiology of America. Cost: free. To order visit our website at medscape.com/shea. Available on the Internet at medscape.com/shea. Key terms: infections and infection control in long-term-care facility; surveillance; isolation; outbreak control; resident-care in long-term care.

Infection Control Practitioners
Epidemiology

Book-Help for the Hospital Epidemiologist. *Infect Control Hosp Epidemiol.* 1995;16:98; 16:166; 16:236; 16:292; 16:348; 16:419; 16:478; 16:512. 3pp; 4pp; 4pp; 8pp; 10pp; 8pp; 5pp; 6pp. 6refs; 7refs; 3refs; 14refs; 13refs; 7refs; 9refs; 8refs. Sponsored by the Society for Healthcare Epidemiology of America. Cost: free. To order visit our website at medscape.com/shea. Available on the Internet at medscape.com/shea. Key terms: introduction to practical healthcare epidemiology; the hospital epidemiologist—practical ideas; preparing for and surviving a JCAHO inspection; employee health and infection control.

Infertility

Infertility. *ACOG Technical Bulletin.* 1989;125. 7pp. 15refs. Sponsored by the American College of Obstetricians and Gynecologists. Cost: free copy. Set of Bulletins $70 + s/h ACOG members, $125 + s/h nonmembers. One-year subscription $55 member, $65 nonmember. To order single copy, call ACOG Resource Center 202 863-2518; to order set or subscription, call ACOG Distribution Center, 1 800 762-2264. Available on the Internet to members only at acog.org.

Infertility/Diagnosis

Unexplained Infertility. 1992. 4pp. 14refs. Sponsored by the American Society for Reproductive Medicine. Cost: $1. To order call ASRM Publication Department 205 978-5000.

Infertility, Male

Male Infertility. *ACOG Technical Bulletin.* 1990;142. 8pp. 26refs. Sponsored by the American College of Obstetricians and Gynecologists. Cost: free copy. Set of Bulletins $70 + s/h ACOG members, $125 + s/h nonmembers. One-year subscription $55 member, $65 nonmember. To order single copy, call ACOG Resource Center 202 863-2518; to order set or subscription, call ACOG Distribution Center, 1 800 762-2264. Available on the Internet to members only at acog.org. Key terms: artificial insemination.

Infertility, Male
Varicocele

Varicocele and Infertility. 1992. 2pp. 4refs. Sponsored by the American Society for Reproductive Medicine. Cost: $1. To order call ASRM Publication Department 205 978-5000.

Infertility, Male/Diagnosis
Sperm-Ovum Interactions

Sperm Penetration Assay in Identifying Male Infertility. *JAMA.* 1985;254:1993-1994. 2pp. Sponsored by the American Medical Association, Diagnostic and Therapeutic Technology Assessment Program. Cost: free copy. DATTA subscription available. To order call AMA Department of Technology Assessment 312 464-4531.

Influenza/Prevention and Control

Prevention and Control of Influenza: Recommendations of the Advisory Committee on Immunization Practices (ACIP). *Morbid Mortal Weekly Report.* 1999;48(no. RR-4). Sponsored by the Centers for Disease Control and Prevention. Cost: $1. To order call US Govt Printing Office 202 783-3238. Available on the Internet at cdc.gov/mmwr/ mmwr_rr.html.

Influenza/Prevention and Control

Prevention and Treatment of Influenza in the Elderly. 1996. Sponsored by the American Geriatrics Society. Cost: free. To order call AGS 212 308-1414.

Informed Consent
Dementia

Informed Consent for Research on Human Subjects with Dementia. 1998. Sponsored by the American Geriatrics Society. Cost: free. To order call AGS 212 308-1414.

Informed Consent
Endoscopy

Informed Consent for Gastrointestinal Endoscopy. *Gastrointest Endosc.* 1988;34(suppl):26s-27s. 2pp. 18refs. Sponsored by the American Society for Gastrointestinal Endoscopy. Cost: free. To order call ASGE 978 526-8330.

Informed Consent
Ethics, Medical

Ethical Dimensions of Informed Consent. *ACOG Committee Opinion.* 1992;108. 8pp. 19refs. Sponsored by the American College of Obstetricians and Gynecologists. Cost: free copy. Set of Opinions $55 + s/h ACOG members, $75 + s/h nonmembers. One-year subscription $55 member, $65 nonmember. To order single copy, call ACOG Resource Center 202 863-2518; to order set or subscription, call ACOG Distribution Center, 1 800 762-2264. Available on the Internet to members only at acog.org.

Infusion Pumps, Implantable

External and Implantable Infusion Pumps. *AHCPR Health Technology Review.* 1994;No. 7 (AHCPR Publication No. 94-0013). 29pp. 82refs. Sponsored by the Federal Agency for Health Care Policy and Research. To order call AHCPR Clearinghouse 1 800 358-9295.

Infusions, Parenteral/Instrumentation
Heparin/Administration and Dosage

Implantable and External Infusion Pumps for the Treatment of Thromboembolic Disease in Outpatients. *Ann Intern Med.* 1984;100:305-306. 2pp. Sponsored by the American College of Physicians. To order call ACP Clinical Efficacy Assessment Project 1 800 523-1546.

Insemination, Artificial/Methods

Intrauterine Insemination. 1991. 5pp. 11refs. Sponsored by the American Society for Reproductive Medicine. Cost: $1. To order call ASRM Publication Department 205 978-5000.

Insomnia/Therapy
Psychotherapy

Practice Parameters for the Nonpharmacological Treatment of Insomnia. *Sleep.* 1999. 10refs. Sponsored by the American Academy of Sleep Medicine. Cost: $30 + s/h for a complete set of current AASM Guidelines. To order call AASM 507 287-6006. Key terms: practice guidelines; practice parameters; stimulus control; progressive muscle relaxation; paradoxical intention.

Insulin Infusion Systems/Standards
Technology Assessment, Biomedical

Reassessment of External Insulin Infusion Pumps. *AHCPR Health Technology Review.* 1990;No. 9 (AHCPR Publication No. 91-0030). 7pp. 44refs. Sponsored by the Federal Agency for Health Care Policy and Research. To order call AHCPR Clearinghouse 1 800 358-9295.

Insurance, Health

Position Paper: Prior Authorization/ Pre-Determination. 1992. 2pp. Sponsored by the American Society of Plastic and Reconstructive Surgeons. To order call ASPRS 847 228-9900.

Insurance, Health,
Reimbursement/Standards
Anesthesia, Obstetrical

Pain Relief During Labor. *ACOG Committee Opinion.* 1993;118. 1pp. 1ref. Sponsored by the American College of Obstetricians and Gynecologists. Cost: free copy. Set of Opinions $55 + s/h ACOG members, $75 + s/h nonmembers. One-year subscription $55 member, $65 nonmember. To order single copy, call ACOG Resource Center 202 863-2518; to order set or subscription, call ACOG Distribution Center, 1 800 762-2264. Available on the Internet to members only at acog.org. Key terms: anesthesia: obstetric; women's rights; labor.

Insurance, Long-Term Care

Financing of Long-Term Care Services, Position Statement. 1993. Sponsored by the American Geriatrics Society. Cost: free. To order call AGS 212 308-1414.

Intensive Care
Respiration, Artificial

Mechanical Ventilation Beyond the ICU. *Chest.* 1998;113(suppl):289S-344S. 55pp. 215refs. Sponsored by the American College of Chest Physicians. Cost: $14. To order call ACCP 1 800 343-2227 or 1 847 498-1400 (credit card orders). Available on the Internet at chestnet.org (Quick Reference Guide). Key terms: mechanical ventilation; discharge planning; home care.

Intensive Care Units
Nutritional Support

Applied Nutrition in ICU Patients. *Chest.* 1997;111:769-778. 10pp. 57refs. Sponsored by the American College of Chest Physicians. Cost: $5. To order call ACCP 1 800 343-2227 or 1 847 498-1400 (credit card orders).

Intensive Care Units
Patient Discharge
Patient Admission

Guidelines for ICU Admission, Discharge, and Triage. *Critical Care Med.* 1999;27:633-638. 6pp. 34refs. Sponsored by the Society of Critical Care Medicine. Cost: Complete Set $60 + s/h SCCM members, $80 + s/h nonmembers; $5 for a single guideline. To order call SCCM 714 282-6000 or access Book Store on the SCCM website. Available free on the Internet at sccm.org. Key terms: critical care; admission; discharge; triage; prioritization.

Intensive Care Units, Pediatric
Guidelines

Guidelines and Levels of Care for Pediatric Intensive Care Units. *Critical Care Med.* 1993;21:1077-1086. 10pp. 1ref. Sponsored by the Society of Critical Care Medicine, American Academy of Pediatrics. Cost: Complete Set $60 + s/h SCCM members, $80 + s/h nonmembers; $5 for a single guideline. To order call SCCM 714 282-6000 or access Book Store on the SCCM website. Available free on the Internet at sccm.org. Key terms: intensive care unit; pediatrics; resuscitation; hospital equipment and supplies; nursing staff.

Intensive Care Units, Pediatric Patient Admission

Guidelines for Developing Admission and Discharge Policies for the Pediatric ICU. *Critical Care Med.* 1999;27:843-845. 3pp. 2refs. Sponsored by the Society of Critical Care Medicine. Cost: Complete Set $60 + s/h SCCM members, $80 + s/h nonmembers; $5 for a single guideline. To order call SCCM 714 282-6000 or access Book Store on the SCCM website. Available free on the Internet at sccm.org. Key terms: admission; discharge; interdisciplinary; physiologic; criteria.

Intensive Care Units/Manpower Critical Care/Manpower

Guidelines on Critical Care Services and Personnel: Recommendations Based on a System of Categorization into Two Levels of Care. *Critical Care Med.* 1999;27:422-426. 5pp. 13refs. Sponsored by the Society of Critical Care Medicine. Cost: Complete Set $60 + s/h SCCM members, $80 + s/h nonmembers; $5 for a single guideline. To order call SCCM 714 282-6000 or access Book Store on the SCCM website. Available free on the Internet at sccm.org. Key terms: critical care services; critical care personnel; guidelines; hospital care levels.

Interferon Alpha-2a/Therapeutic Use Leukemia, Myeloid, Chronic-Phase/Therapy

Alpha-Interferon for Chronic Myelogenous Leukemia. *JAMA.* 1990;264:2137-2140. 4pp. 34refs. Sponsored by the American Medical Association, Diagnostic and Therapeutic Technology Assessment Program. Cost: free copy. DATTA subscription available. To order call AMA Department of Technology Assessment 312 464-4531.

Interferon-Beta/Therapeutic Use Multiple Sclerosis/Drug Therapy

Practice Advisory on Selection of Patients with Multiple Sclerosis for Treatment with Betaseron. *Neurol.* 1994;44:1537-1540. 4pp. 15refs. Sponsored by the American Academy of Neurology. Cost: individual statements are free. To order call AAN Member Service Center 1 800 879-1960. Available on the Internet at aan.com.

Intermittent Positive Pressure Ventilation/Methods

Intermittent Positive Pressure Breathing: Old Technologies Rarely Die. 1993. 14pp. 34refs. Sponsored by the Federal Agency for Health Care Policy and Research. To order call AHCPR Clearinghouse 1 800 358-9295.

Intermittent Positive-Pressure Ventilation/Standards Technology Assessment, Biomedical

Intermittent Positive Pressure Breathing (IPPB) Therapy. *AHCPR Health Technology Assessment.* 1991;No. 1 (AHCPR Publication No. 92-0013). 9pp. 57refs. Sponsored by the Federal Agency for Health Care Policy and Research. To order call AHCPR Clearinghouse 1 800 358-9295.

Internship and Residency Internal Medicine

Curriculum Guidelines on the Care of the Elderly for Internal Medicine Residency Training Programs. 1990. 7pp. 3refs. Sponsored by the American Geriatrics Society. Cost: free. To order call AGS 212 308-1414.

Intervertebral Disk Displacement Lumbar Vertebrae

Herniated Lumbar Disk. *Clinical Policies.* 1996. 7pp. 14refs. Sponsored by the American Academy of Orthopaedic Surgeons, North American Spine Society. Cost: $50 (set of 15) for nonmembers. To order call 1 800 626-6276. Key terms: herniated disk; spine; back pain; paresthesia; American Academy of Orthopaedic Surgeons.

Intervertebral Disk/Surgery Intervertebral Disk Displacement/Surgery

Reassessment of Automated Percutaneous Lumbar Diskectomy for Herniated Disks. *JAMA.* 1991;265:2122-2125. 3pp. 15refs. Sponsored by the American Medical Association, Diagnostic and Therapeutic Technology Assessment Program. Cost: free copy. DATTA subscription available. To order call AMA Department of Technology Assessment 312 464-4531.

Intestinal Diseases/Radiography Tomography, X-ray Computed/Methods

ACR Standard for the Performance of Adult Enteroclysis Examinations. 1999. 6pp. 7refs. Sponsored by the American College of Radiology. Cost: $25 (ACR nonmembers). To order call ACR Dept of Quality Assurance 703 716-7592. Available on the Internet at acr.org. Key terms: lower GI; enteroclysis; radiology; examination; small intestine.

Intestine, Small/Radiography Contrast Media/Administration and Dosage

ACR Standard for the Performance of Per Oral Small Bowel Examinations in Adults. 1999. 5pp. 7refs. Sponsored by the American College of Radiology. Cost: $25 (ACR nonmembers). To order call ACR Dept of Quality Assurance 703 716-7592. Available free on the Internet at acr.org. Key terms: lower GI; small bowel; radiology.

Intestines, Small/Radiography Contrast Media

ACR Standard for the Performance of Pediatric Contrast Examination of the Small Bowel. 1998. 4pp. 9refs. Sponsored by the American College of Radiology. Cost: $25 (ACR nonmembers). To order call ACR Dept of Quality Assurance 703 716-7592. Available free on the Internet at acr.org. Key terms: small bowel; contrast examination; intuseption; malabsorption; pediatric.

Intracranial Pressure Head Injuries/Therapy

Indications for Intracranial Pressure Monitoring. *Guidelines for the Management of Severe Head Injury.* 1996;42-70. 29pp. Sponsored by the American Association of Neurological Surgeons. Cost: $45. To order call AANS 847 692-9500.

Intracranial Pressure Monitoring, Physiology/Standards Head Injuries/Therapy

Intracranial Pressure Monitoring Technology. *Guidelines for the Management of Severe Head Injury.* 1996;77-94. 18pp. Sponsored by the American Association of Neurological Surgeons. Cost: $45. To order call AANS 847 692-9500.

Intraoperative Complications/ Prevention and Control

Lower Urinary Tract Operative Injuries. *ACOG Educational Bulletin.* 1997;238. 6pp. 20refs. Sponsored by the American College of Obstetricians and Gynecologists. Cost: free copy. Set of Bulletins $70 + s/h ACOG members, $125 + s/h nonmembers. One-year subscription $55 member, $65 nonmember. To order single copy, call ACOG Resource Center 202 863-2518; to order set or subscription, call ACOG Distribution Center, 1 800 762-2264. Available on the Internet to members only at acog.org. Key terms: intraoperative complications; postoperative complications; urinary tract/injuries; surgery; ob/gyn.

Intrauterine Devices

Intrauterine Device. *ACOG Technical Bulletin.* 1992;164. 4pp. 16refs. Sponsored by the American College of Obstetricians and Gynecologists. Cost: free copy. Set of Bulletins $70 + s/h ACOG members, $125 + s/h nonmembers. One-year subscription $55 member, $65 nonmember. To order single copy, call ACOG Resource Center 202 863-2518; to order set or subscription, call ACOG Distribution Center, 1 800 762-2264. Available on the Internet to members only at acog.org.

Iodine Radioisotopes/Diagnostic Use Thyroid Neoplasms/ Radionuclide Imaging

Procedure Guideline for Extended Scintigraphy for Differentiated Thyroid Cancer. *J Nuclear Med.* 1996;37:1269-1271. 3pp. 5refs. Sponsored by the Society of Nuclear Medicine. Cost: Free. To order call Bill Uffelman 703 708-9000. Available on the Internet at snm.org. Key terms: thyroid cancer scintigraphy; routine diagnostic tests; radionuclide imaging; thyroid cancer.

Iodine Radioisotopes/Therapeutic Use Thyroid Gland/Radionuclide Imaging

ACR Standard for the Performance of Thyroid Scintigraphy and Uptake Measurements. 1999. 5pp. 9refs. Sponsored by the American College of Radiology. Cost: $25 (ACR nonmembers). To order call ACR Dept of Quality Assurance 703 716-7592. Available free on the Internet at acr.org. Key terms: nuclear medicine; thyroid; uptake.

Iron/Administration and Dosage
Iron/Deficiency

Recommendations to Prevent and Control Iron Deficiency in the United States. *Morbid Mortal Weekly Report*. 1998;47(no. RR-03). Sponsored by the Centers for Disease Control and Prevention. Cost: $1. To order call US Govt Printing Office 202 783-3238.

Ischemia/Surgery
Vascular Surgical Procedures/Methods

Practice Guidelines: Lower Extremity Revascularization. *J Vasc Surg*. 1993;18:280-294. 15pp. 98refs. Sponsored by the Society for Vascular Surgery/ North American Chapter, ICVS. Cost: free. To order call 978 526-8330.

Jaundice, Neonatal/Therapy
Algorithms

Management of Hyperbilirubinemia in the Healthy Term Newborn. *Pediatr*. 1994;94:558-565. 18pp. 31refs. Sponsored by the American Academy of Pediatrics. Cost: $1.95. Discounted set of policies available. To order call 1 800 433-9016.

Jaundice/Diagnosis

Clinical Evaluation of Jaundice: A Guideline of the Patient Care Committee of the American Gastroenterological Association. *JAMA*. 1989;262:3031-3034. 4pp. 42refs. Sponsored by the American Gastroenterological Association. Cost: free. To order call AGA 301 654-2055.

Jaw/Surgery
Insurance, Health

Position Paper: Recommended Criteria for Insurance Coverage of Orthognathic Surgery. 1992. 2pp. Sponsored by the American Society of Plastic and Reconstructive Surgeons. To order call ASPRS 847 228-9900.

Kawasaki Disease (see Mucocutaneous Lymph Node Syndrome)

Keratectomy, Photorefractive
Astigmatism/Surgery

Excimer Laser Photorefractive Keratectomy (PRK) for Myopia and Astigmatism Ophthalmic Procedure Assessment. *Ophthalmology*. 1999;106:422-437. 16pp. 79refs. Sponsored by the American Academy of Ophthalmology. Cost: $11 members, $16 nonmembers. AAO members first copy free upon publication. To order call AAO Order Dept 415 561-8540. Key terms: photorefractive surgery; myopia; astigmatism; laser surgery; refractive surgery.

Keratitis
Eye Infections, Bacterial

Bacterial Keratitis Preferred Practice Pattern. 1995. 19pp. 36refs. Sponsored by the American Academy of Ophthalmology. Cost: $11 members, $16 nonmembers. AAO members first copy free upon publication. To order call AAO Order Dept 415 561-8540. Key terms: eye; bacterial keratitis; external eye disease.

Keratosis/Diagnosis
Melanoma/Diagnosis

Guidelines of Care for Nevi I (Nevocellular Nevi and Seborrheic Keratoses). *J Am Acad Derm*. 1992;26:629-631. 3pp. 19refs. Sponsored by the American Academy of Dermatology. Cost: free copy. To order call Alice Bell 847 330-0230 x333. Available on the Internet at aad.org. Key terms: keratosis; pigmented nevus.

Keratosis/Therapy

Actinic Keratoses. *J Am Acad Derm*. 1995;32:95-98. 4pp. 29refs. Sponsored by the American Academy of Dermatology. Cost: free copy. To order call Alice Bell 847 330-0230 x333. Available on the Internet at aad.org. Key terms: keratosis; diagnosis; etiology; therapy.

Keratotomy, Radial
Myopia/Surgery

Radial Keratotomy for Myopia Ophthalmic Procedure Assessment. *Ophthalmology*. 1993;100:1103-1115. 13pp. 147refs. Sponsored by the American Academy of Ophthalmology. Cost: $11 members, $16 nonmembers. AAO members first copy free upon publication. To order call AAO Order Dept 415 561-8540. Key terms: eye; eye surgery; refractive surgery; RK; myopia.

Keratotomy, Radial
Myopia/Surgery

Reassessment of Radial Keratotomy for Simple Myopia. *JAMA*. 1988;260:264-267. 4pp. Sponsored by the American Medical Association, Diagnostic and Therapeutic Technology Assessment Program. Cost: free copy. DATTA subscription available. To order call AMA Department of Technology Assessment 312 464-4531.

Kidney Calculi/Therapy
Kidney Pelvis

Management of Staghorn Calculi: Summary Report, Report, Patient Guide. 1994. 56pp. 110refs. Sponsored by the American Urological Association. Cost: $42 members, $49 nonmembers. To order write Health Policy Dept, AUA, 1120 N Charles St, Baltimore, MD 21201. Key terms: urinary calculi; kidney calculi; guidelines.

Kidney Calculi/Therapy
Nephrostomy, Percutaneous

Percutaneous Nephrolithotomy for Kidney Stone Removal. *JAMA*. 1984;252:3301-3302. 2pp. Sponsored by the American Medical Association, Diagnostic and Therapeutic Technology Assessment Program. Cost: free copy. DATTA subscription available. To order call AMA Department of Technology Assessment 312 464-4531.

Kidney Cortex/Radionuclide Imaging
Organotechnetium Compounds/
Diagnostic Use

Procedure Guideline for Renal Cortical Scintigraphy in Children. *J Nuclear Med*. 1997;38:1644-1646. 3pp. 11refs. Sponsored by the Society of Nuclear Medicine. Cost: free. To order call Bill Uffelman 703 708-9000. Available on the Internet at snm.org. Key terms: routine diagnostic tests; radionuclide imaging; pediatric; pyelonephritis; vesico-ureteral reflux.

Kidney Diseases/Radionuclide Imaging

ACR Standard for the Performance of Adult and Pediatric Renal Scintigraphy (Revised). 1998. 7pp. 11refs. Sponsored by the American College of Radiology. Cost: $25 (ACR nonmembers). To order call ACR Dept of Quality Assurance 703 716-7592. Available free on the Internet at acr.org. Key terms: kidney disease; nuclear medicine; scintigraphy.

Kidney Failure, Chronic
Dental Care for Chronically Ill/Methods

Oral Health Care Series: Patients with End-Stage Renal Disease. 1996. 12pp. 7refs. Sponsored by the American Dental Association. Cost: $8 ADA members, $12 nonmembers. To order call ADA Dept of Salable Materials 1 800 947-4746.

Kidney Failure, Chronic/Complications
Anemia/Therapy

NKF-DOQI Clinical Practice Guidelines for the Treatment of Anemia of Chronic Renal Failure. 1997. 184pp. Sponsored by the National Kidney Foundation. Cost: $13. To order call NKF 1 800 622-9010. Key terms: hemodialysis adequacy; peritoneal dialysis adequacy; vascular access; anemia management; executive summaries.

Kidney Transplantation/Methods
Pancreas Transplantation/Methods

Simultaneous Pancreas-Kidney and Sequential Pancreas-After-Kidney Transplantation. *AHCPR Health Technology Assessment*. 1995;No. 4 (AHCPR Publication No. 95-0065). 53pp. 110refs. Sponsored by the Federal Agency for Health Care Policy and Research. To order call AHCPR Clearinghouse 1 800 358-9295.

Knee
Pain

Clinical Guideline on Knee Pain (Phases I and II). 1996. 24pp. 102refs. Sponsored by the American Academy of Orthopaedic Surgeons, North American Spine Society. Cost: $10 AAOS member, $20 nonmember. To order call 1 800 626-6276. Available on the Internet free at guidelines.gov. Key terms: knee pain; osteoarthritis; inflammatory arthritis; bursitis/tendonitis; internal derangement.

Knee Joint
Osteoarthritis/Therapy

Guidelines for the Medical Management of Osteoarthritis Part II: Osteoarthritis of the Knee. *Arthritis Rheum*. 1995;38:1541-1546. 6pp. 40refs. Sponsored by the American College of Rheumatology. To order call 404 633-3777. Available free on the Internet at rheumatology.org. Key terms: osteoarthritis; joint; musculoskeletal; drugs; therapy.

Labor, Induced

Induction of Labor. *ACOG Technical Bulletin.*
1995;217. 8pp. 34refs. Sponsored by the American
College of Obstetricians and Gynecologists. Cost: free
copy. Set of Bulletins $70 + s/h ACOG members, $125
+ s/h nonmembers. One-year subscription $55
member, $65 nonmember. To order single copy, call
ACOG Resource Center 202 863-2518; to order set or
subscription, call ACOG Distribution Center,
1 800 762-2264. Available on the Internet to members
only at acog.org. Key terms: labor: induced.

Labor, Premature
Tocolysis

Preterm Labor. *ACOG Technical Bulletin.* 1995;206.
10pp. 65refs. Sponsored by the American College of
Obstetricians and Gynecologists. Cost: free copy. Set
of Bulletins $70 + s/h ACOG members, $125 + s/h
nonmembers. One-year subscription $55 member,
$65 nonmember. To order single copy, call ACOG
Resource Center 202 863-2518; to order set or
subscription, call ACOG Distribution Center,
1 800 762-2264. Available on the Internet to members
only at acog.org.

Laboratory Techniques and Procedures

Methods of Practice Regarding Lab Procedures.
J Allergy Clin Immun. 1978;62:71, Position Statement
No. 4. 1pp. Sponsored by the American Academy of
Allergy, Asthma, and Immunology. Cost: free copy.
To order call 414 272-6071.

Laboratory Techniques and
Procedures/Methods
Lupus Erythematosus,
Systemic/Diagnosis

LE Cell Test. *Am J Clin Pathol.* 1994;101:65-66. 2pp.
9refs. Sponsored by the American Society of Clinical
Pathologists. Cost: free copy. To order call Felicia
Nelson 312 738-1336 x1350. Key terms: anti-nuclear
antibodies; LE cell test; lupus erythematosus;
immune-mediated diseases; SLE.

Laminectomy/Methods
Intervertebral Disk
Displacement/Surgery

Laminectomy and Microlaminectomy for Lumbar Disc
Herniation. *JAMA.* 1990;264:1469-1472. 4pp. 26refs.
Sponsored by the American Medical Association,
Diagnostic and Therapeutic Technology Assessment
Program. Cost: free copy. DATTA subscription
available. To order call AMA Department of
Technology Assessment 312 464-4531.

Laparoscopy

Guidelines for Diagnostic Laparoscopy. *Surgical
Endoscopy.* 1993;7:367-368. 3pp. 15refs. Sponsored by
the Society of American Gastrointestinal and
Endoscopic Surgeons. Cost: free. To order call
310 314-2404. Available on the Internet at sages.org.
Key terms: surgery; diagnostic; laparoscopy.

Laparotomy
Ovarian Neoplasms

Second-Look Laparotomy for Epithelial Ovarian
Cancer. *ACOG Committee Opinion.* 1995;165. 3pp.
11refs. Sponsored by the American College of
Obstetricians and Gynecologists. Cost: free copy. Set
of Opinions $55 + s/h ACOG members, $75 + s/h
nonmembers. One-year subscription $55 member,
$65 nonmember. To order single copy, call ACOG
Resource Center 202 863-2518; to order set or
subscription, call ACOG Distribution Center,
1 800 762-2264. Available on the Internet to members
only at acog.org. Key terms: follow-up.

Laryngeal Diseases/Diagnosis
Nasopharyngeal Diseases/Diagnosis

Laryngoscopy/Nasopharyngoscopy. *Clinical
Indicators Compendium.* 1999. 2pp. Sponsored by
the American Academy of Otolaryngology-Head and
Neck Surgery. Cost: $10 AAO-HNS members, $15
nonmembers. To order write to AAO-HNS, 1 Prince
St, Alexandria, VA 22314 Key terms: laryngoscopy,
nasopharyngoscopy; diagnostic; larynx; pharynx.

Laryngeal Neoplasms/Surgery

Laryngeal Cancer Surgical Practice Guidelines.
Oncology. 1997;11(8). 5pp. 5refs. Sponsored by the
Society of Surgical Oncology. Cost: call 516 424-8900
x316. To order write Oncology, PRR, Inc, 17 Prospect
St, Huntington, NY 11743. Key terms: laryngeal.

Laryngectomy

Laryngectomy. *Clinical Indicators Compendium.*
1999. 2pp. 20refs. Sponsored by the American
Academy of Otolaryngology-Head and Neck Surgery.
Cost: $10 AAO-HNS members, $15 nonmembers. To
order write to AAO-HNS, 1 Prince St, Alexandria, VA
22314. Key terms: neck dissection; larynx; neoplasm;
glottis.

Laser Surgery

Statement on Laser Surgery. *Am Coll Surg Bulletin.*
1991;76(3):12. 1pp. Sponsored by the American
College of Surgeons. Cost: free copy. To order call
ACS Socioeconomic Affairs Dept 312 664-4050.

Laser Surgery
Sleep Apnea Syndromes/Complications

Practice Parameters for the Use of Laser-Assisted Uvulopalatoplasty. *Sleep*. 1994;17(8):744-748. 5pp. 38refs. Sponsored by the American Academy of Sleep Medicine. Cost: $30 + s/h for a complete set of current AASM Guidelines. To order call AASM 507 287-6006. Key terms: practice guidelines; laser surgery; polysomnography; sleep apnea syndromes; snoring.

Lasers/Therapeutic Use
Gastrointestinal Hemorrhage/Surgery

Endoscopic Laser Photocoagulation for Gastrointestinal Hemorrhage. *JAMA*. 1985;253:2732-2733. 2pp. Sponsored by the American Medical Association, Diagnostic and Therapeutic Technology Assessment Program. Cost: free copy. DATTA subscription available. To order call AMA Department of Technology Assessment 312 464-4531.

Lead Poisoning/Diagnosis

Screening for Elevated Lead Levels in Childhood and Pregnancy. *Guide to Clinical Preventive Services, 2nd Ed*. 1996. Sponsored by the US Preventive Services Task Force. To order call Williams & Wilkins 1 800 638-0672.

Lead Poisoning/Prevention and Control
Mass Screening
Lead/Blood

Screening for Elevated Blood Lead Levels. *Pediatr*. 1998;101(6):1072-1078. 7pp. 48refs. Sponsored by the American Academy of Pediatrics. Cost: $1.95. Discounted set of policies available. To order call 1 800 433-9016.

Leukemia, Myeloid, Chronic

Chronic Myelogenous Leukemia. *Blood*. 1999. 40pp. 108refs. Sponsored by the American Society of Hematology. Cost: free. To order call ASH 202 857-1118. Available on the Internet at hematology.org. Key terms: CML; allogenic BMT; hydroxyurea; interferon; leukemia.

Libraries, Medical
Occupational Medicine

Recommended Library for Occupational Physicians. *J Occupation Med*. 1991;33:1997-1300. 4pp. Sponsored by the American College of Occupational and Environmental Medicine. Cost: free copy. To order call Marianne Dreger 847 228-6850 x18.

Life Support Care
Mental Competency

Decisions for Forgoing Life-Sustaining Treatment for Incompetent Patients. *Reports of CEJA*. 1991;2:65-77. 13pp. Sponsored by the American Medical Association, Council on Ethical and Judicial Affairs. Cost: free copy. To order call AMA 312 464-5223.

Lipectomy

Liposuction. *J Am Acad Derm*. 1991;24:489-494. 6pp. 56refs. Sponsored by the American Academy of Dermatology. Cost: free copy. To order call Alice Bell 847 330-0230 x333. Available on the Internet at aad.org. Key terms: lipectomy; methods.

Lipectomy/Standards

Guidelines for Liposuction Surgery. 1997. 6pp. 17refs. Sponsored by the American Academy of Cosmetic Surgery. To order call Kimberly Brown 312 527-6713. Key terms: liposuction; ultrasonic; tumescent; standards; procedures.

Lipoprotein/Blood
Cerebrovascular Disorders

Plasma Concentrations of Lipoprotein (a). *Diagnostic and Therapeutic Technology Assessment (DATTA)*. 1995. 37pp. 120refs. Sponsored by the American Medical Association, Diagnostic and Therapeutic Technology Assessment Program. Cost: free copy. DATTA subscription available. To order call AMA Department of Technology Assessment 312 464-4531.

Liposuction (see Lipectomy)

Lithotripsy
Kidney Calculi

Non-Invasive Extracorporeal Lithotripsy for Disruption of Kidney Stones—UPDATE. *JAMA*. 1984;252:3301. 1pp. Sponsored by the American Medical Association, Diagnostic and Therapeutic Technology Assessment Program. Cost: free copy. DATTA subscription available. To order call AMA Department of Technology Assessment 312 464-4531.

Lithotripsy
Ureteral Calculi/Therapy

Ureteral Stone Management: Ureteroscopy and Extracorporeal Shock Wave Lithotripsy. *JAMA*. 1988;259:1382-1384. 3pp. Sponsored by the American Medical Association, Diagnostic and Therapeutic Technology Assessment Program. Cost: free copy. DATTA subscription available. To order call AMA Department of Technology Assessment 312 464-4531.

Liver Diseases
Pregnancy Complications

Liver Disease in the Pregnant Patient. *Am J Gastroenterol*. 1999;94:1728-1732. 5pp. 61refs. Sponsored by the American College of Gastroenterology. Cost: free copy. To order call ACG 703 820-7400. Available on the Internet at elsevier.com/locate/amjgastro.

Liver Diseases, Alcoholic/Diagnosis
Liver Diseases, Alcoholic/Therapy

Alcoholic Liver Disease. *Am J Gastroenterol*. 1998;93:2022-2036. 14pp. 167refs. Sponsored by the American College of Gastroenterology. Cost: free copy. To order call ACG 703 820-7400.

Liver Diseases/Radionuclide Imaging
Bile Duct Diseases/Radionuclide Imaging

ACR Standard for the Performance of Adult and Pediatric Hepatobiliary Scintigraphy (Revised). 1998. 4pp. 9refs. Sponsored by the American College of Radiology. Cost: $25 (ACR nonmembers). To order call ACR Dept of Quality Assurance 703 716-7592. Available free on the Internet at acr.org. Key terms: liver disease; nuclear medicine; hepatobiliary.

Liver/Radionuclide Imaging
Spleen/Radionuclide Imaging

Procedure Guideline for Hepatic and Splenic Imaging. *J Nuclear Med*. 1998;39:1114-1116. 3pp. 7refs. Sponsored by the Society of Nuclear Medicine. Cost: free. To order call Bill Uffelman 703 708-9000. Available on the Internet at snm.org. Key terms: liver/spleen scintigraphy; liver diseases; spleen; routine diagnostic tests; radionuclide imaging.

Low Back Pain

Clinical Guideline on Low Back Pain (Phases I and II). 1996. 22pp. 127refs. Sponsored by the American Academy of Orthopaedic Surgeons, North American Spine Society. Cost: $10 AAOS member, $20 nonmember. To order call 1 800 626-6276. Available on the Internet free at guidelines.gov. Key terms: low back pain; herniated nucleus pulposus; spondylolysis; lytic spondylolisthesis; spinal stenosis.

Low Back Pain
Manipulation, Spinal

Spinal Manipulation of Low-Back Pain. 1991. R-4025/2. 117pp. Sponsored by RAND, Academic Medical Center Consortium. To order call RAND 310 393-0411 x7002. Key terms: spinal manipulation; appropriateness; treatment outcomes; utilization; complications.

Low Back Pain/Prevention and Control

Counseling to Prevent Low Back Pain. *Guide to Clinical Preventive Services, 2nd Ed*. 1996. Sponsored by the US Preventive Services Task Force. To order call Williams & Wilkins 1 800 638-0672.

Low Back Pain/Therapy

Acute Low Back Pain Problems in Adults. *AHCPR*. 1994;Publication No. 95-0642. 160pp. 360refs. Sponsored by the Federal Agency for Health Care Policy and Research. To order call AHCPR Clearinghouse 1 800 358-9295.

Lumbar Vertebrae/Injury
Sprains and Strains

Low Back Musculoligamentous Injury (Sprain/Strain). *Clinical Policies*. 1996. 5pp. 22refs. Sponsored by the American Academy of Orthopaedic Surgeons, North American Spine Society. Cost: $50 (set of 15) for nonmembers. To order call 1 800 626-6276. Key terms: low back pain; paraspinal muscle spasm; sprain/strain; American Academy of Orthopaedic Surgeons.

Lumbar Vertebrae/Surgery

Lumbar Spine Surgery. 1993. Sponsored by the American Association of Neurological Surgeons. To order call AANS 847 692-9500.

Lung Diseases, Fungal/Drug Therapy
Mycoses/Drug Therapy

Chemotherapy of Pulmonary Mycoses. *Amer Rev Resp Dis*. 1988;138:4. Sponsored by the American Thoracic Society. Cost: $6. To order send check payable to American Thoracic Society, 1740 Broadway, New York, NY 10019-4374; for credit card orders, call 212 315-8863.

Lung Diseases, Obstructive/Diagnosis
Lung Diseases, Obstructive/Therapy

Standards for the Diagnosis and Care of Patients with Chronic Obstructive Pulmonary Disease. *Am J Respir Crit Care Med*. 1995;152:5. Sponsored by the American Thoracic Society. To order send check payable to American Thoracic Society, 1740 Broadway, New York, NY 10019-4374; for credit card orders, call 212 315-8863.

Lung Diseases, Obstructive/ Rehabilitation

Pulmonary Rehabilitation: Joint ACCP/AACVPR Evidence-Based Guideline (with the American Association for Cardiovascular and Pulmonary Rehabilitation). *Chest.* 1997;112(suppl):1363-1396. 33pp. 185refs. Sponsored by the American College of Chest Physicians. Cost: $2. To order call ACCP 1 800 343 2227 or 1 847 498-1400 (credit card orders). Key terms: pulmonary rehabilitation; exercise; COPD; dyspnea ventilatory muscle training.

Lung Diseases, Obstructive/Surgery Pneumonectomy/Statistics and Numerical Data

Lung-Volume Reduction Surgery for End-Stage Chronic Obstructive Pulmonary Disease. *AHCPR Health Technology Assessment.* 1996;No. 10 (AHCPR Publication No. 96-0062). 30pp. 90refs. Sponsored by the Federal Agency for Health Care Policy and Research. To order call AHCPR Clearinghouse 1 800 358-9295.

Lung/Radionuclide Imaging

ACR Standard for the Performance of Pulmonary Scintigraphy. 1999. 5pp. 13refs. Sponsored by the American College of Radiology. Cost: $25 (ACR nonmembers). To order call ACR Dept of Quality Assurance 703 716-7592. Available free on the Internet at acr.org. Key terms: lung disease; nuclear medicine; scintigraphy; pulmonary.

Lung Diseases, Obstructive/Therapy Patient Care Team

Skills of the Health Care Team Involved in Out-of-Hospital Care for Patients with COPD. *Amer Rev Resp Dis.* 1986;135:5. Sponsored by the American Thoracic Society. Cost: $6. To order send check payable to American Thoracic Society, 1740 Broadway, New York, NY 10019-4374; for credit card orders, call 212 315-8863.

Lung Diseases/Diagnosis Referral and Consultation

Essentials of a Pulmonary Consultation. *Amer Rev Resp Dis.* 1987;136:4. Sponsored by the American Thoracic Society. Cost: $4. To order send check payable to American Thoracic Society, 1740 Broadway, New York, NY 10019-4374; for credit card orders, call 212 315-8863.

Lung Diseases/Diagnosis Respiratory Function Tests

Respiratory Function Measurement in Infants: Measurement Conditions. *Am J Respir Crit Care Med.* 1995;152:6. Sponsored by the American Thoracic Society. Cost: $6. To order send check payable to American Thoracic Society, 1740 Broadway, New York, NY 10019-4374; for credit card orders, call 212 315-8863.

Lung Diseases/Prevention and Control Respiratory Function Tests

Preoperative Pulmonary Function Testing. *Ann Intern Med.* 1990;112:793-794. 2pp. 51refs. Sponsored by the American College of Physicians. To order call ACP Clinical Efficacy Assessment Project 1 800 523-1546.

Lung Diseases/Radiography

ACR Standard for the Performance of Pediatric and Adult Bedside (Portable) Chest Radiography (Revised). 1997. 4pp. 24refs. Sponsored by the American College of Radiology. Cost: $25 (ACR nonmembers). To order call ACR Dept of Quality Assurance 703 716-7592. Available free on the Internet at acr.org. Key terms: chest radiography; pediatric; portable; bedside; pulmonary.

Lung Diseases/Radiography

ACR Standard for the Performance of Pediatric and Adult Chest Radiography (Revised). 1997. 4pp. 24refs. Sponsored by the American College of Radiology. Cost: $25 (ACR nonmembers). To order call ACR Dept of Quality Assurance 703 716-7592. Available free on the Internet at acr.org. Key terms: chest radiography; respiratory; pulmonary; pediatric.

Lung Neoplasms/ Prevention and Control Mass Screening

Screening for Lung Cancer. *Ann Intern Med.* 1989;111:232-237. 6pp. 27refs. Sponsored by the American College of Physicians. To order call ACP Clinical Efficacy Assessment Project 1 800 523-1546.

Lung Neoplasms/Surgery

Lung Cancer Surgical Practice Guidelines. *Oncology.* 1997;11(6):899. 5pp. 8refs. Sponsored by the Society of Surgical Oncology. Cost: call 516 424-8900 x316. To order write Oncology, PRR, Inc, 17 Prospect St, Huntington NY 11743. Key terms: lung.

Lung Neoplasms/Therapy
Neoplasm Staging

Staging of Non-Small Cell Lung Cancer (8 variants). 14pp. 23refs. Sponsored by the American College of Radiology. Cost: Vols. 1 & 2 $25 each (ACR members), $75/set (ACR nonmembers). To order call ACR Appropriateness Criteria™ 703 716-7583 x7596. Available free on the Internet at acr.org/f-appcrit.html. Registration required. Key terms: non-small cell lung cancer; staging.

Lung Transplantation
Technology Assessment, Biomedical

Lung Transplantation. *JAMA*. 1993;269:931-936. 6pp. Sponsored by the American Medical Association, Diagnostic and Therapeutic Technology Assessment Program. Cost: free copy. DATTA subscription available. To order call AMA Department of Technology Assessment 312 464-4531.

Lung Transplantation/Standards
Technology Assessment/Biomedical

Single and Double Lung Transplantation. *AHCPR Health Technology Assessment*. 1991;No. 5 (AHCPR Publication No. 92-0028). 15pp. 94refs. Sponsored by the Federal Agency for Health Care Policy and Research. To order call AHCPR Clearinghouse 1 800 358-9295.

Lung/Growth and Development
Respiration

Aspiration Hazards to the Developing Lung. *Amer Rev Resp Dis*. 1985;131:5. Sponsored by the American Thoracic Society. Cost: $4. To order send check payable to American Thoracic Society, 1740 Broadway, New York, NY 10019-4374; for credit card orders, call 212 315-8863.

Lung/Radionuclide Imaging

Procedure Guideline for Lung Scintigraphy. *J Nuclear Med*. 1996;37:1906-1910. 5pp. 6refs. Sponsored by the Society of Nuclear Medicine. Cost: free. To order call Bill Uffelman 703 708-9000. Available on the Internet at snm.org. Key terms: lung scintigraphy; pulmonary embolism; ventilation-perfusion ratio; routine diagnostic tests; radionuclide imaging.

Lupus Erythematosus, Cutaneous/
Drug Therapy

Cutaneous Lupus Erythematosus. *J Am Acad Derm*. 1996;34:830-836. 7pp. 30refs. Sponsored by the American Academy of Dermatology. Cost: free copy. To order call Alice Bell 847 330-0230 x333. Available on the Internet at aad.org. Key terms: cutaneous lupus erythematosus; diagnosis; drug therapy.

Lyme Disease/Diagnosis
Nervous System Diseases/Diagnosis

Practice Parameter: Diagnosis of Patients with Nervous System Lyme Borreliosis (Lyme Disease). *Neurol*. 1996;46:881-882. 2pp. Sponsored by the American Academy of Neurology. Cost: individual statements are free. To order call AAN Member Service Center 1 800 879-1960. Available on the Internet at aan.com.

Lyme Disease/Prevention and Control
Borrelia burgdorferi/Immunology

Recommendations for the Use of Lyme Disease Vaccine Recommendations of the Advisory Committee on Immunization Practices (ACIP). *Morbid Mortal Weekly Report*. 1999;48(no. RR-7). Sponsored by the Centers for Disease Control and Prevention. To order call US Govt Printing Office 202 783-3238. Available on the Internet at cdc.gov/mwr/mmwr_rr.html.

Macular Degeneration

Age-Related Macular Degeneration Preferred Practice Pattern. 1998. 23pp. 56refs. Sponsored by the American Academy of Ophthalmology. Cost: $11 members, $16 nonmembers. AAO members first copy free upon publication. To order call AAO Order Dept 415 561-8540. Key terms: eye; macular degeneration; diagnosis; treatment.

Magnetic Resonance Imaging/
Instrumentation
Nuclear Physics

ACR Standard for Diagnostic Medical Physics Monitoring of MRI Equipment. 1999. 5pp. 13refs. Sponsored by the American College of Radiology. Cost: $25 (ACR nonmembers). To order call ACR Dept of Quality Assurance 703 716-7592. Available free on the Internet at acr.org. Key terms: magnetic resonance; physics; equipment; quality control; monitoring.

Magnetic Resonance Imaging

ACR Standard for the Performance of Magnetic Resonance Imaging (Revised). 1996. 5pp. 26refs. Sponsored by the American College of Radiology. Cost: $25 (ACR nonmembers). To order call ACR Dept of Quality Assurance 703 716-7592. Available free on the Internet at acr.org. Key terms: magnetic resonance; radiology; cross-sectional imaging.

Magnetic Resonance Imaging

Magnetic Resonance Imaging: Prologue. *JAMA*. 1987;258:3283-3285. 3pp. Sponsored by the American Medical Association, Council on Scientific Affairs. Cost: free. To order call Nancy Nolan, AMA, 312 464-5046.

Magnetic Resonance Imaging
Brain Diseases/Diagnosis

Magnetic Resonance Imaging of Brain and Spine. *Ann Intern Med*. 1988;108:474-476. 3pp. Sponsored by the American College of Physicians. To order call ACP Clinical Efficacy Assessment Project 1 800 523-1546.

Magnetic Resonance Imaging
Brain Diseases/Radiography

Update: MRI of the Brain and Spine. 1993. Sponsored by the American College of Physicians. To order call ACP Clinical Efficacy Assessment Project 1 800 523-1546.

Magnetic Resonance Imaging/Methods

Fundamentals of Magnetic Resonance Imaging. *JAMA*. 1987;258:3417-3423. 7pp. Sponsored by the American Medical Association, Council on Scientific Affairs. Cost: free. To order call Nancy Nolan, AMA, 312 464-5046.

Magnetic Resonance Imaging/Methods
Head/Pathology

Magnetic Resonance Imaging of the Head and Neck Region. *JAMA*. 1988;260:3313-3326. 14pp. Sponsored by the American Medical Association, Council on Scientific Affairs. Cost: free. To order call Nancy Nolan, AMA, 312 464-5046.

Magnetoencephalography/Standards

Assessment: Magnetoencephalography (MEG). *Neurol*. 1992;42:1-4. 4pp. 24refs. Sponsored by the American Academy of Neurology. Cost: individual statements are free. To order call AAN Member Service Center 1 800 879-1960. Available on the Internet at aan.com.

Malaria/Prevention and Control
Mefloquine/Administration and Dosage

Revised Dosing Regimen for Malaria Prophylaxis with Mefloquine. *Morbid Mortal Weekly Report*. 1990;39:630. 1pp. Sponsored by the Centers for Disease Control and Prevention. Cost: $1. To order call US Govt Printing Office 202 783-3238.

Malaria/Prevention and Control
Travel

Recommendations for the Prevention of Malaria Among Travelers. *Morbid Mortal Weekly Report*. 1990;39(no. RR-3):1-10. 10pp. 2refs. Sponsored by the Centers for Disease Control and Prevention. Cost: $1. To order call US Govt Printing Office 202 783-3238.

Malpractice
Gynecology/Legislation and Jurisprudence

Coping with the Stress of Malpractice Litigation. *ACOG Committee Opinion*. 1994;150. 1pp. Sponsored by the American College of Obstetricians and Gynecologists. Cost: free copy. Set of Opinions $55 + s/h ACOG members, $75 + s/h nonmembers. One-year subscription $55 member, $65 nonmember. To order single copy, call ACOG Resource Center 202 863-2518; to order set or subscription, call ACOG Distribution Center, 1 800 762-2264. Available on the Internet to members only at acog.org. Key terms: stress; psychological.

Mammography
Breast Neoplasms/Diagnosis

ACR Standard for the Performance of Screening Mammography. 1999. 8pp. 32refs. Sponsored by the American College of Radiology. Cost: $25 (ACR nonmembers). To order call ACR Dept of Quality Assurance 703 716-7592. Available on the Internet at acr.org. Key terms: breast cancer; screening.

Mammography
Breast Neoplasms/Diagnosis

Mammographic Screening for Breast Cancer. *JAMA*. 1987;258:1387-1389. 3pp. Sponsored by the American Medical Association, Diagnostic and Therapeutic Technology Assessment Program. Cost: free copy. DATTA subscription available. To order call AMA Department of Technology Assessment 312 464-4531.

Mammography
Guidelines

Quality Determinants of Mammography. *AHCPR.* 1994;Publication No. 95-0632. 170pp. 300refs. Sponsored by the Federal Agency for Health Care Policy and Research. To order call AHCPR Clearinghouse 1 800 358-9295.

Mammography/Methods

ACR Standard for the Performance of Diagnostic Mammography. 1998. 4pp. 14refs. Sponsored by the American College of Radiology. Cost: $25 (ACR nonmembers). To order call ACR Dept of Quality Assurance 703 716-7592. Available free on the Internet at acr.org. Key terms: breast disease; breast cancer; mammography; diagnostic.

Mammoplasty

Breast Reconstruction. 1994. Sponsored by the American Society of Plastic and Reconstructive Surgeons. Cost: $25 members, $55 nonmembers (full set of guidelines), + s/h. To order call 1 800 766-4955.

Mammoplasty
Insurance, Health
Mastectomy

Position Paper: Recommended Criteria for Insurance Coverage of Breast Reconstruction Following Mastectomy. 1992. 2pp. 3refs. Sponsored by the American Society of Plastic and Reconstructive Surgeons. To order call ASPRS 847 228-9900.

Managed Care Programs
Physician's Role

Physician Responsibility Under Managed Care. *ACOG Committee Opinion.* 1996;170. 5pp. 23refs. Sponsored by the American College of Obstetricians and Gynecologists. Cost: free copy. Set of Opinions $55 + s/h ACOG members, $75 + s/h nonmembers. One-year subscription $55 member, $65 nonmember. To order single copy, call ACOG Resource Center 202 863-2518; to order set or subscription, call ACOG Distribution Center, 1 800 762-2264. Available on the Internet to members only at acog.org. Key terms: physician role; ethics.

Mandatory Reporting
Physician's Role

Mandatory Reporting of Domestic Violence. *ACOG Committee Opinion.* 1998;200. 3pp. 13refs. Sponsored by the American College of Obstetricians and Gynecologists. Cost: free copy. Set of Opinions $55 + s/h ACOG members, $75 + s/h nonmembers. One-year subscription $55 member, $65 nonmember. To order single copy, call ACOG Resource Center 202 863-2518; to order set or subscription, call ACOG Distribution Center, 1 800 762-2264. Available on the Internet to members only at acog.org. Key terms: domestic violence; legislation and jurisprudence; physicians role; physician-patient relations.

Mandibular Fractures

Mandibular Fracture. *Clinical Indicators Compendium.* 1999. 1pp. Sponsored by the American Academy of Otolaryngology-Head and Neck Surgery. Cost: $10 AAO-HNS members, $15 nonmembers. To order write to AAO-HNS, 1 Prince St, Alexandria, VA 22314.

Mannitol
Head Injuries

Mannitol. *Guidelines for the Management of Severe Head Injury.* 1996;115-125. 11pp. Sponsored by the American Association of Neurological Surgeons. Cost: $45. To order call AANS 847 692-9500.

Mass Media
Violence

Physician Guide to Media Violence. 1996. 32pp. Sponsored by the American Medical Association, Division of Health Science. Cost: AMA members $2.25 nonmembers $3. To order call AMA 312 464-5066.

Mass Screening
Mouth Neoplasms

Screening for Oral Cancer. 1996. 2pp. Sponsored by the National Cancer Institute. To order call 1 800 4CA-NCER. Also available on the Internet, at http://cancernet.nci.nih.gov.

Mass Screening
Neoplasms/Prevention and Control

Routine Cancer Screening. *ACOG Committee Opinion.* 1997;185. 5pp. 69refs. Sponsored by the American College of Obstetricians and Gynecologists. Cost: free copy. Set of Opinions $55 + s/h ACOG members, $75 + s/h nonmembers. One-year subscription $55 member, $65 nonmember. To order single copy, call ACOG Resource Center 202 863-2518; to order set or subscription, call ACOG Distribution Center, 1 800 762-2264. Available on the Internet to members only at acog.org. Key terms: mammography; vaginal smears; mass screening; neoplasms: breast; cervix.

Mass Screening
Ovarian Neoplasms

Screening for Ovarian Cancer. 1996. 5pp. Sponsored by the National Cancer Institute. To order call 1 800 4CA-NCER. Also available on the Internet, at http://cancernet.nci.nih.gov.

Mass Screening
Ovarian Neoplasms/
Prevention and Control

Ovarian Cancer: Screening, Treatment, and Follow-up. *NIH Consensus Development Conference Statement.* 1994;12(3):1-30[Conf. No. 96]. 31pp. Sponsored by the National Institutes of Health. Cost: free copy. To order call 1 888 644-2667. Available on the Internet at consensus.nih.gov.

Mass Screening
Prostatic Neoplasms

Screening for Prostate Cancer. 1996. 9pp. Sponsored by the National Cancer Institute. To order call 1 800 4CA-NCER. Also available on the Internet, at http://cancernet.nci.nih.gov.

Mass Screening
Prostatic Neoplasms/Diagnosis

Screening for Prostate Cancer. *Ann Intern Med.* 1997;126:480-484. 5pp. 52refs. Sponsored by the American College of Physicians. To order call ACP Clinical Efficacy Assessment Project 1 800 523-1546.

Mass Screening
Testicular Neoplasms

Screening for Testicular Cancer. 1996. 2pp. Sponsored by the National Cancer Institute. To order call 1 800 4CA-NCER. Also available on the Internet, at http://cancernet.nci.nih.gov.

Mass Screening/Methods
Cervix Neoplasms

Screening for Cervical Cancer. 1996. 4pp. Sponsored by the National Cancer Institute. To order call 1 800 4CA-NCER. Also available on the Internet, at http://cancernet.nci.nih.gov.

Mass Screening/Methods
Colorectal Neoplasms/Diagnosis

Screening for Colorectal Cancer. 1996. 5pp. Sponsored by the National Cancer Institute. To order call 1 800 4CA-NCER. Also available on the Internet, at http://cancernet.nci.nih.gov.

Mass Screening/Methods
Ovarian Neoplasms/
Prevention and Control

Practice Policy Statement: Screening Asymptomatic Women for Ovarian Cancer. *Am J Prev Med.* 1997;13(6):444-446. 3pp. 17refs. Sponsored by the American College of Preventive Medicine. To order reprint address request to ACPM, 1660 L St NW, #206, Washington, DC 20036.

Mass Screening/Methods
Skin Neoplasms/Prevention and Control

Screening for Skin Cancer. 1996. 3pp. Sponsored by the National Cancer Institute. To order call 1 800 4CA-NCER. Also available on the Internet, at http://cancernet.nci.nih.gov.

Mass Screening/Standards
Ovarian Neoplasms/
Prevention and Control

Screening for Ovarian Cancer. *Ann Intern Med.* 1994;121:124-132. 9pp. 83refs. Sponsored by the American College of Physicians. To order call ACP Customer Service 215 351-2600.

Mass Screening/Standards
Skin Neoplasms/Prevention and Control

Practice Policy Statement: Screening for Skin Cancer. *Am J Prev Med.* 1998;14(1):80-82. 3pp. 23refs. Sponsored by the American College of Preventive Medicine. To order reprint address request to ACPM, 1660 L St NW, #206, Washington, DC 20036.

Mastoid/Surgery

Mastoidectomy. *Clinical Indicators Compendium*. 1999. 2pp. 20refs. Sponsored by the American Academy of Otolaryngology-Head and Neck Surgery. Cost: $10 AAO-HNS members, $15 nonmembers. To order write to AAO-HNS, 1 Prince St, Alexandria, VA 22314. Key terms: mastoid; hearing loss; mastoiditis; ossiculoplasty; tympanoplasty.

Maxillary Sinus/Surgery
Maxillary Sinusitis/Surgery

Caldwell-Luc. *Clinical Indicators Compendium*. 1999. 1pp. 20refs. Sponsored by the American Academy of Otolaryngology-Head and Neck Surgery. Cost: $10 AAO-HNS members, $15 nonmembers. To order write to AAO-HNS, 1 Prince St, Alexandria, VA 22314. Key terms: maxillary; antrostomy; sinusitis; sinusotomy.

Maxillofacial Injuries

Trauma. *J Oral & Maxillofacial Surg*. 1995. Sponsored by the American Association of Oral and Maxillofacial Surgeons. To order call AAOMS Publications 1 800 366-6725.

Maxillofacial Injuries
Jaw Fractures/Surgery

LeFort Fractures. *Clinical Indicators Compendium*. 1999. 3pp. Sponsored by the American Academy of Otolaryngology-Head and Neck Surgery. Cost: $10 AAO-HNS members, $15 nonmembers. To order write to AAO-HNS, 1 Prince St, Alexandria, VA 22314. Key terms: midface; cheek; fracture; jaw.

Maxillofacial Injuries/Surgery

Maxillofacial Trauma. *Clinical Practice Guidelines: Plastic and Maxillofacial Surgery*. 1995. 90pp. 170refs. Sponsored by the American Society of Maxillofacial Surgeons. Cost: Maxillofacial Surgery Guidelines $25 for entire set (not sold separately). Binder $10 (price includes shipping). To order call 1 800 766-4955.

Maxillofacial Prosthesis
Maxillofacial Prosthesis Implantation

Dental and Maxillofacial Implant. *J Oral & Maxillofacial Surg*. 1995. Sponsored by the American Association of Oral and Maxillofacial Surgeons. To order call AAOMS Publications 1 800 366-6725.

Measles/Prevention and Control

Measles Prevention: Recommendations of the Immunization Practices Advisory Committee (ACIP). *Morbid Mortal Weekly Report*. 1989;38(S-9). 18pp. 25refs. Sponsored by the Centers for Disease Control and Prevention. Cost: $1. To order call US Govt Printing Office 202 783-3238.

Measles/Prevention and Control
Cross Infection/Prevention and Control

Quality Standard for Assurance of Measles Immunity Among Health Care Workers. *Infect Control Hosp Epidemiol*. 1994;15:193-199. 7pp. 36refs. Sponsored by the Society for Healthcare Epidemiology of America. Cost: free. To order visit our website at medscape.com/shea. Available on the Internet at medscape.com/shea. Key terms: determination of measles immunity among healthcare workers; measles vaccine; efficacy of vaccination; adverse reactions to vaccine; precautions.

Measles/Prevention and Control
Measles Vaccine/Contraindications
HIV Infections

Measles Immunization in HIV-Infected Children (joint with COPA+). *Pediatr*. 1999;103(5):1057-1060. 3pp. 25refs. Sponsored by the American Academy of Pediatrics. Cost: $1.95. Discounted set of policies available. To order call 1 800 433-9016.

Measles/Prevention and Control
World Health

Measles Eradication: Recommendations from a Meeting Cosponsored by the World Health Organization, the Pan American Health Organization, and CDC. *Morbid Mortal Weekly Report*. 1997;46(no. RR-11). Sponsored by the Centers for Disease Control and Prevention. Cost: $1. To order call US Govt Printing Office 202 783-3238.

Medical Records

Improving Patient Records. *Practice-Related Report of the AMA Council on Scientific Affairs*. 1992. Sponsored by the American Medical Association, Council on Scientific Affairs. Cost: free. To order call Nancy Nolan, AMA, 312 464-5046.

Medical Waste

Medical Waste. *Infect Control Hosp Epidemiol.* 1992;13:38-48. 11pp. 60refs. Sponsored by the Society for Healthcare Epidemiology of America. Cost: free. To order visit our website at medscape.com/shea. Available on the Internet at medscape.com/shea. Key terms: defining and characterizing waste; public health implications of waste; real vs perceived health risks; microbiological quality of hospital waste vs household waste; public health and occupational risks.

Medicare

Medicare, Position Statement. 1993. Sponsored by the American Geriatrics Society. Cost: free. To order call AGS 212 308-1414.

Medicare
Reimbursement Mechanisms

Physician Reimbursement Under Medicare, Position Statement. 1993. Sponsored by the American Geriatrics Society. Cost: free. To order call AGS 212 308-1414.

Melanoma
Skin Neoplasms

Melanoma Surgical Practice Guidelines. *Oncology.* 1997;11(9). 6pp. 13refs. Sponsored by the Society of Surgical Oncology. Cost: call 516 424-8900 x316. To order write Oncology, PRR, Inc, 17 Prospect St, Huntington, NY 11743. Key terms: melanoma.

Melanoma/Diagnosis
Skin Neoplasms/Diagnosis

Diagnosis and Treatment of Early Melanoma. *NIH Consensus Development Conference Statement.* 1992;10(1):1-26[Conf. No. 88]. 27pp. Sponsored by the National Institutes of Health. Cost: free copy. To order call 1 888 644-2667. Available on the Internet at consensus.nih.gov.

Melanoma/Therapy
Skin Neoplasms/Therapy

Guidelines of Care for Malignant Melanoma. *J Am Acad Derm.* 1993;28:638-641. 4pp. 15refs. Sponsored by the American Academy of Dermatology. Cost: free copy. To order call Alice Bell 847 330-0230 x333. Available on the Internet at aad.org. Key terms: melanoma; diagnosis; drug therapy; surgery; biopsy.

Meningococcal Infections/
Prevention and Control
Antibiotic Prophylaxis

Control and Prevention of Meningococcal Disease and Control and Prevention of Serogroup C Meningococcal Disease: Evaluation and Management of Suspected Outbreaks. *Morbid Mortal Weekly Report.* 1997;46(no. RR-5). Sponsored by the Centers for Disease Control and Prevention. Cost: $1. To order call US Govt Printing Office 202 783-3238.

Meningomyelocele/Surgery
Meningocele/Surgery

Meningocele or Myelomeningocele Repair. 1993. Sponsored by the American Association of Neurological Surgeons. To order call AANS 847 692-9500.

Menisci, Tibial

Tear, Meniscus of the Knee (Medial and/or Lateral). *Clinical Policies.* 1996. 6pp. 30refs. Sponsored by the American Academy of Orthopaedic Surgeons, North American Spine Society. Cost: $50 (set of 15) for nonmembers. To order call 1 800 626-6276. Key terms: knee pain; thigh muscle atrophy; tear; meniscus of the knee; American Academy of Orthopaedic Surgeons.

Menopause

Management of Menopause. 1993. 7pp. 24refs. Sponsored by the American Society for Reproductive Medicine. Cost: $1. To order call ASRM Publication Department 205 978-5000.

Mental Competency
Resuscitation Orders

Decisions Near the End of Life. *JAMA.* 1992;267:2229-2233. 5pp. Sponsored by the American Medical Association, Council on Ethical and Judicial Affairs. Cost: free copy. To order call AMA 312 464-5223.

Mental Disorders

Altered Mental States. 1998. 16pp. 17refs. Sponsored by the American Medical Directors Association. Cost: $8. To order call 1 800 876-2632 or 410 740-9743.

Mental Disorders Diagnosed in Childhood

Disorders Usually First Diagnosed in Infancy, Childhood, or Adolescence. *Treatments of Psychiatric Disorders, Second Edition, Volume I.* 1995;Section 2. 322pp. 1032refs. Sponsored by the American Psychiatric Association. Cost: $250 for 2-volume set. To order call 1 800 368-5777 order #SPCT8700. Key terms: TPD; disorders; treatment.

Mental Disorders/Diagnosis

Practice Guideline for the Psychiatric Evaluation of Adults. *Am J Psych.* 1995;152(suppl):11. 33pp. 58refs. Sponsored by the American Psychiatric Association. Cost: $22.50. To order call 1 800 368-5777 order #SPCT2304. Key terms: evaluation; adults.

Mental Disorders/Drug Therapy
Mental Disorders/Therapy

General Considerations in Psychiatric Treatment. *Treatments of Psychiatric Disorders, Second Edition, Volume I.* 1995;Section 1. 90pp. 274refs. Sponsored by the American Psychiatric Association. Cost: $250 for 2-volume set. To order call 1 800 368-5777 order #SPCT8700. Key terms: TPD; disorders; treatment.

Mental Health Services
Mental Disorders/Etiology

Mental Health and the Elderly, Position Statement. 1993. Sponsored by the American Geriatrics Society. Cost: free. To order call AGS 212 308-1414.

Metabolic Detoxification, Drug

Detoxification: Principles and Protocols. *Topics in Addiction Medicine: Topics 2 (1997).* 1997. Sponsored by the American Society of Addiction Medicine. Cost: $20. To order call ASAM 1 800 844-8948. Available free on the Internet at asam.org (Public Policies). Key terms: alcoholism; detoxification; addictions.

Middle Ear Ventilation/Methods
Tympanic Membrane/Surgery

Myringotomy and Tympanostomy Tubes. *Clinical Indicators Compendium.* 1999. 1pp. 20refs. Sponsored by the American Academy of Otolaryngology-Head and Neck Surgery. Cost: $10 AAO-HNS members, $15 nonmembers. To order write to AAO-HNS, 1 Prince St, Alexandria, VA 22314. Key terms: tubes; tympanostomy; middle ear; otitis media; hearing loss.

Migraine/Drug Therapy

Management of Migraine Headache. Four Guidelines. 1999. Sponsored by the American Academy of Family Physicians. To order call 1 800 944-0000. Available on the Internet at aafp.org/clinical/.

Minority Groups
Tuberculosis/Prevention and Control

Prevention and Control of Tuberculosis in US Communities with At-Risk Minority Populations. *Morbid Mortal Weekly Report.* 1992;41(no. RR-5):1-11. 12pp. Sponsored by the Centers for Disease Control and Prevention. Cost: $1. To order call US Govt Printing Office 202 783-3238.

Molar/Surgery
Tooth Extraction

Removal of Third Molars. *NIH Consensus Development Conference Statement.* 1979;2(21):65-68[Conf. No. 21]. 5pp. Sponsored by the National Institutes of Health. Cost: free copy. To order call 1 888 644-2667. Available on the Internet at consensus.nih.gov.

Monitoring, Intraoperative/Standards
Nervous System/Physiopathology

Assessment: Intraoperative Neurophysiology. *Neurol.* 1990;40:1644-1646. 3pp. Sponsored by the American Academy of Neurology. Cost: individual statements are free. To order call AAN Member Service Center 1 800 879-1960. Available on the Internet at aan.com.

Monitoring, Physiologic

Standards for Basic Anesthetic Monitoring. *ASA Standards, Guidelines and Statements.* 1998;2-3. 2pp. Sponsored by the American Society of Anesthesiologists. Cost: free copy. To order call ASA 847 825-5586. Available on the Internet at asahq.org. Key terms: oxygenation; ventilation; circulation; body temperature.

Mood Disorders/Therapy

Mood Disorders. *Treatments of Psychiatric Disorders, Second Edition, Volume I.* 1995;Section 6. 285pp. 1018refs. Sponsored by the American Psychiatric Association. Cost: $250 for 2-volume set. To order call 1 800 368-5777 order #SPCT8700. Key terms: TPD; disorders; treatment.

Motor Activity
Sleep Disorders/Physiopathology

Practice Parameters for the Use of Actigraphy in the Clinical Assessment of Sleep Disorders. *Sleep.* 1995;18:285-287. 3pp. 1ref. Sponsored by the American Academy of Sleep Medicine. Cost: $30 + s/h for a complete set of current AASM Guidelines. To order call AASM 507 287-6006. Key terms: actigraphy; insomnia; movement; physiologic monitoring; sleep.

Mouth Diseases/Etiology
Antineoplastic Agents/Adverse Effects

Oral Complications of Cancer Therapies: Diagnosis, Prevention, and Treatment. *NIH Consensus Development Conference Statement.* 1989;7(7):1-11[Conf. No. 73]. 12pp. Sponsored by the National Institutes of Health. Cost: free copy. To order call 1 888 644-2667. Available on the Internet at consensus.nih.gov.

Mouth Neoplasms

Screening for Oral Cancer. *Guide to Clinical Preventive Services, 2nd Ed.* 1996. Sponsored by the US Preventive Services Task Force. To order call Williams & Wilkins 1 800 638-0672.

Mouth Neoplasms/
Prevention and Control
Pharyngeal Neoplasms/
Prevention and Control

Preventing and Controlling Oral and Pharyngeal Cancer Recommendations from a National Strategic Planning Conference. 1998. 47(no. RR-14). Sponsored by the Centers for Disease Control and Prevention. To order call US Govt Printing Office 202 783-3238. Available on the Internet at cdc.gov/mmwr/mmwr_rr.html.

Movement

Guidelines for Safe Movement. *The Osteoporosis Report.* 1997. 5pp. Sponsored by the National Osteoporosis Foundation. Cost: free copy. To order fax Fulfillment Department, NOF, 202 223-2237. Available on the Internet at nof.org. Key terms: posture; movement; activity; do/don'ts.

Mucocutaneous Lymph Node Syndrome/Diagnosis
Mucocutaneous Lymph Node Syndrome/Therapy

Diagnosis and Therapy of Kawasaki Disease in Children. *Circulation.* 1993;87:1776-1780. 5pp. Sponsored by the American Heart Association. Cost: free copy. To order call 1 800 242-8721 (US only) or write to: American Heart Association, Public Inquiries, 7272 Greenville Ave, Dallas TX 75231-4596.

Multiple Chemical Sensitivity/Etiology

Idiopathic Environmental Intolerances. *J Allergy Clin Immun.* 1999;103:36-40, Position Statement No. 35. 5pp. 100refs. Sponsored by the American Academy of Allergy, Asthma, and Immunology. Cost: free copy. To order call 414 272-6071. Available on the Internet at aaaai.org/professional/physicianreference/positionstatements/default.stm.

Multiple Sclerosis/Etiology
Stress, Psychological/Complications
Wounds and Injuries/Complications

The Relationship of MS to Physical Trauma and Psychological Stress. *Neurol.* 1999;52:1737-1745. 9pp. 66refs. Sponsored by the American Academy of Neurology. Cost: individual statements are free. To order call AAN Member Service Center 1 800 879-1960. Available on the Internet at aan.com.

Mumps/Prevention and Control

Mumps Prevention. *Morbid Mortal Weekly Report.* 1989;38:388-400. 13pp. Sponsored by the Centers for Disease Control and Prevention. Cost: $1. To order call US Govt Printing Office 202 783-3238.

Musculoskeletal Diseases/Diagnosis
Physical Examination

Guidelines for the Initial Evaluation of the Adult Patient with Acute Musculoskeletal Symptoms. *Arthritis Rheum.* 1996;39(1):1-8. 8pp. 41refs. Sponsored by the American College of Rheumatology. To order call 404 633-3777. Available free on the Internet at rheumatology.org. Key terms: musculoskeletal; pain; arthritis; tendinitis; rheumatic.

Mycobacterium Infections/Diagnosis Laboratory Techniques and Procedures

Levels of Laboratory Services for Mycobacterial Disease. *Amer Rev Resp Dis*. 1983;128:1. Sponsored by the American Thoracic Society. Cost: $4. To order send check payable to American Thoracic Society, 1740 Broadway, New York, NY 10019-4374; for credit card orders, call 212 315-8863.

Mycobacterium Tuberculosis/ Immunology Tuberculosis/Prevention and Control

Development of New Vaccines for Tuberculosis Recommendations of the Advisory Council for the Elimination of Tuberculosis (ACET). *Morbid Mortal Weekly Report*. 1998;47(no. RR-13). Sponsored by the Centers for Disease Control and Prevention. Cost: $1. To order call US Govt Printing Office 202 783-3238. Available on the Internet at cdc.gov/epo/mmwr/review/ind98_rr.html.

Mycobacterium, Infectious, Atypical

Diagnosis and Treatment of Disease Due to Non-Tuberculous Mycobacteria. *Amer Rev Resp Dis*. 1990;142:4. Sponsored by the American Thoracic Society. Cost: $4. To order send check payable to American Thoracic Society, 1740 Broadway, New York, NY 10019-4374; for credit card orders, call 212 315-8863.

Myelography

ACR Standard for the Performance of Myelography and Cisternography. 1998. 3pp. 14refs. Sponsored by the American College of Radiology. Cost: $25 (ACR nonmembers). To order call ACR Dept of Quality Assurance 703 716-7592. Available free on the Internet at acr.org. Key terms: spinal cord; evaluation; myelography; cisternography.

Myelography

Myelography. 1993. Sponsored by the American Association of Neurological Surgeons. To order call AANS 847 692-9500.

Myocardial Infarction/Drug Therapy Fibrinolytic Agents/Therapeutic Use

Thrombolysis for Evolving Myocardial Infarction. *Ann Intern Med*. 1985;103:463-469. 7pp. Sponsored by the American College of Physicians. To order call ACP Clinical Efficacy Assessment Project 1 800 523-1546.

Myocardial Infarction/ Prevention and Control Aspirin/Therapeutic Use

Aspirin Prophylaxis for the Primary Prevention of Myocardial Infarctions. *Guide to Clinical Preventive Services, 2nd Ed*. 1996. Sponsored by the US Preventive Services Task Force. To order call Williams & Wilkins 1 800 638-0672.

Myocardial Infarction/Therapy

ACC/AHA Guidelines for the Management of Patients with Acute Myocardial Infarction. *J Am Coll Cardiol*. 1996;28. 104pp. 787refs. Sponsored by the American College of Cardiology, American Heart Association. Cost: free copy. To order call Educational Services Department 1 800 257-4740.

Myocardial Infarction/Therapy

Guidelines for the Early Management of Patients with Acute Myocardial Infarction. *Circulation*. 1996;94:2341-2350. 10pp. 787refs. Sponsored by the American Heart Association, American College of Cardiology. Cost: free copy. To order call 1 800 242-8721 (US only) or write to: American Heart Association, Public Inquiries, 7272 Greenville Ave, Dallas TX 75231-4596.

Myocardial Revascularization Postoperative Care

Optimal Risk Factor Management in Patients after Coronary Revascularization. *Circulation*. 1994;90(6):3125-3133. 8pp. 73refs. Sponsored by the American Heart Association. Cost: free copy. To order call 1 800 242-8721 (US only) or write to: American Heart Association, Public Inquiries, 7272 Greenville Ave, Dallas TX 75231-4596.

Myocardium/Metabolism Tomography, Emission-Computed/Methods

Application of Positron Emission Tomography in the Heart. *JAMA*. 1988;259:2438-2445. 8pp. Sponsored by the American Medical Association, Council on Scientific Affairs. Cost: free. To order call Nancy Nolan, AMA, 312 464-5046.

Myoma Infertility

Myomas and Reproductive Dysfunction. 1992. 6pp. 30refs. Sponsored by the American Society for Reproductive Medicine. Cost: $1. To order call ASRM Publication Department 205 978-5000.

Nail Disorders/Therapy

Nail Disorders. *J Am Acad Derm.* 1996;34:529-533. 5pp. 14refs. Sponsored by the American Academy of Dermatology. Cost: free copy. To order call Alice Bell 847 330-0230 x333. Available on the Internet at aad.org. Key terms: nail diseases; diagnosis; therapy.

Nasal Fracture
Orbital Fractures

Septal Fracture. *Clinical Indicators Compendium.* 1999. Sponsored by the American Academy of Otolaryngology-Head and Neck Surgery. Cost: $10 AAO-HNS members, $15 nonmembers. To order write to AAO-HNS, 1 Prince St, Alexandria, VA 22314. Key terms: closed reduction; nasal trauma; septal fracture.

Nasal Septum/Surgery

Septoplasty. *Clinical Indicators Compendium.* 1999. 24pp. 20refs. Sponsored by the American Academy of Otolaryngology-Head and Neck Surgery. Cost: $10 AAO-HNS members, $15 nonmembers. To order write to AAO-HNS, 1 Prince St, Alexandria, VA 22314. Key terms: airway obstruction; nose; polyps; septal perforation; septum.

Neonatal Abstinence Syndrome

Neonatal Drug Withdrawal. *Pediatr.* 1998;101(6):1079-1088. 9pp. 107refs. Sponsored by the American Academy of Pediatrics. Cost: $1.95. Discounted set of policies available. To order call 1 800 433-9016.

Neoplasm Recurrence, Local

Local Regional Recurrence and Salvage Surgery (10 variants). 1996. 15pp. 23refs. Sponsored by the American College of Radiology. Cost: Vols. 1 & 2 $25 each (ACR members); $75/set (ACR nonmembers). To order call ACR Appropriateness Criteria™ 703 716-7583 x7596. Available free on the Internet at acr.org/f-appcrit.html. Key terms: breast neoplasms; local recurrence; salvage mastectomy.

Neoplasms/Diagnosis
Mass Screening

Cancer Screening Overview. 1996. 6pp. Sponsored by the National Cancer Institute. To order call 1 800 4CA-NCER. Also available on the Internet, at http://cancernet.nci.nih.gov.

Neoplasms/Metabolism
Tomography,
Emission-Computed/Methods

Positron Emission Tomography in Oncology. *JAMA.* 1988;259:2126-2131. 6pp. Sponsored by the American Medical Association, Council on Scientific Affairs. Cost: free. To order call Nancy Nolan, AMA, 312 464-5046.

Neoplasms/Radionuclide Imaging
Fludeoxyglucose F 18/Diagnostic Use

Procedure Guideline for Tumor Imaging Using F-18 FDG. *J Nuclear Med.* 1998;39:1302-1305. 4pp. 13refs. Sponsored by the Society of Nuclear Medicine. Cost: free. To order call Bill Uffelman 703 708-9000. Available on the Internet at snm.org. Key terms: positron imaging of malignant disease; fluoride radioisotopes; neoplasm; routine diagnostic tests radionuclide imaging.

Nephrostomy, Percutaneous

ACR Standard for the Performance of Percutaneous Nephrostomy (PCN). 1995. 4pp. 8refs. Sponsored by the American College of Radiology. Cost: $25 (ACR nonmembers). To order call ACR Dept of Quality Assurance 703 716-7592. Available free on the Internet at acr.org. Key terms: kidney disease; percutaneous; nephrostomy.

Nephrostomy, Percutaneous

Credentialing Criteria: Percutaneous Nephrostomy. *JVIR.* 1989;2:59-65. 7pp. Sponsored by the Society of Cardiovascular and Interventional Radiology. Cost: free copy. To order call SCVIR 703 691-1805.

Nerve Block

Nerve Block, Somatic or Sympathetic, with Injection of Diagnostic or Treatment Agent. 1993. Sponsored by the American Association of Neurological Surgeons. To order call AANS 847 692-9500.

Nerve Block/Diagnosis
Neural Conduction

Consensus Criteria for the Diagnosis of Partial Conduction Block. *Muscle Nerve.* 1999;8(suppl):S225-S229. 5pp. 11refs. Sponsored by the American Association of Electrodiagnostic Medicine. Cost: $10 members, $20 nonmembers. To order write AAEM, 421 First Avenue SW, #300E, Rochester, MN 55902. Key terms: conduction block; temporal dispersion.

Nervous System/Ultrasonography

ACR Standard for the Performance of the Pediatric Neurosonology Examination. 1999. 3pp. 8refs. Sponsored by the American College of Radiology. Cost: $25 (ACR nonmembers). To order call ACR Dept of Quality Performance 703 716-7592. Available free on the Internet at acr.org. Key terms: neurologic testing; ultrasound; pediatric; brain.

Nervous System Diseases/Diagnosis
Posture/Physiology

Assessment: Posturography. *Neurol.* 1993;43:1261-1264. 4pp. 45refs. Sponsored by the American Academy of Neurology. Cost: individual statements are free. To order call AAN Member Service Center 1 800 879-1960. Available on the Internet at aan.com.

Nervous System Diseases/Etiology
Vaccination/Adverse Effects

Assessment: Neurologic Risk of Immunization. *Neurol.* 1999;52:1546-1552. 7pp. 30refs. Sponsored by the American Academy of Neurology. Cost: individual statements are free. To order call AAN Member Service Center 1 800 879-1960. Available on the Internet at aan.com.

Nervous System Diseases/Psychology
Neuropsychological Tests

Assessment: Neuropsychological Testing of Adults: Considerations for Neurologists. *Neurol.* 1996;47:592-599. 8pp. 57refs. Sponsored by the American Academy of Neurology. Cost: individual statements are free. To order call AAN Member Service Center 1 800 879-1960. Available on the Internet at aan.com.

Nervous System Diseases/Therapy
Plasmapheresis

Assessment of Plasmapheresis. *Neurol.* 1996;47:840-843. 4pp. 33refs. Sponsored by the American Academy of Neurology. Cost: individual statements are free. To order call AAN Member Service Center 1 800 879-1960. Available on the Internet at aan.com.

Nervous System Diseases/Therapy
Plasmapheresis

Utility of Therapeutic Plasmapheresis for Neurological Disorders. *NIH Consensus Development Conference Statement.* 1986;6(4):1-7[Conf. No. 56]. 8pp. Sponsored by the National Institutes of Health. Cost: free copy. To order call 1 888 644-2667. Available on the Internet at consensus.nih.gov.

Neurofibromatosis I/Therapy
Skin Neoplasms/Therapy

Neurofibromatosis Type 1. *J Am Acad Derm.* 1997;37:625-630. 6pp. 19refs. Sponsored by the American Academy of Dermatology. Cost: free copy. To order call Alice Bell 847 330-0230 x333. Available on the Internet at aad.org. Key terms: genetics; diagnosis; complications; therapy.

Neurologic Examination
Sex Disorders/Diagnosis

Assessment: Neurological Evaluation of Male Sexual Dysfunction. *Neurol.* 1995;45:2287-2292. 6pp. 77refs. Sponsored by the American Academy of Neurology. Cost: individual statements are free. To order call AAN Member Service Center 1 800 879-1960. Available on the Internet at aan.com.

Neurology
Clinical Protocols/Standards

Practice Parameters: Neurologic Evaluation. *Neurol.* 1990;40:871. 1pp. 6refs. Sponsored by the American Academy of Neurology. Cost: individual statements are free. To order call AAN Member Service Center 1 800 879-1960. Available on the Internet at aan.com.

Neurology
Thermography

Assessment: Thermography in Neurologic Practice. *Neurol.* 1990;40:523-525. 3pp. 54refs. Sponsored by the American Academy of Neurology. Cost: individual statements are free. To order call AAN Member Service Center 1 800 879-1960. Available on the Internet at aan.com.

Neuroma, Acoustic/Surgery
Neurosurgical Procedures/Methods

Acoustic Neuroma Surgery. *Clinical Indicators Compendium.* 1999. 3pp. Sponsored by the American Academy of Otolaryngology-Head and Neck Surgery. Cost: $10 AAO-HNS members, $15 nonmembers. To order write to AAO-HNS, 1 Prince St, Alexandria, VA 22314. Key terms: hearing; balance; nerve; neuroma; acoustic.

Nicotine
Substance-Related Disorders/Therapy

Guidelines for the Diagnosis and Treatment of Nicotine Dependence. 1994. 16pp. Sponsored by the American Medical Association, Division of Health Science. Cost: $2. To order call Georgianne Cooper, AMA 312 464-5066.

Nose/Abnormalities

Nasal Deformity. 1993. 6pp. Sponsored by the American Society of Plastic and Reconstructive Surgeons. Cost: $25 members, $55 nonmembers (full set of guidelines), + s/h. To order call 1 800 766-4955.

Nuclear Medicine

ACR Standard for the Diagnostic Medical Physics Performance Monitoring of Nuclear Medicine Equipment. 1998. Sponsored by the American College of Radiology. Cost: $25 (ACR nonmembers). To order call ACR Dept of Quality Assurance 703 716-7592. Available free on the Internet at acr.org. Key terms: nuclear medicine; equipment monitoring; medical physics.

Nuclear Medicine
Practice Guidelines

Guidelines for Guideline Development. *J Nuclear Med*. 1996;37:878-881. 4pp. 12refs. Sponsored by the Society of Nuclear Medicine. Cost: free. To order call Bill Uffelman 703 708-9000. Available on the Internet at snm.org. Key terms: guideline; methodology; consensus; expert opinion; procedures.

Nuclear Warfare

Prevention of Nuclear War, Position Statement. 1993. Sponsored by the American Geriatrics Society. Cost: free. To order call AGS 212 308-1414.

Nursing (see Breast Feeding)

Nursing Care/Standards
Respiratory Tract Diseases/Nursing

Standards of Nursing Care for Adult Patients with Pulmonary Dysfunction. *Amer Rev Resp Dis*. 1991;144:1. Sponsored by the American Thoracic Society. Cost: $4. To order send check payable to American Thoracic Society, 1740 Broadway, New York, NY 10019-4374; for credit card orders, call 212 315-8863.

Nutrition
Women

Nutrition and Women. *ACOG Educational Bulletin*. 1996;229. 12pp. 40refs. Sponsored by the American College of Obstetricians and Gynecologists. Cost: free copy. Set of Bulletins $70 + s/h ACOG members, $125 + s/h nonmembers. One-year subscription $55 member, $65 nonmember. To order single copy, call ACOG Resource Center 202 863-2518; to order set or subscription, call ACOG Distribution Center, 1 800 762-2264. Available on the Internet to members only at acog.org. Key terms: women's health.

Obesity

Localized Adiposity. 1993. 6pp. Sponsored by the American Society of Plastic and Reconstructive Surgeons. Cost: $25 members, $55 nonmembers (full set of guidelines), + s/h. To order call 1 800 766-4955.

Obesity/Complications

Health Implications of Obesity. *NIH Consensus Development Conference Statement*. 1985;5(9):1-7[Conf. No. 49]. 8pp. Sponsored by the National Institutes of Health. Cost: free copy. To order call 1 888 644-2667. Available on the Internet at consensus.nih.gov.

Obesity/Diagnosis

Screening for Obesity. *Guide to Clinical Preventive Services, 2nd Ed*. 1996. Sponsored by the US Preventive Services Task Force. To order call Williams & Wilkins 1 800 638-0672.

Obesity/Prevention and Control
Weight Loss

Methods for Voluntary Weight Loss and Control. *NIH Technology Assessment Conference Statement*. 1992. 29pp. Sponsored by the National Institutes of Health. Cost: free copy. To order call 1 888 644-2667. Available on the Internet at consensus.nih.gov.

Obesity/Therapy

Treatment of Obesity in Adults. *JAMA*. 1988;260:2547-2551. 5pp. Sponsored by the American Medical Association, Council on Scientific Affairs. Cost: free. To order call Nancy Nolan, AMA, 312 464-5046.

Obesity/Therapy
Weight Loss

Bariatric Practice Guidelines. 1998. 1pp. Sponsored by the American Society of Bariatric Physicians. Cost: single copies free, 200/$40. To order call the American Society of Bariatric Physicians 303 770-2526 x10. Key terms: obesity; weight; overweight; preventive health; fat.

Obesity, Morbid/Therapy
Prostheses and Implants

Garren Gastric Bubble for Morbid Obesity. *JAMA*. 1986;256:3282-3284. 3pp. Sponsored by the American Medical Association, Diagnostic and Therapeutic Technology Assessment Program. Cost: free copy. DATTA subscription available. To order call AMA Department of Technology Assessment 312 464-4531.

Obsessive-Compulsive
Disorder/Therapy

Practice Parameters for the Assessment and Treatment of Children and Adolescents with Obsessive-Compulsive Disorder. *J Am Acad Child Adol Psych*. 1998;37(suppl). 18pp. 189refs. Sponsored by the American Academy of Child and Adolescent Psychiatry. Cost: $10 AACAP members/$20 others. To order call Communications Department 202 966-7300. Key terms: obsessive; compulsive; anxiety; tic; cognitive.

Obstetrical Delivery/Methods
Physician's Practice Patterns

Operative Vaginal Delivery. *ACOG Technical Bulletin*. 1994;196. 6pp. 15refs. Sponsored by the American College of Obstetricians and Gynecologists. Cost: free copy. Set of Bulletins $70 + s/h ACOG members, $125 + s/h nonmembers. One-year subscription $55 member, $65 nonmember. To order single copy, call ACOG Resource Center 202 863-2518; to order set or subscription, call ACOG Distribution Center, 1 800 762-2264. Available on the Internet to members only at acog.org. Key terms: vacuum extraction; OB forceps; extraction: obstetrical; shoulder dystocia.

Occupational Health Services
Health Facilities

Guidelines for Employee Health Services in Health Care Institutions. *J Occupation Med*. 1986;28:518-523. 6pp. Sponsored by the American College of Occupational and Environmental Medicine. Cost: free copy. To order call Marianne Dreger 847 228-6850 x18.

Occupational Medicine
Occupational Health

Scope of Occupational and Environmental Health Programs and Practice. *J Occupation Med*. 1992;34:436-440. 5pp. 13refs. Sponsored by the American College of Occupational and Environmental Medicine. Cost: free copy. To order call Marianne Dreger 847 228-6850 x18.

Onychomycosis/Diagnosis, Therapy

Superficial Mycotic Infections of the Skin: Onychomycosis. *J Am Acad Derm*. 1996;34:116-121. 6pp. 42refs. Sponsored by the American Academy of Dermatology. Cost: free copy. To order call Alice Bell 847 330-0230 x333. Available on the Internet at aad.org. Key terms: onychomycosis; diagnosis; therapy.

Oocyte Donation

Guidelines for Gamete Donation. 1993. 9pp. Sponsored by the American Society for Reproductive Medicine. Cost: $5. To order call ASRM Publication Department 205 978-5000.

Operating Room Technicians

Statement on Surgical Assistants. *ACOG Committee Opinion*. 1994;145. 1pp. Sponsored by the American College of Obstetricians and Gynecologists. Cost: free copy. Set of Opinions $55 + s/h ACOG members, $75 + s/h nonmembers. One-year subscription $55 member, $65 nonmember. To order single copy, call ACOG Resource Center 202 863-2518; to order set or subscription, call ACOG Distribution Center, 1 800 762-2264. Available on the Internet to members only at acog.org.

Opioid-Related Disorders/Therapy

Effective Medical Treatment of Opiate Addiction. *NIH Consensus Development Conference Statement*. 1997;15(6):1[Conf. No. 108]. 38pp. 66refs. Sponsored by the National Institutes of Health. Cost: free copy. To order call 1 888 644-2667. Available on the Internet at consensus.nih.gov.

Oral Health
Women's Health

Oral Health Care Series: Women's Oral Health Issues. 1995. 43pp. 108refs. Sponsored by the American Dental Association. Cost: $8 ADA members, $12 nonmembers. To order call ADA Dept of Salable Materials 1 800 947-4776.

Oropharyngeal Neoplasms/Surgery
Mouth Neoplasms/Surgery

Oropharyngeal and Oral Cavity Cancer Surgical Practice Guidelines. *Oncology*. 1997;11(8). 4pp. 6refs. Sponsored by the Society of Surgical Oncology. Cost: call 516 424-8900 x316. To order write Oncology, PRR, Inc, 17 Prospect St, Huntington NY 11743. Key terms: oropharyngeal.

Orthodontic Appliances
Sleep Apnea Syndromes/Therapy

Practice Parameters for the Treatment of Snoring and Obstructive Sleep Apnea with Oral Appliances. *Sleep*. 1995;18(6):511-513. 3pp. 3refs. Sponsored by the American Academy of Sleep Medicine. Cost: $30 + s/h for a complete set of current AASM Guidelines. To order call AASM 507 287-6006. Key terms: activator appliances; orthodontic appliances; removable; sleep apnea syndromes; snoring.

Orthopedic Fixation Devices/Therapy
Leg Length Inequality/Therapy

Distraction/Compression Osteosynthesis with the Ilizarov Device. *JAMA*. 1992;268:2717-2724. 8pp. Sponsored by the American Medical Association, Diagnostic and Therapeutic Technology Assessment Program. Cost: free copy. DATTA subscription available. To order call AMA Department of Technology Assessment 312 464-4531.

Osteoarthritis
Knee Joint

Osteoarthritis (Arthrosis) of the Knee (Degenerative Joint Disease). *Clinical Policies*. 1996. 7pp. 14refs. Sponsored by the American Academy of Orthopaedic Surgeons, North American Spine Society. Cost: $50 (set of 15) for nonmembers. To order call 1 800 626-6276. Key terms: osteoarthritis of the knee; arthrosis of the knee.

Osteoarthritis, Hip

Osteoarthritis of the Hip. *Clinical Policies*. 1996. 5pp. 9refs. Sponsored by the American Academy of Orthopaedic Surgeons, North American Spine Society. Cost: $50 (set of 15) for nonmembers. To order call 1 800 626-6276. Key terms: osteoarthrosis of hip; hip pain; joint cartilage degeneration; American Academy of Orthopaedic Surgeons.

Osteoarthritis, Hip/Therapy

Guidelines for the Medical Management of Osteoarthritis Part I: Osteoarthritis of Hip. *Arthritis Rheum*. 1995;38:1535-1540. 6pp. 40refs. Sponsored by the American College of Rheumatology. To order call 404 633-3777. Available free on the Internet at rheumatology.org. Key terms: osteoarthritis; joint; musculoskeletal; drugs; therapy.

Osteoporosis

Osteoporosis. 1999. 12pp. 16refs. Sponsored by the American Medical Directors Association. Cost: $8. To order call 1 800 876-2632 or 410 740-9743.

Osteoporosis

Osteoporosis. *ACOG Educational Bulletin*. 1998;246. 9pp. 30refs. Sponsored by the American College of Obstetricians and Gynecologists. Cost: free copy. Set of Bulletins $70 + s/h ACOG members, $125 + s/h nonmembers. One-year subscription $55 member, $65 nonmember. To order single copy, call ACOG Resource Center 202 863-2518; to order set or subscription, call ACOG Distribution Center, 1 800 762-2264. Available on the Internet to members only at acog.org. Key terms: osteoporosis; postmenopausal; bone density; ERT.

Osteoporosis, Postmenopausal

Clinical Practice Guidelines for the Treatment of Postmenopausal Osteoporosis. 1996. 27pp. 33refs. Sponsored by the American Association of Clinical Endocrinologists. To order call AACE 904 353-7878. Key terms: osteoporosis; post menopausal; bone disease; low bone mass; calcium.

Osteoporosis, Postmenopausal/Diagnosis

Screening for Postmenopausal Osteoporosis. *Guide to Clinical Preventive Services, 2nd Ed*. 1996. Sponsored by the US Preventive Services Task Force. To order call Williams & Wilkins 1 800 638-0672.

Osteoporosis, Postmenopausal/Diagnosis
Mass Screening

Screening for Osteoporosis. *Ann Intern Med*. 1990;112:516-528. 13pp. 123refs. Sponsored by the American College of Physicians. To order call ACP Clinical Efficacy Assessment Project 1 800 523-1546.

Osteoporosis/Prevention and Control

Physician's Guide to Prevention and Treatment of Osteoporosis. *Self-Published NOF (National Osteoporosis Foundation)*. 1998. 30pp. Sponsored by the National Osteoporosis Foundation. Cost: free copy. To order fax Fulfillment Department, NOF, 202 223-2237. Available on the Internet at nof.org. Key terms: osteoporosis; diagnosis; risk factors; testing; recommendations.

Otorhinolaryngologic Surgical Procedures
Pharynx/Surgery
Uvula/Surgery

Uvulopalatopharyngoplasty. *Clinical Indicators Compendium*. 1999. 1pp. 20refs. Sponsored by the American Academy of Otolaryngology-Head and Neck Surgery. Cost: $10 AAO-HNS members, $15 nonmembers. To order write to AAO-HNS, 1 Prince St, Alexandria, VA 22314. Key terms: snoring; sleep apnea; uvulectomy; polysomnography; airway.

Ovarian Neoplasms

Cancer of the Ovary. *ACOG Educational Bulletin*. 1998;250. 10pp. 20refs. Sponsored by the American College of Obstetricians and Gynecologists. Cost: free copy. Set of Bulletins $70 + s/h ACOG members, $125 + s/h nonmembers. One-year subscription $55 member, $65 nonmember. To order single copy, call ACOG Resource Center 202 863-2518; to order set or subscription, call ACOG Distribution Center, 1 800 762-2264. Available on the Internet to members only at acog.org. Key terms: ovarian neoplasm.

Ovarian Neoplasms/Diagnosis

Screening for Ovarian Cancer. *Guide to Clinical Preventive Services, 2nd Ed*. 1996. Sponsored by the US Preventive Services Task Force. To order call Williams & Wilkins 1 800 638-0672.

Ovarian Neoplasms/Diagnosis
Medical Oncology/Methods

Ovarian Cancer Surgical Practice Guidelines. *Oncology*. 1997;11(6):896. 7pp. 15refs. Sponsored by the Society of Surgical Oncology. Cost: call 516 424-8900 x316. To order write Oncology, PRR, Inc, 17 Prospect St, Huntington NY 11743. Key terms: ovarian.

Ovariectomy

Prophylactic Oophorectomy. *ACOG Technical Bulletin*. 1987;111. 4pp. 26refs. Sponsored by the American College of Obstetricians and Gynecologists. Cost: free copy. Set of Bulletins $70 + s/h ACOG members, $125 + s/h nonmembers. One-year subscription $55 member, $65 nonmember. To order single copy, call ACOG Resource Center 202 863-2518; to order set or subscription, call ACOG Distribution Center, 1 800 762-2264. Available on the Internet to members only at acog.org. Key terms: ovarian neoplasms: D&C.

Ovulation Induction/Methods
Menotropins/Therapeutic Use

Induction of Ovulation with Human Menopausal Gonadotropins. 1993. 7pp. 40refs. Sponsored by the American Society for Reproductive Medicine. Cost: $1. To order call ASRM Publication Department 205 978-5000.

Pacemaker, Artificial

Indications for the Use of Permanently Implanted Cardiac Pacemakers. *Am Coll Surg Bulletin*. 1986;71:26. 1pp. Sponsored by the American College of Surgeons. Cost: free copy. To order call ACS Socioeconomic Affairs Dept 312 664-4050.

Pain, Intractable/Drug Therapy
Neoplasms/Complications

Management of Cancer Pain. *AHCPR*. 1994;Publication No. 94-0592. 257pp. 526refs. Sponsored by the Federal Agency for Health Care Policy and Research. To order call AHCPR Clearinghouse 1 800 358-9295.

Pain, Intractable/Radiotherapy
Bone Neoplasms/Radiotherapy

Procedure Guideline for Bone Pain Treatment. *J Nuclear Med*. 1996;37:881-884. 4pp. 9refs. Sponsored by the Society of Nuclear Medicine. Cost: free. To order call Bill Uffelman 703 708-9000. Available on the Internet at snm.org. Key terms: bone metastasis; radiation therapy; strontium-89; palliation; neoplasm metastasis.

Pain/Drug Therapy

The Management of Chronic Pain in Older Persons. *J Am Ger Soc*. 1998;46:635-651. 27pp. Sponsored by the American Geriatrics Society. Cost: free. To order call AGS 212 308-1414.

Pain/Therapy

Acute Pain Management: Operative or Medical Procedures and Trauma. *AHCPR*. 1992;Publication No. 92-0032. 145pp. 127refs. Sponsored by the Federal Agency for Health Care Policy and Research. To order call AHCPR Clearinghouse 1 800 358-9295.

Pain/Therapy

Integrated Approach to the Management of Pain. *NIH Consensus Development Conference Statement*. 1986;6(3):1-8[Conf. No. 55]. 9pp. Sponsored by the National Institutes of Health. Cost: free copy. To order call 1 888 644-2667. Available on the Internet at consensus.nih.gov.

Pain/Therapy

Practice Guidelines for Chronic Pain Management. *Anesthesiology*. 1997;86:995-1004. 10pp. 376refs. Sponsored by the American Society of Anesthesiologists. Cost: free copy. To order call ASA 847 825-5586. Available on the Internet at asahq.org. Key terms: chronic pain management.

Pain/Therapy
Insomnia/Therapy

The Integration of Behavioral and Relaxation Approaches into the Treatment of Chronic Pain and Insomnia. *NIH Technology Assessment Conference Statement*. 1995. 34pp. 86refs. Sponsored by the National Institutes of Health. Cost: free copy. To order call 1 888 644-2667. Available on the Internet at consensus.nih.gov.

Pamphlets
Spouse Abuse

Domestic Violence. *ACOG Technical Bulletin*. 1995;209. 10pp. 38refs. Sponsored by the American College of Obstetricians and Gynecologists. Cost: free copy. Set of Bulletins $70 + s/h ACOG members, $125 + s/h nonmembers. One-year subscription $55 member, $65 nonmember. To order single copy, call ACOG Resource Center 202 863-2518; to order set or subscription, call ACOG Distribution Center, 1 800 762-2264. Available on the Internet to members only at acog.org.

Pancreas Transplantation

Isolated Pancreas Transplantation. *AHCPR Health Technology Review*. 1995;No. 11 (AHCPR Publication No. 95-0068). 15pp. 45refs. Sponsored by the Federal Agency for Health Care Policy and Research. To order call AHCPR Clearinghouse 1 800 358-9295.

Pancreas Transplantation/Physiology

Pancreas Transplants. *JAMA*. 1991;265:510-514. 5pp. 39refs. Sponsored by the American Medical Association, Diagnostic and Therapeutic Technology Assessment Program. Cost: free copy. DATTA subscription available. To order call AMA Department of Technology Assessment 312 464-4531.

Pancreatic Neoplasms/Diagnosis

Screening for Pancreatic Cancer. *Guide to Clinical Preventive Services, 2nd Ed*. 1996. Sponsored by the US Preventive Services Task Force. To order call Williams & Wilkins 1 800 638-0672.

Pancreatic Neoplasms/Epidemiology
Pancreatic Neoplasms/Diagnosis

Epidemiology, Diagnosis, and Treatment of Pancreatic Ductal Adenocarcinoma. *Gastroenterology*. 1999. Sponsored by the American Gastroenterological Association. Cost: free. To order call AGA 301 643-2055.

Pancreatic Neoplasms/Surgery

Pancreatic Cancer Surgical Practice Guidelines. *Oncology*. 1997;11(7):1074. 6pp. 12refs. Sponsored by the Society of Surgical Oncology. Cost: call 516 424-8900 x316. To order write Oncology, PRR, Inc, 17 Prospect St, Huntington NY 11743. Key terms: pancreatic.

Panic Disorder/Drug Therapy

Practice Guideline for the Treatment of Patients with Panic Disorder. 1998. Sponsored by the American Psychiatric Association. Cost: $22.50. To order call 1 800 368-5777 order #SPCT2311.

Panic Disorder/Therapy

Treatment of Panic Disorder. *NIH Consensus Development Conference Statement*. 1991;9(2):1-24[Conf. No. 85]. 25pp. Sponsored by the National Institutes of Health. Cost: free copy. To order call 1 888 644-2667. Available on the Internet at consensus.nih.gov.

Papillomavirus, Human
Tumor Virus Infections/Therapy

Warts: HPV. *J Am Acad Derm*. 1995;32:98-103. 5pp. 24refs. Sponsored by the American Academy of Dermatology. Cost: free copy. To order call Alice Bell 847 330-0230 x333. Available on the Internet at aad.org. Key terms: human papillomavirus; diagnosis; therapy; patient education.

Paracentesis
Ultrasonography

ACR Standard for Imaging-Guided Percutaneous Drainage or Aspiration of Fluid Collections in Adults. 1999. 5pp. 9refs. Sponsored by the American College of Radiology. Cost: $25 (ACR nonmembers). To order call ACR Dept of Quality Assurance 703 716-7592. Available free on the Internet at acr.org. Key terms: transthoracic; catheter drainage; percutaneous; abscess; fluid collections.

Paranasal Sinuses/Surgery
Surgical Procedures, Endoscopic

Endoscopic Sinus Surgery, Adult. *Clinical Indicators Compendium.* 1999. 1pp. 20refs. Sponsored by the American Academy of Otolaryngology-Head and Neck Surgery. Cost: $10 AAO-HNS members, $15 nonmembers. To order write to AAO-HNS, 1 Prince St, Alexandria, VA 22314.

Paranasal Sinuses/Surgery
Surgical Procedures, Endoscopic

Endoscopic Sinus Surgery, Pediatric. *Clinical Indicators Compendium.* 1999. Sponsored by the American Academy of Otolaryngology-Head and Neck Surgery. Cost: $10 AAO-HNS members, $15 nonmembers. To order write to AAO-HNS, 1 Prince St, Alexandria, VA 22314.

Parathyroid Glands/
Radionuclide Imaging

ACR Standard for the Performance of Parathyroid Scintigraphy. 1999. 5pp. 4refs. Sponsored by the American College of Radiology. Cost: $25 (ACR nonmembers). To order call ACR Dept of Quality Assurance 703 716-7592. Available free on the Internet at acr.org. Key terms: nuclear medicine; parathyroid; scintigraphy.

Parathyroid Glands/
Radionuclide Imaging
Radiopharmaceuticals/Diagnostic Use

Procedure Guideline for Parathyroid Scintigraphy. *J Nuclear Med.* 1998;39:1111-1114. 4pp. 16refs. Sponsored by the Society of Nuclear Medicine. Cost: free. To order call Bill Uffelman 703 708-9000. Available on the Internet at snm.org. Key terms: parathyroid; scintigraphy; hyperparathyroidism; routine diagnostic tests; radionuclide imaging.

Parenteral Nutrition

Peripheral Parenteral Nutrition. *Diagnostic and Therapeutic Technology Assessment (DATTA).* 1995. 16pp. 60refs. Sponsored by the American Medical Association, Diagnostic and Therapeutic Technology Assessment Program. Cost: free copy. DATTA subscription available. To order call AMA Department of Technology Assessment 312 464-4531.

Parenteral Nutrition, Total

Statement on Guidelines for Total Parenteral Nutrition. *Digest Dsi Sci.* 1989;34:489-496. 8pp. 70refs. Sponsored by the American Gastroenterological Association. Cost: free. To order call AGA 301 654-2055.

Parenteral Nutrition, Total
Surgical Procedures, Operative

Perioperative Parenteral Nutrition. *Ann Intern Med.* 1987;107:252-253. 2pp. Sponsored by the American College of Physicians. To order call ACP Clinical Efficacy Assessment Project 1 800 523-1546.

Parkinson's Disease/Drug Therapy
Antiparkinson Agents/Therapy

Practice Parameters: Initial Therapy of Parkinson's Disease. *Neurol.* 1993;43:1296-1297. 2pp. Sponsored by the American Academy of Neurology. Cost: individual statements are free. To order call AAN Member Service Center 1 800 879-1960. Available on the Internet at aan.com.

Parotid Neoplasms/Surgery

Parotid Gland Cancer Surgical Practice Guidelines. *Oncology.* 1997;11(8). 5pp. 5refs. Sponsored by the Society of Surgical Oncology. Cost: call 516 424-8900 x316. To order write Oncology, PRR, Inc, 17 Prospect St, Huntington NY 11743. Key terms: parotid.

Particle Accelerators
Radioisotopes/Diagnostic Use

Cyclotrons and Radiopharmaceuticals in Positron Emission Tomography. *JAMA.* 1988;259:1854-1860. 7pp. Sponsored by the American Medical Association, Council on Scientific Affairs. Cost: free. To order call Nancy Nolan, AMA, 312 464-5046.

Pathology, Clinical/Methods
Pathology, Clinical/standards

Stat Testing? A Guideline for Meeting Clinician Turnaround Time Requirements. *Am J Clin Pathol.* 1996;105:671-675. 5pp. 13refs. Sponsored by the American Society of Clinical Pathologists. Cost: free copy. To order call Felicia Nelson 312 738-1336 x1350. Key terms: stat testing; turnaround time; urgent care.

Patient Care Team
Interprofessional Relations

Guidelines for Implementing Collaborative Practice. 1995. 41pp. Sponsored by the American College of Obstetricians and Gynecologists. Cost: $20 + s/h members; $30 + s/h nonmembers per copy. To order call ACOG Distribution Center, 1 800 762-2264. Available on the Internet to members only at acog.org. Key terms: interprofessional relations; advanced practice nurses; NPs; CNMs.

Patient Isolation
Infection Control
Hospitals/Standards

The Revised CDC Guidelines for Isolation Precautions in Hospitals: Implications for Pediatrics. *Pediatr.* 1998;101(3):e13. 4pp. 2refs. Sponsored by the American Academy of Pediatrics. Cost: $1.95. Discounted set of policies available. To order call 1 800 433-9016.

Pelvic Neoplasms/Diagnosis
Magnetic Resonance Imaging

Magnetic Resonance Imaging of the Abdomen and Pelvis. *JAMA.* 1989;261:420-433. 14pp. Sponsored by the American Medical Association, Council on Scientific Affairs. Cost: free. To order call Nancy Nolan, AMA, 312 464-5046.

Pelvic Pain/Therapy

Chronic Pelvic Pain. *ACOG Technical Bulletin.* 1996;223. 9pp. 46refs. Sponsored by the American College of Obstetricians and Gynecologists. Cost: free copy. Set of Bulletins $70 + s/h ACOG members, $125 + s/h nonmembers. One-year subscription $55 member, $65 nonmember. To order single copy, call ACOG Resource Center 202 863-2518; to order set or subscription, call ACOG Distribution Center, 1 800 762-2264. Available on the Internet to members only at acog.org.

Peptic Ulcer/Diagnosis
Endoscopy

Role of Endoscopy in the Management of the Patient with Peptic Ulcer Disease: Guidelines for Clinical Application. *Gastrointest Endosc.* 1988;34(suppl):21s-22s. 2pp. 20refs. Sponsored by the American Society for Gastrointestinal Endoscopy. Cost: free. To order call ASGE 978 526-8330.

Perimetry/Methods
Vision Disorders/Diagnosis

Automated Perimetry Ophthalmic Procedure Assessment. *Ophthalmology.* 1996;103:1144-1165. 22pp. 15refs. Sponsored by the American Academy of Ophthalmology. Cost: $11 members, $16 nonmembers. AAO members first copy free upon publication. To order call AAO Order Dept 415 561-8540. Key terms: eye; perimetry; automated perimetry.

Perinatal Care
Practice Guidelines

Guidelines for Perinatal Care. 1997. 4th Edition. 411pp. Sponsored by the American College of Obstetricians and Gynecologists. Cost: $60/copy + $12 s/h (one book). To order call ACOG Distribution Center 1 800 762-2264. Key terms: prenatal care; postnatal care; intrapartum care.

Periodontal Diseases/
Prevention and Control
Tooth Diseases/Prevention and Control

Counseling to Prevent Dental and Periodontal Disease. *Guide to Clinical Preventive Services, 2nd Ed.* 1996. Sponsored by the US Preventive Services Task Force. To order call Williams & Wilkins 1 800 638-0672.

Peripheral Nerves/Surgery

Peripheral Nerve Surgery. 1993. Sponsored by the American Association of Neurological Surgeons. To order call AANS 847 692-9500.

Peripheral Vascular Diseases/Diagnosis

Screening for Peripheral Arterial Disease. *Guide to Clinical Preventive Services, 2nd Ed.* 1996. Sponsored by the US Preventive Services Task Force. To order call Williams & Wilkins 1 800 638-0672.

Peripheral Vascular Diseases/Ultrasonography

ACR Standard for the Performance of the Peripheral Arterial Ultrasound Examination (Revised). 1997. 4pp. 16refs. Sponsored by the American College of Radiology. Cost: $25 (ACR nonmembers). To order call ACR Dept of Quality Assurance 703 716-7592. Available free on the Internet at acr.org. Key terms: arterial; ultrasound; Doppler; vascular; occlusive disease.

Peripheral Vascular Diseases/Ultrasonography Venous Insufficiency/Ultrasonography

ACR Standard for the Performance of the Peripheral Venous Ultrasound Examination (Revised). 1997. 3pp. 13refs. Sponsored by the American College of Radiology. Cost: $25 (ACR nonmembers). To order call ACR Dept of Quality Assurance 703 716-7592. Available free on the Internet at acr.org. Key terms: peripheral; venous; ultrasound; thrombosis; Doppler.

Peritoneal Dialysis/Standards

NKF-DOQI Clinical Practice Guidelines for Peritoneal Dialysis Adequacy. 1997. 224pp. 137refs. Sponsored by the National Kidney Foundation. Cost: $13. To order call NKF 1 800 622-9010. Key terms: hemodialysis adequacy; peritoneal dialysis adequacy; vascular access; anemia management; executive summaries.

Persistent Vegetative State

Practice Parameter: Assessment and Management of Patients in the Persistent Vegetative State. *Neurol.* 1995;45:1015-1018. 4pp. 2refs. Sponsored by the American Academy of Neurology. Cost: individual statements are free. To order call AAN Member Service Center 1 800 879-1960. Available on the Internet at aan.com.

Personality Disorders/Drug Therapy Personality Disorders/Therapy

Personality Disorders. *Treatments of Psychiatric Disorders, Second Edition, Volume II.* 1995;Section 11. 150pp. 381refs. Sponsored by the American Psychiatric Association. Cost: $250 for 2-volume set. To order call 1 800 368-5777 order #SPCT8700. Key terms: TPD; disorders; treatment.

Personnel Administration, Hospital HIV Seropositivity

Revised: Management of Health Care Workers Who Are Infected with HIV, HBV, HCV, and Other Blood-borne Pathogens. *Infect Control Hosp Epidemiol.* 1997;18:349. 15pp. 111refs. Sponsored by the Society for Healthcare Epidemiology of America. Cost: free. To order visit our website at medscape.com/shea. Available on the Internet at medscape.com/shea. Key terms: practice issues; disclosure issues; exposure management; testing issues.

Pertussis Vaccine

Acellular Pertussis Vaccine: Recommendations for Use as the Initial Series in Infants and Children. *Pediatr.* 1997;99(2):282-288. 7pp. 21refs. Sponsored by the American Academy of Pediatrics. Cost: $1.95. Discounted set of policies available. To order call 1 800 433-9016.

Pertussis Vaccine/Adverse Effects Convulsions/Etiology

Pertussis Immunization: Family History of Convulsions and Use of Antipyretics—Supplementary ACIP Statement. *Morbid Mortal Weekly Report.* 1987;36:281-282. 2pp. Sponsored by the Centers for Disease Control and Prevention. Cost: $1. To order call US Govt Printing Office 202 783-3238.

Pharyngitis/Diagnosis Streptococcal Infections

Diagnosis and Management of Group A Streptococcal Pharyngitis: A Practice Guideline. *Clin Inf Dis.* 1997;25:574. 10pp. 58refs. Sponsored by the Infectious Diseases Society of America. To obtain request from medical library or download via the Internet. Available on the Internet at idsociety.org/practice.

Pharyngitis/Microbiology Streptococcal Infections/Diagnosis

Throat Cultures and Rapid Tests for Diagnosis of Group A Streptococcal Pharyngitis. *Ann Intern Med.* 1986;105:892-896. 5pp. Sponsored by the American College of Physicians. To order call ACP Clinical Efficacy Assessment Project 1 800 523-1546.

Phenylketonuria/Diagnosis

Screening for Phenylketonuria. *Guide to Clinical Preventive Services, 2nd Ed.* 1996. Sponsored by the US Preventive Services Task Force. To order call Williams & Wilkins 1 800 638-0672.

Phenytoin
Substance Withdrawal Syndrome

The Role of Phenytoin in the Management of Alcohol Withdrawal. *Topic in Addiction Medicine: Topics 1 (1995).* 1994. 16pp. 61refs. Sponsored by the American Society of Addiction Medicine. Cost: $20. To order call PMDS 301 656-3920. Available free on the Internet at asam.org (Practice Guidelines). Key terms: alcoholism; addiction; withdrawal.

Phototherapy
Sleep Disorders/Therapy

Practice Parameters for the Use of Light Therapy in the Treatment of Sleep Disorders. 1999;5:641-660. 20pp. 49refs. Sponsored by the American Academy of Sleep Medicine. Cost: $30 + s/h for a complete set of current AASM Guidelines. To order call AASM 507 287-6006. Key terms: practice guidelines; practice parameters; light therapy; sleep disorders; delayed sleep phase syndrome.

Physical Fitness
Mass Screening

Recommendations for Cardiovascular Screening, Staffing and the Emergency Policies at Health/Fitness Facilities. *Circulation.* 1998;97:2283-2293. 11pp. 31refs. Sponsored by the American Heart Association. Cost: free copy. To order call 1 800 242-8721 (US only) or write to: American Heart Association, Public Inquiries, 7272 Greenville Ave, Dallas TX 75231-4596.

Physician's Practice Patterns

Preferred Practice Patterns. *Minnesota Academy of Otolaryngology-Head and Neck Surgery.* 1995. 16pp. 70refs. Sponsored by the Minnesota Academy of Otolaryngology-Head & Neck Surgery. Cost: $25. To order e-mail: rlampright@mnmeo.org. Available on the Internet at mnmeo.org.

Physician's Practice Patterns
Spine/Surgery
Surgical Procedures, Laparoscopic

Guidelines for Collaborative Practice in Endoscopic/Thoracoscopic Spinal Surgery for the General Surgeon. *SAGES Publication.* 1996;19. 6pp. 3refs. Sponsored by the Society of American Gastrointestinal and Endoscopic Surgeons. Cost: free. To order call 310 314-2404. Available on the Internet at sages.org. Key terms: surgery; collaborative; spine; endoscopy; thoracoscopy.

Physician's Role
Domestic Violence

Physicians and Domestic Violence. *JAMA.* 1992;267:3190-3193. 4pp. Sponsored by the American Medical Association, Council on Ethical and Judicial Affairs. Cost: free copy. To order call AMA 312 464-5223.

Physician's Role
Long-Term Care

Physician's Role in the Long-Term Care Facility, Position Statement. 1993. Sponsored by the American Geriatrics Society. Cost: free. To order call AGS 212 308-1414.

Physician's Role
Substance-Related Disorders/
Prevention and Control

Tobacco, Alcohol, and Other Drugs: The Role of the Pediatrician in Prevention and Management of Substance Abuse. *Pediatr.* 1998;101(1):125-128. 4pp. 28refs. Sponsored by the American Academy of Pediatrics. Cost: $1.95. Discounted set of policies available. To order call 1 800 433-9016.

Physicians
Public Relations

Guidelines for Relationships with Industry. *ACOG Committee Opinion.* 1997;182. 2pp. 2refs. Sponsored by the American College of Obstetricians and Gynecologists. Cost: free copy. Set of Opinions $55 + s/h ACOG members, $75 + s/h nonmembers. One-year subscription $55 member, $65 nonmember. To order single copy, call ACOG Resource Center 202 863-2518; to order set or subscription, call ACOG Distribution Center, 1 800 762-2264. Available on the Internet to members only at acog.org. Key terms: ob/gyn; ethics: medical; conflict of interest.

Piedra/Diagnosis
Piedra/Therapy

Superficial Mycotic Infections of the Skin: Piedra. *J Am Acad Derm.* 1996;34:122-124. 3pp. 7refs. Sponsored by the American Academy of Dermatology. Cost: free copy. To order call Alice Bell 847 330-0230 x333. Available on the Internet at aad.org. Key terms: piedra; diagnosis; therapy.

Pit and Fissure Sealants/Therapeutic Use
Dental Caries/Prevention and Control

Dental Sealants in the Prevention of Tooth Decay. *NIH Consensus Development Conference Statement.* 1983;4(11):1-18[Conf. No. 40]. 19pp. Sponsored by the National Institutes of Health. Cost: free copy. To order call 1 888 644-2667. Available on the Internet at consensus.nih.gov.

Pituitary Neoplasms/Surgery
Hypophysectomy

Hypophysectomy, Transsphenoidal or Transnasal, for Hypophysectomy or Excision of Pituitary Tumor. 1993. Sponsored by the American Association of Neurological Surgeons. To order call AANS 847 692-9500.

Placenta/Pathology
Pathology, Surgical/Methods

Practice Guideline for Examination of the Placenta. *Arch Path Lab Med.* 1997;121:449-476. 28pp. 66refs. Sponsored by the College of American Pathologists. Cost: reprints: free. To order call CAP 1 800 323-4040 x7378. Key terms: placenta; fetus; obstetrics; pathology.

Placenta/Pathology
Placental Diseases/Diagnosis

Placental Pathology. *ACOG Committee Opinion.* 1993;125. 2pp. 1ref. Sponsored by the American College of Obstetricians and Gynecologists. Cost: free copy. Set of Opinions $55 + s/h ACOG members, $75 + s/h nonmembers. One-year subscription $55 member, $65 nonmember. To order single copy, call ACOG Resource Center 202 863-2518; to order set or subscription, call ACOG Distribution Center, 1 800 762-2264. Available on the Internet to members only at acog.org. Key terms: placental diseases; placental pathology.

Plague/Prevention and Control
Vaccination/Standards

Prevention of Plague. *Morbid Mortal Weekly Report.* 1996;45(no. RR-14). Sponsored by the Centers for Disease Control and Prevention. Cost: $1. To order call US Govt Printing Office 202 783-3238.

Plasmapheresis

Therapeutic Apheresis, Part I. Background and Nonrenal Indications. *Diagnostic and Therapeutic Technology Assessment (DATTA).* 1996. 20pp. 27refs. Sponsored by the American Medical Association, Diagnostic and Therapeutic Technology Assessment Program. Cost: free copy. DATTA subscription available. To order call AMA Department of Technology Assessment 312 464-4531.

Plasmapheresis
Kidney Diseases

Therapeutic Apheresis, Part II. Renal Indications. *Diagnostic and Therapeutic Technology Assessment (DATTA).* 1996. 13pp. 18refs. Sponsored by the American Medical Association, Diagnostic and Therapeutic Technology Assessment Program. Cost: free copy. DATTA subscription available. To order call AMA Department of Technology Assessment 312 464-4531.

Pleural Effusion/Etiology
Punctures

Diagnostic Thoracentesis in Pleural Biopsy. *Clinical Policies.* 1991;103:799-802. 3pp. Sponsored by the American College of Physicians. Cost: $15 (set of 15) for nonmembers. To order call ACP Clinical Efficacy Assessment Project 1 800 523-1546.

Pneumococcal Infections/Drug Therapy
Antibiotics/Therapeutic Use

Therapy for Children with Invasive Pneumococcal Infections. *Pediatr.* 1997;99(2):289-299. 11pp. 82refs. Sponsored by the American Academy of Pediatrics. Cost: $1.95. Discounted set of policies available. To order call 1 800 433-9016.

Pneumococcal Infections/
Prevention and Control
Bacterial Vaccines

Prevention of Pneumococcal Disease. *Morbid Mortal Weekly Report.* 1997;46(no. RR-8). Sponsored by the Centers for Disease Control and Prevention. Cost: $1. To order call US Govt Printing Office 202 783-3238.

Pneumoconiosis/Etiology
Silicic Acid/Adverse Effects

Health Effects of Tremolite. *Amer Rev Resp Dis.* 1990;142:6. Sponsored by the American Thoracic Society. Cost: $4. To order send check payable to American Thoracic Society, 1740 Broadway, New York, NY 10019-4374; for credit card orders, call 212 315-8863.

Pneumonia, Pneumocystis carinii/ Prevention and Control
HIV Infections/Prevention and Control
AIDS-Related Opportunistic Infections/ Prevention and Control

1995 Revised Guidelines for Prophylaxis Against Pneumocystis carinii Pneumonia for Children Infected with or Perinatally Exposed to Human Immunodeficiency Virus. *Morbid Mortal Weekly Report*. 1995;44(no. RR-4). Sponsored by the Centers for Disease Control and Prevention. Cost: $1. To order call US Govt Printing Office 202 783-3238.

Pneumonia/Diagnosis
Pneumonia/Therapy

Guidelines for the Initial Management of Adults with Community-Acquired Pneumonia: Diagnosis, Assessment of Severity, and Initial Antimicrobial Therapy. *Amer Rev Resp Dis*. 1993;148:5. Sponsored by the American Thoracic Society. Cost: $6. To order send check payable to American Thoracic Society, 1740 Broadway, New York, NY 10019-4374; for credit card orders, call 212 315-8863.

Poliomyelitis/Prevention and Control
Poliovirus Vaccine, Oral

Poliomyelitis Prevention: Revised Recommendations for Use of Inactivated and Live Oral Poliovirus Vaccines. *Pediatr*. 1999;103(1):172-172. 2pp. Sponsored by the American Academy of Pediatrics. Cost: $1.95. Discounted set of policies available. To order call 1 800 433-9016.

Poliomyelitis/Prevention and Control
Poliovirus Vaccine/ Administration and Dosage

Poliomyelitis Prevention in the United States: Introduction of a Sequential Vaccination Schedule of Inactivated Poliovirus Vaccine Followed by Oral Poliovirus Vaccine. *Morbid Mortal Weekly Report*. 1997;46(no. RR-3). Sponsored by the Centers for Disease Control and Prevention. Cost: $1. To order call US Govt Printing Office 202 783-3238.

Polychlorinated Biphenyls/Analysis
Milk, Human/Chemistry
Breast Feeding

PCBs in Breast Milk. *Pediatr*. 1997;94(1):122-123. 2pp. 13refs. Sponsored by the American Academy of Pediatrics. Cost: $1.95. Discounted set of policies available. To order call 1 800 433-9016.

Polysomnography/Instrumentation
Sleep Apnea Syndromes/Diagnosis

Practice Parameters for the Use of Portable Recording in the Assessment of Obstructive Sleep Apnea. *Sleep*. 1994;17(4):372-377. 6pp. 1ref. Sponsored by the American Academy of Sleep Medicine. Cost: $30 + s/h for a complete set of current AASM Guidelines. To order call AASM 507 287-6006. Key terms: durable medical equipment; equipment and supplies; guidelines; monitoring; physiologic-polysomnography.

Polysomnography/Methods
Sleep Apnea Syndromes/Diagnosis

Practice Parameters for the Indications for Polysomnography and Related Procedures. *Sleep*. 1997;20(6):406-422. 17pp. 12refs. Sponsored by the American Academy of Sleep Medicine. Cost: $30 + s/h for a complete set of current AASM Guidelines. To order call AASM 507 287-6006. Key terms: polysomnography; sleep apnea syndrome; sleep disorders; narcolepsy; parasomnias.

Polytetrafluoroethylene/ Therapeutic Use
Urinary Incontinence

Teflon Injections for Urinary Incontinence. *JAMA*. 1993;269:2975-2980. 6pp. Sponsored by the American Medical Association, Diagnostic and Therapeutic Technology Assessment Program. Cost: free copy. DATTA subscription available. To order call AMA Department of Technology Assessment 312 464-4531.

Population Surveillance/Methods
HIV Infections/Epidemiology

Surveillance of Pediatric HIV Infection. *Pediatr*. 1998;101:315. 5pp. 32refs. Sponsored by the American Academy of Pediatrics. Cost: $1.95. Discounted set of policies available. To order call 1 800 433-9016.

Portasystemic Shunt, Surgical

Transjugular Intrahepatic Portosystemic Shunt (TIPS). *JAMA*. 1995;273(23):1824-1830. 7pp. 28refs. Sponsored by the American Medical Association, Diagnostic and Therapeutic Technology Assessment Program. Cost: free copy. DATTA subscription available. To order call AMA Department of Technology Assessment 312 464-4531.

Positive Pressure Respiration/Standards
Sleep Apnea Syndromes/Therapy

Indications and Standards for the Use of Nasal Continuous Positive Airway Pressure (CPAP) in Sleep Apnea Syndromes. *Am J Respir Crit Care Med*. 1994;150:6. Sponsored by the American Thoracic Society. Cost: $6. To order send check payable to American Thoracic Society, 1740 Broadway, New York, NY 10019-4374; for credit card orders, call 212 315-8863.

Postpartum Hemorrhage

Postpartum Hemorrhage. *ACOG Educational Bulletin*. 1998;243. 8pp. 35refs. Sponsored by the American College of Obstetricians and Gynecologists. Cost: free copy. Set of Bulletins $70 + s/h ACOG members, $125 + s/h nonmembers. One-year subscription $55 member, $65 nonmember. To order single copy, call ACOG Resource Center 202 863-2518; to order set or subscription, call ACOG Distribution Center, 1 800 762-2264. Available on the Internet to members only at acog.org. Key terms: uterine hemorrhage; puerperal disorders.

Posture
Sudden Infant Death/
Prevention and Control

Positioning and Sudden Infant Death Syndrome (SIDS). *Pediatr*. 1996;98(suppl):1216-1218. 3pp. 9refs. Sponsored by the American Academy of Pediatrics. Cost: $1.95. Discounted set of policies available. To order call 1 800 433-9016.

Practice Guidelines

Executive Summaries of the NKF-DOQI Clinical Practice Guidelines. 1997. 120pp. Sponsored by the National Kidney Foundation. Cost: $15. To order call NKF 1 800 622-9010. Key terms: hemodialysis adequacy; peritoneal dialysis adequacy; vascular access; anemia management; executive summaries.

Practice Guidelines

Guideline Implementation. 1998. 24pp. 18refs. Sponsored by the American Medical Directors Association. Cost: $10. To order call 1 800 876-2632 or 410 740-9743.

Practice Guidelines

One Set Color Laminated Clinical Guidelines. 1996. Sponsored by the American Academy of Orthopaedic Surgeons, North American Spine Society. Cost: $50 AAOS member, $100 nonmember. To order call 1 800 626-6276. Available on the Internet free at guidelines.gov.

Practice Guidelines

One Set Color Paper Clinical Guidelines. 1996. Sponsored by the American Academy of Orthopaedic Surgeons, North American Spine Society. Cost: $30 AAOS member, $60 nonmember. To order call 1 800 626-6276. Available on the Internet free at guidelines.gov.

Practice Guidelines

Practice Guideline Book. 1996. 361pp. Sponsored by the American Psychiatric Association. Cost: $54.95 (hardcover), $43.50 (paperback). To order call 1 800 368-5777 (hardcover order #SPCT2305; paperback order #SPTC2306). Key terms: eating disorders; major depressive disorder; bipolar disorder; substance abuse disorders; psychiatric evaluation.

Practice Guidelines
Eating Disorders

Practice Guideline for Eating Disorders. *Am J Psych*. 1993;150(2):212-28. 16pp. 182refs. Sponsored by the American Psychiatric Association. Cost: $22.50. To order call 1 800 368-5777 order #SPCT2300. Key terms: eating disorders.

Practice Guidelines
Nuclear Medicine

Society of Nuclear Medicine Procedure Guidelines Manual 1999. 1999. 165pp. Sponsored by the Society of Nuclear Medicine. Cost: $35 + s/h. To order call Bill Uffelman 703 708-9000. Available on the Internet at snm.org. Key terms: guidelines diagnostic tests; radionuclide imaging; radiation therapy; procedures.

Practice Guidelines
Pancreatitis/Therapy

Practice Guidelines in Acute Pancreatitis. *Am J Gastroenterol*. 1997;92:377-386. 10pp. 38refs. Sponsored by the American College of Gastroenterology. Cost: free copy. To order call ACG 703 820-7400.

Preanesthestic Medication
Preoperative Care/Standards

Basic Standards for Preanesthesia Care. *ASA Standards, Guidelines and Statements.* 1998;2. 1pp. Sponsored by the American Society of Anesthesiologists. Cost: free copy. To order call ASA 847 825-5586. Available on the Internet at asahq.org. Key terms: preanesthesia care.

Pre-Eclampsia/Diagnosis

Screening for Preeclampsia. *Guide to Clinical Preventive Services, 2nd Ed.* 1996. Sponsored by the US Preventive Services Task Force. To order call Williams & Wilkins 1 800 638-0672.

Pregnancy
Vaccination

Immunization During Pregnancy. *ACOG Technical Bulletin.* 1991;160. 10pp. 44refs. Sponsored by the American College of Obstetricians and Gynecologists. Cost: free copy. Set of Bulletins $70 + s/h ACOG members, $125 + s/h nonmembers. One-year subscription $55 member, $65 nonmember. To order single copy, call ACOG Resource Center 202 863-2518; to order set or subscription, call ACOG Distribution Center, 1 800 762-2264. Available on the Internet to members only at acog.org. Key terms: pregnancy complications; infections: prevention and control; prenatal care.

Pregnancy Complications
Epilepsy/Drug Therapy

Seizure Disorders in Pregnancy. *ACOG Educational Bulletin.* 1997;231. 8pp. 46refs. Sponsored by the American College of Obstetricians and Gynecologists. Cost: free copy. Set of Bulletins $70 + s/h ACOG members, $125 + s/h nonmembers. One-year subscription $55 member, $65 nonmember. To order single copy, call ACOG Resource Center 202 863-2518; to order set or subscription, call ACOG Distribution Center, 1 800 762-2264. Available on the Internet to members only at acog.org. Key terms: pregnancy complications; cardiovascular.

Pregnancy Complications
Lung Diseases

Pulmonary Disease in Pregnancy. *ACOG Technical Bulletin.* 1996;224. 9pp. 22refs. Sponsored by the American College of Obstetricians and Gynecologists. Cost: free copy. Set of Bulletins $70 + s/h ACOG members, $125 + s/h nonmembers. One-year subscription $55 member, $65 nonmember. To order single copy, call ACOG Resource Center 202 863-2518; to order set or subscription, call ACOG Distribution Center, 1 800 762-2264. Available on the Internet to members only at acog.org. Key terms: pregnancy complications.

Pregnancy Complications
Substance-Related Disorders

Substance Abuse in Pregnancy. *ACOG Technical Bulletin.* 1994;195. 7pp. 47refs. Sponsored by the American College of Obstetricians and Gynecologists. Cost: free copy. Set of Bulletins $70 + s/h ACOG members, $125 + s/h nonmembers. One-year subscription $55 member, $65 nonmember. To order single copy, call ACOG Resource Center 202 863-2518; to order set or subscription, call ACOG Distribution Center, 1 800 762-2264. Available on the Internet to members only at acog.org. Key terms: pregnancy complications.

Pregnancy Complications
Thyroid Diseases

Thyroid Disease in Pregnancy. *ACOG Technical Bulletin.* 1993;181. 7pp. 38refs. Sponsored by the American College of Obstetricians and Gynecologists. Cost: free copy. Set of Bulletins $70 + s/h ACOG members, $125 + s/h nonmembers. One-year subscription $55 member, $65 nonmember. To order single copy, call ACOG Resource Center 202 863-2518; to order set or subscription, call ACOG Distribution Center, 1 800 762-2264. Available on the Internet to members only at acog.org. Key terms: pregnancy complications.

Pregnancy Complications, Cardiovascular

Cardiac Disease in Pregnancy. *ACOG Technical Bulletin*. 1992;168. 8pp. 26refs. Sponsored by the American College of Obstetricians and Gynecologists. Cost: free copy. Set of Bulletins $70 + s/h ACOG members, $125 + s/h nonmembers. One-year subscription $55 member, $65 nonmember. To order single copy, call ACOG Resource Center 202 863-2518; to order set or subscription, call ACOG Distribution Center, 1 800 762-2264. Available on the Internet to members only at acog.org. Key terms: pregnancy complications; vascular.

Pregnancy Complications, Cardiovascular Hypertension

Working Group Report on High Blood Pressure in Pregnancy. *PB 95-217311*. 1991. 38pp. Sponsored by the National Heart, Lung, and Blood Institute. Cost: $19.50. To order contact the NHLBI Information Center, PO Box 30105, Bethesda, MD 20824-0105, 301 251-1222.

Pregnancy Complications, Cardiovascular/Therapy Hypertension/Therapy

Hypertension in Pregnancy. *ACOG Technical Bulletin*. 1996;219. 8pp. 59refs. Sponsored by the American College of Obstetricians and Gynecologists. Cost: free copy. Set of Bulletins $70 + s/h ACOG members, $125 + s/h nonmembers. One-year subscription $55 member, $65 nonmember. To order single copy, call ACOG Resource Center 202 863-2518; to order set or subscription, call ACOG Distribution Center, 1 800 762-2264. Available on the Internet to members only at acog.org. Key terms: pre-eclampsia; HELLP syndrome.

Pregnancy Complications, Infectious Virus Diseases

Perinatal Viral and Parasitic Infections. *ACOG Technical Bulletin*. 1993;177. 8pp. 28refs. Sponsored by the American College of Obstetricians and Gynecologists. Cost: free copy. Set of Bulletins $70 + s/h ACOG members, $125 + s/h nonmembers. One-year subscription $55 member, $65 nonmember. To order single copy, call ACOG Resource Center 202 863-2518; to order set or subscription, call ACOG Distribution Center, 1 800 762-2264. Available on the Internet to members only at acog.org. Key terms: pregnancy complications; infections: parasitic; viral; vertical transmission.

Pregnancy Complications, Infectious/Drug Therapy Antibiotics/Therapeutic Use

Antimicrobial Therapy for Obstetric Patients. *ACOG Educational Bulletin*. 1998;245. 10pp. 35refs. Sponsored by the American College of Obstetricians and Gynecologists. Cost: free copy. Set of Bulletins $70 + s/h ACOG members, $125 + s/h nonmembers. One-year subscription $55 member, $65 nonmember. To order single copy, call ACOG Resource Center 202 863-2518; to order set or subscription, call ACOG Distribution Center, 1 800 762-2264. Available on the Internet to members only at acog.org. Key terms: antibiotics; obstetrics.

Pregnancy Complications/Surgery Surgical Procedures, Laparoscopic/Standards

Guidelines for Laparoscopic Surgery During Pregnancy. *Surgical Endoscopy*. 1998;12:189-190. 2pp. 22refs. Sponsored by the Society of American Gastrointestinal and Endoscopic Surgeons. Cost: free. To order call 310 314-2404. Available on the Internet at sages.org. Key terms: surgery; laparoscopy; pregnancy.

Pregnancy Complications/Therapy Pregnancy, Prolonged

Management of Postterm Pregnancy. *ACOG Practice Patterns*. 1997;6. 6pp. 21refs. Sponsored by the American College of Obstetricians and Gynecologists. Cost: free copy. Multiples of 25: $20 + s/h member, $30 + s/h nonmember. To order single copy, call ACOG Resource Center 202 863-2518; to order set or subscription, call ACOG Distribution Center, 1 800 762-2264. Available on the Internet to members only at acog.org. Key terms: pregnancy; prolonged; labor; induced.

Pregnancy in Diabetes

Diabetes and Pregnancy. *ACOG Technical Bulletin*. 1994;200. 8pp. 47refs. Sponsored by the American College of Obstetricians and Gynecologists. Cost: free copy. Set of Bulletins $70 + s/h ACOG members, $125 + s/h nonmembers. One-year subscription $55 member, $65 nonmember. To order single copy, call ACOG Resource Center 202 863-2518; to order set or subscription, call ACOG Distribution Center, 1 800 762-2264. Available on the Internet to members only at acog.org. Key terms: pregnancy in diabetes; gestational diabetes.

Pregnancy Outcome
Ultrasonography, Prenatal

Ultrasound Screening: Implications of the RADIUS Study. *NIH Technology Assessment Conference Statement.* 1993. Sponsored by the National Institutes of Health. Cost: free copy. To order call 1 888 644-2667. Available on the Internet at consensus.nih.gov.

Pregnancy, Ectopic/Diagnosis
Pregnancy, Ectopic/Drug Therapy

Early Diagnosis and Management of Ectopic Pregnancy. 1992. 3pp. 12refs. Sponsored by the American Society for Reproductive Medicine. Cost: $1. To order call ASRM Publication Department 205 978-5000.

Pregnancy, Multiple
Prenatal Care

Special Problems of Multiple Gestation. *ACOG Educational Bulletin.* 1998;253. 11pp. 65+refs. Sponsored by the American College of Obstetricians and Gynecologists. Cost: free copy. Set of Bulletins $70 + s/h ACOG members, $125 + s/h nonmembers. One-year subscription $55 member, $65 nonmember. To order single copy, call ACOG Resource Center 202 863-2518; to order set or subscription, call ACOG Distribution Center, 1 800 762-2264. Available on the Internet to members only at acog.org. Key terms: multiple pregnancy.

Pregnancy, Tubal/Diagnosis
Methotrexate/Therapeutic Use

Medical Management of Tubal Pregnancy. *ACOG Practice Bulletin.* 1998;3. 7pp. 31refs. Sponsored by the American College of Obstetricians and Gynecologists. Cost: free copy. Set of Bulletins $70 + s/h ACOG members, $125 + s/h nonmembers. One-year subscription $55 member, $65 nonmember. To order single copy, call ACOG Resource Center 202 863-2518; to order set or subscription, call ACOG Distribution Center, 1 800 762-2264. Available on the Internet to members only at acog.org. Key terms: tubal pregnancy; ectopic pregnancy; methotrexate.

Pregnancy, Unwanted
Contraception/Methods

Counseling to Prevent Unintended Pregnancy. *Guide to Clinical Preventive Services, 2nd Ed.* 1996. Sponsored by the US Preventive Services Task Force. To order call Williams & Wilkins 1 800 638-0672.

Pregnancy/Immunology
Rh Isoimmunizations

Management of Isoimmunization in Pregnancy. *ACOG Educational Bulletin.* 1996;227. 8pp. 35refs. Sponsored by the American College of Obstetricians and Gynecologists. Cost: free copy. Set of Bulletins $70 + s/h ACOG members, $125 + s/h nonmembers. One-year subscription $55 member, $65 nonmember. To order single copy, call ACOG Resource Center 202 863-2518; to order set or subscription, call ACOG Distribution Center, 1 800 762-2264. Available on the Internet to members only at acog.org. Key terms: Rh.

Premenopause
Delivery of Health Care

Health Maintenance for Perimenopausal Women. *ACOG Technical Bulletin.* 1995;210. 10pp. 37refs. Sponsored by the American College of Obstetricians and Gynecologists. Cost: free copy. Set of Bulletins $70 + s/h ACOG members, $125 + s/h nonmembers. One-year subscription $55 member, $65 nonmember. To order single copy, call ACOG Resource Center 202 863-2518; to order set or subscription, call ACOG Distribution Center, 1 800 762-2264. Available on the Internet to members only at acog.org. Key terms: premenopause; menopause; postmenopause; women's health services.

Premenstrual Syndrome/Therapy

Premenstrual Syndrome. *ACOG Committee Opinion.* 1995;155. 4pp. 23refs. Sponsored by the American College of Obstetricians and Gynecologists. Cost: free copy. Set of Opinions $55 + s/h ACOG members, $75 + s/h nonmembers. One-year subscription $55 member, $65 nonmember. To order single copy, call ACOG Resource Center 202 863-2518; to order set or subscription, call ACOG Distribution Center, 1 800 762-2264. Available on the Internet to members only at acog.org.

Prenatal Care

Prenatal Care. 1992. JR-05. 73pp. 383refs. Sponsored by RAND, Academic Medical Center Consortium. To order call RAND 310 393-0411 x7002. Key terms: prenatal care; appropriateness; treatment outcomes; utilization; complications.

Prenatal Care/Standards

Scope of Services for Uncomplicated Obstetric Care. *ACOG Committee Opinion*. 1996;175. 1pp. Sponsored by the American College of Obstetricians and Gynecologists. Cost: free copy. Set of Opinions $55 + s/h ACOG members, $75 + s/h nonmembers. One-year subscription $55 member, $65 nonmember. To order single copy, call ACOG Resource Center 202 863-2518; to order set or subscription, call ACOG Distribution Center, 1 800 762-2264. Available on the Internet to members only at acog.org. Key terms: reimbursement; prenatal care; delivery.

Prescriptions, Drug
Drugs, Non-Prescription

Conversion of Prescription Drugs to Over-the-Counter Designation, Position Statement. 1993. Sponsored by the American Geriatrics Society. Cost: free. To order call AGS 212 308-1414.

Prescriptions, Drug
Therapeutic Equivalency

Position Statement: Therapeutic Substitution. 1990. 2pp. Sponsored by the American College of Cardiology. Cost: free copy. To order call Educational Services Department 1 800 257-4740.

Preventive Health Services
Health Policy

Summary of Policy Recommendations for Periodic Health Examination. 1999. 14pp. Sponsored by the American Academy of Family Physicians. To order call AAFP Order Department 1 800 944-0000, order #962. Available on the Internet at aafp.org/clinical/. Key terms: health maintenance; screening; immunizations; counseling; family practice.

Preventive Medicine
Immunization Schedule

Practice Policy Statement: Adult Immunization. *Am J Prev Med*. 1998;14(2):156-158. 3pp. 17refs. Sponsored by the American College of Preventive Medicine. To order reprint address request to ACPM, 1660 L St NW, #206, Washington, DC 20036.

Preventive Medicine/Standards
Prostatic Neoplasms/
Prevention and Control

Practice Policy Statement: Screening for Prostate Cancer in American Men. *Am J Prev Med*. 1997;15:81-84. Sponsored by the American College of Preventive Medicine. To order reprint address request to ACPM, 1660 L St NW, #206, Washington, DC 20036.

Primary Health Care
Preventive Health Services

Primary and Preventive Care. *Primary Care Review*. 1997;1. 10pp. Sponsored by the American College of Obstetricians and Gynecologists. Cost: single copy available without charge; $25 copies. To order call ACOG Resource Center 202 863-2518. Available free on the Internet at acog.org. Key terms: primary health care; women's health services; primary prevention; mass screening; age factors.

Primary Prevention/Methods
Tuberculosis/Prevention and Control

Future Research in Tuberculosis: Prospects and Priorities for Elimination. *Amer Rev Resp Dis*. 1986;136:3. Sponsored by the American Thoracic Society. Cost: $4. To order send check payable to American Thoracic Society, 1740 Broadway, New York, NY 10019-4374; for credit card orders, call 212 315-8863.

Prisons
Tuberculosis/Prevention and Control

Prevention and Control of Tuberculosis in Correctional Facilities. *Morbid Mortal Weekly Report*. 1996;45(no. RR-8). Sponsored by the Centers for Disease Control and Prevention. Cost: $1. To order call US Govt Printing Office 202 783-3238.

Probability Theory
Diagnostic Tests, Routine

Probability Theory in the Use of Diagnostic Tests: Application to Critical Study of the Literature. *Ann Intern Med*. 1986;104:60-66. 7pp. Sponsored by the American College of Physicians. To order call ACP Clinical Efficacy Assessment Project 1 800 523-1546.

Professional Competence
Electrodiagnosis

Who Is Qualified to Practice Electrodiagnostic Medicine?. *Muscle Nerve*. 1999;8(suppl):S263-S265. 3pp. 5refs. Sponsored by the American Association of Electrodiagnostic Medicine. Cost: free. To order write AAEM, 421 First Avenue SW, #300E, Rochester, MN 55902. Available on the Internet at aaem.net/pdffiles/who_is_qualified.pdf. Key terms: electrodiagnostic; qualifications; needle electromyography; nerve conduction studies.

Program Development
Suicide/Prevention and Control

Programs for Prevention of Suicide Among Adolescents and Young Adults. *Morbid Mortal Weekly Report.* 1994;43(no. RR-6). Sponsored by the Centers for Disease Control and Prevention. Cost: $1. To order call US Govt Printing Office 202 783-3238.

Program Development
Tuberculosis/Prevention and Control

Recommendations of the Hospital Infection Control Practice Advisory Committee: Essential Components of a Tuberculosis Prevention and Control Program; Screening for Tuberculosis and Tuberculosis Infection in High-Risk Populations. *Morbid Mortal Weekly Report.* 1995;44(no. RR-11). Sponsored by the Centers for Disease Control and Prevention. Cost: $1. To order call US Govt Printing Office 202 783-3238.

Prostatic Diseases/Ultrasonography

ACR Standard for the Performance of the Ultrasound Examination of the Prostate (and Surrounding Structures) (Revised). 1996. 3pp. 23refs. Sponsored by the American College of Radiology. Cost: $25 (ACR nonmembers). To order call ACR Dept of Quality Assurance 703 716-7592. Available free on the Internet at acr.org. Key terms: ultrasound; prostate.

Prostatic Hyperplasia/Diagnosis
Prostatic Hyperplasia/Surgery

Benign Prostatic Hyperplasia: Diagnosis and Treatment. *AHCPR.* 1994;Publication No. 94-0582. 225pp. 324refs. Sponsored by the Federal Agency for Health Care Policy and Research. To order call AHCPR Clearinghouse 1 800 358-9295.

Prostatic Neoplasms

Locally Advanced (high risk) Prostate Cancer (6 variants). 1996. 13pp. 31refs. Sponsored by the American College of Radiology. Cost: Vols. 1 & 2 $25 each (ACR members); $75/set (ACR nonmembers). To order call ACR Appropriateness Criteria™ 703 716-7583 x7596. Available free on the Internet at acr.org/f-appcrit.html. Key terms: prostate cancer; advanced; radiotherapy; prostatectomy.

Prostatic Neoplasms

Management of Localized Prostate Cancer. 1995. 88pp. 165refs. Sponsored by the American Urological Association. Cost: $52 members, $67 nonmembers. To order write Health Policy Dept, AUA, 1120 N Charles St, Baltimore, MD, 21201. Key terms: prostatic neoplasms; prostatectomy; radiotherapy; prachytherapy; guidelines.

Prostatic Neoplasms
Brachytherapy

Permanent Source Brachytherapy for Prostate Cancer (8 variants). 1996. 15pp. 30refs. Sponsored by the American College of Radiology. Cost: Vols. 1 & 2 $25 each (ACR members); $75/set (ACR nonmembers). To order call ACR Appropriateness Criteria™ 703 716-7583 x7596. Available free on the Internet at acr.org/f-appcrit.html. Key terms: prostate cancer; brachytherapy.

Prostatic Neoplasms
Lymph Nodes

Node-Positive Prostate Cancer (3 variants). 1996. 7pp. 22refs. Sponsored by the American College of Radiology. Cost: Vols. 1 & 2 $25 each (ACR members); $75/set (ACR nonmembers). To order call ACR Appropriateness Criteria™ 703 716-7583 x7596. Available free on the Internet at acr.org/f-appcrit.html. Key terms: prostate cancer; lymph node; radiotherapy; hormone treatment.

Prostatic Neoplasms
Neoplasm Staging

Staging Evaluation for Patients with Adenocarcinoma of the Prostate (10 variants). 1996. 17pp. 46refs. Sponsored by the American College of Radiology. Cost: Vols. 1 & 2 $25 each (ACR members); $75/set (ACR nonmembers). To order call ACR Appropriateness Criteria™ 703 716-7583 x7596. Available free on the Internet at acr.org/f-appcrit.html. Key terms: prostate cancer; staging; adenocarcinoma.

Prostatic Neoplasms/Radiotherapy

Definitive External Beam Irradiation in Stage T1, T2 Carcinoma of the Prostate (9 variants). *Int J Radiat Oncol Biol Phys.* 1999;43(1):125-168. 25pp. 118refs. Sponsored by the American College of Radiology. Cost: Vols. 1 & 2 $25 each (ACR members), $75/set (ACR nonmembers). To order call ACR Appropriateness Criteria™ 703 716-7583 x7596. Available free on the Internet at acr.org/f-appcrit.html. Registration required. Key terms: prostate cancer; prostatectomy; radiotherapy.

Prostatic Neoplasms/Radiotherapy

Postradical Prostatectomy Irradiation in Carcinoma of the Prostate (11 variants). 1996. 23pp. 76refs. Sponsored by the American College of Radiology. Cost: Vols. 1 & 2 $25 each (ACR members); $75/set (ACR nonmembers). To order call ACR Appropriateness Criteria™ 703 716-7583 x7596. Available free on the Internet at acr.org/f-appcrit.html. Key terms: prostate cancer; radical prostatectomy; radiotherapy.

Prostatic Neoplasms/Radiotherapy
Radiotherapy Planning, Computer-Assisted/Methods

Treatment Planning for Clinically Localized Prostate Cancer (4 variants). 1996. 13pp. 30refs. Sponsored by the American College of Radiology. Cost: Vols. 1 & 2 $25 each (ACR members), $75/set (ACR nonmembers). To order call ACR Appropriateness Criteria™ 703 716-7583 x7596. Available free on the Internet at acr.org/f-appcrit.html. Registration required. Key terms: prostate cancer; localized; treatment planning.

Prostatic Neoplasms/Surgery

Prostate Cancer Surgical Practice Guidelines. *Oncology*. 1997;11(6):907. 6pp. 20refs. Sponsored by the Society of Surgical Oncology. Cost: call 516 424-8900 x316. To order write Oncology, PRR, Inc, 17 Prospect St, Huntington NY 11743. Key terms: prostate.

Prothrombin Time
Blood Coagulation Tests

Diagnostic Uses of the Activated Partial Thromboplastin Time and Prothrombin Time. *Ann Intern Med*. 1986;104:810-816. 7pp. Sponsored by the American College of Physicians. To order call ACP Clinical Efficacy Assessment Project 1 800 523-1546.

Psoriasis/Therapy

Guidelines of Care for Psoriasis. *J Am Acad Derm*. 1993;28:632-637. 6pp. 83refs. Sponsored by the American Academy of Dermatology. Cost: free copy. To order call Alice Bell 847 330-0230 x333. Available on the Internet at aad.org. Key terms: psoriasis; diagnosis; drug therapy; dermatologic agents; ambulatory care.

Psychology/Methods
Diabetes Mellitus/Therapy

Practical Psychology for Diabetes Clinicians. 1996. 200pp. Sponsored by the American Diabetes Association. Cost: $24.95. To order call 1 800 232-6733; online bookstore: merchant.diabetes. org. Available on the Internet at merchant.diabetes. org. Key terms: behavioral; diabetes: development; treatment; prevention.

Psychotherapy/Methods

Alternative Psychological Methods in Patient Care. *Practice-Related Report of the AMA Council on Scientific Affairs*. 1990. 19pp. 104refs. Sponsored by the American Medical Association, Council on Scientific Affairs. Cost: free. To order call Nancy Nolan, AMA, 312 464-5046.

Psychotropic Drugs/Therapeutic Use
Nursing Homes/Standards

Psychotherapeutic Medications in the Nursing Home. 1992. Sponsored by the American Geriatrics Society. Cost: free. To order call AGS 212 308-1414.

Public Health/Legislation and Jurisprudence
Tuberculosis/Prevention and Control

Tuberculosis Control Laws—United States, 1993. *Morbid Mortal Weekly Report*. 1993;42(no. RR-15). Sponsored by the Centers for Disease Control and Prevention. Cost: $1. To order call US Govt Printing Office 202 783-3238.

Puerperium
Sterilization, Tubal

Postpartum Tubal Sterilization. *ACOG Committee Opinion*. 1992;105. 1pp. Sponsored by the American College of Obstetricians and Gynecologists. Cost: free copy. Set of Opinions $55 + s/h ACOG members, $75 + s/h nonmembers. One-year subscription $55 member, $65 nonmember. To order single copy, call ACOG Resource Center 202 863-2518; to order set or subscription, call ACOG Distribution Center, 1 800 762-2264. Available on the Internet to members only at acog.org.

Pulmonary Diffusing Capacity
Respiratory Function Tests/Standards

DLCO—Recommendations for a Standard Technique. *Am J Respir Crit Care Med*. 1995;152:6. Sponsored by the American Thoracic Society. To order send check payable to American Thoracic Society, 1740 Broadway, New York, NY 10019-4374; for credit card orders, call 212 315-8863.

Pulmonary Diffusing Capacity Respiratory Function Tests/Standards

Single Breath Carbon Monoxide Diffusing Capacity (Transfer Factor). *Am J Respir Crit Care Med.* 1995;152. Sponsored by the American Thoracic Society. To order send check payable to American Thoracic Society, 1740 Broadway, New York, NY 10019-4374; for credit card orders, call 212 315-8863.

Pulmonary Disease (Specialty)/Trends

Future Directions for Research on Disease of the Lung. *Am J Respir Crit Care Med.* 1995;152:5. Sponsored by the American Thoracic Society. To order send check payable to American Thoracic Society, 1740 Broadway, New York, NY 10019-4374; for credit card orders, call 212 315-8863.

Pulmonary Embolism/ Prevention and Control Thrombophlebitis/ Prevention and Control

Prevention of Venous Thrombosis and Pulmonary Embolism. *NIH Consensus Development Conference Statement.* 1986;6(2):1-8[Conf. No. 54]. 9pp. Sponsored by the National Institutes of Health. Cost: free copy. To order call 1 888 644-2667. Available on the Internet at consensus.nih.gov.

Quality Assurance, Health Care

Manual of Psychiatric Quality Assurance. 1992. 254pp. 210refs. Sponsored by the American Psychiatric Association. Cost: $27.50. To order call 1 800 368-5777 order #SPCT2232. Key terms: manual; quality; assurance.

Quality Assurance, Health Care Obstetrics/Standards

Quality Assessment and Improvement in Obstetrics and Gynecology. 1994. 113pp. 8refs. Sponsored by the American College of Obstetricians and Gynecologists. Cost: $30 + s/h members; $45 + s/h nonmembers per copy. To order call ACOG Distribution Center, 1 800 762-2264. Available on the Internet to members only at acog.org.

Quality Assurance, Health Care/Standards Infection Control

Interim Report of the Quality Indicator Study Group. *Infect Control Hosp Epidemiol.* 1994;15:265-268. 4pp. 11refs. Sponsored by the Society for Healthcare Epidemiology of America. Cost: free. To order visit our website at medscape.com/shea. Available on the Internet at medscape.com/shea. Key terms: superficial incisions SSI; deep incisional SSI; organ/space SSI; SSI involving more than one specific site; comparing hospital SSI data to NNIS system SSI data.

Quality of Healthcare Eye Diseases/Drug Therapy

Quality of Ophthalmic Care. 1988. 3pp. Sponsored by the American Academy of Ophthalmology. Cost: $11 members, $16 nonmembers. AAO members first copy free upon publication. To order call AAO Order Dept 415 561-8540.

Rabies/Prevention and Control

Compendium of Animal Rabies Control, 1998 National Association of State Public Health Veterinarians, Inc. *Morbid Mortal Weekly Report.* 1998;47(no. RR-9). Sponsored by the Centers for Disease Control and Prevention. To order call US Govt Printing Office. Available on the Internet at cdc.gov/epo/mmwr/preview/ind98_rr.html.

Rabies Vaccine Immunoglobulins, Intravenous/ Therapeutic Use

Human Rabies Prevention—United States, 1999 Recommendations of the Advisory Committee on Immunization Practices (ACIP). *Morbid Mortal Weekly Report.* 1998;48(no. RR-1). 19pp. 86refs. Sponsored by the Centers for Disease Control and Prevention. Cost: $1. To order call US Govt Printing Office 202 783-3238. Available on the Internet at cdc.gov/mmwr/mmwr_rr.html.

Radiation Oncology

ACR Standard for Radiation Oncology Physics for External Beam Therapy (Revised). 1999. 9pp. 9refs. Sponsored by the American College of Radiology. Cost: $25 ACR nonmembers. To order call ACR Dept of Quality Assurance 703 716-7592. Available free on the Internet at acr.org. Key terms: radiation oncology; physics; external beam.

Radiation Oncology/Standards

ACR Standard for Communication: Radiation Oncology. 1999. 19pp. 10refs. Sponsored by the American College of Radiology. Cost: $25 (ACR nonmembers). To order call ACR Dept of Quality Assurance 703 716-7592. Available free on the Internet at acr.org. Key terms: radiation oncology; reporting; communication; documentation; therapy.

Radiation Oncology/Standards

ACR Standard for Radiation Oncology. 1999. 12pp. 5refs. Sponsored by the American College of Radiology. Cost: $25 (ACR nonmembers). To order call ACR Dept of Quality Assurance 703 716-7592. Available free on the Internet at acr.org. Key terms: radiation oncology; external beam; brachytherapy.

Radical Neck Dissection

Radical Neck Dissection. *Clinical Indicators Compendium.* 1999. 1pp. 20refs. Sponsored by the American Academy of Otolaryngology-Head and Neck Surgery. Cost: $10 AAO-HNS members, $15 nonmembers. To order write to AAO-HNS, 1 Prince St, Alexandria, VA 22314. Key terms: malignancy; neck; dissection; lymphadenectomy; laryngectomy.

Radioallergosorbent Test

RAST Marketing. 1979, Position Statement No. 5. 1pp. Sponsored by the American Academy of Allergy, Asthma, and Immunology. Cost: free copy. To order call 414 272-6071.

Radioallergosorbent Tests
IgE/Diagnostic Use

Use of Radioallergosorbent and IgE Tests in Practice. *J Allergy Clin Immun.* 1980;66:431, Position Statement No. 6. 1pp. Sponsored by the American Academy of Allergy, Asthma, and Immunology. Cost: free copy. To order call 414 272-6071.

Radiography

ACR Standard for the Performance of General (Plain) Radiography. 1996. 5pp. 12refs. Sponsored by the American College of Radiology. Cost: $25 (ACR nonmembers). To order call ACR Dept of Quality Assurance 703 716-7592. Available free on the Internet at acr.org. Key terms: radiology; general.

Radiography, Interventional

Guidelines for Establishing a Quality Assurance Program in Vascular and Interventional Radiology. 1989. 12pp. 25refs. Sponsored by the Society of Cardiovascular and Interventional Radiology. Cost: free copy. To order call SCVIR 703 691-1805.

Radioisotope Renography
Angiotensin-Converting Enzyme
Inhibitors/Diagnostic Use
Hypertension, Renovascular/
Radionuclide Imaging

Radionuclide Scintirenography in the Evaluation of Patients with Hypertension. *J Am Coll Cardiol.* 1993;21:838-839. 2pp. 10refs. Sponsored by the American College of Cardiology. Cost: free copy. To order call Educational Services Department 1 800 257-4740.

Radioisotopes/Therapeutic Use

ACR Standard for the Performance of Therapy with Unsealed Radionuclide Sources. 1996. 7pp. 18refs. Sponsored by the American College of Radiology. Cost: $25 (ACR nonmembers). To order call ACR Dept of Quality Assurance 703 716-7592. Available free on the Internet at acr.org. Key terms: hyperthyroidism; cancer; radionuclide; implant; palliation.

Radiology, Interventional
Biopsy, Needle/Methods

Quality Improvement Guidelines for Image-Guided Percutaneous Biopsy in Adults. *JVIR.* 1996;7:943-946. 8pp. 32refs. Sponsored by the Society of Cardiovascular and Interventional Radiology. Cost: free copy. To order call SCVIR 703 691-1805. Key terms: biopsies; interventional radiology.

Radiology, Interventional/
Instrumentation
Equipment Design

General Principles for Evaluation of New Interventional Technologies and Devices. *JVIR.* 1997;8:133-136. 4pp. 21refs. Sponsored by the Society of Cardiovascular and Interventional Radiology. Cost: free copy. To order call SCVIR 703 691-1805. Key terms: interventional procedures; technology; radiology and radiologists; research; statistical analysis.

Radionuclide Imaging/Standards

Procedure Guideline for General Imaging. *J Nuclear Med.* 1996;37:2087-2092. 6pp. 4refs. Sponsored by the Society of Nuclear Medicine. Cost: free. To order call Bill Uffelman 703 708-9000. Available on the Internet at snm.org. Key terms: guidelines; routine diagnostic tests; radionuclide imaging; nuclear medicine imaging; practice guideline.

Radiopharmaceuticals/Diagnostic Use

Procedure Guideline for Use of Radiopharmaceuticals. *J Nuclear Med.* 1996;37:2092-2094. 3pp. 8refs. Sponsored by the Society of Nuclear Medicine. Cost: free. To order call Bill Uffelman 703 708-9000. Available on the Internet at snm.org. Key terms: radiopharmaceuticals; guidelines; routine diagnostic tests; radionuclide imaging; scintigraphic studies.

Radiopharmaceuticals/Therapeutic Use

ACR Standard for the Performance of Clinical Procedures Using Radiopharmaceuticals (Revised). 1998. 11pp. 8refs. Sponsored by the American College of Radiology. Cost: $25 (ACR nonmembers). To order call ACR Dept of Quality Assurance 703 716-7592. Available free on the Internet at acr.org. Key terms: radiopharmaceutical imaging.

Radiosurgery
Biopsy

Stereotactic Lesion Creation. 1993. Sponsored by the American Association of Neurological Surgeons. To order call AANS 847 692-9500.

Radiosurgery
Brachytherapy

Stereotactic Procedure for Brachytherapy. 1993. Sponsored by the American Association of Neurological Surgeons. To order call AANS 847 692-9500.

Radiosurgery
Brain Diseases
Biopsy

Stereotactic Procedure for Biopsy, Aspiration, Excision of Intracranial Lesion. 1993. Sponsored by the American Association of Neurological Surgeons. To order call AANS 847 692-9500.

Radiosurgery
Brain/Surgery

Stereotactic Procedure for Radiosurgery of Brain or Skull Base. 1994. Sponsored by the American Association of Neurological Surgeons. To order call AANS 847 692-9500.

Radiosurgery
Electrodes
Cerebral Cortex

Stereotactic Introduction of Subcortical Electrodes. 1993. Sponsored by the American Association of Neurological Surgeons. To order call AANS 847 692-9500.

Radiosurgery
Tomography, X-ray Computed

Stereotactic Procedure With or Without CAT Guidance. 1993. Sponsored by the American Association of Neurological Surgeons. To order call AANS 847 692-9500.

Radiotherapy

ACR Standard for 3D External Beam Radiation Planning and Conformal Therapy. 1997. 4pp. 18refs. Sponsored by the American College of Radiology. Cost: $25 (ACR nonmembers). To order call ACR Dept of Quality Assurance 703 716-7592. Available free on the Internet at acr.org. Key terms: radiation oncology; treatment planning; 3D.

Radius Fractures

Distal Radius Fracture. *Clinical Policies.* 1996. 7pp. 12refs. Sponsored by the American Academy of Orthopaedic Surgeons, North American Spine Society. Cost: $50 (set of 15) for nonmembers. To order call 1 800 626-6276. Key terms: distal radius fracture; wrist deformity; wrist pain; American Academy of Orthopaedic Surgeons.

Rape

Sexual Assault. *ACOG Educational Bulletin.* 1997;242. 8pp. 25refs. Sponsored by the American College of Obstetricians and Gynecologists. Cost: free copy. Set of Bulletins $70 + s/h ACOG members, $125 + s/h nonmembers. One-year subscription $55 member, $65 nonmember. To order single copy, call ACOG Resource Center 202 863-2518; to order set or subscription, call ACOG Distribution Center, 1 800 762-2264. Available on the Internet to members only at acog.org. Key terms: rape.

Rape
Adolescence

Adolescent Victims of Sexual Assault. *ACOG Educational Bulletin.* 1998;252. 5pp. 30refs. Sponsored by the American College of Obstetricians and Gynecologists. Cost: $20 + s/h members; $30 + s/h nonmembers per copy. To order call ACOG Distribution Center, 1 800 762-2264. Available on the Internet to members only at acog.org. Key terms: adolescent health services; rape; incest.

Rape/Prevention and Control
Rape/Rehabilitation

Strategies for the Treatment and Prevention of Sexual Assault. 1995. 38pp. Sponsored by the American Medical Association, Division of Health Science. Cost: AMA members $2.25 nonmembers $3. To order call AMA 312 464-5066.

RAST (See Radioallergosorbent Test)

Reconstructive Surgical Procedures
Oral Surgical Procedures

Maxillofacial Cosmetic Surgery. *J Oral & Maxillofacial Surg.* 1995. Sponsored by the American Association of Oral and Maxillofacial Surgeons. To order call AAOMS Publications 1 800 366-6725.

Reconstructive Surgical Procedures
Surgery, Oral

Reconstructive Surgery. *J Oral & Maxillofacial Surg.* 1995. Sponsored by the American Association of Oral and Maxillofacial Surgeons. To order call AAOMS Publications 1 800 366-6725.

Rectal Fissure/Surgery

Fistula-in-Ano. *Dis Colon Rectum.* 1996. Sponsored by the American Society of Colon and Rectal Surgeons. Cost: free. To order write ASCRS, 85 W Algonquin Rd, #550, Arlington Hts, IL 60005.

Rectal Neoplasms

Locally Unresectable Rectal Cancer (7 variants). 1998. 12pp. 26refs. Sponsored by the American College of Radiology. Cost: Vols. 1 & 2 $25 each (ACR members); $75/set (ACR nonmembers). To order call ACR Appropriateness Criteria™ 703 716-7583 x7596. Available free on the Internet at acr.org/f-appcrit.html. Key terms: rectal cancer; unresectable; chemotherapy; radiotherapy.

Rectal Neoplasms
Neoplasm Metastasis

Rectal Cancer: Presentation with Metastatic and Locally Advanced Disease (8 variants). 1998. 14pp. 18refs. Sponsored by the American College of Radiology. Cost: Vols. 1 & 2 $25 each (ACR members); $75/set (ACR nonmembers). To order call ACR Appropriateness Criteria™ 703 716-7583 x7596. Available free on the Internet at acr.org/f-appcrit.html. Key terms: rectal cancer; palliative care; metastases.

Rectal Neoplasms/Surgery

Management of Resectable Rectal Cancer (6 variants). 1998. 10pp. 15refs. Sponsored by the American College of Radiology. Cost: Vols. 1 & 2 $25 each (ACR members); $75/set (ACR nonmembers). To order call ACR Appropriateness Criteria™ 703 716-7583 x7596. Available free on the Internet at acr.org/f-appcrit.html. Key terms: rectal; colorectal cancer; resectable; radiotherapy; chemotherapy.

Rectum/Surgery
Ambulatory Surgical Procedures

Practice Parameters for Ambulatory Anorectal Surgery. *Dis Colon Rectum.* 1991;34(3):285-286. 2pp. Sponsored by the American Society of Colon and Rectal Surgeons. Cost: free. To order write ASCRS, 85 W Algonquin Rd, #550, Arlington Hts, IL 60005.

Refractive Errors

Refractive Errors Preferred Practice Patterns. 1997. 39pp. 208refs. Sponsored by the American Academy of Ophthalmology. Cost: $11 members, $16 nonmembers. AAO members first copy free upon publication. To order call AAO Order Dept 415 561-8540. Key terms: eye; refraction; eyeglasses; contact lenses.

Rehabilitation
Geriatrics

Geriatric Rehabilitation, Position Statement. 1993. Sponsored by the American Geriatrics Society. Cost: free. To order call AGS 212 308-1414.

Reminder Systems,
Vaccination/Utilization

Use of Reminder and Recall Systems by Vaccination Providers to Increase Vaccination Rates. 1999. Sponsored by the American Academy of Family Physicians. To order call 1 800 944-0000. Available on the Internet at aafp.org/clinical/.

Research
Animal Welfare

Animals in Medical Research. *Amer Rev Resp Dis.* 1991;144:4. Sponsored by the American Thoracic Society. Cost: $4. To order send check payable to American Thoracic Society, 1740 Broadway, New York, NY 10019-4374; for credit card orders, call 212 315-8863.

Research
Geriatrics

Research and Geriatric Medicine, Position Statement. 1993. Sponsored by the American Geriatrics Society. Cost: free. To order call AGS 212 308-1414.

Respiration Disorders/Therapy
Physician Executives

Medical Director of Respiratory Care. *Amer Rev Resp Dis*. 1988;138:4. Sponsored by the American Thoracic Society. Cost: $4. To order send check payable to American Thoracic Society, 1740 Broadway, New York, NY 10019-4374; for credit card orders, call 212 315-8863.

Respiration, Artificial

Mechanical Ventilation. *Chest*. 1993;104:1833-1859. 27pp. 158refs. Sponsored by the American College of Chest Physicians. Cost: $5. To order call ACCP 1 800 343-2227 or 1 847 498-1400 (credit card orders). Key terms: mechanical ventilation; pulmonary disease.

Respiration, Artificial/Standards
Respiratory Insufficiency/Therapy

Guidelines for Standards of Care for Patients with Acute Respiratory Failure on Mechanical Ventilatory Support. *Critical Care Med*. 1991;19:275-278. 4pp. 2refs. Sponsored by the Society of Critical Care Medicine. Cost: Complete Set $60 + s/h SCCM members, $80 + s/h nonmembers; $5 for a single guideline. To order call SCCM 714 282-6000 or access Book Store on the SCCM website. Available free on the Internet at sccm.org.

Respiratory Function Tests
Abbreviations

Respiratory Function Measurement in Infants: Symbols, Abbreviations, and Units (SI Units). *Am J Respir Crit Care Med*. 1995;152:6. Sponsored by the American Thoracic Society. Cost: $6. To order send check payable to American Thoracic Society, 1740 Broadway, New York, NY 10019-4374; for credit card orders, call 212 315-8863.

Respiratory Function Tests
Quality Assurance, Health Care

Quality Assurance in Pulmonary Function Laboratories. *Amer Rev Resp Dis*. 1986;134:3. Sponsored by the American Thoracic Society. Cost: $4. To order send check payable to American Thoracic Society, 1740 Broadway, New York, NY 10019-4374; for credit card orders, call 212 315-8863.

Respiratory Function Tests/Standards

Lung Function Testing: Selection of References Values and Interpretive Strategies. *Amer Rev Resp Dis*. 1991;144:5. Sponsored by the American Thoracic Society. Cost: $6. To order send check payable to American Thoracic Society, 1740 Broadway, New York, NY 10019-4374; for credit card orders, call 212 315-8863.

Respiratory Syncytial Virus Infections/
Prevention and Control
Antibodies, Monoclonal/Therapeutic Use
Immunoglobulins, Intravenous/
Therapeutic Use

Prevention of Respiratory Syncytial Virus Infections: Indications for the Use of Palivizumab and Update on the Use of RSV-IGIV. *Pediatr*. 1998;102(5):1211-1216. 5pp. 21refs. Sponsored by the American Academy of Pediatrics. Cost: $1.95. Discounted set of policies available. To order call 1 800 433-9016.

Respiratory Syncytial Virus
Infections/Therapy
Immunoglobulins, Intravenous

Respiratory Syncytial Virus Immune Globulin Intravenous: Indications for Use. *Pediatr*. 1997;99(4):645-650. 6pp. 44refs. Sponsored by the American Academy of Pediatrics. Cost: $1.95. Discounted set of policies available. To order call 1 800 433-9016.

Respiratory Therapy
Licensure

Licensure of Respiratory Therapy Technical Personnel. *ATS News*. 1981. Sponsored by the American Thoracic Society. Cost: $4. To order send check payable to American Thoracic Society, 1740 Broadway, New York, NY 10019-4374; for credit card orders, call 212 315-8863.

Respiratory Tract
Diseases/Physiopathology
Respiratory Mechanics

Respiratory Mechanics in Infants: Physiologic Evaluation in Health and Disease. *Amer Rev Resp Dis*. 1993;147:2. Sponsored by the American Thoracic Society. Cost: $6. To order send check payable to American Thoracic Society, 1740 Broadway, New York, NY 10019-4374; for credit card orders, call 212 315-8863.

Restless Legs/Therapy

The Treatment of Restless Legs Syndrome and Periodic Limb Movements. *Sleep.* 1999. 33refs. Sponsored by the American Academy of Sleep Medicine. Cost: $30 + s/h for a complete set of current AASM Guidelines. To order call AASM 507 287-6006. Key terms: Practice guidelines; practice parameters; sleep disorders; restless legs syndrome; periodic limb movement disorder.

Restraint, Physical

Guidelines for Restraint Use. 1997. Sponsored by the American Geriatrics Society. Cost: free. To order call AGS 212 308-1414.

Restraint, Physical

The Use of Physical Restraint Interventions for Children and Adolescents in the Acute Care Setting. *Pediatr.* 1997;99:497. 2pp. 6refs. Sponsored by the American Academy of Pediatrics. Cost: $1.95. Discounted set of policies available. To order call 1 800 433-9016.

Restraint, Physical
Long-Term Care

Guidelines for the Use of Restraints in Long Term Care Facilities. *Reports of CEJA.* 1989;1:57-61. 5pp. Sponsored by the American Medical Association, Council on Ethical and Judicial Affairs. Cost: free copy. To order call AMA 312 464-5223.

Resuscitation
Emergency Medical Services

Recommended Guidelines for Uniform Reporting of Pediatric Advanced Life Support: The Pediatric Utstein Style. *Circulation.* 1995;92(7):2006-2020. 14pp. 60refs. Sponsored by the American Heart Association. Cost: free copy. To order call 1 800 242-8721 (US only) or write to: American Heart Association, Public Inquiries, 7272 Greenville Ave, Dallas TX 75231-4596.

Resuscitation Orders

Guidelines for the Appropriate Use of Do-Not-Resuscitate Orders. *JAMA.* 1991;265:1868-1871. 4pp. Sponsored by the American Medical Association, Council on Ethical and Judicial Affairs. Cost: free copy. To order call AMA 312 464-5223.

Retinal Detachment

Repair of Rhegmatogenous Retinal Detachments Ophthalmic Procedure Assessment. *Ophthalmology.* 1996;103:1313-1324. 12pp. 90refs. Sponsored by the American Academy of Ophthalmology. Cost: $11 members, $16 nonmembers. AAO members first copy free upon publication. To order call AAO Order Dept 415 561-8540. Key terms: eye; retina; retinal detachment.

Retroperitoneal Space/Ultrasonography
Abdomen/Ultrasonography
Kidney Diseases/Ultrasonography

ACR Standard for the Performance of Abdominal, Renal, or Retroperitoneal Ultrasound Examination in Infants, Children, and Adults. 1997. 4pp. 37refs. Sponsored by the American College of Radiology. Cost: $25 (ACR nonmembers). To order call ACR Dept of Quality Assurance 703 716-7592. Available free on the Internet at acr.org. Key terms: ultrasound: abdominal; renal; retroperitoneal; children; infants.

Rh Isoimmunization/
Prevention and Control
Rho(D) Immuno globulin/
Administration and Dosage

Prevention of Rh D Alloimmunization. *ACOG Technical Bulletin.* 1999;4. 8pp. 58refs. Sponsored by the American College of Obstetricians and Gynecologists. Cost: free copy. Set of Bulletins $70 + s/h ACOG members, $125 + s/h nonmembers. One-year subscription $55 member, $65 nonmember. To order single copy, call ACOG Resource Center 202 863-2518; to order set or subscription, call ACOG Distribution Center, 1 800 762-2264. Available on the Internet to members only at acog.org. Key terms: Rh D immunoglobulin; Rh isoimmunization; Rh-HR blood groups; hemolytic disease of newborn.

Rheumatic Fever/Diagnosis
Streptococcal Infections/Diagnosis

Guidelines for the Diagnosis of Rheumatic Fever: Jones Criteria, Updated 1992. *Circulation.* 1993;87:302-307. 6pp. 9refs. Sponsored by the American Heart Association. Cost: free copy. To order call 1 800 242-8721 (US only) or write to: American Heart Association, Public Inquiries, 7272 Greenville Ave, Dallas TX 75231-4596.

Rheumatic Fever/
Prevention and Control
Streptococcal Infections

Treatment of Acute Streptococcal Pharyngitis and Prevention of Rheumatic Fever. *Circulation.* 1995;96(4):758-764. 6pp. 58refs. Sponsored by the American Heart Association. Cost: free copy. To order call 1 800 242-8721 (US only) or write to: American Heart Association, Public Inquiries, 7272 Greenville Ave, Dallas TX 75231-4596.

Rhinitis, Allergic, Perennial
Hypersensitivity

Allergy Testing for Allergic Rhinitus. *Clinical Indicators Compendium.* 1999. 4pp. Sponsored by the American Academy of Otolaryngology-Head and Neck Surgery. Cost: $10 AAO-HNS members, $15 nonmembers. To order write to AAO-HNS, 1 Prince St, Alexandria, VA 22314. Key terms: SET; allergy; rhinitus; in vitro; immunotherapy.

Rhinitis, Allergic, Perennial
Practice Guidelines

Allergic Rhinitis Clinical Practice Guideline. *Otolaryngology-Head and Neck Surgery.* 1996. Sponsored by the American Academy of Otolaryngic Allergy. Cost: free copy. To order call AAOA 301 588-1800.

Rhinitis/Diagnosis
Rhinitis/Therapy

Diagnosis and Management of Rhinitis: Parameter Documents of the Joint Task…. *Ann Allergy Asthma Immun.* 1998;81:S463-S518. 55pp. Sponsored by the American Academy of Allergy, Asthma, and Immunology; American College of Allergy, Asthma, and Immunology; Joint Council of Allergy, Asthma, and Immunology. Cost: free copy. To order call 847 934-1918. Available on the Internet at jcaai.org.

Rhinoplasty

Rhinoplasty. *Clinical Indicators Compendium.* 1999. 1pp. 20refs. Sponsored by the American Academy of Otolaryngology-Head and Neck Surgery. Cost: $10 AAO-HNS members, $15 nonmembers. To order write to AAO-HNS, 1 Prince St, Alexandria, VA 22314. Key terms: nose; septal repair; deviated septum; sinusitis.

Ribavirin/Therapeutic Use
Respiratory Syncytial Virus Infections

Reassessment of Indications for Ribavirin Therapy in Respiratory Syncytial Virus Infections. *Pediatr.* 1996;97(1):137-140. 4pp. 28refs. Sponsored by the American Academy of Pediatrics. Cost: $1.95. Discounted set of policies available. To order call 1 800 433-9016.

Risk Management

Risk Management. 1992. 19pp. Sponsored by the American Society for Gastrointestinal Endoscopy. Cost: $10. To order call ASGE 978 526-8330.

Rotavirus/Immunology
Gastroenteritis/Virology

Rotavirus Vaccine for the Prevention of Rotavirus Gastroenteritis Among Children Recommendations of the Advisory Committee on Immunization Practices (ACIP). 1999;48(no. RR-2). Sponsored by the Centers for Disease Control and Prevention. To order call US Govt Printing Office 202 783-3238. Available on the Internet at cdc.gov/mmwr/mmwr_rr.html.

Rotavirus/Immunology
Viral Vaccines/Therapeutic Use

Prevention of Rotavirus Disease: Guidelines for Use of Rotavirus Vaccine. *Pediatr.* 1998;102(6):1483-1491. 8pp. 73refs. Sponsored by the American Academy of Pediatrics. Cost: $1.95. Discounted set of policies available. To order call 1 800 433-9016.

Rubella Syndrome, Congenital
Pregnancy Complications, Infectious

Rubella, Congenital and Pregnancy. *ACOG Technical Bulletin.* 1992;171. 6pp. 18refs. Sponsored by the American College of Obstetricians and Gynecologists. Cost: free copy. Set of Bulletins $70 + s/h ACOG members, $125 + s/h nonmembers. One-year subscription $55 member, $65 nonmember. To order single copy, call ACOG Resource Center 202 863-2518; to order set or subscription, call ACOG Distribution Center, 1 800 762-2264. Available on the Internet to members only at acog.org. Key terms: pregnancy complications; infections; rubella vaccine.

Rubella/Diagnosis

Screening for Rubella. *Guide to Clinical Preventive Services, 2nd Ed.* 1996. Sponsored by the US Preventive Services Task Force. To order call Williams & Wilkins 1 800 638-0672.

Rubella/Prevention and Control
Vaccination

Rubella Prevention: Recommendations of the Immunization Practices Advisory Committee. *Morbid Mortal Weekly Report.* 1990;39(no. RR-15):1-18. 18pp. 66refs. Sponsored by the Centers for Disease Control and Prevention. Cost: $1. To order call US Govt Printing Office 202 783-3238.

Schizophrenia/Therapy

Practice Guideline for the Treatment of Patients with Schizophrenia. *Am J Psych.* 1997;154(suppl):4. 63pp. 581refs. Sponsored by the American Psychiatric Association. Cost: $22.50. To order call 1 800 368-5777 order #SPCT2309. Key terms: schizophrenia.

Schizophrenia/Therapy
Psychotic Disorders/Therapy

Schizophrenia and Other Psychotic Disorders. *Treatments of Psychiatric Disorders, Second Edition, Volume I.* 1995;Section 5. 184pp. 776refs. Sponsored by the American Psychiatric Association. Cost: $250 for 2-volume set. To order call 1 800 368-5777 order # SPCT8700. Key terms: TPD; disorders; treatment.

Schizophrenia, Childhood/Therapy

Practice Parameters for the Assessment and Treatment of Children and Adolescents with Schizophrenia. *J Am Acad Child Adol Psych.* 1994;34(5):616-635. 20pp. 89refs. Sponsored by the American Academy of Child and Adolescent Psychiatry. Cost: $10 AACAP members/$20 others. To order call Communications Department 202 966-7300. Key terms: schizophrenia; children; adolescents; psychosis; practice parameters.

Scleroderma, Systemic/Therapy

Scleroderma and Sclerodermoid Disorders. *J Am Acad Derm.* 1996;35:609 614. 6pp. 22refs. Sponsored by the American Academy of Dermatology. Cost: free copy. To order call Alice Bell 847 330-0230 x333. Available on the Internet at aad.org. Key terms: systemic scleroderma; circumscribed scleroderma; therapy.

Sclerotherapy
Telangiectasis/Therapy

Sclerotherapy Treatment of Varicose and Telangiectatic Leg Veins. *J Am Acad Derm.* 1996;34:523-528. 6pp. 23refs. Sponsored by the American Academy of Dermatology. Cost: free copy. To order call Alice Bell 847 330-0230 x333. Available on the Internet at aad.org. Key terms: sclerotherapy; telangiectasis; varicose veins; methods.

Scoliosis/Diagnosis

Screening for Adolescent Idiopathic Scoliosis. *Guide to Clinical Preventive Services, 2nd Ed.* 1996. Sponsored by the US Preventive Services Task Force. To order call Williams & Wilkins 1 800 638-0672.

Scrotum/Ultrasonography

ACR Standard for the Performance of a Scrotal Ultrasound Examination. 1997. 2pp. 7refs. Sponsored by the American College of Radiology. Cost: $25 (ACR nonmembers). To order call ACR Dept of Quality Assurance 703 716-7592. Available free on the Internet at acr.org. Key terms: scrotal; ultrasound; testes; epididymis.

Second Hand Smoke (see Tobacco Smoke Pollution)

Seizures/Radiography
Emergency Medicine

Practice Parameter: Neuroimaging in the Emergency Patient Presenting with Seizure (Summary Statement). *Ann Emerg Med.* 1996;28:114-118. 5pp. Sponsored by the American College of Emergency Physicians. Cost: ACEP members free copy, fee nonmembers. To order call ACEP 1 800 798-1822 x6. Key terms: neuroimaging; seizure; emergency.

Seizures/Radiography
Neurology

Practice Parameter: Neuroimaging in the Emergency Patient Presenting with Seizure. *Neurol.* 1996;47:288-291. 4pp. Sponsored by the American Academy of Neurology, American College of Emergency Physicians, American Association of Neurological Surgeons, American Society of Neuroradiology. Cost: individual statements are free. To order call AAN Member Service Center 1 800 879-1960. Available on the Internet at aan.com. Key terms: neuroimaging and seizure (emergency seizure patient).

Seizures, Febrile/Therapy
Practice Guidelines

Treatment of Febrile Seizures. *Pediatr.* 1999. Sponsored by the American Academy of Pediatrics. Cost: $1.95. Discounted set of policies available. To order call 1 800 433-9016.

Self-Help Devices

Guidelines for the Use of Assistive Technology: Evaluation, Referral, Prescription. 1994. 58pp. 33refs. Sponsored by the American Medical Association, Division of Health Science. Cost: $5 single copy, $100 for packages of 25. To order call Georgianne Cooper, AMA 312 464-5066.

Sepsis
Hemodynamics

Practice Parameters for Hemodynamic Support of Sepsis in Adult Patients. *Critical Care Med.* 1999;27:639-660. 12pp. 196refs. Sponsored by the Society of Critical Care Medicine. Cost: Complete Set $60 + s/h SCCM members, $80 + s/h nonmembers; $10 for a single guideline. To order call SCCM 714 282-6000 or access Book Store on the SCCM website. Available free on the Internet at sccm.org. Key terms: hemodynamic; sepsis; fluid resuscitation; vasopressor therapy; inotropic therapy.

Septicemia/Therapy
Multiple Organ Failure/Therapy

Definitions for Sepsis and Organ Failure and Guidelines for the Use of Innovative Therapies in Sepsis. *Chest.* 1992;101:1644-1655. 12pp. 45refs. Sponsored by the American College of Chest Physicians. Cost: $5. To order call ACCP 1 800 343-2227 or 1 847 498-1400 (credit card orders). Key terms: sepsis; organ failure.

Serotum/Radionuclide Imaging

ACR Standard for the Performance of Scrotal Scintigraphy. 1999. 4pp. 6refs. Sponsored by the American College of Radiology. Cost: $25 (ACR nonmembers). To order call ACR Dept of Quality Assurance 703 716-7592. Available free on the Internet at acr.org. Key terms: nuclear medicine; scrotal; scintigraphy.

Sex Disorders

Clinical Practice Guidelines for Male Sexual Dysfunction. *Endocrine Practice.* 1998. 16pp. 110refs. Sponsored by the American Association of Clinical Endocrinologists. To order call AACE 904 353-7878. Key terms: libido; ejaculation; penis; sexual dysfunction; erection.

Sex Disorders

Sexual Dysfunction. *ACOG Technical Bulletin.* 1995;211. 12pp. 25refs. Sponsored by the American College of Obstetricians and Gynecologists. Cost: free copy. Set of Bulletins $70 + s/h ACOG members, $125 + s/h nonmembers. One-year subscription $55 member, $65 nonmember. To order single copy, call ACOG Resource Center 202 863-2518; to order set or subscription, call ACOG Distribution Center, 1 800 762-2264. Available on the Internet to members only at acog.org. Key terms: sex disorders; frigidity.

Sex Preselection
Ethics, medical

Sex Selection. *ACOG Committee Opinion.* 1996;177. 4pp. 20refs. Sponsored by the American College of Obstetricians and Gynecologists. Cost: free copy. Set of Opinions $55 + s/h ACOG members, $75 + s/h nonmembers. One-year subscription $55 member, $65 nonmember. To order single copy, call ACOG Resource Center 202 863-2518; to order set or subscription, call ACOG Distribution Center, 1 800 762-2264. Available on the Internet to members only at acog.org. Key terms: ethics; medical.

Sexual Abstinence

Limitations of Abstinence-Only Sexuality Education. *ACOG Statement of Policy.* 1998;74. 2pp. 5refs. Sponsored by the American College of Obstetricians and Gynecologists. Cost: free copy. To order single copy, call ACOG Resource Center 202 863-2518; to order set or subscription, call ACOG Distribution Center, 1 800 762-2264. Available on the Internet to members only at acog.org. Key terms: sex education; abstinence.

Sexually Transmitted Diseases/Therapy
Practice Guidelines

1998 Guidelines for Treatment of Sexually Transmitted Disease. *Morbid Mortal Weekly Report.* 1998;47(no. RR-01). Sponsored by the Centers for Disease Control and Prevention. Cost: $1. To order call US Govt Printing Office 202 783-3238.

Shock, Hemorrhagic/Therapy
Pregnancy Complications, Cardiovascular/Therapy

Hemorrhagic Shock. *ACOG Educational Bulletin.* 1997;235. 8pp. 15refs. Sponsored by the American College of Obstetricians and Gynecologists. Cost: free copy. Set of Bulletins $70 + s/h ACOG members, $125 + s/h nonmembers. One-year subscription $55 member, $65 nonmember. To order single copy, call ACOG Resource Center 202 863-2518; to order set or subscription, call ACOG Distribution Center, 1 800 762-2264. Available on the Internet to members only at acog.org. Key terms: hemorrhage; postpartum.

Shock, Septic

Septic Shock. *ACOG Technical Bulletin.* 1995;204. 8pp. 24refs. Sponsored by the American College of Obstetricians and Gynecologists. Cost: free copy. Set of Bulletins $70 + s/h ACOG members, $125 + s/h nonmembers. One-year subscription $55 member, $65 nonmember. To order single copy, call ACOG Resource Center 202 863-2518; to order set or subscription, call ACOG Distribution Center, 1 800 762-2264. Available on the Internet to members only at acog.org.

Shoulder/Ultrasonography

ACR Standard for the Performance of a Shoulder Ultrasound Examination. 1998. 2pp. 11refs. Sponsored by the American College of Radiology. Cost: $23 (ACR nonmembers). To order call ACR Dept of Quality Assurance 703 716-7592. Available free on the Internet at acr.org. Key terms: shoulder; ultrasound; rotator cuff.

Shoulder Pain

Clinical Guideline on Shoulder Pain. 1996. 13pp. 71refs. Sponsored by the American Academy of Orthopaedic Surgeons, North American Spine Society. Cost: $10 AAOS member, $20 nonmember. To order call 1 800 626-6276. Available on the Internet free at guidelines.gov. Key terms: shoulder pain; frozen shoulder; rotator cuff impingement; glenohumeral instability; arthritis of the glenohumeral joint.

Sickle Cell (see Anemia, Sickle Cell)

Sigmoidoscopy

Rigid and Flexible Sigmoidoscopies. *JAMA.* 1990;264:89. 1pp. Sponsored by the American Medical Association, Diagnostic and Therapeutic Technology Assessment Program. Cost: free copy. DATTA subscription available. To order call AMA Department of Technology Assessment 312 464-4531.

Sigmoidoscopy
Rectal Neoplasms/Diagnosis

Flexible Sigmoidoscopy: Guidelines for Clinical Application. *Gastrointest Endosc.* 1988;34(suppl):16s-17s. 2pp. 17refs. Sponsored by the American Society for Gastrointestinal Endoscopy. Cost: free. To order call ASGE 978 526-8330.

Signal Processing, Computer-Assisted

ACR Standard for Digital Image Data Management. 1998. 8pp. 12refs. Sponsored by the American College of Radiology. Cost: $25 (ACR nonmembers). To order call ACR Dept of Quality Assurance 703 716-7592. Available free on the Internet at acr.org. Key terms: PACS; digital imaging; archiving; image acquisition.

Sinusitis/Diagnosis
Sinusitis/Therapy

Parameters for the Diagnosis and Management of Sinusitis. *J Allergy Clin Immun.* 1998;102:S107-S144. 37pp. Sponsored by the American Academy of Allergy, Asthma, and Immunology; American College of Allergy, Asthma, and Immunology; Joint Council of Allergy, Asthma, and Immunology. Cost: free copy. To order call 847 934-1918. Available on the Internet at aai.org.

SIV
Laboratory Infection/
Prevention and Control

Guidelines to Prevent Simian Immunodeficiency Virus Infection in Laboratory Workers and Animal Handlers. *Morbid Mortal Weekly Report.* 1988;37:693-704. 12pp. Sponsored by the Centers for Disease Control and Prevention. Cost: $1. To order call US Govt Printing Office 202 783-3238.

Skin/Pathology
Skin Diseases

Skin Lesions. 1994. Sponsored by the American Society of Plastic and Reconstructive Surgeons. Cost: $25 members, $55 nonmembers (full set of guidelines), + s/h. To order call 1 800 766-4955.

Skin/Surgery
Surgical Flaps

Complex Closures, Flaps, and Grafts. *J Am Acad Derm.* 1996;34:703-708. 6pp. 21refs. Sponsored by the American Academy of Dermatology. Cost: free copy. To order call Alice Bell 847 330-0230 x333. Available on the Internet at aad.org. Key terms: skin transplantation; adverse effects; methods; surgical flaps.

Skin Aging
Sunlight/Adverse Effects

Photoaging/Photodamage. *J Am Acad Derm.* 1996;35:462-464. 3pp. 20refs. Sponsored by the American Academy of Dermatology. Cost: free copy. To order call Alice Bell 847 330-0230 x333. Available on the Internet at aad.org. Key terms: skin aging; skin care; sunlight; adverse effects.

Skin Diseases/Drug Therapy
Phototherapy

Phototherapy and Photochemotherapy. *J Am Acad Derm.* 1994;31:643-648. 6pp. 39refs. Sponsored by the American Academy of Dermatology. Cost: free copy. To order call Alice Bell 847 330-0230 x333. Available on the Internet at aad.org. Key terms: phototherapy; photochemotherapy; adverse effects; methods.

Skin Diseases/Etiology
Sunlight/Adverse Effects

Sunlight, Ultraviolet Radiation, and the Skin. *NIH Consensus Development Conference Statement.* 1989;7(8):1-29[Conf. No. 74]. 30pp. Sponsored by the National Institutes of Health. Cost: free copy. To order call 1 888 644-2667. Available on the Internet at consensus.nih.gov.

Skin Neoplasms/Diagnosis

Screening for Skin Cancer. *Guide to Clinical Preventive Services, 2nd Ed.* 1996. Sponsored by the US Preventive Services Task Force. To order call Williams & Wilkins 1 800 638-0672.

Skin Neoplasms/Surgery
Mohs Surgery

Guidelines of Care for Mohs Micrographic Surgery. *J Am Acad Derm.* 1995;33:271-278. 8pp. 30refs. Sponsored by the American Academy of Dermatology. Cost: free copy. To order call Alice Bell 847 330-0230 x333. Available on the Internet at aad.org. Key terms: basal cell carcinoma; squamous cell carcinoma; skin neoplasms; surgery.

Skin Test End-Point Titration

Skin Titration (Rinkel Method). *J Allergy Clin Immun.* 1981;67:333-338, Position Statement No. 8— Controversial Techniques. 2pp. 9refs. Sponsored by the American Academy of Allergy, Asthma, and Immunology. Cost: free copy. To order call 414 272-6071.

Skull/Surgery

Cranial Base Surgery. *Clinical Practice Guidelines: Plastic and Maxillofacial Surgery.* 1995. 28pp. 9refs. Sponsored by the American Society of Maxillofacial Surgeons. Cost: Maxillofacial Surgery Guidelines $25 for entire set (not sold separately). Binder $10 (price includes shipping). To order call 1 800 766-4955.

Sleep Apnea Syndromes
Accidents, Traffic

Sleep Apnea: Sleepiness and Driving Risk. *Am J Respir Crit Care Med.* 1994;145:5. Sponsored by the American Thoracic Society. Cost: $6. To order send check payable to American Thoracic Society, 1740 Broadway, New York, NY 10019-4374; for credit card orders, call 212 315-8863.

Sleep Apnea Syndromes/Surgery
Pulmonary Ventilation

Practice Parameters for the Treatment of Obstructive Sleep Apnea in Adults: The Efficacy of Surgical Modifications of the Upper Airway. *Sleep.* 1996;19(2):152-155. 4pp. 6refs. Sponsored by the American Academy of Sleep Medicine. Cost: $30 + s/h for a complete set of current AASM Guidelines. To order call AASM 507 287-6006. Key terms: practice guidelines; sleep apnea syndromes; surgery; snoring; sleep disorders.

Sleep Disorders/Diagnosis
Monitoring, Physiologic/Standards

Polysomnography and Sleep Disorder Centers. *AHCPR Health Technology Assessment.* 1991;No. 4 (AHCPR Publication No. 92-0027). 22pp. 54refs. Sponsored by the Federal Agency for Health Care Policy and Research. To order call AHCPR Clearinghouse 1 800 358-9295.

Sleep Disorders/Diagnosis
Sleep Disorders/Therapy

Assessment: Techniques Associated with the Diagnosis and Management of Sleep Disorders. *Neurol.* 1992;42:269-275. 7pp. 59refs. Sponsored by the American Academy of Neurology. Cost: individual statements are free. To order call AAN Member Service Center 1 800 879-1960. Available on the Internet at aan.com.

Sleep Disorders/Drug Therapy

Sleep Disorders. *Treatments of Psychiatric Disorders, Second Edition, Volume II*. 1995;Section 12. 60pp. 137refs. Sponsored by the American Psychiatric Association. Cost: $250 for 2-volume set. To order call 1 800 368-5777 order #SPCT8700. Key terms: TPD; disorders; treatment.

Sleep Disorders/Therapy

Treatment of Sleep Disorders of Older People. *NIH Consensus Development Conference Statement*. 1990;8(3):1-22[Conf. No. 78]. 23pp. Sponsored by the National Institutes of Health. Cost: free copy. To order call 1 888 644-2667. Available on the Internet at consensus.nih.gov.

Smallpox Vaccine

Vaccinia (Smallpox) Vaccine. *Morbid Mortal Weekly Report*. 1991;40(no. RR-14):1-10. 11pp. Sponsored by the Centers for Disease Control and Prevention. Cost: $1. To order call US Govt Printing Office 202 783-3238.

Smoking
Cardiovascular Diseases

Cigarette Smoking, Cardiovascular Disease, and Stroke. *Circulation*. 1997;96:3243-3247. 5pp. 36refs. Sponsored by the American Heart Association. Cost: free copy. To order call 1 800 242-8721 (US only) or write to: American Heart Association, Public Inquiries, 7272 Greenville Ave, Dallas TX 75231-4596.

Smoking/Adverse Effects
Physician's Role

Smoking and Health: Physician Responsibility. *Chest*. 1995;108:1118-1121. 4pp. 15refs. Sponsored by the American College of Chest Physicians. Cost: $3. To order call ACCP 1 800 343-2227 or 1 847 498-1400 (credit card orders). Key terms: smoking; tobacco; physician behavior.

Smoking/Adverse Effects
Women's Health

Smoking and Women's Health. *ACOG Educational Bulletin*. 1997;240. 12pp. 44refs. Sponsored by the American College of Obstetricians and Gynecologists. Cost: free copy. Set of Bulletins $70 + s/h ACOG members, $125 + s/h nonmembers. One-year subscription $55 member, $65 nonmember. To order single copy, call ACOG Resource Center 202 863-2518; to order set or subscription, call ACOG Distribution Center, 1 800 762-2264. Available on the Internet to members only at acog.org. Key terms: smoking; women's health; infertility; female; abortion.

Smoking Cessation

Smoking Cessation. *AHCPR*. 1996;Publication No. 96-0692. 125pp. 144refs. Sponsored by the Federal Agency for Health Care Policy and Research. To order call AHCPR Clearinghouse 1 800 358-9295.

Social Responsibility
Asbestosis

Public Responsibility in Asbestos-Associated Diseases. *ATS News*. 1983. Sponsored by the American Thoracic Society. Cost: $4. To order send check payable to American Thoracic Society, 1740 Broadway, New York, NY 10019-4374; for credit card orders, call 212 315-8863.

Soft Tissue Neoplasms
Sarcoma

Soft Tissue Sarcoma Surgical Practice Guidelines. *Oncology*. 1997;11(9). 6pp. 16refs. Sponsored by the Society of Surgical Oncology. Cost: call 516 424-8900 x316. To order write Oncology, PRR, Inc, 17 Prospect St, Huntington NY 11743. Key terms: sarcoma.

Somatoform Disorders
Factitious Disorders

Somatoform and Factitious Disorders. *Treatments of Psychiatric Disorders, Second Edition, Volume II*. 1995;Section 8. 126pp. 420refs. Sponsored by the American Psychiatric Association. Cost: $250 for 2-volume set. To order call 1 800 368-5777 order #SPCT8700. Key terms: TPD; disorders; treatment.

Somatotropin

Bovine Somatotropin. *NIH Technology Assessment Conference Statement*. 1990. 16pp. Sponsored by the National Institutes of Health. Cost: free copy. To order call 1 888 644-2667. Available on the Internet at consensus.nih.gov.

Somatotropin/Therapeutic Use

Clinical Practice Guidelines for Growth Hormone Use in Adults and Children. 1998. 14pp. 12refs. Sponsored by the American Association of Clinical Endocrinologists. To order call AACE 904 353-7878. Key terms: hormones; growth hormone deficiency; Turner syndrome; growth delay; short stature.

Somatotropins, Recombinant/ Adverse Effects
Somatotropins, Recombinant/ Therapeutic Use

Considerations Related to the Use of Recombinant Human Growth Hormone in Children. *Pediatr.* 1997;99(1):122-129. 8pp. 72refs. Sponsored by the American Academy of Pediatrics. Cost: $1.95. Discounted set of policies available. To order call 1 800 433-9016.

Speech Therapy
Otitis Media with Effusion

Speech Therapy for Otitis Media with Effusion. *Diagnostic and Therapeutic Technology Assessment (DATTA).* 1996. 14pp. 36refs. Sponsored by the American Medical Association, Diagnostic and Therapeutic Technology Assessment Program. Cost: free copy. DATTA subscription available. To order call AMA Department of Technology Assessment 312 464-4531.

Speech Therapy/Methods
Music

Assessment: Melodic Intonation Therapy. *Neurol.* 1994;44:566-568. 3pp. 8refs. Sponsored by the American Academy of Neurology. Cost: individual statements are free. To order call AAN Member Service Center 1 800 879-1960. Available on the Internet at aan.com.

Spinal Cord Injuries/Complications
Labor Complications/Therapy

Obstetric Management of Patients with Spinal Cord Injury. *ACOG Committee Opinion.* 1993;121. 2pp. 7refs. Sponsored by the American College of Obstetricians and Gynecologists. Cost: free copy. Set of Opinions $55 + s/h ACOG members, $75 + s/h nonmembers. One-year subscription $55 member, $65 nonmember. To order single copy, call ACOG Resource Center 202 863-2518; to order set or subscription, call ACOG Distribution Center, 1 800 762-2264. Available on the Internet to members only at acog.org. Key terms: pregnancy complications.

Spinal Cord Neoplasms
Laminectomy

Cervical, Thoracic, or Lumbar Laminectomy for Tumor. *Neurosurgical Case Screening Guidelines.* 1989;4pp. Sponsored by the American Association of Neurological Surgeons. Cost: $50 for set of guidelines. To order call AANS 847 692-9500.

Spinal Disorders/Ultrasonography
Back Pain
Spinal Nerve Roots

Review of the Literature on Spinal Ultrasound for the Evaluation of Back Pain and Radicular Disorders. *Neurol.* 1998;51:343-344. 2pp. 12refs. Sponsored by the American Academy of Neurology. Cost: individual statements are free. To order call AAN Member Service Center 1 800 879-1960. Available on the Internet at aan.com.

Spinal Fusion
Electrical Stimulation

Electrical Bone-Growth Stimulation and Spinal Fusion. *AHCPR Health Technology Review.* 1994;No. 8 (AHCPR Publication No. 94-0014). 6pp. 16refs. Sponsored by the Federal Agency for Health Care Policy and Research. To order call AHCPR Clearinghouse 1 800 358-9295.

Spinal Osteophytosis
Electromyography

Practice Parameter for Needle Electromyographic Evaluation of Patients with Suspected Cervical Radiculopathy. *Muscle Nerve.* 1999;8(suppl):S209-S221. 13pp. 59refs. Sponsored by the American Association of Electrodiagnostic Medicine. Cost: $10 members, $20 nonmembers. To order write AAEM, 421 First Avenue SW, #300E, Rochester, MN 55902. Key terms: cervical radiculopathy; electrodiagnosis; EMG; electromyography; spinal root compression.

Spinal Puncture

Practice Parameters: Lumbar Puncture. *Neurol.* 1993;43:625-627. 3pp. Sponsored by the American Academy of Neurology. Cost: individual statements are free. To order call AAN Member Service Center 1 800 879-1960. Available on the Internet at aan.com.

Spinal Puncture

Spinal Puncture. 1993. Sponsored by the American Association of Neurological Surgeons. To order call AANS 847 692-9500.

Spinal Stenosis

Lumbar Spinal Stenosis. *Clinical Policies.* 1996. 6pp. 15refs. Sponsored by the American Academy of Orthopaedic Surgeons, North American Spine Society. Cost: $50 (set of 15) for nonmembers. To order call 1 800 626-6276. Key terms: lumbar spinal stenosis; back pain; sciatica; thigh/calf pain; American Academy of Orthopaedic Surgeons.

Spirometry
Workplace

Spirometry in the Workplace. *J Occupation Med.* 1992;34:559-561. 3pp. 13refs. Sponsored by the American College of Occupational and Environmental Medicine. Cost: free copy. To order call Marianne Dreger 847 228-6850 x18.

Spirometry/Standards
Lung Volume Measurements

Standardization of Spirometry. *Am J Respir Crit Care Med.* 1995;152:3. Sponsored by the American Thoracic Society. Cost: $6. To order send check payable to American Thoracic Society, 1740 Broadway, New York, NY 10019-4374; for credit card orders, call 212 315-8863.

Spleen/Radionuclide Imaging
Liver/Radionuclide Imaging

ACR Standard for the Performance of Liver/Spleen Scintigraphy. 1996. 6pp. 17refs. Sponsored by the American College of Radiology. Cost: $25 (ACR nonmembers). To order call ACR Dept of Quality Assurance 703 716-7592. Available free on the Internet at acr.org. Key terms: nuclear medicine; liver; spleen; scintigraphy.

Sports
Physical Examination

Cardiovascular Preparticipation Screening of Competitive Athletes: Addendum. *Circulation.* 1998;97:2294. 1pp. Sponsored by the American Heart Association. Cost: free copy. To order call 1 800 242-8721 (US only) or write to: American Heart Association, Public Inquiries, 7272 Greenville Ave, Dallas TX 75231-4596.

Stapes Surgery

Stapedectomy. *Clinical Indicators Compendium.* 1999. 1pp. 20refs. Sponsored by the American Academy of Otolaryngology-Head and Neck Surgery. Cost: $10 AAO-HNS members, $15 nonmembers. To order write to AAO-HNS, 1 Prince St, Alexandria, VA 22314. Key terms: stapes; conductive hearing loss; tympanic membrane; otosclerosis.

Stereotaxic Techniques
Biopsy, Needle/Methods
Breast Neoplasms/Pathology

ACR Standard for the Performance of Stereotactically-Guided Breast Interventional Procedures. 1996. 11pp. 14refs. Sponsored by the American College of Radiology. Cost: $25 (ACR nonmembers). To order call ACR Dept of Quality Assurance 703 716-7592. Available free on the Internet at acr.org. Key terms: breast disease; breast surgery; imaging-guided; interventional.

Stereotaxic Techniques/Standards

ACR Standard for the Performance of Stereotactic Radiation Therapy/Radiosurgery. 1997. 5pp. 13refs. Sponsored by the American College of Radiology. Cost: $25 (ACR nonmembers). To order call ACR Dept of Quality Assurance 703 716-7592. Available free on the Internet at acr.org. Key terms: radiation oncology; radiosurgery; stereotactic.

Sterilization Reversal
Vasovasostomy

Vasectomy Reversal. 1992. 5pp. 13refs. Sponsored by the American Society for Reproductive Medicine. Cost: $1. To order call ASRM Publication Department 205 978-5000.

Sterilization, Sexual
Counseling

Sterilization. *ACOG Technical Bulletin.* 1996;222. 7pp. 52refs. Sponsored by the American College of Obstetricians and Gynecologists. Cost: free copy. Set of Bulletins $70 + s/h ACOG members, $125 + s/h nonmembers. One-year subscription $55 member, $65 nonmember. To order single copy, call ACOG Resource Center 202 863-2518; to order set or subscription, call ACOG Distribution Center, 1 800 762-2264. Available on the Internet to members only at acog.org. Key terms: vasectomy; sexual; tubal.

Stomach/Surgery
Obesity, Morbid/Surgery

Gastrointestinal Surgery for Severe Obesity. *NIH Consensus Development Conference Statement.* 1991;9(1):1-20[Conf. No. 84]. 21pp. Sponsored by the National Institutes of Health. Cost: free copy. To order call 1 888 644-2667. Available on the Internet at consensus.nih.gov.

Stomach Neoplasms

Screening for Gastric Cancer. 1996. 3pp. Sponsored by the National Cancer Institute. To order call 1 800 4CA-NCER. Also available on the Internet, at http://cancernet.nci.nih.gov.

Stomach Neoplasms/Surgery

Gastric Cancer Surgical Practice Guidelines. *Oncology.* 1997;11(7). 6pp. 29refs. Sponsored by the Society of Surgical Oncology. Cost: call 516 424-8900 x316. To order write Oncology, PRR, Inc, 17 Prospect St, Huntington NY 11743. Key terms: gastric.

Stomatognathic Diseases/Pathology

Pathology. *J Oral & Maxillofacial Surg.* 1995. Sponsored by the American Association of Oral and Maxillofacial Surgeons. To order call AAOMS Publications 1 800 366-6725.

Streptococcal Infections/Etiology
Streptococcal Infections/Epidemiology
Streptococcus Pyogenes/Pathology

Severe Invasive Group A Streptococcal Infections: A Subject Review. *Pediatr.* 1998;101:136. 5pp. 32refs. Sponsored by the American Academy of Pediatrics. Cost: $1.95. Discounted set of policies available. To order call 1 800 433-9016.

Streptococcal Infections/ Prevention and Control Disease Transmission, Vertical/ Prevention and Control

Prevention of Early-Onset Group B Streptococcal Disease in Newborns. *ACOG Committee Opinion.* 1996;173. 8pp. 47refs. Sponsored by the American College of Obstetricians and Gynecologists. Cost: free copy. Set of Opinions $55 + s/h ACOG members, $75 + s/h nonmembers. One-year subscription $55 member, $65 nonmember. To order single copy, call ACOG Resource Center 202 863-2518; to order set or subscription, call ACOG Distribution Center, 1 800 762-2264. Available on the Internet to members only at acog.org. Key terms: strep infections; vertical transmission.

Streptococcal Infections/ Prevention and Control Penicillius/Therapeutic Use

Revised Guidelines for Prevention of Early-onset Group-B Streptococcal (GBS) Infection. *Pediatr.* 1997;99:489. 8pp. 33refs. Sponsored by the American Academy of Pediatrics. Cost: $1.95. Discounted set of policies available. To order call 1 800 433-9016.

Stress Disorders, Post-Trauma

Practice Parameters for the Assessment and Treatment of Children and Adolescents with Post-Traumatic Stress Disorder. *J Am Acad Child Adol Psych.* 1998;37(suppl). 25pp. 300refs. Sponsored by the American Academy of Child and Adolescent Psychiatry. Cost: $10 AACAP members/$20 others. To order call Communications Department 202 966-7300. Key terms: child and adolescent psychiatry; post-traumatic stress disorder; trauma-focused therapy.

Stroke (see Cerbrovascular Disorders)

Substance Abuse (See Substance-Related Disorders)

Substance-Related Disorders

Substance Abuse. *ACOG Technical Bulletin.* 1994;194. 7pp. 13refs. Sponsored by the American College of Obstetricians and Gynecologists. Cost: free copy. Set of Bulletins $70 + s/h ACOG members, $125 + s/h nonmembers. One-year subscription $55 member, $65 nonmember. To order single copy, call ACOG Resource Center 202 863-2518; to order set or subscription, call ACOG Distribution Center, 1 800 762-2264. Available on the Internet to members only at acog.org.

Substance-Related Disorders/Diagnosis
Substance-Related Disorders/Therapy

Practice Parameters for the Assessment and Treatment of Children and Adolescents with Substance Use Disorders. *J Am Acad Child Adol Psych.* 1997;3610 (suppl): 1405-1565. 16pp. 101refs. Sponsored by the American Academy of Child and Adolescent Psychiatry. Cost: $10 AACAP members/$20 others. To order call Communications Department 202 966-7300. Key terms: substance abuse; dependence; adolescents; children; evaluation.

Substance-Related Disorders/ Rehabilitation

Patient Placement Criteria for the Treatment of Substance-Related Disorders (2nd Ed.). 1996. 206pp. 155refs. Sponsored by the American Society of Addiction Medicine. Cost: $55. To order call ASAM 1 800 844-8948.

Substance-Related Disorders/Therapy

Substance-Related Disorders. *Treatments of Psychiatric Disorders, Second Edition, Volume I.* 1995;Section 4. 308pp. 819refs. Sponsored by the American Psychiatric Association. Cost: $250 for 2-volume set. To order call 1 800 368-5777 order #SPCT8700. Key terms: TPD; disorders; treatment.

Substance Withdrawal Syndrome/ Drug Therapy
Alcoholism

Pharmacological Management of Alcohol Withdrawal. *JAMA.* 1997;278(2):144-151. 8pp. 175refs. Sponsored by the American Society of Addiction Medicine. Cost: free. To order call ASAM 301 656-3920. Available free on the Internet at asam.org (Practice Guidelines). Key terms: alcoholism; pharmacology; addictions; withdrawal.

Sudden Infant Death
Investigative Techniques

Guidelines for Death Scene Investigation of Sudden, Unexplained Infant Deaths. *Morbid Mortal Weekly Report.* 1996;45(no. RR-10). Sponsored by the Centers for Disease Control and Prevention. Cost: $1. To order call US Govt Printing Office 202 783-3238.

Suicide, Assisted
Euthanasia

Physician Assisted Suicide and Voluntary Active Euthanasia, Position Statement. 1998. Sponsored by the American Geriatrics Society. Cost: free. To order call AGS 212 308-1414.

Suicide/Prevention and Control

Screening for Suicide Risk. *Guide to Clinical Preventive Services, 2nd Ed.* 1996. Sponsored by the US Preventive Services Task Force. To order call Williams & Wilkins 1 800 638-0672.

Suicide/Prevention and Control
Adolescent Behavior

Prevention of Adolescent Suicide. *ACOG Committee Opinion.* 1997;190. 3pp. 11refs. Sponsored by the American College of Obstetricians and Gynecologists. Cost: free copy. Set of Opinions $55 + s/h ACOG members, $75 + s/h nonmembers. One-year subscription $55 member, $65 nonmember. To order single copy, call ACOG Resource Center 202 863-2518; to order set or subscription, call ACOG Distribution Center, 1 800 762-2264. Available on the Internet to members only at acog.org. Key terms: adolescent behavior; adolescent health services; suicide.

Surgery, Oral
Surgery, Plastic

Maxillofacial Surgery (Including Orthognathic Surgery and Skeletal Aesthetic Enhancement). *Clinical Practice Guidelines: Plastic and Maxillofacial Surgery.* 1995. 28pp. 35refs. Sponsored by the American Society of Maxillofacial Surgeons. Cost: Maxillofacial Surgery Guidelines $25 for entire set (not sold separately). Binder $10 (price includes shipping). To order call 1 800 766-4955.

Surgery, Oral/Standards

Parameters of Care (Revision). *J Oral & Maxillofacial Surg.* 1995;539(suppl):5. Sponsored by the American Association of Oral and Maxillofacial Surgeons. To order call AAOMS Publications 1 800 366-6725.

Surgery, Oral/Standards
Temporomandibular Joint/Surgery

Temporomandibular Joint Surgery. *J Oral & Maxillofacial Surg.* 1995. Sponsored by the American Association of Oral and Maxillofacial Surgeons. To order call AAOMS Publications 1 800 366-6725.

Surgical Procedures, Laparoscopic
Laparoscopy

Operative Laparoscopy. *ACOG Educational Bulletin.* 1997;239. 4pp. 18refs. Sponsored by the American College of Obstetricians and Gynecologists. Cost: free copy. Set of Bulletins $70 + s/h ACOG members, $125 + s/h nonmembers. One-year subscription $55 member, $65 nonmember. To order single copy, call ACOG Resource Center 202 863-2518; to order set or subscription, call ACOG Distribution Center, 1 800 762-2264. Available on the Internet to members only at acog.org. Key terms: surgery; laparoscopic; surgery; gynecologic.

Surgical Procedures, Laparoscopic/Education

Position Statement on Advanced Laparoscopic Training. *SAGES Publication.* 1997;25. 1pp. Sponsored by the Society of American Gastrointestinal and Endoscopic Surgeons. Cost: free. To order call 310 314-2404. Available on the Internet at sages.org. Key terms: surgery; laparoscopy; training.

Surgical Procedures, Laparoscopic/Standards

SAGES Position Statement—Global Statement on New Procedures. *SAGES Publication.* 1998. 1pp. Sponsored by the Society of American Gastrointestinal and Endoscopic Surgeons. Cost: free. To order call 310 314-2404. Available on the Internet at sages.org. Key terms: surgery; new; procedures; consent.

Surgical Procedures, Operative Parenteral Nutrition, Total

Parenteral Nutrition in Patients Receiving Cancer Chemotherapy. *Ann Intern Med.* 1989;110:734-736. 3pp. 25refs. Sponsored by the American College of Physicians. To order call ACP Clinical Efficacy Assessment Project 1 800 523-1546.

Surgical Wound Infection/Classification Cross Infection/Classification

1992 Modification of CDC Definitions of Surgical Wound Infections. *Infect Control Hosp Epidemiol.* 1992;13:606-608. 3pp. 6refs. Sponsored by the Society for Healthcare Epidemiology of America. Cost: free. To order visit our website at medscape.com/shea. Available on the Internet at medscape.com/shea. Key terms: surgical site infection (SSI); superficial incisional SSI; SSI involving more than one specific site; organ/space SSI.

Surgical Wound Infection/Epidemiology

Consensus Paper on the Surveillance of Surgical Wound Infection. *Infect Control Hosp Epidemiol.* 1992;13:599-605. 7pp. 54refs. Sponsored by the Society for Healthcare Epidemiology of America. Cost: free. To order visit our website at medscape.com/shea. Available on the Internet at medscape.com/shea. Key terms: surgical wound infection task force; surveillance in hospitals; surveillance after discharge; surveillance of minor and outpatient procedures; stratification of SWI data by risk factors.

Surrogate Mothers Ethics, Medical

Ethical Issues in Surrogate Motherhood. *ACOG Committee Opinion.* 1990;88. 6pp. 2refs. Sponsored by the American College of Obstetricians and Gynecologists. Cost: free copy. Set of Opinions $55 + s/h ACOG members, $75 + s/h nonmembers. One-year subscription $55 member, $65 nonmember. To order single copy, call ACOG Resource Center 202 863-2518; to order set or subscription, call ACOG Distribution Center, 1 800 762-2264. Available on the Internet to members only at acog.org.

Sympathectomy

Sympathectomy. 1993. Sponsored by the American Association of Neurological Surgeons. To order call AANS 847 692-9500.

Syphilis, Congenital/ Prevention and Control

Guidelines for the Prevention and Control of Congenital Syphilis. *Morbid Mortal Weekly Report.* 1988;37(S-1). 13pp. Sponsored by the Centers for Disease Control and Prevention. Cost: $1. To order call US Govt Printing Office 202 783-3238.

Syphilis/Diagnosis

Screening for Syphilis. *Guide to Clinical Preventive Services, 2nd Ed.* 1996. Sponsored by the US Preventive Services Task Force. To order call Williams & Wilkins 1 800 638-0672.

Syphilis/Diagnosis

Syphilis Tests in Diagnostic and Therapeutic Decision Making. *Ann Intern Med.* 1986;104:368-376. 9pp. Sponsored by the American College of Physicians. To order call ACP Clinical Efficacy Assessment Project 1 800 523-1546.

Tamoxifen/Adverse Effects Endometrial Neoplasms/ Chemically Induced

Tamoxifen and Endometrial Cancer. *ACOG Committee Opinion.* 1996;169. 3pp. 10refs. Sponsored by the American College of Obstetricians and Gynecologists. Cost: free copy. Set of Opinions $55 + s/h ACOG members, $75 + s/h nonmembers. One-year subscription $55 member, $65 nonmember. To order single copy, call ACOG Resource Center 202 863-2518; to order set or subscription, call ACOG Distribution Center, 1 800 762-2264. Available on the Internet to members only at acog.org.

Tartrazine

Tartrazine. 1977. Position Statement No. 3. 1pp. Sponsored by the American Academy of Allergy, Asthma, and Immunology. Cost: free copy. To order call 414 272-6071.

Tay-Sachs Disease/Diagnosis Heterozygote Detection/Methods

Screening for Tay-Sachs Disease. *ACOG Committee Opinion*. 1995;162. 2pp. 1ref. Sponsored by the American College of Obstetricians and Gynecologists. Cost: free copy. Set of Opinions $55 + s/h ACOG members, $75 + s/h nonmembers. One-year subscription $55 member, $65 nonmember. To order single copy, call ACOG Resource Center 202 863-2518; to order set or subscription, call ACOG Distribution Center, 1 800 762-2264. Available on the Internet to members only at acog.org. Key terms: genetic screening.

Telemedicine
Surgery

Guidelines for the Surgical Practice of Telemedicine. 1996;21. 8pp. 18refs. Sponsored by the Society of American Gastrointestinal and Endoscopic Surgeons. Cost: free. To order call 310 314-2404. Available on the Internet at sages.org. Key terms: surgery; telemedicine.

Teleradiology

ACR Standard for Teleradiology (Revised). 1998. 9pp. 45refs. Sponsored by the American College of Radiology. Cost: $25 (ACR nonmembers). To order call ACR Dept of Quality Assurance 703 716-7592. Available free on the Internet at acr.org. Key terms: teleradiology.

Temporomandibular Joint/Surgery

Temporomandibular Joint. *Clinical Practice Guidelines: Plastic and Maxillofacial Surgery*. 1995. 22pp. 72refs. Sponsored by the American Society of Maxillofacial Surgeons. Cost: Maxillofacial Surgery Guidelines $25 for entire set (not sold separately). Binder $10 (price includes shipping). To order call 1 800 766-4955.

Temporomandibular Joint Disorders/Diagnosis
Temporomandibular Joint Disorders/Therapy

Guidelines for Diagnosis and Management of Disorders Involving the Temporomandibular Joint and Related Musculoskeletal Structures (Revision). 1994. 4pp. 85refs. Sponsored by the American Society of Temporomandibular Joint Surgeons, American Society of Maxillofacial Surgeons. To order call ASTJS 612 930-0988.

Temporomandibular Joint Disorders/Diagnosis
Temporomandibular Joint Disorders/Therapy

Management of Temporomandibular Disorders. *NIH Technology Assessment Conference Statement*. 1996. 38pp. 77refs. Sponsored by the National Institutes of Health. Cost: free copy. To order call 1 888 644-2667. Available on the Internet at consensus.nih.gov.

Tennis Elbow

Lateral Epicondylitis of the Elbow. *Clinical Policies*. 1996. 6pp. 15refs. Sponsored by the American Academy of Orthopaedic Surgeons, North American Spine Society. Cost: $50 (set of 15) for nonmembers. To order call 1 800 626-6276. Key terms: elbow pain; tennis elbow; forearm extensors; radial tunnel syndrome; American Academy of Orthopaedic Surgeons.

Tenosynovitis

DeQuervain's Stenosing Tenosynovitis. *Clinical Policies*. 1996. 5pp. 14refs. Sponsored by the American Academy of Orthopaedic Surgeons, North American Spine Society. Cost: $50 (set of 15) for nonmembers. To order call 1 800 626-6276. Key terms: DeQuervain's stenosing tenosynovitis; wrist; thumb; American Academy of Orthopaedic Surgeons.

Teratology

Teratology. *ACOG Educational Bulletin*. 1997;236. 8pp. 3refs. Sponsored by the American College of Obstetricians and Gynecologists. Cost: free copy. Set of Bulletins $70 + s/h ACOG members, $125 + s/h nonmembers. One-year subscription $55 member, $65 nonmember. To order single copy, call ACOG Resource Center 202 863-2518; to order set or subscription, call ACOG Distribution Center, 1 800 762-2264. Available on the Internet to members only at acog.org. Key terms: teratogens.

Terminal Care

The Care of Dying Patients, Position Statement. 1998. Sponsored by the American Geriatrics Society. Cost: free. To order call AGS 212 308-1414.

Therapeutics
Education, Medical

Improving Medical Education in Therapeutics. *Ann Intern Med*. 1988;108:145-147. 3pp. Sponsored by the American College of Physicians. To order call ACP Clinical Efficacy Assessment Project 1 800 523-1546.

Thoracic Diseases
Ethics

The Potential for Conflict of Interest of Members of the American Thoracic Society. *Amer Rev Resp Dis.* 1988;137:2. Sponsored by the American Thoracic Society. Cost: $4. To order send check payable to American Thoracic Society, 1740 Broadway, New York, NY 10019-4374; for credit card orders, call 212 315-8863.

Thoracic Vertebrae/Surgery

Thoracic Spine Surgery. 1993. Sponsored by the American Association of Neurological Surgeons. To order call AANS 847 692-9500.

Thromboembolism
Pregnancy Complications, Cardiovascular

Thromboembolism in Pregnancy. *ACOG Educational Bulletin.* 1997;234. 10pp. 56refs. Sponsored by the American College of Obstetricians and Gynecologists. Cost: free copy. Set of Bulletins $70 + s/h ACOG members, $125 + s/h nonmembers. One-year subscription $55 member, $65 nonmember. To order single copy, call ACOG Resource Center 202 863-2518; to order set or subscription, call ACOG Distribution Center, 1 800 762-2264. Available on the Internet to members only at acog.org. Key terms: embolism and thrombosis; pregnancy complications; cardiovascular.

Thrombophlebitis
Postoperative Complications

Global Statement on Deep Venous Thrombosis Prophylaxis during Laparoscopic Surgery. 1998. 1pp. 6refs. Sponsored by the Society of American Gastrointestinal and Endoscopic Surgeons. Cost: free. To order call 310 314-2404. Available on the Internet at sages.org. Key terms: DVT; laparoscopic; surgery.

Thyroid Diseases/Diagnosis
Mass Screening

Screening for Thyroid Disease. *Ann Intern Med.* 1990;112:840-849. 10pp. 80refs. Sponsored by the American College of Physicians. To order call ACP Clinical Efficacy Assessment Project 1 800 523-1546.

Thyroid Diseases/Diagnosis
Thyroid Function Tests

American Thyroid Association Guidelines for Use of Laboratory Tests in Thyroid Disorders. *JAMA.* 1990;263:1529-1532. 4pp. 31refs. Sponsored by the American Thyroid Association. Cost: free. To order request as a fax from 202 882-7813. Available on the Internet at thyroid.org.

Thyroid Diseases/Radionuclide Imaging

Procedure Guideline for Thyroid Uptake Measurement. *J Nuclear Med.* 1996;37:1266-1268. 3pp. 9refs. Sponsored by the Society of Nuclear Medicine. Cost: free. To order call Bill Uffelman 703 708-9000. Available on the Internet at snm.org. Key terms: routine diagnostic tests; thyroid uptake measurement; radionuclide imaging; thyroid gland; hyperthyroidism.

Thyroid Diseases/Radionuclide Imaging
Iodine Radioisotopes/Diagnostic Use

Procedure Guideline for Thyroid Scintigraphy. *J Nuclear Med.* 1996;37:1264-1266. 3pp. 9refs. Sponsored by the Society of Nuclear Medicine. Cost: free. To order call Bill Uffelman 703 708-9000. Available on the Internet at snm.org. Key terms: thyroid scintigraphy; routine diagnostic tests; radionuclide imaging; thyroid cancer; thyroid gland.

Thyroid Diseases/Ultrasonography
Parathyroid Diseases/Ultrasonography

ACR Standard for the Performance of the Thyroid and Parathyroid Ultrasound Examination (Revised). 1998. 5pp. 9refs. Sponsored by the American College of Radiology. Cost: $25 (ACR nonmembers). To order call ACR Dept of Quality Assurance 703 716-7592. Available free on the Internet at acr.org. Key terms: thyroid; parathyroid; ultrasound.

Thyroid Gland/Radionuclide Imaging

ACR Standard for the Performance of Thyroid Scintigraphy and Uptake Measurements. 1995. 5pp. 9refs. Sponsored by the American College of Radiology. Cost: $25 (ACR nonmembers). To order call ACR Dept of Quality Assurance 703 716-7592. Available free on the Internet at acr.org. Key terms: nuclear medicine; thyroid; uptake.

Thyroid Neoplasms/Surgery

Thyroid Cancer Surgical Practice Guidelines. *Oncology.* 1997;11(8). 5pp. 5refs. Sponsored by the Society of Surgical Oncology. Cost: call 516 424-8900 x316. To order write Oncology, PRR, Inc, 17 Prospect St, Huntington NY 11743. Key terms: thyroid.

Thyroid Neoplasms/Therapy
Practice Guidelines

AACE Clinical Practice Guidelines for the Management of Thyroid Carcinoma. *Endocrine Practice*. 1997;3(1):60-71. 12pp. 33refs. Sponsored by the American Association of Clinical Endocrinologists. To order call AACE 904 353-7878. Key terms: thyroid; carcinoma; cancer; neck-mass; impalpable lesion.

Thyroid Neoplasms/Therapy
Thyroid Nodule/Therapy

Treatment Guidelines for Patients with Thyroid Nodules and Well-Differentiated Thyroid Cancer. *Arch Intern Med*. 1996;156:2165-2172. 8pp. 21refs. Sponsored by the American Thyroid Association. Cost: free. To order request as a fax from 718 882-6085. Available on the Internet at thyroid.org. Key terms: thyroid; nodule; goiter; cancer; treatment.

Thyroid Nodule/Diagnosis
Diagnosis, Differential

Diagnostic Evaluation of the Differential Diagnosis of Thyroid Nodules. *Practice-Related Report of the AMA Council on Scientific Affairs*. 1991. Sponsored by the American Medical Association, Council on Scientific Affairs. Cost: free. To order call Nancy Nolan, AMA, 312 464-5046.

Thyroid Nodule/Diagnosis
Thyroid Nodule/Therapy

Clinical Practice Guidelines for the Diagnosis and Management of Thyroid Nodules. 1996. 8pp. 16refs. Sponsored by the American Association of Clinical Endocrinologists. To order call AACE 904 353-7878. Key terms: thyroid; gland; nodules; thyroiditis; hyperthyroidism/hypothyroidism.

Thyroidectomy

Thyroidectomy. *Clinical Indicators Compendium*. 1999. Sponsored by the American Academy of Otolaryngology-Head and Neck Surgery. Cost: $10 AAO-HNS members, $15 nonmembers. To order write to AAO-HNS, 1 Prince St, Alexandria, VA 22314.

Tinea/Drug Therapy

Superficial Mycotic Infections of the Skin: Tinea corporis, Tinea cruris, Tinea faciei, Tinea manuum, and Tinea pedis. *J Am Acad Derm*. 1996;34:282-286. 5pp. 22refs. Sponsored by the American Academy of Dermatology. Cost: free copy. To order call Alice Bell 847 330-0230 x333. Available on the Internet at aad.org. Key terms: tinea; diagnosis; drug therapy; antifungal agents.

Tinea Versicolor/Drug Therapy

Superficial Mycotic Infections of the Skin: Pityriasis (tinea) versicolor. *J Am Acad Derm*. 1996;34:287-289. 3pp. 19refs. Sponsored by the American Academy of Dermatology. Cost: free copy. To order call Alice Bell 847 330-0230 x333. Available on the Internet at aad.org. Key terms: tinea versicolor; diagnosis; antifungal agents.

Tobacco Smoke Pollution

Fact Sheet: "Facts About Second Hand Smoke." *ATS News*. 1993. Sponsored by the American Thoracic Society. Cost: $1. To order send check payable to American Thoracic Society, 1740 Broadway, New York, NY 10019-4374; for credit card orders, call 212 315-8863.

Tobacco Smoke Pollution/
Adverse Effects
Respiratory Tract Diseases/Etiology

Environmental Tobacco Smoke: A Hazard to Children. *Pediatr*. 1997;99:639. 4pp. 59refs. Sponsored by the American Academy of Pediatrics. Cost: $1.95. Discounted set of policies available. To order call 1 800 433-9016.

Tobacco Use Disorder/
Prevention and Control
Health Education

Counseling to Prevent Tobacco Use. *Guide to Clinical Preventive Services, 2nd Ed*. 1996. Sponsored by the US Preventive Services Task Force. To order call Williams & Wilkins 1 800 638-0672.

Tobacco Use Disorder/Therapy

Practical Guideline for the Treatment of Patients with Nicotine Dependence. *Am J Psych*. 1996;153(suppl): 10. 31pp. 219refs. Sponsored by the American Psychiatric Association. Cost: $22.50. To order call 1 800 368-5777 order #SPCT2308. Key terms: nicotine.

Tomography/X-ray Computed
Radiography, Thoracic

ACR Standard for the Performance of Thoracic Computed Tomography in Adults and Children. 1998. 8pp. 25refs. Sponsored by the American College of Radiology. Cost: $25 (ACR nonmembers). To order call ACR Dept of Quality Assurance 703 716-7592. Available free on the Internet at acr.org. Key terms: thoracic; computed tomography; chest; pulmonary.

Tomography, Emission Computed/Instrumentation

Instrumentation in Positron Emission Tomography. *JAMA*. 1988;259:1531-1536. 6pp. Sponsored by the American Medical Association, Council on Scientific Affairs. Cost: free. To order call Nancy Nolan, AMA, 312 464-5046.

Tomography, Emission-Computed/Standards

Assessment: Positron Emission Tomography. *Neurol*. 1991;41:163-167. 5pp. 67refs. Sponsored by the American Academy of Neurology. Cost: individual statements are free. To order call AAN Member Service Center 1 800 879-1960. Available on the Internet at aan.com.

Tomography, X-ray Computed

ACR Standard for Diagnostic Medical Physics Performance Monitoring of Computed Tomography Equipment. 1998. Sponsored by the American College of Radiology. Cost: $25 (ACR nonmembers). To order call ACR Dept of Quality Assurance 703 716-7592. Available free on the Internet at acr.org. Key terms: CT; equipment monitoring; medical physics.

Tomography, X-ray Computed

ACR Standard for the Performance of Computed Tomography of the Abdomen and Pelvis (Revised). 1997. 4pp. 5refs. Sponsored by the American College of Radiology. Cost: $25 (ACR nonmembers). To order call ACR Dept of Quality Assurance 703 716-7592. Available free on the Internet at acr.org. Key terms: computed tomography; abdominal; pelvic.

Tomography, X-ray Computed

Performance/Interpretation Qualifications: Computed Tomography. 1991. Sponsored by the American Academy of Neurology. Cost: individual statements are free. To order call AAN Member Service Center 1 800 879-1960. Available on the Internet at aan.com.

Tomography, X-ray Computed Nervous System Diseases/Radiography

ACR Standard for the Performance of Computed Tomography in Neuroradiologic Imaging in Adults and Children. 1998. 7pp. 56refs. Sponsored by the American College of Radiology. Cost: $25 (ACR nonmembers). To order call ACR Dept of Quality Assurance 703 716-7592. Key terms: neuroradiology; brain; spine; CT; neuroimaging.

Tooth Extraction Oral Surgical Procedures

Dentoalveolar Surgery. *J Oral & Maxillofacial Surg*. 1995. Sponsored by the American Association of Oral and Maxillofacial Surgeons. To order call AAOMS Publications 1 800 366-6725.

Trabeculectomy/Methods Glaucoma, Open-Angle/Surgery

Laser Trabeculoplasty for Primary Open-Angle Glaucoma Ophthalmic Procedure Assessment. *Ophthalmology*. 1996;103:1706-1712. 7pp. 62refs. Sponsored by the American Academy of Ophthalmology. Cost: $11 members, $16 nonmembers. AAO members first copy free upon publication. To order call AAO Order Dept 415 561-8540. Key terms: eye; glaucoma; laser surgery; open-angle glaucoma; trabeculoplasty.

Tracheostomy

Tracheostomy. *Clinical Indicators Compendium*. 1999. 1pp. 20refs. Sponsored by the American Academy of Otolaryngology-Head and Neck Surgery. Cost: $10 AAO-HNS members, $15 nonmembers. To order write to AAO-HNS, 1 Prince St, Alexandria, VA 22314. Key terms: trachea; larynx; ventilation.

Transients and Migrants Tuberculosis, Pulmonary/ Prevention and Control

Prevention and Control of Tuberculosis in Migrant Farm Workers. *Morbid Mortal Weekly Report*. 1992;41(no. RR-10):1-14. 15pp. Sponsored by the Centers for Disease Control and Prevention. Cost: $1. To order call US Govt Printing Office 202 783-3238.

Treatment Refusal Adolescent Psychology Levonorgestrel

Adolescents' Right to Refuse Long-Term Contraceptives. *ACOG Committee Opinion*. 1994;139. 2pp. 6refs. Sponsored by the American College of Obstetricians and Gynecologists. Cost: free copy. Set of Opinions $55 + s/h ACOG members, $75 + s/h nonmembers. One-year subscription $55 member, $65 nonmember. To order single copy, call ACOG Resource Center 202 863-2518; to order set or subscription, call ACOG Distribution Center, 1 800 762-2264. Available on the Internet to members only at acog.org. Key terms: informed consent; Norplant; Depo-Provera; health services for adolescents.

Treatment Refusal
Informed Consent

Informed Refusal. *ACOG Committee Opinion.*
1995;166. 2pp. 3refs. Sponsored by the American
College of Obstetricians and Gynecologists. Cost: free
copy. Set of Opinions $55 + s/h ACOG members, $75
+ s/h nonmembers. One-year subscription $55
member, $65 nonmember. To order single copy, call
ACOG Resource Center 202 863-2518; to order set or
subscription, call ACOG Distribution Center,
1 800 762-2264. Available on the Internet to members
only at acog.org.

Trephining
Brain Diseases/Surgery

Puncture, Burr Holes, Twist Drill, or Trephine for
Drainage for Exploration. 1993. Sponsored by the
American Association of Neurological Surgeons. To
order call AANS 847 692-9500.

Trephining
Brain Diseases/Surgery
Drainage

Puncture, Burr Holes, Twist Drill, or Trephine for
Drainage for Aspiration. 1993. Sponsored by the
American Association of Neurological Surgeons. To
order call AANS 847 692-9500.

Trephining
Brain Diseases/Surgery
Injections, Intraventricular

Puncture, Burr Holes, Twist Drill, or Trephine for
Drainage for Intracranial Injection. 1993. Sponsored
by the American Association of Neurological
Surgeons. To order call AANS 847 692-9500.

Trephining
Hematoma, Subdural

Burr Holes or Twist Drill for Intracranial Hematoma.
1993. Sponsored by the American Association of
Neurological Surgeons. To order call AANS
847 692-9500.

Trephining
Skull Fractures/Surgery

Craniotomy or Burr Holes for Skull Fracture, Open or
Depressed. 1993. Sponsored by the American
Association of Neurological Surgeons. To order call
AANS 847 692-9500.

Trephining
Wounds, Penetrating

Craniotomy or Burr Holes for Penetrating Cranial
Wound. 1993. Sponsored by the American Association
of Neurological Surgeons. To order call AANS
847 692-9500.

Trigeminal Ganglion
Radiosurgery

Stereotactic Lesion Creation in Gasserian Ganglion or
Trigeminal Tract. 1993. Sponsored by the American
Association of Neurological Surgeons. To order call
AANS 847 692-9500.

Trophoblastic Neoplasms/Therapy
Uterine Neoplasms/Diagnosis

Management of Gestational Trophoblastic Neoplasia.
ACOG Technical Bulletin. 1993;178. 8pp. 23refs.
Sponsored by the American College of Obstetricians
and Gynecologists. Cost: free copy. Set of Bulletins
$70 + s/h ACOG members, $125 + s/h nonmembers.
One-year subscription $55 member, $65 nonmember.
To order single copy, call ACOG Resource Center
202 863-2518; to order set or subscription, call ACOG
Distribution Center, 1 800 762-2264. Available on the
Internet to members only at acog.org.

Tuberculin
Nursing Homes

Two-Step PPD Testing for Nursing Home Patients on
Admission. 1997. Sponsored by the American
Geriatrics Society. Cost: free. To order call AGS
212 308-1414.

Tuberculin Test

The Tuberculin Skin Test. *Amer Rev Resp Dis.*
1981;124:3. Sponsored by the American Thoracic
Society. Cost: $4. To order send check payable to
American Thoracic Society, 1740 Broadway, New
York, NY 10019-4374; for credit card orders, call
212 315-8863.

Tuberculin Test
Tuberculosis/Prevention and Control

Update on Tuberculosis Skin Testing of Children.
Pediatr. 1996;97(2):282-284. 3pp. 11refs. Sponsored
by the American Academy of Pediatrics. Cost: $1.95.
Discounted set of policies available. To order call
1 800 433-9016.

Tuberculosis/Prevention and Control

Strategic Plan for the Elimination of Tuberculosis in the United States. *Morbid Mortal Weekly Report.* 1989;38:269-272. 4pp. Sponsored by the Centers for Disease Control and Prevention. Cost: $1. To order call US Govt Printing Office 202 783-3238.

Tuberculosis, Pulmonary/Diagnosis

Diagnostic Standards and Classification of Tuberculosis. *Amer Rev Resp Dis.* 1990;142:3. Sponsored by the American Thoracic Society, Centers for Disease Control and Prevention. Cost: $6. To order send check payable to American Thoracic Society, 1740 Broadway, New York, NY 10019-4374; for credit card orders, call 212 315-8863.

Tuberculosis, Pulmonary/ Prevention and Control

Control of Tuberculosis in the U.S. *Amer Rev Resp Dis.* 1992;146:6. Sponsored by the American Thoracic Society. Cost: $6. To order send check payable to American Thoracic Society, 1740 Broadway, New York, NY 10019-4374; for credit card orders, call 212 315-8863.

Tuberculosis, Pulmonary/ Prevention and Control Virus Diseases/Complications

1997 USPHS/IDSA Guidelines for the Prevention of Opportunistic Infections in Patients Infected with Human Immunodeficiency Virus: Disease-Specific Recommendations. *Clin Infec Dis.* 1997;25(suppl 3):S313. 23pp. 15refs. Sponsored by the Infectious Diseases Society of America. To obtain, request from medical library or download via the Internet. Available on the Internet at idsociety.org/practice.

Tuberculosis, Pulmonary/ Prevention and Control Virus Diseases/Complications

Preface to the 1997 USPHS/IDSA Guidelines for the Prevention of Opportunistic Infections in Persons with Human Immunodeficiency Virus: Disease-Specific Recommendations. *Clin Infec Dis.* 1997;25(suppl 3):S299. 14pp. 107refs. Sponsored by the Infectious Diseases Society of America. To obtain, request from medical library or download via the Internet. Available on the Internet at idsociety.org/practice.

Tumor Markers, Biological/Analysis Colorectal Neoplasms/Diagnosis Breast Neoplasms/Diagnosis

1998 Update of Recommendations for the Use of Tumor Markers in Breast and Colorectal Cancer. *J Clin Oncol.* 1999;16:793-795. 3pp. 3refs. Sponsored by the American Society of Clinical Oncology. Cost: free copy. To order call ASCO 703 299-0150 or e-mail: guidelines@asco.org. Available free on the Internet at asco.org.

Turbinates/Surgery

Inferior Turbinectomy. *Clinical Indicators Compendium.* 1999. 1pp. 20refs. Sponsored by the American Academy of Otolaryngology-Head and Neck Surgery. Cost: $10 AAO-HNS members, $15 nonmembers. To order write to AAO-HNS, 1 Prince St, Alexandria, VA 22314. Key terms: sinusitis; hypertrophy; ablation; excision; turbinate.

Tympanoplasty

Tympanoplasty. *Clinical Indicators Compendium.* 1999. 2pp. 20refs. Sponsored by the American Academy of Otolaryngology-Head and Neck Surgery. Cost: $10 AAO-HNS members, $15 nonmembers. To order write to AAO-HNS, 1 Prince St, Alexandria, VA 22314. Key terms: myringoplasty; antrostomy; middle-ear; tympanic membrane; mastoidectomy.

Typhoid/Immunization Typhoid-Paratyphoid Vaccines/ Administration and Dosage

Typhoid Immunization. *Morbid Mortal Weekly Report.* 1994;43(no. RR-14). Sponsored by the Centers for Disease Control and Prevention. Cost: $1. To order call US Govt Printing Office 202 783-3238.

Ulnar Nerve Compression Syndrome/Surgery

Ulnar Nerve Transposition. 1993. Sponsored by the American Association of Neurological Surgeons. To order call AANS 847 692-9500.

Ultrafiltration/Methods Kidney Failure, Acute/Therapy

Continuous Arteriovenous Hemofiltration (CAVH) for Fluid Removal. *JAMA.* 1985;253:1325-1326. 2pp. Sponsored by the American Medical Association, Diagnostic and Therapeutic Technology Assessment Program. Cost: free copy. DATTA subscription available. To order call AMA Department of Technology Assessment 312 464-4531.

Ultrasonography

Diagnostic Ultrasonography: Clinical Interpretation. *Practice-Related Report of the AMA Council on Scientific Affairs.* 1990. 19pp. 41refs. Sponsored by the American Medical Association, Council on Scientific Affairs. Cost: free. To order call Nancy Nolan, AMA, 312 464-5046.

Ultrasonography
Diagnostic Imaging

ACR Standard for Performing and Interpreting Diagnostic Ultrasound Examinations (Revised). 1996. 2pp. Sponsored by the American College of Radiology. Cost: $25 (ACR nonmembers). To order call ACR Dept of Quality Assurance 703 716-7592. Available free on the Internet at acr.org. Key terms: ultrasound; diagnostic; qualifications.

Ultrasonography
Heart Diseases/Ultrasonography

Ultrasonic Imaging of the Heart. *Practice-Related Report of the AMA Council on Scientific Affairs.* 1990. 20pp. 33refs. Sponsored by the American Medical Association, Council on Scientific Affairs. Cost: free. To order call Nancy Nolan, AMA, 312 464-5046.

Ultrasonography
Prostatic Neoplasms/Diagnosis

Reassessment of Transrectal Ultrasonography. *JAMA.* 1990;263:1563. 1pp. Sponsored by the American Medical Association, Diagnostic and Therapeutic Technology Assessment Program. Cost: free copy. DATTA subscription available. To order call AMA Department of Technology Assessment 312 464-4531.

Ultrasonography, Mammary
Biopsy, Needle/Methods

ACR Standard for the Performance of Ultrasound-Guided Breast Interventional Procedures. 1996. 9pp. 16refs. Sponsored by the American College of Radiology. Cost: $25 (ACR nonmembers). To order call ACR Dept of Quality Assurance 703 716-7592. Available free on the Internet at acr.org. Key terms: ultrasound; breast procedures; interventional.

Ultrasonography, Prenatal

ACR Standard for the Performance of Antepartum Obstetrical Ultrasound. 1999. 9pp. 9refs. Sponsored by the American College of Radiology. Cost: $25 (ACR nonmembers). To order call ACR Dept of Quality Assurance 703 716-7592. Available free on the Internet at acr.org. Key terms: antepartum; obstetrical; ultrasound; fetal.

Ultrasonography, Prenatal

Ultrasonography in Pregnancy. *ACOG Technical Bulletin.* 1993;187. Sponsored by the American College of Obstetricians and Gynecologists. Cost: free copy. Set of Bulletins $70 + s/h ACOG members, $125 + s/h nonmembers. One-year subscription $55 member, $65 nonmember. To order single copy, call ACOG Resource Center 202 863-2518; to order set or subscription, call ACOG Distribution Center, 1 800 762-2264. Available on the Internet to members only at acog.org. Key terms: ultrasound; prenatal.

Ultrasonography, Prenatal
Abnormalities/Ultrasonography

Routine Ultrasound in Low-Risk Pregnancy. *ACOG Practice Patterns.* 1997;5. 6pp. 12refs. Sponsored by the American College of Obstetricians and Gynecologists. Cost: free copy. Multiples of 25: $20 + s/h member, $30 + s/h nonmember. To order single copy, call ACOG Resource Center 202 863-2518; to order set or subscription, call ACOG Distribution Center, 1 800 762-2264. Available on the Internet to members only at acog.org. Key terms: ultrasonography; prenatal; prenatal care; costs and cost analysis; technology assessment.

Ultrasonography, Prenatal/Methods

Screening Ultrasonography in Pregnancy. *Guide to Clinical Preventive Services, 2nd Ed.* 1996. Sponsored by the US Preventive Services Task Force. To order call Williams & Wilkins 1 800 638-0672.

Ultrasonography/Instrumentation

Status of Medical Diagnostic Ultrasound Instrumentation. *Practice-Related Report of the AMA Council on Scientific Affairs.* 1990. 13pp. 9refs. Sponsored by the American Medical Association, Council on Scientific Affairs. Cost: free. To order call Nancy Nolan, AMA, 312 464-5046.

Ultrasonography/Instrumentation
Data Display/Standards

New Ultrasound Output Display Standards. *ACOG Committee Opinion.* 1996;180. 2pp. 3refs. Sponsored by the American College of Obstetricians and Gynecologists. Cost: free copy. Set of Opinions $55 + s/h ACOG members, $75 + s/h nonmembers. One-year subscription $55 member, $65 nonmember. To order single copy, call ACOG Resource Center 202 863-2518; to order set or subscription, call ACOG Distribution Center, 1 800 762-2264. Available on the Internet to members only at acog.org. Key terms: ultrasound; prenatal; technology assessment; biomedical.

Ultrasonography/Standards

ACR Standard for Diagnostic Medical Physics Performance Monitoring of Real Time B-Mode Ultrasound Equipment. 1999. 5pp. 10refs. Sponsored by the American College of Radiology. Cost: $25 (ACR nonmembers). To order call ACR Dept of Quality Assurance 703 716-7592. Available free on the Internet at acr.org. Key terms: ultrasound; monitoring; physics; quality control; equipment.

Ultrasonography/Trends

Future of Ultrasonography. *Practice-Related Report of the AMA Council on Scientific Affairs.* 1990. 15pp. 51refs. Sponsored by the American Medical Association, Council on Scientific Affairs. Cost: free. To order call Nancy Nolan, AMA, 312 464-5046.

Ultraviolet Rays/Adverse Effects Skin Neoplasms/Prevention and Control

Practice Policy Statement: Skin Protection from Ultraviolet Light Exposure. *Am J Prev Med.* 1998;14(1):83-86. 4pp. 46refs. Sponsored by the American College of Preventive Medicine. To order reprint address request to ACPM, 1660 L St NW, #206, Washington, DC 20036.

United States

The American Health Care System. *J Allergy Clin Immun.* 1995;95:797-800, Position Statement No. 27. Sponsored by the American Academy of Allergy, Asthma, and Immunology. Cost: free copy. To order call 414 272-6071.

United States Department of Veterans Affairs Geriatrics

The Role of the Veterans Administration in the Care of the Elderly, Position Statement. 1993. Sponsored by the American Geriatrics Society. Cost: free. To order call AGS 212 308-1414.

United States Occupational Safety and Health Administration Endoscopy/Standards

OSHA Regulations—Requirements for Endoscopic Practice. 1993. Sponsored by the American Society for Gastrointestinal Endoscopy. To order call ASGE 978 526-8330.

Ureteral Calculi/Therapy

Management of Ureteral Calculi. 1997. 80pp. 327refs. Sponsored by the American Urological Association. Cost: $49 members, $69 nonmembers. To order write Health Policy Dept, AUA, 1120 N Charles St, Baltimore, MD 21201. Key terms: urinary calculi; ureteral calculi.

Ureteral Calculi/Therapy Lithotripsy

Ureteral Stone Management: Ureteroscopy and Ultrasonic Lithotripsy. *JAMA.* 1988;259:1557-1559. 3pp. Sponsored by the American Medical Association, Diagnostic and Therapeutic Technology Assessment Program. Cost: free copy. DATTA subscription available. To order call AMA Department of Technology Assessment 312 464-4531.

Urinary Calculi/Therapy

Lithotripsy. *Ann Intern Med.* 1985;103:626-629. 4pp. Sponsored by the American College of Physicians. To order call ACP Clinical Efficacy Assessment Project 1 800 523-1546.

Urinary Incontinence

Urinary Incontinence. 1996. 12pp. 41refs. Sponsored by the American Medical Directors Association. Cost: $8. To order call 1 800 876-2632 or 410 740-9743.

Urinary Incontinence

Urinary Incontinence in Adults. *NIH Consensus Development Conference Statement.* 1988;7(5):1-32[Conf. No. 71]. 33pp. Sponsored by the National Institutes of Health. Cost: free copy. To order call 1 888 644-2667. Available on the Internet at consensus.nih.gov.

Urinary Incontinence Urinary Incontinence, Stress

Urinary Incontinence and UI Stress. *ACOG Technical Bulletin.* 1995;213. 12pp. 32refs. Sponsored by the American College of Obstetricians and Gynecologists. Cost: free copy. Set of Bulletins $70 + s/h ACOG members, $125 + s/h nonmembers. One-year subscription $55 member, $65 nonmember. To order single copy, call ACOG Resource Center 202 863-2518; to order set or subscription, call ACOG Distribution Center, 1 800 762-2264. Available on the Internet to members only at acog.org.

Urinary Incontinence, Stress/Surgery

Surgical Treatment of Female Stress Urinary Incontinence. 1997. 80pp. 282refs. Sponsored by the American Urological Association. Cost: $49 members, $69 nonmembers. To order write Health Policy Dept, AUA, 1120 N Charles St, Baltimore, MD, 21201. Key terms: urinary incontinence; stress incontinence; guidelines.

Urinary Incontinence/Therapy

Urinary Incontinence in Adults: Acute and Chronic Management. *AHCPR.* 1996;Publication No. 96-0682. 154pp. 463refs. Sponsored by the Federal Agency for Health Care Policy and Research. To order call AHCPR Clearinghouse 1 800 358-9295.

Urinary Tract Infections/Diagnosis
Urinary Tract Infections/Therapy

Diagnosis and Management of Urinary Tract Infection. *Pediatr.* 1999;103:843-852. 10pp. 53refs. Sponsored by the American Academy of Pediatrics. To order call 1 800 433-9016.

Urine

Urine Autoinjection (Autogenous Urine Immunization). *J Allergy Clin Immun.* 1981;67:333-338, Position Statement No. 8—Controversial Techniques. 2pp. 6refs. Sponsored by the American Academy of Allergy, Asthma, and Immunology. Cost: free copy. To order call 414 272-6071.

Urine/Analysis
Urinary Tract Infections/Diagnosis

Urinalysis and Urine Culture in Women with Dysuria. *Ann Intern Med.* 1986;104:212-218. 7pp. Sponsored by the American College of Physicians. To order call ACP Clinical Efficacy Assessment Project 1 800 523-1546.

Urography

ACR Standards for Adult Cystography and Urethrography (Revised). 1996. 3pp. 6refs. Sponsored by the American College of Radiology. Cost: $25 (ACR nonmembers). To order call ACR Dept of Quality Assurance 703 716-7592. Available free on the Internet at acr.org. Key terms: radiology; cystography; urethrography.

Urography/Standards

ACR Standard for the Performance of Excretory Urography. 1999. 7pp. 8refs. Sponsored by the American College of Radiology. Cost: $25 (ACR nonmembers). To order call ACR Dept of Quality Assurance 703 716-7592. Available free on the Internet at acr.org. Key terms: kidney disease; urography; excretory.

Uterine Hemorrhage/Diagnosis

Dysfunctional Uterine Bleeding. *ACOG Technical Bulletin.* 1989;134. 5pp. 18refs. Sponsored by the American College of Obstetricians and Gynecologists. Cost: free copy. Set of Bulletins $70 + s/h ACOG members, $125 + s/h nonmembers. One-year subscription $55 member, $65 nonmember. To order single copy, call ACOG Resource Center 202 863-2518; to order set or subscription, call ACOG Distribution Center, 1 800 762-2264. Available on the Internet to members only at acog.org. Key terms: menorrhagia.

Uterine Hemorrhage/Diagnosis
Clinical Protocols

Vaginal Bleeding. *Ann Emerg Med.* 1997;29:435-458. 24pp. 53refs. Sponsored by the American College of Emergency Physicians. Cost: ACEP members free copy, fee nonmembers. To order call ACEP 1 800 798-1822 x6. Key terms: vaginal bleeding; Emergency Department; postmenarchal patients.

Uterine Monitoring
Home Nursing

Home Uterine Monitoring. *AHCPR Health Technology Review.* 1992;No. 1 (AHCPR Publication No. 92-0064). 5pp. 21refs. Sponsored by the Federal Agency for Health Care Policy and Research. To order call AHCPR Clearinghouse 1 800 358-9295.

Uterine Monitoring
Labor, Premature/
Prevention and Control

Home Uterine Activity Monitoring. *ACOG Committee Opinion.* 1996;172. 7pp. 32refs. Sponsored by the American College of Obstetricians and Gynecologists. Cost: free copy. Set of Opinions $55 + s/h ACOG members, $75 + s/h nonmembers. One-year subscription $55 member, $65 nonmember. To order single copy, call ACOG Resource Center 202 863-2518; to order set or subscription, call ACOG Distribution Center, 1 800 762-2264. Available on the Internet to members only at acog.org.

Uterine Neoplasms
Leiomyoma

Uterine Leiomyomata. *ACOG Technical Bulletin.* 1994;192. 9pp. 39refs. Sponsored by the American College of Obstetricians and Gynecologists. Cost: free copy. Set of Bulletins $70 + s/h ACOG members, $125 + s/h nonmembers. One-year subscription $55 member, $65 nonmember. To order single copy, call ACOG Resource Center 202 863-2518; to order set or subscription, call ACOG Distribution Center, 1 800 762-2264. Available on the Internet to members only at acog.org. Key terms: uterine diseases.

Uterine Prolapse
Urogenital Diseases/Therapy

Pelvic Organ Prolapse. *ACOG Technical Bulletin.* 1995;214. 8pp. 35refs. Sponsored by the American College of Obstetricians and Gynecologists. Cost: free copy. Set of Bulletins $70 + s/h ACOG members, $125 + s/h nonmembers. One-year subscription $55 member, $65 nonmember. To order single copy, call ACOG Resource Center 202 863-2518; to order set or subscription, call ACOG Distribution Center, 1 800 762-2264. Available on the Internet to members only at acog.org. Key terms: uterine prolapse.

Vaccination
Adolescent Health Services

Immunization of Adolescents. *Pediatr.* 1997;99:479. 10pp. 34refs. Sponsored by the American Academy of Pediatrics. Cost: $1.95. Discounted set of policies available. To order call 1 800 433-9016.

Vaccination/Economics
Financing, Government/Legislation and Jurisprudence

Compensation for Vaccine-Related Injuries. *Ann Intern Med.* 1984;101:559-561. 3pp. Sponsored by the American College of Physicians. To order call ACP Clinical Efficacy Assessment Project 1 800 523-1546.

Vaccination/Standards
Measles/Prevention and Control

Measles, Mumps, and Rubella—Vaccine Use and Strategies for Elimination of Measles, Rubella, and Congenital Rubella Syndrome and Control of Mumps: Recommendations of the Advisory Committee on Immunization Practices (ACIP). *Morbid Mortal Weekly Report.* 1998;47(no. RR-8). Sponsored by the Centers for Disease Control and Prevention. To order call US Govt Printing Office. Available on the Internet at cdc.gov/epo/mmwr/preview/ind98_rr.html.

Vaccines, Combined
Immunization

Combination Vaccines for Childhood Immunization (joint with CDC and AAFP). *Pediatr.* 1999;103(5):1064-1077. 14pp. 80refs. Sponsored by the American Academy of Pediatrics. Cost: $1.95. Discounted set of policies available. To order call 1 800 433-9016.

Vacuum Extraction, Obstetrical/ Instrumentation
Obstetrics/Standards

Delivery by Vacuum Extraction. *ACOG Committee Opinion.* 1998;208. 1pp. Sponsored by the American College of Obstetricians and Gynecologists. Cost: free copy. Set of Bulletins $70 + s/h ACOG members, $125 + s/h nonmembers. One-year subscription $55 member, $65 nonmember. To order single copy, call ACOG Resource Center 202 863-2518; to order set or subscription, call ACOG Distribution Center, 1 800 762-2264. Available on the Internet to members only at acog.org. Key terms: vacuum extraction; obstetrical; extraction.

Vaginal Birth After Cesarean

Rate of Vaginal Births after Cesarean Delivery. *ACOG Committee Opinion.* 1996;179. 2pp. Sponsored by the American College of Obstetricians and Gynecologists. Cost: free copy. Set of Opinions $55 + s/h ACOG members, $75 + s/h nonmembers. One-year subscription $55 member, $65 nonmember. To order single copy, call ACOG Resource Center 202 863-2518; to order set or subscription, call ACOG Distribution Center, 1 800 762-2264. Available on the Internet to members only at acog.org. Key terms: UBAC; data interpretation.

Vaginal Birth After Cesarean/Standards

Vaginal Birth after Previous Cesarean Delivery. *ACOG Practice Bulletin.* 1999;5. 7pp. 71refs. Sponsored by the American College of Obstetricians and Gynecologists. Cost: free copy. Set of Opinions $55 + s/h ACOG members, $75 + s/h nonmembers. One-year subscription $55 member, $65 nonmember. To order single copy, call ACOG Resource Center 202 863-2518; to order set or subscription, call ACOG Distribution Center, 1 800 762-2264. Available on the Internet to members only at acog.org. Key terms: vaginal birth after cesarean.

Vaginal Smears

Cervical Cytology: Evaluation and Management of Abnormalities. *ACOG Technical Bulletin.* 1993;183. 8pp. 26refs. Sponsored by the American College of Obstetricians and Gynecologists. Cost: free copy. Set of Bulletins $70 + s/h ACOG members, $125 + s/h nonmembers. One-year subscription $55 member, $65 nonmember. To order single copy, call ACOG Resource Center 202 863-2518; to order set or subscription, call ACOG Distribution Center, 1 800 762-2264. Available on the Internet to members only at acog.org. Key terms: vaginal smears.

Vaginal Smears
Cervix Neoplasms/
Prevention and Control

Recommendations on Frequency of Pap Test Screening. *ACOG Committee Opinion.* 1995;152. 2pp. Sponsored by the American College of Obstetricians and Gynecologists. Cost: free copy. Set of Opinions $55 + s/h ACOG members, $75 + s/h nonmembers. One-year subscription $55 member, $65 nonmember. To order single copy, call ACOG Resource Center 202 863-2518; to order set or subscription, call ACOG Distribution Center, 1 800 762-2264. Available on the Internet to members only at acog.org. Key terms: vaginal smears; time factors.

Vaginitis

Vaginitis. *ACOG Technical Bulletin.* 1996;226. 9pp. 50refs. Sponsored by the American College of Obstetricians and Gynecologists. Cost: free copy. Set of Bulletins $70 + s/h ACOG members, $125 + s/h nonmembers. One-year subscription $55 member, $65 nonmember. To order single copy, call ACOG Resource Center 202 863-2518; to order set or subscription, call ACOG Distribution Center, 1 800 762-2264. Available on the Internet to members only at acog.org.

Vaginosis, Bacterial/Diagnosis
Labor, Premature/
Prevention and Control

Bacterial Vaginosis Screening for Prevention of Preterm Delivery. *ACOG Committee Opinion.* 1998;198. 2pp. 5refs. Sponsored by the American College of Obstetricians and Gynecologists. Cost: free copy. Set of Opinions $55 + s/h ACOG members, $75 + s/h nonmembers. One-year subscription $55 member, $65 nonmember. To order single copy, call ACOG Resource Center 202 863-2518; to order set or subscription, call ACOG Distribution Center, 1 800 762-2264. Available on the Internet to members only at acog.org. Key terms: bacterial vaginosis: labor; premature; prevention and control; pregnancy complications; infectious.

Vascular Surgical Procedures/Standards
Clinical Trials/Methods

Clinical Research and Vascular Surgery. *J Vasc Surg.* 1992;15:867-903. 37pp. Sponsored by the Society for Vascular Surgery/North American Chapter, ICVS. Cost: free. To order call 978 526-8330.

Version, Fetal

External Cephalic Version. *ACOG Practice Patterns.* 1997;4. 8pp. 33refs. Sponsored by the American College of Obstetricians and Gynecologists. Cost: free copy. Multiples of 25: $20 + s/h member, $30 + s/h nonmember. To order single copy, call ACOG Resource Center 202 863-2518; to order set or subscription, call ACOG Distribution Center, 1 800 762-2264. Available on the Internet to members only at acog.org. Key terms: breech presentation; version; fetal; costs and cost analysis.

Vesicoureteral Reflux/Therapy

Management of Primary Vesicoureteral Reflux in Children. 1997. 96pp. 168refs. Sponsored by the American Urological Association. Cost: $49 members, $69 nonmembers. To order write Health Policy Dept, AUA, 1120 N Charles St, Baltimore, MD 21201. Key terms: vesicoureteral reflux; kidney; ureter; bladder; outcome assessment.

Violence
Physician's Role

Violence Against Women. *JAMA.* 1992;267:3184-3189. 6pp. Sponsored by the American Medical Association, Council on Scientific Affairs. Cost: free. To order call Nancy Nolan, AMA, 312 464-5046.

Violence/Prevention and Control

Counseling to Prevent Youth Violence. *Guide to Clinical Preventive Services, 2nd Ed.* 1996. Sponsored by the US Preventive Services Task Force. To order call Williams & Wilkins 1 800 638-0672.

Virus Diseases/Etiology Adrenal Cortex Hormones/ Administration and Dosage

Inhaled Corticosteroids and Severe Viral Infections. *J Allergy Clin Immun.* 1993;91:223-228, Position Statement No. 23. 6pp. 29refs. Sponsored by the American Academy of Allergy, Asthma, and Immunology. Cost: free copy. To order call 414 272-6071.

Vision Disorders/Diagnosis

Screening for Visual Impairment. *Guide to Clinical Preventive Services, 2nd Ed.* 1996. Sponsored by the US Preventive Services Task Force. To order call Williams & Wilkins 1 800 638-0672.

Vision Screening/Standards Diabetic Retinopathy/ Prevention and Control

Screening for Diabetic Retinopathy. *Ann Intern Med.* 1992;116:683-685. 3pp. Sponsored by the American College of Physicians, American Academy of Ophthalmology, American Diabetes Association. To order call ACP Clinical Efficacy Assessment Project 1 800 523-1546.

Vision, Subnormal

Rehabilitation: The Management of Adult Patients with Low Vision Preferred Practice Pattern. 1994. 18pp. 16refs. Sponsored by the American Academy of Ophthalmology. Cost: $11 members, $16 nonmembers. AAO members first copy free upon publication. To order call AAO Order Dept 415 561-8540. Key terms: eye; visual performance; visual function.

Vitamins/Administration and Dosage

Vitamin Preparations as Dietary Supplements and as Therapeutic Agents. *JAMA.* 1987;257:1929-1936. 8pp. Sponsored by the American Medical Association, Council on Scientific Affairs. Cost: free. To order call Nancy Nolan, AMA, 312 464-5046.

Vitiligo/Therapy

Vitiligo. *J Am Acad Derm.* 1996;35:620-626. 7pp. 30refs. Sponsored by the American Academy of Dermatology. Cost: free copy. To order call Alice Bell 847 330-0230 x333. Available on the Internet at aad.org. Key terms: vitiligo; drug therapy; surgery; PUVA; skin transplantation.

Vitreous Detachment

Management of Posterior Vitreous Detachment, Retinal Breaks, and Lattica Degeneration Preferred Practice Pattern. 1998. 24pp. 60refs. Sponsored by the American Academy of Ophthalmology. Cost: $11 members, $16 nonmembers. AAO members first copy free upon publication. To order call AAO Order Dept 415 561-8540. Key terms: eye; retina; retinal detachment; treatment.

Voluntary Health Organizations

Voluntary Health Organizations. 1976;Position Statement No. 3. 1pp. Sponsored by the American Academy of Allergy, Asthma, and Immunology. Cost: free copy. To order call 414 272-6071.

Vulvar Diseases/Classification Epithelium/Pathology

Vulvar Nonneoplastic Epithelial Disorders. *ACOG Educational Bulletin.* 1998;241. Sponsored by the American College of Obstetricians and Gynecologists. Cost: free copy. Set of Bulletins $70 + s/h ACOG members, $125 + s/h nonmembers. One-year subscription $55 member, $65 nonmember. To order single copy, call ACOG Resource Center 202 863-2518; to order set or subscription, call ACOG Distribution Center, 1 800 762-2264. Available on the Internet to members only at acog.org. Key terms: vulvar disease.

Vulvar Neoplasms

Vulvar Cancer. *ACOG Technical Bulletin.* 1993;186. 8pp. 30refs. Sponsored by the American College of Obstetricians and Gynecologists. Cost: free copy. Set of Bulletins $70 + s/h ACOG members, $125 + s/h nonmembers. One-year subscription $55 member, $65 nonmember. To order single copy, call ACOG Resource Center 202 863-2518; to order set or subscription, call ACOG Distribution Center, 1 800 762-2264. Available on the Internet to members only at acog.org. Key terms: vulvar neoplasms.

Warfarin

The Use of Oral Anticoagulants (warfarin) in the Elderly. 1995. Sponsored by the American Geriatrics Society. Cost: free. To order call AGS 212 308-1414.

Wolff-Parkinson-White Syndrome/Surgery Catheter Ablation

Ablation of Accessory Pathways in Wolff-Parkinson-White Syndrome. *JAMA*. 1987;258:384-386. 3pp. Sponsored by the American Medical Association, Diagnostic and Therapeutic Technology Assessment Program. Cost: free copy. DATTA subscription available. To order call AMA Department of Technology Assessment 312 464-4531.

Women's Health

Guidelines for Women's Health Care. 1995. Sponsored by the American College of Obstetricians and Gynecologists. Cost: $40 + s/h members; $50 + s/h nonmembers per copy. To order call ACOG Distribution Center, 1 800 762-2264. Available on the Internet to members only at acog.org.

Wounds and Injuries/Surgery Trauma Centers/Classification

Resources for Optimal Care of the Injured Patient. 1990. 79pp. Sponsored by the American College of Surgeons. Cost: $10 per copy. To order call ACS Office of Public Info 312 664-4050.

Wounds, Nonpenetrating/Diagnosis Emergency Medical Services/Standards

Acute Blunt Trauma. *Ann Emerg Med*. 1998;31:422-454. 33pp. 99refs. Sponsored by the American College of Emergency Physicians. Cost: ACEP members free copy, fee nonmembers. To order call ACEP 1 800 798-1822 x6. Key terms: acute blunt trauma; 12 years and older; Emergency Department.

Wrist Joint/Pathology

Clinical Guideline on Wrist Pain. 1996. 9pp. 20refs. Sponsored by the American Academy of Orthopaedic Surgeons, North American Spine Society. Cost: $10 AAOS member, $20 nonmember. To order call 1 800 626-6276. Available on the Internet free at guidelines.gov. Key terms: wrist pain; tendonitis; carpal tunnel syndrome; ligamentous injury; arthritis (degenerative).

Section II
Clinical Practice
Guidelines
by Sponsor

American Academy of Allergy, Asthma, and Immunology

Adverse Effects and Complications of Treatment With Beta-Adrenergic Agonist Drugs. In Section I, see: Adrenergic Beta-Agonists/Adverse Effects.

Allergen Skin Testing. In Section I, see: Allergens/Analysis.

Allergen Standardization. In Section I, see: Allergens.

Anaphylaxis in Schools and Other Child-Care Settings. In Section I, see: Anaphylaxis/Prevention and Control.

Beta-Adrenergic Blockers, Immunotherapy and Skin Testing. In Section I, see: Adrenergic Beta-Antagonists/Adverse Effects.

Candidiasis Hypersensitivity Syndrome. In Section I, see: Candidiasis/Immunology.

Carotid Body Resection. In Section I, see: Carotid Body/Surgery.

Clinical Ecology. In Section I, see: Air Pollutants/Adverse Effects.

Conference Participation. In Section I, see: Congresses.

Cytotoxicity Testing (Bryan's Testing). In Section I, see: Cytotoxicity, Immunologic.

Environmental Allergen Avoidance in Allergic Asthma. In Section I, see: Allergens/Adverse Effects.

Epinephrine Injection. In Section I, see: Epinephrine/Therapeutic Use.

Guidelines to Minimize the Risk from Systemic Reactions Caused by Immunotherapy with Allergenic Extracts. In Section I, see: Desensitization, Immunologic/Adverse Effects.

Idiopathic Environmental Intolerances. In Section I, see: Multiple Chemical Sensitivity/Etiology.

Inhaled Beta-Adrenergic Agonists in Asthma. In Section I, see: Asthma/Drug Therapy.

Inhaled Corticosteroids and Severe Viral Infections. In Section I, see: Virus Diseases/Etiology.

Measurement of Circulating IgG and IgE Food-Immune Complexes. In Section I, see: Antigen-Antibody Complex/Analysis.

Measurement of Specific and Nonspecific IgG4 Levels as Diagnostic and Prognostic Tests for Clinical Allergy. In Section I, see: Hypersensitivity/Diagnosis.

Methods of Practice Regarding Lab Procedures. In Section I, see: Laboratory Techniques and Procedures.

Participation in Meetings Advocating Unproven Techniques. In Section I, see: Hypersensitivity.

Personnel and Equipment to Treat Systemic Reactions Caused by Immunotherapy with Allergenic Extracts. In Section I, see: Allergens/Administration and Dosage.

Provocative Testing (Sublingual). In Section I, see: Hypersensitivity/Diagnosis.

Provocative and Neutralization Testing (Subcutaneous). In Section I, see: Food Hypersensitivity/Diagnosis.

RAST Marketing. In Section I, see: Radioallergosorbent Test.

Remote Practice of Allergy. In Section I, see: Delivery of Health Care.

Role of Allergists in Hospitals. In Section I, see: Allergy and Immunology.

Role of the Allergist/Immunologist as a Subspecialist. In Section I, see: Allergy and Immunology/Trends.

Safety and Appropriate Use of Salmeterol in the Treatment of Asthma. In Section I, see: Adrenergic Beta-Agonists/Pharmacology.

Skin Testing and Radioallergosorbent Testing (RAST) for Diagnosis of Specific Allergens Responsible for IgE Mediated Diseases. In Section I, see: IgE/Metabolism.

Skin Titration (Rinkel Method). In Section I, see: Skin Test End-Point Titration.

Some Untested Diagnostic and Therapeutic Procedures in Clinical Allergy. In Section I, see: Hypersensitivity/Diagnosis.

Statement on Resuscitative Equipment. In Section I, see: Allergy and Immunology.

Statement on the Question of Allergy to Fluoride as Used in the Fluoridation of Community Water Supplies. In Section I, see: Fluorides/Immunology.

Tartrazine. In Section I, see: Tartrazine.

The Discontinuation of Hymenoptera Venon Immunotherapy. In Section I, see: Hymenoptera/Immunology.

The Future of the Subspecialty of Allergy and Immunology. In Section I, see: Allergy and Immunology/Education.

The Waiting Period After Allergen Skin Testing and Immunotherapy. In Section I, see: Allergens/Diagnostic Use.

Training Program Directors Committee Position Statement on Health Care Reform. In Section I, see: Allergy and Immunology/Manpower.

Unproven Procedures for Diagnosis and Treatment of Allergic and Immunologic Diseases. In Section I, see: Hypersensitivity/Diagnosis.

Urine Autoinjection (Autogenous Urine Immunization). In Section I, see: Urine.

Use of Anhydrous Theophylline in the Management of Asthma. In Section I, see: Allergens/Diagnostic Use.

Use of Antihistamines in Patients with Asthma. In Section I, see: Asthma/Therapy.

Use of Epinephrine in the Treatment of Anaphylaxis. In Section I, see: Anaphylaxis/Drug Therapy.

Use of In Vitro Tests for IgE Antibody in the Specific Diagnosis of IgE Mediated Disorders and the Formulation of Allergen Immunotherapy. In Section I, see: Allergens/Therapeutic Use.

Use of Inhaled Medications in School by Students with Asthma. In Section I, see: Asthma/Drug Therapy.

Use of Radioallergosorbent and IgE Tests in Practice. In Section I, see: Radioallergosorbent Tests.

Voluntary Health Organizations. In Section I, see: Voluntary Health Organizations.

American Academy of Allergy, Asthma, and Immunology; American College of Allergy, Asthma, and Immunology; Joint Council of Allergy, Asthma, and Immunology

Algorithm for the Diagnosis and Management of Asthma. In Section I, see: Asthma/Diagnosis.

Allergen Immunotherapy. In Section I, see: Immunotherapy/Standards.

Allergy Diagnostic Testing. In Section I, see: Hypersensitivity/Diagnosis.

Diagnosis and Management of Immunodeficiency. In Section I, see: Immunologic Deficiency Syndromes/ Diagnosis.

Diagnosis and Management of Rhinitis: Parameter Documents of the Joint Task…. In Section I, see: Rhinitis/Diagnosis.

Diagnosis and Treatment of Asthma. In Section I, see: Hypersensitivity/Diagnosis.

Disease Management of Atopic Dermatitis: A Practice Parameter. In Section I, see: Dermatitis, Atopic/ Therapy.

Parameters for the Diagnosis and Management of Sinusitis. In Section I, see: Sinusitis/Diagnosis.

Stinging Insect Hypersensitivity: A Practice Parameter. In Section I, see: Hypersensitivity/Therapy.

The Diagnosis and Management of Anaphylaxis. In Section I, see: Anaphylaxis/Diagnosis.

American Academy of Child and Adolescent Psychiatry

Practice Parameters for Child Custody Evaluation. In Section I, see: Child Custody/Legislation and Jurisprudence.

Practice Parameters for the Assessment and Treatment of Children and Adolescents with Anxiety Disorders. In Section I, see: Anxiety Disorders.

Practice Parameters for the Assessment and Treatment of Children and Adolescents with Attention Deficit Hyperactivity Disorder. In Section I, see: Attention Deficit Disorder with Hyperactivity/Diagnosis.

Practice Parameters for the Assessment and Treatment of Children and Adolescents with Bipolar Disorder. In Section I, see: Bipolar Disorder.

Practice Parameters for the Assessment and Treatment of Children and Adolescents with Conduct Disorder. In Section I, see: Conduct Disorder/Diagnosis.

Practice Parameters for the Assessment and Treatment of Children and Adolescents with Obsessive-Compulsive Disorder. In Section I, see: Obsessive-Compulsive Disorder/Therapy.

Practice Parameters for the Assessment and Treatment of Children and Adolescents with Post-Traumatic Stress Disorder. In Section I, see: Stress Disorders, Post-Trauma.

Practice Parameters for the Assessment and Treatment of Children and Adolescents with Schizophrenia. In Section I, see: Schizophrenia, Childhood/Therapy.

Practice Parameters for the Assessment and Treatment of Children and Adolescents with Substance Use Disorders. In Section I, see: Substance-Related Disorders/Diagnosis.

Practice Parameters for the Forensic Evaluation of Children and Adolescents Who May Have Been Physically or Sexually Abused. In Section I, see: Child Abuse/Diagnosis.

Sponsor

Practice Parameters for the Psychiatric Assessment of Children and Adolescents. In Section I, see: Adolescent Psychiatry.

Practice Parameters for the Psychiatric Assessment of Infants and Toddlers. In Section I, see: Child Psychiatry.

American Academy of Cosmetic Surgery

Guidelines for Liposuction Surgery. In Section I, see: Lipectomy/Standards.

American Academy of Dermatology

Actinic Keratoses. In Section I, see: Keratosis/ Therapy.

Androgenetic Alopecia. In Section I, see: Alopecia/ Therapy.

Complex Closures, Flaps, and Grafts. In Section I, see: Skin/Surgery.

Contact Dermatitis. In Section I, see: Dermatitis, Contact/Therapy.

Cryosurgery. In Section I, see: Cryosurgery.

Cutaneous Adverse Drug Reactions. In Section I, see: Drug Eruptions/Therapy.

Cutaneous Lupus Erythematosus. In Section I, see: Lupus Erythematosus, Cutaneous/Drug Therapy.

Dermabrasion. In Section I, see: Dermabrasion.

Dermatologic Conditions in Patients Infected with Human Immunodeficiency Virus (HIV). In Section I, see: HIV Infections/Complications.

Dermatomyositis. In Section I, see: Dermatomyositis/ Therapy.

Guidelines of Care for Acne Vulgaris (including Guidelines for Prescribing Isotretinoin in the Tx of Female Acne Patients of Childbearing Potential). In Section I, see: Acne Vulgaris/Therapy.

Guidelines of Care for Alopecia Areata. In Section I, see: Alopecia Areata.

Guidelines of Care for Atopic Dermatitis. In Section I, see: Dermatitis, Atopic/Therapy.

Guidelines of Care for Basal Cell Carcinoma. In Section I, see: Carcinoma, Basal Cell/Therapy.

Guidelines of Care for Chemical Peeling. In Section I, see: Chemexfoliation.

Guidelines of Care for Cutaneous Squamous Cell Carcinoma. In Section I, see: Carcinoma, Squamous Cell/Therapy.

Guidelines of Care for Local and Regional Anesthesia in Cutaneous Surgery. In Section I, see: Anesthesia, Conduction.

Guidelines of Care for Malignant Melanoma. In Section I, see: Melanoma/Therapy.

Guidelines of Care for Mohs Micrographic Surgery. In Section I, see: Skin Neoplasms/Surgery.

Guidelines of Care for Nevi I (Nevocellular Nevi and Seborrheic Keratoses). In Section I, see: Keratosis/ Diagnosis.

Guidelines of Care for Office Surgical Facilities, Part I. In Section I, see: Ambulatory Surgical Procedures/ Standards.

Guidelines of Care for Office Surgical Facilities, Part II. In Section I, see: Ambulatory Care Facilities/ Classification.

Guidelines of Care for Psoriasis. In Section I, see: Psoriasis/Therapy.

Hemangiomas of Infancy. In Section I, see: Hemangioma/Etiology.

Liposuction. In Section I, see: Lipectomy.

Nail Disorders. In Section I, see: Nail Disorders/ Therapy.

Neurofibromatosis Type 1. In Section I, see: Neurofibromatosis I/Therapy.

Non-Melanocytic Nevi, Hamartomas and Potentially Malignant Lesions, Part II. In Section I, see: Hamartoma/Therapy.

Photoaging/Photodamage. In Section I, see: Skin Aging.

Phototherapy and Photochemotherapy. In Section I, see: Skin Diseases/Drug Therapy.

Recommendations for Credentialing and Privileging. In Section I, see: Credentialing.

Scleroderma and Sclerodermoid Disorders. In Section I, see: Scleroderma, Systemic/Therapy.

Sclerotherapy Treatment of Varicose and Telangiectatic Leg Veins. In Section I, see: Sclerotherapy.

Soft Tissue Augmentation (3): Gelatin Matrix Implant. In Section I, see: Biocompatible Materials.

Soft Tissue Augmentation Collagen Implant. In Section I, see: Collagen.

Soft Tissue Augmentation Fat Transplantation. In Section I, see: Adipose Tissue/Transplantation.

Superficial Mycotic Infections of the Skin: Mucocutaneous Candidiasis. In Section I, see: Candidiasis, Chronic Mucocutaneous/Drug Therapy.

Superficial Mycotic Infections of the Skin: Onychomycosis. In Section I, see: Onychomycosis/Diagnosis, Therapy.

Superficial Mycotic Infections of the Skin: Piedra. In Section I, see: Piedra/Diagnosis.

Superficial Mycotic Infections of the Skin: Pityriasis (tinea) versicolor. In Section I, see: Tinea Versicolor/Drug Therapy.

Superficial Mycotic Infections of the Skin: Tinea capitis and Tinea barbae. In Section I, see: Facial Dermatoses/Microbiology.

Superficial Mycotic Infections of the Skin: Tinea corporis, Tinea cruris, Tinea faciei, Tinea manuum, and Tinea pedis. In Section I, see: Tinea/Drug Therapy.

Topical Glucocorticosteroids. In Section I, see: Dermatologic Agents/Therapy.

Vitiligo. In Section I, see: Vitiligo/Therapy.

Warts: HPV. In Section I, see: Papillomavirus, Human.

American Academy of Family Physicians

Fluoridation of Public Water Supplies. In Section I, see: Fluoridation/Standards.

Management of Migraine Headache. In Section I, see: Migraine/Drug Therapy.

Minor Closed Head Trauma in Children. In Section I, see: Head Injuries, Closed.

Neonatal Circumcision. In Section I, see: Circumcision.

Summary of Policy Recommendations for Periodic Health Examination. In Section I, see: Preventive Health Services.

The Benefits and Risks of Controlling Blood Glucose Levels in Patients with Type 2 Diabetes Mellitus. In Section I, see: Blood Glucose.

Trial of Labor versus Elective Repeat Cesarean Section for the Woman with a Previous Cesarean Section. In Section I, see: Cesarean Section, Repeat.

Use of Reminder and Recall Systems by Vaccination Providers to Increase Vaccination Rates. In Section I, see: Reminder Systems, Vaccination/Utilization.

American Academy of Neurology

Assessment of Brain SPECT. In Section I, see: Brain/Radionuclide Imaging.

Assessment of Plasmapheresis. In Section I, see: Nervous System Diseases/Therapy.

Assessment of Vagus Nerve Stimulation for Epilepsy. In Section I, see: Epilepsy/Therapy.

Assessment: Clinical Autonomic Testing. In Section I, see: Autonomic Nervous System/Physiopathology.

Assessment: Dermatomal Somatosensory Evoked Potentials. In Section I, see: Evoked Potentials, Somatosensory.

Assessment: DTP Vaccination. In Section I, see: Diptheria-Tetanus-Pertussis Vaccine/Adverse Effects.

Assessment: Electronystagmography. In Section I, see: Electronystagmography.

Assessment: Intensive EEG/Video Monitoring for Epilepsy. In Section I, see: Electroencephalography.

Assessment: Intraoperative Neurophysiology. In Section I, see: Monitoring, Intraoperative/Standards.

Assessment: Magnetoencephalography (MEG). In Section I, see: Magnetoencephalography/Standards.

Assessment: Melodic Intonation Therapy. In Section I, see: Speech Therapy/Methods.

Assessment: Neurologic Risk of Immunization. In Section I, see: Nervous System Diseases/Etiology.

Assessment: Neurological Evaluation of Male Sexual Dysfunction. In Section I, see: Neurologic Examination.

Assessment: Neuropsychological Testing of Adults: Considerations for Neurologists. In Section I, see: Nervous System Diseases/Psychology.

Assessment: Positron Emission Tomography. In Section I, see: Tomography, Emission-Computed/Standards.

Assessment: Posturography. In Section I, see: Nervous System Diseases/Diagnosis.

Assessment: Techniques Associated with the Diagnosis and Management of Sleep Disorders. In Section I, see: Sleep Disorders/Diagnosis.

Assessment: The Clinical Usefulness of Botulinum Toxin-A in Treating Neurological Disorders. In Section I, see: Botulinum Toxins/Therapeutic Use.

Assessment: Thermography in Neurologic Practice. In Section I, see: Neurology.

Assessment: Transcranial Doppler. In Section I, see: Cerebral Arteries/Physiopathology.

Driving Following an Unprovoked Generalized Single Tonic Clonic Seizure. In Section I, see: Epilepsy, Tonic-Clonic.

Evaluation and Management of Intracranial Mass Lesions in AIDS. In Section I, see: AIDS-Related Opportunistic Infections/Diagnosis.

Generic Substitution for Antiepileptic Medication. In Section I, see: Anticonvulsants/Standards.

Genetic Testing Alert. In Section I, see: Genetic Screening.

Guidelines for Prevention of Transmissions of HIV Type I in Neurologic Practice. In Section I, see: Acquired Immunodeficiency Syndrome/Complications.

Interim Assessment: Carotid Endarterectomy. In Section I, see: Carotid Arteries/Surgery.

Performance/Interpretation Qualifications: Computed Tomography. In Section I, see: Tomography, X-ray Computed.

Practice Advisory on Selection of Patients with Multiple Sclerosis for Treatment with Betaseron. In Section I, see: Interferon-Beta/Therapeutic Use.

Practice Advisory on the Treatment of Amyotrophic Lateral Sclerosis with Riluzole. In Section I, see: Amyotrophic Lateral Sclerosis/Drug Therapy.

Practice Advisory: The Use of Felbamate in the Treatment of Patients with Intractable Epilepsy. In Section I, see: Anticonvulsants/Therapeutic Use.

Practice Advisory: Thrombolytic Therapy for Acute Ischemic Stroke (rt-PA)—Summary Statement. In Section I, see: Cerebral Ischemia/Drug Therapy.

Practice Parameter for Electrodiagnostic Studies in Carpal Tunnel Syndrome. In Section I, see: Carpal Tunnel Syndrome/Diagnosis.

Practice Parameter: A Guideline for Discontinuing Antiepileptic Drugs in Seizure-Free Patients. In Section I, see: Anticonvulsants/Therapeutic Use.

Practice Parameter: Assessment and Management of Patients in the Persistent Vegetative State. In Section I, see: Persistent Vegetative State.

Practice Parameter: Determining Brain Death in Adults. In Section I, see: Brain Death/Diagnosis.

Practice Parameter: Diagnosis and Evaluation of Dementia. In Section I, see: Dementia/Diagnosis.

Practice Parameter: Diagnosis of Patients with Nervous System Lyme Borreliosis (Lyme Disease). In Section I, see: Lyme Disease/Diagnosis.

Practice Parameter: Electrodiagnostic Studies in Lunar Neuropathy at the Elbow. In Section I, see: Electrodiagnosis.

Practice Parameter: Electroencephalogram in the Evaluation of Headache. In Section I, see: Headache/Physiopathology.

Practice Parameter: Management Issues for Women with Epilepsy. In Section I, see: Anticonvulsants/Adverse Effects.

Practice Parameter: The Care of the Patient with Amyotrophic Lateral Sclerosis (an evidence-based review). In Section I, see: Amyotrophic Lateral Sclerosis/Therapy.

Practice Parameter: The Management of Concussion in Sports. In Section I, see: Athletic Injuries/Therapy.

Practice Parameters: Appropriate Use of Ergotamine and Dihydroergotamine in the Treatment of Migraine and Status Migrainosus. In Section I, see: Dihydroergotamine/Therapeutic Use.

Practice Parameters: Carpal Tunnel Syndrome. In Section I, see: Carpal Tunnel Syndrome/Diagnosis.

Practice Parameters: Initial Therapy of Parkinson's Disease. In Section I, see: Parkinson's Disease/Drug Therapy.

Practice Parameters: Lumbar Puncture. In Section I, see: Spinal Puncture.

Practice Parameters: MRI in the Evaluation of Low Back Syndrome. In Section I, see: Back Pain/Diagnosis.

Practice Parameters: Neurologic Evaluation. In Section I, see: Neurology.

Practice Parameters: Utility of Neuroimaging in the Evaluation of Headache in Patients with Normal Neurologic Examinations. In Section I, see: Headache/Diagnosis.

Research Criteria for Diagnosis of Chronic Inflammatory Demyelinating Polyneuropathy (CIDP). In Section I, see: Demyelinating Diseases/Diagnosis.

Review of the Literature on Spinal Ultrasound for the Evaluation of Back Pain and Radicular Disorders. In Section I, see: Spinal Disorders/Ultrasonography.

Silicone Breast Implants and Neurologic Disorders. In Section I, see: Breast Implants/Adverse Effects.

Stroke Prevention in Patients with Nonvalvular Atrial Fibrillation. In Section I, see: Cerebrovascular Disorders/Prevention and Control.

The Relationship of MS to Physical Trauma and Psychological Stress. In Section I, see: Multiple Sclerosis/Etiology.

Training Guidelines for the Use of Botulinum Toxin for the Treatment of Neurologic Disorders. In Section I, see: Botulinum Toxins/Therapeutic Use.

American Academy of Neurology, American Clinical Neurophysiology Society

Assessment of Digital EEG, Quantitive EEG, and EEG Brain Mapping. In Section I, see: Brain/Physiology.

American Academy of Neurology, American College of Emergency Physicians, American Association of Neurological Surgeons, American Society of Neuroradiology

Practice Parameter: Neuroimaging in the Emergency Patient Presenting with Seizure. In Section I, see: Seizures/Radiography.

American Academy of Ophthalmology

Age-Related Macular Degeneration Preferred Practice Pattern. In Section I, see: Macular Degeneration.

Amblyopia Preferred Practice Pattern. In Section I, see: Amblyopia.

Automated Lamellar Keratoplasty Preliminary Procedure Assessment. In Section I, see: Cornea/Surgery.

Automated Perimetry Ophthalmic Procedure Assessment. In Section I, see: Perimetry/Methods.

Bacterial Keratitis Preferred Practice Pattern. In Section I, see: Keratitis.

Blepharitis Preferred Practice Pattern. In Section I, see: Blepharitis.

Cataract in the Adult Eye. In Section I, see: Cataract.

Comprehensive Adult Eye Evaluation Preferred Practice Pattern. In Section I, see: Eye Diseases/Diagnosis.

Conjunctivitis Preferred Practice Pattern. In Section I, see: Conjunctivitis.

Corneal Endothelial Photography Ophthalmic Procedure Assessment. In Section I, see: Endothelium, Corneal.

Corneal Opacification Preferred Practice Pattern. In Section I, see: Corneal Opacity.

Corneal Topography Opthalamic Procedure Assessment. In Section I, see: Corneal Topography.

Diabetic Retinopathy Preferred Practice Patterns. In Section I, see: Diabetic Retinopathy.

Dry Eye Syndrome. In Section I, see: Dry Eye Syndromes.

Epikeratoplasty Ophthalmic Procedure Assessment. In Section I, see: Epikeratophakia.

Esotropia Preferred Practice Pattern. In Section I, see: Esotropia.

Excimer Laser Photorefractive Keratectomy (PRK) for Myopia and Astigmatism Ophthalmic Procedure Assessment. In Section I, see: Keratectomy, Photorefractive.

Functional Indications for Upper and Lower Eyelid Blepharoplasty Ophthalmic Procedure Assessment. In Section I, see: Blepharoplasty.

Indocyanine Green Angiography Ophthalmic Procedure Assessment. In Section I, see: Indocyanine Green.

Laser Blepharoplasty and Skin Resurfacing Ophthalmic Procedure Assessment. In Section I, see: Blepharoplasty.

Laser Peripheral Iridotomy for Pupillary-Block Glaucoma Ophthalmic Procedure Assessment. In Section I, see: Glaucoma, Angle-Closure/Surgery.

Laser Trabeculoplasty for Primary Open-Angle Glaucoma Ophthalmic Procedure Assessment. In Section I, see: Trabeculectomy/Methods.

Management of Posterior Vitreous Detachment, Retinal Breaks, and Lattica Degeneration Preferred Practice Pattern. In Section I, see: Vitreous Detachment.

Nd: YAG Photodisruptors Ophthalmic Procedure Assessment. In Section I, see: Anterior Eye Segment/Surgery.

Optic Nerve Head and Retinal Fiber Analysis Ophthalmic Procedure Assessment. In Section I, see: Diagnostic Techniques, Ophthalmological/Diagnosis.

Pediatric Eye Evaluations. In Section I, see: Eye Diseases/Prevention and Control.

Primary Angle-Closure Glaucoma Preferred Practice Pattern. In Section I, see: Glaucoma, Angle-Closure.

Primary Open-Angle Glaucoma. In Section I, see: Glaucoma, Open-Angle.

Primary Open-Angle Glaucoma Suspect Preferred Practice Pattern. In Section I, see: Glaucoma, Open-Angle/Diagnosis.

Sponsor

Punctal Occlusion for the Dry Eye Ophthalmic Procedure Assessment. In Section I, see: Dry Eye Syndromes/Surgery.

Quality of Ophthalmic Care. In Section I, see: Quality of Healthcare.

Radial Keratotomy for Myopia Ophthalmic Procedure Assessment. In Section I, see: Keratotomy, Radial.

Ready-to-Wear Reading Glasses Ophthalmic Procedure Assessment. In Section I, see: Eyeglasses/ Standards.

Refractive Errors Preferred Practice Patterns. In Section I, see: Refractive Errors.

Rehabilitation: The Management of Adult Patients with Low Vision Preferred Practice Pattern. In Section I, see: Vision, Subnormal.

Repair of Rhegmatogenous Retinal Detachments Ophthalmic Procedure Assessment. In Section I, see: Retinal Detachment.

American Academy of Orthopaedic Surgeons, North American Spine Society

Clinical Guideline on Ankle Injury. In Section I, see: Ankle Injuries.

Clinical Guideline on Hip Pain. In Section I, see: Hip Joint.

Clinical Guideline on Knee Pain (Phases I and II). In Section I, see: Knee.

Clinical Guideline on Low Back Pain (Phases I and II). In Section I, see: Low Back Pain.

Clinical Guideline on Shoulder Pain. In Section I, see: Shoulder Pain.

Clinical Guideline on Wrist Pain. In Section I, see: Wrist Joint/Pathology.

DeQuervain's Stenosing Tenosynovitis. In Section I, see: Tenosynovitis.

Distal Radius Fracture. In Section I, see: Radius Fractures.

Femoral Neck Fracture (Adult). In Section I, see: Femoral Neck Fractures.

Hallux Valgus. In Section I, see: Hallux Valgus.

Herniated Lumbar Disk. In Section I, see: Intervertebral Disk Displacement.

Lateral Epicondylitis of the Elbow. In Section I, see: Tennis Elbow.

Low Back Musculoligamentous Injury (Sprain/Strain). In Section I, see: Lumbar Vertebrae/Injury.

Lumbar Spinal Stenosis. In Section I, see: Spinal Stenosis.

One Set Color Laminated Clinical Guidelines. In Section I, see: Practice Guidelines.

One Set Color Paper Clinical Guidelines. In Section I, see: Practice Guidelines.

Osteoarthritis (Arthrosis) of the Knee (Degenerative Joint Disease). In Section I, see: Osteoarthritis.

Osteoarthritis of the Hip. In Section I, see: Osteoarthritis, Hip.

Pes Planus (Congenital, Acquired, Flexible and Rigid). In Section I, see: Flatfoot.

Proximal Humeral Fracture. In Section I, see: Humerus/Injuries.

Tear, Meniscus of the Knee (Medial and/or Lateral). In Section I, see: Menisci, Tibial.

Ulnar Collateral Ligament Injury of the Thumb. In Section I, see: Collateral Ligaments/Injuries.

American Academy of Otolaryngic Allergy

Allergic Rhinitis Clinical Practice Guideline. In Section I, see: Rhinitis, Allergic, Perennial.

Practice Guidelines for Respiratory Allergy. In Section I, see: Hypersensitivity.

American Academy of Otolaryngology– Head and Neck Surgery

Acoustic Neuroma Surgery. In Section I, see: Neuroma, Acoustic/Surgery.

Adenoidectomy. In Section I, see: Adenoidectomy.

Allergy Testing for Allergic Rhinitus. In Section I, see: Rhinitis, Allergic, Perennial.

Auditory Brainstem Response. In Section I, see: Evoked Potentials, Auditory.

Caldwell-Luc. In Section I, see: Maxillary Sinus/ Surgery.

Diagnostic Nasal Endoscopy. In Section I, see: Endoscopy.

Endoscopic Sinus Surgery, Pediatric. In Section I, see: Paranasal Sinuses/Surgery.

Endoscopic Sinus Surgery, Adult. In Section I, see: Paranasal Sinuses/Surgery.

Ethmoidectomy. In Section I, see: Ethmoid Sinus/ Surgery.

Inferior Turbinectomy. In Section I, see: Turbinates/ Surgery.

Laryngectomy. In Section I, see: Laryngectomy.

Laryngoscopy/Nasopharyngoscopy. In Section I, see: Laryngeal Diseases/Diagnosis.

LeFort Fractures. In Section I, see: Maxillofacial Injuries.

Mandibular Fracture. In Section I, see: Mandibular Fractures.

Mastoidectomy. In Section I, see: Mastoid/Surgery.

Myringotomy and Tympanostomy Tubes. In Section I, see: Middle Ear Ventilation/Methods.

Radical Neck Dissection. In Section I, see: Radical Neck Dissection.

Rhinoplasty. In Section I, see: Rhinoplasty.

Septal Fracture. In Section I, see: Nasal Fracture.

Septoplasty. In Section I, see: Nasal Septum/Surgery.

Stapedectomy. In Section I, see: Stapes Surgery.

Thyroidectomy. In Section I, see: Thyroidectomy.

Tonsillectomy, Adenoidectomy, Adenotonsillectomy. In Section I, see: Adenoidectomy.

Tracheostomy. In Section I, see: Tracheostomy.

Tympanoplasty. In Section I, see: Tympanoplasty.

Uvulopalatopharyngoplasty. In Section I, see: Otorhinolaryngologic Surgical Procedures.

American Academy of Pediatrics

Acellular Pertussis Vaccine: Recommendations for Use as the Initial Series in Infants and Children. In Section I, see: Pertussis Vaccine.

Breastfeeding and the Use of Human Milk. In Section I, see: Breast Feeding.

Cholesterol in Childhood. In Section I, see: Cholesterol/Blood.

Circumcision Policy Statement (formerly, Report of the Task Force on Circumcision). In Section I, see: Circumcision.

Combination Vaccines for Childhood Immunization (joint with CDC and AAFP). In Section I, see: Vaccines, Combined.

Considerations Related to the Use of Recombinant Human Growth Hormone in Children. In Section I, see: Somatotropins, Recombinant/Adverse Effects.

Diagnosis and Management of Urinary Tract Infection. In Section I, see: Urinary Tract Infections/ Diagnosis.

Drugs for Pediatric Emergencies. In Section I, see: Emergency Treatment/Methods.

Environmental Tobacco Smoke: A Hazard to Children. In Section I, see: Tobacco Smoke Pollution/Adverse Effects.

Evaluation and Medical Treatment of the HIV-Exposed Infant. In Section I, see: HIV Infections/ Prevention and Control.

Evaluation and Preparation of Pediatric Patients Undergoing Anesthesia. In Section I, see: Anesthesia.

Female Genital Mutilation. In Section I, see: Circumcision, Female.

Gonorrhea in Prepubertal Children. In Section I, see: Gonorrhea.

Guidance for Effective Discipline. In Section I, see: Child Behavior.

Guidelines for the Pediatric Perioperative Anesthesia Environment. In Section I, see: Anesthesia.

Hepatitis C Virus Infection. In Section I, see: Hepatitis C.

Hospital Discharge of the High-Risk Neonate. In Section I, see: Infant, Premature, Diseases/Nursing.

Hospital Stay for Healthy Term Newborns. In Section I, see: Infant, Newborn.

Immunization of Adolescents. In Section I, see: Vaccination.

Long-term Treatment of the Child with Simple Febrile Seizures. In Section I, see: Fever/Drug Therapy.

Management of Acute Gastroenteritis in Young Children. In Section I, see: Gastroenteritis/Therapy.

Management of Hyperbilirubinemia in the Healthy Term Newborn. In Section I, see: Jaundice, Neonatal/ Therapy.

Measles Immunization in HIV-Infected Children (joint with COPA+). In Section I, see: Measles/Prevention and Control.

Neonatal Drug Withdrawal. In Section I, see: Neonatal Abstinence Syndrome.

Neurodiagnostic Evaluation of a First, Simple Febrile Seizure in Children. In Section I, see: Convulsions.

PCBs in Breast Milk. In Section I, see: Polychlorinated Biphenyls/Analysis.

Poliomyelitis Prevention: Revised Recommendations for Use of Inactivated and Live Oral Poliovirus Vaccines. In Section I, see: Poliomyelitis/Prevention and Control.

Positioning and Sudden Infant Death Syndrome (SIDS). In Section I, see: Posture.

Prevention of Hepatitis A Infections: Guidelines for Use of Hepatitis A Vaccine and Immune Globulin. In Section I, see: Hepatitis A/Prevention and Control.

Prevention of Respiratory Syncytial Virus Infections: Indications for the Use of Palivizumab and update on the Use of RSV-IGIV. In Section I, see: Respiratory Syncytial Virus Infections/Prevention and Control.

Prevention of Rotavirus Disease: Guidelines for Use of Rotavirus Vaccine. In Section I, see: Rotavirus/Immunology.

Reassessment of Indications for Ribavirin Therapy in Respiratory Syncytial Virus Infections. In Section I, see: Ribavirin/Therapeutic Use.

Recommended Childhood Immunization Schedule—United States, January–December 1999. In Section I, see: Immunization Schedule.

Respiratory Syncytial Virus Immune Globulin Intravenous: Indications for Use. In Section I, see: Respiratory Syncytial Virus Infections/Therapy.

Revised Guidelines for Prevention of Early-onset Group-B Streptococcal (GBS) Infection. In Section I, see: Streptococcal Infections/Prevention and Control.

Screening for Elevated Blood Lead Levels. In Section I, see: Lead Poisoning/Prevention and Control.

Screening Infants and Young Children for Developmental Disabilities. In Section I, see: Developmental Disabilities/Diagnosis.

Severe Invasive Group A Streptococcal Infections: A Subject Review. In Section I, see: Streptococcal Infections/Etiology.

Surveillance of Pediatric HIV Infection. In Section I, see: Population Surveillance/Methods.

The Pediatrician's Role in Disaster Preparedness. In Section I, see: Disasters.

The Revised CDC Guidelines for Isolation Precautions in Hospitals: Implications for Pediatrics. In Section I, see: Patient Isolation.

The Role of Home Visitation Programs in Improving Health Outcomes for Children and Families. In Section I, see: Home Care Services/Economics.

The Use of Physical Restraint Interventions for Children and Adolescents in the Acute Care Setting. In Section I, see: Restraint, Physical.

Therapy for Children with Invasive Pneumococcal Infections. In Section I, see: Pneumococcal Infections/Drug Therapy.

Tobacco, Alcohol, and Other Drugs: The Role of the Pediatrician in Prevention and Management of Substance Abuse. In Section I, see: Physician's Role.

Treatment of Febrile Seizures. In Section I, see: Seizures, Febrile/Therapy.

Update on Tuberculosis Skin Testing of Children. In Section I, see: Tuberculin Test.

American Academy of Physical Medicine and Rehabilitation

Practice Parameter: Antiepileptic Drug Treatment of Posttraumatic Seizures. In Section I, see: Anticonvulsants/Therapeutic Use.

American Academy of Sleep Medicine

Practice Parameters for the Indications for Polysomnography and Related Procedures. In Section I, see: Polysomnography/Methods.

Practice Parameters for the Nonpharmacological Treatment of Insomnia. In Section I, see: Insomnia/Therapy.

Practice Parameters for the Treatment of Obstructive Sleep Apnea in Adults: The Efficacy of Surgical Modifications of the Upper Airway. In Section I, see: Sleep Apnea Syndromes/Surgery.

Practice Parameters for the Treatment of Snoring and Obstructive Sleep Apnea with Oral Appliances. In Section I, see: Orthodontic Appliances.

Practice Parameters for the Use of Actigraphy in the Clinical Assessment of Sleep Disorders. In Section I, see: Motor Activity.

Practice Parameters for the Use of Laser-Assisted Uvulopalatoplasty. In Section I, see: Laser Surgery.

Practice Parameters for the Use of Light Therapy in the Treatment of Sleep Disorders. In Section I, see: Phototherapy.

Practice Parameters for the Use of Polysomnography in the Evaluation of Insomnia. In Section I, see: Guidelines.

Practice Parameters for the Use of Portable Recording in the Assessment of Obstructive Sleep Apnea. In Section I, see: Polysomnography/Instrumentation.

Practice Parameters for the Use of Stimulants in the Treatment of Narcolepsy. In Section I, see: Central Nervous System Stimulants/Therapeutic Use.

The Treatment of Restless Legs Syndrome and Periodic Limb Movements. In Section I, see: Restless Legs/Therapy.

American Association of Clinical Endocrinologists

AACE Clinical Practice Guidelines for the Management of Thyroid Carcinoma. In Section I, see: Thyroid Neoplasms/Therapy.

Clinical Practice Guidelines for Growth Hormone Use in Adults and Children. In Section I, see: Somatotropin/Therapeutic Use.

Clinical Practice Guidelines for Male Sexual Dysfunction. In Section I, see: Sex Disorders.

Clinical Practice Guidelines for the Diagnosis and Management of Thyroid Nodules. In Section I, see: Thyroid Nodule/Diagnosis.

Clinical Practice Guidelines for the Evaluation and Treatment of Hyperthyroidism and Hypothyroidism. In Section I, see: Hyperthyroidism/Therapy.

Clinical Practice Guidelines for the Evaluation and Treatment of Hypogonadism in Adult Male Patients. In Section I, see: Hypogonadism/Diagnosis.

Clinical Practice Guidelines for the Treatment of Postmenopausal Osteoporosis. In Section I, see: Osteoporosis, Postmenopausal.

Management of Diabetes Mellitus. In Section I, see: Diabetes Mellitus/Drug Therapy.

American Association of Electrodiagnostic Medicine

Consensus Criteria for the Diagnosis of Partial Conduction Block. In Section I, see: Nerve Block/Diagnosis.

Electrodiagnostic Techniques. In Section I, see: Electrodiagnosis/Methods.

Guidelines for Ethical Behavior Relating to Clinical Practice Issues in Electrodiagnostic Medicine. In Section I, see: Electrodiagnosis/Standards.

Guidelines for Outcome Studies in Electrodiagnostic Medicine. In Section I, see: Electrodiagnosis.

Guidelines for Somatosensory Evoked Potentials. In Section I, see: Evoked Potentials, Somatosensory/Physiology.

Guidelines in Electrodiagnostic Medicine. In Section I, see: Electrodiagnosis.

Job Descriptions for Electrodiagnostic Technologists. In Section I, see: Electrodiagnosis.

Practice Parameter for Electrodiagnostic Studies in Carpal Tunnel Syndrome. In Section I, see: Carpal Tunnel Syndrome/Diagnosis.

Practice Parameter for Needle Electromyographic Evaluation of Patients with Suspected Cervical Radiculopathy. In Section I, see: Spinal Osteophytosis.

Practice Parameters for Electrodiagnostic Studies in Ulnar Neuropathy at the Elbow. In Section I, see: Electrodiagnosis.

Recommended Policy for Electrodiagnostic Medicine. In Section I, see: Electrodiagnostic.

Responsibilities of an Electrodiagnostic Technologist. In Section I, see: Allied Health Personnel.

Risks in Electrodiagnostic Medicine. In Section I, see: Electrodiagnosis.

Somatosensory Evoked Potentials: Clinical Uses. In Section I, see: Evoked Potentials, Somatosensory.

Technology Review: Dynamic Electromyography in Gait and Motion Analysis. In Section I, see: Electromyography.

Technology Review: Nervepace Digital Electroneurometer. In Section I, see: Computers.

Technology Review: The Neurometer Currrent Perception Threshold (CPT). In Section I, see: Electrodiagnosis.

Technology Review: The Use of Surface EMG in the Diagnosis and Treatment of Nerve and Muscle Disorders. In Section I, see: Electromyography.

The Electrodiagnostic Medicine Consultation. In Section I, see: Electrodiagnosis.

The Electrodiagnostic Medicine Consultation. In Section I, see: Electrodiagnosis.

The Scope of Electrodiagnostic Medicine. In Section I, see: Electrodiagnosis.

Who Is Qualified to Practice Electrodiagnostic Medicine? In Section I, see: Professional Competence.

American Association of Neurological Surgeons

Angiography, Cerebral or Cervical. In Section I, see: Cerebral Angiography.

Barbiturates. In Section I, see: Head Injuries/Drug Therapy.

Brain-Specific Treatments in the Initial Resuscitation of the Head Injury Patient. In Section I, see: Head Injuries/Therapy.

Burr Holes or Twist Drill for Intracranial Hematoma. In Section I, see: Trephining.

Carpal Tunnel Release. In Section I, see: Carpal Tunnel Syndrome/Surgery.

Cerebral Perfusion Pressure Monitoring. In Section I, see: Brain Injuries/Physiopathology.

Cerebrospinal Fluid Shunting Procedure. In Section I, see: Cerebrospinal Fluid Shunts.

Cervical Spine Surgery. In Section I, see: Cervical Vertebrae/Surgery.

Cervical, Thoracic, or Lumbar Laminectomy for Tumor. In Section I, see: Spinal Cord Neoplasms.

Craniostenosis (Synostosis) Surgery. In Section I, see: Craniosynostoses/Surgery.

Craniotomy for Hypophysectomy or Pituitary Tumor. In Section I, see: Craniotomy.

Craniotomy for Intracranial Aneurysm or AVM. In Section I, see: Craniotomy.

Craniotomy for Tumor of Brain or Associated Structures, or Brain Abscess. In Section I, see: Brain Abscess/Surgery.

Craniotomy or Burr Holes for Penetrating Cranial Wound. In Section I, see: Trephining.

Craniotomy or Burr Holes for Skull Fracture, Open or Depressed. In Section I, see: Trephining.

Critical Pathway for the Treatment of Established Intracranial Hypertension. In Section I, see: Head Injuries/Therapy.

Evaluation and Management of Closed Head Injuries. In Section I, see: Head Injuries, Closed/Diagnosis.

Hyperventilation. In Section I, see: Head Injuries.

Hypophysectomy, Transsphenoidal or Transnasal, for Hypophysectomy or Excision of Pituitary Tumor. In Section I, see: Pituitary Neoplasms/Surgery.

Indications for Intracranial Pressure Monitoring. In Section I, see: Intracranial Pressure.

Intracranial Pressure Monitoring Technology. In Section I, see: Intracranial Pressure Monitoring, Physiology/Standards.

Intracranial Pressure Treatment Threshold. In Section I, see: Head Injuries/Therapy.

Lumbar Spine Surgery. In Section I, see: Lumbar Vertebrae/Surgery.

Mannitol. In Section I, see: Mannitol.

Meningocele or Myelomeningocele Repair. In Section I, see: Meningomyelocele/Surgery.

Myelography. In Section I, see: Myelography.

Nerve Block, Somatic or Sympathetic, with Injection of Diagnostic or Treatment Agent. In Section I, see: Nerve Block.

Nutritional Support. In Section I, see: Brain Injuries/Therapy.

Peripheral Nerve Surgery. In Section I, see: Peripheral Nerves/Surgery.

Prophylactic Anticonvulsants. In Section I, see: Anticonvulsants.

Puncture, Burr Holes, Twist Drill, or Trephine for Drainage for Aspiration. In Section I, see: Trephining.

Puncture, Burr Holes, Twist Drill, or Trephine for Drainage for Exploration. In Section I, see: Trephining.

Puncture, Burr Holes, Twist Drill, or Trephine for Drainage for Intracranial Injection. In Section I, see: Trephining.

Resuscitation of Blood Pressure and Oxygenation. In Section I, see: Head Injuries/Physiopathology.

Spinal Puncture. In Section I, see: Spinal Puncture.

Stereotactic Introduction of Subcortical Electrodes. In Section I, see: Radiosurgery.

Stereotactic Lesion Creation. In Section I, see: Radiosurgery.

Stereotactic Lesion Creation in Gasserian Ganglion or Trigeminal Tract. In Section I, see: Trigeminal Ganglion.

Stereotactic Procedure for Biopsy, Aspiration, Excision of Intracranial Lesion. In Section I, see: Radiosurgery.

Stereotactic Procedure for Brachytherapy. In Section I, see: Radiosurgery.

Stereotactic Procedure for Radiosurgery of Brain or Skull Base. In Section I, see: Radiosurgery.

Stereotactic Procedure With or Without CAT Guidance. In Section I, see: Radiosurgery.

Steroids. In Section I, see: Head Injuries/Drug Therapy.

Surgery of Craniofacial Anomalies. In Section I, see: Craniofacial Abnormalities/Surgery.

Surgical Procedures for Managing Extradural or Subdural Hematomas by Burr Hole or Twist Drill Evacuation. In Section I, see: Hematoma, Epidural/Surgery.

Sympathectomy. In Section I, see: Sympathectomy.

Thoracic Spine Surgery. In Section I, see: Thoracic Vertebrae/Surgery.

Trauma Systems, Pre-Hospital Care, and the Neurosurgeon. In Section I, see: Head Injuries/Surgery.

Ulnar Nerve Transposition. In Section I, see: Ulnar Nerve Compression Syndrome/Surgery.

American Association of Oral and Maxillofacial Surgeons

Anesthesia in Outpatient Facilities. In Section I, see: Anesthesia, Dental.

Antibiotic Therapy. In Section I, see: Antibiotics/Standards.

Dental and Maxillofacial Implant. In Section I, see: Maxillofacial Prosthesis.

Dentoalveolar Surgery. In Section I, see: Tooth Extraction.

Maxillofacial Cosmetic Surgery. In Section I, see: Reconstructive Surgical Procedures.

Orthognathic, Cleft, Craniofacial Surgery and Adjunctive Procedures. In Section I, see: Cleft Lip/Surgery

Parameters of Care (Revision). In Section I, see: Surgery, Oral/Standards.

Pathology. In Section I, see: Stomatognathic Diseases/Pathology.

Reconstructive Surgery. In Section I, see: Reconstructive Surgical Procedures.

Temporomandibular Joint Surgery. In Section I, see: Surgery, Oral/Standards.

Trauma. In Section I, see: Maxillofacial Injuries.

American Cancer Society

American Cancer Society Guidelines for Screening and Surveillance for Early Detection of Colorectal Polyps and Cancer: Update 1997. In Section I, see: Colonic Polyps/Diagnosis.

American Cancer Society Guidelines for the Early Detection of Breast Cancer: Update 1997. In Section I, see: Breast Neoplasms/Radiography.

American College of Cardiology

24th Bethesda Conference Report: Cardiac Transplantation. In Section I, see: Heart Transplantation.

25th Bethesda Conference Report: Future Personnel Needs for Cardiovascular Health Care. In Section I, see: Health Services Needs and Demand.

ACC Core Cardiology Training Symposium (COCATS) Guidelines for Training in Adult Cardiovascular Medicine. In Section I, see: Cardiology/Education.

Cardiovascular Abnormalities in the Athlete: Recommendations Regarding Eligibility for Competition. In Section I, see: Cardiovascular Diseases/Diagnosis.

Cardiovascular Disease in the Elderly. In Section I, see: Cardiovascular Diseases.

Congenital Heart Disease After Childhood: An Expanding Patient Population. In Section I, see: Heart Defects, Congenital.

Emergency Cardiac Care. In Section I, see: Emergency Medical Services.

Ethics in Cardiovascular Medicine. In Section I, see: Cardiology.

Expert Consensus Document: Signal-Averaged Electrocardiography. In Section I, see: Electrocardiography/Methods.

Insurability and Employability of the Patient with Ischemic Heart Disease. In Section I, see: Coronary Disease/Economics.

Noninvasive Diagnostic Instrumentation for Assessment of Cardiovascular Disease in the Young. In Section I, see: Cardiovascular Diseases/Diagnosis.

Noninvasive Technology in the Assessment of Ventricular Function. In Section I, see: Heart Diseases/Diagnosis.

Position Statement: Access to Cardiovascular Care. In Section I, see: Cardiovascular Diseases/Therapy.

Position Statement: Ambulatory Blood Pressure Monitoring. In Section I, see: Blood Pressure Monitors/Standards.

Position Statement: Cardiac Angiography Without Cine Film: Creating a "Tower of Babel" in the Cardiac Catheterization Laboratory. In Section I, see: Cineangiography.

Position Statement: Chelation Therapy (Reapproved). In Section I, see: Chelation Therapy.

Position Statement: Clinical Trials. In Section I, see: Clinical Trials.

Position Statement: Doppler Echocardiography in the Human Fetus. In Section I, see: Echocardiography, Doppler.

Position Statement: Early Defibrillation. In Section I, see: Electric Countershock/Methods.

Position Statement: Early Triage of Patients with Chest Discomfort, Approaches to. In Section I, see: Chest Pain/Diagnosis.

Position Statement: Heart Rate Variability for Risk Stratification of Life-Threatening Arrhythmias. In Section I, see: Arrhythmia/Physiopathology.

Position Statement: In-Hospital Cardiac Monitoring of Adults for Detection of Arrhythmia. In Section I, see: Arrhythmia/Diagnosis.

Position Statement: Indications for Implantation of the Automatic Implanted Cardioverter Defibrillator. In Section I, see: Electric Countershock/Instrumentation.

Position Statement: Interventional Catheterization Procedures and Cardiothoracic Surgical Consultation. In Section I, see: Heart Catheterization/Standards.

Position Statement: Physician Recertification. In Section I, see: Certification.

Position Statement: Preventive Cardiology and Atherosclerotic Disease. In Section I, see: Atherosclerosis/Prevention and Control.

Position Statement: Recommendations for Development and Maintenance of Competence in Coronary Interventional Procedures. In Section I, see: Clinical Competence/Standards.

Position Statement: Recommendations for Peripheral Transluminal Angioplasty: Training and Facilities. In Section I, see: Angioplasty, Balloon/Standards.

Position Statement: Recommendations for Training in Vascular Medicine. In Section I, see: Education, Medical, Graduate/Standards.

Position Statement: Same Day Surgical Admission. In Section I, see: Cardiac Surgical Procedures.

Position Statement: Therapeutic Substitution. In Section I, see: Prescriptions, Drug.

Position Statement: Training in Adult Clinical Cardiac Electrophysiology. In Section I, see: Electrophysiology/Education.

Position Statement: Use of Nonionic or Low Osmolar Contrast Agents in Cardiovascular Procedures. In Section I, see: Cardiovascular Diseases/Radiography.

Radionuclide Scintirenography in the Evaluation of Patients with Hypertension. In Section I, see: Radioisotope Renography.

Sudden Cardiac Death. In Section I, see: Death, Sudden.

Trends in the Practice of Cardiology: Implications for Manpower. In Section I, see: Cardiology/Manpower.

Use of Radiographic Devices by Cardiologists. In Section I, see: Fluoroscopy.

American College of Cardiology, American College of Physicians, American Heart Association

Clinical Competence in Ambulatory Electrocardiography. In Section I, see: Clinical Competence/Standards.

Clinical Competence in Elective Direct Current (DC) Cardioversion. In Section I, see: Clinical Competence/Standards.

Clinical Competence in Electrophysiologic Studies. In Section I, see: Clinical Competence/Standards.

Clinical Competence in Insertion of a Temporary Transvenous Ventricular Pacemaker. In Section I, see: Clinical Competence/Standards.

American College of Cardiology, American Heart Association

ACC/AHA Guidelines and Indications for Coronary Artery Bypass Graft Surgery. In Section I, see: Coronary Bypass.

ACC/AHA Guidelines for Cardiac Catheterization and Cardiac Catheterization Laboratories. In Section I, see: Heart Catheterization/Standards.

ACC/AHA Guidelines for Clinical Intracardiac Electrophysiologic and Catheter Ablation Procedures (Revision of 1989 Guidelines). In Section I, see: Catheter Ablation.

ACC/AHA Guidelines for Clinical Use of Cardiac Radionuclide Imaging (Revision of 1986 Report). In Section I, see: Coronary Disease/Radionuclide Imaging.

ACC/AHA Guidelines for Electrocardiography. In Section I, see: Cardiovascular Diseases/Diagnosis.

ACC/AHA Guidelines for Exercise Testing (Revision of 1986 Report). In Section I, see: Exercise Test.

ACC/AHA Guidelines for Implantation of Cardiac Pacemakers and Antiarrhythmia Devices. In Section I, see: Arrhythmia/Therapy.

ACC/AHA Guidelines for Percutaneous Transluminal Coronary Angioplasty (Revision of 1988 Guidelines). In Section I, see: Coronary Disease/Therapy.

ACC/AHA Guidelines for Perioperative Cardiovascular Evaluation of Noncardiac Surgery. In Section I, see: Cardiovascular Diseases/Prevention and Control.

ACC/AHA Guidelines for the Clinical Application of Echocardiography (Revision). In Section I, see: Echocardiography.

ACC/AHA Guidelines for the Management of Heart Failure. In Section I, see: Heart Failure, Congestive/Therapy.

ACC/AHA Guidelines for the Management of Patients with Acute Myocardial Infarction. In Section I, see: Myocardial Infarction/Therapy.

American College of Chest Physicians

Applied Nutrition in ICU Patients. In Section I, see: Intensive Care Units.

Assessment of Asthma in the Workplace. In Section I, see: Asthma/Diagnosis.

Definitions for Sepsis and Organ Failure and Guidelines for the Use of Innovative Therapies in Sepsis. In Section I, see: Septicemia/Therapy.

Ethical and Moral Guidelines for the Initiation, Continuation, and Withdrawal of Intensive Care. In Section I, see: Ethics, Medical.

Fifth ACCP Consensus Conference on Antithrombotic Therapy. In Section I, see: Fibrinolytic Agents/Therapeutic Use.

Institutional Infection Control Measures for Tuberculosis in the Era of Multiple Drug Resistance. In Section I, see: Infection Control.

Managing Cough as a Defense Mechanism and as a Symptom. In Section I, see: Cough.

Mechanical Ventilation. In Section I, see: Respiration, Artificial.

Mechanical Ventilation Beyond the ICU. In Section I, see: Intensive Care.

Primary Pulmonary Hypertension. In Section I, see: Hypertension, Pulmonary.

Pulmonary Rehabilitation: Joint ACCP/AACVPR Evidence-Based Guideline (with the American Association for Cardiovascular and Pulmonary Rehabilitation). In Section I, see: Lung Diseases, Obstructive/Rehabilitation.

Smoking and Health: Physician Responsibility. In Section I, see: Smoking/Adverse Effects.

American College of Emergency Physicians

Acute Blunt Trauma. In Section I, see: Wounds, Nonpenetrating/Diagnosis.

Acute Toxic Ingestion or Dermal or Inhalation Exposure. In Section I, see: Emergency Medicine/Methods.

Clinical Policy for the Initial Approach to Adolescents and Adults Presenting to the Emergency Department with a Chief Complaint of Headache. In Section I, see: Headache/Diagnosis.

Clinical Policy for the Initial Approach to Adults Presenting with a Chief Complaint of Chest Pain, with No History of Trauma. In Section I, see: Chest Pain/Etiology.

Clinical Policy for the Initial Approach to Patients Presenting with a Chief Complaint of Seizure Who Are Not in Status Epilepticus. In Section I, see: Emergency Medicine.

Clinical Policy for the Initial Approach to Patients Presenting with Altered Mental Status. In Section I, see: Cognition Disorders/Etiology.

Nontraumatic Acute Abdominal Pain. In Section I, see: Abdomen, Acute/Diagnosis.

Pediatric Fever. In Section I, see: Clinical Protocols.

Penetrating Extremity Trauma. In Section I, see: Emergency Treatment/Standards.

Practice Parameter: Neuroimaging in the Emergency Patient Presenting with Seizure (Summary Statement). In Section I, see: Seizures/Radiography.

Procedural Sedation and Analgesia in the Emergency Department. In Section I, see: Conscious Sedation/Methods.

Vaginal Bleeding. In Section I, see: Uterine Hemorrhage/Diagnosis.

American College of Gastroenterology

A Guideline for the Treatment and Prevention of NSAID-Induced Ulcers. In Section I, see: Anti-Inflammatory Agents, Non-Steroidal/Adverse Effects.

Alcoholic Liver Disease. In Section I, see: Liver Diseases, Alcoholic/Diagnosis.

Crohn's Disease. In Section I, see: Crohn Disease/Diagnosis.

Diagnosis and Treatment of Esophageal Diseases Associated with HIV Infection. In Section I, see: Aids-Related Opportunistic Infections/Diagnosis.

Diagnosis and Treatment of Gastrointestinal Bleeding Secondary to Portal Hypertension. In Section I, see: Esophageal and Gastric Varices/Complications.

Esophageal Cancer. In Section I, see: Esophageal Neoplasms/Diagnosis.

Guidelines for the Diagnosis and Management of Clostridium-Difficile-Associated Diarrhea and Colitis. In Section I, see: Clostridium Difficile Diarrhea/Microbiology.

Guidelines for the Management of Helicobacter Pylori Infection. In Section I, see: Helicobacter Infections/Therapy.

Guidelines on Acute Infectious Diarrhea in Adults. In Section I, see: Communicable Diseases/Diagnosis.

Liver Disease in the Pregnant Patient. In Section I, see: Liver Diseases.

Management of Polyps of the Colon. In Section I, see: Colonic Polyps/Diagnosis, Therapy.

Management of the Adult Patient with Acute Lower GI Bleeding. In Section I, see: Gastrointestinal Hemorrhage/Diagnosis.

Medical Treatment of Peptic Ulcer Disease Practice Guidelines. In Section I, see: Anti-Ulcer Agents/Therapeutic Use.

Polyp Guideline: Diagnosis, Treatment and Surveillance for Patients with Nonfamilial Colorectal Polyps. In Section I, see: Colonic Polyps/Therapy.

Ulcerative Colitis. In Section I, see: Colitis, Ulcerative/Diagnosis.

Updated Guidelines for the Guidelines for the Diagnosis and Treatment of Gastroesophageal Reflux Disease. In Section I, see: Gastroesophageal Reflux/Diagnosis.

American College of Obstetricians and Gynecologists

Abortion, Induced. In Section I, see: Abortion, Induced.

Absence of Endocervical Cells on a Pap Test. In Section I, see: Cervix Uteri/Pathology.

Access to Health Care for Women with Physical Disabilities. In Section I, see: Disabled Persons.

Adolescent Victims of Sexual Assault. In Section I, see: Rape.

Adolescents' Right to Refuse Long-Term Contraceptives. In Section I, see: Treatment Refusal.

Advanced Paternal Age: Risks to the Fetus. In Section I, see: Fetal Diseases/Genetics.

Amenorrhea. In Section I, see: Amenorrhea.

Anesthesia for Emergency Deliveries. In Section I, see: Anesthesia, Obstetrical.

Antenatal Corticosteroid Therapy for Fetal Maturation. In Section I, see: Fetal Membranes, Premature Rupture.

Antepartum Fetal Surveillance. In Section I, see: Fetal Diseases/Diagnosis.

Antibiotics and Gynecologic Infections. In Section I, see: Adnexitis/Drug Therapy.

Anticoagulation with Low-Molecular-Weight Heparin during Pregnancy. In Section I, see: Heparin, Low-Molecular-Weight/Therapeutic Use.

Antimicrobial Therapy for Obstetric Patients. In Section I, see: Pregnancy Complications, Infectious/Drug Therapy.

Antiphospholipid Syndrome. In Section I, see: Antiphospholipid Syndrome.

Assessment of Fetal Lung Maturity. In Section I, see: Fetal Organ Maturity.

Bacterial Vaginosis Screening for Prevention of Preterm Delivery. In Section I, see: Vaginosis, Bacterial/Diagnosis.

Blood Component Therapy. In Section I, see: Blood Component Transfusion.

Breast-Ovarian Cancer Screening. In Section I, see: Breast Neoplasms/Diagnosis.

Breastfeeding and the Risk of Hepatitis C Virus Transmission. In Section I, see: Breast Feeding.

Cancer of the Ovary. In Section I, see: Ovarian Neoplasms.

Carcinoma of the Breast. In Section I, see: Breast Neoplasms/Diagnosis.

Carcinoma of the Endometrium. In Section I, see: Adenocarcinoma.

Cardiac Disease in Pregnancy. In Section I, see: Pregnancy Complications, Cardiovascular.

Cervical Cytology: Evaluation and Management of Abnormalities. In Section I, see: Vaginal Smears.

Chorionic Villus Sampling. In Section I, see: Chorionic Villi Sampling.

Genetic Evaluation of Stillbirths and Neonatal Deaths. In Section I, see: Fetal Death/Genetics.

Genetic Screening for Hemoglobinopathies. In Section I, see: Hemoglobinopathies/Genetics.

Genetic Screening of Gamete Donors. In Section I, see: Genetic Screening/Standards.

Genetic Technologies. In Section I, see: Genetic Techniques.

Genital Human Papillomavirus Infections. In Section I, see: Genital Diseases/Female.

Guidelines for Diagnostic Imaging During Pregnancy. In Section I, see: Diagnostic Imaging.

Guidelines for Implementing Collaborative Practice. In Section I, see: Patient Care Team.

Guidelines for Perinatal Care. In Section I, see: Perinatal Care.

Guidelines for Relationships with Industry. In Section I, see: Physicians.

Guidelines for Women's Health Care. In Section I, see: Women's Health.

Gynecologic Ultrasonography. In Section I, see: Genital Diseases, Female/Ultrasonography.

Health Maintenance for Perimenopausal Women. In Section I, see: Premenopause.

Hemorrhagic Shock. In Section I, see: Shock, Hemorrhagic/Therapy.

Hepatitis B Immunization for Adolescents. In Section I, see: Hepatitis B Vaccines.

Hepatitis Virus Infections in Obstetrician-Gynecologists. In Section I, see: Disease Transmission.

Home Uterine Activity Monitoring. In Section I, see: Uterine Monitoring.

Hormonal Contraception. In Section I, see: Contraceptives, Oral, Hormonal/Adverse Effects.

Hormone Replacement Therapy. In Section I, see: Hormone Replacement Therapy.

Human Immunodeficiency Virus Infection: Physician's Responsibilities. In Section I, see: HIV Infections/Therapy.

Hyperandrogenic Anovulation. In Section I, see: Anovulation/Etiology.

Hypertension in Pregnancy. In Section I, see: Pregnancy Complications, Cardiovascular/Therapy.

Hysteroscopy. In Section I, see: Hysteroscopy.

Immunization During Pregnancy. In Section I, see: Pregnancy.

Inappropriate Use of the Terms Fetal Distress and Birth Asphyxia. In Section I, see: Asphyxia Neonatorum/Classification.

Incidental Appendectomy. In Section I, see: Appendectomy.

Induction of Labor. In Section I, see: Labor, Induced.

Infertility. In Section I, see: Infertility.

Informed Refusal. In Section I, see: Treatment Refusal.

Institutional Responsibility to Provide Legal Representation. In Section I, see: Ethics Committees/Legislation and Jurisprudence.

Intrauterine Device. In Section I, see: Intrauterine Devices.

Invasive Hemodynamic Monitoring in Obstetrics and Gynecology. In Section I, see: Hemodynamics/Physiology.

Laparoscopically Assisted Vaginal Hysterectomy. In Section I, see: Hysterectomy, Vaginal.

Length of Stay for Gynecologic Procedures. In Section I, see: Gynecologic Surgical Procedures/Standards.

Limitations of Abstinence-Only Sexuality Education. In Section I, see: Sexual Abstinence.

Lower Urinary Tract Operative Injuries. In Section I, see: Intraoperative Complications/Prevention and Control.

Male Infertility. In Section I, see: Infertility, Male.

Management of Breech Presentation. In Section I, see: Breech Presentation.

Management of Gestational Trophoblastic Neoplasia. In Section I, see: Trophoblastic Neoplasms/Therapy.

Management of Isoimmunization in Pregnancy. In Section I, see: Pregnancy/Immunology.

Management of Postterm Pregnancy. In Section I, see: Pregnancy Complications/Therapy.

Managing the Anovulatory State: Medical Induction of Ovulation. In Section I, see: Anovulation/Drug Therapy.

Mandatory Reporting of Domestic Violence. In Section I, see: Mandatory Reporting.

Maternal Serum Screening. In Section I, see: Alpha-Fetoproteins/Analysis.

Medical Management of Tubal Pregnancy. In Section I, see: Pregnancy, Tubal/Diagnosis.

Methods of Midtrimester Abortion. In Section I, see: Abortion, Induced.

Monitoring during Induction of Labor with Dinoprostone. In Section I, see: Dinoprostone.

New Pap Test Screening Techniques. In Section I, see: Cervix Neoplasms/Diagnosis.

New Ultrasound Output Display Standards. In Section I, see: Ultrasonography/Instrumentation.

Nonmalignant Conditions of the Breast. In Section I, see: Breast Diseases.

Nonselective Embryo Reduction: Ethical Guidance for the Obstetrician-Gynecologist. In Section I, see: Ethics, Medical.

Nutrition and Women. In Section I, see: Nutrition.

Obstetric Analgesia and Anesthesia. In Section I, see: Analgesia, Obstetrical.

Obstetric Aspects of Trauma Management. In Section I, see: Abdominal Injuries.

Obstetric Management of Patients with Spinal Cord Injury. In Section I, see: Spinal Cord Injuries/Complications.

Obstetrician-Gynecologists' Ethical Responsibilities, Concerns, and Risks Pertaining to Adoption. In Section I, see: Adoption.

Operative Laparoscopy. In Section I, see: Surgical Procedures, Laparoscopic.

Operative Vaginal Delivery. In Section I, see: Obstetrical Delivery/Methods.

Osteoporosis. In Section I, see: Osteoporosis.

Pain Relief During Labor. In Section I, see: Insurance, Health, Reimbursement/Standards.

Patient Choice and the Maternal-Fetal Relationship. In Section I, see: Choice Behavior.

Pediatric Gynecologic Disorders. In Section I, see: Genital Diseases, Female/Diagnosis.

Pelvic Organ Prolapse. In Section I, see: Uterine Prolapse.

Perinatal and Infant Mortality Statistics. In Section I, see: Infant Mortality.

Perinatal Care at the Threshold of Fetal Viability. In Section I, see: Fetal Viability.

Perinatal Viral and Parasitic Infections. In Section I, see: Pregnancy Complications, Infectious.

Physician Responsibility Under Managed Care. In Section I, see: Managed Care Programs.

Physician/Patient Responsibility for Follow-Up of Diagnosis and Treatment. In Section I, see: Continuity Of Patient Care.

Placental Pathology. In Section I, see: Placenta/Pathology.

Postpartum Hemorrhage. In Section I, see: Postpartum Hemorrhage.

Postpartum Tubal Sterilization. In Section I, see: Puerperium.

Preconceptional Care. In Section I, see: Fertilization.

Preembryo Research: History, Scientific Background, and Ethical Considerations. In Section I, see: Embryo.

Premature Rupture of Membranes. In Section I, see: Fetal Membranes, Premature Rupture.

Premenstrual Syndrome. In Section I, see: Premenstrual Syndrome/Therapy.

Preterm Labor. In Section I, see: Labor, Premature.

Prevention of Adolescent Suicide. In Section I, see: Suicide/Prevention and Control.

Prevention of Early-Onset Group B Streptococcal Disease in Newborns. In Section I, see: Streptococcal Infections/Prevention and Control.

Prevention of Rh D Alloimmunization. In Section I, see: Rh Isoimmunization/Prevention and Control.

Primary and Preventive Care. In Section I, see: Primary Health Care.

Prophylactic Oophorectomy. In Section I, see: Ovariectomy.

Pulmonary Disease in Pregnancy. In Section I, see: Pregnancy Complications.

Quality Assessment and Improvement in Obstetrics and Gynecology. In Section I, see: Quality Assurance, Health Care.

Rate of Vaginal Births after Cesarean Delivery. In Section I, see: Vaginal Birth After Cesarean.

Recertification. In Section I, see: Certification.

Recommendations on Frequency of Pap Test Screening. In Section I, see: Vaginal Smears.

Recommended Core Educational Guidelines for Family Practice Residents: Maternity and Gynecologic Care. In Section I, see: Family Practice/Education.

Role of Loop Electrosurgical Excision Procedure in the Evaluation of Abnormal Pap Test Results. In Section I, see: Electrosurgery.

Role of the Obstetrician-Gynecologist in the Diagnosis and Treatment of Breast Disease. In Section I, see: Breast Diseases/Diagnosis.

Routine Cancer Screening. In Section I, see: Mass Screening.

Routine Storage of Umbilical Cord Blood for Potential Future Transplantation. In Section I, see: Fetal Blood.

Routine Ultrasound in Low-Risk Pregnancy. In Section I, see: Ultrasonography, Prenatal.

Rubella, Congenital and Pregnancy. In Section I, see: Rubella Syndrome, Congenital.

Safety of Oral Contraceptives for Teenagers. In Section I, see: Contraceptives, Oral/Adverse Effects.

Scheduled Cesarean Delivery and the Prevention of Vertical Transmission of HIV Infection. In Section I, see: Cesarean Section.

Scope of Services for Uncomplicated Obstetric Care. In Section I, see: Prenatal Care/Standards.

Screening for Canavan Disease. In Section I, see: Canavan Disease/Diagnosis.

Screening for Tay-Sachs Disease. In Section I, see: Tay-Sachs Disease/Diagnosis.

Second-Look Laparotomy for Epithelial Ovarian Cancer. In Section I, see: Laparotomy.

Seizure Disorders in Pregnancy. In Section I, see: Pregnancy Complications.

Septic Shock. In Section I, see: Shock, Septic.

Sex Selection. In Section I, see: Sex Preselection.

Sexual Assault. In Section I, see: Rape.

Sexual Dysfunction. In Section I, see: Sex Disorders.

Sexual Misconduct in the Practice of Obstetrics and Gynecology: Ethical Considerations. In Section I, see: Ethics, Medical.

Shoulder Dystocia. In Section I, see: Dystocia.

Smoking and Women's Health. In Section I, see: Smoking/Adverse Effects.

Special Problems of Multiple Gestation. In Section I, see: Pregnancy, Multiple.

Statement on Surgical Assistants. In Section I, see: Operating Room Technicians.

Sterilization. In Section I, see: Sterilization, Sexual.

Sterilization of Women, Including Those with Mental Disabilities. In Section I, see: Ethics, Medical.

Substance Abuse. In Section I, see: Substance-Related Disorders.

Substance Abuse in Pregnancy. In Section I, see: Pregnancy Complications.

Tamoxifen and Endometrial Cancer. In Section I, see: Tamoxifen/Adverse Effects.

Teratology. In Section I, see: Teratology.

Thromboembolism in Pregnancy. In Section I, see: Thromboembolism.

Thyroid Disease in Pregnancy. In Section I, see: Pregnancy Complications.

Tubal Ligation with Cesarean Delivery. In Section I, see: Cesarean Section.

Ultrasonography in Pregnancy. In Section I, see: Ultrasonography, Prenatal.

Umbilical Artery Blood Acid-Base Analysis. In Section I, see: Acid-Base Equilibrium.

Urinary Incontinence and UI Stress. In Section I, see: Urinary Incontinence.

Use and Abuse of the Apgar Score. In Section I, see: Apgar Score.

Uterine Leiomyomata. In Section I, see: Uterine Neoplasms.

Utility of Antepartum Umbilical Artery Doppler Velocimetry in Intrauterine Growth Restriction. In Section I, see: Fetal Growth Retardation/ Ultrasonography.

Utility of Umbilical Cord Blood Acid-Base Assessment. In Section I, see: Acid-Base Equilibrium.

Vaginal Birth after Previous Cesarean Delivery. In Section I, see: Vaginal Birth After Cesarean/Standards.

Vaginitis. In Section I, see: Vaginitis.

Viral Hepatitis in Pregnancy. In Section I, see: Hepatitis, Viral, Human/Diagnosis.

Vitamin A Supplementation During Pregnancy. In Section I, see: Dietary Supplements.

Vulvar Cancer. In Section I, see: Vulvar Neoplasms.

Vulvar Nonneoplastic Epithelial Disorders. In Section I, see: Vulvar Diseases/Classification.

Women and Exercise. In Section I, see: Exercise.

American College of Occupational and Environmental Medicine

Drug Screening in the Workplace: Ethical Guidelines. In Section I, see: Drug Screening.

Guidelines for Employee Health Services in Health Care Institutions. In Section I, see: Occupational Health Services.

Recommended Library for Occupational Physicians. In Section I, see: Libraries, Medical.

Scope of Occupational and Environmental Health Programs and Practice. In Section I, see: Occupational Medicine.

Spirometry in the Workplace. In Section I, see: Spirometry.

American College of Physicians

AIDS and Infection with HIV. In Section I, see: HIV Seropositivity.

Apheresis in Chronic Inflammatory Demyelinating Polyneuropathy and in Renal Transplantation. In Section I, see: Demyelinating Diseases/Therapy.

Automated Ambulatory Blood Pressure Monitoring. In Section I, see: Blood Pressure Monitoring, Ambulatory.

Biochemical Profiles: Applications in Ambulatory Screening and Preadmission Testing of Adults. In Section I, see: Blood Chemical Analysis.

Biofeedback for Gastrointestinal Disorders. In Section I, see: Biofeedback (Psychology).

Biofeedback for Headaches. In Section I, see: Biofeedback (Psychology).

Biofeedback for Hypertension. In Section I, see: Biofeedback (Psychology).

Biofeedback for Neuromuscular Disorders. In Section I, see: Biofeedback (Psychology).

Blood Cultures. In Section I, see: Bacteriological Techniques.

Carcinoembryonic Antigen. In Section I, see: Carcinoembryonic Antigen/Analysis.

Carotid Endarterectomy. In Section I, see: Endarterectomy.

Cholesterol Screening (Update). In Section I, see: Cholesterol/Blood.

Clinical Competence in Percutaneous Renal Biopsy. In Section I, see: Biopsy Needle/Standards.

Common Screening Tests. In Section I, see: Diagnostic Tests, Routine.

Compensation for Vaccine-Related Injuries. In Section I, see: Vaccination/Economics.

Complete Blood Count and Leukocyte Differential Count: An Approach to Their Rational Application. In Section I, see: Blood Cell Count.

Dexamethasone Suppression Test for the Detection, Diagnosis, and Management of Depression. In Section I, see: Dexamethasone/Diagnostic Use.

Diagnostic Endocardial Electrical Recording and Stimulation. In Section I, see: Endocardium/Physiology.

Diagnostic Evaluation of Carotid Arteries. In Section I, see: Carotid Artery Diseases/Diagnosis.

Diagnostic Spinal Tap. In Section I, see: Cerebrospinal Fluid.

Diagnostic Thoracentesis in Pleural Biopsy. In Section I, see: Pleural Effusion/Etiology.

Diagnostic Uses of the Activated Partial Thromboplastin Time and Prothrombin Time. In Section I, see: Prothrombin Time.

Eating Disorders: Anorexia Nervosa and Bulimia: Position Paper. In Section I, see: Bulimia.

Endoscopic Sclerotherapy for Esophageal Varices. In Section I, see: Esophageal and Gastric Varices/Therapy.

Endoscopy in the Evaluation of Dyspepsia. In Section I, see: Dyspepsia/Etiology.

Erythrocyte Sedimentation Rate: Guidelines for Rational Use. In Section I, see: Blood Sedimentation.

Evaluation of Patients after Recent Acute Myocardial Infarction. In Section I, see: Heart Function Tests/Methods.

Exercise Thallium-201 Myocardial Perfusion Scintigraphy in the Diagnosis of Coronary Artery Disease. In Section I, see: Exercise Test.

Financing Care of Patients with AIDS. In Section I, see: Delivery of Health Care/Economics.

Glycosylated Hemoglobin Assays in the Management and Diagnosis of Diabetes Mellitus. In Section I, see: Diabetes Mellitus/Blood.

Guide for Adult Immunization, 2nd Edition. In Section I, see: Immunization.

Guidelines for Counseling Postmenopausal Women about Preventive Hormone Therapy. In Section I, see: Estrogen Replacement Therapy.

Guidelines for Risk Stratification after Myocardial Infarction. In Section I, see: Hospitalization.

Hepatitis B Vaccine. In Section I, see: Hepatitis B/Prevention and Control.

Sponsor

Hormone Therapy to Prevent Disease and Prolong Life in Postmenopausal Women. In Section I, see: Estrogen Replacement Therapy.

How to Study the Gallbladder. In Section I, see: Cholecystitis/Diagnosis.

Implantable and External Infusion Pumps for the Treatment of Thromboembolic Disease in Outpatients. In Section I, see: Infusions, Parenteral/Instrumentation.

Improving Medical Education in Therapeutics. In Section I, see: Therapeutics.

Indications for Arterial Blood Gas Analysis. In Section I, see: Blood Gas Analysis.

Indications for Holter Monitoring. In Section I, see: Electrocardiography, Ambulatory.

Indications for Red Blood Transfusion. In Section I, see: Anemia/Therapy.

Lithotripsy. In Section I, see: Urinary Calculi/Therapy.

Magnetic Resonance Imaging of Brain and Spine. In Section I, see: Magnetic Resonance Imaging.

Management of Gallstones. In Section I, see: Cholelithiasis/Therapy.

Management of Hypertension after Ambulatory Blood Pressure Monitoring. In Section I, see: Hypertension/Prevention and Control.

Medical Treatment for Stroke Prevention. In Section I, see: Cerebrovascular Disorders/Prevention and Control.

Parenteral Nutrition in Patients Receiving Cancer Chemotherapy. In Section I, see: Surgical Procedures, Operative.

Percutaneous Transluminal Angioplasty. In Section I, see: Angioplasty, Transluminal, Percutaneous.

Performance of Ergonovine Provocative Testing for Coronary Artery Spasm. In Section I, see: Ergonovine/Diagnostic Use.

Perioperative Parenteral Nutrition. In Section I, see: Parenteral Nutrition, Total.

Pneumococcal Vaccine. In Section I, see: Bacterial Vaccines.

Preoperative Pulmonary Function Testing. In Section I, see: Lung Diseases/Prevention and Control.

Probability Theory in the Use of Diagnostic Tests: Application to Critical Study of the Literature. In Section I, see: Probability Theory.

Safety and Efficacy of Ambulatory Cardiac Catheterization in Hospital and Freestanding Setting. In Section I, see: Heart Catheterization/Methods.

Screening for Asymptomatic Coronary Artery Disease: The Resting Electrocardiogram. In Section I, see: Electrocardiography.

Screening for Breast Cancer. In Section I, see: Breast Neoplasms/Prevention and Control.

Screening for Cervical Cancer. In Section I, see: Cervix Neoplasms/Epidemiology.

Screening for Colorectal Cancer. In Section I, see: Colorectal Neoplasms/Diagnosis.

Screening for Diabetes Mellitus in Apparently Healthy, Asymptomatic Adults. In Section I, see: Diabetes Mellitus/Prevention and Control.

Screening for Hypertension. In Section I, see: Hypertension/Prevention and Control.

Screening for Lung Cancer. In Section I, see: Lung Neoplasms/Prevention and Control.

Screening for Osteoporosis. In Section I, see: Osteoporosis, Postmenopausal/Diagnosis.

Screening for Ovarian Cancer. In Section I, see: Mass Screening/Standards.

Screening for Prostate Cancer. In Section I, see: Mass Screening.

Screening for Thyroid Disease. In Section I, see: Thyroid Diseases/Diagnosis.

Screening Low Risk, Asymptomatic Adults for Cardiac Risk Factors: Serum Cholesterol and Triglycerides. In Section I, see: Coronary Disease/Prevention and Control.

Selected Methods for the Management of Diabetes Mellitus. In Section I, see: Diabetes Mellitus/Therapy.

Serum Electrolytes, Serum Osmolality, Blood Urea Nitrogen, and Serum Creatinine. In Section I, see: Diagnostic Tests/Routine.

Serum Enzyme Assays in the Diagnosis of Acute Myocardial Infarction: Recommendations Based on a Quantitative Analysis. In Section I, see: Enzyme Tests.

Suggested Technique for Fecal Occult Blood Testing and Interpretation in Colorectal Cancer Screening. In Section I, see: Colorectal Neoplasms/Prevention and Control.

Syphilis Tests in Diagnostic and Therapeutic Decision Making. In Section I, see: Syphilis/Diagnosis.

Throat Cultures and Rapid Tests for Diagnosis of Group A Streptococcal Pharyngitis. In Section I, see: Pharyngitis/Microbiology.

Thrombolysis for Evolving Myocardial Infarction. In Section I, see: Myocardial Infarction/Drug Therapy.

Update: MRI of the Brain and Spine. In Section I, see: Magnetic Resonance Imaging.

Urinalysis and Urine Culture in Women with Dysuria. In Section I, see: Urine/Analysis.

Utility of Routine Chest Radiographs. In Section I, see: Diagnostic Tests, Routine.

Utility of the Routine Electrocardiogram Before Surgery and on General Hospital Admission: Critical Review and New Guidelines. In Section I, see: Diagnostic Tests, Routine.

American College of Physicians, American Academy of Ophthalmology, American Diabetes Association

Screening for Diabetic Retinopathy. In Section I, see: Vision Screening/Standards.

American College of Physicians, American College of Cardiology, American Heart Association

Clinical Competence in Hemodynamic Monitoring. In Section I, see: Clinical Competence/Standards.

American College of Physicians, Blue Cross/Blue Shield Association

Common Diagnostic Tests: Use and Interpretation, 2nd edition. In Section I, see: Diagnostic Tests, Routine.

American College of Preventive Medicine

Practice Policy Statement: Adult Immunization. In Section I, see: Preventive Medicine.

Practice Policy Statement: Cervical Cancer Screening. In Section I, see: Cervix Neoplasms.

Practice Policy Statement: Childhood Immunizations. In Section I, see: Immunization Schedule.

Practice Policy Statement: Screening Asymptomatic Women for Ovarian Cancer. In Section I, see: Mass Screening/Methods.

Practice Policy Statement: Screening for Prostate Cancer in American Men. In Section I, see: Preventive Medicine/Standards.

Practice Policy Statement: Screening for Skin Cancer. In Section I, see: Mass Screening/Standards.

Practice Policy Statement: Screening Mammography for Breast Cancer. In Section I, see: Breast Neoplasms/Prevention and Control.

Practice Policy Statement: Skin Protection from Ultraviolet Light Exposure. In Section I, see: Ultraviolet Rays/Adverse Effects.

American College of Radiology

ACR Standard for 3D External Beam Radiation Planning and Conformal Therapy. In Section I, see: Radiotherapy.

ACR Standard for Brachytherapy Physics: Manually Loaded Sources. In Section I, see: Brachytherapy.

ACR Standard for Communication: Radiation Oncology. In Section I, see: Radiation Oncology/Standards.

ACR Standard for Continuing Medical Education (CME) (Revised). In Section I, see: Education, Medical, Continuing/Standards.

ACR Standard for Diagnostic Medical Physics Monitoring of MRI Equipment. In Section I, see: Magnetic Resonance Imaging/Instrumentation.

ACR Standard for Diagnostic Medical Physics Performance Monitoring of Computed Tomography Equipment. In Section I, see: Tomography, X-ray Computed.

ACR Standard for Diagnostic Medical Physics Performance Monitoring of Real Time B-Mode Ultrasound Equipment. In Section I, see: Ultrasonography/Standards.

ACR Standard for Digital Image Data Management. In Section I, see: Signal Processing, Computer-Assisted.

ACR Standard for Imaging-Guiding Percutaneous Drainage or Aspiration of Fluid Collections in Adults. In Section I, see: Paracentesis.

ACR Standard for Performing and Interpreting Diagnostic Ultrasound Examinations (Revised). In Section I, see: Ultrasonography.

ACR Standard for Radiation Oncology. In Section I, see: Radiation Oncology/Standards.

ACR Standard for Radiation Oncology Physics for External Beam Therapy (Revised). In Section I, see: Radiation Oncology.

ACR Standard for Skeletal Surveys in Children. In Section I, see: Bone and Bones/Radiography.

ACR Standard for Teleradiology (Revised). In Section I, see: Teleradiology.

ACR Standard for the Diagnostic Medical Physics Performance Monitoring of Nuclear Medicine Equipment. In Section I, see: Nuclear Medicine.

ACR Standard for the Performance of a Scrotal Ultrasound Examination. In Section I, see: Scrotum/Ultrasonography.

ACR Standard for the Performance of a Shoulder Ultrasound Examination. In Section I, see: Shoulder/Ultrasonography.

ACR Standard for the Performance of Abdominal, Renal, or Retroperitoneal Ultrasound Examination in Infants, Children, and Adults. In Section I, see: Retroperitoneal Space/Ultrasonography.

ACR Standard for the Performance of Adult and Pediatric Hepatobiliary Scintigraphy (Revised). In Section I, see: Liver Diseases/Radionuclide Imaging.

ACR Standard for the Performance of Adult and Pediatric Renal Scintigraphy (Revised). In Section I, see: Kidney Diseases/Radionuclide Imaging.

ACR Standard for the Performance of Adult Barium Enema Examinations. In Section I, see: Barium Sulfate/Diagnostic Use.

ACR Standard for the Performance of Adult Enteroclysis Examinations. In Section I, see: Intestinal Diseases/Radiography.

ACR Standard for the Performance of Adult Esophagrams & Upper Gastrointestinal Examinations. In Section I, see: Endoscopy, Gastrointestinal.

ACR Standard for the Performance of Antepartum Obstetrical Ultrasound. In Section I, see: Ultrasonography/Prenatal.

ACR Standard for the Performance of an Ultrasound Examination of the Extracranial Cerebrovascular System (Revised). In Section I, see: Carotid Artery Diseases/Ultrasonography.

ACR Standard for the Performance of Breast Ultrasound Examination. In Section I, see: Breast Diseases/Ultrasonography.

ACR Standard for the Performance of Cardiac Scintigraphy. In Section I, see: Coronary Disease/Radionuclide Imaging.

ACR Standard for the Performance of Cerebral Scintigraphy. In Section I, see: Brain/Radionuclide Imaging.

ACR Standard for the Performance of Clinical Procedures Using Radiopharmaceuticals (Revised). In Section I, see: Radiopharmaceuticals/Therapeutic Use.

ACR Standard for the Performance of Computed Tomography in Neuroradiologic Imaging in Adults and Children. In Section I, see: Tomography, X-ray Computed.

ACR Standard for the Performance of Computed Tomography of the Abdomen and Pelvis (Revised). In Section I, see: Tomography, X-ray Computed.

ACR Standard for the Performance of Diagnostic Mammography. In Section I, see: Mammography/Methods.

ACR Standard for the Performance of Dual Energy X-ray Absorptiometry (DXA). In Section I, see: Absorptiometry, Photon.

ACR Standard for the Performance of Excretory Urography. In Section I, see: Urography/Standards.

ACR Standard for the Performance of Gastrointestinal Scintigraphy. In Section I, see: Gastrointestinal System/Radionuclide Imaging.

ACR Standard for the Performance of General (Plain) Radiography. In Section I, see: Radiography.

ACR Standard for the Performance of Hepatobiliary Scintigraphy. In Section I, see: Biliary Tract/Radionuclide Imaging.

ACR Standard for the Performance of High-Dose-Rate Brachytherapy. In Section I, see: Brachytherapy.

ACR Standard for the Performance of Imaging-Guided Percutaneous Needle Biopsy in Adults. In Section I, see: Biopsy, Needle/Methods.

ACR Standard for the Performance of Liver/Spleen Scintigraphy. In Section I, see: Spleen/Radionuclide Imaging.

ACR Standard for the Performance of Low-Dose-Rate Brachytherapy. In Section I, see: Brachytherapy.

ACR Standard for the Performance of Magnetic Resonance Imaging (Revised). In Section I, see: Magnetic Resonance Imaging.

ACR Standard for the Performance of Myelography and Cisternography. In Section I, see: Myelography.

ACR Standard for the Performance of Parathyroid Scintigraphy. In Section I, see: Parathyroid Glands/Radionuclide Imaging.

ACR Standard for the Performance of Pediatric and Adult Bedside (Portable) Chest Radiography (Revised). In Section I, see: Lung Diseases/Radiography.

ACR Standard for the Performance of Pediatric and Adult Chest Radiography (Revised). In Section I, see: Lung Diseases/Radiography.

ACR Standard for the Performance of Pediatric Contrast Enema. In Section I, see: Contrast Media.

ACR Standard for the Performance of Pediatric Contrast Examination of the Small Bowel. In Section I, see: Intestines, Small/Radiography.

ACR Standard for the Performance of Pediatric Contrast Examinations of the Upper Gastrointestinal Tract. In Section I, see: Contrast Media.

ACR Standard for the Performance of Per Oral Small Bowel Examinations in Adults. In Section I, see: Intestine, Small/Radiography.

ACR Standard for the Performance of Percutaneous Nephrostomy (PCN). In Section I, see: Nephrostomy, Percutaneous.

ACR Standard for the Performance of Pulmonary Scintigraphy. In Section I, see: Lung/Radionuclide Imaging.

ACR Standard for the Performance of Radiography of the Cervical Spine in Children and Adults. In Section I, see: Cervical Vertebrae/Radiography.

ACR Standard for the Performance of Radionuclide Cystography. In Section I, see: Bladder/Radionuclide Imaging.

ACR Standard for the Performance of Scintigraphy for Infections and Inflammations. In Section I, see: Bacterial Infections/Radionuclide Imaging.

ACR Standard for the Performance of Screening Mammography. In Section I, see: Mammography.

ACR Standard for the Performance of Scrotal Scintigraphy. In Section I, see: Scrotum/Radionuclide Imaging.

ACR Standard for the Performance of Skeletal Scintigraphy (Revised). In Section I, see: Bone Diseases/Radionuclide Imaging.

ACR Standard for the Performance of Stereotactic Radiation Therapy/Radiosurgery. In Section I, see: Stereotaxic Techniques/Standards.

ACR Standard for the Performance of Stereotactically-Guided Breast Interventional Procedures. In Section I, see: Stereotaxic Techniques.

ACR Standard for the Performance of the Pediatric Neurosonology Examination. In Section I, see: Nervous System/Ultrasonography.

ACR Standard for the Performance of the Peripheral Arterial Ultrasound Examination (Revised). In Section I, see: Peripheral Vascular Diseases/Ultrasonography.

ACR Standard for the Performance of the Peripheral Venous Ultrasound Examination (Revised). In Section I, see: Peripheral Vascular Diseases/Ultrasonography.

ACR Standard for the Performance of the Thyroid and Parathyroid Ultrasound Examination (Revised). In Section I, see: Thyroid Diseases/Ultrasonography.

ACR Standard for the Performance of the Ultrasound Examination for Detection of Developmental Dysplasia of the Hip. In Section I, see: Hip Dislocation, Congenital/Ultrasonography.

ACR Standard for the Performance of the Ultrasound Examination of the Female Pelvis. In Section I, see: Genital Diseases, Female/Diagnosis

ACR Standard for the Performance of the Ultrasound Examination of the Prostate (and Surrounding Structures) (Revised). In Section I, see: Prostatic Diseases/Ultrasonography.

ACR Standard for the Performance of Therapy with Unsealed Radionuclide Sources. In Section I, see: Radioisotopes/Therapeutic Use.

ACR Standard for the Performance of Thoracic Computed Tomography in Adults and Children. In Section I, see: Tomography, X-ray Computed.

ACR Standard for the Performance of Thyroid Scintigraphy and Uptake Measurements. In Section I, see: Iodine Radioisotopes/Therapeutic Use.

ACR Standard for the Performance of Tumor Scintigraphy (with Gamma Cameras). In Section I, see: Gamma Cameras.

ACR Standard for the Performance of Ultrasound-Guided Breast Interventional Procedures. In Section I, see: Ultrasonography, Mammary.

ACR Standard for the Performance of Voiding Cystourethrography in Children. In Section I, see: Bladder/Radiography.

ACR Standards for Adult Cystography and Urethrography (Revised). In Section I, see: Urography.

ACR Standards on Communication—Diagnostic Radiology. In Section I, see: Diagnostic Imaging.

Anal Cancer (6 variants). In Section I, see: Anus Neoplasms/Therapy.

Bone Metastases (25 variants). In Section I, see: Bone Neoplasms/Secondary.

Conservative Surgery and Radiation in the Treatment of Stage I and II Carcinoma of the Breast (9 variants). In Section I, see: Breast Neoplasms/Diagnosis.

Definitive External Beam Irradiation in Stage T1, T2 Carcinoma of the Prostate (9 variants). In Section I, see: Prostatic Neoplasms/Radiotherapy.

Ductal Carcinoma in Situ and Microinvasive Disease (10 variants). In Section I, see: Carcinoma, Infiltrating Duct.

Follow-Up of Non-Small-Cell Lung Carcinoma (5 variants). In Section I, see: Carcinoma, Non-Small-Cell Lung.

Local Regional Recurrence and Salvage Surgery (10 variants). In Section I, see: Neoplasm Recurrence, Local.

Locally Advanced (high risk) Prostate Cancer (6 variants). In Section I, see: Prostatic Neoplasms.

Locally Advanced Breast Cancer (5 variants). In Section I, see: Breast Neoplasms.

Locally Unresectable Rectal Cancer (7 variants). In Section I, see: Rectal Neoplasms.

Management of Resectable Rectal Cancer (6 variants). In Section I, see: Rectal Neoplasms/Surgery.

Neoadjuvant Therapy for Marginally Resectable (Clinical N2) Non-Small-Cell Lung Carcinoma (1 variant). In Section I, see: Carcinoma, Non-Small-Cell Lung/Surgery.

Node-Positive Prostate Cancer (3 variants). In Section I, see: Prostatic Neoplasms.

Non-Aggressive, Non-Surgical Treatment of Inoperable Non-Small-Cell Lung Cancer. In Section I, see: Carcinoma, Non-Small-Cell Lung/Therapy.

Non-Small-Cell Lung Carcinoma, Non-Surgical Aggressive Therapy (8 variants). In Section I, see: Carcinoma, Non-Small-Cell Lung/Therapy.

Permanent Source Brachytherapy for Prostate Cancer (8 variants). In Section I, see: Prostatic Neoplasms.

Postmastectomy Radiotherapy (15 variants). In Section I, see: Breast Neoplasms/Radiotherapy.

Postoperative Radiotherapy in Non-Small-Cell Lung Cancer (18 variants). In Section I, see: Carcinoma, Non-Small-Cell Lung/Radiotherapy.

Postradical Prostatectomy Irradiation in Carcinoma of the Prostate (11 variants). In Section I, see: Prostatic Neoplasms/Radiotherapy.

Rectal Cancer: Presentation with Metastatic and Locally Advanced Disease (8 variants). In Section I, see: Rectal Neoplasms.

Staging Evaluation for Patients with Adenocarcinoma of the Prostate (10 variants). In Section I, see: Prostatic Neoplasms.

Staging of Non-Small-Cell Lung Cancer (8 variants). In Section I, see: Lung Neoplasms/Therapy.

Standard for Diagnostic Arteriography in Adults. In Section I, see: Angiography.

Treatment Planning for Clinically Localized Prostate Cancer (4 variants). In Section I, see: Prostatic Neoplasms/Radiotherapy.

American College of Radiology, American College of Surgeons, College of American Pathologists, Society of Surgical Oncology

Standards for Diagnosis and Management of Invasive Breast Carcinoma (Revised). In Section I, see: Breast Neoplasms.

Standards for Management of Ductal Carcinoma In Situ (DCIS) (Revised). In Section I, see: Carcinoma In Situ.

American College of Rheumatology

Guidelines for Monitoring Drug Therapy in Rheumatoid Arthritis. In Section I, see: Arthritis, Rheumatoid/Drug Therapy.

Guidelines for the Initial Evaluation of the Adult Patient with Acute Musculoskeletal Symptoms. In Section I, see: Musculoskeletal Diseases/Diagnosis.

Guidelines for the Management of Rheumatoid Arthritis. In Section I, see: Arthritis, Rheumatoid/Therapy.

Guidelines for the Medical Management of Osteoarthritis Part I: Osteoarthritis of Hip. In Section I, see: Osteoarthritis, Hip/Therapy.

Guidelines for the Medical Management of Osteoarthritis Part II: Osteoarthritis of the Knee. In Section I, see: Knee Joint.

Methotrexate for Rheumatoid Arthritis: Suggested Guidelines for Monitoring Liver Toxicity. In Section I, see: Arthritis, Rheumatoid/Drug Therapy.

Recommendations for the Prevention and Treatment of Glucocorticoid-Induced Osteoporosis. In Section I, see: Glucocorticoids/Adverse Effects.

American College of Rheumatology, Infectious Diseases Society of America

Empiric Parenteral Antibiotic Treatment of Patients with Fibromyalgia and a Positive Serologic Result for Lyme Disease. In Section I, see: Antibiotics/Administration and Dosage.

American College of Surgeons

Guidelines for Minimal Standards in Cardiac Surgery. In Section I, see: Heart Diseases/Surgery.

Indications for the Use of Permanently Implanted Cardiac Pacemakers. In Section I, see: Pacemaker, Artificial.

Resources for Optimal Care of the Injured Patient. In Section I, see: Wounds and Injuries/Surgery.

Statement on Laparoscopic Cholecystectomy. In Section I, see: Cholecystectomy, Laparoscopic.

Statement on Laser Surgery. In Section I, see: Laser Surgery.

American Dental Association

Dental Practice Parameters. In Section I, see: Dentistry/Standards.

Oral Health Care Series: Chemically Dependent Patients. In Section I, see: Dental Care For Chronically Ill/Methods.

Oral Health Care Series: Head and Neck Cancer Patients Receiving Radiation Therapy. In Section I, see: Head and Neck Neoplasms/Radiotherapy.

Oral Health Care Series: Patients Receiving Cancer Chemotherapy. In Section I, see: Antineoplastic Agents.

Oral Health Care Series: Patients with Cardiovascular Disease. In Section I, see: Cardiovascular Diseases/Therapy.

Oral Health Care Series: Patients with Diabetes. In Section I, see: Dental Care for Chronically Ill/Methods.

Oral Health Care Series: Patients with End-Stage Renal Disease. In Section I, see: Kidney Failure, Chronic.

Oral Health Care Series: Patients with Hepatic Disease. In Section I, see: Dental Care for Chronically Ill/Methods.

Oral Health Care Series: Patients with Physical and Mental Disorders. In Section I, see: Dental Care for Disabled.

Oral Health Care Series: Women's Oral Health Issues. In Section I, see: Oral Health.

American Diabetes Association

American Diabetes Association Guide to Diabetes Coding. In Section I, see: Forms and Records Control.

American Diabetes Association Guide to Medical Nutrition Therapy for Diabetes. In Section I, see: Diet Therapy.

Clinical Practice Recommendations. In Section I, see: Diabetes Mellitus/Therapy.

Diabetes Medical Nutrition Therapy. In Section I, see: Diabetic Diet.

Diabetes: 1996 Vital Statistics. In Section I, see: Diabetes Mellitus/Epidemiology.

Intensive Diabetes Management, 2nd Edition. In Section I, see: Diabetes Mellitus/Drug Therapy.

Medical Management of Insulin-Dependent (Type 1) Diabetes, 3rd Edition. In Section I, see: Diabetes Mellitus, Insulin-Dependent.

Medical Management of Non-Insulin-Dependent (Type 2) Diabetes, 4th Edition. In Section I, see: Diabetes Mellitus, Non-Insulin-Dependent.

Medical Management of Pregnancy Complicated by Diabetes, 2nd Edition. In Section I, see: Diabetes, Gestational.

Practical Psychology for Diabetes Clinicians. In Section I, see: Psychology/Methods.

The Health Professional's Guide to Diabetes and Exercise. In Section I, see: Diabetes Mellitus.

Therapy for Diabetes Mellitus and Related Disorders, 3rd Edition. In Section I, see: Diabetes Mellitus/Therapy.

American Gastroenterological Association

A Primer on Outcomes Research for the Gastroenterologist: Report of the AGA Taskforce on Outcomes Research. In Section I, see: Gastroenterology.

Anorectal Testing Techniques. In Section I, see: Anus Diseases/Diagnosis.

Chronic Diarrhea. In Section I, see: Diarrhea/Therapy.

Clinical Esophageal pH Recording. In Section I, see: Esophageal Diseases/Diagnosis.

Clinical Evaluation of Jaundice: A Guideline of the Patient Care Committee of the American Gastroenterological Association. In Section I, see: Jaundice/Diagnosis.

Clinical Use of Esophageal Manometry. In Section I, see: Esophagus/Physiology.

Colorectal Cancer Screening. In Section I, see: Colorectal Neoplasms/Prevention and Control.

Sponsor

Detection and Surveillance of Colorectal Cancer. In Section I, see: Colorectal Neoplasms/Diagnosis.

Epidemiology, Diagnosis, and Treatment of Pancreatic Ductal Adenocarcinoma. In Section I, see: Pancreatic Neoplasms/Epidemiology.

Evaluation of Dyspepsia. In Section I, see: Dyspepsia/ Diagnosis.

Guidelines for the Management of Malnutrition and Cachexia, Chronic Diarrhea, and Hepatobiliary Disease in Patients with HIV Infection. In Section I, see: Cachexia/Therapy.

Guidelines for the Use of Enteral Nutrition. In Section I, see: Enteral Nutrition.

Guidelines for Training in Gallstone Lithotripsy. In Section I, see: Education, Medical, Continuing/ Standards.

Hospital Credentialing Standards for Physicians who Perform Endoscopies. In Section I, see: Credentialing/ Standards.

Irritable Bowel Syndrome. In Section I, see: Colonic Diseases, Functional/Diagnosis.

List of Available Gastroenterology Training Programs. In Section I, see: Education, Medical, Graduate.

Management of Oropharyngeal Dysphagia. In Section I, see: Deglutition Disorders.

Management of Patients with Dysphagia Caused by Benign Disorders of the Distal Esophagus. In Section I, see: Deglutition Disorders/Etiology.

Statement on Guidelines for Total Parenteral Nutrition. In Section I, see: Parenteral Nutrition, Total.

American Geriatrics Society

Alcohol Use Disorders in Older Adults, Pocket Guide. In Section I, see: Alcoholism.

Care Management, Position Statement. In Section I, see: Care Management.

Clinical Practice Guidelines Bibliography. In Section I, see: Bibliography.

Comprehensive Geriatric Assessment for the Older Patient, Position Statement. In Section I, see: Geriatric Assessment.

Conversion of Prescription Drugs to Over-the-Counter Designation, Position Statement. In Section I, see: Prescriptions, Drug.

Curriculum Guidelines on the Care of the Elderly for Internal Medicine Residency Training Programs. In Section I, see: Internship and Residency.

Drug Evaluation and Surveillance, Position Statement. In Section I, see: Drug Evaluation.

Education in Geriatric Medicine, Position Statement. In Section I, see: Education, Medical.

Financing of Long-Term Care Services, Position Statement. In Section I, see: Insurance, Long-Term Care.

Geriatric Rehabilitation, Position Statement. In Section I, see: Rehabilitation.

Guidelines for Fellowship Training Programs in Geriatric Medicine. In Section I, see: Geriatrics.

Guidelines for Restraint Use. In Section I, see: Restraint, Physical.

Home Care and Home Care Reimbursement, Position Statement. In Section I, see: Home Care Services.

Implementation of Geriatric Medicine Fellowship Guidelines: Suggestions for Program Directors. In Section I, see: Education, Medical, Graduate.

Informed Consent for Research on Human Subjects with Dementia. In Section I, see: Informed Consent.

Making Treatment Decisions for Incapacitated Elderly Patients without Advance Directives, Position Statement. In Section I, see: Decision Making.

Medical Treatment Decisions Concerning Elderly People, Position Statement. In Section I, see: Decision Making.

Medicare, Position Statement. In Section I, see: Medicare.

Mental Health and the Elderly, Position Statement. In Section I, see: Mental Health Services.

Oral Anticoagulation for Older Adults, Pocket Guide. In Section I, see: Anticoagulants.

Physician Assisted Suicide and Voluntary Active Euthanasia, Position Statement. In Section I, see: Suicide, Assisted.

Physician Reimbursement Under Medicare, Position Statement. In Section I, see: Medicare.

Physician's Role in the Long-Term Care Facility, Position Statement. In Section I, see: Physician's Role.

Prevention and Treatment of Influenza in the Elderly. In Section I, see: Influenza/Prevention and Control.

Prevention of Nuclear War, Position Statement. In Section I, see: Nuclear Warfare.

Psychotherapeutic Medications in the Nursing Home. In Section I, see: Psychotropic Drugs/Therapeutic Use.

Public Financing of Catastrophic Care for the Older Patient, Position Statement. In Section I, see: Health Services Needs and Demands/Economics.

Rational Allocation of Medical Care. In Section I, see: Health Care Rationing.

Regulation of Nursing Facilities, Position Statement. In Section I, see: Facility Regulation and Control.

Research and Geriatric Medicine, Position Statement. In Section I, see: Research.

Screening for Cervical Carcinoma in Elderly Women. In Section I, see: Cervix Neoplasms.

The Care of Dying Patients, Position Statement. In Section I, see: Terminal Care.

The Management of Chronic Pain in Older Persons. In Section I, see: Pain/Drug Therapy.

The Role of Physicians in House Calls in Geriatric Practice. In Section I, see: House Calls.

The Role of the Veterans Administration in the Care of the Elderly, Position Statement. In Section I, see: United States Department of Veterans Affairs.

The Training of Geriatrics Fellows in Rehabilitation. In Section I, see: Education, Medical, Graduate.

The Use of Drugs of Questionable Efficacy in the Elderly, Position Statement. In Section I, see: Drugs, Prescription.

The Use of Oral Anticoagulants (warfarin) in the Elderly. In Section I, see: Warfarin.

Two-Step PPD Testing for Nursing Home Patients on Admission. In Section I, see: Tuberculin.

American Heart Association

Antimicrobial Treatment of Infective Endocarditis Due to Viridans Streptococci, Enterococci, and Staphylococci. In Section I, see: Endocarditis, Bacterial/Drug Therapy.

Aspirin as a Therapeutic Agent in Cardiovascular Disease. In Section I, see: Aspirin/Therapeutic Use.

Cardiac Positron Emission Tomography. In Section I, see: Coronary Disease/Radionuclide Imaging.

Cardiac Rehabilitation Programs. In Section I, see: Cardiovascular Diseases/Rehabilitation.

Cardiac Transplantation: Recipient Selection, Donor Procurement, and Medical Follow-Up. In Section I, see: Cardiology.

Cardiovascular Disease in Women. In Section I, see: Cardiovascular Diseases/Epidemiology.

Cardiovascular Preparticipation Screening of Competitive Athletes: Addendum. In Section I, see: Sports.

Carotid Stenting and Angioplasty. In Section I, see: Angioplasty, Balloon.

Cigarette Smoking, Cardiovascular Disease, and Stroke. In Section I, see: Smoking.

Clinical Investigation of Antiarrhythmic Devices. In Section I, see: Arrhythmia/Prevention and Control.

Diagnosis and Therapy of Kawasaki Disease in Children. In Section I, see: Mucocutaneous Lymph Node Syndrome/Diagnosis.

Exercise Standards. In Section I, see: Exercise Test.

Guide to Anticoagulant Therapy. In Section I, see: Heparin/Therapeutic Use.

Guideline for Clinical Use of Cardiac Radionuclide Imaging. In Section I, see: Coronary Disease/ Radionuclide Imaging.

Guidelines and Indications for Coronary Artery Bypass Graft Surgery. In Section I, see: Coronary Artery Bypass/Methods.

Guidelines for Carotid Endarterectomy. In Section I, see: Carotid Artery Diseases/Surgery.

Guidelines for Electrocardiography. In Section I, see: Cardiovascular Diseases/Diagnosis.

Guidelines for Evaluation and Management of Common Congenital Cardiac Problems in Infants, Children, and Adolescents. In Section I, see: Heart Defects, Congenital/Diagnosis.

Guidelines for Long-Term Management of Patients with Kawasaki Disease. In Section I, see: Cardiology.

Guidelines for Percutaneous Transluminal Coronary Angioplasty. In Section I, see: Coronary Disease/ Therapy.

Guidelines for Peripheral Percutaneous Transluminal Angioplasty of the Abdominal Aorta and Lower Extremity Vessels. In Section I, see: Angioplasty, Balloon.

Guidelines for the Diagnosis of Rheumatic Fever: Jones Criteria, Updated 1992. In Section I, see: Rheumatic Fever/Diagnosis.

Guidelines for the Evaluation and Management of Heart Failure. In Section I, see: Heart Failure, Congestive/Diagnosis.

Guidelines for the Management of Aneurysmal Subarachnoid Hemorrhage. In Section I, see: Aneurysm, Ruptured/Therapy.

Guidelines for the Management of Patients with Acute Ischemic Stroke. In Section I, see: Cerebral Ischemia/Therapy.

Guidelines for the Management of Transient Ischemic Attacks. In Section I, see: Cerebral Ischemia, Transient/Therapy.

Human Blood Pressure Determination by Sphygmomanometry. In Section I, see: Blood Pressure Determination/Methods.

Instrumentation and Practice Standards of Electrocardiographic Monitoring in Special Care Units. In Section I, see: Electrocardiography/Instrumentation.

Insurability of the Adolescent and Young Adult with Heart Disease. In Section I, see: Heart Defects, Congenital/Economics.

Low-Energy Biphasic Waveform Defibrillation. In Section I, see: Electric Countershock.

Obesity and Heart Disease. In Section I, see: Heart Diseases/Etiology.

Optimal Resources for the Examination and Endovascular Treatment of Peripheral and Visceral Vascular Systems. In Section I, see: Angiography/Standards.

Optimal Risk Factor Management in Patients after Coronary Revascularization. In Section I, see: Myocardial Revascularization.

Pediatric Therapeutic Cardiac Catheterization. In Section I, see: Heart Catheterization.

Practice Guideline: Cardiac Catheterization and Cardiac Catheterization Laboratories. In Section I, see: Heart Catheterization/Standards.

Preventing Heart Attack and Death in Patients with Coronary Disease. In Section I, see: Coronary Diseases/Complications.

Prevention of Bacterial Endocarditis: Recommendations by the American Heart Association. In Section I, see: Endocarditis, Bacterial/Prevention and Control.

Primary Prevention of Coronary Heart Disease: A Guidance from Framingham. In Section I, see: Coronary Diseases/Prevention and Control.

Recommendations for Cardiovascular Screening, Staffing and the Emergency Policies at Health/Fitness Facilities. In Section I, see: Physical Fitness.

Recommendations for Standardization and Specifications in Automated Electrocardiography:

Bandwidth and Digital Signal Processing. In Section I, see: Electrocardiography/Standards.

Recommended Guidelines for Uniform Reporting of Data from Out-of-Hospital Cardiac Arrest: The Utstein Style. In Section I, see: Emergency Medical Services/Standards.

Recommended Guidelines for Uniform Reporting of Pediatric Advanced Life Support: The Pediatric Utstein Style. In Section I, see: Resuscitation.

Selection and Treatment of Candidates for Heart Transplantation. In Section I, see: Heart Diseases/Surgery.

The American Heart Association Stroke Outcome Classification. In Section I, see: Cerebrovascular Disorders/Classification.

The American Heart Association Stroke Outcome Classification Executive Summary. In Section I, see: Cerebrovascular Disorders/Classification.

Treatment of Acute Streptococcal Pharyngitis and Prevention of Rheumatic Fever. In Section I, see: Rheumatic Fever/Prevention and Control.

American Heart Association, American College of Cardiology

Clinical Competence in Ambulatory Electrocardiography. In Section I, see: Clinical Competence.

Guidelines for Clinical Intracardiac Electrophysiologic and Catheter Ablation Procedures. In Section I, see: Catheter Ablation.

Guidelines for Exercise Testing. In Section I, see: Cardiology/Standards.

Guidelines for Implantation of Cardiac Pacemakers and Antiarrhythmia Devices. In Section I, see: Arrhythmia/Therapy.

Guidelines for the Clinical Application of Echocardiography. In Section I, see: Echocardiography.

Guidelines for the Early Management of Patients with Acute Myocardial Infarction. In Section I, see: Myocardial Infarction/Therapy.

Perioperative Cardiovascular Evaluation for Non-Cardiac Surgery. In Section I, see: Cardiovascular Diseases/Physiopathology.

American In Vitro Allergy/ Immunology Society

The Clinical Utility and Appropriate Use of In Vitro Allergy Testing. In Section I, see: Hypersensitivity.

American Medical Association, Council on Ethical and Judicial Affairs

Confidential Care for Minors. In Section I, see: Confidentiality.

Confidentiality of HIV Status on Autopsy Reports. In Section I, see: Autopsy.

Decisions for Forgoing Life-Sustaining Treatment for Incompetent Patients. In Section I, see: Life Support Care.

Decisions Near the End of Life. In Section I, see: Mental Competency.

Ethical Issues in Health Care System Reform. In Section I, see: Ethics.

Ethical Issues in the Growing AIDS Crisis. In Section I, see: Ethics, Medical.

Guidelines for the Appropriate Use of Do-Not-Resuscitate Orders. In Section I, see: Resuscitation Orders.

Guidelines for the Use of Restraints in Long Term Care Facilities. In Section I, see: Restraint, Physical.

Informing Families of a Patient's Death: Guidelines for the Involvement of Medical Students. In Section I, see: Death.

Physicians and Domestic Violence. In Section I, see: Physician's Role.

Treatment Decisions for Seriously Ill Newborns. In Section I, see: Decision Making.

American Medical Association, Council on Scientific Affairs

Alternative Psychological Methods in Patient Care. In Section I, see: Psychotherapy/Methods.

Alternatives to Animal Use in Biomedical Research. In Section I, see: Animal Testing Alternatives.

Application of Positron Emission Tomography in the Heart. In Section I, see: Myocardium/Metabolism.

Autopsy. In Section I, see: Autopsy.

Aversion Therapy. In Section I, see: Aversive Therapy.

Carpal Tunnel Syndrome. In Section I, see: Carpal Tunnel Syndrome/Surgery.

Clinical Ecology. In Section I, see: Air Pollutants/Adverse Effects.

Comorbidity. In Section I, see: Comorbidity.

Corneal Transplantation. In Section I, see: Cornea/Transplantation.

Cyclotrons and Radiopharmaceuticals in Positron Emission Tomography. In Section I, see: Particle Accelerators.

Diagnostic Evaluation of the Differential Diagnosis of Thyroid Nodules. In Section I, see: Thyroid Nodule/Diagnosis.

Diagnostic Ultrasonography: Clinical Interpretation. In Section I, see: Ultrasonography.

Dietary Fiber and Health. In Section I, see: Dietary Fiber/Therapeutic Use.

Dyslexia. In Section I, see: Dyslexia.

Elder Abuse and Neglect. In Section I, see: Elder Abuse.

Fundamentals of Magnetic Resonance Imaging. In Section I, see: Magnetic Resonance Imaging/Methods.

Future of Ultrasonography. In Section I, see: Ultrasonography/Trends.

Guidelines for Clinical Assessment and Management of Alcoholism in the Elderly. In Section I, see: Alcoholism/Therapy.

Helmets and Preventing Motorcycle and Bicycle-Related Injuries. In Section I, see: Head Protective Devices/Standards.

Improving Patient Records. In Section I, see: Medical Records.

Instrumentation in Positron Emission Tomography. In Section I, see: Tomography, Emission Computed/Instrumentation.

Introduction to the Management of Immunosuppression. In Section I, see: Immunosuppression/Methods.

Magnetic Resonance Imaging of the Abdomen and Pelvis. In Section I, see: Pelvic Neoplasms/Diagnosis.

Magnetic Resonance Imaging of the Cardiovascular System. In Section I, see: Cardiovascular Diseases/Diagnosis.

Magnetic Resonance Imaging of the Central Nervous System. In Section I, see: Central Nervous System Diseases/Diagnosis.

Magnetic Resonance Imaging of the Head and Neck Region. In Section I, see: Magnetic Resonance Imaging/Methods.

Magnetic Resonance Imaging: Prologue. In Section I, see: Magnetic Resonance Imaging.

Mammography Screening in Asymptomatic Women Forty Years and Older. In Section I, see: Breast Neoplasms/Prevention and Control.

Modern Component Usage in Transfusion Therapy, 1992. In Section I, see: Blood Component Transfusion.

Positron Emission Tomography—A New Approach to Brain Chemistry. In Section I, see: Brain Chemistry.

Positron Emission Tomography in Oncology. In Section I, see: Neoplasms/Metabolism.

Recognition and Treatment of Depression in Medical Practice. In Section I, see: Depressive Disorder/Diagnosis.

Status of Medical Diagnostic Ultrasound Instrumentation. In Section I, see: Ultrasonography/Instrumentation.

Systemic Therapy for Breast Cancer. In Section I, see: Breast Neoplasms/Drug Thereapy.

Treatment of Depression by Primary Care Physicians: Pharmacological Approaches. In Section I, see: Depressive Disorder.

Treatment of Depression by Primary Care Physicians: Psychotherapeutic Treatments for Depression. In Section I, see: Depression/Therapy.

Treatment of Obesity in Adults. In Section I, see: Obesity/Therapy.

Ultrasonic Evaluation of the Fetus. In Section I, see: Fetal Diseases/Ultrasonography.

Ultrasonic Imaging of the Abdomen: Report of the Ultrasonography Task Force. In Section I, see: Abdomen/Ultrasonography.

Ultrasonic Imaging of the Heart. In Section I, see: Ultrasonography.

Ultrasonic Imaging of the Vascular System. In Section I, see: Blood Vessels/Ultrasonography.

Violence Against Women. In Section I, see: Violence.

Vitamin Preparations as Dietary Supplements and as Therapeutic Agents. In Section I, see: Vitamins/Administration and Dosage.

Vitro Tests for Allergy. In Section I, see: Hypersensitivity/Diagnosis.

Vivo Diagnostic Testing and Immunotherapy for Allergy: Part I. In Section I, see: Desensitization, Immunologic.

Vivo Diagnostic Testing and Immunotherapy for Allergy: Part II. In Section I, see: Desensitization, Immunologic.

American Medical Association, Diagnostic and Therapeutic Technology Assessment Program

Ablation of Accessory Pathways in Wolff-Parkinson-White Syndrome. In Section I, see: Wolff-Parkinson-White Syndrome/Surgery.

Aerosolized Pentamidine for HIV Patients. In Section I, see: HIV Infections/Complications.

Allogeneic Bone Marrow Transplantation for Chronic Myelogenous Leukemia. In Section I, see: Bone Marrow Transplantation.

Alpha-Interferon for Chronic Myelogenous Leukemia. In Section I, see: Interferon Alpha-2a/Therapeutic Use.

Angelchik Antireflux Prosthesis Treatment of Gastroesophageal Reflux. In Section I, see: Gastroesophageal Reflux/Surgery.

Cardiac Rehabilitation Services. In Section I, see: Heart Diseases/Rehabilitation.

Chelation Therapy (with EDTA) for Atherosclerosis. In Section I, see: Chelating Agents/Therapeutic Use.

Chorionic Villus Sampling: A Reassessment. In Section I, see: Chorionic Villi Sampling.

Continuous Ambulatory Esophageal pH Monitoring in the Evaluation of Patients with Gastroesophageal Reflux. In Section I, see: Gastroesophageal Reflux/Diagnosis.

Continuous Arteriovenous Hemofiltration (CAVH) for Fluid Removal. In Section I, see: Ultrafiltration/Methods.

Distraction/Compression Osteosynthesis with the Ilizarov Device. In Section I, see: Orthopedic Fixation Devices/Therapy.

Dorsal Rhizotomy. In Section I, see: Cerebral Palsy/Surgery.

Endoscopic Balloon Dilation of the Prostate. In Section I, see: Balloon Dilation.

Endoscopic Electrocoagulation for Gastrointestinal Hemorrhage. In Section I, see: Electrocoagulation/Methods.

Endoscopic Laser Photocoagulation for Gastrointestinal Hemorrhage. In Section I, see: Lasers/Therapeutic Use.

Endoscopic Release of the Carpal Ligament. In Section I, see: Carpal Tunnel Syndrome/Surgery.

Endoscopic Thermal Coagulation for Gastrointestinal Hemorrhage. In Section I, see: Electrocoagulation/Methods.

Endoscopic Topical Therapy for Gastrointestinal Hemorrhage. In Section I, see: Gastrointestinal Hemorrhage/Therapy.

Endovascular Atherectomy for Coronary Artery Disease: Directional Coronary Atherectomy. In Section I, see: Coronary Disease/Surgery.

Gamete Intrafallopian Transfer (GIFT). In Section I, see: Gamete Intrafallopian Transfer.

Garren Gastric Bubble for Morbid Obesity. In Section I, see: Obesity, Morbid/Therapy.

Gastric Restrictive Surgery. In Section I, see: Gastric Bypass.

Growth Hormone for Short Stature. In Section I, see: Body Height.

Human Papillomavirus DNA Testing in the Management of Cervical Neoplasia. In Section I, see: Cervix Neoplasms/Microbiology.

Hyperthermia as Adjuvant Treatment for Recurrent Breast Cancer and Primary Malignant Glioma. In Section I, see: Breast Neoplasms/Therapy.

Image-Guided Breast Biopsy. In Section I, see: Biopsy, Needle/Methods.

Immuno-Augmentative Therapy for Cancer. In Section I, see: Immunotherapy/Methods.

Immunochemiluminometric Assays (ICMA) of Thyroid-Stimulating Hormone (TSH) for the Diagnosis of Thyroid Disorders and for Monitoring Response to Therapy. In Section I, see: Chemiluminescence.

Intracavernous Pharmacotherapy for Impotence: Papaverine and Phentolamine. In Section I, see: Impotence/Drug Therapy.

Laminectomy and Microlaminectomy for Lumbar Disc Herniation. In Section I, see: Laminectomy/Methods.

Laparoscopic Cholecystectomy. In Section I, see: Cholecystectomy/Methods.

Laparoscopic Herniorrhaphy. In Section I, see: Hernia, Inguinal/Surgery.

Laparoscopic Nissen Fundoplication. In Section I, see: Fundoplication/Methods.

Laser Ablation of the Endometrium. In Section I, see: Endometrium/Surgery.

Lung Transplantation. In Section I, see: Lung Transplantation.

Mammographic Screening for Breast Cancer. In Section I, see: Mammography.

Maternal Serum Alpha-Fetoprotein Testing for Down's Syndrome. In Section I, see: Alpha-Fetoproteins/Blood.

Measurement of Bone Density with Dual Energy X-ray Absorptiometry (DEXA). In Section I, see: Bone Density.

Microsurgical Reconstruction for Brachial Plexus Injury. In Section I, see: Brachial Plexus/Injuries.

Myocardial Perfusion Imaging Utilizing Single-Photon Emission-Computed Tomography (SPECT). In Section I, see: Coronary Disease/Diagnosis.

Non-Invasive Extracorporeal Lithotripsy for Disruption of Kidney Stones—UPDATE. In Section I, see: Lithotripsy.

Pancreas Transplants. In Section I, see: Pancreas Transplantation/Physiology.

Pedicle Screw Fixation System for Spinal Instability. In Section I, see: Bone Screws.

Penile Implants for Erectile Impotence. In Section I, see: Impotence/Surgery.

Percutaneous Nephrolithotomy for Kidney Stone Removal. In Section I, see: Kidney Calculi/Therapy.

Peripheral Parenteral Nutrition. In Section I, see: Parenteral Nutrition.

Plasma Concentrations of Lipoprotein (a). In Section I, see: Lipoprotein/Blood.

Prophylactic Treatment of Opportunistic Infections in HIV-Positive Patients: Toxoplasma gondii Prophylaxis. In Section I, see: HIV Seropositivity.

Radiofrequency Catheter Ablation of Aberrant Conducting Pathways of the Heart. In Section I, see: Catheter Ablation.

Reassessment of Autologous Bone Marrow Transplantation. In Section I, see: Bone Marrow Transplantation.

Reassessment of Automated Percutaneous Lumbar Diskectomy for Herniated Disks. In Section I, see: Intervertebral Disk/Surgery.

Reassessment of BCG Immunotherapy in Bladder Cancer. In Section I, see: Bladder Neoplasms/Therapy.

Reassessment of Cardiokymography for the Diagnosis of Coronary Artery Disease. In Section I, see: Coronary Disease/Diagnosis.

Reassessment of Radial Keratotomy for Simple Myopia. In Section I, see: Keratotomy, Radial.

Reassessment of Transrectal Ultrasonography. In Section I, see: Ultrasonography.

Rigid and Flexible Sigmoidoscopies. In Section I, see: Sigmoidoscopy.

Speech Therapy for Otitis Media with Effusion. In Section I, see: Speech Therapy.

Sperm Penetration Assay in Identifying Male Infertility. In Section I, see: Infertility, Male/Diagnosis.

Surrogate Markers of Progressive HIV Disease. In Section I, see: HIV Infections/Immunology.

Teflon Injections for Urinary Incontinence. In Section I, see: Polytetrafluoroethylene/Therapeutic Use.

Therapeutic Apheresis, Part I. Background and Nonrenal Indications. In Section I, see: Plasmapheresis.

Therapeutic Apheresis, Part II. Renal Indications. In Section I, see: Plasmapheresis.

Transjugular Intrahepatic Portosystemic Shunt (TIPS). In Section I, see: Portasystemic Shunt, Surgical.

Ureteral Stone Management: Ureteroscopy and Extracorporeal Shock Wave Lithotripsy. In Section I, see: Lithotripsy.

Ureteral Stone Management: Ureteroscopy and Ultrasonic Lithotripsy. In Section I, see: Ureteral Calculi/Therapy.

Use of Plasma Concentrations of Apolipoproteins. In Section I, see: Apolipoproteins B/Blood.

Vasoactive Intracavernous Pharmacotherapy for Impotence: Intracavernous Injection of Prostaglandin E1. In Section I, see: Alprostadil/Therapeutic Use.

American Medical Association, Division of Health Science

Alcoholism in the Elderly: Diagnosis, Treatment, and Prevention. In Section I, see: Alcoholism/Prevention and Control.

Child Physical Abuse and Neglect. In Section I, see: Child Abuse.

Child Sexual Abuse. In Section I, see: Child Abuse, Sexual.

Diagnostic and Treatment Guidelines on Mental Health Effects of Family Violence. In Section I, see: Domestic Violence.

Domestic Violence: A Directory of Protocols for Healthcare Providers. In Section I, see: Domestic Violence.

Guidelines for Adolescent Preventive Services. In Section I, see: Adolescent Health Services/Organization and Administration.

Guidelines for the Diagnosis and Treatment of Nicotine Dependence. In Section I, see: Nicotine.

Guidelines for the Medical Management of the Home Care Patient. In Section I, see: Home Care Services.

Guidelines for the Use of Assistive Technology: Evaluation, Referral, Prescription. In Section I, see: Self-Help Devices.

Guides to the Evaluation of Permanent Impairment. In Section I, see: Disability Evaluation.

Hepatitis Guidelines. In Section I, see: Hepatitis.

HIV Blood Test Counseling: AMA Physician Guidelines, 2nd Edition. In Section I, see: HIV Infections/Diagnosis.

Physician Guide to HIV Prevention. In Section I, see: HIV Infections/Prevention and Control.

Physician Guide to Media Violence. In Section I, see: Mass Media.

Strategies for the Treatment and Prevention of Sexual Assault. In Section I, see: Rape/Prevention and Control.

American Medical Directors Association

Altered Mental States. In Section I, see: Mental Disorders.

Dementia. In Section I, see: Dementia.

Depression. In Section I, see: Depression.

Falls and Fall Risk. In Section I, see: Accidental Falls.

Guideline Implementation. In Section I, see: Practice Guidelines.

Heart Failure. In Section I, see: Heart Failure, Congestive/Mortality.

Osteoporosis. In Section I, see: Osteoporosis.

Pharmacotherapy Companion to the 1996 Depression Clinical Practice Guideline. In Section I, see: Depression.

Pressure Ulcers. In Section I, see: Decubitus Ulcer.

Urinary Incontinence. In Section I, see: Urinary Incontinence.

American Psychiatric Association

Anxiety Disorders, Dissociative Disorders, and Adjustment Disorders. In Section I, see: Anxiety Disorders.

Delirium, Dementia, Amnesia, and Other Cognitive Disorders. In Section I, see: Delirium.

Disorders of Impulse Control. In Section I, see: Impulse Control Disorders/Drug Therapy.

Disorders Usually First Diagnosed in Infancy, Childhood, or Adolescence. In Section I, see: Mental Disorders Diagnosed in Childhood.

Eating Disorders. In Section I, see: Anorexia Nervosa.

General Considerations in Psychiatric Treatment. In Section I, see: Mental Disorders/Drug Therapy.

Manual of Psychiatric Quality Assurance. In Section I, see: Quality Assurance, Health Care.

Mood Disorders. In Section I, see: Mood Disorders/ Therapy.

Personality Disorders. In Section I, see: Personality Disorders/Drug Therapy.

Practice Guideline Book. In Section I, see: Practice Guidelines.

Practice Guideline for Eating Disorders. In Section I, see: Practice Guidelines.

Practice Guideline for Major Depressive Disorder in Adults. In Section I, see: Depressive Disorder Therapy.

Practice Guideline for the Psychiatric Evaluation of Adults. In Section I, see: Mental Disorders/Diagnosis.

Practice Guideline for the Treatment of Patients with Alzheimer's Disease and Other Dementias of Late Life. In Section I, see: Alzheimer's Disease/Therapy.

Practice Guideline for the Treatment of Patients with Bipolar Disorder. In Section I, see: Bipolar Disorder/ Therapy.

Practice Guideline for the Treatment of Patients with Delirium. In Section I, see: Delirium/Therapy.

Practice Guideline for the Treatment of Patients with Nicotine Dependence. In Section I, see: Tobacco Use Disorder/Therapy.

Practice Guideline for the Treatment of Patients with Panic Disorder. In Section I, see: Panic Disorder/Drug Therapy.

Practice Guideline for the Treatment of Patients with Schizophrenia. In Section I, see: Schizophrenia/ Therapy.

Practice Guideline for the Treatment of Patients with Substance Use Disorders: Alcohol, Cocaine, Opioids. In Section I, see: Cocaine-Related Disorders/Therapy.

Practice of ECT: Recommendations for Treatment, Training, and Privileging. In Section I, see: Electroconvulsive Therapy/Education.

Schizophrenia and Other Psychotic Disorders. In Section I, see: Schizophrenia/Therapy.

Sexual and Gender Identity Disorders. In Section I, see: Gender Identity/Therapy.

Sleep Disorders. In Section I, see: Sleep Disorders/ Drug Therapy.

Somatoform and Factitious Disorders. In Section I, see: Somatoform Disorders.

Substance-Related Disorders. In Section I, see: Substance-Related Disorders/Therapy.

American Society for Gastrointestinal Endoscopy

Appropriate Use of Gastrointestinal Endoscopy. In Section I, see: Endoscopy, Gastrointestinal.

Conscious Sedation and Monitoring of Patients Undergoing GI Endoscopic Procedures. In Section I, see: Endoscopy, Gastrointestinal.

Diagnostic and Therapeutic Procedures. In Section I, see: Diagnosis.

Endoscopic Therapy of Biliary Tract and Pancreatic Diseases. In Section I, see: Biliary Tract Diseases/ Therapy.

Esophageal Dilation. In Section I, see: Balloon Dilation/Methods.

Flexible Sigmoidoscopy: Guidelines for Clinical Application. In Section I, see: Sigmoidoscopy.

Guideline for Management of Ingested Foreign Bodies. In Section I, see: Endoscopy, Gastrointestinal.

Guidelines for Establishment of Gastrointestinal Endoscopy Areas. In Section I, see: Endoscopy.

Infection Control During Gastrointestinal Endoscopy: Guidelines for Clinical Application. In Section I, see: Cross-Infection/Prevention and Control.

Informed Consent for Gastrointestinal Endoscopy. In Section I, see: Informed Consent.

Methods of Granting Hospital Privileges to Perform Gastrointestinal Endoscopy. In Section I, see: Endoscopy, Gastrointestinal.

Monitoring of Patients Undergoing Gastrointestinal Endoscopic Procedures. In Section I, see: Endoscopy, Gastrointestinal.

OSHA Regulations—Requirements for Endoscopic Practice. In Section I, see: United States Occupational Safety and Health Administration.

Preparation of Patients for Gastrointestinal Endoscopy: Guidelines for Clinical Application. In Section I, see: Gastroscopy.

Proctoring and Hospital Endoscopy Privileges. In Section I, see: Endoscopy, Gastrointestinal/Standards.

Quality Assurance of Gastrointestinal Endoscopy. In Section I, see: Endoscopy, Gastrointestinal.

Risk Management. In Section I, see: Risk Management.

Role of Colonoscopy in the Management of Patients with Colonic Polyps: Guidelines for Clinical Application. In Section I, see: Colonic Polyps/Diagnosis.

Role of Colonoscopy in the Management of Patients with Inflammatory Bowel Disease: Guidelines for Clinical Application. In Section I, see: Colitis, Ulcerative/Diagnosis.

Role of Endoscopic Sclerotherapy in the Management of Variceal Bleeding: Guidelines for Clinical Application. In Section I, see: Esophageal and Gastric Varices/Drug Therapy.

Role of Endoscopy in Diseases of the Biliary Tract and Pancreas: Guidelines for Clinical Application. In Section I, see: Biliary Tract Diseases/Diagnosis.

Role of Endoscopy in the Management of Acute Nonvariceal Upper Gastrointestinal Bleeding. In Section I, see: Endoscopy, Gastrointestinal.

Role of Endoscopy in the Management of Esophagitis. In Section I, see: Esophagitis, Peptic/Diagnosis.

Role of Endoscopy in the Management of the Patient with Peptic Ulcer Disease: Guidelines for Clinical Application. In Section I, see: Peptic Ulcer/Diagnosis.

Role of Endoscopy in the Management of Upper Gastrointestinal Hemorrhage. In Section I, see: Endoscopy.

Role of Endoscopy in the Patient with Lower Gastrointestinal Bleeding: Guidelines for Clinical Application. In Section I, see: Colonoscopy.

Role of Endoscopy in the Surveillance of Premalignant Conditions of the Upper Gastrointestinal Tract: Guidelines for Clinical Application. In Section I, see: Esophageal Neoplasms/Diagnosis.

Role of Laparoscopy in the Diagnosis and Management of Gastrointestinal Disease: Guidelines for Clinical Application. In Section I, see: Gastrointestinal Diseases/Diagnosis.

Role of Percutaneous Endoscopic Gastrostomy: Guidelines for Clinical Application. In Section I, see: Enteral Nutrition.

Standards of Practice of Gastrointestinal Endoscopy. In Section I, see: Education, Medical.

Statement on Endoscopic Training. In Section I, see: Endoscopy/Education.

Statement on Role of Short Courses in Endoscopic Training. In Section I, see: Endoscopy/Education.

The Role of Screening Tests Before Gastrointestinal Endoscopic Procedures. In Section I, see: Endoscopy, Gastrointestinal.

Tissue Sampling and Analysis. In Section I, see: Biopsy/Standards.

American Society for Reproductive Medicine

Age Related Infertility. In Section I, see: Aging/Physiology.

Contraceptive Choices. In Section I, see: Contraceptive Agents.

Current Evaluation and Treatment of Amenorrhea. In Section I, see: Amenorrhea/Diagnosis.

Early Diagnosis and Management of Ectopic Pregnancy. In Section I, see: Pregnancy, Ectopic/Diagnosis.

Evaluation and Treatment of Androgen Excess. In Section I, see: Androgens/Adverse Effects.

Evaluation and Treatment of Endometriosis. In Section I, see: Endometriosis/Diagnosis.

Guidelines for Gamete Donation. In Section I, see: Oocyte Donation.

Guidelines for Human Embryology and Human Andrology Laboratories. In Section I, see: Embryology.

Induction of Ovulation with Clomiphene Citrate. In Section I, see: Clomiphene/Therapeutic Use.

Induction of Ovulation with Human Menopausal Gonadotropins. In Section I, see: Ovulation Induction/Methods.

Intrauterine Insemination. In Section I, see: Insemination, Artificial/Methods.

Management of Menopause. In Section I, see: Menopause.

Myomas and Reproductive Dysfunction. In Section I, see: Myoma.

Recurrent Pregnancy Loss. In Section I, see: Abortion, Habitual.

Tubal Disease. In Section I, see: Fallopian Tube Diseases.

Unexplained Infertility. In Section I, see: Infertility/Diagnosis.

Use of Bromocriptine. In Section I, see: Bromocriptine/Therapeutic Use.

Varicocele and Infertility. In Section I, see: Infertility, Male.

Vasectomy Reversal. In Section I, see: Sterilization Reversal.

American Society of Addiction Medicine

Detoxification: Principles and Protocols. In Section I, see: Metabolic Detoxification, Drug.

Patient Placement Criteria for the Treatment of Substance-Related Disorders (2nd Ed.). In Section I, see: Substance-Related Disorders/Rehabilitation.

Pharmacological Management of Alcohol Withdrawal. In Section I, see: Substance Withdrawal Syndrome/Drug Therapy.

The Role of Phenytoin in the Management of Alcohol Withdrawal. In Section I, see: Phenytoin.

American Society of Anesthesiologists

Basic Standards for Preanesthesia Care. In Section I, see: Preanesthestic Medication.

Practice Guidelines for Acute Pain in the Perioperative Setting. In Section I, see: Analgesia/Standards.

Practice Guidelines for Chronic Pain Management. In Section I, see: Pain/Therapy.

Practice Guidelines for Management of the Difficult Airway. In Section I, see: Anesthesia.

Practice Guidelines for Obstetrical Anesthesia. In Section I, see: Anesthesia, Obstetrical/Standards.

Practice Guidelines for Perioperative Transesophageal Echocardiography. In Section I, see: Echocardiography, Transesophageal/Standards.

Practice Guidelines for Preoperative Fasting and the Use of Pharmacologic Agents to Reduce the Risk of Pulmonary Aspiration. In Section I, see: Anesthesiology/Standards.

Practice Guidelines for Pulmonary Artery Catheterization Monitoring. In Section I, see: Catheterization, Swan-Ganz.

Practice Guidelines for Sedation and Analgesia by Non-Anesthesiologists. In Section I, see: Analgesia/Standards.

Standards for Basic Anesthetic Monitoring. In Section I, see: Monitoring, Physiologic.

Standards for Postanesthesia Care. In Section I, see: Anesthesia Recovery Period.

Statement on Routine Preoperative Laboratory and Diagnostic Screening. In Section I, see: Diagnostic Tests, Routine.

American Society of Bariatric Physicians

Anorectic Usage Guidelines. In Section I, see: Appetite Depressants/Therapeutic Use.

Bariatric Practice Guidelines. In Section I, see: Obesity/Therapy.

American Society of Clinical Oncology

1997 Update of Recommendations for the Use of Hematopoietic Colony-Stimulating Factors. In Section I, see: Colony-Stimulating Factors/Therapeutic Use.

1998 Update of Recommendations for the Use of Tumor Markers in Breast and Colorectal Cancer. In Section I, see: Tumor Markers, Biological/Analysis.

1998 Update of Recommended Breast Cancer Surveillance Guidelines. In Section I, see: Breast Neoplasms/Diagnosis.

Clinical Practice Guidelines for the Treatment of Unresectable Non-Small-Cell Lung Cancer. In Section I, see: Carcinoma, Non-Small-Cell Lung.

Recommended Breast Cancer Surveillance Guidelines. In Section I, see: Breast Neoplasms/Diagnosis.

The Use of Chemotherapy and Radiotherapy Protectants. In Section I, see: Antineoplastic Agents/Antagonists and Inhibitors.

Use of Anti-Emetic Agents. In Section I, see: Antiemetics/Therapeutic Use.

American Society of Clinical Pathologists

Breast Frozen Section Biopsies. In Section I, see: Breast/Pathology.

CAP/ASCP Position Paper: The Preoperative Bleeding Time Test Lacks Clinical Benefit. In Section I, see: Bleeding Time.

Critical Values. In Section I, see: Critical Care/Standards.

LE Cell Test. In Section I, see: Laboratory Techniques and Procedures/Methods.

Prevention of Transfusion-Associated CMV Infection. In Section I, see: Cytomegalovirus/Prevention and Control.

Screening Test for Dyslipidemia. In Section I, see: Hyperlipidemia/Prevention and Control.

Stat Testing? A Guideline for Meeting Clinician Turnaround Time Requirements. In Section I, see: Pathology, Clinical/Methods.

Use of Irradiated Blood Components. In Section I, see: Blood Cells/Radiation Effects.

Utilizing Monospecific Antihuman Globulin to Test Blood-Group Compatibility. In Section I, see: Antibodies, Anti-Idiotypic/Immunology.

American Society of Colon and Rectal Surgeons

Fistula-in-Ano. In Section I, see: Rectal Fissure/Surgery.

Practice Parameters for Ambulatory Anorectal Surgery. In Section I, see: Rectum/Surgery.

Practice Parameters for Anal Fissure. In Section I, see: Fissure in Anus/Therapy.

Practice Parameters for Antibiotic Prophylaxis to Prevent Infective Endocarditis of Infected Prosthesis During Colon and Rectal Surgery. In Section I, see: Antibiotics/Therapeutic Use.

Practice Parameters for Sigmoid Diverticulitis. In Section I, see: Diverticulitis, Colonic/Therapy.

Practice Parameters for the Detection of Colorectal Neoplasms. In Section I, see: Colorectal Neoplasms/Diagnosis.

Practice Parameters for the Treatment of Hemorrhoids. In Section I, see: Hemorrhoids/Therapy.

Practice Parameters for Treatment of Rectal Carcinoma. In Section I, see: Colorectal Surgery.

American Society of Hematology

Chronic Myelogenous Leukemia. In Section I, see: Leukemia, Myeloid, Chronic.

Idiopathic Thrombocytopenic Purpura. In Section I, see: Autoimmune Diseases/Therapy.

American Society of Maxillofacial Surgeons

Cleft Lip and Cleft Palate. In Section I, see: Cleft Lip/Surgery.

Cranial Base Surgery. In Section I, see: Skull/Surgery.

Craniosynostosis (Including Syndromal Craniosynostosis, Brachycephaly, Plagiocephaly,

Trigonocephaly, Scaphocephaly). In Section I, see: Craniosynostoses.

Maxillofacial Surgery (Including Orthognathic Surgery and Skeletal Aesthetic Enhancement). In Section I, see: Surgery, Oral.

Maxillofacial Trauma. In Section I, see: Maxillofacial Injuries/Surgery.

Temporomandibular Joint. In Section I, see: Temporomandibular Joint/Surgery.

American Society of Plastic and Reconstructive Surgeons

Abdominoplasty. In Section I, see: Abdominal Muscles/Surgery.

Breast Reconstruction. In Section I, see: Mammoplasty.

Dupuytren's Contracture. In Section I, see: Dupuytren's Contracture.

Ear Deformity: Prominent Ears. In Section I, see: Ear, External/Abnormalities.

Eyelid Surgery. In Section I, see: Eyelids/Surgery.

Female Breast Hypertrophy/Breast Reduction. In Section I, see: Breast/Pathology.

Female Breast Hypoplasia/Breast Augmentation. In Section I, see: Breast/Abnormalities.

Gynecomastia. In Section I, see: Gynecomastia.

Localized Adiposity. In Section I, see: Obesity.

Nasal Deformity. In Section I, see: Nose/Abnormalities.

Position Paper: Prior Authorization/Pre-Determination. In Section I, see: Insurance, Health.

Position Paper: Recommended Criteria for Insurance Coverage of Blepharoplasty. In Section I, see: Blepharoplasty.

Position Paper: Recommended Criteria for Insurance Coverage of Breast Reconstruction Following Mastectomy. In Section I, see: Mammoplasty.

Position Paper: Recommended Criteria for Insurance Coverage of Cleft Lip and Palate Surgery. In Section I, see: Cleft Lip/Surgery.

Position Paper: Recommended Criteria for Insurance Coverage of Orthognathic Surgery. In Section I, see: Jaw/Surgery.

Position Paper: Recommended Criteria for Insurance Coverage of Prophylactic Mastectomy. In Section I, see: Breast Neoplasms/Prevention and Control.

Position Paper: Recommended Criteria for Insurance Coverage of Re-Operation on Women with Breast Implants. In Section I, see: Breast Implants.

Pressure Sores. In Section I, see: Decubitus Ulcer.

Skin Lesions. In Section I, see: Skin/Pathology.

American Society of Temporomandibular Joint Surgeons, American Society of Maxillofacial Surgeons

Guidelines for Diagnosis and Management of Disorders Involving the Temporomandibular Joint and Related Musculoskeletal Structures (Revision). In Section I, see: Temporomandibular Joint Disorders/ Diagnosis.

American Thoracic Society

Animals in Medical Research. In Section I, see: Research.

Aspiration Hazards to the Developing Lung. In Section I, see: Lung/Growth and Development.

Chemotherapy of Pulmonary Mycoses. In Section I, see: Lung Diseases, Fungal/Drug Therapy.

Clinical Role of Bronchoalveolar Lavage. In Section I, see: Bronchoalveolar Lavage Fluid.

Computer Guidelines for Pulmonary Laboratories. In Section I, see: Computers/Standards.

Control of Tuberculosis in the U.S. In Section I, see: Tuberculosis, Pulmonary/Prevention and Control.

Diagnosis and Treatment of Disease Due to Non-Tuberculous Mycobacteria. In Section I, see: Mycobacterium, Infectious, Atypical.

Diagnosis of Non-Malignant Disease Related to Asbestos. In Section I, see: Asbestos/Adverse Effects.

DLCO—Recommendations for a Standard Technique. In Section I, see: Pulmonary Diffusing Capacity

Environmental Controls and Lung Disease. In Section I, see: Air Pollution/Prevention and Control.

Essentials of a Pulmonary Consultation. In Section I, see: Lung Diseases/Diagnosis.

Fact Sheet: "Facts About Second Hand Smoke." In Section I, see: Tobacco Smoke Pollution.

Flexible Endoscopy of the Pediatric Airway. In Section I, see: Bronchoscopy.

Fungal Infections in HIV-Infected Persons. In Section I, see: AIDS-Related Opportunistic Infections/ Pathology.

Future Directions for Research on Disease of the Lung. In Section I, see: Pulmonary Disease (Specialty)/Trends.

Future Research in Tuberculosis: Prospects and Priorities for Elimination. In Section I, see: Primary Prevention/Methods.

Guidelines as to What Constitutes an Adverse Respiratory Health Effect, with Special Reference to Epidemiologic Studies of Air Pollution. In Section I, see: Air Pollution/Adverse Effects.

Guidelines for Percutaneous Transthoracic Needle Biopsy. In Section I, see: Biopsy, Needle/Methods.

Guidelines for the Approach to the Patient with Severe Hereditary Alpha-1-Antitrypsin Deficiency. In Section I, see: Alpha 1-Antitrypsin/Deficiency.

Guidelines for the Evaluation of Impairment/ Disability in Patients with Asthma. In Section I, see: Asthma/Diagnosis.

Guidelines for the Initial Management of Adults with Community-Acquired Pneumonia: Diagnosis, Assessment of Severity, and Initial Antimicrobial Therapy. In Section I, see: Pneumonia/Diagnosis.

Guidelines for Thoracentesis and Needle Biopsy of the Pleura. In Section I, see: Biopsy, Needle/Methods.

Health Effects of Tremolite. In Section I, see: Pneumoconiosis/Etiology.

Home Mechanical Ventilation of Pediatric Patients. In Section I, see: Home Care Services.

Indications and Standards for Cardiopulmonary Sleep Studies. In Section I, see: Heart/Physiology.

Indications and Standards for the Use of Nasal Continuous Positive Airway Pressure (CPAP) in Sleep Apnea Syndromes. In Section I, see: Positive Pressure Respiration/Standards.

Laboratory Diagnosis of Mycotic Infections and Specific Fungal Infections. In Section I, see: Fungi/ Isolation and Purification.

Levels of Laboratory Services for Mycobacterial Disease. In Section I, see: Mycobacterium Infections/ Diagnosis.

Licensure of Respiratory Therapy Technical Personnel. In Section I, see: Respiratory Therapy.

Lung Function Testing: Selection of References Values and Interpretive Strategies. In Section I, see: Respiratory Function Tests/Standards.

Medical Director of Respiratory Care. In Section I, see: Respiration Disorders/Therapy.

Mycobacteriosis and Acquired Immunodeficiency Syndrome. In Section I, see: Acquired Immunodeficiency Syndrome/Complications.

Physicians and the Pharmaceutical Industry. In Section I, see: Drug Industry.

Progress at the Interface of Inflammation and Asthma: Report of the ALA/ATS. In Section I, see: Asthma.

Public Responsibility in Asbestos Associated Diseases. In Section I, see: Social Responsibility.

Pulmonary Function Laboratory Personnel Qualifications. In Section I, see: Health Manpower/Standards.

Quality Assurance in Pulmonary Function Laboratories. In Section I, see: Respiratory Function Tests.

Research Priorities in Respiratory Nursing. In Section I, see: Clinical Nursing Research.

Respiratory Function Measurement in Infants: Measurement Conditions. In Section I, see: Lung Diseases/Diagnosis.

Respiratory Function Measurement in Infants: Symbols, Abbreviations, and Units (SI Units). In Section I, see: Respiratory Function Tests.

Respiratory Mechanics in Infants: Physiologic Evaluation in Health and Disease. In Section I, see: Respiratory Tract Diseases/Physiopathology.

Role of Pulmonary and Critical Care Medicine Physician in the American Health Care System. In Section I, see: Critical Care.

Single Breath Carbon Monoxide Diffusing Capacity (Transfer Factor). In Section I, see: Pulmonary Diffusing Capacity.

Skills of the Health Care Team Involved in Out-of-Hospital Care for Patients with COPD. In Section I, see: Lung Diseases, Obstructive/Therapy.

Sleep Apnea: Sleepiness, and Driving Risk. In Section I, see: Sleep Apnea Syndromes.

Standardization of Spirometry. In Section I, see: Spirometry/Standards.

Standards for the Diagnosis and Care of Patients with Chronic Obstructive Pulmonary Disease. In Section I, see: Lung Diseases, Obstructive/Diagnosis.

Standards of Nursing Care for Adult Patients with Pulmonary Dysfunction. In Section I, see: Nursing Care/Standards.

The Potential for Conflict of Interest of Members of the American Thoracic Society. In Section I, see: Thoracic Diseases.

The Report on the ATS Workshop on the Health Effects of Atmospheric Acids and Their Precursors. In Section I, see: Acid Rain/Adverse Effects.

The Tuberculin Skin Test. In Section I, see: Tuberculin Test.

Treatment of Tuberculosis and Tuberculosis Infection in Adults and Children. In Section I, see: Antitubercular Agents/Therapeutic Use.

Withdrawing and Withholding Life-Sustaining Therapy. In Section I, see: Euthanasia, Passive.

American Thoracic Society, Centers for Disease Control and Prevention

Diagnostic Standards and Classification of Tuberculosis. In Section I, see: Tuberculosis, Pulmonary/Diagnosis.

American Thyroid Association

American Thyroid Association Guidelines for Use of Laboratory Tests in Thyroid Disorders. In Section I, see: Thyroid Diseases/Diagnosis.

Treatment Guidelines for Patients wih Hyperthyroidism and Hypothyroidism. In Section I, see: Hyperthyroidism/Therapy.

Treatment Guidelines for Patients with Thyroid Nodules and Well-Differentiated Thyroid Cancer. In Section I, see: Thyroid Neoplasms/Therapy.

American Urological Association

Management of Localized Prostate Cancer. In Section I, see: Prostatic Neoplasms.

Management of Primary Vesicoureteral Reflux in Children. In Section I, see: Vesicoureteral Reflux/Therapy.

Management of Staghorn Calculi: Summary Report, Report, Patient Guide. In Section I, see: Kidney Calculi/Therapy.

Management of Ureteral Calculi. In Section I, see: Ureteral Calculi/Therapy.

Surgical Treatment of Female Stress Urinary Incontinence. In Section I, see: Urinary Incontinence, Stress/Surgery.

Treatment of Organic Erectile Dysfunction. In Section I, see: Impotence/Therapy.

Arthroscopy Association of North America

Suggested Guidelines for the Practice of Arthroscopic Surgery. In Section I, see: Arthroscopy.

Centers for Disease Control and Prevention

1988 Agent Summary Statement for Human Immunodeficiency Virus and Report on Laboratory-Acquired Infection with Human Immunodeficiency Virus. In Section I, see: Acquired Immunodeficiency Syndrome.

1993 Revised Classification System for HIV Infection and Expanded Surveillance Case Definition for AIDS Among Adolescents and Adults. In Section I, see: Acquired Immunodeficiency Syndrome/Epidemiology.

1994 Revised Classification System for Human Immunodeficiency Virus Infection in Children Less Than 3 Years of Age. In Section I, see: HIV Infections/Classification.

1995 Revised Guidelines for Prophylaxis Against Pneumocystis carinii Pneumonia for Children Infected with or Perinatally Exposed to Human Immunodeficiency Virus. In Section I, see: Pneumonia, Pneumocystis carinii/Prevention and Control.

1997 Revised Guidelines for Performing CD4+ T-Cell Determinations in Persons Infected with Human Immunodeficiency Virus (HIV). In Section I, see: CD4 Lymphocyte Count.

1997 USPHS/IDSA Guidelines for the Prevention of Opportunistic Infections in Persons Infected with Human Immunodeficiency Virus. In Section I, see: AIDS-Related Opportunistic Infections/Prevention and Control.

1998 Guidelines for Treatment of Sexually Transmitted Disease. In Section I, see: Sexually Transmitted Diseases/Therapy.

Anergy Skin Testing and Preventive Therapy for HIV-Infected Persons: Revised Recommendations. In Section I, see: AIDS-Related Opportunistic Infections/Prevention and Control.

Appendix—Characteristics of Available Antiretroviral Drugs. In Section I, see: Anti-HIV Agents.

Appendix—First-Line Drugs for HIV Postexposure Prophylaxis (PEP). In Section I, see: Health Personnel.

Appendix—Recommended Treatment Options for Persons with Human Immunodeficiency Virus-Related Tuberculosis Infection and Disease. In Section I, see:

Appendix A—Methods for Diagnosing Avian Chlamydiosis. In Section I, see: Chlamydia psittaci.

Appendix B—Treatment Options for Pet Birds with Avian Chlamydiosis. In Section I, see: Bird Diseases/Prevention and Control.

AIDS-Related Opportunistic Infections/Prevention and Control.

Case Definitions for Infectious Conditions Under Public Health Surveillance. In Section I, see: Disease Notification.

CDC Criteria for Anemia in Children and Childbearing-Aged Women. In Section I, see: Anemia, Hypochromic/Diagnosis.

Chlamydia Trachomatis Infections: Policy Guidelines for Prevention and Control. In Section I, see: Chlamydia Infections/Prevention and Control.

Chorionic Villus Sampling and Amniocentesis: Recommendations for Prenatal Counseling. In Section I, see: Amniocentesis.

Combination Vaccines for Childhood Immunization Recommendations of the Advisory Committee on Immunization Practices (ACIP), the American Academy of Pediatrics (AAP), and the American Academy of Family Physicians (AAFP). In Section I, see: Immunization.

Compendium of Animal Rabies Control, 1998 National Association of State Public Health Veterinarians Inc. In Section I, see: Rabies/Prevention and Control.

Compendium of Measures to Control Chlamydia psittaci Infection Among Humans (Psittacosis) and Pet Birds (Avian Chlamydiosis). In Section I, see: Bird Diseases/Prevention and Control.

Compendium of Psittacosis (Chlamydiosis) Control, 1997. In Section I, see: Bird Diseases/Prevention and Control.

Control and Prevention of Meningococcal Disease and Control and Prevention of Serogroup C Meningococcal Disease: Evaluation and Management of Suspected Outbreaks. In Section I, see: Meningococcal Infections/Prevention and Control.

Development of New Vaccines for Tuberculosis Recommendations of the Advisory Council for the Elimination of Tuberculosis (ACET). In Section I, see: Mycobacterium Tuberculosis/Immunology.

Diphtheria, Tetanus, and Pertussis: Recommendations for Vaccine Use and Other Preventive Measures: Recommendations of the Immunization Practices Advisory Committee (ACIP). In Section I, see: Diphtheria-Tetanus-Pertussis Vaccine/Administration and Dosage.

General Recommendations on Immunization. In Section I, see: Immunization/Standards.

Guidelines for Death Scene Investigation of Sudden, Unexplained Infant Deaths. In Section I, see: Sudden Infant Death.

Guidelines for Preventing Transmission of Human Immunodeficiency Virus Through Transplantation of Human Tissue and Organs. In Section I, see: HIV Infections/Prevention and Control.

Guidelines for Prevention of Nosocomial Pneumonia. In Section I, see: Cross Infection/Prevention and Control.

Guidelines for Prevention of Transmission of Human Immunodeficiency Virus and Hepatitis B Virus to Health-Care and Public-Safety Workers. In Section I, see: Acquired Immunodeficiency Syndrome/Transmission.

Guidelines for Prophylaxis Against Pneumocystis carinii Pneumonia for Persons Infected with Human Immunodeficiency Virus. In Section I, see: Acquired Immunodeficiency Syndrome/Complications.

Guidelines for the Prevention and Control of Congenital Syphilis. In Section I, see: Syphilis, Congenital/Prevention and Control.

Guidelines for the Use of Antiretroviral Agents in Pediatric HIV Infection. In Section I, see: Anti-HIV Agents/Therapeutic Use.

Guidelines to Prevent Simian Immunodeficiency Virus Infection in Laboratory Workers and Animal Handlers. In Section I, see: SIV.

Haemophilus b Conjugate Vaccines for Prevention of Haemophilus Influenza Type b Disease Among Infants and Children Two Months of Age and Older: Recommendations of the Immunization Practices Advisory Committee. In Section I, see: Haemophilus Infections/Prevention and Control.

Hantavirus Infection—Southwestern United States: Interim Recommendations for Risk Reduction. In Section I, see: Bunyaviridae Infections/Prevention and Control.

Hepatitis B Virus: A Comprehensive Strategy for Eliminating Transmission in the United States Through Universal Childhood Vaccination. In Section I, see: Hepatitis B/Immunology.

HIV Prevention Through Early Detection and Treatment of Other Sexually Transmitted Disease—United States. In Section I, see: HIV Infections/Prevention and Control.

Human Rabies Prevention—United States, 1999 Recommendations of the Advisory Committee on Immunization Practices (ACIP). In Section I, see: Rabies Vaccine.

Hypothermia Prevention. In Section I, see: Hypothermia/Prevention and Control.

Immunization of Children Infected with Human Immunodeficiency Virus-Supplement. In Section I, see: Acquired Immunodeficiency Syndrome/Immunology.

Immunization of Health-Care Workers. In Section I, see: Health Personnel/Standards.

Inactivated Japanese Encephalitis Virus Vaccine. In Section I, see: Encephalitis, Japanese/Prevention and Control.

Initial Therapy for Tuberculosis in the Era of Multidrug Resistance. In Section I, see: Antitubercular Agents/Therapeutic Use.

Injury-Control Recommendations: Bicycle Helmets. In Section I, see: Bicycling.

Laboratory Management of Agents Associated with Hantavirus Pulmonary Syndrome: Interim Biosafety Guidelines. In Section I, see: Bunyaviridae Infections/Prevention and Control.

Management of Patients with Suspected Viral Hemorrhagic Fever. In Section I, see: Hemorrhagic Fevers, Viral/Diagnosis.

Management of Possible Sexual, Injecting-Drug-Use, or Other Nonoccupational Exposure to HIV, Including Considerations Related to Antiretroviral Therapy Public Health Service Statement. In Section I, see: Anti-HIV Agents/Therapeutic Use.

Mandatory Reporting of Infectious Diseases by Clinicians and Mandatory Reporting of Occupational Diseases by Clinicians. In Section I, see: Communicable Disease Control/Legislation and Jurisprudence.

Measles Eradication: Recommendations from a Meeting Cosponsored by the World Health Organization, the Pan American Health Organization, and CDC. In Section I, see: Measles/Prevention and Control.

Sponsor

Public Health Service Guidelines for the Management of Health-Care Worker Exposure to HIV and Recommendations for Postexposure Prophylaxis. In Section I, see: Health Personnel.

Public Health Service Inter-Agency Guidelines for Screening Donors of Blood, Plasma, Organs, Tissues, and Semen for Evidence of Hepatitis B and Hepatitis C. In Section I, see: Blood Donors.

Public Health Service Report on Fluoride Benefits and Risks. In Section I, see: Dental Caries/Prevention and Control.

Public Health Service Statement on Management of Occupational Exposure to HIV, Including Considerations Regarding Zidovudine Postexposure Use. In Section I, see: Acquired Immunodeficiency Syndrome/Prevention and Control.

Public Health Service Task Force Recommendations for the Use of Antiretroviral Drugs in Pregnant Women Infected with HIV-1 for Maternal Health and for Reducing Perinatal HIV-1 Transmission in the United States. In Section I, see: Anti-HIV Agents/Therapeutic Use.

Recommendations for Collection of Laboratory Specimens Associated with Outbreaks of Gastroenteritis. In Section I, see: Disease Outbreaks.

Recommendations for Counseling Persons Infected with Human T-Lymphotrophic Virus, Types I and II. In Section I, see: HTLV-I Infections.

Recommendations for Diagnosing and Treating Syphilis in HIV-Infected Patients. In Section I, see: Acquired Immunodeficiency Syndrome/Complications.

Recommendations for HIV Testing Services for Inpatients and Outpatients in Acute-Care Settings; and Technical Guidance on HIV Counseling. In Section I, see: AIDS.

Recommendations for Human Immunodeficiency Virus Counseling and Voluntary Testing for Pregnant Women. In Section I, see: Disease Transmission, Vertical/Prevention and Control.

Recommendations for Preventing the Spread of Vancomycin Resistance. In Section I, see: Antibiotics, Glycopeptide/Pharmacology.

Recommendations for Preventing Transmission of Human Immunodeficiency Virus and Hepatitis B Virus to Patients During Exposure-Prone Invasive Procedures. In Section I, see: Health Manpower.

Recommendations for Prevention and Control of Hepatitis C Virus (HCV) Infection and HCV-Related

Chronic Disease. In Section I, see: Hepatitis C, Chronic/Prevention and Control.

Recommendations for Prevention and Control of Tuberculosis Among Foreign-Born Persons Report of the Working Group on Tuberculosis Among Foreign-Born Persons. In Section I, see: Communicable Disease Control/Standards.

Recommendations for Prevention and Management of Chlamydia trachomatis Infections, 1993. In Section I, see: Chlamydia Trachomatis.

Recommendations for Prevention of HIV Transmission in Health-Care Settings. In Section I, see: Acquired Immunodeficiency Syndrome/Prevention and Control.

Recommendations for Prophylaxis Against Pneumocystis carinii Pneumonia for Adults and Adolescents Infected with Human Immunodeficiency Virus. In Section I, see: HIV Infections/Complications.

Recommendations for Protecting Human Health Against Potential Adverse Effects of Long-Term Exposure to Low Doses of Chemical Warfare Agents. In Section I, see: Chemical Warfare Agents/Adverse Effects.

Recommendations for the Prevention of Malaria Among Travelers. In Section I, see: Malaria/Prevention and Control.

Recommendations for the Use of Folic Acid to Reduce the Number of Cases of Spina Bifida and Other Neural Tube Defects. In Section I, see: Folic Acid/Therapeutic Use.

Recommendations for the Use of Lyme Disease Vaccine Recommendations of the Advisory Committee on Immunization Practices (ACIP). In Section I, see: Lyme Disease/Prevention and Control.

Recommendations for Use of Haemophilus b Conjugate Vaccines and a Combined Diphtheria, Tetanus, Pertussis, and Haemophilus b Vaccine. In Section I, see: Haemophilus Vaccines/Administration and Dosage.

Recommendations of the Hospital Infection Control Practice Advisory Committee: Essential Components of a Tuberculosis Prevention and Control Program; Screening for Tuberculosis and Tuberculosis Infection in High-Risk Populations. In Section I, see: Program Development.

Recommendations of the International Task Force for Disease Eradication. In Section I, see: Communicable Disease Control.

Recommendations of the US Public Health Service Task Force on the Use of Zidovudine to Reduce Perinatal Transmission of Human Immunodeficiency Virus. In Section I, see: HIV Infections/Prevention and Control.

Recommendations to Prevent and Control Iron Deficiency in the United States. In Section I, see: Iron/Administration and Dosage.

Recommended Infection-Control Practices for Dentistry. In Section I, see: Dentistry/Standards.

Report of the NIH Panel to Define Principles of Therapy of HIV Infection and Guidelines for the Use of Antiretroviral Agents in HIV-Infected Adults and Adolescents. In Section I, see: Anti-HIV Agents/Therapeutic Use.

Revised Dosing Regimen for Malaria Prophylaxis with Mefloquine. In Section I, see: Malaria/Prevention and Control.

Rotavirus Vaccine for the Prevention of Rotavirus Gastroenteritis Among Children Recommendations of the Advisory Committee on Immunization Practices (ACIP). In Section I, see: Rotavirus/Immunology.

Rubella Prevention: Recommendations of the Immunization Practices Advisory Committee. In Section I, see: Rubella/Prevention and Control.

Strategic Plan for the Elimination of Tuberculosis in the United States. In Section I, see: Tuberculosis/Prevention and Control.

Transmission of HIV Through Bone Transplantation: Case Report and Public Health Recommendation. In Section I, see: Acquired Immunodeficiency Syndrome/Immunology.

Treatment with Quinidine Gluconate of Persons with Severe Plasmodium Falciparum Infection: Discontinuation of Parenteral Quinine from CDC Drug Service. In Section I, see: Antimalarials/Administration and Dosage.

Tuberculosis Control Laws—United States, 1993. In Section I, see: Public Health/Legislation and Jurisprudence.

Typhoid Immunization. In Section I, see: Typhoid/Immunization.

Update: Vaccine Side Effects, Adverse Reactions, Contraindications, and Precautions. In Section I, see: Bacterial Vaccines/Adverse Effects.

US Public Health Service Guidelines for Testing and Counseling Blood and Plasma Donors for Human Immunodeficiency Virus Type 1 Antigen. In Section I, see: Blood Banks/Standards.

Uses of Vaccines and Immune Globulins in Persons with Altered Immunocompetence. In Section I, see: Immunizations, Passive/Standards.

USPHS/IDSA Guidelines for the Prevention of Opportunistic Infections in Persons Infected with Human Immunodeficiency Virus: A Summary. In Section I, see: AIDS-Related Opportunistic Infections/Prevention and Control.

Vaccinia (Smallpox) Vaccine. In Section I, see: Smallpox Vaccine.

Yellow Fever Vaccine: Recommendations of the Immunization Practices Advisory Panel (ACIP). In Section I, see: Immunization.

Centers for Disease Control and Prevention, American College of Sports Medicine

Physical Activity and Public Health. In Section I, see: Health Promotion.

College of American Pathologists

Autopsy Procedures for Brain, Spinal Cord and Neuromuscular System. In Section I, see: Autopsy/Standards.

Practice Guideline for Examination of the Placenta. In Section I, see: Placenta/Pathology.

Practice Guidelines for Autopsy Pathology: Autopsy Performance (Reaffirmed, 1996). In Section I, see: Autopsy/Standards.

Practice Guidelines for Autopsy Pathology: Autopsy Reporting. In Section I, see: Autopsy/Standards.

Practice Guidelines for Autopsy Pathology: Perinatal and Pediatric Autopsy. In Section I, see: Autopsy/Methods.

Practice Parameter for Hereditary Hemochromatosis. In Section I, see: Hemochromatosis/Genetics.

Practice Parameter for the Use of Fresh-Frozen Plasma, Cryoprecipitate, and Platelets. In Section I, see: Blood Component Transfusion/Standards.

Practice Parameter for the Use of Red Blood Cell Transfusions. In Section I, see: Erythrocyte Transfusion.

Practice Parameter on Laboratory Panel Testing for Screening and Case Finding in Asymptomatic Adults. In Section I, see: Diagnostic Tests, Routine.

Federal Agency for Health Care Policy and Research

Acute Low Back Pain Problems in Adults. In Section I, see: Low Back Pain/Therapy.

Acute Pain Management: Operative or Medical Procedures and Trauma. In Section I, see: Pain/Therapy.

Alzheimer's Disease. In Section I, see: Alzheimer Disease.

Autologous Peripheral Stem-Cell Transplantation. In Section I, see: Hematopoietic Stem-Cell Transplantation.

Benign Prostatic Hyperplasia: Diagnosis and Treatment. In Section I, see: Prostatic Hyperplasia/Diagnosis.

Bone Densitometry: Patients Receiving Prolonged Steroid Therapy. In Section I, see: Bone Density.

Cardiac Rehabilitation. In Section I, see: Coronary Disease/Rehabilitation.

Cardiac Rehabilitation Programs. In Section I, see: Cardiovascular Diseases/Rehabilitation.

Carotid Endarterectomy (Revised). In Section I, see: Endarterectomy, Carotid.

Cataract in Adults: Management of Functional Impairment. In Section I, see: Cataract/Therapy.

Cochlear Implantation in Outpatient Settings. In Section I, see: Cochlear Implantation.

Depression in Primary Care: Volume I: Detection and Diagnosis; Volume II: Treatment of Major Depression. In Section I, see: Depressive Disorder/Diagnosis.

Electrical Bone-Growth Stimulation and Spinal Fusion. In Section I, see: Spinal Fusion.

Electroencephalographic (EEG) Video Monitoring. In Section I, see: Electroencephalography/Methods.

External and Implantable Infusion Pumps. In Section I, see: Infusion Pumps, Implantable.

Extracranial-Intracranial Bypass to Reduce the Risk of Ischemic Stroke. In Section I, see: Cerebral Ischemia/Prevention and Control.

Heart Failure: Evaluation and Care of Patients with Left-Ventricular Systolic Dysfunction. In Section I, see: Heart Failure, Congestive/Therapy.

Hematopoietic Stem-Cell Transplantation in Multiple Myeloma. In Section I, see: Hematopoietic Stem-Cell Transplantation.

Home Uterine Monitoring. In Section I, see: Uterine Monitoring.

Hyperthermia Alone or Combined with Chemotherapy for the Treatment of Cancer. In Section I, see: Hyperthermia, Induced/Standards.

Implantation of the Automatic Cardioverter-Defibrillator—Non-Inducibility of Ventricular Tachyarrhythmia as a Patient Selection Criteria. In Section I, see: Defibrillators, Implantable.

Institutional and Patient Criteria for Heart-Lung Transplantation. In Section I, see: Heart-Lung Transplantation.

Intermittent Positive Pressure Breathing (IPPB) Therapy. In Section I, see: Intermittent Positive-Pressure Ventilation/Standards.

Intermittent Positive Pressure Breathing: Old Technologies Rarely Die. In Section I, see: Intermittent Positive Pressure Ventilation/Methods.

Isolated Pancreas Transplantation. In Section I, see: Pancreas Transplantation.

Laboratory Tests in End-Stage Renal Disease Patients Undergoing Dialysis. In Section I, see: Hemodialysis.

Lung-Volume Reduction Surgery for End-Stage Chronic Obstructive Pulmonary Disease. In Section I, see: Lung Diseases, Obstructive/Surgery.

Management of Cancer Pain. In Section I, see: Pain, Intractable/Drug Therapy.

Measuring Cardiac Output by Electrical Bioimpedance. In Section I, see: Cardiac Output.

Polysomnography and Sleep Disorder Centers. In Section I, see: Sleep Disorders/Diagnosis.

Post-Stroke Rehabilitation. In Section I, see: Cerebrovascular Disorders/Rehabilitation.

Pressure Ulcers in Adults: Prediction and Prevention. In Section I, see: Decubitus Ulcer/Prevention and Control.

Procuren: A Platelet-Derived Wound Healing Formula. In Section I, see: Blood Platelets.

Protein A Columns for Immune Thrombocytopenia. In Section I, see: Autoimmune Diseases/Therapy.

Quality Determinants of Mammography. In Section I, see: Mammography.

Reassessment of External Insulin Infusion Pumps. In Section I, see: Insulin Infusion Systems/Standards.

Salivary Electrostimulation in Sjogren's Syndrome. In Section I, see: Electric Stimulation Therapy/Methods.

Sickle Cell Disease: Screening, Diagnosis, Management, and Counseling in Newborns and Infants. In Section I, see: Anemia, Sickle Cell/Diagnosis.

Simultaneous Pancreas-Kidney and Sequential Pancreas-After-Kidney Transplantation. In Section I, see: Kidney Transplantation/Methods.

Single and Double Lung Transplantation. In Section I, see: Lung Transplantation/Standards.

Smoking Cessation. In Section I, see: Smoking Cessation.

Surface/Specialty Coil Devices and Gating Techniques in Magnetic Resonance Imaging. In Section I, see: Gated Blood-Pool Imaging/Standards.

Treatment of Pressure Ulcers. In Section I, see: Decubitus Ulcer/Nursing Care.

Unstable Angina: Diagnosis and Management. In Section I, see: Angina, Unstable/Diagnosis.

Urinary Incontinence in Adults: Acute and Chronic Management. In Section I, see: Urinary Incontinence/Therapy.

Infectious Diseases Society of America

1997 USPHS/IDSA Guidelines for the Prevention of Opportunistic Infections in Patients Infected with Human Immunodeficiency Virus: Disease-Specific Recommendations. In Section I, see:.Tuberculosis, Pulmonary/Prevention and Control.

Antiendotoxin Monoclonal Antibodies for Gram-Negative Sepsis. In Section I, see: Antibodies, Monoclonal/Therapeutic Use.

Community-Aquired Pneumonia in Adults: Guidelines for Management. In Section I, see: Community-Acquired Infections.

Diagnosis and Management of Group A Streptococcal Pharyngitis: A Practice Guideline. In Section I, see: Pharyngitis/Diagnosis.

Guidelines for the Use of Antimicrobial Agents in Neutropenic Patients with Unexplained Fever. In Section I, see: Agranulocytosis/Complications.

Guidelines for the Use of Systemic Glucocorticosteroids in the Management of Selected Infections. In Section I, see: Glucocorticoids/Therapeutic Use.

Hospital Pharmacists and Infectious Disease Specialists. In Section I, see: Communicable Diseases.

Practice Guidelines for Community-Based Parenteral Anti-Infective Therapy. In Section I, see: Anti-Infective Agents/Administration and Dosage.

Practice Guidelines for Evaluating New Fever in Critically Ill Adult Patients. In Section I, see: Critical Illness.

Practice Guidelines for Infectious Diseases: Rationale for Work in Progress. In Section I, see: Infection.

Preface to the 1997 USPHS/IDSA Guidelines for the Prevention of Opportunistic Infections in Persons with Human Immunodeficiency Virus: Disease-Specific Recommendations. In Section I, see: Tuberculosis, Pulmonary/Prevention and Control.

Primary Care of Patients Infected with Human Immunodeficiency Virus. In Section I, see: HIV Infections/Theory.

Purpose of Quality Standards for Infectious Diseases. In Section I, see: Infection/Therapy.

Quality Standard for Assurance of Measles Immunity Among Health Care Workers. In Section I, see: Health Personnel/Standards.

Quality Standard for the Treatment of Bacteremia. In Section I, see: Bacteremia/Drug Therapy.

Quality Standards for Immunization. In Section I, see: Communicable Disease Control.

Society for Healthcare Epidemiology of America and Infectious Diseases Society of America Joint Committee on the Prevention of Antimicrobial Resistance: Guidelines for the Prevention of Antimicrobial Resistance in Hospitals. In Section I, see: Drug Resistance, Microbial.

Kentucky Diabetic Retinopathy Group

Guidelines for Eye Care in Patients with Diabetes Mellitus. In Section I, see: Diabetes Mellitus/Complications.

Minnesota Academy of Otolaryngology-Head and Neck Surgery

Preferred Practice Patterns. In Section I, see: Physician's Practice Patterns.

National Cancer Institute

Cancer Screening Overview. In Section I, see: Neoplasms/Diagnosis.

Screening for Breast Cancer for Health Professionals. In Section I, see: Breast Neoplasms.

Screening for Cervical Cancer. In Section I, see: Mass Screening/Methods.

Screening for Colorectal Cancer. In Section I, see: Mass Screening/Methods.

Screening for Gastric Cancer. In Section I, see: Stomach Neoplasms.

Screening for Oral Cancer. In Section I, see: Mass Screening.

Screening for Ovarian Cancer. In Section I, see: Mass Screening.

Screening for Prostate Cancer. In Section I, see: Mass Screening.

Screening for Skin Cancer. In Section I, see: Mass Screening/Methods.

Screening for Testicular Cancer. In Section I, see: Mass Screening.

National Eye Institute

Photocoagulation for Diabetic Retinopathy. In Section I, see: Diabetic Retinopathy/Surgery.

National Heart, Lung, and Blood Institute

Guidelines for the Diagnosis and Management of Asthma. In Section I, see: Asthma/Diagnosis.

NCEP Report of the Expert Panel on Blood Cholesterol Levels in Children and Adolescents. In Section I, see: Cholesterol/Blood.

Second Report of the Expert Panel on Detection, Evaluation, and Treatment of High Blood Cholesterol in Adults. In Section I, see: Hypercholesterolemia/Drug Therapy.

Sixth Report of the Joint National Committee on Detection, Evaluation, and Treatment of High Blood Pressure (JNC VI). In Section I, see: Hypertension/Diagnosis.

Transfusion Alert: Use of Autologous Blood. In Section I, see: Blood Transfusion, Autologous.

Working Group Report on High Blood Pressure in Pregnancy. In Section I, see: Pregnancy Complications, Cardiovascular.

Working Group Report on Hypertension in the Elderly. In Section I, see: Hypertension.

Working Group Report on Management of Asthma During Pregnancy. In Section I, see: Asthma/Therapy.

Working Group Report on Primary Prevention of Hypertension. In Section I, see: Hypertension/Prevention and Control.

Working Report on Hypertension in Diabetes. In Section I, see: Diabetes Mellitus/Complications.

National Institutes of Health

Acupuncture. In Section I, see: Acupuncture.

Adjuvant Therapy for Patients with Colon and Rectum Cancer. In Section I, see: Colonic Neoplasms/Therapy.

Anesthesia and Sedation in the Dental Office. In Section I, see: Anesthesia, Dental.

Bioelectrical Impedance Analysis in Body Composition Measurement. In Section I, see: Body Composition.

Bovine Somatotropin. In Section I, see: Somatotropin.

Breast Cancer Screening for Women Ages 40-49. In Section I, see: Breast Neoplasms/Prevention and Control.

Cervical Cancer. In Section I, see: Cervix Neoplasms/Diagnosis.

Clinical Use of Botulinum Toxin. In Section I, see: Botulinum Toxins/Therapeutic Use.

Cochlear Implants in Adults and Children. In Section I, see: Cochlear Implants.

Critical Care Medicine. In Section I, see: Critical Care.

Defined Diets and Childhood Hyperactivity. In Section I, see: Attention Deficit Disorder with Hyperactivity/Drug Therapy.

Dental Implants. In Section I, see: Dental Implantation.

Dental Sealants in the Prevention of Tooth Decay. In Section I, see: Pit and Fissure Sealants/Therapeutic Use.

Diagnosis and Management of Asymptomatic Primary Hyperparathyroidism. In Section I, see: Hyperparathyroidism/Therapy.

Diagnosis and Treatment of Attention Deficit Hyperactivity Disorder (ADHD). In Section I, see: Attention Deficit Disorder with Hyperactivity/Diagnosis.

Diagnosis and Treatment of Depression in Late Life. In Section I, see: Depression/Diagnosis.

Diagnosis and Treatment of Early Melanoma. In Section I, see: Melanoma/Diagnosis.

Diet and Exercise in Non-Insulin-Dependent Diabetes Mellitus. In Section I, see: Diabetes Mellitus, Non-Insulin-Dependent/Diet Therapy.

Differential Diagnosis of Dementing Diseases. In Section I, see: Dementia/Diagnosis.

Early Identification of Hearing Impairment in Infants and Young Children. In Section I, see: Hearing Disorders/Prevention and Control.

Early Stage Breast Cancer. In Section I, see: Breast Neoplasms/Therapy.

Effect of Corticosteroids for Fetal Maturation on Perinatal Outcomes. In Section I, see: Adrenal Cortex Hormones/Therapeutic Use.

Treatment of Panic Disorder. In Section I, see: Panic Disorder/Therapy.

Treatment of Sleep Disorders of Older People. In Section I, see: Sleep Disorders/Therapy.

Triglyceride, High Density Lipoprotein, and Coronary Heart Disease. In Section I, see: Coronary Disease/Epidemiology.

Ultrasound Screening: Implications of the RADIUS Study. In Section I, see: Pregnancy Outcome.

Urinary Incontinence in Adults. In Section I, see: Urinary Incontinence.

Utility of Therapeutic Plasmapheresis for Neurological Disorders. In Section I, see: Nervous System Diseases/Therapy.

National Kidney Foundation

Executive Summaries of the NKF-DOQI Clinical Practice Guidelines. In Section I, see: Practice Guidelines.

National Kidney Foundation Report on Dialyzer Reuse. In Section I, see: Disposable Equipment/Standards.

NKF-DOQI Clinical Practice Guidelines for Hemodialysis Adequacy. In Section I, see: Hemodialysis/Standards.

NKF-DOQI Clinical Practice Guidelines for Peritoneal Dialysis Adequacy. In Section I, see: Peritoneal Dialysis/Standards.

NKF-DOQI Clinical Practice Guidelines for the Treatment of Anemia of Chronic Renal Failure. In Section I, see: Kidney Failure, Chronic/Complications.

NKF-DOQI Clinical Practice Guidelines for Vascular Access. In Section I, see: Arteriovenous Shunt, Surgical.

Screening of Microalbuminuria in Patients with Diabetes. In Section I, see: Albuminuria/Diagnosis.

National Osteoporosis Foundation

Clinical Indications for Bone Mass Measurements. In Section I, see: Bone Density.

Guidelines for Safe Movement. In Section I, see: Movement.

Physician's Guide to Prevention and Treatment of Osteoporosis. In Section I, see: Osteoporosis/Prevention and Control.

RAND

Cataract Surgery. In Section I, see: Cataract Extraction.

Hysterectomy. In Section I, see: Hysterectomy.

RAND, Academic Medical Center Consortium

Abdominal Aortic Aneurysm Surgery. In Section I, see: Aortic Aneurysm, Abdominal/Surgery.

Coronary Artery Bypass Graft Surgery and Percutaneous Transluminal Coronary Angioplasty. In Section I, see: Coronary Artery Bypass.

Prenatal Care. In Section I, see: Prenatal Care.

Spinal Manipulation of Low-Back Pain. In Section I, see: Low Back Pain.

RAND, Academic Medical Center Consortium, American Medical Association

Coronary Angiography. In Section I, see: Coronary Angiography.

Coronary Artery Bypass Graft. In Section I, see: Coronary Artery Bypass.

Percutaneous Transluminal Coronary Angioplasty. In Section I, see: Angioplasty, Transluminal, Percutaneous.

Renal Physicians Association

Adequacy of Hemodialysis. In Section I, see: Hemodialysis.

Society for Healthcare Epidemiology of America

1992 Modification of CDC Definitions of Surgical Wound Infections. In Section I, see: Surgical Wound Infection/Classification.

An Approach to the Evaluation of Quality Indicators of the Outcome of Care in Hospitalized Patients with a Focus on Nosocomial Infection Indicators. In Section I, see: Cross Infection/Epidemiology.

Antimicrobial Use in Long Term Care Facilities and Antimicrobial Resistance in Long Term Care Facilities. In Section I, see: Drug Resistance, Microbial.

Book-Help for the Hospital Epidemiologist. In Section I, see: Infection Control Practitioners.

Clostridium difficile–Associated Diarrhea and Colitis. In Section I, see: Clostridium Infections.

Consensus Panel on Infrastructure and Essential Activities of Hospital Epidemiology and Infection Control Programs. In Section I, see: Epidemiologic Studies.

Consensus Paper on the Surveillance of Surgical Wound Infection. In Section I, see: Surgical Wound Infection/Epidemiology.

Description of Case-Mix Adjusters by Severity of Illness Working Group of the Society for Healthcare Epidemiologists of America (SHEA). In Section I, see: Cross Infection/Economics.

Guidelines for the Prevention of Antimicrobial Resistance in Hospitals (SHEA/ISDA Joint Statement). In Section I, see: Drug Resistance, Microbial.

How to Select and Interpret Molecular Strain Typing Methods for Epi Studies of Bacterial Infections: A Review for Healthcare Epidemiologists. In Section I, see: Bacterial Typing Techniques.

Infection Prevention and Control in the Long-Term-Care Facility. In Section I, see: Infection Control/Standards.

Interim Report of the Quality Indicator Study Group. In Section I, see: Quality Assurance, Health Care/Standards.

"Look Back" Notifications for HIV/HBV-Positive Healthcare Workers. In Section I, see: Infection Control/Methods.

Medical Waste. In Section I, see: Medical Waste.

Quality Standard for Antimicrobial Prophylaxis in Surgical Procedures. In Section I, see: Antibiotics/Therapeutic Use.

Quality Standard for Assurance of Measles Immunity Among Health Care Workers. In Section I, see: Measles/Prevention and Control.

Quality Standard for the Treatment of Bacteremia. In Section I, see: Bacteremia/Drug Therapy.

Requirements for Infrastructure and Essential Activities of Infection Control and Epidemiology in Hospitals: A Consensus Panel Report. In Section I, see: Cross Infection/Prevention and Control.

Revised: Management of Health Care Workers Who Are Infected with HIV, HBV, HCV, and Other Blood-borne Pathogens. In Section I, see: Personnel Administration, Hospital.

The HIV-Infected Healthcare Worker. In Section I, see: Health Occupations.

Society for Vascular Surgery/North American Chapter, ICVS

Carotid Endarterectomy: Practice Guidelines Report of the Ad Hoc Committee. In Section I, see: Endarterectomy, Carotid/Standards.

Clinical Research and Vascular Surgery. In Section I, see: Vascular Surgical Procedures/Standards.

Practice Guidelines: Lower Extremity Revascularization. In Section I, see: Ischemia/Surgery.

Recommended Indications for Operative Treatment of Abdominal Aortic Aneurysms. In Section I, see: Aortic Aneurysm/Diagnosis.

Society of American Gastrointestinal and Endoscopic Surgeons

Advanced Laparoscopy into Surgical Residency Training. In Section I, see: Curriculum.

Framework for Post-Residency Surgical Education & Training. In Section I, see: Education, Medical, Continuing/Standards.

Global Statement on Deep Venous Thrombosis Prophylaxis during Laparoscopic Surgery. In Section I, see: Thrombophlebitis.

Granting of Privileges for Gastrointestinal Endoscopy by Surgeons. In Section I, see: Credentialing.

Granting of Ultrasonography Privileges for Surgeons. In Section I, see: Credentialing.

Guidelines for Collaborative Practice in Endoscopic/Thoracoscopic Spinal Surgery for the General Surgeon. In Section I, see: Physician's Practice Patterns.

Guidelines for Diagnostic Laparoscopy. In Section I, see: Laparoscopy.

Guidelines for Granting of Privileges for Laparoscopic and Thoracoscopic General Surgery. In Section I, see: Credentialing.

Guidelines for Laparoscopic Surgery During Pregnancy. In Section I, see: Pregnancy Complications/Surgery.

Guidelines for Office Endoscopic Services. In Section I, see: Ambulatory Care/Standards.

Guidelines for Surgical Treatment of Gastroesophageal Reflux Disease (GERD). In Section I, see: Gastroesophageal Reflux/Surgery.

Guidelines for the Clinical Application of Laparoscopic Biliary Tract Surgery. In Section I, see: Biliary Tract Surgical Procedures.

Guidelines for the Surgical Practice of Telemedicine. In Section I, see: Telemedicine.

Guidelines for Training in Diagnostic and Therapeutic Endoscopic Retrograde Cholangiopancreatography (ERCP). In Section I, see: Cholangiopancreatography, Endosopic, Retrograde.

Position Statement on Advanced Laparoscopic Training. In Section I, see: Surgical Procedures, Laparoscopic/Education.

SAGES Position Statement—Global Statement on New Procedures. In Section I, see: Surgical Procedures, Laparoscopic/Standards.

SAGES Position Statement—Laparoscopic Appendectomy. In Section I, see: Appendectomy/ Methods.

Society of Cardiovascular and Interventional Radiology

Angioplasty Standard of Practice. In Section I, see: Angioplasty, Balloon/Standards.

Credentialing Criteria: Percutaneous Nephrostomy. In Section I, see: Nephrostomy, Percutaneous.

Credentialing Criteria: Peripheral and Visceral Arteriography. In Section I, see: Angiography.

Credentialing Criteria: Peripheral, Renal and Visceral Percutaneous Transluminal Angioplasty. In Section I, see: Angioplasty, Balloon/Standards.

General Principles for Evaluation of New Interventional Technologies and Devices. In Section I, see: Radiology, Interventional/Instrumentation.

Guidelines for Establishing a Quality Assurance Program in Vascular and Interventional Radiology. In Section I, see: Radiography, Interventional.

Guidelines for Percutaneous Transluminal Angioplasty. In Section I, see: Angioplasty, Transluminal, Percutaneous, Coronary.

Guidelines for the Development and Use of Transluminally Placed Endovascular Prosthetic Grafts in the Arterial System. In Section I, see: Blood Vessel Prosthesis.

Quality Improvement Guidelines for Adult Percutaneous Abscess and Fluid Drainage. In Section I, see: Abscess/Therapy.

Quality Improvement Guidelines for Central Venous Access. In Section I, see: Catheterization, Central Venous.

Quality Improvement Guidelines for Dialysis Access. In Section I, see: Hemodialysis/Instrumentation.

Quality Improvement Guidelines for Image-Guided Percutaneous Biopsy in Adults. In Section I, see: Radiology, Interventional.

Quality Improvement Guidelines for Percutaneous Transcatheter Embolization. In Section I, see: Embolization, Therapeutic/Standards.

Quality Improvement Guidelines for Percutaneous Transhepatic Cholangiography and Biliary Drainage. In Section I, see: Cholangiography/Standards.

Reporting Standards for Clinical Evaluation of New Peripheral Arterial Revascularization Devices. In Section I, see: Angioplasty/Standards.

Reporting Standards on Transjugular Intrahepatic Portosystemic Shunts (TIPS). In Section I, see: Documentation/Standards.

SCVIR HIV/Bloodborne Pathogens Guidelines. In Section I, see: Bloodborne Pathogens.

Society of Critical Care Medicine

Guidelines for Advanced Training for Physicians in Critical Care. In Section I, see: Clinical Competence/ Standards.

Guidelines for Developing Admission and Discharge Policies for the Pediatric ICU. In Section I, see: Intensive Care Units, Pediatric.

Guidelines for Granting Privileges for the Performance of Procedures in Critically Ill Patients. In Section I, see: Critical Care.

Guidelines for ICU Admission, Discharge, and Triage. In Section I, see: Intensive Care Units.

Guidelines for Intensive Care Unit Design. In Section I, see: Hospital Design and Construction.

Guidelines for Resident Training in Critical Care Medicine. In Section I, see: Critical Care.

Guidelines for Standards of Care for Patients with Acute Repiratory Failure on Mechanical Ventilatory Support. In Section I, see: Respiration, Artificial/ Standards.

Guidelines for the Definition of an Intensivist and the Practice of Critical Care Medicine. In Section I, see: Critical Care/Standards.

Guidelines for the Transfer of Critically Ill Patients. In Section I, see: Critical Care/Standards.

Guidelines on Admission and Discharge for Adult Intermediate Care Units. In Section I, see: Hospital Units.

Guidelines on Critical Care Services and Personnel: Recommendations Based on a System of Categorization into Two Levels of Care. In Section I, see: Intensive Care Units/Manpower.

Practice Parameters for Evaluating New Fever in Critically Ill Adult Patients. In Section I, see: Fever/ Diagnosis.

Practice Parameters for Hemodynamic Support of Sepsis in Adult Patients. In Section I, see: Sepsis.

Practice Parameters for Intraveneous Analgesia and Sedation for Patients in the Intensive Care Unit: An Executive Summary. In Section I, see: Analgesia.

Practice Parameters for Sustained Neuromuscular Blockade in the Adult Critically Ill Patient: An Executive Summary. In Section I, see: Critical Care.

Society of Critical Care Medicine, American Academy of Pediatrics

Guidelines and Levels of Care for Pediatric Intensive Care Units. In Section I, see: Intensive Care Units, Pediatric.

Society of Nuclear Medicine

Guidelines for Guideline Development. In Section I, see: Nuclear Medicine.

Procedure Guideline for Bone Pain Treatment. In Section I, see: Pain, Intractable/Radiotherapy.

Procedure Guideline for Bone Scintigraphy. In Section I, see: Bone and Bones/Radionuclide Imaging.

Procedure Guideline for Brain Perfusion Single Photon Emission Computed Tomography (SPECT) Using Tc99m Radiopharmaceuticals. In Section I, see: Brain/Radionuclide Imaging.

Procedure Guideline for Breast Scintigraphy. In Section I, see: Breast Neoplasms/Radionuclide Imaging.

Procedure Guideline for C-14 Urea Breath Test. In Section I, see: Breath Tests.

Procedure Guideline for Diagnosis of Renovascular Hypertension. In Section I, see: Hypertension, Renovascular/Radionuclide Imaging.

Procedure Guideline for Diuretic Renography in Children. In Section I, see: Diuretics/Diagnostic Use.

Procedure Guideline for Extended Scintigraphy for Differentiated Thyroid Cancer. In Section I, see: Iodine Radioisotopes/Diagnostic Use.

Procedure Guideline for Gallium Scintigraphy in Inflammation. In Section I, see: Gallium Radioisotopes/Diagnostic Use.

Procedure Guideline for Gallium Scintigraphy in the Evaluation of Malignant Disease. In Section I, see: Gallium Radioisotopes.

Procedure Guideline for Gastric Emptying and Motility. In Section I, see: Gastric Emptying.

Procedure Guideline for Gastrointestinal Bleeding and Meckel's Diverticulum Scintigraphy. In Section I, see: Gastrointestinal Hemorrhage/Radionuclide Imaging.

Procedure Guideline for Gated Equilibrium Radionuclide Ventriculography. In Section I, see: Gated Blood-Pool Imaging.

Procedure Guideline for General Imaging. In Section I, see: Radionuclide Imaging/Standards.

Procedure Guideline for Hepatic and Splenic Imaging. In Section I, see: Liver/Radionuclide Imaging.

Procedure Guideline for Hepatobiliary Scintigraphy. In Section I, see: Biliary Tract Diseases/Radionuclide Imaging.

Procedure Guideline for In-111 Leukocyte Scintigraphy for Suspected Infection/Inflammation. In Section I, see: Indium Radioisotopes/Diagnostic Use.

Procedure Guideline for Lung Scintigraphy. In Section I, see: Lung/Radionuclide Imaging.

Procedure Guideline for Myocardial Perfusion Imaging. In Section I, see: Coronary Disease/Radionuclide Imaging.

Procedure Guideline for Parathyroid Scintigraphy. In Section I, see: Parathyroid Glands/Radionuclide Imaging.

Procedure Guideline for Pediatric Sedation in Nuclear Medicine. In Section I, see: Hypnotics and Sedatives.

Procedure Guideline for Radionuclide Cystography in Children. In Section I, see: Bladder/Radionuclide Imaging.

Procedure Guideline for Renal Cortical Scintigraphy in Children. In Section I, see: Kidney Cortex/Radionuclide Imaging.

Procedure Guideline for Tc-99m Hexametazime (HMPAO) Labeled Leukocyte Scintigraphy for Suspected Infection/Inflammation. In Section I, see: Infection/Radionuclide Imaging.

Procedure Guideline for Thyroid Scintigraphy. In Section I, see: Thyroid Diseases/Radionuclide Imaging.

Procedure Guideline for Thyroid Uptake Measurement. In Section I, see: Thyroid Diseases/Radionuclide Imaging.

Procedure Guideline for Tumor Imaging Using F-18 FDG. In Section I, see: Neoplasms/Radionuclide Imaging.

Procedure Guideline for Use of Radiopharmaceuticals. In Section I, see: Radiopharmaceuticals/Diagnostic Use.

Society of Nuclear Medicine Procedure Guidelines Manual 1999. In Section I, see: Practice Guidelines.

Sponsor

Society of Surgical Oncology

Breast Cancer Surgical Practice Guidelines. In Section I, see: Breast Neoplasms/Surgery.

Colorectal Cancer Surgical Practice Guidelines. In Section I, see: Colorectal Neoplasms/Surgery.

Esophageal Cancer Surgical Practice Guidelines. In Section I, see: Esophageal Neoplasms/Surgery.

Gastric Cancer Surgical Practice Guidelines. In Section I, see: Stomach Neoplasms/Surgery.

Laryngeal Cancer Surgical Practice Guidelines. In Section I, see: Laryngeal Neoplasms/Surgery.

Lung Cancer Surgical Practice Guidelines. In Section I, see: Lung Neoplasms/Surgery.

Melanoma Surgical Practice Guidelines. In Section I, see: Melanoma.

Oropharyngeal and Oral Cavity Cancer Surgical Practice Guidelines. In Section I, see: Oropharyngeal Neoplasms/Surgery.

Ovarian Cancer Surgical Practice Guidelines. In Section I, see: Ovarian Neoplasms/Diagnosis.

Pancreatic Cancer Surgical Practice Guidelines. In Section I, see: Pancreatic Neoplasms/Surgery.

Parotid Gland Cancer Surgical Practice Guidelines. In Section I, see: Parotid Neoplasms/Surgery.

Prostate Cancer Surgical Practice Guidelines. In Section I, see: Prostatic Neoplasms/Surgery.

Soft Tissue Sarcoma Surgical Practice Guidelines. In Section I, see: Soft Tissue Neoplasms.

Thyroid Cancer Surgical Practice Guidelines. In Section I, see: Thyroid Neoplasms/Surgery.

US Pharmacopeia/Micromedex, Inc.

Advice for the Patient. In Section I, see: Asthma.

Approved Drug Products and Legal Requirements. In Section I, see: Drug Approval.

Common Cold. In Section I, see: Common Cold/Drug Therapy.

Drug Information for the Health Care Professional. In Section I, see: Drug Information Services.

US Preventive Services Task Force

Adult Immunizations. In Section I, see: Immunization.

Aspirin Prophylaxis for the Primary Prevention of Myocardial Infarctions. In Section I, see: Myocardial Infarction/Prevention and Control.

Aspirin Prophylaxis in Pregnancy. In Section I, see: Aspirin/Administration and Dosage.

Childhood Immunizations. In Section I, see: Immunization.

Counseling to Prevent Dental and Periodontal Disease. In Section I, see: Periodontal Diseases/Prevention and Control.

Counseling to Prevent Gynecologic Cancers. In Section I, see: Genital Neoplasm, Female/Prevention and Control.

Counseling to Prevent Household and Recreational Injuries. In Section I, see: Accident Prevention.

Counseling to Prevent Human Immunodeficiency Virus Infection and Other Sexually Transmitted Diseases. In Section I, see: HIV Infections/Prevention and Control.

Counseling to Prevent Low Back Pain. In Section I, see: Low Back Pain/Prevention and Control.

Counseling to Prevent Motor Vehicle Injuries. In Section I, see: Accidents, Traffic/Prevention and Control.

Counseling to Prevent Tobacco Use. In Section I, see: Tobacco Use Disorder/Prevention and Control.

Counseling to Prevent Unintended Pregnancy. In Section I, see: Pregnancy, Unwanted.

Counseling to Prevent Youth Violence. In Section I, see: Violence/Prevention and Control.

Counseling to Promote a Healthy Diet. In Section I, see: Diet.

Counseling to Promote Physical Activity. In Section I, see: Exercise.

Intrapartum Electronic Fetal Monitoring. In Section I, see: Fetal Monitoring.

Postexposure Prophylaxis for Selected Infectious Diseases. In Section I, see: Communicable Diseases/Prevention and Control.

Postmenopausal Hormone Prophylaxis. In Section I, see: Hormone Replacement Therapy.

Screening for Abdominal Aortic Aneurysm. In Section I, see: Aortic Aneurysm, Abdominal/Diagnosis.

Screening for Adolescent Idiopathic Scoliosis. In Section I, see: Scoliosis/Diagnosis.

Screening for Asymptomatic Bacteriuria. In Section I, see: Bacteriuria/Diagnosis.

Screening for Asymptomatic Carotid Artery Stenosis. In Section I, see: Carotid Stenosis/Diagnosis.

Screening for Asymptomatic Coronary Artery Disease. In Section I, see: Coronary Disease/Diagnosis.

Screening for Cervical Cancer. In Section I, see: Cervix Neoplasms.

Screening for Chlamydial Infection. In Section I, see: Chlamydia Infections/Diagnosis.

Screening for Colorectal Cancer. In Section I, see: Colorectal Neoplasms/Diagnosis.

Screening for Congenital Hypothyroidism. In Section I, see: Cretinism/Diagnosis.

Screening for Dementia. In Section I, see: Dementia/Diagnosis.

Screening for Diabetes Mellitus. In Section I, see: Diabetes Mellitus/Diagnosis.

Screening for Down Syndrome. In Section I, see: Down Syndrome/Prevention and Control.

Screening for Elevated Lead Levels in Childhood and Pregnancy. In Section I, see: Lead Poisoning/Diagnosis.

Screening for Family Violence. In Section I, see: Domestic Violence.

Screening for Glaucoma. In Section I, see: Glaucoma/Diagnosis.

Screening for Gonorrhea. In Section I, see: Gonorrhea/Diagnosis.

Screening for Hearing Impairment. In Section I, see: Hearing Disorders/Diagnosis.

Screening for Hemoglobinopathies. In Section I, see: Hemoglobinopathies/Prevention and Control.

Screening for High Blood Cholesterol and Other Lipid Abnormalities. In Section I, see: Hypercholesterolemia/Diagnosis.

Screening for Human Immunodeficiency Virus Infection. In Section I, see: HIV Infections/Diagnosis.

Screening for Obesity. In Section I, see: Obesity/Diagnosis.

Screening for Oral Cancer. In Section I, see: Mouth Neoplasms.

Screening for Ovarian Cancer. In Section I, see: Ovarian Neoplasms/Diagnosis.

Screening for Pancreatic Cancer. In Section I, see: Pancreatic Neoplasms/Diagnosis.

Screening for Peripheral Arterial Disease. In Section I, see: Peripheral Vascular Diseases/Diagnosis.

Screening for Phenylketonuria. In Section I, see: Phenylketonuria/Diagnosis.

Screening for Postmenopausal Osteoporosis. In Section I, see: Osteoporosis, Postmenopausal/Diagnosis.

Screening for Preeclampsia. In Section I, see: Preeclampsia/Diagnosis.

Screening for Problem Drinking. In Section I, see: Alcoholism/Diagnosis.

Screening for Rubella. In Section I, see: Rubella/Diagnosis.

Screening for Skin Cancer. In Section I, see: Skin Neoplasms/Diagnosis.

Screening for Suicide Risk. In Section I, see: Suicide/Prevention and Control.

Screening for Syphilis. In Section I, see: Syphilis/Diagnosis.

Screening for Visual Impairment. In Section I, see: Vision Disorders/Diagnosis.

Screening Ultrasonography in Pregnancy. In Section I, see: Ultrasonography, Prenatal/Methods.

Section III
Clinical Practice
Guidelines by Title

1988 Agent Summary Statement for Human Immunodeficiency Virus and Report on Laboratory-Acquired Infection with Human Immunodeficiency Virus. In Section I, see: Acquired Immunodeficiency Syndrome.

1992 Modification of CDC Definitions of Surgical Wound Infections. In Section I, see: Surgical Wound Infection/Classification.

1993 Revised Classification System for HIV Infection and Expanded Surveillance Case Definition for AIDS Among Adolescents and Adults. In Section I, see: Acquired Immunodeficiency Syndrome/Epidemiology.

1994 Revised Classification System for Human Immunodeficiency Virus Infection in Children Less Than 3 Years of Age. In Section I, see: HIV Infections/Classification.

1995 Revised Guidelines for Prophylaxis Against Pneumocystis carinii Pneumonia for Children Infected with or Perinatally Exposed to Human Immunodeficiency Virus. In Section I, see: Pneumonia, Pneumocystis carinii/Prevention and Control.

1997 Revised Guidelines for Performing CD4+ T-Cell Determinations in Persons Infected with Human Immunodeficiency Virus (HIV). In Section I, see: Cd4 Lymphocyte Count.

1997 Update of Recommendations for the Use of Hematopoietic Colony-Stimulating Factors. In Section I, see: Colony-Stimulating Factors/Therapeutic Use.

1998 Update of Recommendations for the Use of Tumor Markers in Breast and Colorectal Cancer. In Section I, see: Tumor Markers, Biological/Analysis.

1997 USPHS/IDSA Guidelines for the Prevention of Opportunistic Infections in Persons Infected with Human Immunodeficiency Virus. In Section I, see: Tuberculosis, Pulmonary/Prevention and Control Virus Diseases/Complications

1998 Guidelines for Treatment of Sexually Transmitted Disease. In Section I, see: Sexually Transmitted Diseases/Therapy.

1998 Update of Recommended Breast Cancer Surveillance Guidelines. In Section I, see: Breast Neoplasms/Diagnosis.

24th Bethesda Conference Report: Cardiac Transplantation. In Section I, see: Heart Transplantation.

25th Bethesda Conference Report: Future Personnel Needs for Cardiovascular Health Care. In Section I, see: Health Services Needs and Demand.

A

A Guideline for the Treatment and Prevention of NSAID-Induced Ulcers. In Section I, see: Anti-Inflammatory Agents, Non-Steroidal/Adverse Effects.

A Primer on Outcomes Research for the Gastroenterologist: Report of the AGA Taskforce on Outcomes Research. In Section I, see: Gastroenterology.

AACE Clinical Practice Guidelines for the Management of Thyroid Carcinoma. In Section I, see: Thyroid Neoplasms/Therapy.

Abdominal Aortic Aneurysm Surgery. In Section I, see: Aortic Aneurysm, Abdominal/Surgery.

Abdominoplasty. In Section I, see: Abdominal Muscles/Surgery.

Ablation of Accessory Pathways in Wolff-Parkinson-White Syndrome. In Section I, see: Wolff-Parkinson-White Syndrome/Surgery.

Abortion, Induced. In Section I, see: Abortion, Induced.

Absence of Endocervical Cells on a Pap Test. In Section I, see: Cervix Uteri/Pathology.

ACC Core Cardiology Training Symposium (COCATS) Guidelines for Training in Adult Cardiovascular Medicine. In Section I, see: Cardiology/Education.

ACC/AHA Guidelines and Indications for Coronary Artery Bypass Graft Surgery. In Section I, see: Coronary Bypass.

ACC/AHA Guidelines for Cardiac Catheterization and Cardiac Catheterization Laboratories. In Section I, see: Heart Catheterization/Standards.

ACC/AHA Guidelines for Clinical Intracardiac Electrophysiologic and Catheter Ablation Procedures (Revision of 1989 Guidelines). In Section I, see: Catheter Ablation.

ACC/AHA Guidelines for Clinical Use of Cardiac Radionuclide Imaging (Revision of 1986 Report). In Section I, see: Coronary Disease/Radionuclide Imaging.

ACC/AHA Guidelines for Electrocardiography. In Section I, see: Cardiovascular Diseases/Diagnosis.

ACC/AHA Guidelines for Exercise Testing (Revision of 1986 Report). In Section I, see: Exercise Test.

ACC/AHA Guidelines for Implantation of Cardiac Pacemakers and Antiarrhythmia Devices. In Section I, see: Arrhythmia/Therapy.

ACR Standard for the Performance of an Ultrasound Examination of the Extracranial Cerebrovascular System (Revised). In Section I, see: Carotid Artery Diseases/Ultrasonography.

ACR Standard for the Performance of Antepartum Obstetrical Ultrasound. In Section I, see: Ultrasonography, Prenatal.

ACR Standard for the Performance of Breast Ultrasound Examination. In Section I, see: Breast Diseases/Ultrasonography.

ACR Standard for the Performance of Cardiac Scintigraphy. In Section I, see: Coronary Disease/Radionuclide Imaging.

ACR Standard for the Performance of Cerebral Scintigraphy. In Section I, see: Brain/Radionuclide Imaging.

ACR Standard for the Performance of Clinical Procedures Using Radiopharmaceuticals (Revised). In Section I, see: Radiopharmaceuticals/Therapeutic Use.

ACR Standard for the Performance of Computed Tomography in Neuroradiologic Imaging in Adults and Children. In Section I, see: Tomography, X-ray Computed.

ACR Standard for the Performance of Computed Tomography of the Abdomen and Pelvis (Revised). In Section I, see: Tomography, X-ray Computed.

ACR Standard for the Performance of Diagnostic Mammography. In Section I, see: Mammography/Methods.

ACR Standard for the Performance of Dual Energy X-ray Absorptiometry (DXA). In Section I, see: Absorptiometry, Photon.

ACR Standard for the Performance of Excretory Urography. In Section I, see: Urography/Standards.

ACR Standard for the Performance of Gastrointestinal Scintigraphy. In Section I, see: Gastrointestinal System/Radionuclide Imaging.

ACR Standard for the Performance of General (Plain) Radiography. In Section I, see: Radiography.

ACR Standard for the Performance of Hepatobiliary Scintigraphy. In Section I, see: Biliary Tract/Radionuclide Imaging.

ACR Standard for the Performance of High-Dose-Rate Brachytherapy. In Section I, see: Brachytherapy.

ACR Standard for the Performance of Imaging-Guided Percutaneous Needle Biopsy in Adults. In Section I, see: Biopsy, Needle/Methods.

ACR Standard for the Performance of Liver/Spleen Scintigraphy. In Section I, see: Spleen/Radionuclide Imaging.

ACR Standard for the Performance of Low-Dose-Rate Brachytherapy. In Section I, see: Brachytherapy.

ACR Standard for the Performance of Magnetic Resonance Imaging (Revised). In Section I, see: Magnetic Resonance Imaging.

ACR Standard for the Performance of Myelography and Cisternography. In Section I, see: Myelography.

ACR Standard for the Performance of Parathyroid Scintigraphy. In Section I, see: Parathyroid Glands/Radionuclide Imaging.

ACR Standard for the Performance of Pediatric and Adult Bedside (Portable) Chest Radiography (Revised). In Section I, see: Lung Diseases/Radiography.

ACR Standard for the Performance of Pediatric and Adult Chest Radiography (Revised). In Section I, see: Lung Diseases/Radiography.

ACR Standard for the Performance of Pediatric Contrast Enema. In Section I, see: Contrast Media.

ACR Standard for the Performance of Pediatric Contrast Examination of the Small Bowel. In Section I, see: Intestines, Small/Radiography.

ACR Standard for the Performance of Pediatric Contrast Examinations of the Upper Gastrointestinal Tract. In Section I, see: Contrast Media.

ACR Standard for the Performance of Per Oral Small Bowel Examinations in Adults. In Section I, see: Intestine, Small/Radiography.

ACR Standard for the Performance of Percutaneous Nephrostomy (PCN). In Section I, see: Nephrostomy, Percutaneous.

ACR Standard for the Performance of Pulmonary Scintigraphy. In Section I, see: Lung/Radionuclide Imaging.

ACR Standard for the Performance of Radiography of the Cervical Spine in Children and Adults. In Section I, see: Cervical Vertebrae/Radiography.

ACR Standard for the Performance of Radionuclide Cystography. In Section I, see: Bladder/Radionuclide Imaging.

ACR Standard for the Performance of Scintigraphy for Infections and Inflammations. In Section I, see: Bacterial Infections/Radionuclide Imaging.

ACR Standard for the Performance of Screening Mammography. In Section I, see: Mammography.

ACR Standard for the Performance of Scrotal Scintigraphy. In Section I, see: Scrotum/Radionuclide Imaging.

ACR Standard for the Performance of Skeletal Scintigraphy (Revised). In Section I, see: Bone Diseases/Radionuclide Imaging.

ACR Standard for the Performance of Stereotactic Radiation Therapy/Radiosurgery. In Section I, see: Stereotaxic Techniques/Standards.

ACR Standard for the Performance of Stereotactically-Guided Breast Interventional Procedures. In Section I, see: Stereotaxic Techniques.

ACR Standard for the Performance of the Pediatric Neurosonology Examination. In Section I, see: Nervous System/Ultrasonography.

ACR Standard for the Performance of the Peripheral Arterial Ultrasound Examination (Revised). In Section I, see: Peripheral Vascular Diseases/Ultrasonography.

ACR Standard for the Performance of the Peripheral Venous Ultrasound Examination (Revised). In Section I, see: Peripheral Vascular Diseases/Ultrasonography.

ACR Standard for the Performance of the Thyroid and Parathyroid Ultrasound Examination (Revised). In Section I, see: Thyroid Diseases/Ultrasonography.

ACR Standard for the Performance of the Ultrasound Examination for Detection of Developmental Dysplasia of the Hip. In Section I, see: Hip Dislocation, Congenital/Ultrasonography.

ACR Standard for the Performance of the Ultrasound Examination of the Female Pelvis. In Section I, see: Genital Diseases, Female/Diagnosis.

ACR Standard for the Performance of the Ultrasound Examination of the Prostate (and Surrounding Structures) (Revised). In Section I, see: Prostatic Diseases/Ultrasonography.

ACR Standard for the Performance of Therapy with Unsealed Radionuclide Sources. In Section I, see: Radioisotopes/Therapeutic Use.

ACR Standard for the Performance of Thoracic Computed Tomography in Adults and Children. In Section I, see: Tomography, X-ray Computed.

ACR Standard for the Performance of Thyroid Scintigraphy and Uptake Measurements. In Section I, see: Iodine Radioisotopes/Therapeutic Use.

ACR Standard for the Performance of Tumor Scintigraphy (with Gamma Cameras). In Section I, see: Gamma Cameras.

ACR Standard for the Performance of Ultrasound-Guided Breast Interventional Procedures. In Section I, see: Ultrasonography, Mammary.

ACR Standard for the Performance of Voiding Cystourethrography in Children. In Section I, see: Bladder/Radiography.

ACR Standard on Communication—Diagnostic Radiology. In Section I, see: Diagnostic Imaging.

Actinic Keratoses. In Section I, see: Keratosis/Therapy.

Acupuncture. In Section I, see: Acupuncture.

Acute Blunt Trauma. In Section I, see: Wounds, Nonpenetrating/Diagnosis.

Acute Low Back Pain Problems in Adults. In Section I, see: Low Back Pain/Therapy.

Acute Pain Management: Operative or Medical Procedures and Trauma. In Section I, see: Pain/Therapy.

Acute Toxic Ingestion or Dermal or Inhalation Exposure. In Section I, see: Emergency Medicine/Methods.

Adenoidectomy. In Section I, see: Adenoidectomy.

Adequacy of Hemodialysis. In Section I, see: Hemodialysis.

Adjuvant Therapy for Patients with Colon and Rectum Cancer. In Section I, see: Colonic Neoplasms/Therapy.

Adolescent Victims of Sexual Assault. In Section I, see: Rape.

Adolescents' Right to Refuse Long-Term Contraceptives. In Section I, see: Treatment Refusal.

Adult Immunizations. In Section I, see: Immunization.

Advanced Laparoscopy into Surgical Residency Training. In Section I, see: Curriculum.

Advanced Paternal Age: Risks to the Fetus. In Section I, see: Fetal Diseases/Genetics.

Adverse Effects and Complications of Treatment With Beta-Adrenergic Agonist Drugs. In Section I, see: Adrenergic Beta-Agonists/Adverse Effects.

Advice for the Patient. In Section I, see: Asthma.

Aerosolized Pentamidine for HIV Patients. In Section I, see: HIV Infections/Complications.

Age Related Infertility. In Section I, see: Aging/Physiology.

Age-Related Macular Degeneration Preferred Practice Pattern. In Section I, see: Macular Degeneration.

AIDS and Infection with HIV. In Section I, see: HIV Seropositivity.

Alcohol Use Disorders in Older Adults, Pocket Guide. In Section I, see: Alcoholism.

Alcoholic Liver Disease. In Section I, see: Liver Diseases, Alcoholic/Diagnosis.

Alcoholism in the Elderly: Diagnosis, Treatment, and Prevention. In Section I, see: Alcoholism/Prevention and Control.

Algorithm for the Diagnosis and Management of Asthma. In Section I, see: Asthma/Diagnosis.

Allergen Immunotherapy. In Section I, see: Immunotherapy/Standards.

Allergen Skin Testing. In Section I, see: Allergens/Analysis.

Allergen Standardization. In Section I, see: Allergens.

Allergic Rhinitis Clinical Practice Guideline. In Section I, see: Rhinitis, Allergic, Perennial.

Allergy Diagnostic Testing. In Section I, see: Hypersensitivity/Diagnosis.

Allergy Testing for Allergic Rhinitus. In Section I, see: Rhinitis, Allergic, Perennial.

Allogeneic Bone Marrow Transplantation for Chronic Myelogenous Leukemia. In Section I, see: Bone Marrow Transplantation.

Alpha-Interferon for Chronic Myelogenous Leukemia. In Section I, see: Interferon Alpha-2a/Therapeutic Use.

Altered Mental States. In Section I, see: Mental Disorders.

Alternative Psychological Methods in Patient Care. In Section I, see: Psychotherapy/Methods.

Alternatives to Animal Use in Biomedical Research. In Section I, see: Animal Testing Alternatives.

Alzheimer's Disease. In Section I, see: Alzheimer Disease.

Amblyopia Preferred Practice Pattern. In Section I, see: Amblyopia.

Amenorrhea. In Section I, see: Amenorrhea.

American Cancer Society Guidelines for Screening and Surveillance for Early Detection of Colorectal Polyps and Cancer: Update 1997. In Section I, see: Colonic Polyps/Diagnosis.

American Cancer Society Guidelines for the Early Detection of Breast Cancer: Update 1997. In Section I, see: Breast Neoplasms/Radiography.

American Diabetes Association Guide to Diabetes Coding. In Section I, see: Forms and Records Control.

American Diabetes Association Guide to Medical Nutrition Therapy for Diabetes. In Section I, see: Diet Therapy.

American Thyroid Association Guidelines for Use of Laboratory Tests in Thyroid Disorders. In Section I, see: Thyroid Diseases/Diagnosis.

An Approach to the Evaluation of Quality Indicators of the Outcome of Care in Hospitalized Patients with a Focus on Nosocomial Infection Indicators. In Section I, see: Cross Infection/Epidemiology.

Anal Cancer (6 variants). In Section I, see: Anus Neoplasms/Therapy.

Anaphylaxis in Schools and Other Child-Care Settings. In Section I, see: Anaphylaxis/Prevention and Control.

Androgenetic Alopecia. In Section I, see: Alopecia/Therapy.

Anergy Skin Testing and Preventive Therapy for HIV-Infected Persons: Revised Recommendations. In Section I, see: AIDS-Related Opportunistic Infections/Prevention and Control.

Anesthesia and Sedation in the Dental Office. In Section I, see: Anesthesia, Dental.

Anesthesia for Emergency Deliveries. In Section I, see: Anesthesia, Obstetrical.

Anesthesia in Outpatient Facilities. In Section I, see: Anesthesia, Dental.

Angelchik Antireflux Prosthesis Treatment of Gastroesophageal Reflux. In Section I, see: Gastroesophageal Reflux/Surgery.

Angiography, Cerebral or Cervical. In Section I, see: Cerebral Angiography.

Angioplasty Standard of Practice. In Section I, see: Angioplasty, Balloon/Standards.

Animals in Medical Research. In Section I, see: Research.

Anorectal Testing Techniques. In Section I, see: Anus Diseases/Diagnosis.

Anorectic Usage Guidelines. In Section I, see: Appetite Depressants/Therapeutic Use.

Title

Assessment: Melodic Intonation Therapy. In Section I, see: Speech Therapy/Methods.

Assessment: Neurologic Risk of Immunization. In Section I, see: Nervous System Diseases/Etiology.

Assessment: Neurological Evaluation of Male Sexual Dysfunction. In Section I, see: Neurologic Examination.

Assessment: Neuropsychological Testing of Adults: Considerations for Neurologists. In Section I, see: Nervous System Diseases/Psychology.

Assessment: Positron Emission Tomography. In Section I, see: Tomography, Emission-Computed/Standards.

Assessment: Posturography. In Section I, see: Nervous System Diseases/Diagnosis.

Assessment: Techniques Associated with the Diagnosis and Management of Sleep Disorders. In Section I, see: Sleep Disorders/Diagnosis.

Assessment: The Clinical Usefulness of Botulinum Toxin-A in Treating Neurological Disorders. In Section I, see: Botulinum Toxins/Therapeutic Use.

Assessment: Thermography in Neurologic Practice. In Section I, see: Neurology.

Assessment: Transcranial Doppler. In Section I, see: Cerebral Arteries/Physiopathology.

Auditory Brainstem Response. In Section I, see: Evoked Potentials, Auditory.

Autologous Peripheral Stem-Cell Transplantation. In Section I, see: Hematopoietic Stem-Cell Transplantation.

Automated Ambulatory Blood Pressure Monitoring. In Section I, see: Blood Pressure Monitoring, Ambulatory.

Automated Lamellar Keratoplasty Preliminary Procedure Assessment. In Section I, see: Cornea/Surgery.

Automated Perimetry Ophthalmic Procedure Assessment. In Section I, see: Perimetry/Methods.

Autopsy. In Section I, see: Autopsy.

Autopsy Procedures for Brain, Spinal Cord and Neuromuscular System. In Section I, see: Autopsy/Standards.

Aversion Therapy. In Section I, see: Aversive Therapy.

B

Bacterial Keratitis Preferred Practice Pattern. In Section I, see: Keratitis.

Bacterial Vaginosis Screening for Prevention of Preterm Delivery. In Section I, see: Vaginosis, Bacterial/Diagnosis.

Barbiturates. In Section I, see: Head Injuries/Drug Therapy.

Bariatric Practice Guidelines. In Section I, see: Obesity/Therapy.

Basic Standards for Preanesthesia Care. In Section I, see: Preanesthestic Medication.

Benign Prostatic Hyperplasia: Diagnosis and Treatment. In Section I, see: Prostatic Hyperplasia/Diagnosis.

Beta-Adrenergic Blockers, Immunotherapy and Skin Testing. In Section I, see: Adrenergic Beta-Antagonists/Adverse Effects.

Biochemical Profiles: Applications in Ambulatory Screening and Preadmission Testing of Adults. In Section I, see: Blood Chemical Analysis.

Bioelectrical Impedance Analysis in Body Composition Measurement. In Section I, see: Body Composition.

Biofeedback for Gastrointestinal Disorders. In Section I, see: Biofeedback (Psychology).

Biofeedback for Headaches. In Section I, see: Biofeedback (Psychology).

Biofeedback for Hypertension. In Section I, see: Biofeedback (Psychology).

Biofeedback for Neuromuscular Disorders. In Section I, see: Biofeedback (Psychology).

Blepharitis Preferred Practice Pattern. In Section I, see: Blepharitis.

Blood Component Therapy. In Section I, see: Blood Component Transfusion.

Blood Cultures. In Section I, see: Bacteriological Techniques.

Bone Densitometry: Patients Receiving Prolonged Steroid Therapy. In Section I, see: Bone Density.

Bone Metastases (25 variants). In Section I, see: Bone Neoplasms/Secondary.

Book-Help for the Hospital Epidemiologist. In Section I, see: Infection Control Practitioners.

Bovine Somatotropin. In Section I, see: Somatotropin.

Brain-Specific Treatments in the Initial Resuscitation of the Head Injury Patient. In Section I, see: Head Injuries/Therapy.

Breast Cancer Screening for Women Ages 40-49. In Section I, see: Breast Neoplasms/Prevention and Control.

Breast Cancer Surgical Practice Guidelines. In Section I, see: Breast Neoplasms/Surgery.

Breast Frozen Section Biopsies. In Section I, see: Breast/Pathology.

Breast Reconstruction. In Section I, see: Mammoplasty.

Breast-Ovarian Cancer Screening. In Section I, see: Breast Neoplasms/Diagnosis.

Breastfeeding and the Risk of Hepatitis C Virus Transmission. In Section I, see: Breast Feeding.

Breastfeeding and the Use of Human Milk. In Section I, see: Breast Feeding.

Burr Holes or Twist Drill for Intracranial Hematoma. In Section I, see: Trephining.

C

Caldwell-Luc. In Section I, see: Maxillary Sinus/ Surgery.

Cancer of the Ovary. In Section I, see: Ovarian Neoplasms.

Cancer Screening Overview. In Section I, see: Neoplasms/Diagnosis.

Candidiasis Hypersensitivity Syndrome. In Section I, see: Candidiasis/Immunology.

CAP/ASCP Position Paper: The Preoperative Bleeding Time Test Lacks Clinical Benefit. In Section I, see: Bleeding Time.

Carcinoembryonic Antigen. In Section I, see: Carcinoembryonic Antigen/Analysis.

Carcinoma of the Breast. In Section I, see: Breast Neoplasms/Diagnosis.

Carcinoma of the Endometrium. In Section I, see: Adenocarcinoma.

Cardiac Disease in Pregnancy. In Section I, see: Pregnancy Complications, Cardiovascular.

Cardiac Positron Emission Tomography. In Section I, see: Coronary Disease/Radionuclide Imaging.

Cardiac Rehabilitation. In Section I, see: Coronary Disease/Rehabilitation.

Cardiac Rehabilitation Programs. In Section I, see: Cardiovascular Diseases/Rehabilitation.

Cardiac Rehabilitation Programs. In Section I, see: Cardiovascular Diseases/Rehabilitation.

Cardiac Rehabilitation Services. In Section I, see: Heart Diseases/Rehabilitation.

Cardiac Transplantation: Recipient Selection, Donor Procurement, and Medical Follow-Up. In Section I, see: Cardiology.

Cardiovascular Abnormalities in the Athlete: Recommendations Regarding Eligibility for Competition. In Section I, see: Cardiovascular Diseases/Diagnosis.

Cardiovascular Disease in the Elderly. In Section I, see: Cardiovascular Diseases.

Cardiovascular Disease in Women. In Section I, see: Cardiovascular Diseases/Epidemiology.

Cardiovascular Preparticipation Screening of Competitive Athletes: Addendum. In Section I, see: Sports.

Care Management, Position Statement. In Section I, see: Care Management.

Carotid Body Resection. In Section I, see: Carotid Body/Surgery.

Carotid Endarterectomy. In Section I, see: Endarterectomy.

Carotid Endarterectomy (Revised). In Section I, see: Endarterectomy, Carotid.

Carotid Endarterectomy: Practice Guidelines Report of the Ad Hoc Committee. In Section I, see: Endarterectomy, Carotid/Standards.

Carotid Stenting and Angioplasty. In Section I, see: Angioplasty, Balloon.

Carpal Tunnel Release. In Section I, see: Carpal Tunnel Syndrome/Surgery.

Carpal Tunnel Syndrome. In Section I, see: Carpal Tunnel Syndrome/Surgery.

Case Definitions for Infectious Conditions Under Public Health Surveillance. In Section I, see: Disease Notification.

Cataract in Adults: Management of Functional Impairment. In Section I, see: Cataract/Therapy.

Cataract in the Adult Eye. In Section I, see: Cataract.

Cataract Surgery. In Section I, see: Cataract Extraction.

CDC Criteria for Anemia in Children and Childbearing-Aged Women. In Section I, see: Anemia, Hypochromic/Diagnosis.

Cerebral Perfusion Pressure Monitoring. In Section I, see: Brain Injuries/Physiopathology.

Cerebrospinal Fluid Shunting Procedure. In Section I, see: Cerebrospinal Fluid Shunts.

Cervical Cancer. In Section I, see: Cervix Neoplasms/Diagnosis.

Cervical Cytology: Evaluation and Management of Abnormalities. In Section I, see: Vaginal Smears.

Cervical Spine Surgery. In Section I, see: Cervical Vertebrae/Surgery.

Cervical, Thoracic, or Lumbar Laminectomy for Tumor. In Section I, see: Spinal Cord Neoplasms.

Chelation Therapy (with EDTA) for Atherosclerosis. In Section I, see: Chelating Agents/Therapeutic Use.

Chemotherapy of Pulmonary Mycoses. In Section I, see: Lung Diseases, Fungal/Drug Therapy.

Child Physical Abuse and Neglect. In Section I, see: Child Abuse.

Child Sexual Abuse. In Section I, see: Child Abuse, Sexual.

Childhood Immunizations. In Section I, see: Immunization.

Chlamydia Trachomatis Infections: Policy Guidelines for Prevention and Control. In Section I, see: Chlamydia Infections/Prevention and Control.

Cholesterol in Childhood. In Section I, see: Cholesterol/Blood.

Cholesterol Screening (Update). In Section I, see: Cholesterol/Blood.

Chorionic Villus Sampling. In Section I, see: Chorionic Villi Sampling.

Chorionic Villus Sampling and Amniocentesis: Recommendations for Prenatal Counseling. In Section I, see: Amniocentesis.

Chorionic Villus Sampling: A Reassessment. In Section I, see: Chorionic Villi Sampling.

Chronic Diarrhea. In Section I, see: Diarrhea/Therapy.

Chronic Myelogenous Leukemia. In Section I, see: Leukemia, Myeloid, Chronic.

Chronic Pelvic Pain. In Section I, see: Pelvic Pain/Therapy.

Cigarette Smoking, Cardiovascular Disease, and Stroke. In Section I, see: Smoking.

Circumcision Policy Statement (formerly, Report of the Task Force on Circumcision). In Section I, see: Circumcision.

Cleft Lip and Cleft Palate. In Section I, see: Cleft Lip/Surgery.

Clinical Competence in Ambulatory Electrocardiography. In Section I, see: Clinical Competence/Standards.

Clinical Competence in Elective Direct Current (DC) Cardioversion. In Section I, see: Clinical Competence/Standards.

Clinical Competence in Electrophysiologic Studies. In Section I, see: Clinical Competence/Standards.

Clinical Competence in Hemodynamic Monitoring. In Section I, see: Clinical Competence/Standards.

Clinical Competence in Insertion of a Temporary Transvenous Ventricular Pacemaker. In Section I, see: Clinical Competence/Standards.

Clinical Competence in Percutaneous Renal Biopsy. In Section I, see: Biopsy Needle/Standards.

Clinical Completence in Ambulatory Electrocardiography. In Section I, see: Clinical Competence.

Clinical Ecology. In Section I, see: Air Pollutants/Adverse Effects.

Clinical Ecology. In Section I, see: Air Pollutants/Adverse Effects.

Clinical Esophageal pH Recording. In Section I, see: Esophageal Diseases/Diagnosis.

Clinical Evaluation of Jaundice: A Guideline of the Patient Care Committee of the American Gastroenterological Association. In Section I, see: Jaundice/Diagnosis.

Clinical Guideline on Ankle Injury. In Section I, see: Ankle Injuries.

Clinical Guideline on Hip Pain. In Section I, see: Hip Joint.

Clinical Guideline on Knee Pain (Phases I and II). In Section I, see: Knee.

Clinical Guideline on Low Back Pain (Phases I and II). In Section I, see: Low Back Pain.

Clinical Guideline on Shoulder Pain. In Section I, see: Shoulder Pain.

Compendium of Measures to Control Chlamydia psittaci Infection Among Humans (Psittacosis) and Pet Birds (Avian Chlamydiosis). In Section I, see: Bird Diseases/Prevention and Control.

Compendium of Psittacosis (Chlamydiosis) Control, 1997. In Section I, see: Bird Diseases/Prevention and Control.

Compensation for Vaccine-Related Injuries. In Section I, see: Vaccination/Economics.

Complete Blood Count and Leukocyte Differential Count: An Approach to Their Rational Application. In Section I, see: Blood Cell Count.

Complex Closures, Flaps, and Grafts. In Section I, see: Skin/Surgery.

Comprehensive Adult Eye Evaluation Preferred Practice Pattern. In Section I, see: Eye Diseases/Diagnosis.

Comprehensive Geriatric Assessment for the Older Patient, Position Statement. In Section I, see: Geriatric Assessment.

Computer Guidelines for Pulmonary Laboratories. In Section I, see: Computers/Standards.

Condom Availability for Adolescents. In Section I, see: Condoms/Supply and Distribution.

Conference Participation. In Section I, see: Congresses.

Confidential Care for Minors. In Section I, see: Confidentiality.

Confidentiality in Adolescent Health Care. In Section I, see: Confidentiality.

Confidentiality of HIV Status on Autopsy Reports. In Section I, see: Autopsy.

Congenital Heart Disease After Childhood: An Expanding Patient Population. In Section I, see: Heart Defects, Congenital.

Conjunctivitis Preferred Practice Pattern. In Section I, see: Conjunctivitis.

Conscious Sedation and Monitoring of Patients Undergoing GI Endoscopic Procedures. In Section I, see: Endoscopy, Gastrointestinal.

Consensus Criteria for the Diagnosis of Partial Conduction Block. In Section I, see: Nerve Block/Diagnosis.

Consensus Panel on Infrastructure and Essential Activities of Hospital Epidemiology and Infection Control Programs. In Section I, see: Epidemiologic Studies.

Consensus Paper on the Surveillance of Surgical Wound Infection. In Section I, see: Surgical Wound Infection/Epidemiology.

Conservative Surgery and Radiation in the Treatment of Stage I and II Carcinoma of the Breast (9 variants). In Section I, see: Breast Neoplasms/Diagnosis.

Considerations Related to the Use of Recombinant Human Growth Hormone in Children. In Section I, see: Somatotropins, Recombinant/Adverse Effects.

Contact Dermatitis. In Section I, see: Dermatitis, Contact/Therapy.

Continuous Ambulatory Esophageal pH Monitoring in the Evaluation of Patients with Gastroesophageal Reflux. In Section I, see: Gastroesophageal Reflux/Diagnosis.

Continuous Arteriovenous Hemofiltration (CAVH) for Fluid Removal. In Section I, see: Ultrafiltration/Methods.

Contraceptive Choices. In Section I, see: Contraceptive Agents.

Contraceptives and Congenital Anomalities. In Section I, see: Abnormalities/Etiology.

Control and Prevention of Meningococcal Disease and Control and Prevention of Serogroup C Meningococcal Disease: Evaluation and Management of Suspected Outbreaks. In Section I, see: Meningococcal Infections/Prevention and Control.

Control of Tuberculosis in the U.S. In Section I, see: Tuberculosis, Pulmonary/Prevention and Control.

Conversion of Prescription Drugs to Over-the-Counter Designation, Position Statement. In Section I, see: Prescriptions, Drug.

Coping with the Stress of Malpractice Litigation. In Section I, see: Malpractice.

Corneal Endothelial Photography Ophthalmic Procedure Assessment. In Section I, see: Endothelium, Corneal.

Corneal Opacification Preferred Practice Pattern. In Section I, see: Corneal Opacity.

Corneal Topography Opthalamic Procedure Assessment. In Section I, see: Corneal Topography.

Corneal Transplantation. In Section I, see: Cornea/Transplantation.

Coronary Angiography. In Section I, see: Coronary Angiography.

Coronary Artery Bypass Graft. In Section I, see: Coronary Artery Bypass.

Coronary Artery Bypass Graft Surgery and Percutaneous Transluminal Coronary Angioplasty. In Section I, see: Coronary Artery Bypass.

Cost Containment in Medical Care. In Section I, see: Delivery of Health Care/Economics.

Counseling to Prevent Dental and Periodontal Disease. In Section I, see: Periodontal Diseases/Prevention and Control.

Counseling to Prevent Gynecologic Cancers. In Section I, see: Genital Neoplasm, Female/Prevention and Control.

Counseling to Prevent Household and Recreational Injuries. In Section I, see: Accident Prevention.

Counseling to Prevent Human Immunodeficiency Virus Infection and Other Sexually Transmitted Diseases. In Section I, see: HIV Infections/Prevention and Control.

Counseling to Prevent Low Back Pain. In Section I, see: Low Back Pain/Prevention and Control.

Counseling to Prevent Motor Vehicle Injuries. In Section I, see: Accidents, Traffic/Prevention and Control.

Counseling to Prevent Tobacco Use. In Section I, see: Tobacco Use Disorder/Prevention and Control.

Counseling to Prevent Unintended Pregnancy. In Section I, see: Pregnancy, Unwanted.

Counseling to Prevent Youth Violence. In Section I, see: Violence/Prevention and Control.

Counseling to Promote a Healthy Diet. In Section I, see: Diet.

Counseling to Promote Physical Activity. In Section I, see: Exercise.

Cranial Base Surgery. In Section I, see: Skull/Surgery.

Craniostenosis (Synostosis) Surgery. In Section I, see: Craniosynostoses/Surgery.

Craniosynostosis (Including Syndromal Craniosynostosis, Brachycephaly, Plagiocephaly, Trigonocephaly, Scaphocephaly). In Section I, see: Craniosynostoses.

Craniotomy for Hypophysectomy or Pituitary Tumor. In Section I, see: Craniotomy.

Craniotomy for Intracranial Aneurysm or AVM. In Section I, see: Craniotomy.

Craniotomy for Tumor of Brain or Associated Structures, or Brain Abscess. In Section I, see: Brain Abscess/Surgery.

Craniotomy or Burr Holes for Penetrating Cranial Wound. In Section I, see: Trephining.

Craniotomy or Burr Holes for Skull Fracture, Open or Depressed. In Section I, see: Trephining.

Credentialing Criteria: Percutaneous Nephrostomy. In Section I, see: Nephrostomy, Percutaneous.

Credentialing Criteria: Peripheral and Visceral Arteriography. In Section I, see: Angiography.

Credentialing Criteria: Peripheral, Renal and Visceral Percutaneous Transluminal Angioplasty. In Section I, see: Angioplasty, Balloon/Standards.

Critical Care Medicine. In Section I, see: Critical Care.

Critical Pathway for the Treatment of Established Intracranial Hypertension. In Section I, see: Head Injuries/Therapy.

Critical Values. In Section I, see: Critical Care/Standards.

Crohn's Disease. In Section I, see: Crohn Disease/Diagnosis.

Cryosurgery. In Section I, see: Cryosurgery.

Cultural Competency in Health Care. In Section I, see: Cultural Diversity.

Current Evaluation and Treatment of Amenorrhea. In Section I, see: Amenorrhea/Diagnosis.

Current Status of Cystic Fibrosis Carrier Screening. In Section I, see: Cystic Fibrosis/Genetics.

Curriculum Guidelines on the Care of the Elderly for Internal Medicine Residency Training Programs. In Section I, see: Internship and Residency.

Cutaneous Adverse Drug Reactions. In Section I, see: Drug Eruptions/Therapy.

Cutaneous Lupus Erythematosus. In Section I, see: Lupus Erythematosus, Cutaneous/Drug Therapy.

Cyclotrons and Radiopharmaceuticals in Positron Emission Tomography. In Section I, see: Particle Accelerators.

Cytotoxicity Testing (Bryan's Testing). In Section I, see: Cytotoxicity, Immunologic.

D

Deception. In Section I, see: Deception.

Decisions for Forgoing Life-Sustaining Treatment for Incompetent Patients. In Section I, see: Life Support Care.

Decisions Near the End of Life. In Section I, see: Mental Competency.

Defined Diets and Childhood Hyperactivity. In Section I, see: Attention Deficit Disorder with Hyperactivity/Drug Therapy.

Definitions for Sepsis and Organ Failure and Guidelines for the Use of Innovative Therapies in Sepsis. In Section I, see: Septicemia/Therapy.

Definitive External Beam Irradiation in Stage T1, T2 Carcinoma of the Prostate (9 variants). In Section I, see: Prostatic Neoplasms/Radiotherapy.

Delineation of Obstetric-Gynecologic Primary Care Practice. In Section I, see: Family Practice/Standards.

Delirium, Dementia, Amnesia, and Other Cognitive Disorders. In Section I, see: Delirium.

Delivery by Vacuum Extraction. In Section I, see: Vacuum Extraction, Obstetrical/Instrumentation.

Dementia. In Section I, see: Dementia.

Dental and Maxillofacial Implant. In Section I, see: Maxillofacial Prosthesis.

Dental Implants. In Section I, see: Dental Implantation.

Dental Practice Parameters. In Section I, see: Dentistry/Standards.

Dental Sealants in the Prevention of Tooth Decay. In Section I, see: Pit and Fissure Sealants/Therapeutic Use.

Dentoalveolar Surgery. In Section I, see: Tooth Extraction.

Depression. In Section I, see: Depression.

Depression in Primary Care: Volume I: Detection and Diagnosis; Volume II: Treatment of Major Depression. In Section I, see: Depressive Disorder/Diagnosis.

Depression in Women's Health. In Section I, see: Depressive Disorder.

DeQuervain's Stenosing Tenosynovitis. In Section I, see: Tenosynovitis.

Dermabrasion. In Section I, see: Dermabrasion.

Dermatologic Conditions in Patients Infected with Human Immunodeficiency Virus (HIV). In Section I, see: HIV Infections/Complications.

Dermatomyositis. In Section I, see: Dermatomyositis/Therapy.

Description of Case-Mix Adjusters by Severity of Illness Working Group of the Society for Healthcare

Epidemiologists of America (SHEA). In Section I, see: Cross Infection/Economics.

Detection and Surveillance of Colorectal Cancer. In Section I, see: Colorectal Neoplasms/Diagnosis.

Detoxification: Principles and Protocols. In Section I, see: Metabolic Detoxification, Drug.

Development of New Vaccines for Tuberculosis Recommendations of the Advisory Council for the Elimination of Tuberculosis (ACET). In Section I, see: Mycobacterium Tuberculosis/Immunology.

Dexamethasone Suppression Test for the Detection, Diagnosis, and Management of Depression. In Section I, see: Dexamethasone/Diagnostic Use.

Diabetes and Pregnancy. In Section I, see: Pregnancy in Diabetes.

Diabetes Medical Nutrition Therapy. In Section I, see: Diabetic Diet.

Diabetes: 1996 Vital Statistics. In Section I, see: Diabetes Mellitus/Epidemiology.

Diabetic Retinopathy Preferred Practice Patterns. In Section I, see: Diabetic Retinopathy.

Diagnosis and Management of Asymptomatic Primary Hyperparathyroidism. In Section I, see: Hyperparathyroidism/Therapy.

Diagnosis and Management of Fetal Death. In Section I, see: Fetal Death/Diagnosis.

Diagnosis and Management of Group A Streptococcal Pharyngitis: A Practice Guideline. In Section I, see: Pharyngitis/Diagnosis.

Diagnosis and Management of Immunodeficiency. In Section I, see: Immunologic Deficiency Syndromes/Diagnosis.

Diagnosis and Management of Invasive Cervical Carcinomas. In Section I, see: Cervix Neoplasms/Diagnosis.

Diagnosis and Management of Rhinitis: Parameter Documents of the Joint Task.... In Section I, see: Rhinitis/Diagnosis.

Diagnosis and Management of Urinary Tract Infection. In Section I, see: Urinary Tract Infections/Diagnosis.

Diagnosis and Therapy of Kawasaki Disease in Children. In Section I, see: Mucocutaneous Lymph Node Syndrome/Diagnosis.

Diagnosis and Treatment of Asthma. In Section I, see: Hypersensitivity/Diagnosis.

Diagnosis and Treatment of Attention Deficit Hyperactivity Disorder (ADHD). In Section I, see: Attention Deficit Disorder with Hyperactivity/Diagnosis.

Diagnosis and Treatment of Depression in Late Life. In Section I, see: Depression/Diagnosis.

Diagnosis and Treatment of Disease Due to Non-Tuberculous Mycobacteria. In Section I, see: Mycobacterium, Infectious, Atypical.

Diagnosis and Treatment of Early Melanoma. In Section I, see: Melanoma/Diagnosis.

Diagnosis and Treatment of Esophageal Diseases Associated with HIV Infection. In Section I, see: AIDS-Related Opportunistic Infections/Diagnosis.

Diagnosis and Treatment of Gastrointestinal Bleeding Secondary to Portal Hypertension. In Section I, see: Esophageal and Gastric Varices/Complications.

Diagnosis of Non-Malignant Disease Related to Asbestos. In Section I, see: Asbestos/Adverse Effects.

Diagnostic and Therapeutic Procedures. In Section I, see: Diagnosis.

Diagnostic and Treatment Guidelines on Mental Health Effects of Family Violence. In Section I, see: Domestic Violence.

Diagnostic Endocardial Electrical Recording and Stimulation. In Section I, see: Endocardium/Physiology.

Diagnostic Evaluation of Carotid Arteries. In Section I, see: Carotid Artery Diseases/Diagnosis.

Diagnostic Evaluation of the Differential Diagnosis of Thyroid Nodules. In Section I, see: Thyroid Nodule/Diagnosis.

Diagnostic Nasal Endoscopy. In Section I, see: Endoscopy.

Diagnostic Spinal Tap. In Section I, see: Cerebrospinal Fluid.

Diagnostic Standards and Classification of Tuberculosis. In Section I, see: Tuberculosis, Pulmonary/Diagnosis.

Diagnostic Thoracentesis in Pleural Biopsy. In Section I, see: Pleural Effusion/Etiology.

Diagnostic Ultrasonography: Clinical Interpretation. In Section I, see: Ultrasonography.

Diagnostic Uses of the Activated Partial Thromboplastin Time and Prothrombin Time. In Section I, see: Prothrombin Time.

Diet and Exercise in Non-Insulin-Dependent Diabetes Mellitus. In Section I, see: Diabetes Mellitus, Non-Insulin-Dependent/Diet Therapy.

Dietary Fiber and Health. In Section I, see: Dietary Fiber/Therapeutic Use.

Diethylstilbestrol 1993. In Section I, see: Diethylstilbestrol.

Differential Diagnosis of Dementing Diseases. In Section I, see: Dementia/Diagnosis.

Diphtheria, Tetanus, and Pertussis: Recommendations for Vaccine Use and Other Preventive Measures: Recommendations of the Immunization Practices Advisory Committee (ACIP). In Section I, see: Diphtheria-Tetanus-Pertussis Vaccine/Administration and Dosage.

Disease Management of Atopic Dermatitis: A Practice Parameter. In Section I, see: Dermatitis, Atopic/Therapy.

Disorders of Impulse Control. In Section I, see: Impulse Control Disorders/Drug Therapy.

Disorders Usually First Diagnosed in Infancy, Childhood, or Adolescence. In Section I, see: Mental Disorders Diagnosed in Childhood.

Distal Radius Fracture. In Section I, see: Radius Fractures.

Distraction/Compression Osteosynthesis with the Ilizarov Device. In Section I, see: Orthopedic Fixation Devices/Therapy.

DLCO—Recommendations for a Standard Technique. In Section I, see: Pulmonary Diffusing Capacity.

Domestic Violence. In Section I, see: Pamphlets.

Domestic Violence: A Directory of Protocols for Healthcare Providers. In Section I, see: Domestic Violence.

Dorsal Rhizotomy. In Section I, see: Cerebral Palsy/Surgery.

Driving Following an Unprovoked Generalized Single Tonic Clonic Seizure. In Section I, see: Epilepsy, Tonic-Clonic.

Drug Evaluation and Surveillance, Position Statement. In Section I, see: Drug Evaluation.

Drug Information for the Health Care Professional. In Section I, see: Drug Information Services.

Drug Screening in the Workplace: Ethical Guidelines. In Section I, see: Drug Screening.

Drugs for Pediatric Emergencies. In Section I, see: Emergency Treatment/Methods.

Dry Eye Syndrome. In Section I, see: Dry Eye Syndromes.

Ductal Carcinoma in Situ and Microinvasive Disease (10 variants). In Section I, see: Carcinoma, Infiltrating Duct.

Dupuytren's Contracture. In Section I, see: Dupuytren's Contracture.

Dysfunctional Uterine Bleeding. In Section I, see: Uterine Hemorrhage/Diagnosis.

Dyslexia. In Section I, see: Dyslexia.

Dystocia and the Augmentation of Labor. In Section I, see: Dystocia/Therapy.

E

Ear Deformity: Prominent Ears. In Section I, see: Ear, External/Abnormalities.

Early Diagnosis and Management of Ectopic Pregnancy. In Section I, see: Pregnancy, Ectopic/Diagnosis.

Early Identification of Hearing Impairment in Infants and Young Children. In Section I, see: Hearing Disorders/Prevention and Control.

Early Pregnancy Loss. In Section I, see: Abortion, Habitual.

Early Stage Breast Cancer. In Section I, see: Breast Neoplasms/Therapy.

Eating Disorders. In Section I, see: Anorexia Nervosa.

Eating Disorders: Anorexia Nervosa and Bulimia: Position Paper. In Section I, see: Bulimia.

Education in Geriatric Medicine, Position Statement. In Section I, see: Education, Medical.

Effect of Corticosteroids for Fetal Maturation on Perinatal Outcomes. In Section I, see: Adrenal Cortex Hormones/Therapeutic Use.

Effective Medical Treatment of Opiate Addiction. In Section I, see: Opioid-Related Disorders/Therapy.

Effects and Side Effects of Dental Restorative Materials. In Section I, see: Dental Materials/Adverse Effects.

Elder Abuse and Neglect. In Section I, see: Elder Abuse.

Electrical Bone-Growth Stimulation and Spinal Fusion. In Section I, see: Spinal Fusion.

Electroconvulsive Therapy. In Section I, see: Electroconvulsive Therapy.

Electrodiagnostic Techniques. In Section I, see: Electrodiagnosis/Methods.

Electroencephalographic (EEG) Video Monitoring. In Section I, see: Electroencephalography/Methods.

Emergency Cardiac Care. In Section I, see: Emergency Medical Services.

Emergency Contraception. In Section I, see: Contraceptives, Postcoital.

Empiric Parenteral Antibiotic Treatment of Patients with Fibromyalgia and a Positive Serologic Result for Lyme Disease. In Section I, see: Antibiotics/Administration and Dosage.

End-of-Life Decision Making: Understanding the Goals of Care. In Section I, see: Decision Making.

Endometriosis. In Section I, see: Endometriosis.

Endorsement of Institutional Ethics Committees. In Section I, see: Ethics, Institutional.

Endoscope Sinus Surgery, Pediatric. In Section I, see: Paranasal Sinuses/Surgery.

Endoscopic Balloon Dilation of the Prostate. In Section I, see: Balloon Dilation.

Endoscopic Electrocoagulation for Gastrointestinal Hemorrhage. In Section I, see: Electrocoagulation/Methods.

Endoscopic Laser Photocoagulation for Gastrointestinal Hemorrhage. In Section I, see: Lasers/Therapeutic Use.

Endoscopic Release of the Carpal Ligament. In Section I, see: Carpal Tunnel Syndrome/Surgery.

Endoscopic Sclerotherapy for Esophageal Varices. In Section I, see: Esophageal and Gastric Varices/Therapy.

Endoscopic Sinus Surgery, Adult. In Section I, see: Paranasal Sinuses/Surgery.

Endoscopic Therapy of Biliary Tract and Pancreatic Diseases. In Section I, see: Biliary Tract Diseases/Therapy.

Endoscopic Thermal Coagulation for Gastrointestinal Hemorrhage. In Section I, see: Electrocoagulation/Methods.

Endoscopic Topical Therapy for Gastrointestinal Hemorrhage. In Section I, see: Gastrointestinal Hemorrhage/Therapy.

Endoscopy in the Evaluation of Dyspepsia. In Section I, see: Dyspepsia/Etiology.

Exercise Thallium-201 Myocardial Perfusion Scintigraphy in the Diagnosis of Coronary Artery Disease. In Section I, see: Exercise Test.

Expert Consensus Document: Signal-Averaged Electrocardiography. In Section I, see: Electrocardiography/Methods.

External and Implantable Infusion Pumps. In Section I, see: Infusion Pumps, Implantable.

External Cephalic Version. In Section I, see: Version, Fetal.

Extracranial-Intracranial Bypass to Reduce the Risk of Ischemic Stroke. In Section I, see: Cerebral Ischemia/ Prevention and Control.

Eyelid Surgery. In Section I, see: Eyelids/Surgery.

F

Fact Sheet: "Facts About Second Hand Smoke." In Section I, see: Tobacco Smoke Pollution.

Falls and Fall Risk. In Section I, see: Accidental Falls.

Female Breast Hypertrophy/Breast Reduction. In Section I, see: Breast/Pathology.

Female Breast Hypoplasia/Breast Augmentation. In Section I, see: Breast/Abnormalities.

Female Genital Mutilation. In Section I, see: Circumcision, Female.

Female Genital Mutilation. In Section I, see: Circumcision, Female.

Femoral Neck Fracture (Adult). In Section I, see: Femoral Neck Fractures.

Fetal and Neonatal Neurologic Injury. In Section I, see: Cerebral Palsy/Etiology.

Fetal Fibronectin Preterm Labor Risk Test. In Section I, see: Fibronectins/Analysis.

Fetal Heart Rate Patterns: Monitoring, Interpretation, and Management. In Section I, see: Fetal Monitoring.

Fetal Macrosomia. In Section I, see: Fetal Macrosomia.

Fifth ACCP Consensus Conference on Antithrombotic Therapy. In Section I, see: Fibrinolytic Agents/ Therapeutic Use.

Financial Influences on Mode of Delivery. In Section I, see: Delivery/Economics.

Financing Care of Patients with AIDS. In Section I, see: Delivery of Health Care/Economics.

Financing of Long-Term Care Services, Position Statement. In Section I, see: Insurance, Long-Term Care.

Fistula-in-Ano. In Section I, see: Rectal Fissure/ Surgery.

Flexible Endoscopy of the Pediatric Airway. In Section I, see: Bronchoscopy.

Flexible Sigmoidoscopy: Guidelines for Clinical Application. In Section I, see: Sigmoidoscopy.

Fluoridation of Public Water Supplies. In Section I, see: Fluoridation/Standards.

Follow-Up of Non-Small-Cell Lung Carinoma (5 variants). In Section I, see: Carcinoma, Non-Small-Cell Lung.

Fragile X-Syndrome. In Section I, see: Fragile X-Syndrome/Diagnosis.

Framework for Post-Residency Surgical Education and Training. In Section I, see: Education, Medical, Continuing/Standards.

Fresh Frozen Plasma: Indications and Risks. In Section I, see: Blood Transfusion.

Functional Indications for Upper and Lower Eyelid Blepharoplasty Ophthalmic Procedure Assessment. In Section I, see: Blepharoplasty.

Fundamentals of Magnetic Resonance Imaging. In Section I, see: Magnetic Resonance Imaging/Methods.

Fungal Infections in HIV-Infected Persons. In Section I, see: AIDS-Related Opportunistic Infections/ Pathology.

Future Directions for Research on Disease of the Lung. In Section I, see: Pulmonary Disease (Specialty)/Trends.

Future of Ultrasonography. In Section I, see: Ultrasonography/Trends.

Future Research in Tuberculosis: Prospects and Priorities for Elimination. In Section I, see: Primary Prevention/Methods.

G

Gallstones and Laparoscopic Cholecystectomy. In Section I, see: Cholecystectomy, Laparoscopic.

Gamete Intrafallopian Transfer (GIFT). In Section I, see: Gamete Intrafallopian Transfer.

Garren Gastric Bubble for Morbid Obesity. In Section I, see: Obesity, Morbid/Therapy.

Gastric Cancer Surgical Practice Guidelines. In Section I, see: Stomach Neoplasms/Surgery.

Gastric Restrictive Surgery. In Section I, see: Gastric Bypass.

Gastrointestinal Surgery for Severe Obesity. In Section I, see: Stomach/Surgery.

Gaucher Disease: Current Issues in Diagnosis and Treatment. In Section I, see: Gaucher's Disease/Diagnosis.

General Considerations in Psychiatric Treatment. In Section I, see: Mental Disorders/Drug Therapy.

General Principles for Evaluation of New Interventional Technologies and Devices. In Section I, see: Radiology, Interventional/Instrumentation.

General Recommendations on Immunization. In Section I, see: Immunization/Standards.

Generic Substitution for Antiepileptic Medication. In Section I, see: Anticonvulsants/Standards.

Genetic Evaluation of Stillbirths and Neonatal Deaths. In Section I, see: Fetal Death/Genetics.

Genetic Screening for Hemoglobinopathies. In Section I, see: Hemoglobinopathies/Genetics.

Genetic Screening of Gamete Donors. In Section I, see: Genetic Screening/Standards.

Genetic Technologies. In Section I, see: Genetic Techniques.

Genetic Testing Alert. In Section I, see: Genetic Screening.

Genetic Testing for Cystic Fibrosis. In Section I, see: Cystic Fibrosis/Genetics.

Genital Human Papillomavirus Infections. In Section I, see: Genital Diseases/Female.

Geriatric Assessment Methods for Clinical Decision-Making. In Section I, see: Decision Making.

Geriatric Rehabilitation, Position Statement. In Section I, see: Rehabilitation.

Global Statement on Deep Venous Thrombosis Prophylaxis during Laparoscopic Surgery. In Section I, see: Thrombophlebitis.

Glycosylated Hemoglobin Assays in the Management and Diagnosis of Diabetes Mellitus. In Section I, see: Diabetes Mellitus/Blood.

Gonorrhea in Prepubertal Children. In Section I, see: Gonorrhea.

Granting of Privileges for Gastrointestinal Endoscopy by Surgeons. In Section I, see: Credentialing.

Granting of Ultrasonography Privileges for Surgeons. In Section I, see: Credentialing.

Growth Hormone for Short Stature. In Section I, see: Body Height.

Guidance for Effective Discipline. In Section I, see: Child Behavior.

Guide for Adult Immunization, 2nd Edition. In Section I, see: Immunization.

Guide to Anticoagulant Therapy. In Section I, see: Heparin/Therapeutic Use.

Guideline for Clinical Use of Cardiac Radionuclide Imaging. In Section I, see: Coronary Disease/Radionuclide Imaging.

Guideline for Management of Ingested Foreign Bodies. In Section I, see: Endoscopy, Gastrointestinal.

Guideline Implementation. In Section I, see: Practice Guidelines.

Guidelines and Indications for Coronary Artery Bypass Graft Surgery. In Section I, see: Coronary Artery Bypass/Methods.

Guidelines and Levels of Care for Pediatric Intensive Care Units. In Section I, see: Intensive Care Units, Pediatric.

Guidelines as to What Constitutes an Adverse Respiratory Health Effect, with Special Reference to Epidemiologic Studies of Air Pollution. In Section I, see: Air Pollution/Adverse Effects.

Guidelines for Adolescent Preventive Services. In Section I, see: Adolescent Health Services/Organization and Administration.

Guidelines for Advanced Training for Physicians in Critical Care. In Section I, see: Clinical Competence/Standards.

Guidelines for Carotid Endarterectomy. In Section I, see: Carotid Artery Diseases/Surgery.

Guidelines for Clinical Assessment and Management of Alcoholism in the Elderly. In Section I, see: Alcoholism/Therapy.

Guidelines for Clinical Intracardiac Electrophysiologic and Catheter Ablation Procedures. In Section I, see: Catheter Ablation.

Guidelines for Collaborative Practice in Endoscopic/Thoracoscopic Spinal Surgery for the General Surgeon. In Section I, see: Physician's Practice Patterns.

Guidelines for Counseling Postmenopausal Women about Preventive Hormone Therapy. In Section I, see: Estrogen Replacement Therapy.

Guidelines for Death Scene Investigation of Sudden, Unexplained Infant Deaths. In Section I, see: Sudden Infant Death.

Guidelines for Developing Admission and Discharge Policies for the Pediatric ICU. In Section I, see: Intensive Care Units, Pediatric.

Guidelines for Diagnosis and Management of Disorders Involving the Temporomandibular Joint and Related Musculoskeletal Structures (Revision). In Section I, see: Temporomandibular Joint Disorders/Diagnosis.

Guidelines for Diagnostic Imaging During Pregnancy. In Section I, see: Diagnostic Imaging.

Guidelines for Diagnostic Laparoscopy. In Section I, see: Laparoscopy.

Guidelines for Electrocardiography. In Section I, see: Cardiovascular Diseases/Diagnosis.

Guidelines for Employee Health Services in Health Care Institutions. In Section I, see: Occupational Health Services.

Guidelines for Establishing a Quality Assurance Program in Vascular and Interventional Radiology. In Section I, see: Radiography, Interventional.

Guidelines for Establishment of Gastrointestinal Endoscopy Areas. In Section I, see: Endoscopy.

Guidelines for Ethical Behavior Relating to Clinical Practice Issues in Electrodiagnostic Medicine. In Section I, see: Electrodiagnosis/Standards.

Guidelines for Evaluation and Management of Common Congenital Cardiac Problems in Infants, Children, and Adolescents. In Section I, see: Heart Defects, Congenital/Diagnosis.

Guidelines for Exercise Testing. In Section I, see: Cardiology/Standards.

Guidelines for Eye Care in Patients with Diabetes Mellitus. In Section I, see: Diabetes Mellitus/Complications.

Guidelines for Fellowship Training Programs in Geriatric Medicine. In Section I, see: Geriatrics.

Guidelines for Gamete Donation. In Section I, see: Oocyte Donation.

Guidelines for Granting of Privileges for Laparoscopic and Thoracoscopic General Surgery. In Section I, see: Credentialing.

Guidelines for Granting Privileges for the Performance of Procedures in Critically Ill Patients. In Section I, see: Critical Care.

Guidelines for Guideline Development. In Section I, see: Nuclear Medicine.

Guidelines for Human Embryology and Human Andrology Laboratories. In Section I, see: Embryology.

Guidelines for ICU Admission, Discharge, and Triage. In Section I, see: Intensive Care Units.

Guidelines for Implantation of Cardiac Pacemakers and Antiarrhythmia Devices. In Section I, see: Arrhythmia/Therapy.

Guidelines for Implementing Collaborative Practice. In Section I, see: Patient Care Team.

Guidelines for Intensive Care Unit Design. In Section I, see: Hospital Design and Construction.

Guidelines for Laparoscopic Surgery During Pregnancy. In Section I, see: Pregnancy Complications/Surgery.

Guidelines for Liposuction Surgery. In Section I, see: Lipectomy/Standards.

Guidelines for Long-Term Management of Patients with Kawasaki Disease. In Section I, see: Cardiology.

Guidelines for Minimal Standards in Cardiac Surgery. In Section I, see: Heart Diseases/Surgery.

Guidelines for Monitoring Drug Therapy in Rheumatoid Arthritis. In Section I, see: Arthritis, Rheumatoid/Drug Therapy.

Guidelines for Office Endoscopic Services. In Section I, see: Ambulatory Care/Standards.

Guidelines for Outcome Studies in Electrodiagnostic Medicine. In Section I, see: Electrodiagnosis.

Guidelines for Percutaneous Transluminal Angioplasty. In Section I, see: Angioplasty, Transluminal, Percutaneous, Coronary.

Guidelines for Percutaneous Transluminal Coronary Angioplasty. In Section I, see: Coronary Disease/Therapy.

Guidelines for Percutaneous Transthoracic Needle Biopsy. In Section I, see: Biopsy, Needle/Methods.

Guidelines for Perinatal Care. In Section I, see: Perinatal Care.

Guidelines for Peripheral Percutaneous Transluminal Angioplasty of the Abdominal Aorta and Lower Extremity Vessels. In Section I, see: Angioplasty, Balloon.

Guidelines for Preventing Transmission of Human Immunodeficiency Virus Through Transplantation of Human Tissue and Organs. In Section I, see: HIV Infections/Prevention and Control.

Guidelines for Prevention of Nosocomial Pneumonia. In Section I, see: Cross Infection/Prevention and Control.

Guidelines for Prevention of Transmission of Human Immunodeficiency Virus and Hepatitis B Virus to Health-Care and Public-Safety Workers. In Section I, see: Acquired Immunodeficiency Syndrome/ Transmission.

Guidelines for Prevention of Transmissions of HIV Type I in Neurologic Practice. In Section I, see: Acquired Immunodeficiency Syndrome/ Complications.

Guidelines for Prophylaxis Against Pneumocystis carinii Pneumonia for Persons Infected with Human Immunodeficiency Virus. In Section I, see: Acquired Immunodeficiency Syndrome/Complications.

Guidelines for Relationships with Industry. In Section I, see: Physicians.

Guidelines for Resident Training in Critical Care Medicine. In Section I, see: Critical Care.

Guidelines for Restraint Use. In Section I, see: Restraint, Physical.

Guidelines for Risk Stratification after Myocardial Infarction. In Section I, see: Hospitalization.

Guidelines for Safe Movement. In Section I, see: Movement.

Guidelines for Somatosensory Evoked Potentials. In Section I, see: Evoked Potentials, Somatosensory/ Physiology.

Guidelines for Standards of Care for Patients with Acute Repiratory Failure on Mechanical Ventilatory Support. In Section I, see: Respiration, Artificial/ Standards.

Guidelines for Surgical Treatment of Gastroesophageal Reflux Disease (GERD). In Section I, see: Gastroesophageal Reflux/Surgery.

Guidelines for the Approach to the Patient with Severe Hereditary Alpha-1-Antitrypsin Deficiency. In Section I, see: Alpha 1-Antitrypsin/Deficiency.

Guidelines for the Appropriate Use of Do-Not-Resuscitate Orders. In Section I, see: Resuscitation Orders.

Guidelines for the Clinical Application of Echocardiography. In Section I, see: Echocardiography.

Guidelines for the Clinical Application of Laparoscopic Biliary Tract Surgery. In Section I, see: Biliary Tract Surgical Procedures.

Guidelines for the Definition of an Intensivist and the Practice of Critical Care Medicine. In Section I, see: Critical Care/Standards.

Guidelines for the Development and Use of Transluminally Placed Endovascular Prosthetic Grafts in the Arterial System. In Section I, see: Blood Vessel Prosthesis.

Guidelines for the Diagnosis and Management of Asthma. In Section I, see: Asthma/Diagnosis.

Guidelines for the Diagnosis and Management of Clostridium-Difficile-Associated Diarrhea and Colitis. In Section I, see: Clostridium Difficile Diarrhea/ Microbiology.

Guidelines for the Diagnosis and Treatment of Nicotine Dependence. In Section I, see: Nicotine.

Guidelines for the Diagnosis of Rheumatic Fever: Jones Criteria, Updated 1992. In Section I, see: Rheumatic Fever/Diagnosis.

Guidelines for the Early Management of Patients with Acute Myocardial Infarction. In Section I, see: Myocardial Infarction/Therapy.

Guidelines for the Evaluation and Management of Heart Failure. In Section I, see: Heart Failure, Congestive/Diagnosis.

Guidelines for the Evaluation of Impairment/ Disability in Patients with Asthma. In Section I, see: Asthma/Diagnosis.

Guidelines for the Initial Evaluation of the Adult Patient with Acute Musculoskeletal Symptoms. In Section I, see: Musculoskeletal Diseases/Diagnosis.

Guidelines for the Initial Management of Adults with Community-Acquired Pneumonia: Diagnosis, Assessment of Severity, and Initial Antimicrobial Therapy. In Section I, see: Pneumonia/Diagnosis.

Guidelines for the Management of Aneurysmal Subarachnoid Hemorrhage. In Section I, see: Aneurysm, Ruptured/Therapy.

Guidelines for the Management of Helicobacter Pylori Infection. In Section I, see: Helicobacter Infections/ Therapy.

Guidelines for the Management of Malnutrition and Cachexia, Chronic Diarrhea, and Hepatobiliary Disease in Patients with HIV Infection. In Section I, see: Cachexia/Therapy.

Guidelines for the Management of Patients with Acute Ischemic Stroke. In Section I, see: Cerebral Ischemia/Therapy.

Guidelines for the Management of Rheumatoid Arthritis. In Section I, see: Arthritis, Rheumatoid/Therapy.

Guidelines for the Management of Transient Ischemic Attacks. In Section I, see: Cerebral Ischemia, Transient/Therapy.

Guidelines for the Medical Management of Osteoarthritis Part I: Osteoarthritis of Hip. In Section I, see: Osteoarthritis, Hip/Therapy.

Guidelines for the Medical Management of Osteoarthritis Part II: Osteoarthritis of the Knee. In Section I, see: Knee Joint.

Guidelines for the Medical Management of the Home Care Patient. In Section I, see: Home Care Services.

Guidelines for the Pediatric Perioperative Anesthesia Environment. In Section I, see: Anesthesia.

Guidelines for the Prevention and Control of Congenital Syphilis. In Section I, see: Syphilis, Congenital/Prevention and Control.

Guidelines for the Prevention of Antimicrobial Resistance in Hospitals (SHEA/ISDA Joint Statement). In Section I, see: Drug Resistance, Microbial.

Guidelines for the Surgical Practice of Telemedicine. In Section I, see: Telemedicine.

Guidelines for the Transfer of Critically Ill Patients. In Section I, see: Critical Care/Standards.

Guidelines for the Use of Antimicrobial Agents in Neutropenic Patients with Unexplained Fever. In Section I, see: Agranulocytosis/Complications.

Guidelines for the Use of Antiretroviral Agents in Pediatric HIV Infection. In Section I, see: Anti-HIV Agents/Therapeutic Use.

Guidelines for the Use of Assistive Technology: Evaluation, Referral, Prescription. In Section I, see: Self-Help Devices.

Guidelines for the Use of Enteral Nutrition. In Section I, see: Enteral Nutrition.

Guidelines for the Use of Restraints in Long Term Care Facilities. In Section I, see: Restraint, Physical.

Guidelines for the Use of Systemic Glucocorticosteroids in the Management of Selected Infections. In Section I, see: Glucocorticoids/Therapeutic Use.

Guidelines for Thoracentesis and Needle Biopsy of the Pleura. In Section I, see: Biopsy, Needle/Methods.

Guidelines for Training in Diagnostic and Therapeutic Endoscopic Retrograde Cholangiopancreatography (ERCP). In Section I, see: Cholangiopancreatography, Endosopic, Retrograde.

Guidelines for Training in Gallstone Lithotripsy. In Section I, see: Education, Medical, Continuing/Standards.

Guidelines for Women's Health Care. In Section I, see: Women's Health.

Guidelines in Electrodiagnostic Medicine. In Section I, see: Electrodiagnosis.

Guidelines of Care for Acne Vulgaris (including Guidelines for Prescribing Isotretinoin in the Tx of Female Acne Patients of Childbearing Potential). In Section I, see: Acne Vulgaris/Therapy.

Guidelines of Care for Alopecia Areata. In Section I, see: Alopecia Areata.

Guidelines of Care for Atopic Dermatitis. In Section I, see: Dermatitis, Atopic/Therapy.

Guidelines of Care for Basal Cell Carcinoma. In Section I, see: Carcinoma, Basal Cell/Therapy.

Guidelines of Care for Chemical Peeling. In Section I, see: Chemexfoliation.

Guidelines of Care for Cutaneous Squamous Cell Carcinoma. In Section I, see: Carcinoma, Squamous Cell/Therapy.

Guidelines of Care for Local and Regional Anesthesia in Cutaneous Surgery. In Section I, see: Anesthesia, Conduction.

Guidelines of Care for Malignant Melanoma. In Section I, see: Melanoma/Therapy.

Guidelines of Care for Mohs Micrographic Surgery. In Section I, see: Skin Neoplasms/Surgery.

Guidelines of Care for Nevi I (Nevocellular Nevi and Seborrheic Keratoses). In Section I, see: Keratosis/Diagnosis.

Guidelines of Care for Office Surgical Facilities, Part I. In Section I, see: Ambulatory Surgical Procedures/Standards.

Guidelines of Care for Office Surgical Facilities, Part II. In Section I, see: Ambulatory Care Facilities/Classification.

Guidelines of Care for Psoriasis. In Section I, see: Psoriasis/Therapy.

Guidelines on Acute Infectious Diarrhea in Adults. In Section I, see: Communicable Diseases/Diagnosis.

Guidelines on Admission and Discharge for Adult Intermediate Care Units. In Section I, see: Hospital Units.

Guidelines on Critical Care Services and Personnel: Recommendations Based on a System of Categorization into Two Levels of Care. In Section I, see: Intensive Care Units/Manpower.

Guidelines to Minimize the Risk from Systemic Reactions Caused by Immunotherapy with Allergenic Extracts. In Section I, see: Desensitization, Immunologic/Adverse Effects.

Guidelines to Prevent Simian Immunodeficiency Virus Infection in Laboratory Workers and Animal Handlers. In Section I, see: SIV.

Guides to the Evaluation of Permanent Impairment. In Section I, see: Disability Evaluation.

Gynecologic Ultrasonography. In Section I, see: Genital Diseases, Female/Ultrasonography.

Gynecomastia. In Section I, see: Gynecomastia.

H

Haemophilus b Conjugate Vaccines for Prevention of Haemophilus Influenza Type b Disease Among Infants and Children Two Months of Age and Older: Recommendations of the Immunization Practices Advisory Committee. In Section I, see: Haemophilus Infections/Prevention and Control.

Hallux Valgus. In Section I, see: Hallux Valgus.

Hantavirus Infection—Southwestern United States: Interim Recommendations for Risk Reduction. In Section I, see: Bunyaviridae Infections/Prevention and Control.

Health Effects of Tremolite. In Section I, see: Pneumoconiosis/Etiology.

Health Implications of Obesity. In Section I, see: Obesity/Complications.

Health Maintenance for Perimenopausal Women. In Section I, see: Premenopause.

Heart Failure. In Section I, see: Heart Failure, Congestive/Mortality.

Heart Failure: Evaluation and Care of Patients with Left-Ventricular Systolic Dysfunction. In Section I, see: Heart Failure, Congestive/Therapy.

Helicobacter pylori. In Section I, see: Helicobacter Infections.

Helmets and Preventing Motorcycle and Bicycle-Related Injuries. In Section I, see: Head Protective Devices/Standards.

Hemangiomas of Infancy. In Section I, see: Hemangioma/Etiology.

Hematopoietic Stem-Cell Transplantation in Multiple Myeloma. In Section I, see: Hematopoietic Stem-Cell Transplantation.

Hemorrhagic Shock. In Section I, see: Shock, Hemorrhagic/Therapy.

Hepatitis B Immunization for Adolescents. In Section I, see: Hepatitis B Vaccines.

Hepatitis B Vaccine. In Section I, see: Hepatitis B/Prevention and Control.

Hepatitis B Virus: A Comprehensive Strategy for Eliminating Transmission in the United States Through Universal Childhood Vaccination. In Section I, see: Hepatitis B/Immunology.

Hepatitis C Virus Infection. In Section I, see: Hepatitis C.

Hepatitis Guidelines. In Section I, see: Hepatitis.

Hepatitis Virus Infections in Obstetrician-Gynecologists. In Section I, see: Disease Transmission.

Herniated Lumbar Disk. In Section I, see: Intervertebral Disk Displacement.

HIV Blood Test Counseling: AMA Physician Guidelines, 2nd Edition. In Section I, see: HIV Infections/Diagnosis.

HIV Prevention Through Early Detection and Treatment of Other Sexually Transmitted Disease—United States. In Section I, see: HIV Infections/Prevention and Control.

Home Care and Home Care Reimbursement, Position Statement. In Section I, see: Home Care Services.

Home Mechanical Ventilation of Pediatric Patients. In Section I, see: Home Care Services.

Home Uterine Activity Monitoring. In Section I, see: Uterine Monitoring.

Home Uterine Monitoring. In Section I, see: Uterine Monitoring.

Hormonal Contraception. In Section I, see: Contraceptives, Oral, Hormonal/Adverse Effects.

Hormone Replacement Therapy. In Section I, see: Hormone Replacement Therapy.

Hormone Therapy to Prevent Disease and Prolong Life in Postmenopausal Women. In Section I, see: Estrogen Replacement Therapy.

Hospital Credentialing Standards for Physicians who Perform Endoscopies. In Section I, see: Credentialing/Standards.

Hospital Discharge of the High-Risk Neonate. In Section I, see: Infant, Premature, Diseases/Nursing.

Hospital Pharmacists and Infectious Disease Specialists. In Section I, see: Communicable Diseases.

Hospital Stay for Healthy Term Newborns. In Section I, see: Infant, Newborn.

How to Select and Interpret Molecular Strain Typing Methods for Epi Studies of Bacterial Infections: A Review for Healthcare Epidemiologists. In Section I, see: Bacterial Typing Techniques.

How to Study the Gallbladder. In Section I, see: Cholecystitis/Diagnosis.

Human Blood Pressure Determination by Sphygmomanometry. In Section I, see: Blood Pressure Determination/Methods.

Human Immunodeficiency Virus Infection: Physician's Responsibilities. In Section I, see: HIV Infections/Therapy.

Human Papillomavirus DNA Testing in the Management of Cervical Neoplasia. In Section I, see: Cervix Neoplasms/Microbiology.

Human Rabies Prevention—United States, 1999 Recommendations of the Advisory Committee on Immunization Practices (ACIP). In Section I, see: Rabies Vaccine.

Hyperandrogenic Anovulation. In Section I, see: Anovulation/Etiology.

Hypertension in Pregnancy. In Section I, see: Pregnancy Complications, Cardiovascular/Therapy.

Hyperthermia Alone or Combined with Chemotherapy for the Treatment of Cancer. In Section I, see: Hyperthermia, Induced/Standards.

Hyperthermia as Adjuvant Treatment for Recurrent Breast Cancer and Primary Malignant Glioma. In Section I, see: Breast Neoplasms/Therapy.

Hyperventilation. In Section I, see: Head Injuries.

Hypophysectomy, Transsphenoidal or Transnasal, for Hypophysectomy or Excision of Pituitary Tumor. In Section I, see: Pituitary Neoplasms/Surgery.

Hypothermia Prevention. In Section I, see: Hypothermia/Prevention and Control.

Hysterectomy. In Section I, see: Hysterectomy.

Hysteroscopy. In Section I, see: Hysteroscopy.

I

Idiopathic Environmental Intolerances. In Section I, see: Multiple Chemical Sensitivity/Etiology.

Idiopathic Thrombocytopenic Purpura. In Section I, see: Autoimmune Diseases/Therapy.

Image-Guided Breast Biopsy. In Section I, see: Biopsy, Needle/Methods.

Immunization During Pregnancy. In Section I, see: Pregnancy.

Immunization of Adolescents. In Section I, see: Vaccination.

Immunization of Children Infected with Human Immunodeficiency Virus-Supplement. In Section I, see: Acquired Immunodeficiency Syndrome/Immunology.

Immunization of Health-Care Workers. In Section I, see: Health Personnel/Standards.

Immuno-Augmentative Therapy for Cancer. In Section I, see: Immunotherapy/Methods.

Immunochemiluminometric Assays (ICMA) of Thyroid-Stimulating Hormone (TSH) for the Diagnosis of Thyroid Disorders and for Monitoring Response to Therapy. In Section I, see: Chemiluminescence.

Implantable and External Infusion Pumps for the Treatment of Thromboembolic Disease in Outpatients. In Section I, see: Infusions, Parenteral/Instrumentation.

Implantation of the Automatic Cardioverter-Defibrillator—Non-Inducibility of Ventricular Tachyarrhythmia as a Patient Selection Criteria. In Section I, see: Defibrillators, Implantable.

Implementation of Geriatric Medicine Fellowship Guidelines: Suggestions for Program Directors. In Section I, see: Education, Medical, Graduate.

Impotence. In Section I, see: Impotence.

Improving Clinical and Consumer Use of Blood Pressure Measuring Devices. In Section I, see: Blood Pressure Determination/Instrumentation.

Improving Medical Education in Therapeutics. In Section I, see: Therapeutics.

Improving Patient Records. In Section I, see: Medical Records.

Inactivated Japanese Encephalitis Virus Vaccine. In Section I, see: Encephalitis, Japanese/Prevention and Control.

Inappropriate Use of the Terms Fetal Distress and Birth Asphyxia. In Section I, see: Asphyxia Neonatorum/Classification.

Incidental Appendectomy. In Section I, see: Appendectomy.

Indications and Standards for Cardiopulmonary Sleep Studies. In Section I, see: Heart/Physiology.

Indications and Standards for the Use of Nasal Continuous Positive Airway Pressure (CPAP) in Sleep Apnea Syndromes. In Section I, see: Positive Pressure Respiration/Standards.

Indications for Arterial Blood Gas Analysis. In Section I, see: Blood Gas Analysis.

Indications for Holter Monitoring. In Section I, see: Electrocardiography, Ambulatory.

Indications for Intracranial Pressure Monitoring. In Section I, see: Intracranial Pressure.

Indications for Red Blood Transfusion. In Section I, see: Anemia/Therapy.

Indications for the Use of Permanently Implanted Cardiac Pacemakers. In Section I, see: Pacemaker, Artificial.

Indocyanine Green Angiography Ophthalmic Procedure Assessment. In Section I, see: Indocyanine Green.

Induction of Labor. In Section I, see: Labor, Induced.

Induction of Ovulation with Clomiphene Citrate. In Section I, see: Clomiphene/Therapeutic Use.

Induction of Ovulation with Human Menopausal Gonadotropins. In Section I, see: Ovulation Induction/Methods.

Infantile Apnea and Home Monitoring. In Section I, see: Apnea/Prevention and Control.

Infection Control During Gastrointestinal Endoscopy: Guidelines for Clinical Application. In Section I, see: Cross-Infection/Prevention and Control.

Infection Prevention and Control in the Long-Term-Care Facility. In Section I, see: Infection Control/Standards.

Infectious Disease Testing for Blood Transfusions. In Section I, see: Blood Transfusion.

Inferior Turbinectomy. In Section I, see: Turbinates/Surgery.

Infertility. In Section I, see: Infertility.

Informed Consent for Gastrointestinal Endoscopy. In Section I, see: Informed Consent.

Informed Consent for Research on Human Subjects with Dementia. In Section I, see: Informed Consent.

Informed Refusal. In Section I, see: Treatment Refusal.

Informing Families of a Patient's Death: Guidelines for the Involvement of Medical Students. In Section I, see: Death.

Inhaled Beta-Adrenergic Agonists in Asthma. In Section I, see: Asthma/Drug Therapy.

Inhaled Corticosteroids and Severe Viral Infections. In Section I, see: Virus Diseases/Etiology.

Initial Therapy for Tuberculosis in the Era of Multidrug Resistance. In Section I, see: Antitubercular Agents/Therapeutic Use.

Injury-Control Recommendations: Bicycle Helmets. In Section I, see: Bicycling.

Institutional and Patient Criteria for Heart-Lung Transplantation. In Section I, see: Heart-Lung Transplantation.

Institutional Infection Control Measures for Tuberculosis in the Era of Multiple Drug Resistance. In Section I, see: Infection Control.

Institutional Responsibility to Provide Legal Representation. In Section I, see: Ethics Committees/Legislation and Jurisprudence.

Instrumentation and Practice Standards of Electrocardiographic Monitoring in Special Care Units. In Section I, see: Electrocardiography/Instrumentation.

Instrumentation in Positron Emission Tomography. In Section I, see: Tomography, Emission Computed/Instrumentation.

Insurability and Employability of the Patient with Ischemic Heart Disease. In Section I, see: Coronary Disease/Economics.

Insurability of the Adolescent and Young Adult with Heart Disease. In Section I, see: Heart Defects, Congenital/Economics.

Integrated Approach to the Management of Pain. In Section I, see: Pain/Therapy.

Intensive Diabetes Management, 2nd Edition. In Section I, see: Diabetes Mellitus/Drug Therapy.

Interim Assessment: Carotid Endarterectomy. In Section I, see: Carotid Arteries/Surgery.

Interim Report of the Quality Indicator Study Group. In Section I, see: Quality Assurance, Health Care/Standards.

Intermittent Positive Pressure Breathing (IPPB) Therapy. In Section I, see: Intermittent Positive-Pressure Ventilation/Standards.

Intermittent Positive Pressure Breathing: Old Technologies Rarely Die. In Section I, see: Intermittent Positive Pressure Ventilation/Methods.

Interventions to Prevent HIV Risk Behaviors. In Section I, see: HIV Infections/Epidemiology.

Intracavernous Pharmacotherapy for Impotence: Papaverine and Phentolamine. In Section I, see: Impotence/Drug Therapy.

Intracranial Pressure Monitoring Technology. In Section I, see: Intracranial Pressure Monitoring, Physiology/Standards.

Intracranial Pressure Treatment Threshold. In Section I, see: Head Injuries/Therapy.

Intrapartum Electronic Fetal Monitoring. In Section I, see: Fetal Monitoring.

Intrauterine Device. In Section I, see: Intrauterine Devices.

Intrauterine Insemination. In Section I, see: Insemination, Artificial/Methods.

Intravenous Immunoglobulin. In Section I, see: Immunization, Passive.

Introduction to the Management of Immunosuppression. In Section I, see: Immunosuppression/Methods.

Invasive Hemodynamic Monitoring in Obstetrics and Gynecology. In Section I, see: Hemodynamics/Physiology.

Irritable Bowel Syndrome. In Section I, see: Colonic Diseases, Functional/Diagnosis.

Isolated Pancreas Transplantation. In Section I, see: Pancreas Transplantation.

J

Job Descriptions for Electrodiagnostic Technologists. In Section I, see: Electrodiagnosis.

L

Laboratory Diagnosis of Mycotic Infections and Specific Fungal Infections. In Section I, see: Fungi/Isolation and Purification.

Laboratory Management of Agents Associated with Hantavirus Pulmonary Syndrome: Interim Biosafety Guidelines. In Section I, see: Bunyaviridae Infections/Prevention and Control.

Laboratory Tests in End-Stage Renal Disease Patients Undergoing Dialysis. In Section I, see: Hemodialysis.

Laminectomy and Microlaminectomy for Lumbar Disc Herniation. In Section I, see: Laminectomy/Methods.

Laparoscopic Cholecystectomy. In Section I, see: Cholecystectomy/Methods.

Laparoscopic Herniorrhaphy. In Section I, see: Hernia, Inguinal/Surgery.

Laparoscopic Nissen Fundoplication. In Section I, see: Fundoplication/Methods.

Laparoscopically Assisted Vaginal Hysterectomy. In Section I, see: Hysterectomy, Vaginal.

Laryngeal Cancer Surgical Practice Guidelines. In Section I, see: Laryngeal Neoplasms/Surgery.

Laryngectomy. In Section I, see: Laryngectomy.

Laryngoscopy/Nasopharyngoscopy. In Section I, see: Laryngeal Diseases/Diagnosis.

Laser Ablation of the Endometrium. In Section I, see: Endometrium/Surgery.

Laser Blepharoplasty and Skin Resurfacing Ophthalmic Procedure Assessment. In Section I, see: Blepharoplasty.

Laser Peripheral Iridotomy for Pupillary-Block Glaucoma Ophthalmic Procedure Assessment. In Section I, see: Glaucoma, Angle-Closure/Surgery.

Laser Trabeculoplasty for Primary Open-Angle Glaucoma Ophthalmic Procedure Assessment. In Section I, see: Trabeculectomy/Methods.

Lateral Epicondylitis of the Elbow. In Section I, see: Tennis Elbow.

LE Cell Test. In Section I, see: Laboratory Techniques and Procedures/Methods.

LeFort Fractures. In Section I, see: Maxillofacial Injuries.

Length of Stay for Gynecologic Procedures. In Section I, see: Gynecologic Surgical Procedures/Standards.

Levels of Laboratory Services for Mycobacterial Disease. In Section I, see: Mycobacterium Infections/ Diagnosis.

Licensure of Respiratory Therapy Technical Personnel. In Section I, see: Respiratory Therapy.

Limitations of Abstinence-Only Sexuality Education. In Section I, see: Sexual Abstinence.

Liposuction. In Section I, see: Lipectomy.

List of Available Gastroenterology Training Programs. In Section I, see: Education, Medical, Graduate.

Lithotripsy. In Section I, see: Urinary Calculi/Therapy.

Liver Disease in the Pregnant Patient. In Section I, see: Liver Diseases.

Local Regional Recurrence and Salvage Surgery (10 variants). In Section I, see: Neoplasm Recurrence, Local.

Localized Adiposity. In Section I, see: Obesity.

Locally Advanced (high risk) Prostate Cancer (6 variants). In Section I, see: Prostatic Neoplasms.

Locally Advanced Breast Cancer (5 variants). In Section I, see: Breast Neoplasms.

Locally Unresectable Rectal Cancer (7 variants). In Section I, see: Rectal Neoplasms.

Long-term Treatment of the Child with Simple Febrile Seizures. In Section I, see: Fever/Drug Therapy.

"Look Back" Notifications for HIV/HBV-Positive Healthcare Workers. In Section I, see: Infection Control/Methods.

Low Back Musculoligamentous Injury (Sprain/Strain). In Section I, see: Lumbar Vertebrae/Injury.

Low-Energy Biphasic Waveform Defibrillation. In Section I, see: Electric Countershock.

Lower Urinary Tract Operative Injuries. In Section I, see: Intraoperative Complications/Prevention and Control.

Lowering Blood Cholesterol to Prevent Heart Disease. In Section I, see: Cholesterol/Blood.

Lumbar Spinal Stenosis. In Section I, see: Spinal Stenosis.

Lumbar Spine Surgery. In Section I, see: Lumbar Vertebrae/Surgery.

Lung Cancer Surgical Practice Guidelines. In Section I, see: Lung Neoplasms/Surgery.

Lung Function Testing: Selection of References Values and Interpretive Strategies. In Section I, see: Respiratory Function Tests/Standards.

Lung Transplantation. In Section I, see: Lung Transplantation.

Lung-Volume Reduction Surgery for End-Stage Chronic Obstructive Pulmonary Disease. In Section I, see: Lung Diseases, Obstructive/Surgery.

M

Magnetic Resonance Imaging of Brain and Spine. In Section I, see: Magnetic Resonance Imaging.

Magnetic Resonance Imaging of the Abdomen and Pelvis. In Section I, see: Pelvic Neoplasms/Diagnosis.

Magnetic Resonance Imaging of the Cardiovascular System. In Section I, see: Cardiovascular Diseases/ Diagnosis.

Magnetic Resonance Imaging of the Central Nervous System. In Section I, see: Central Nervous System Diseases/Diagnosis.

Magnetic Resonance Imaging of the Head and Neck Region. In Section I, see: Magnetic Resonance Imaging/Methods.

Magnetic Resonance Imaging: Prologue. In Section I, see: Magnetic Resonance Imaging.

Making Treatment Decisions for Incapacitated Elderly Patients without Advance Directives, Position Statement. In Section I, see: Decision Making.

Male Infertility. In Section I, see: Infertility, Male.

Mammographic Screening for Breast Cancer. In Section I, see: Mammography.

Mammography Screening in Asymptomatic Women Forty Years and Older. In Section I, see: Breast Neoplasms/Prevention and Control.

Management of Acute Gastroenteritis in Young Children. In Section I, see: Gastroenteritis/Therapy.

Management of Breech Presentation. In Section I, see: Breech Presentation.

Management of Cancer Pain. In Section I, see: Pain, Intractable/Drug Therapy.

Management of Diabetes Mellitus. In Section I, see: Diabetes Mellitus/Drug Therapy.

Management of Gallstones. In Section I, see: Cholelithiasis/Therapy.

Management of Gestational Trophoblastic Neoplasia. In Section I, see: Trophoblastic Neoplasms/Therapy.

Management of Hepatitis C. In Section I, see: Hepatitis C/Therapy.

Management of Hyperbilirubinemia in the Healthy Term Newborn. In Section I, see: Jaundice, Neonatal/Therapy.

Management of Hypertension after Ambulatory Blood Pressure Monitoring. In Section I, see: Hypertension/Prevention and Control.

Management of Isoimmunization in Pregnancy. In Section I, see: Pregnancy/Immunology.

Management of Localized Prostate Cancer. In Section I, see: Prostatic Neoplasms.

Management of Menopause. In Section I, see: Menopause.

Management of Migraine Headache. In Section I, see: Migraine/Drug Therapy.

Management of Oropharyngeal Dysphagia. In Section I, see: Deglutition Disorders.

Management of Patients with Dysphagia Caused by Benign Disorders of the Distal Esophagus. In Section I, see: Deglutition Disorders/Etiology.

Management of Patients with Suspected Viral Hemorrhagic Fever. In Section I, see: Hemorrhagic Fevers, Viral/Diagnosis.

Management of Polyps of the Colon. In Section I, see: Colonic Polyps/Diagnosis, Therapy.

Management of Possible Sexual, Injecting-Drug-Use, or Other Nonoccupational Exposure to HIV, Including Considerations Related to Antiretroviral Therapy Public Health Service Statement. In Section I, see: Anti-HIV Agents/Therapeutic Use.

Management of Posterior Vitreous Detachment, Retinal Breaks, and Lattica Degeneration Preferred Practice Pattern. In Section I, see: Vitreous Detachment.

Management of Postterm Pregnancy. In Section I, see: Pregnancy Complications/Therapy.

Management of Primary Vesicoureteral Reflux in Children. In Section I, see: Vesicoureteral Reflux/Therapy.

Management of Resectable Rectal Cancer (6 variants). In Section I, see: Rectal Neoplasms/Surgery.

Management of Staghorn Calculi: Summary Report, Report, Patient Guide. In Section I, see: Kidney Calculi/Therapy.

Management of Temporomandibular Disorders. In Section I, see: Temporomandibular Joint Disorders/Diagnosis.

Management of the Adult Patient with Acute Lower GI Bleeding. In Section I, see: Gastrointestinal Hemorrhage/Diagnosis.

Management of Ureteral Calculi. In Section I, see: Ureteral Calculi/Therapy.

Managing Cough as a Defense Mechanism and as a Symptom. In Section I, see: Cough.

Managing the Anovulatory State: Medical Induction of Ovulation. In Section I, see: Anovulation/Drug Therapy.

Mandatory Reporting of Domestic Violence. In Section I, see: Mandatory Reporting.

Mandatory Reporting of Infectious Diseases by Clinicians and Mandatory Reporting of Occupational Diseases by Clinicians. In Section I, see: Communicable Disease Control/Legislation and Jurisprudence.

Mandibular Fracture. In Section I, see: Mandibular Fractures.

Mannitol. In Section I, see: Mannitol.

Manual of Psychiatric Quality Assurance. In Section I, see: Quality Assurance, Health Care.

Mastoidectomy. In Section I, see: Mastoid/Surgery.

Maternal Serum Alpha-Fetoprotein Testing for Down's Syndrome. In Section I, see: Alpha-Fetoproteins/Blood.

Maternal Serum Screening. In Section I, see: Alpha-Fetoproteins/Analysis.

Maxillofacial Cosmetic Surgery. In Section I, see: Reconstructive Surgical Procedures.

Maxillofacial Surgery (Including Orthognathic Surgery and Skeletal Aesthetic Enhancement). In Section I, see: Surgery, Oral.

Maxillofacial Trauma. In Section I, see: Maxillofacial Injuries/Surgery.

Measles Eradication: Recommendations from a Meeting Cosponsored by the World Health Organization, the Pan American Health Organization, and CDC. In Section I, see: Measles/Prevention and Control.

Measles Immunization in HIV-Infected Children (joint with COPA+). In Section I, see: Measles/Prevention and Control.

Measles, Mumps, and Rubella—Vaccine Use and Strategies for Elimination of Measles, Rubella, and Congenital Rubella Syndrome and Control of Mumps: Recommendations of the Advisory Committee on Immunization Practices (ACIP). In Section I, see: Vaccination/Standards.

Measles Prevention: Recommendations of the Immunization Practices Advisory Committee (ACIP). In Section I, see: Measles/Prevention and Control.

Measurement of Bone Density with Dual Energy X-ray Absorptiometry (DEXA). In Section I, see: Bone Density.

Measurement of Circulating IgG and IgE Food-Immune Complexes. In Section I, see: Antigen-Antibody Complex/Analysis.

Measurement of Circulating IgG and IgE Food-Immune Complexes. In Section I, see: Antigen-Antibody Complex/Analysis.

Measurement of Specific and Nonspecific IgG4 Levels as Diagnostic and Prognostic Tests for Clinical Allergy. In Section I, see: Hypersensitivity/Diagnosis.

Measuring Cardiac Output by Electrical Bioimpedance. In Section I, see: Cardiac Output.

Mechanical Ventilation. In Section I, see: Respiration, Artificial.

Mechanical Ventilation Beyond the ICU. In Section I, see: Intensive Care.

Medical Director of Respiratory Care. In Section I, see: Respiration Disorders/Therapy.

Medical Management of Insulin-Dependent (Type 1) Diabetes, 3rd Edition. In Section I, see: Diabetes Mellitus, Insulin-Dependent.

Medical Management of Non-Insulin-Dependent (Type 2) Diabetes, 4th Edition. In Section I, see: Diabetes Mellitus, Non-Insulin-Dependent.

Medical Management of Pregnancy Complicated by Diabetes, 2nd Edition. In Section I, see: Diabetes, Gestational.

Medical Management of Tubal Pregnancy. In Section I, see: Pregnancy, Tubal/Diagnosis.

Medical Treatment Decisions Concerning Elderly People, Position Statement. In Section I, see: Decision Making.

Medical Treatment for Stroke Prevention. In Section I, see: Cerebrovascular Disorders/Prevention and Control.

Medical Treatment of Peptic Ulcer Disease Practice Guidelines. In Section I, see: Anti-Ulcer Agents/Therapeutic Use.

Medical Waste. In Section I, see: Medical Waste.

Medicare, Position Statement. In Section I, see: Medicare.

Melanoma Surgical Practice Guidelines. In Section I, see: Melanoma.

Meningocele or Myelomeningocele Repair. In Section I, see: Meningomyelocele/Surgery.

Mental Health and the Elderly, Position Statement. In Section I, see: Mental Health Services.

Methods for Voluntary Weight Loss and Control. In Section I, see: Obesity/Prevention and Control.

Methods of Granting Hospital Privileges to Perform Gastrointestinal Endoscopy. In Section I, see: Endoscopy, Gastrointestinal.

Methods of Midtrimester Abortion. In Section I, see: Abortion, Induced.

Methods of Practice Regarding Lab Procedures. In Section I, see: Laboratory Techniques and Procedures.

Methotrexate for Rheumatoid Arthritis: Suggested Guidelines for Monitoring Liver Toxicity. In Section I, see: Arthritis, Rheumatoid/Drug Therapy.

Microsurgical Reconstruction for Brachial Plexus Injury. In Section I, see: Brachial Plexus/Injuries.

Minor Closed Head Trauma in Children. In Section I, see: Head Injuries, Closed.

Modern Component Usage in Transfusion Therapy, 1992. In Section I, see: Blood Component Transfusion.

Monitoring during Induction of Labor with Dinoprostone. In Section I, see: Dinoprostone.

Monitoring of Patients Undergoing Gastrointestinal Endoscopic Procedures. In Section I, see: Endoscopy, Gastrointestinal.

Mood Disorders. In Section I, see: Mood Disorders/Therapy.

Mood Disorders: Pharmacologic Prevention of Recurrences. In Section I, see: Affective Disorders, Psychotic/Prevention and Control.

Morbidity and Mortality of Dialysis. In Section I, see: Hemodialysis.

Mumps Prevention. In Section I, see: Mumps/Prevention and Control.

Mycobacteriosis and Acquired Immunodeficiency Syndrome. In Section I, see: Acquired Immunodeficiency Syndrome/Complications.

Myelography. In Section I, see: Myelography.

Myocardial Perfusion Imaging Utilizing Single-Photon Emission-Computed Tomography (SPECT). In Section I, see: Coronary Disease/Diagnosis.

Myomas and Reproductive Dysfunction. In Section I, see: Myoma.

Myringotomy and Tympanostomy Tubes. In Section I, see: Middle Ear Ventilation/Methods.

N

Nail Disorders. In Section I, see: Nail Disorders/ Therapy.

Nasal Deformity. In Section I, see: Nose/ Abnormalities.

National Action Plan to Combat Multidrug-Resistant Tuberculosis. In Section I, see: Antitubercular Agents/ Therapeutic Use.

National Kidney Foundation Report on Dialyzer Reuse. In Section I, see: Disposable Equipment/ Standards.

NCEP Report of the Expert Panel on Blood Cholesterol Levels in Children and Adolescents. In Section I, see: Cholesterol/Blood.

Nd: YAG Photodisruptors Ophthalmic Procedure Assessment. In Section I, see: Anterior Eye Segment/ Surgery.

Neoadjuvant Therapy for Marginally Resectable (Clinical N2) Non-Small-Cell Lung Carcinoma (1 variant). In Section I, see: Carcinoma, Non-Small-Cell Lung/Surgery.

Neonatal Circumcision. In Section I, see: Circumcision.

Neonatal Drug Withdrawal. In Section I, see: Neonatal Abstinence Syndrome.

Nerve Block, Somatic or Sympathetic, with Injection of Diagnostic or Treatment Agent. In Section I, see: Nerve Block.

Neurodiagnostic Evaluation of a First, Simple Febrile Seizure in Children. In Section I, see: Convulsions.

Neurofibromatosis Type 1. In Section I, see: Neurofibromatosis I/Therapy.

New Pap Test Screening Techniques. In Section I, see: Cervix Neoplasms/Diagnosis.

New Ultrasound Output Display Standards. In Section I, see: Ultrasonography/Instrumentation.

Newborn Screening for Cystic Fibrosis: A Paradigm for Public Health Genetics Policy Development. In Section I, see: Cystic Fibrosis/Prevention and Control.

Newborn Screening for Sickle Cell Disease and Other Hemoglobinopathies. In Section I, see: Anemia, Sickle Cell/Epidemiology.

NKF-DOQI Clinical Practice Guidelines for Hemodialysis Adequacy. In Section I, see: Hemodialysis/Standards.

NKF-DOQI Clinical Practice Guidelines for Peritoneal Dialysis Adequacy. In Section I, see: Peritoneal Dialysis/Standards.

NKF-DOQI Clinical Practice Guidelines for the Treatment of Anemia of Chronic Renal Failure. In Section I, see: Kidney Failure, Chronic/Complications.

NKF-DOQI Clinical Practice Guidelines for Vascular Access. In Section I, see: Arteriovenous Shunt, Surgical.

Node-Positive Prostate Cancer (3 variants). In Section I, see: Prostatic Neoplasms.

Noise and Hearing Loss. In Section I, see: Hearing Loss, Noise-Induced.

Non-Aggressive, Non-Surgical Treatment of Inoperable Non-Small-Cell Lung Cancer. In Section I, see: Carcinoma, Non-Small-Cell Lung/Therapy.

Non-Invasive Extracorporeal Lithotripsy for Disruption of Kidney Stones—UPDATE. In Section I, see: Lithotripsy.

Non-Melanocytic Nevi, Hamartomas and Potentially Malignant Lesions, Part II. In Section I, see: Hamartoma/Therapy.

Non-Small-Cell Lung Carcinoma, Non-Surgical Aggressive Therapy (8 variants). In Section I, see: Carcinoma, Non-Small-Cell Lung/Therapy.

Noninvasive Diagnostic Instrumentation for Assessment of Cardiovascular Disease in the Young. In Section I, see: Cardiovascular Diseases/Diagnosis.

Noninvasive Technology in the Assessment of Ventricular Function. In Section I, see: Heart Diseases/Diagnosis.

Nonmalignant Conditions of the Breast. In Section I, see: Breast Diseases.

Nonselective Embryo Reduction: Ethical Guidance for the Obstetrician-Gynecologist. In Section I, see: Ethics, Medical.

Nontraumatic Acute Abdominal Pain. In Section I, see: Abdomen, Acute/Diagnosis.

Nutrition and Women. In Section I, see: Nutrition.

Nutritional Support. In Section I, see: Brain Injuries/Therapy.

O

Obesity and Heart Disease. In Section I, see: Heart Diseases/Etiology.

Obstetric Analgesia and Anesthesia. In Section I, see: Analgesia, Obstetrical.

Obstetric Aspects of Trauma Management. In Section I, see: Abdominal Injuries.

Obstetric Management of Patients with Spinal Cord Injury. In Section I, see: Spinal Cord Injuries/Complications.

Obstetrician-Gynecologists' Ethical Responsibilities, Concerns, and Risks Pertaining to Adoption. In Section I, see: Adoption.

One Set Color Laminated Clinical Guidelines. In Section I, see: Practice Guidelines.

One Set Color Paper Clinical Guidelines. In Section I, see: Practice Guidelines.

Operative Laparoscopy. In Section I, see: Surgical Procedures, Laparoscopic.

Operative Vaginal Delivery. In Section I, see: Obstetrical Delivery/Methods.

Optic Nerve Head and Retinal Fiber Analysis Ophthalmic Procedure Assessment. In Section I, see: Diagnostic Techniques, Ophthalmological/Diagnosis.

Optimal Calcium Intake. In Section I, see: Calcium/Administration and Dosage.

Optimal Resources for the Examination and Endovascular Treatment of Peripheral and Visceral Vascular Systems. In Section I, see: Angiography/Standards.

Optimal Risk Factor Management in Patients after Coronary Revascularization. In Section I, see: Myocardial Revascularization.

Oral Anticoagulation for Older Adults, Pocket Guide. In Section I, see: Anticoagulants.

Oral Complications of Cancer Therapies: Diagnosis, Prevention, and Treatment. In Section I, see: Mouth Diseases/Etiology.

Oral Health Care Series: Chemically Dependent Patients. In Section I, see: Dental Care For Chronically Ill/Methods.

Oral Health Care Series: Head and Neck Cancer Patients Receiving Radiation Therapy. In Section I, see: Head and Neck Neoplasms/Radiotherapy.

Oral Health Care Series: Patients Receiving Cancer Chemotherapy. In Section I, see: Antineoplastic Agents.

Oral Health Care Series: Patients with Cardiovascular Disease. In Section I, see: Cardiovascular Diseases/Therapy.

Oral Health Care Series: Patients with Diabetes. In Section I, see: Dental Care for Chronically Ill/Methods.

Oral Health Care Series: Patients with End-Stage Renal Disease. In Section I, see: Kidney Failure, Chronic.

Oral Health Care Series: Patients with Hepatic Disease. In Section I, see: Dental Care for Chronically Ill/Methods.

Oral Health Care Series: Patients with Physical and Mental Disorders. In Section I, see: Dental Care for Disabled.

Oral Health Care Series: Women's Oral Health Issues. In Section I, see: Oral Health.

Oropharyngeal and Oral Cavity Cancer Surgical Practice Guidelines. In Section I, see: Oropharyngeal Neoplasms/Surgery.

Orthognathic, Cleft, Craniofacial Surgery and Adjunctive Procedures. In Section I, see: Cleft Lip/Surgery.

OSHA Regulations—Requirements for Endoscopic Practice. In Section I, see: United States Occupational Safety and Health Administration.

Osteoarthritis (Arthrosis) of the Knee (Degenerative Joint Disease). In Section I, see: Osteoarthritis.

Osteoarthritis of the Hip. In Section I, see: Osteoarthritis, Hip.

Osteoporosis. In Section I, see: Osteoporosis.

Ovarian Cancer Surgical Practice Guidelines. In Section I, see: Ovarian Neoplasms/Diagnosis.

Ovarian Cancer: Screening, Treatment, and Follow-up. In Section I, see: Mass Screening.

P

Pain Relief During Labor. In Section I, see: Insurance, Health, Reimbursement/Standards.

Pancreas Transplants. In Section I, see: Pancreas Transplantation/Physiology.

Pancreatic Cancer Surgical Practice Guidelines. In Section I, see: Pancreatic Neoplasms/Surgery.

Parameters for the Diagnosis and Management of Sinusitis. In Section I, see: Sinusitis/Diagnosis.

Parameters of Care (Revision). In Section I, see: Surgery, Oral/Standards.

Parenteral Nutrition in Patients Receiving Cancer Chemotherapy. In Section I, see: Surgical Procedures, Operative.

Parotid Gland Cancer Surgical Practice Guidelines. In Section I, see: Parotid Neoplasms/Surgery.

Participation in Meetings Advocating Unproven Techniques. In Section I, see: Hypersensitivity.

Pathology. In Section I, see: Stomatognathic Diseases/Pathology.

Patient Choice and the Maternal-Fetal Relationship. In Section I, see: Choice Behavior.

Patient Placement Criteria for the Treatment of Substance-Related Disorders (2nd Ed.). In Section I, see: Substance-Related Disorders/Rehabilitation.

PCBs in Breast Milk. In Section I, see: Polychlorinated Biphenyls/Analysis.

Pediatric Eye Evaluations. In Section I, see: Eye Diseases/Prevention and Control.

Pediatric Fever. In Section I, see: Clinical Protocols.

Pediatric Gynecologic Disorders. In Section I, see: Genital Diseases, Female/Diagnosis.

Pediatric Therapeutic Cardiac Catheterization. In Section I, see: Heart Catheterization.

Pedicle Screw Fixation System for Spinal Instability. In Section I, see: Bone Screws.

Pelvic Inflammatory Disease: Guidelines for Prevention and Management. In Section I, see: Adnexitis/Prevention and Control.

Pelvic Organ Prolapse. In Section I, see: Uterine Prolapse.

Penetrating Extremity Trauma. In Section I, see: Emergency Treatment/Standards.

Penile Implants for Erectile Impotence. In Section I, see: Impotence/Surgery.

Percutaneous Nephrolithotomy for Kidney Stone Removal. In Section I, see: Kidney Calculi/Therapy.

Percutaneous Transluminal Angioplasty. In Section I, see: Angioplasty, Transluminal, Percutaneous.

Percutaneous Transluminal Coronary Angioplasty. In Section I, see: Angioplasty, Transluminal, Percutaneous.

Performance of Ergonovine Provocative Testing for Coronary Artery Spasm. In Section I, see: Ergonovine/Diagnostic Use.

Performance/Interpretation Qualifications: Computed Tomography. In Section I, see: Tomography, X-ray Computed.

Perinatal and Infant Mortality Statistics. In Section I, see: Infant Mortality.

Perinatal Care at the Threshold of Fetal Viability. In Section I, see: Fetal Viability.

Perinatal Viral and Parasitic Infections. In Section I, see: Pregnancy Complications, Infectious.

Perioperative Cardiovascular Evaluation for Non-Cardiac Surgery. In Section I, see: Cardiovascular Diseases/Physiopathology.

Perioperative Parenteral Nutrition. In Section I, see: Parenteral Nutrition, Total.

Perioperative Red Cell Transfusion. In Section I, see: Blood Component Transfusion.

Peripheral Nerve Surgery. In Section I, see: Peripheral Nerves/Surgery.

Peripheral Parenteral Nutrition. In Section I, see: Parenteral Nutrition.

Permanent Source Brachytherapy for Prostate Cancer (8 variants). In Section I, see: Prostatic Neoplasms.

Personality Disorders. In Section I, see: Personality Disorders/Drug Therapy.

Personnel and Equipment to Treat Systemic Reactions Caused by Immunotherapy with Allergenic Extracts. In Section I, see: Allergens/Administration and Dosage.

Pertussis Immunization: Family History of Convulsions and Use of Antipyretics—Supplementary ACIP Statement. In Section I, see: Pertussis Vaccine/Adverse Effects.

Pertussis Vaccination: Acellular Pertussis Vaccine for Reinforcing and Booster Use—Supplementary ACIP Statement. In Section I, see: Diphtheria-Tetanus-Pertussis Vaccine.

Position Statement: Access to Cardiovascular Care. In Section I, see: Cardiovascular Diseases/Therapy.

Position Statement: Ambulatory Blood Pressure Monitoring. In Section I, see: Blood Pressure Monitors/Standards.

Position Statement: Cardiac Angiography Without Cine Film: Creating a "Tower of Babel" in the Cardiac Catheterization Laboratory. In Section I, see: Cineangiography.

Position Statement: Chelation Therapy (Reapproved). In Section I, see: Chelation Therapy.

Position Statement: Clinical Trials. In Section I, see: Clinical Trials.

Position Statement: Doppler Echocardiography in the Human Fetus. In Section I, see: Echocardiography, Doppler.

Position Statement: Early Defibrillation. In Section I, see: Electric Countershock/Methods.

Position Statement: Early Triage of Patients with Chest Discomfort, Approaches to. In Section I, see: Chest Pain/Diagnosis.

Position Statement: Heart Rate Variability for Risk Stratification of Life-Threatening Arrhythmias. In Section I, see: Arrhythmia/Physiopathology.

Position Statement: In-Hospital Cardiac Monitoring of Adults for Detection of Arrhythmia. In Section I, see: Arrhythmia/Diagnosis.

Position Statement: Indications for Implantation of the Automatic Implanted Cardioverter Defibrillator. In Section I, see: Electric Countershock/Instrumentation.

Position Statement: Interventional Catheterization Procedures and Cardiothoracic Surgical Consultation. In Section I, see: Heart Catheterization/Standards.

Position Statement: Physician Recertification. In Section I, see: Certification.

Position Statement: Preventive Cardiology and Atherosclerotic Disease. In Section I, see: Atherosclerosis/Prevention and Control.

Position Statement: Recommendations for Development and Maintenance of Competence in Coronary Interventional Procedures. In Section I, see: Clinical Competence/Standards.

Position Statement: Recommendations for Peripheral Transluminal Angioplasty: Training and Facilities. In Section I, see: Angioplasty, Balloon/Standards.

Position Statement: Recommendations for Training in Vascular Medicine. In Section I, see: Education, Medical, Graduate/Standards.

Position Statement: Same Day Surgical Admission. In Section I, see: Cardiac Surgical Procedures.

Position Statement: Therapeutic Substitution. In Section I, see: Prescriptions, Drug.

Position Statement: Training in Adult Clinical Cardiac Electrophysiology. In Section I, see: Electrophysiology/Education.

Position Statement: Use of Nonionic or Low Osmolar Contrast Agents in Cardiovascular Procedures. In Section I, see: Cardiovascular Diseases/Radiography.

Positioning and Sudden Infant Death Syndrome (SIDS). In Section I, see: Posture.

Positron Emission Tomography—A New Approach to Brain Chemistry. In Section I, see: Brain Chemistry.

Positron Emission Tomography in Oncology. In Section I, see: Neoplasms/Metabolism.

Post-Stroke Rehabilitation. In Section I, see: Cerebrovascular Disorders/Rehabilitation.

Postexposure Prophylaxis for Selected Infectious Diseases. In Section I, see: Communicable Diseases/ Prevention and Control.

Postmastectomy Radiotherapy (15 variants). In Section I, see: Breast Neoplasms/Radiotherapy.

Postmenopausal Hormone Prophylaxis. In Section I, see: Hormone Replacement Therapy.

Postoperative Radiotherapy in Non-Small-Cell Lung Cancer (18 variants). In Section I, see: Carcinoma, Non-Small-Cell Lung/Radiotherapy.

Postpartum Hemorrhage. In Section I, see: Postpartum Hemorrhage.

Postpartum Tubal Sterilization. In Section I, see: Puerperium.

Postradical Prostatectomy Irradiation in Carcinoma of the Prostate (11 variants). In Section I, see: Prostatic Neoplasms/Radiotherapy.

Practical Psychology for Diabetes Clinicians. In Section I, see: Psychology/Methods.

Practice Advisory on Selection of Patients with Multiple Sclerosis for Treatment with Betaseron. In Section I, see: Interferon-Beta/Therapeutic Use.

Practice Advisory on the Treatment of Amyotrophic Lateral Sclerosis with Riluzole. In Section I, see: Amyotrophic Lateral Sclerosis/Drug Therapy.

Practice Advisory: The Use of Felbamate in the Treatment of Patients with Intractable Epilepsy. In Section I, see: Anticonvulsants/Therapeutic Use.

Practice Advisory: Thrombolytic Therapy for Acute Ischemic Stroke (rt-PA)—Summary Statement. In Section I, see: Cerebral Ischemia/Drug Therapy.

Practice Guideline Book. In Section I, see: Practice Guidelines.

Practice Guideline for Eating Disorders. In Section I, see: Practice Guidelines.

Practice Guideline for Examination of the Placenta. In Section I, see: Placenta/Pathology.

Practice Guideline for Major Depressive Disorder in Adults. In Section I, see: Depressive Disorder Therapy.

Practice Guideline for the Psychiatric Evaluation of Adults. In Section I, see: Mental Disorders/Diagnosis.

Practice Guideline for the Treatment of Patients with Alzheimer's Disease and Other Dementias of Late Life. In Section I, see: Alzheimer's Disease/Therapy.

Practice Guideline for the Treatment of Patients with Bipolar Disorder. In Section I, see: Bipolar Disorder/Therapy.

Practice Guideline for the Treatment of Patients with Delirium. In Section I, see: Delirium/Therapy.

Practice Guideline for the Treatment of Patients with Nicotine Dependence. In Section I, see: Tobacco Use Disorder/Therapy.

Practice Guideline for the Treatment of Patients with Panic Disorder. In Section I, see: Panic Disorder/Drug Therapy.

Practice Guideline for the Treatment of Patients with Schizophrenia. In Section I, see: Schizophrenia/Therapy.

Practice Guideline for Treatment of Patients with Substance Use Disorders: Alcohol, Cocaine, Opioids. In Section I, see: Cocaine-Related Disorders/Therapy.

Practice Guideline: Cardiac Catheterization and Cardiac Catheterization Laboratories. In Section I, see: Heart Catheterization/Standards.

Practice Guidelines for Acute Pain in the Perioperative Setting. In Section I, see: Analgesia/Standards.

Practice Guidelines for Autopsy Pathology: Autopsy Performance (Reaffirmed, 1996). In Section I, see: Autopsy/Standards.

Practice Guidelines for Autopsy Pathology: Autopsy Reporting. In Section I, see: Autopsy/Standards.

Practice Guidelines for Autopsy Pathology: Perinatal and Pediatric Autopsy. In Section I, see: Autopsy/Methods.

Practice Guidelines for Chronic Pain Management. In Section I, see: Pain/Therapy.

Practice Guidelines for Community-Based Parenteral Anti-Infective Therapy. In Section I, see: Anti-Infective Agents/Administration and Dosage.

Practice Guidelines for Evaluating New Fever in Critically Ill Adult Patients. In Section I, see: Critical Illness.

Practice Guidelines for Infectious Diseases: Rationale for Work in Progress. In Section I, see: Infection.

Practice Guidelines for Management of the Difficult Airway. In Section I, see: Anesthesia.

Practice Guidelines for Obstetrical Anesthesia. In Section I, see: Anesthesia, Obstetrical/Standards.

Practice Guidelines for Perioperative Transesophageal Echocardiography. In Section I, see: Echocardiography, Transesophageal/Standards.

Practice Guidelines for Preoperative Fasting and the Use of Pharmacologic Agents to Reduce the Risk of Pulmonary Aspiration. In Section I, see: Anesthesiology/Standards.

Practice Guidelines for Pulmonary Artery Catheterization Monitoring. In Section I, see: Catheterization, Swan-Ganz,

Practice Guidelines for Respiratory Allergy. In Section I, see: Hypersensitivity.

Practice Guidelines for Sedation and Analgesia by Non-Anesthesiologists. In Section I, see: Analgesia/Standards.

Practice Guidelines: Lower Extremity Revascularization. In Section I, see: Ischemia/Surgery.

Practice of ECT. Recommendations for Treatment, Training, and Privileging. In Section I, see: Electroconvulsive Therapy/Education.

Practice Parameter for Electrodiagnostic Studies in Carpal Tunnel Syndrome. In Section I, see: Carpal Tunnel Syndrome/Diagnosis.

Practice Parameter for Electrodiagnostic Studies in Carpal Tunnel Syndrome. In Section I, see: Carpal Tunnel Syndrome/Diagnosis.

Practice Parameter for Hereditary Hemochromatosis. In Section I, see: Hemochromatosis/Genetics.

Practice Parameter for Needle Electromyographic Evaluation of Patients with Suspected Cervical Radiculopathy. In Section I, see: Spinal Osteophytosis.

Practice Parameter for the Use of Fresh-Frozen Plasma, Cryoprecipitate, and Platelets. In Section I, see: Blood Component Transfusion/Standards.

Practice Parameter for the Use of Red Blood Cell Transfusions. In Section I, see: Erythrocyte Transfusion.

Practice Parameter on Laboratory Panel Testing for Screening and Case Finding in Asymptomatic Adults. In Section I, see: Diagnostic Tests, Routine.

Practice Parameter: A Guideline for Discontinuing Antiepileptic Drugs in Seizure-Free Patients. In Section I, see: Anticonvulsants/Therapeutic Use.

Practice Parameter: Antiepileptic Drug Treatment of Posttraumatic Seizures. In Section I, see: Anticonvulsants/Therapeutic Use.

Practice Parameter: Assessment and Management of Patients in the Persistent Vegetative State. In Section I, see: Persistent Vegetative State.

Practice Parameter: Determining Brain Death in Adults. In Section I, see: Brain Death/Diagnosis.

Practice Parameter: Diagnosis and Evaluation of Dementia. In Section I, see: Dementia/Diagnosis.

Practice Parameter: Diagnosis of Patients with Nervous System Lyme Borreliosis (Lyme Disease). In Section I, see: Lyme Disease/Diagnosis.

Practice Parameter: Electrodiagnostic Studies in Lunar Neuropathy at the Elbow. In Section I, see: Electrodiagnosis.

Practice Parameter: Electroencephalogram in the Evaluation of Headache. In Section I, see: Headache/Physiopathology.

Practice Parameter: Management Issues for Women with Epilepsy. In Section I, see: Anticonvulsants/Adverse Effects.

Practice Parameter: Neuroimaging in the Emergency Patient Presenting with Seizure. In Section I, see: Seizures/Radiography.

Practice Parameter: Neuroimaging in the Emergency Patient Presenting with Seizure (Summary Statement). In Section I, see: Seizures/Radiography.

Practice Parameter: The Care of the Patient with Amyotrophic Lateral Sclerosis (an evidence-based review). In Section I, see: Amyotrophic Lateral Sclerosis/Therapy.

Practice Parameter: The Management of Concussion in Sports. In Section I, see: Athletic Injuries/Therapy.

Practice Parameters for Ambulatory Anorectal Surgery. In Section I, see: Rectum/Surgery.

Practice Parameters for Anal Fissure. In Section I, see: Fissure in Anus/Therapy.

Practice Parameters for Antibiotic Prophylaxis to Prevent Infective Endocarditis of Infected Prosthesis During Colon and Rectal Surgery. In Section I, see: Antibiotics/Therapeutic Use.

Practice Parameters for Child Custody Evaluation. In Section I, see: Child Custody/Legislation and Jurisprudence.

Practice Parameters for Electrodiagnostic Studies in Ulnar Neuropathy at the Elbow. In Section I, see: Electrodiagnosis.

Practice Parameters for Evaluating New Fever in Critically Ill Adult Patients. In Section I, see: Fever/Diagnosis.

Practice Parameters for Hemodynamic Support of Sepsis in Adult Patients. In Section I, see: Sepsis.

Practice Parameters for Intraveneous Analgesia and Sedation for Patients in the Intensive Care Unit: An Executive Summary. In Section I, see: Analgesia.

Practice Parameters for Sigmoid Diverticulitis. In Section I, see: Diverticulitis, Colonic/Therapy.

Practice Parameters for Sustained Neuromuscular Blockade in the Adult Critically Ill Patient: An Executive Summary. In Section I, see: Critical Care.

Practice Parameters for the Assessment and Treatment of Children and Adolescents with Anxiety Disorders. In Section I, see: Anxiety Disorders.

Practice Parameters for the Assessment and Treatment of Children and Adolescents with Attention Deficit Hyperactivity Disorder. In Section I, see: Attention Deficit Disorder with Hyperactivity/Diagnosis.

Practice Parameters for the Assessment and Treatment of Children and Adolescents with Bipolar Disorder. In Section I, see: Bipolar Disorder.

Practice Parameters for the Assessment and Treatment of Children and Adolescents with Conduct Disorder. In Section I, see: Conduct Disorder/Diagnosis.

Practice Parameters for the Assessment and Treatment of Children and Adolescents with Obsessive-Compulsive Disorder. In Section I, see: Obsessive-Compulsive Disorder/Therapy.

Practice Parameters for the Assessment and Treatment of Children and Adolescents with Post-Traumatic Stress Disorder. In Section I, see: Stress Disorders, Post-Trauma.

Practice Parameters for the Assessment and Treatment of Children and Adolescents with Schizophrenia. In Section I, see: Schizophrenia, Childhood/Therapy.

Practice Parameters for the Assessment and Treatment of Children and Adolescents with Substance Use Disorders. In Section I, see: Substance-Related Disorders/Diagnosis.

Practice Parameters for the Detection of Colorectal Neoplasms. In Section I, see: Colorectal Neoplasms/Diagnosis.

Practice Parameters for the Forensic Evaluation of Children and Adolescents Who May Have Been Physically or Sexually Abused. In Section I, see: Child Abuse/Diagnosis.

Practice Parameters for the Indications for Polysomnography and Related Procedures. In Section I, see: Polysomnography/Methods.

Practice Parameters for the Nonpharmacological Treatment of Insomnia. In Section I, see: Insomnia/Therapy.

Practice Parameters for the Psychiatric Assessment of Children and Adolescents. In Section I, see: Adolescent Psychiatry.

Practice Parameters for the Psychiatric Assessment of Infants and Toddlers. In Section I, see: Child Psychiatry.

Practice Parameters for the Treatment of Hemorrhoids. In Section I, see: Hemorrhoids/Therapy.

Practice Parameters for the Treatment of Obstructive Sleep Apnea in Adults: The Efficacy of Surgical Modifications of the Upper Airway. In Section I, see: Sleep Apnea Syndromes/Surgery.

Practice Parameters for the Treatment of Snoring and Obstructive Sleep Apnea with Oral Appliances. In Section I, see: Orthodontic Appliances.

Practice Parameters for the Use of Actigraphy in the Clinical Assessment of Sleep Disorders. In Section I, see: Motor Activity.

Practice Parameters for the Use of Laser-Assisted Uvulopalatoplasty. In Section I, see: Laser Surgery.

Practice Parameters for the Use of Light Therapy in the Treatment of Sleep Disorders. In Section I, see: Phototherapy.

Practice Parameters for the Use of Polysomnography in the Evaluation of Insomnia. In Section I, see: Guidelines.

Practice Parameters for the Use of Portable Recording in the Assessment of Obstructive Sleep Apnea. In Section I, see: Polysomnography/Instrumentation.

Practice Parameters for the Use of Stimulants in the Treatment of Narcolepsy. In Section I, see: Central Nervous System Stimulants/Therapeutic Use.

Practice Parameters for Treatment of Rectal Carcinoma. In Section I, see: Colorectal Surgery.

Practice Parameters: Appropriate Use of Ergotamine and Dihydroergotamine in the Treatment of Migraine and Status Migrainosus. In Section I, see: Dihydroergotamine/Therapeutic Use.

Practice Parameters: Carpal Tunnel Syndrome. In Section I, see: Carpal Tunnel Syndrome/Diagnosis.

Practice Parameters: Initial Therapy of Parkinson's Disease. In Section I, see: Parkinson's Disease/Drug Therapy.

Practice Parameters: Lumbar Puncture. In Section I, see: Spinal Puncture.

Practice Parameters: MRI in the Evaluation of Low Back Syndrome. In Section I, see: Back Pain/Diagnosis.

Practice Parameters: Neurologic Evaluation. In Section I, see: Neurology.

Practice Parameters: Utility of Neuroimaging in the Evaluation of Headache in Patients with Normal Neurologic Examinations. In Section I, see: Headache/Diagnosis.

Practice Policy Statement: Adult Immunization. In Section I, see: Preventive Medicine.

Practice Policy Statement: Cervical Cancer Screening. In Section I, see: Cervix Neoplasms.

Practice Policy Statement: Childhood Immunizations. In Section I, see: Immunization Schedule.

Practice Policy Statement: Screening Asymptomatic Women for Ovarian Cancer. In Section I, see: Mass Screening/Methods.

Practice Policy Statement: Screening for Prostate Cancer in American Men. In Section I, see: Preventive Medicine/Standards.

Practice Policy Statement: Screening for Skin Cancer. In Section I, see: Mass Screening/Standards.

Title

Practice Policy Statement: Screening Mammography for Breast Cancer. In Section I, see: Breast Neoplasms/Prevention and Control.

Practice Policy Statement: Skin Protection from Ultraviolet Light Exposure. In Section I, see: Ultraviolet Rays/Adverse Effects.

Preconceptional Care. In Section I, see: Fertilization.

Preembryo Research: History, Scientific Background, and Ethical Considerations. In Section I, see: Embryo.

Preface to the 1997 USPHS/IDSA Guidelines for the Prevention of Opportunistic Infections in Persons with Human Immunodeficiency Virus: Disease-Specific Recommendations. In Section I, see: Tuberculosis, Pulmonary/Prevention and Control.

Preferred Practice Patterns. In Section I, see: Physician's Practice Patterns.

Premature Rupture of Membranes. In Section I, see: Fetal Membranes, Premature Rupture.

Premenstrual Syndrome. In Section I, see: Premenstrual Syndrome/Therapy.

Prenatal Care. In Section I, see: Prenatal Care.

Preoperative Pulmonary Function Testing. In Section I, see: Lung Diseases/Prevention and Control.

Preparation of Patients for Gastrointestinal Endoscopy: Guidelines for Clinical Application. In Section I, see: Gastroscopy.

Pressure Sores. In Section I, see: Decubitus Ulcer.

Pressure Ulcers. In Section I, see: Decubitus Ulcer.

Pressure Ulcers in Adults: Prediction and Prevention. In Section I, see: Decubitus Ulcer/Prevention and Control.

Preterm Labor. In Section I, see: Labor, Premature.

Preventing and Controlling Oral and Pharyngeal Cancer Recommendations from a National Strategic Planning Conference. In Section I, see: Mouth Neoplasms/Prevention and Control.

Preventing Heart Attack and Death in Patients with Coronary Disease. In Section I, see: Coronary Diseases/Complications.

Prevention and Control of Influenza: Recommendations of the Advisory Committee on Immunization Practices (ACIP). In Section I, see: Influenza/Prevention and Control.

Prevention and Control of Influenza: Recommendations of the Advisory Committee on Immunization Practices (ACIP). In Section I, see: Influenza Vaccine.

Prevention and Control of Tuberculosis Among Homeless Persons. In Section I, see: Homeless Persons.

Prevention and Control of Tuberculosis in Correctional Facilities. In Section I, see: Prisons.

Prevention and Control of Tuberculosis in Facilities Providing Long-Term Care to the Elderly: Recommendations of the Advisory Committee for the Elimination of Tuberculosis. In Section I, see: Homes for the Elderly.

Prevention and Control of Tuberculosis in Migrant Farm Workers. In Section I, see: Transients and Migrants.

Prevention and Control of Tuberculosis in US Communities with At-Risk Minority Populations. In Section I, see: Minority Groups.

Prevention and Treatment of Influenza in the Elderly. In Section I, see: Influenza/Prevention and Control.

Prevention and Treatment of Tuberculosis Among Patients Infected with Human Immunodeficiency Virus: Principles of Therapy and Revised Recommendations. In Section I, see: AIDS-Related Opportunistic Infections/Prevention and Control.

Prevention of Adolescent Suicide. In Section I, see: Suicide/Prevention and Control.

Prevention of Bacterial Endocarditis: Recommendations by the American Heart Association. In Section I, see: Endocarditis, Bacterial/Prevention and Control.

Prevention of Early-Onset Group B Streptococcal Disease in Newborns. In Section I, see: Streptococcal Infections/Prevention and Control.

Prevention of Hepatitis A Infections: Guidelines for Use of Hepatitis A Vaccine and Immune Globulin. In Section I, see: Hepatitis A/Prevention and Control.

Prevention of Hepatitis A Through Active or Passive Immunization. In Section I, see: Hepatitis A/Prevention and Control.

Prevention of Nuclear War, Position Statement. In Section I, see: Nuclear Warfare.

Prevention of Perinatal Group B Streptococcal Disease: A Public Health Perspective. In Section I, see: Antibiotic Prophylaxis.

Prevention of Plague. In Section I, see: Plague/Prevention and Control.

Prevention of Pneumococcal Disease. In Section I, see: Pneumococcal Infections/Prevention and Control.

Title

Procedure Guideline for Parathyroid Scintigraphy. In Section I, see: Parathyroid Glands/Radionuclide Imaging.

Procedure Guideline for Pediatric Sedation in Nuclear Medicine. In Section I, see: Hypnotics and Sedatives.

Procedure Guideline for Radionuclide Cystography in Children. In Section I, see: Bladder/Radionuclide Imaging.

Procedure Guideline for Renal Cortical Scintigraphy in Children. In Section I, see: Kidney Cortex/Radionuclide Imaging.

Procedure Guideline for Tc-99m Hexametazime (HMPAO) Labeled Leukocyte Scintigraphy for Suspected Infection/Inflammation. In Section I, see: Infection/Radionuclide Imaging.

Procedure Guideline for Thyroid Scintigraphy. In Section I, see: Thyroid Diseases/Radionuclide Imaging.

Procedure Guideline for Thyroid Uptake Measurement. In Section I, see: Thyroid Diseases/Radionuclide Imaging.

Procedure Guideline for Tumor Imaging Using F-18 FDG. In Section I, see: Neoplasms/Radionuclide Imaging.

Procedure Guideline for Use of Radiopharmaceuticals. In Section I, see: Radiopharmaceuticals/Diagnostic Use.

Proctoring and Hospital Endoscopy Privileges. In Section I, see: Endoscopy, Gastrointestinal/Standards.

Procuren: A Platelet-Derived Wound Healing Formula. In Section I, see: Blood Platelets.

Programs for Prevention of Suicide Among Adolescents and Young Adults. In Section I, see: Program Development.

Progress at the Interface of Inflammation and Asthma: Report of the ALA/ATS. In Section I, see: Asthma.

Prophylactic Anticonvulsants. In Section I, see: Anticonvulsants.

Prophylactic Oophorectomy. In Section I, see: Ovariectomy.

Prophylactic Treatment of Opportunistic Infections in HIV-Positive Patients: Toxoplasma gondii Prophylaxis. In Section I, see: HIV Seropositivity.

Prostate Cancer Surgical Practice Guidelines. In Section I, see: Prostatic Neoplasms/Surgery.

Protection Against Viral Hepatitis: Recommendations of the Immunization Practices Advisory Committee

(ACIP). In Section I, see: Hepatitis, Viral, Human/Prevention and Control.

Protein A Columns for Immune Thrombocytopenia. In Section I, see: Autoimmune Diseases/Therapy.

Provocative and Neutralization Testing (Subcutaneous). In Section I, see: Food Hypersensitivity/Diagnosis.

Provocative Testing (Sublingual). In Section I, see: Food Hypersensitivity/Diagnosis.

Proximal Humeral Fracture. In Section I, see: Humerus/Injuries.

Psychotherapeutic Medications in the Nursing Home. In Section I, see: Psychotropic Drugs/Therapeutic Use.

Public Financing of Catastrophic Care for the Older Patient, Position Statement. In Section I, see: Health Services Needs and Demands/Economics.

Public Health Service Guidelines for Counseling and Antibody Testing to Prevent HIV Infection and AIDS. In Section I, see: Acquired Immunodeficiency Syndrome/Prevention and Control.

Public Health Service Guidelines for the Management of Health-Care Worker Exposure to HIV and Recommendations for Postexposure Prophylaxis. In Section I, see: Health Personnel.

Public Health Service Inter-Agency Guidelines for Screening Donors of Blood, Plasma, Organs, Tissues, and Semen for Evidence of Hepatitis B and Hepatitis C. In Section I, see: Blood Donors.

Public Health Service Report on Fluoride Benefits and Risks. In Section I, see: Dental Caries/Prevention and Control.

Public Health Service Statement on Management of Occupational Exposure to HIV, Including Considerations Regarding Zidovudine Postexposure Use. In Section I, see: Acquired Immunodeficiency Syndrome/Prevention and Control.

Public Health Service Task Force Recommendations for the Use of Antiretroviral Drugs in Pregnant Women Infected with HIV-1 for Maternal Health and for Reducing Perinatal HIV-1 Transmission in the United States. In Section I, see: Anti-HIV Agents/Therapeutic Use.

Public Responsibility in Asbestos-Associated Diseases. In Section I, see: Social Responsibility.

Pulmonary Disease in Pregnancy. In Section I, see: Pregnancy Complications.

Pulmonary Function Laboratory Personnel Qualifications. In Section I, see: Health Manpower/Standards.

Pulmonary Rehabilitation: Joint ACCP/AACVPR Evidence-Based Guideline (with the American Association for Cardiovascular and Pulmonary Rehabilitation). In Section I, see: Lung Diseases, Obstructive/Rehabilitation.

Punctal Occlusion for the Dry Eye Ophthalmic Procedure Assessment. In Section I, see: Dry Eye Syndromes/Surgery.

Puncture, Burr Holes, Twist Drill, or Trephine for Drainage for Aspiration. In Section I, see: Trephining.

Puncture, Burr Holes, Twist Drill, or Trephine for Drainage for Exploration. In Section I, see: Trephining.

Puncture, Burr Holes, Twist Drill, or Trephine for Drainage for Intracranial Injection. In Section I, see: Trephining.

Purpose of Quality Standards for Infectious Diseases. In Section I, see: Infection/Therapy.

Q

Quality Assessment and Improvement in Obstetrics and Gynecology. In Section I, see: Quality Assurance, Health Care.

Quality Assurance in Pulmonary Function Laboratories. In Section I, see: Respiratory Function Tests.

Quality Assurance of Gastrointestinal Endoscopy. In Section I, see: Endoscopy, Gastrointestinal.

Quality Determinants of Mammography. In Section I, see: Mammography.

Quality Improvement Guidelines for Adult Percutaneous Abscess and Fluid Drainage. In Section I, see: Abscess/Therapy.

Quality Improvement Guidelines for Central Venous Access. In Section I, see: Catheterization, Central Venous.

Quality Improvement Guidelines for Dialysis Access. In Section I, see: Hemodialysis/Instrumentation.

Quality Improvement Guidelines for Image-Guided Percutaneous Biopsy in Adults. In Section I, see: Radiology, Interventional.

Quality Improvement Guidelines for Percutaneous Transcatheter Embolization. In Section I, see: Embolization, Therapeutic/Standards.

Quality Improvement Guidelines for Percutaneous Transhepatic Cholangiography and Biliary Drainage. In Section I, see: Cholangiography/Standards.

Quality of Ophthalmic Care. In Section I, see: Quality of Healthcare.

Quality Standard for Antimicrobial Prophylaxis in Surgical Procedures. In Section I, see: Antibiotics/Therapeutic Use.

Quality Standard for Assurance of Measles Immunity Among Health Care Workers. In Section I, see: Measles/Prevention and Control.

Quality Standard for Assurance of Measles Immunity Among Health Care Workers. In Section I, see: Health Personnel/Standards.

Quality Standard for the Treatment of Bacteremia. In Section I, see: Bacteremia/Drug Therapy.

Quality Standard for the Treatment of Bacteremia. In Section I, see: Bacteremia/Drug Therapy.

Quality Standards for Immunization. In Section I, see: Communicable Disease Control.

R

Radial Keratotomy for Myopia Ophthalmic Procedure Assessment. In Section I, see: Keratotomy, Radial.

Radical Neck Dissection. In Section I, see: Radical Neck Dissection.

Radiofrequency Catheter Ablation of Aberrant Conducting Pathways of the Heart. In Section I, see: Catheter Ablation.

Radionuclide Scintirenography in the Evaluation of Patients with Hypertension. In Section I, see: Radioisotope Renography.

RAST Marketing. In Section I, see: Radioallergosorbent Test.

Rate of Vaginal Births after Cesarean Delivery. In Section I, see: Vaginal Birth After Cesarean.

Rational Allocation of Medical Care. In Section I, see: Health Care Rationing.

Ready-to-Wear Reading Glasses Ophthalmic Procedure Assessment. In Section I, see: Eyeglasses/Standards.

Reassessment of Autologous Bone Marrow Transplantation. In Section I, see: Bone Marrow Transplantation.

Reassessment of Automated Percutaneous Lumbar Diskectomy for Herniated Disks. In Section I, see: Intervertebral Disk/Surgery.

Reassessment of BCG Immunotherapy in Bladder Cancer. In Section I, see: Bladder Neoplasms/ Therapy.

Reassessment of Cardiokymography for the Diagnosis of Coronary Artery Disease. In Section I, see: Coronary Disease/Diagnosis.

Reassessment of External Insulin Infusion Pumps. In Section I, see: Insulin Infusion Systems/Standards.

Reassessment of Indications for Ribavirin Therapy in Respiratory Syncytial Virus Infections. In Section I, see: Ribavirin/Therapeutic Use.

Reassessment of Radial Keratotomy for Simple Myopia. In Section I, see: Keratotomy, Radial.

Reassessment of Transrectal Ultrasonography. In Section I, see: Ultrasonography.

Recertification. In Section I, see: Certification.

Recognition and Treatment of Depression in Medical Practice. In Section I, see: Depressive Disorder/ Diagnosis.

Recommendations for Cardiovascular Screening, Staffing and the Emergency Policies at Health/Fitness Facilities. In Section I, see: Physical Fitness.

Recommendations for Collection of Laboratory Specimens Associated with Outbreaks of Gastroenteritis. In Section I, see: Disease Outbreaks.

Recommendations for Counseling Persons Infected with Human T-Lymphotrophic Virus, Types I and II. In Section I, see: HTLV-I Infections.

Recommendations for Credentialing and Privileging. In Section I, see: Credentialing.

Recommendations for Diagnosing and Treating Syphilis in HIV-Infected Patients. In Section I, see: Acquired Immunodeficiency Syndrome/ Complications.

Recommendations for HIV Testing Services for Inpatients and Outpatients in Acute-Care Settings; and Technical Guidance on HIV Counseling. In Section I, see: AIDS.

Recommendations for Human Immunodeficiency Virus Counseling and Voluntary Testing for Pregnant Women. In Section I, see: Disease Transmission, Vertical/Prevention and Control.

Recommendations for Preventing the Spread of Vancomycin Resistance. In Section I, see: Antibiotics, Glycopeptide/Pharmacology.

Recommendations for Preventing Transmission of Human Immunodeficiency Virus and Hepatitis B Virus to Patients During Exposure-Prone Invasive Procedures. In Section I, see: Health Manpower.

Recommendations for Prevention and Control of Hepatitis C Virus (HCV) Infection and HCV-Related Chronic Disease. In Section I, see: Hepatitis C, Chronic/Prevention and Control.

Recommendations for Prevention and Control of Tuberculosis Among Foreign-Born Persons Report of the Working Group on Tuberculosis Among Foreign-Born Persons. In Section I, see: Communicable Disease Control/Standards.

Recommendations for Prevention and Management of Chlamydia trachomatis Infections, 1993. In Section I, see: Chlamydia Trachomatis.

Recommendations for Prevention of HIV Transmission in Health-Care Settings. In Section I, see: Acquired Immunodeficiency Syndrome/ Prevention and Control.

Recommendations for Prophylaxis Against Pneumocystis carinii Pneumonia for Adults and Adolescents Infected with Human Immunodeficiency Virus. In Section I, see: HIV Infections/Complications.

Recommendations for Protecting Human Health Against Potential Adverse Effects of Long-Term Exposure to Low Doses of Chemical Warfare Agents. In Section I, see: Chemical Warfare Agents/Adverse Effects.

Recommendations for Standardization and Specifications in Automated Electrocardiography: Bandwidth and Digital Signal Processing. In Section I, see: Electrocardiography/Standards.

Recommendations for the Prevention and Treatment of Glucocorticoid-Induced Osteoporosis. In Section I, see: Glucocorticoids/Adverse Effects.

Recommendations for the Prevention of Malaria Among Travelers. In Section I, see: Malaria/ Prevention and Control.

Recommendations for the Use of Folic Acid to Reduce the Number of Cases of Spina Bifida and Other Neural Tube Defects. In Section I, see: Folic Acid/ Therapeutic Use.

Recommendations for the Use of Lyme Disease Vaccine Recommendations of the Advisory Committee on Immunization Practices (ACIP). In Section I, see: Lyme Disease/Prevention and Control.

Recommendations for Use of Haemophilus b Conjugate Vaccines and a Combined Diphtheria, Tetanus, Pertussis, and Haemophilus b Vaccine. In Section I, see: Haemophilus Vaccines/Administration and Dosage.

Recommendations of the Hospital Infection Control Practice Advisory Committee: Essential Components of a Tuberculosis Prevention and Control Program; Screening for Tuberculosis and Tuberculosis Infection in High-Risk Populations. In Section I, see: Program Development.

Recommendations of the International Task Force for Disease Eradication. In Section I, see: Communicable Disease Control.

Recommendations of the US Public Health Service Task Force on the Use of Zidovudine to Reduce Perinatal Transmission of Human Immunodeficiency Virus. In Section I, see: HIV Infections/Prevention and Control.

Recommendations on Frequency of Pap Test Screening. In Section I, see: Vaginal Smears.

Recommendations to Prevent and Control Iron Deficiency in the United States. In Section I, see: Iron/Administration and Dosage.

Recommended Breast Cancer Surveillance Guidelines. In Section I, see: Breast Neoplasms/Diagnosis.

Recommended Childhood Immunization Schedule—United States, January–December 1999. In Section I, see: Immunization Schedule.

Recommended Core Educational Guidelines for Family Practice Residents: Maternity and Gynecologic Care. In Section I, see: Family Practice/Education.

Recommended Guidelines for Uniform Reporting of Data from Out-of-Hospital Cardiac Arrest: The Utstein Style. In Section I, see: Emergency Medical Services/Standards.

Recommended Guidelines for Uniform Reporting of Pediatric Advanced Life Support: The Pediatric Utstein Style. In Section I, see: Resuscitation.

Recommended Indications for Operative Treatment of Abdominal Aortic Aneurysms. In Section I, see: Aortic Aneurysm/Diagnosis.

Recommended Infection-Control Practices for Dentistry. In Section I, see: Dentistry/Standards.

Recommended Library for Occupational Physicians. In Section I, see: Libraries, Medical.

Recommended Policy for Electrodiagnostic Medicine. In Section I, see: Electrodiagnostic.

Reconstructive Surgery. In Section I, see: Reconstructive Surgical Procedures.

Rectal Cancer: Presentation with Metastatic and Locally Advanced Disease (8 variants). In Section I, see: Rectal Neoplasms.

Recurrent Pregnancy Loss. In Section I, see: Abortion, Habitual.

Refractive Errors Preferred Practice Patterns. In Section I, see: Refractive Errors.

Regulation of Nursing Facilities, Position Statement. In Section I, see: Facility Regulation and Control.

Rehabilitation of Persons with Traumatic Brain Injury. In Section I, see: Brain Injuries/Rehabilitation.

Rehabilitation: The Management of Adult Patients with Low Vision Preferred Practice Pattern. In Section I, see: Vision, Subnormal.

Remote Practice of Allergy. In Section I, see: Delivery of Health Care.

Removal of Third Molars. In Section I, see: Molar/Surgery.

Repair of Rhegmatogenous Retinal Detachments Ophthalmic Procedure Assessment. In Section I, see: Retinal Detachment.

Report of the NIH Panel to Define Principles of Therapy of HIV Infection and Guidelines for the Use of Antiretroviral Agents in HIV-Infected Adults and Adolescents. In Section I, see: Anti-HIV Agents/Therapeutic Use.

Reporting Standards for Clinical Evaluation of New Peripheral Arterial Revascularization Devices. In Section I, see: Angioplasty/Standards.

Reporting Standards on Transjugular Intrahepatic Portosystemic Shunts (TIPS). In Section I, see: Documentation/Standards.

Requirements for Infrastructure and Essential Activities of Infection Control and Epidemiology in Hospitals: A Consensus Panel Report. In Section I, see: Cross Infection/Prevention and Control.

Research and Geriatric Medicine, Position Statement. In Section I, see: Research.

Research Criteria for Diagnosis of Chronic Inflammatory Demyelinating Polyneuropathy (CIDP). In Section I, see: Demyelinating Diseases/Diagnosis.

Research Priorities in Respiratory Nursing. In Section I, see: Clinical Nursing Research.

Resources for Optimal Care of the Injured Patient. In Section I, see: Wounds and Injuries/Surgery.

Respiratory Function Measurement in Infants: Measurement Conditions. In Section I, see: Lung Diseases/Diagnosis.

Respiratory Function Measurement in Infants: Symbols, Abbreviations, and Units (SI Units). In Section I, see: Respiratory Function Tests.

Respiratory Mechanics in Infants: Physiologic Evaluation in Health and Disease. In Section I, see: Respiratory Tract Diseases/Physiopathology.

Respiratory Syncytial Virus Immune Globulin Intravenous: Indications for Use. In Section I, see: Respiratory Syncytial Virus Infections/Therapy.

Responsibilities of an Electrodiagnostic Technologist. In Section I, see: Allied Health Personnel.

Resuscitation of Blood Pressure and Oxygenation. In Section I, see: Head Injuries/Physiopathology.

Review of the Literature on Spinal Ultrasound for the Evaluation of Back Pain and Radicular Disorders. In Section I, see: Spinal Disorders/Ultrasonography.

Revised Dosing Regimen for Malaria Prophylaxis with Mefloquine. In Section I, see: Malaria/Prevention and Control.

Revised Guidelines for Prevention of Early-onset Group-B Streptococcal (GBS) Infection. In Section I, see: Streptococcal Infections/Prevention and Control.

Revised: Management of Health Care Workers Who Are Infected with HIV, HBV, HCV, and Other Blood-borne Pathogens. In Section I, see: Personnel Administration, Hospital.

Rhinoplasty. In Section I, see: Rhinoplasty.

Rigid and Flexible Sigmoidoscopies. In Section I, see: Sigmoidoscopy.

Risk Management. In Section I, see: Risk Management.

Risks in Electrodiagnostic Medicine. In Section I, see: Electrodiagnosis.

Role of Allergists in Hospitals. In Section I, see: Allergy and Immunology.

Role of Colonoscopy in the Management of Patients with Colonic Polyps: Guidelines for Clinical Application. In Section I, see: Colonic Polyps/Diagnosis.

Role of Colonoscopy in the Management of Patients with Inflammatory Bowel Disease: Guidelines for Clinical Application. In Section I, see: Colitis, Ulcerative/Diagnosis.

Role of Endoscopic Sclerotherapy in the Management of Variceal Bleeding: Guidelines for Clinical Application. In Section I, see: Esophageal and Gastric Varices/Drug Therapy.

Role of Endoscopy in Diseases of the Biliary Tract and Pancreas: Guidelines for Clinical Application. In Section I, see: Biliary Tract Diseases/Diagnosis.

Role of Endoscopy in the Management of Acute Nonvariceal Upper Gastrointestinal Bleeding. In Section I, see: Endoscopy, Gastrointestinal.

Role of Endoscopy in the Management of Esophagitis. In Section I, see: Esophagitis, Peptic/Diagnosis.

Role of Endoscopy in the Management of the Patient with Peptic Ulcer Disease: Guidelines for Clinical Application. In Section I, see: Peptic Ulcer/Diagnosis.

Role of Endoscopy in the Management of Upper Gastrointestinal Hemorrhage. In Section I, see: Endoscopy.

Role of Endoscopy in the Patient with Lower Gastrointestinal Bleeding: Guidelines for Clinical Application. In Section I, see: Colonoscopy.

Role of Endoscopy in the Surveillance of Premalignant Conditions of the Upper Gastrointestinal Tract: Guidelines for Clinical Application. In Section I, see: Esophageal Neoplasms/Diagnosis.

Role of Laparoscopy in the Diagnosis and Management of Gastrointestinal Disease: Guidelines for Clinical Application. In Section I, see: Gastrointestinal Diseases/Diagnosis.

Role of Loop Electrosurgical Excision Procedure in the Evaluation of Abnormal Pap Test Results. In Section I, see: Electrosurgery.

Role of Percutaneous Endoscopic Gastrostomy: Guidelines for Clinical Application. In Section I, see: Enteral Nutrition.

Role of Pulmonary and Critical Care Medicine Physician in the American Health Care System. In Section I, see: Critical Care.

Role of the Allergist/Immunologist as a Subspecialist. In Section I, see: Allergy and Immunology/Trends.

Role of the Obstetrician-Gynecologist in the Diagnosis and Treatment of Breast Disease. In Section I, see: Breast Diseases/Diagnosis.

Rotavirus Vaccine for the Prevention of Rotavirus Gastroenteritis Among Children Recommendations of the Advisory Committee on Immunization Practices (ACIP). In Section I, see: Rotavirus/Immunology.

Routine Cancer Screening. In Section I, see: Mass Screening.

Routine Storage of Umbilical Cord Blood for Potential Future Transplantation. In Section I, see: Fetal Blood.

Routine Ultrasound in Low-Risk Pregnancy. In Section I, see: Ultrasonography, Prenatal.

Rubella Prevention: Recommendations of the Immunization Practices Advisory Committee. In Section I, see: Rubella/Prevention and Control.

Rubella, Congenital and Pregnancy. In Section I, see: Rubella Syndrome, Congenital.

S

Safety and Appropriate Use of Salmeterol in the Treatment of Asthma. In Section I, see: Adrenergic Beta-Agonists/Pharmacology.

Safety and Efficacy of Ambulatory Cardiac Catheterization in Hospital and Freestanding Setting. In Section I, see: Heart Catheterization/Methods.

Safety of Oral Contraceptives for Teenagers. In Section I, see: Contraceptives, Oral/Adverse Effects.

SAGES Position Statement—Global Statement on New Procedures. In Section I, see: Surgical Procedures, Laparoscopic/Standards.

SAGES Position Statement—Laparoscopic Appendectomy. In Section I, see: Appendectomy/Methods.

Salivary Electrostimulation in Sjogren's Syndrome. In Section I, see: Electric Stimulation Therapy/Methods.

Scheduled Cesarean Delivery and the Prevention of Vertical Transmission of HIV Infection. In Section I, see: Cesarean Section.

Schizophrenia and Other Psychotic Disorders. In Section I, see: Schizophrenia/Therapy.

Scleroderma and Sclerodermoid Disorders. In Section I, see: Scleroderma, Systemic/Therapy.

Sclerotherapy Treatment of Varicose and Telangiectatic Leg Veins. In Section I, see: Sclerotherapy.

Scope of Occupational and Environmental Health Programs and Practice. In Section I, see: Occupational Medicine.

Scope of Services for Uncomplicated Obstetric Care. In Section I, see: Prenatal Care/Standards.

Screening for Abdominal Aortic Aneurysm. In Section I, see: Aortic Aneurysm, Abdominal/Diagnosis.

Screening for Adolescent Idiopathic Scoliosis. In Section I, see: Scoliosis/Diagnosis.

Screening for Asymptomatic Bacteriuria. In Section I, see: Bacteriuria/Diagnosis.

Screening for Asymptomatic Carotid Artery Stenosis. In Section I, see: Carotid Stenosis/Diagnosis.

Screening for Asymptomatic Coronary Artery Disease. In Section I, see: Coronary Disease/Diagnosis.

Screening for Asymptomatic Coronary Artery Disease: The Resting Electrocardiogram. In Section I, see: Electrocardiography.

Screening for Breast Cancer. In Section I, see: Breast Neoplasms/Prevention and Control.

Screening for Breast Cancer for Health Professionals. In Section I, see: Breast Neoplasms.

Screening for Canavan Disease. In Section I, see: Canavan Disease/Diagnosis.

Screening for Cervical Cancer. In Section I, see: Cervix Neoplasms/Epidemiology.

Screening for Cervical Cancer. In Section I, see: Mass Screening/Methods.

Screening for Cervical Cancer. In Section I, see: Cervix Neoplasms.

Screening for Cervical Carcinoma in Elderly Women. In Section I, see: Cervix Neoplasms.

Screening for Chlamydial Infection. In Section I, see: Chlamydia Infections/Diagnosis.

Screening for Colorectal Cancer. In Section I, see: Mass Screening/Methods.

Screening for Colorectal Cancer. In Section I, see: Colorectal Neoplasms/Diagnosis.

Screening for Colorectal Cancer. In Section I, see: Colorectal Neoplasms/Diagnosis.

Screening for Congenital Hypothyroidism. In Section I, see: Cretinism/Diagnosis.

Screening for Dementia. In Section I, see: Dementia/Diagnosis.

Screening for Diabetes Mellitus. In Section I, see: Diabetes Mellitus/Diagnosis.

Screening for Diabetes Mellitus in Apparently Healthy, Asymptomatic Adults. In Section I, see: Diabetes Mellitus/Prevention and Control.

Screening for Diabetic Retinopathy. In Section I, see: Vision Screening/Standards.

Screening for Down Syndrome. In Section I, see: Down Syndrome/Prevention and Control.

Screening for Elevated Blood Lead Levels. In Section I, see: Lead Poisoning/Prevention and Control.

Screening for Elevated Lead Levels in Childhood and Pregnancy. In Section I, see: Lead Poisoning/Diagnosis.

Screening for Family Violence. In Section I, see: Domestic Violence.

Screening for Gastric Cancer. In Section I, see: Stomach Neoplasms.

Screening for Glaucoma. In Section I, see: Glaucoma/Diagnosis.

Screening for Gonorrhea. In Section I, see: Gonorrhea/Diagnosis.

Screening for Hearing Impairment. In Section I, see: Hearing Disorders/Diagnosis.

Screening for Hemoglobinopathies. In Section I, see: Hemoglobinopathies/Prevention and Control.

Screening for High Blood Cholesterol and Other Lipid Abnormalities. In Section I, see: Hypercholesterolemia/Diagnosis.

Screening for Human Immunodeficiency Virus Infection. In Section I, see: HIV Infections/Diagnosis.

Screening for Hypertension. In Section I, see: Hypertension/Prevention and Control.

Screening for Lung Cancer. In Section I, see: Lung Neoplasms/Prevention and Control.

Screening for Obesity. In Section I, see: Obesity/Diagnosis.

Screening for Oral Cancer. In Section I, see: Mass Screening.

Screening for Oral Cancer. In Section I, see: Mouth Neoplasms.

Screening for Osteoporosis. In Section I, see: Osteoporosis, Postmenopausal/Diagnosis.

Screening for Ovarian Cancer. In Section I, see: Mass Screening/Standards.

Screening for Ovarian Cancer. In Section I, see: Mass Screening.

Screening for Ovarian Cancer. In Section I, see: Ovarian Neoplasms/Diagnosis.

Screening for Pancreatic Cancer. In Section I, see: Pancreatic Neoplasms/Diagnosis.

Screening for Peripheral Arterial Disease. In Section I, see: Peripheral Vascular Diseases/Diagnosis.

Screening for Phenylketonuria. In Section I, see: Phenylketonuria/Diagnosis.

Screening for Postmenopausal Osteoporosis. In Section I, see: Osteoporosis, Postmenopausal/Diagnosis.

Screening for Preeclampsia. In Section I, see: Pre-eclampsia/Diagnosis.

Screening for Problem Drinking. In Section I, see: Alcoholism/Diagnosis.

Screening for Prostate Cancer. In Section I, see: Mass Screening.

Screening for Rubella. In Section I, see: Rubella/Diagnosis.

Screening for Skin Cancer. In Section I, see: Skin Neoplasms/Diagnosis.

Screening for Skin Cancer. In Section I, see: Mass Screening/Methods.

Screening for Suicide Risk. In Section I, see: Suicide/Prevention and Control.

Screening for Syphilis. In Section I, see: Syphilis/Diagnosis.

Screening for Tay-Sachs Disease. In Section I, see: Tay-Sachs Disease/Diagnosis.

Screening for Testicular Cancer. In Section I, see: Mass Screening.

Screening for Thyroid Disease. In Section I, see: Thyroid Diseases/Diagnosis.

Screening for Visual Impairment. In Section I, see: Vision Disorders/Diagnosis.

Screening Infants and Young Children for Developmental Disabilities. In Section I, see: Developmental Disabilities/Diagnosis.

Screening Low Risk, Asymptomatic Adults for Cardiac Risk Factors: Serum Cholesterol and Triglycerides. In Section I, see: Coronary Disease/Prevention and Control.

Screening of Microalbuminuria in Patients with Diabetes. In Section I, see: Albuminuria/Diagnosis.

Screening Test for Dyslipidemia. In Section I, see: Hyperlipidemia/Prevention and Control.

Screening Ultrasonography in Pregnancy. In Section I, see: Ultrasonography, Prenatal/Methods.

SCVIR HIV/Bloodborne Pathogens Guidelines. In Section I, see: Bloodborne Pathogens.

Second Report of the Expert Panel on Detection, Evaluation, and Treatment of High Blood Cholesterol in Adults. In Section I, see: Hypercholesterolemia/Drug Therapy.

Second-Look Laparotomy for Epithelial Ovarian Cancer. In Section I, see: Laparotomy.

Seizure Disorders in Pregnancy. In Section I, see: Pregnancy Complications.

Selected Methods for the Management of Diabetes Mellitus. In Section I, see: Diabetes Mellitus/Therapy.

Selection and Treatment of Candidates for Heart Transplantation. In Section I, see: Heart Diseases/Surgery.

Septal Fracture. In Section I, see: Nasal Fracture.

Septic Shock. In Section I, see: Shock, Septic.

Septoplasty. In Section I, see: Nasal Septum/Surgery.

Serum Electrolytes, Serum Osmolality, Blood Urea Nitrogen, and Serum Creatinine. In Section I, see: Diagnostic Tests/Routine.

Serum Enzyme Assays in the Diagnosis of Acute Myocardial Infarction: Recommendations Based on a Quantitative Analysis. In Section I, see: Enzyme Tests.

Severe Invasive Group A Streptococcal Infections: A Subject Review. In Section I, see: Streptococcal Infections/Etiology.

Sex Selection. In Section I, see: Sex Preselection.

Sexual and Gender Identity Disorders. In Section I, see: Gender Identity/Therapy.

Sexual Assault. In Section I, see: Rape.

Sexual Dysfunction. In Section I, see: Sex Disorders.

Sexual Misconduct in the Practice of Obstetrics and Gynecology: Ethical Considerations. In Section I, see: Ethics, Medical.

Shoulder Dystocia. In Section I, see: Dystocia.

Sickle Cell Disease: Screening, Diagnosis, Management, and Counseling in Newborns and Infants. In Section I, see: Anemia, Sickle Cell/Diagnosis.

Silicone Breast Implants and Neurologic Disorders. In Section I, see: Breast Implants/Adverse Effects.

Simultaneous Pancreas-Kidney and Sequential Pancreas-After-Kidney Transplantation. In Section I, see: Kidney Transplantation/Methods.

Single and Double Lung Transplantation. In Section I, see: Lung Transplantation/Standards.

Single Breath Carbon Monoxide Diffusing Capacity (Transfer Factor). In Section I, see: Pulmonary Diffusing Capacity.

Sixth Report of the Joint National Committee on Detection, Evaluation, and Treatment of High Blood Pressure (JNC VI). In Section I, see: Hypertension/Diagnosis.

Skills of the Health Care Team Involved in Out-of-Hospital Care for Patients with COPD. In Section I, see: Lung Diseases, Obstructive/Therapy.

Skin Lesions. In Section I, see: Skin/Pathology.

Skin Testing and Radioallergosorbent Testing (RAST) for Diagnosis of Specific Allergens Responsible for IgE Mediated Diseases. In Section I, see: IgE/Metabolism.

Skin Titration (Rinkel Method). In Section I, see: Skin Test End-Point Titration.

Sleep Apnea: Sleepiness, and Driving Risk. In Section I, see: Sleep Apnea Syndromes.

Sleep Disorders. In Section I, see: Sleep Disorders/Drug Therapy.

Smoking and Health: Physician Responsibility. In Section I, see: Smoking/Adverse Effects.

Smoking and Women's Health. In Section I, see: Smoking/Adverse Effects.

Smoking Cessation. In Section I, see: Smoking Cessation.

Society for Healthcare Epidemiology of America and Infectious Diseases Society of America Joint Committee on the Prevention of Antimicrobial Resistance: Guidelines for the Prevention of Antimicrobial Resistance in Hospitals. In Section I, see: Drug Resistance, Microbial.

Society of Nuclear Medicine Procedure Guidelines Manual 1999. In Section I, see: Practice Guidelines.

Soft Tissue Augmentation (3): Gelatin Matrix Implant. In Section I, see: Biocompatible Materials.

Soft Tissue Augmentation Collagen Implant. In Section I, see: Collagen.

Soft Tissue Augmentation Fat Transplantation. In Section I, see: Adipose Tissue/Transplantation.

Soft Tissue Sarcoma Surgical Practice Guidelines. In Section I, see: Soft Tissue Neoplasms.

Somatoform and Factitious Disorders. In Section I, see: Somatoform Disorders.

Somatosensory Evoked Potentials: Clinical Uses. In Section I, see: Evoked Potentials, Somatosensory.

Some Untested Diagnostic and Therapeutic Procedures in Clinical Allergy. In Section I, see: Hypersensitivity/Diagnosis.

Special Problems of Multiple Gestation. In Section I, see: Pregnancy, Multiple.

Speech Therapy for Otitis Media with Effusion. In Section I, see: Speech Therapy.

Sperm Penetration Assay in Identifying Male Infertility. In Section I, see: Infertility, Male/Diagnosis.

Spinal Manipulation of Low-Back Pain. In Section I, see: Low Back Pain.

Spinal Puncture. In Section I, see: Spinal Puncture.

Spirometry in the Workplace. In Section I, see: Spirometry.

Staging Evaluation for Patients with Adenocarcinoma of the Prostate (10 variants). In Section I, see: Prostatic Neoplasms.

Staging of Non-Small Cell Lung Cancer (8 variants). In Section I, see: Lung Neoplasms/Therapy.

Standard for Diagnostic Arteriography in Adults. In Section I, see: Angiography.

Standardization of Spirometry. In Section I, see: Spirometry/Standards.

Standards for Basic Anesthetic Monitoring. In Section I, see: Monitoring, Physiologic.

Standards for Diagnosis and Management of Invasive Breast Carcinoma (Revised). In Section I, see: Breast Neoplasms.

Standards for Management of Ductal Carcinoma In Situ (DCIS) (Revised). In Section I, see: Carcinoma In Situ.

Standards for Postanesthesia Care. In Section I, see: Anesthesia Recovery Period.

Standards for the Diagnosis and Care of Patients with Chronic Obstructive Pulmonary Disease. In Section I, see: Lung Diseases, Obstructive/Diagnosis.

Standards of Nursing Care for Adult Patients with Pulmonary Dysfunction. In Section I, see: Nursing Care/Standards.

Standards of Practice of Gastrointestinal Endoscopy. In Section I, see: Education, Medical.

Stapedectomy. In Section I, see: Stapes Surgery.

Stat Testing? A Guideline for Meeting Clinician Turnaround Time Requirements. In Section I, see: Pathology, Clinical/Methods.

Statement on Endoscopic Training. In Section I, see: Endoscopy/Education.

Statement on Guidelines for Total Parenteral Nutrition. In Section I, see: Parenteral Nutrition, Total.

Statement on Laparoscopic Cholecystectomy. In Section I, see: Cholecystectomy, Laparoscopic.

Statement on Laser Surgery. In Section I, see: Laser Surgery.

Statement on Resuscitative Equipment. In Section I, see: Allergy and Immunology.

Statement on Role of Short Courses in Endoscopic Training. In Section I, see: Endoscopy/Education.

Statement on Routine Preoperative Laboratory and Diagnostic Screening. In Section I, see: Diagnostic Tests, Routine.

Statement on Surgical Assistants. In Section I, see: Operating Room Technicians.

Statement on the Question of Allergy to Fluoride as Used in the Fluoridation of Community Water Supplies. In Section I, see: Fluorides/Immunology.

Status of Medical Diagnostic Ultrasound Instrumentation. In Section I, see: Ultrasonography/ Instrumentation.

Stereotactic Introduction of Subcortical Electrodes. In Section I, see: Radiosurgery.

Stereotactic Lesion Creation. In Section I, see: Radiosurgery.

Stereotactic Lesion Creation in Gasserian Ganglion or Trigeminal Tract. In Section I, see: Trigeminal Ganglion.

Stereotactic Procedure for Biopsy, Aspiration, Excision of Intracranial Lesion. In Section I, see: Radiosurgery.

Stereotactic Procedure for Brachytherapy. In Section I, see: Radiosurgery.

Stereotactic Procedure for Radiosurgery of Brain or Skull Base. In Section I, see: Radiosurgery.

Stereotactic Procedure With or Without CAT Guidance. In Section I, see: Radiosurgery.

Sterilization. In Section I, see: Sterilization, Sexual.

Sterilization of Women, Including Those with Mental Disabilities. In Section I, see: Ethics, Medical.

Steroids. In Section I, see: Head Injuries/Drug Therapy.

Stinging Insect Hypersensitivity: A Practice Parameter. In Section I, see: Hypersensitivity/Therapy.

Strategic Plan for the Elimination of Tuberculosis in the United States. In Section I, see: Tuberculosis/Prevention and Control.

Strategies for the Treatment and Prevention of Sexual Assault. In Section I, see: Rape/Prevention and Control.

Stroke Prevention in Patients with Nonvalvular Atrial Fibrillation. In Section I, see: Cerebrovascular Disorders/Prevention and Control.

Substance Abuse. In Section I, see: Substance-Related Disorders.

Substance Abuse in Pregnancy. In Section I, see: Pregnancy Complications.

Substance-Related Disorders. In Section I, see: Substance-Related Disorders/Therapy.

Sudden Cardiac Death. In Section I, see: Death, Sudden.

Suggested Guidelines for the Practice of Arthroscopic Surgery. In Section I, see: Arthroscopy.

Suggested Technique for Fecal Occult Blood Testing and Interpretation in Colorectal Cancer Screening. In Section I, see: Colorectal Neoplasms/Prevention and Control.

Summary of Policy Recommendations for Periodic Health Examination. In Section I, see: Preventive Health Services.

Sunlight, Ultraviolet Radiation, and the Skin. In Section I, see: Skin Diseases/Etiology.

Superficial Mycotic Infections of the Skin: Mucocutaneous Candidiasis. In Section I, see: Candidiasis, Chronic Mucocutaneous/Drug Therapy.

Superficial Mycotic Infections of the Skin: Onychomycosis. In Section I, see: Onychomycosis/Diagnosis, Therapy.

Superficial Mycotic Infections of the Skin: Piedra. In Section I, see: Piedra/Diagnosis.

Superficial Mycotic Infections of the Skin: Pityriasis (tinea) versicolor. In Section I, see: Tinea Versicolor/Drug Therapy.

Superficial Mycotic Infections of the Skin: Tinea capitis and Tinea barbae. In Section I, see: Facial Dermatoses/Microbiology.

Superficial Mycotic Infections of the Skin: Tinea corporis, Tinea cruris, Tinea faciei, Tinea manuum, and Tinea pedis. In Section I, see: Tinea/Drug Therapy.

Surface/Specialty Coil Devices and Gating Techniques in Magnetic Resonance Imaging. In Section I, see: Gated Blood-Pool Imaging/Standards.

Surgery for Epilepsy. In Section I, see: Epilepsy/Surgery.

Surgery of Craniofacial Anomalies. In Section I, see: Craniofacial Abnormalities/Surgery.

Surgical Procedures for Managing Extradural or Subdural Hematomas by Burr Hole or Twist Drill Evacuation. In Section I, see: Hematoma, Epidural/Surgery.

Surgical Treatment of Female Stress Urinary Incontinence. In Section I, see: Urinary Incontinence, Stress/Surgery.

Surrogate Markers of Progressive HIV Disease. In Section I, see: HIV Infections/Immunology.

Surveillance of Pediatric HIV Infection. In Section I, see: Population Surveillance/Methods.

Sympathectomy. In Section I, see: Sympathectomy.

Syphilis Tests in Diagnostic and Therapeutic Decision Making. In Section I, see: Syphilis/Diagnosis.

Systemic Therapy for Breast Cancer. In Section I, see: Breast Neoplasms/Drug Thereapy.

T

Tamoxifen and Endometrial Cancer. In Section I, see: Tamoxifen/Adverse Effects.

Tartrazine. In Section I, see: Tartrazine.

Tear, Meniscus of the Knee (Medial and/or Lateral). In Section I, see: Menisci, Tibial.

Technology Review: Dynamic Electromyography in Gait and Motion Analysis. In Section I, see: Electromyography.

Technology Review: Nervepace Digital Electroneurometer. In Section I, see: Computers.

Technology Review: The Neurometer Currrent Perception Threshold (CPT). In Section I, see: Electrodiagnosis.

Technology Review: The Use of Surface EMG in the Diagnosis and Treatment of Nerve and Muscle Disorders. In Section I, see: Electromyography.

Teflon Injections for Urinary Incontinence. In Section I, see: Polytetrafluoroethylene/Therapeutic Use.

Temporomandibular Joint. In Section I, see: Temporomandibular Joint/Surgery.

Temporomandibular Joint Surgery. In Section I, see: Surgery, Oral/Standards.

Teratology. In Section I, see: Teratology.

The American Heart Association Stroke Outcome Classification. In Section I, see: Cerebrovascular Disorders/Classification.

The American Heart Association Stroke Outcome Classification Executive Summary. In Section I, see: Cerebrovascular Disorders/Classification.

The Benefits and Risks of Controlling Blood Glucose Levels in Patients with Type 2 Diabetes Mellitus. In Section I, see: Blood Glucose.

The Care of Dying Patients, Position Statement. In Section I, see: Terminal Care.

The Clinical Utility and Appropriate Use of In Vitro Allergy Testing. In Section I, see: Hypersensitivity.

The Diagnosis and Management of Anaphylaxis. In Section I, see: Anaphylaxis/Diagnosis.

The Discontinuation of Hymenoptera Venon Immunotherapy. In Section I, see: Hymenoptera/ Immunology.

The Electrodiagnostic Medicine Consultation. In Section I, see: Electrodiagnosis.

The Electrodiagnostic Medicine Consultation. In Section I, see: Electrodiagnosis.

The Future of the Subspecialty of Allergy and Immunology. In Section I, see: Allergy and Immunology/Education.

The Health Professional's Guide to Diabetes and Exercise. In Section I, see: Diabetes Mellitus.

The HIV-Infected Healthcare Worker. In Section I, see: Health Occupations.

The Integration of Behavioral and Relaxation Approaches into the Treatment of Chronic Pain and Insomnia. In Section I, see: Pain/Therapy.

The Management of Chronic Pain in Older Persons. In Section I, see: Pain/Drug Therapy.

The Pediatrician's Role in Disaster Preparedness. In Section I, see: Disasters.

The Potential for Conflict of Interest of Members of the American Thoracic Society. In Section I, see: Thoracic Diseases.

The Relationship of MS to Physical Trauma and Psychological Stress. In Section I, see: Multiple Sclerosis/Etiology.

The Report on the ATS Workshop on the Health Effects of Atmospheric Acids and Their Precursors. In Section I, see: Acid Rain/Adverse Effects.

The Revised CDC Guidelines for Isolation Precautions in Hospitals: Implications for Pediatrics. In Section I, see: Patient Isolation.

The Role of Home Visitation Programs in Improving Health Outcomes for Children and Families. In Section I, see: Home Care Services/Economics.

The Role of Phenytoin in the Management of Alcohol Withdrawal. In Section I, see: Phenytoin.

The Role of Physicians in House Calls in Geriatric Practice. In Section I, see: House Calls.

The Role of Screening Tests Before Gastrointestinal Endoscopic Procedures. In Section I, see: Endoscopy, Gastrointestinal.

The Role of the Veterans Administration in the Care of the Elderly, Position Statement. In Section I, see: United States Department of Veterans Affairs.

The Scope of Electrodiagnostic Medicine. In Section I, see: Electrodiagnosis.

The Training of Geriatrics Fellows in Rehabilitation. In Section I, see: Education, Medical, Graduate.

The Treatment of Restless Legs Syndrome and Periodic Limb Movements. In Section I, see: Restless Legs/Therapy.

The Tuberculin Skin Test. In Section I, see: Tuberculin Test.

The Use of Chemotherapy and Radiotherapy Protectants. In Section I, see: Antineoplastic Agents/ Antagonists and Inhibitors.

The Use of Drugs of Questionable Efficacy in the Elderly, Position Statement. In Section I, see: Drugs, Prescription.

The Use of Oral Anticoagulants (warfarin) in the Elderly. In Section I, see: Warfarin.

The Use of Physical Restraint Interventions for Children and Adolescents in the Acute Care Setting. In Section I, see: Restraint, Physical.

The Waiting Period After Allergen Skin Testing and Immunotherapy. In Section I, see: Allergens/ Diagnostic Use.

Therapeutic Apheresis, Part I. Background and Nonrenal Indications. In Section I, see: Plasmapheresis.

Therapeutic Apheresis, Part II. Renal Indications. In Section I, see: Plasmapheresis.

Trends in the Practice of Cardiology: Implications for Manpower. In Section I, see: Cardiology/Manpower.

Trial of Labor versus Elective Repeat Cesarean Section for the Woman with a Previous Cesarean Section. In Section I, see: Cesarean Section, Repeat.

Triglyceride, High Density Lipoprotein, and Coronary Heart Disease. In Section I, see: Coronary Disease/Epidemiology.

Tubal Disease. In Section I, see: Fallopian Tube Diseases.

Tubal Ligation with Cesarean Delivery. In Section I, see: Cesarean Section.

Tuberculosis Control Laws—United States, 1993. In Section I, see: Public Health/Legislation and Jurisprudence.

Two-Step PPD Testing for Nursing Home Patients on Admission. In Section I, see: Tuberculin.

Tympanoplasty. In Section I, see: Tympanoplasty.

Typhoid Immunization. In Section I, see: Typhoid/Immunization.

U

Ulcerative Colitis. In Section I, see: Colitis, Ulcerative/Diagnosis.

Ulnar Collateral Ligament Injury of the Thumb. In Section I, see: Collateral Ligaments/Injuries.

Ulnar Nerve Transposition. In Section I, see: Ulnar Nerve Compression Syndrome/Surgery.

Ultrasonic Evaluation of the Fetus. In Section I, see: Fetal Diseases/Ultrasonography.

Ultrasonic Imaging of the Abdomen: Report of the Ultrasonography Task Force. In Section I, see: Abdomen/Ultrasonography.

Ultrasonic Imaging of the Heart. In Section I, see: Ultrasonography.

Ultrasonic Imaging of the Vascular System. In Section I, see: Blood Vessels/Ultrasonography.

Ultrasonography in Pregnancy. In Section I, see: Ultrasonography, Prenatal.

Ultrasound Screening: Implications of the RADIUS Study. In Section I, see: Pregnancy Outcome.

Umbilical Artery Blood Acid-Base Analysis. In Section I, see: Acid-Base Equilibrium.

Unexplained Infertility. In Section I, see: Infertility/Diagnosis.

Unproven Procedures for Diagnosis and Treatment of Allergic and Immunologic Diseases. In Section I, see: Hypersensitivity/Diagnosis.

Unstable Angina: Diagnosis and Management. In Section I, see: Angina, Unstable/Diagnosis.

Update on Tuberculosis Skin Testing of Children. In Section I, see: Tuberculin Test.

Update: MRI of the Brain and Spine. In Section I, see: Magnetic Resonance Imaging.

Update: Vaccine Side Effects, Adverse Reactions, Contraindications, and Precautions. In Section I, see: Bacterial Vaccines/Adverse Effects.

Updated Guidelines for the Guidelines for the Diagnosis and Treatment of Gastroesophageal Reflux Disease. In Section I, see: Gastroesophageal Reflux/Diagnosis.

Ureteral Stone Management: Ureteroscopy and Extracorporeal Shock Wave Lithotripsy. In Section I, see: Lithotripsy.

Ureteral Stone Management: Ureteroscopy and Ultrasonic Lithotripsy. In Section I, see: Ureteral Calculi/Therapy.

Urinalysis and Urine Culture in Women with Dysuria. In Section I, see: Urine/Analysis.

Urinary Incontinence. In Section I, see: Urinary Incontinence.

Urinary Incontinence and UI Stress. In Section I, see: Urinary Incontinence.

Urinary Incontinence in Adults. In Section I, see: Urinary Incontinence.

Urinary Incontinence in Adults: Acute and Chronic Management. In Section I, see: Urinary Incontinence/Therapy.

Urine Autoinjection (Autogenous Urine Immunization). In Section I, see: Urine.

US Public Health Service Guidelines for Testing and Counseling Blood and Plasma Donors for Human Immunodeficiency Virus Type 1 Antigen. In Section I, see: Blood Banks/Standards.

Use and Abuse of the Apgar Score. In Section I, see: Apgar Score.

Use of Anhydrous Theophylline in the Management of Asthma. In Section I, see: Allergens/Diagnostic Use.

Use of Anti-Emetic Agents. In Section I, see: Antiemetics/Therapeutic Use.

Use of Antihistamines in Patients with Asthma. In Section I, see: Asthma/Therapy.

Use of Bromocriptine. In Section I, see: Bromocriptine/Therapeutic Use.

Use of Epinephrine in the Treatment of Anaphylaxis. In Section I, see: Anaphylaxis/Drug Therapy.

Use of In Vitro Tests for IgE Antibody in the Specific Diagnosis of IgE Mediated Disorders and the Formulation of Allergen Immunotherapy. In Section I, see: Allergens/Therapeutic Use.

Use of Inhaled Medications in School by Students with Asthma. In Section I, see: Asthma/Drug Therapy.

Use of Irradiated Blood Components. In Section I, see: Blood Cells/Radiation Effects.

Use of Plasma Concentrations of Apolipoproteins. In Section I, see: Apolipoproteins B/Blood.

Use of Radioallergosorbent and IgE Tests in Practice. In Section I, see: Radioallergosorbent Tests.

Use of Radiographic Devices by Cardiologists. In Section I, see: Fluoroscopy.

Use of Reminder and Recall Systems by Vaccination Providers to Increase Vaccination Rates. In Section I, see: Reminder Systems, Vaccination/Utilization.

Uses of Vaccines and Immune Globulins in Persons with Altered Immunocompetence. In Section I, see: Immunizations, Passive/Standards.

USPHS/IDSA Guidelines for the Prevention of Opportunistic Infections in Persons Infected with Human Immunodeficiency Virus: A Summary. In Section I, see: AIDS-Related Opportunistic Infections/Prevention and Control.

Uterine Leiomyomata. In Section I, see: Uterine Neoplasms.

Utility of Antepartum Umbilical Artery Doppler Velocimetry in Intrauterine Growth Restriction. In Section I, see: Fetal Growth Retardation/Ultrasonography.

Utility of Routine Chest Radiographs. In Section I, see: Diagnostic Tests, Routine.

Utility of the Routine Electrocardiogram Before Surgery and on General Hospital Admission: Critical Review and New Guidelines. In Section I, see: Diagnostic Tests, Routine.

Utility of Therapeutic Plasmapheresis for Neurological Disorders. In Section I, see: Nervous System Diseases/Therapy.

Utility of Umbilical Cord Blood Acid-Base Assessment. In Section I, see: Acid-Base Equilibrium.

Utilizing Monospecific Antihuman Globulin to Test Blood-Group Compatibility. In Section I, see: Antibodies, Anti-Idiotypic/Immunology.

Uvulopalatopharyngoplasty. In Section I, see: Otorhinolaryngologic Surgical Procedures.

V

Vaccinia (Smallpox) Vaccine. In Section I, see: Smallpox Vaccine.

Vaginal Birth after Previous Cesarean Delivery. In Section I, see: Vaginal Birth After Cesarean/Standards.

Vaginal Bleeding. In Section I, see: Uterine Hemorrhage/Diagnosis.

Vaginitis. In Section I, see: Vaginitis.

Varicocele and Infertility. In Section I, see: Infertility, Male.

Vasectomy Reversal. In Section I, see: Sterilization Reversal.

Vasoactive Intracavernous Pharmacotherapy for Impotence: Intracavernous Injection of Prostaglandin E1. In Section I, see: Alprostadil/Therapeutic Use.

Violence Against Women. In Section I, see: Violence.

Viral Hepatitis in Pregnancy. In Section I, see: Hepatitis, Viral, Human/Diagnosis.

Vitamin A Supplementation During Pregnancy. In Section I, see: Dietary Supplements.

Vitamin Preparations as Dietary Supplements and as Therapeutic Agents. In Section I, see: Vitamins/Administration and Dosage.

Vitiligo. In Section I, see: Vitiligo/Therapy.

Vitro Tests for Allergy. In Section I, see: Hypersensitivity/Diagnosis.

Vivo Diagnostic Testing and Immunotherapy for Allergy: Part I. In Section I, see: Desensitization, Immunologic.

Vivo Diagnostic Testing and Immunotherapy for Allergy: Part II. In Section I, see: Desensitization, Immunologic.

Voluntary Health Organizations. In Section I, see: Voluntary Health Organizations.

Vulvar Cancer. In Section I, see: Vulvar Neoplasms.

Vulvar Nonneoplastic Epithelial Disorders. In Section I, see: Vulvar Diseases/Classification.

W

Warts: HPV. In Section I, see: Papillomavirus, Human.

Who Is Qualified to Practice Electrodiagnostic Medicine?. In Section I, see: Professional Competence.

Withdrawing and Withholding Life-Sustaining Therapy. In Section I, see: Euthanasia, Passive.

Women and Exercise. In Section I, see: Exercise.

Working Group Report on High Blood Pressure in Pregnancy. In Section I, see: Pregnancy Complications, Cardiovascular.

Working Group Report on Hypertension in the Elderly. In Section I, see: Hypertension.

Working Group Report on Management of Asthma During Pregnancy. In Section I, see: Asthma/Therapy.

Working Group Report on Primary Prevention of Hypertension. In Section I, see: Hypertension/ Prevention and Control.

Working Report on Hypertension in Diabetes. In Section I, see: Diabetes Mellitus/Complications.

Y

Yellow Fever Vaccine: Recommendations of the Immunization Practices Advisory Panel (ACIP). In Section I, see: Immunization.

Section IV
Clinical Practice
Guidelines
In Development

American Academy of Child and Adolescent Psychiatry

Title: Practice Parameters for the Assessment and Treatment of Children and Adolescents with Autism and Pervasive Developmental Disorders. *Reference:* Date of publication to be determined. *J Am Acad Child Adol Psych.* For further information contact sponsor. *Contact(s):* Elizabeth Sloan 202-966-7300.

Title: Practice Parameters for the Assessment and Treatment of Children and Adolescents with Depressive Disorders. *Reference:* 1998-1999. *J Am Acad Child Adol Psych.* For further information contact sponsor. *Contact(s):* Elizabeth Sloan 202-966-7300.

Title: Practice Parameters for the Assessment and Treatment of Children and Adolescents with Language and Learning Disorders. *Reference:* 1998-1999. *J Am Acad Child Adol Psych.* For further information contact sponsor. *Contact(s):* Elizabeth Sloan 202-966-7300.

Title: Practice Parameters for the Assessment and Treatment of Children and Adolescents with Mental Retardation. *Reference:* Date of publication to be determined. *J Am Acad Child Adol Psych.* For further information contact sponsor. *Contact(s):* Elizabeth Sloan 202-966-7300.

Title: Practice Parameters for the Assessment and Treatment of Children and Adolescents with Tourette's Disorder. *Reference:* Date of publication to be determined. *J Am Acad Child Adol Psych.* For further information contact sponsor. *Contact(s):* Elizabeth Sloan 202-966-7300.

American Academy of Family Physicians, American Academy of Pediatrics

Title: Pediatric Head Trauma. *Reference:* Date of publication to be determined. *Source information not available.* For further information contact sponsor. *Contact(s):* Bellinda Schoof 816-333-9700, x5560.

American Academy of Ophthalmology

Title: Artificial Drainage Devices in the Management of Glaucoma Ophthalmic Procedure Assessment. *Reference:* Date of publication to be determined. *Source information not available.* For further information contact sponsor. *Contact(s):* Nancy Collins, RN 415-447-0302.

Title: Automated Perimetry Ophthalmic Procedure Assessment. *Reference:* 2000. *Source information not available.* For further information contact sponsor. *Contact(s):* Flora Lum, MD 415-561-8592.

Title: Bacterial Keratitis Preferred Practice Pattern. *Reference:* 2000. *Source information not available.* For further information contact sponsor. *Contact(s):* Flora Lum, MD 415-561-8592.

Title: Corneal Intrastromal Rings Ophthalmic Procedure Preliminary Assessment. *Reference:* Date of publication to be determined. *Source information not available.* For further information contact sponsor. *Contact(s):* Nancy Collins, RN 415-447-0302.

Title: Corneal Opacification Preferred Practice Pattern. *Reference:* 2000. *Source information not available.* For further information contact sponsor. *Contact(s):* Flora Lum, MD 415-561-8592.

Title: Cyclophotocoagulation Ophthalmic Procedure Assessment. *Reference:* Date of publication to be determined. *Source information not available.* For further information contact sponsor. *Contact(s):* Nancy Collins, RN 415-447-0302.

Title: Laser In-Situ Keratomileusis (LASIK) Ophthalmic Procedure Assessment. *Reference:* Date of publication to be determined. *Source information not available.* For further information contact sponsor. *Contact(s):* Flora Lum, MD 415-561-8592.

Title: Macular Translocation Ophthalmic Procedure Preliminary Assessment. *Reference:* Date of publication to be determined. *Source information not available.* For further information contact sponsor. *Contact(s):* Nancy Collins, RN 415-447-0302.

Title: Phacotrabeculectomy Ophthalmic Procedure Assessment. *Reference:* Date of publication to be determined. *Source information not available.* For further information contact sponsor. *Contact(s):* Nancy Collins, RN 415-447-0302.

Title: Primary Angle-Closure Glaucoma Preferred Practice Pattern. *Reference:* 2000. *Source information not available.* For further information contact sponsor. *Contact(s):* Flora Lum, MD 415-561-8592.

Title: Primary Open-Angle Glaucoma. *Reference:* 2000. *Source information not available.* For further information contact sponsor. *Contact(s):* Nancy Collins, RN, 415-447-0302.

Title: Primary Open-Angle Glaucoma Suspect Preferred Practice Pattern. *Reference:* 2000. *Source information not available.* For further information contact sponsor. *Contact(s):* Flora Lum, MD 415-561-8592.

Title: Surgical Management of Macular Holes Ophthalmic Procedure Assessment. *Reference:* Date of publication to be determined. *Source information not available.* For further information contact sponsor. *Contact(s):* Nancy Collins, RN 415-447-0302.

American Academy of Pediatrics

Title: Diagnosis and Evaluation of Attention-Deficit/ Hyperactivity Disorder. *Reference:* Date of publication to be determined. *Source information not available.* For further information contact sponsor. *Contact(s):* Carla Herrerias, MPH 847-981-4317.

Title: Diagnosis of Developmental Dysplasia of the Hip. *Reference:* Date of publication to be determined. *Source information not available.* For further information contact sponsor. *Contact(s):* Carla Herrerias, MPH 847-981-4317.

Title: Management of Diabetes Mellitus. *Reference:* Date of publication to be determined. *Source information not available.* For further information contact sponsor. *Contact(s):* Carla Herrerias, MPH 847-981-4317.

Title: Management of Fever of Unknown Origin in Children 3-36 months. *Reference:* Date of publication to be determined. *Source information not available.* For further information contact sponsor. *Contact(s):* Carla Herrerias, MPH 847-981-4317.

Title: Management of Minor Head Trauma. *Reference:* Date of publication to be determined. *Source information not available.* For further information contact sponsor. *Contact(s):* Carla Herrerias, MPH 847-981-4317.

Title: Management of Serious Head Injury. *Reference:* Date of publication to be determined. *Source information not available.* For further information contact sponsor. *Contact(s):* Carla Herrerias, MPH 847-981-4317.

Title: Management of Wheezing in Young Children. *Reference:* Date of publication to be determined. *Source information not available.* For further information contact sponsor. *Contact(s):* Carla Herrerias, MPH 847-981-4317.

American Academy of Sleep Medicine

Title: Practice Parameters for the Evaluation of Insomnia. *Reference:* Date of publication to be determined. *Sleep.* For further information contact sponsor. *Contact(s):* AASM 507-287-6006.

Title: The Clinical Use of the Multiple Sleep Latency Test. *Reference:* Date of publication to be determined. *Source information not available.* For further information contact sponsor. *Contact(s):* AASM 507-287-6006.

American Association of Electrodiagnostic Medicine

Title: Amyotrophic Lateral Sclerosis (ALS). *Reference:* 1998-1999. *Source information not available.* For further information contact sponsor. *Contact(s):* AAEM 507-288-0100.

Title: Cervical Radiculopathies. *Reference:* 1998-1999. *Source information not available.* For further information contact sponsor. *Contact(s):* AAEM 507-288-0100.

Title: Idiopathic Polyneuritis (Guillain-Barre Syndrome). *Reference:* 1998-1999. *Source information not available.* For further information contact sponsor. *Contact(s):* AAEM 507-288-0100.

Title: Lumbosacral Radiculopathies. *Reference:* 1998-1999. *Source information not available.* For further information contact sponsor. *Contact(s):* AAEM 507-288-0100.

Title: Myasthenia Gravis. *Reference:* 1998-1999. *Source information not available.* For further information contact sponsor. *Contact(s):* AAEM 507-288-0100.

American Association of Oral and Maxillofacial Surgeons

Title: Par Path 2000 (Revision). *Reference:* 2000. *J Oral & Maxillofacial Surg.* For further information contact sponsor. *Contact(s):* Mary Allaite 1-800-822-6637, x315.

American Cancer Society

Title: American Cancer Society Guidelines for the Cancer-Related Checkup: An Update. *Reference:* Date of publication to be determined. *Source information not available.* For further information contact sponsor. *Contact(s):* ACS 404-320-3333.

Title: Guidelines for the Cancer-Related Checkup: Prostate and Endometrial Cancers. *Reference:* Date of publication to be determined. *Ca-A Cancer J for Clinicians.* For further information contact sponsor. *Contact(s):* Robert A. Smith, PhD 404-329-7610.

American College of Cardiology, American Heart Association

Title: ACC/AHA Guidelines for Ambulatory Electrocardiography (Revision). *Reference:* Date of publication to be determined. *Source information not available.* For further information contact sponsor. *Contact(s):* Educational Services Department 1-800-257-4740.

Title: ACC/AHA Guidelines for Coronary Angiography (Revision). *Reference:* Date of publication to be determined. *Source information not available.* For further information contact sponsor. *Contact(s):* Educational Services Department 1-800-257-4740.

Title: ACC/AHA Guidelines for Implantation of Cardiac Pacemakers and Antiarrhythmia Devices (Revision). *Reference:* Date of publication to be determined. *Source information not available.* For further information contact sponsor. *Contact(s):* Educational Services Department 1-800-257-4740.

Title: ACC/AHA Guidelines for Valvular Heart Disease. *Reference:* Date of publication to be determined. *Source information not available.* For further information contact sponsor. *Contact(s):* Educational Services Department 1-800-257-4740.

American College of Emergency Physicians

Title: Asymptomatic Hypertension. *Reference:* 2000. *Ann Emerg Med.* For further information contact sponsor. *Contact(s):* Rhonda Whitson 1-800-798-1822, x3231.

Title: Pneumonia. *Reference:* 2000. *Ann Emerg Med.* For further information contact sponsor. *Contact(s):* Rhonda Whitson 1-800-798-1822, x3231.

Title: Syncope. *Reference:* 2000. *Ann Emerg Med.* For further information contact sponsor. *Contact(s):* Rhonda Whitson 1-800-798-1822, x3231.

American College of Gastroenterology

Title: Management of Crohn's Disease in Adults. *Reference:* Date of publication to be determined. *Source information not available.* For further information contact sponsor. *Contact(s):* ACG 703-820-7400.

Title: Polyp Guideline: Diagnosis, Treatment and Surveillance for Patients with Nonfamilial Colorectal Polyps. *Reference:* Date of publication to be determined. *Source information not available.* For further information contact sponsor. *Contact(s):* ACG 703-820-7400.

Title: Ulcerative Colitis Practice Guidelines in Adults. *Reference:* Date of publication to be determined. *Source information not available.* For further information contact sponsor. *Contact(s):* ACG 703-820-7400.

American College of Preventive Medicine

Title: Colon Cancer Screening. *Reference:* Date of publication to be determined. *Source information not available.* For further information contact sponsor. *Contact(s):* Andrew Keenan 202-466-2044.

Title: Counseling on Hormone Replacement for Peri and Postmenopausal Women. *Reference:* 1999. *Source information not available.* For further information contact sponsor. *Contact(s):* Andrew Keenan 202-466-2044.

Title: Counseling on Physical Activity. *Reference:* Date of publication to be determined. *Source information not available.* For further information contact sponsor. *Contact(s):* Andrew Keenan 202-466-2044.

Title: Counseling on Unintended Pregnancy. *Reference:* Date of publication to be determined. *Source information not available.* For further information contact sponsor. *Contact(s):* Andrew Keenan 202-466-2044.

Title: Domestic Violence Screening. *Reference:* Date of publication to be determined. *Source information not available.* For further information contact sponsor. *Contact(s):* Andrew Keenan 202-466-2044.

Title: Genetic Screening for Cancer. *Reference:* Date of publication to be determined. *Source information not available.* For further information contact sponsor. *Contact(s):* Andrew Keenan 202-466-2044.

Title: Hepatitis A Vaccination. *Reference:* Date of publication to be determined. *Source information not available.* For further information contact sponsor. *Contact(s):* Andrew Keenan 202-466-2044.

Title: Physician Prescribing of Antioxidant Supplements to Prevent Cancer and Heart Disease. *Reference:* Date of publication to be determined. *Source information not available.* For further information contact sponsor. *Contact(s):* Andrew Keenan 202-466-2044.

Title: Physician Recommendations for Weight Loss. *Reference:* Date of publication to be determined. *Source information not available.* For further information contact sponsor. *Contact(s):* Andrew Keenan 202-466-2044.

Title: Screening for Chlamydia Trachomatis. *Reference:* Date of publication to be determined. *Source information not available.* For further information contact sponsor. *Contact(s):* Andrew Keenan 202-466-2044.

Title: Screening for H. pylori in High Risk Groups. *Reference:* Date of publication to be determined. *Source information not available.* For further information contact sponsor. *Contact(s):* Andrew Keenan 202-466-2044.

Title: Screening for Hemochromatosis. *Reference:* Date of publication to be determined. *Source information not available.* For further information contact sponsor. *Contact(s):* Andrew Keenan 202-466-2044.

Title: Screening for Hepatitis C. *Reference:* Date of publication to be determined. *Source information not available.* For further information contact sponsor. *Contact(s):* Andrew Keenan 202-466-2044.

Title: Screening for Lead Poisoning. *Reference:* Date of publication to be determined. *Source information not available.* For further information contact sponsor. *Contact(s):* Andrew Keenan 202-466-2044.

Title: Screening for Osteoporosis in Asymptomatic Women. *Reference:* Date of publication to be determined. *Source information not available.* For further information contact sponsor. *Contact(s):* Andrew Keenan 202-466-2044.

Title: Screening for Testicular Cancer. *Reference:* Date of publication to be determined. *Source information not available.* For further information contact sponsor. *Contact(s):* Andrew Keenan 202-466-2044.

Title: Tobacco Cessation Counseling. *Reference:* Date of publication to be determined. *Source information not available.* For further information contact sponsor. *Contact(s):* Andrew Keenan 202-466-2044.

Title: Varicella Vaccination. *Reference:* Date of publication to be determined. *Source information not available.* For further information contact sponsor. *Contact(s):* Andrew Keenan 202-466-2044.

American College of Radiology

Title: ACR Standard for Use of Conscious Sedation. *Reference:* Date of publication to be determined. *Source information not available.* For further information contact sponsor. *Contact(s):* Sandra Bjork, RN, JD 703-648-8987.

Title: Conservative Surgery and Radiation in the Treatment of Stage I and II Carcinoma of the Breast (9 variants). *Reference:* Date of publication to be determined. *Source information not available.* For further information contact sponsor. *Contact(s):* Christine Waldrip 703-648-8959.

Title: Definitive External Beam Irradiation in Stage T1, T2 Carcinoma of the Prostate (9 variants). *Reference:* Date of publication to be determined. *Source information not available.* For further information contact sponsor. *Contact(s):* Christine Waldrip 703-648-8959.

Title: Ductal Carcinoma in Situ and Microinvasive Disease (10 variants). *Reference:* Date of publication to be determined. *Source information not available.* For further information contact sponsor. *Contact(s):* Christine Waldrip 703-648-8959.

Title: Follow-Up of Hodgkin's Disease (7 variants). *Reference:* Date of publication to be determined. *Source information not available.* For further information contact sponsor. *Contact(s):* Christine Waldrip 703-648-8959.

Title: Follow-Up of Non-Small-Cell Lung Carinoma (5 variants). *Reference:* Date of publication to be determined. *Source information not available.* For further information contact sponsor. *Contact(s):* Christine Waldrip 703-648-8959.

Title: Hodgkin's Disease, Favorable Clinical Stage I and II. *Reference:* Date of publication to be determined. *Source information not available.* For further information contact sponsor. *Contact(s):* Christine Waldrip 703-648-8959.

Title: Hodgkin's Disease, Unfavorable Clinical Stage I and II. *Reference:* Date of publication to be determined. *Source information not available.* For further information contact sponsor. *Contact(s):* Christine Waldrip 703-648-8959.

Title: Local Regional Recurrence and Salvage Surgery (10 variants). *Reference:* Date of publication to be determined. *Source information not available.* For further information contact sponsor. *Contact(s):* Christine Waldrip 703-648-8959.

Title: Locally Advanced (high risk) Prostate Cancer (8 variants). *Reference:* Date of publication to be determined. *Source information not available.* For further information contact sponsor. *Contact(s):* Christine Waldrip 703-648-8959.

Title: Locally Advanced Breast Cancer (5 variants). *Reference:* Date of publication to be determined. *Source information not available.* For further information contact sponsor. *Contact(s):* Christine Waldrip 703-648-8959.

Title: Management of Resectable Rectal Cancer (6 variants). *Reference:* Date of publication to be determined. *Source information not available.* For further information contact sponsor. *Contact(s):* Christine Waldrip 703-648-8959.

Title: Multiple Brain Metastases (5 variants). *Reference:* Date of publication to be determined. *Source information not available.* For further information contact sponsor. *Contact(s):* Christine Waldrip 703-648-8959.

Title: Neoadjuvant Therapy for Marginally Resectable (Clinical N2) Non-Small-Cell Lung Carcinoma (1 variant). *Reference:* Date of publication to be determined. *Source information not available.* For further information contact sponsor. *Contact(s):* Christine Waldrip 703-648-8959.

Title: Node-Positive Prostate Cancer (3 variants). *Reference:* Date of publication to be determined. *Source information not available.* For further information contact sponsor. *Contact(s):* Christine Waldrip 703-648-8959.

Title: Non-Aggressive, Non-Surgical Treatment of Inoperable Non-Small-Cell Lung Cancer. *Reference:* Date of publication to be determined. *Source information not available.* For further information contact sponsor. *Contact(s):* Christine Waldrip 703-648-8959.

Title: Non-Small-Cell Lung Carcinoma, Non-Surgical Aggressive Therapy (8 variants). *Reference:* Date of publication to be determined. *Source information not available.* For further information contact sponsor. *Contact(s):* Christine Waldrip 703-648-8959.

Title: Pediatric Hodgkin's Disease. *Reference:* Date of publication to be determined. *Source information not available.* For further information contact sponsor. *Contact(s):* Christine Waldrip 703-648-8959.

Title: Permanent Source Brachytherapy for Prostate Cancer (8 variants). *Reference:* Date of publication to be determined. *Source information not available.* For further information contact sponsor. *Contact(s):* Christine Waldrip 703-648-8959.

Title: Post-Irradiation Management and Retreatment of Brain Metastases (9 variants). *Reference:* Date of publication to be determined. *Source information not available.* For further information contact sponsor. *Contact(s):* Christine Waldrip 703-648-8959.

Title: Postmastectomy Radiotherapy (15 variants). *Reference:* Date of publication to be determined. *Source information not available.* For further information contact sponsor. *Contact(s):* Christine Waldrip 703-648-8959.

Title: Postoperative Radiotherapy in Non-Small-Cell Lung Cancer (18 variants). *Reference:* Date of publication to be determined. *Source information not available.* For further information contact sponsor. *Contact(s):* Christine Waldrip 703-648-8959.

Title: Postradical Prostatectomy Irradiation in Carcinoma of the Prostate (11 variants). *Reference:* Date of publication to be determined. *Source information not available.* For further information contact sponsor. *Contact(s):* Christine Waldrip 703-648-8959.

Title: Pre-irradiation Evaluation and Management for Brain Metastases (21 variants). *Reference:* Date of publication to be determined. *Source information not available.* For further information contact sponsor. *Contact(s):* Christine Waldrip 703-648-8959.

Title: Recurrent Hodgkin's Disease. *Reference:* Date of publication to be determined. *Source information not available.* For further information contact sponsor. *Contact(s):* Christine Waldrip 703-648-8959.

Title: Solitary Brain Metastasis (14 variants). *Reference:* Date of publication to be determined. *Source information not available.* For further information contact sponsor. *Contact(s):* Christine Waldrip 703-648-8959.

Title: Stage III and IV Hodgkin's Disease Treatment Guidelines (7 variants). *Reference:* Date of publication to be determined. *Source information not available.* For further information contact sponsor. *Contact(s):* Christine Waldrip 703-648-8959.

Title: Staging Evaluation for Patients with Adenocarcinoma of the Prostate (10 variants). *Reference:* Date of publication to be determined. *Source information not available.* For further information contact sponsor. *Contact(s):* Christine Waldrip 703-648-8959.

Title: Staging Evaluation for Patients with Hodgkin's Disease (10 variants). *Reference:* Date of publication to be determined. *Source information not available.* For further information contact sponsor. *Contact(s):* Christine Waldrip 703-648-8959.

Title: Staging of Non-Small-Cell Lung Cancer (8 variants). *Reference:* Date of publication to be determined. *Source information not available.* For further information contact sponsor. *Contact(s):* Christine Waldrip 703-648-8959.

Title: Treatment Planning for Clinically Localized Prostate Cancer (4 variants). *Reference:* Date of publication of publication to be determined. *Source information not available.* For further information contact sponsor. *Contact(s):* Christine Waldrip 703-648-8959.

American College of Radiology, Society of Cardiovascular and Interventional Radiology, American Society of Neurology, American Society of Interventional and Therapeutic Neuroradiology

Title: Standard for the Performance of Diagnostic Cervicocerebral Angiography. *Reference:* 1999. *Source information not available.* For further information contact sponsor. *Contact(s):* Sandra Bjork, RN, JD 703-648-8987.

American College of Rheumatology

Title: Immunological Testing Guidelines. *Reference:* 1998-1999. *Source information not available.* For further information contact sponsor. *Contact(s):* Steven Echard 404-633-3777.

American Gastroenterological Association

Title: Celiac Sprue. *Reference:* Date of publication to be determined. *Source information not available.* For further information contact sponsor. *Contact(s):* Wendy Cohen 301-654-2055.

Title: Chronic Pancreatitis. *Reference:* Date of publication to be determined. *Source information not available.* For further information contact sponsor. *Contact(s):* Wendy Cohen 301-654-2055.

Title: Constipation. *Reference:* Date of publication to be determined. *Source information not available.* For further information contact sponsor. *Contact(s):* Wendy Cohen 301-654-2055.

Title: Food Allergies. *Reference:* Date of publication to be determined. *Source information not available.* For further information contact sponsor. *Contact(s):* Wendy Cohen 301-654-2055.

Title: Gastrointestinal Ischemia. *Reference:* Date of publication to be determined. *Source information not available.* For further information contact sponsor. *Contact(s):* Wendy Cohen 301-654-2055.

Title: Hemorrhoids and Anal Fissures. *Reference:* Date of publication to be determined. *Source information not available.* For further information contact sponsor. *Contact(s):* Wendy Cohen 301-654-2055.

Title: Impact of Dietary Fiber on Colon Cancer Occurrence. *Reference:* Date of publication to be determined. *Source information not available.* For further information contact sponsor. *Contact(s):* Wendy Cohen 301-654-2055.

Title: Nausea and Vomiting. *Reference:* Date of publication to be determined. *Source information not available.* For further information contact sponsor. *Contact(s):* Wendy Cohen 301-654-2055.

Title: Occult GI Bleeding. *Reference:* Date of publication to be determined. *Source information not available.* For further information contact sponsor. *Contact(s):* Wendy Cohen 301-654-2055.

American In Vitro Allergy/ Immunology Society

Title: Practice Parameters. *Reference:* 1998-1999. *Source information not available.* For further information contact sponsor. *Contact(s):* Russell Williams, MD 201-816-1289.

American Medical Association, Diagnostic and Therapeutic Technology Assessment Program

Title: Laparoscopic Hysterectomy. *Reference:* Date of publication to be determined. *Source information not available.* For further information contact sponsor. *Contact(s):* Deloris Collins 312-464-4531.

Title: Laser Bullectomy. *Reference:* Date of publication to be determined. *Source information not available.* For further information contact sponsor. *Contact(s):* Deloris Collins 312-464-4531.

Title: Open Lung Reduction Surgery. *Reference:* Date of publication to be determined. *Source information not available.* For further information contact sponsor. *Contact(s):* Deloris Collins 312-464-4531.

American Medical Directors Association

Title: Chronic Pain Management in the Long-Term Care Setting. *Reference:* 1999. *Source information not available.* For further information contact sponsor. *Contact(s):* Cindy Hock, CPG Project Manager, 410-740-9743.

Title: Therapy Companion to the 1996 Pressure Ulcer Clinical Practice Guideline. *Reference:* 1999. *Source information not available.* For further information contact sponsor. *Contact(s):* Cindy Hock, CPG Project Manager, 410-740-9743.

American Medical Directors Association, American Health Care Association

Title: Osteoporosis. *Reference:* 1998-1999. *Source information not available.* For further information contact sponsor. *Contact(s):* Cindy Hock, CPG Project Manager, 410-740-9743.

American Psychiatric Association

Title: Practice Guideline for Geriatric Care. *Reference:* 1999. *Source information not available.* For further information contact sponsor. *Contact(s):* Deborah Zarin, MD, Leslie Seigle 202-682-6288.

Title: Practice Guideline for the Treatment of Patients with Eating Disorders (Revision). *Reference:* 1998-1999. *Source information not available.* For further information contact sponsor. *Contact(s):* Deborah Zarin, MD, Leslie Seigle 202-682-6288.

Title: Practice Guideline for the Treatment of Patients with HIV/AIDS. *Reference:* 2000. *Source information not available.* For further information contact sponsor. *Contact(s):* Deborah Zarin, MD, Leslie Seigle 202-682-6288.

Title: Practice Guideline for the Treatment of Patients with Major Depressive Disorder (Revision). *Reference:* 1998-1999. *Source information not available.* For further information contact sponsor. *Contact(s):* Deborah Zarin, MD, Leslie Seigle 202-682-6288.

American Society of Clinical Oncology

Title: 1999 Update of Clinical Practice Guidelines for the Treatment of Unresectable Non-Small-Cell Lung Cancer. *Reference:* 2000. *J Clin Oncol.* For further information contact sponsor. *Contact(s):* Jennifer Padberg 703-299-0150.

Title: 1999 Update of Recommendations for the Use of Hematopoietic Colony-Stimulating Factors. *Reference:* 2000. *J Clin Oncol.* For further information contact sponsor. *Contact(s):* Jennifer Padberg 703-299-0150.

In Development

Title: 1999 Update of Recommendations for the Use of Tumor Markers in Breast and Colorectal Cancer. *Reference:* 2000. *J Clin Oncol.* For further information contact sponsor. *Contact(s):* Jennifer Padberg 703-299-0150.

Title: Adjuvant Hormonal Therapy After Treatment of Localized Prostate Cancer. *Reference:* 2000. *J Clin Oncol.* For further information contact sponsor. *Contact(s):* Jennifer Padberg 703-299-0150.

Title: Adjuvant Radiation Therapy After Mastectomy. *Reference:* 2000. *J Clin Oncol.* For further information contact sponsor. *Contact(s):* Jennifer Padberg 703-299-0150.

Title: Establishing a Threshold for Platelet Transfusion. *Reference:* 2000. *J Clin Oncol.* For further information contact sponsor. *Contact(s):* Jennifer Padberg 703-299-0150.

Title: Larynx Preservation. *Reference:* 2000. *J Clin Oncol.* For further information contact sponsor. *Contact(s):* Jennifer Padberg 703-299-0150.

Title: The Use of Bisphosphonates. *Reference:* 1999. *J Clin Oncol.* For further information contact sponsor. *Contact(s):* Jennifer Padberg 703-299-0150.

Title: Treatment of Metastatic Prostate Cancer. *Reference:* 2000. *J Clin Oncol.* For further information contact sponsor. *Contact(s):* Jennifer Padberg 703-299-0150.

Title: Treatment of Metastatic Prostate Cancer. *Reference:* 2000. *J Clin Oncol.* For further information contact sponsor. *Contact(s):* Jennifer Padberg 703-299-0150.

Title: Use of Anti-Emetic Agents. *Reference:* 1999. *J Clin Oncol.* For further information contact sponsor. *Contact(s):* Jennifer Padberg 703-299-0150.

American Society of Clinical Pathologists

Title: Utilization of Rh Immune Globulin. *Reference:* Date of publication to be determined. *Source information not available.* For further information contact sponsor. *Contact(s):* Barbara Hoffman 312-738-4880.

American Society of Hematology

Title: Chronic Myelogenous Leukemia. *Reference:* Date of publication to be determined. *Blood.* For further information contact sponsor. *Contact(s):* ASH 202-857-1118.

American Society of Maxillofacial Surgeons

Title: Cosmetic Surgery for the Craniomaxillofacial Region. *Reference:* 1998-1999. *Source information not available.* For further information contact sponsor. *Contact(s):* Cathy Hay 847-228-8375.

American Society of Plastic and Reconstructive Surgeons

Title: Aesthetic Laser Surgery. *Reference:* 1998-1999. *Source information not available.* For further information contact sponsor. *Contact(s):* Pat Farrell 847-228-9900, x339.

Title: Explantation of Breast Implants. *Reference:* 1998-1999. *Source information not available.* For further information contact sponsor. *Contact(s):* Pat Farrell 847-228-9900, x339.

Title: Lower Extremity Ulceration. *Reference:* 1998-1999. *Source information not available.* For further information contact sponsor. *Contact(s):* Pat Farrell 847-228-9900, x339.

American Thyroid Association

Title: American Thyroid Association Guidelines for Use of Laboratory Tests in Thyroid Disorders. *Reference:* Date of publication to be determined. *Source information not available.* For further information contact sponsor.

Title: Treatment Guidelines for Patients with Hyperthyroidism and Hypothyroidism. *Reference:* Date of publication to be determined. *Source information not available.* For further information contact sponsor.

American Urological Association

Title: Benign Prostatic Hyperplasia: An Update. *Reference:* 2001. *Source information not available.* For further information contact sponsor. *Contact(s):* AUA 410-223-4310.

Title: Management of Interstitial Cystitis. *Reference:* Date of publication to be determined. *Source information not available.* For further information contact sponsor. *Contact(s):* AUA 410-223-4310.

Title: Management of Superficial Bladder Cancer. *Reference:* 1999. *Source information not available.* For further information contact sponsor. *Contact(s):* AUA 410-223-4310.

Title: Treatment of Organic Erectile Dysfunction: An Update. *Reference:* Date of publication to be determined. *Source information not available.* For further information contact sponsor. *Contact(s):* AUA 410-223-4310.

College of American Pathologists

Title: Practice Guideline for Review of Blood Films by a Physician. *Reference:* Date of publication to be determined. *Source information not available.* For further information contact sponsor. *Contact(s):* Barbara J Barrett 1-800-323-4040, x7513.

Title: Practice Guideline for the Platelet Refractory Patient. *Reference:* Date of publication to be determined. *Source information not available.* For further information contact sponsor. *Contact(s):* Barbara J Barrett 1-800-323-4040, x7513.

Title: Practice Guidelines for Forensic Pathology. *Reference:* Date of publication to be determined. *Source information not available.* For further information contact sponsor. *Contact(s):* Barbara J Barrett 1-800-323-4040, x7513.

Title: Practice Parameter for the Recognition, Management, and Prevention of Adverse Consequences of Blood Transfusion. *Reference:* Date of publication to be determined. *Source information not available.* For further information contact sponsor. *Contact(s):* Barbara J Barrett 1-800-323-4040, x7513.

Minnesota Academy of Otolaryngology-Head & Neck Surgery

Title: Preferred Practice Patterns. *Reference:* Date of publication to be determined. *Source information not available.* For further information contact sponsor. *Contact(s):* Robyn Lampright 612-378-1875.

North American Spine Society

Title: North American Spine Society Phase III Clinical Guidelines for Multidisciplinary Spine Care Specialists—Herniated Disc. *Reference:* Date of publication to be determined. *Source information not available.* For further information contact sponsor. *Contact(s):* Pam Hayden 815-675-0021.

Title: North American Spine Society Phase III Clinical Guidelines for Multidisciplinary Spine Care Specialists—Spinal Stenosis. *Reference:* Date of publication to be determined. *Source information not available.* For further information contact sponsor. *Contact(s):* Pam Hayden 815-675-0021.

Title: North American Spine Society Phase III Clinical Guidelines for Multidisciplinary Spine Care Specialists—Spondylolysis, Lytic Spondylolisthesis or Degenerative Spondylolisthesis/Stenosis. *Reference:* Date of publication to be determined. *Source information not available.* For further information contact sponsor. *Contact(s):* Pam Hayden 815-675-0021.

Title: North American Spine Society Phase III Clinical Guidelines for Multidisciplinary Spine Care Specialists—Unremitting Low Back Pain. *Reference:* Date of publication to be determined. *Source information not available.* For further information contact sponsor. *Contact(s):* Pam Hayden 815-675-0021.

Society of American Gastrointestinal and Endoscopic Surgeons

Title: Guidelines for the Clinical Application of Laparoscopic Biliary Tract Surgery. *Reference:* Date of publication to be determined. *Source information not available.* For further information contact sponsor. *Contact(s):* Kelly Wettengel 310-314-2404.

Title: Guidelines for Training in Diagnostic and Therapeutic Endoscopic Retrograde Cholangiopancreatography (ERCP). *Reference:* Date of publication to be determined. *Source information not available.* For further information contact sponsor. *Contact(s):* Kelly Wettengel 310-314-2404.

Society of Cardiovascular and Interventional Radiology

Title: Quality Improvement Guidelines for Arterial Stent. *Reference:* Date of publication to be determined. *Source information not available.* For further information contact sponsor. *Contact(s):* SCVIR 703-691-1805.

Title: Quality Improvement Guidelines for Neuroangiography. *Reference:* 1998-1999. *Source information not available.* For further information contact sponsor. *Contact(s):* SCVIR 703-691-1805.

Society of Critical Care Medicine

Title: Clinical Practice Guidelines for Management of Intravenous Catheter Infections. *Reference:* Date of publication to be determined. *Source information not available.* For further information contact sponsor. *Contact(s):* Charm Kohlenberger 714-282-6046 or e-mail charm@sccm.org.

Title: Clinical Practice Guidelines for the Care of Pediatric Patients with Hemodynamic Instability Associated with Sepsis. *Reference:* Date of publication to be determined. *Source information not available.* For further information contact sponsor. *Contact(s):* Charm Kohlenberger 714-282-6046 or e-mail charm@sccm.org.

Title: Clinical Practice Guidelines for Weaning from Mechanical Ventilation. *Reference:* Date of publication to be determined. *Source information not available.* For further information contact sponsor. *Contact(s):* Charm Kohlenberger 714-282-6046 or e-mail charm@sccm.org.

Title: Clinical Practice Parameters for the Care of Pediatric Patients with Acute Respiratory Failure on Mechanical Ventilatory Support. *Reference:* Date of publication to be determined. *Source information not available.* For further information contact sponsor. *Contact(s):* Charm Kohlenberger 714-282-6046 or e-mail charm@sccm.org.

Title: Guidelines for Admission and Discharge for the Pediatric Intermediate Intensive Care Unit. *Reference:* Date of publication to be determined. *Source information not available.* For further information contact sponsor. *Contact(s):* Charm Kohlenberger 714-282-6046 or e-mail charm@sccm.org.

Title: Guidelines for Critical Care Pharmacy Services. *Reference:* Date of publication to be determined. *Source information not available.* For further information contact sponsor. *Contact(s):* Charm Kohlenberger 714-282-6046 or e-mail charm@sccm.org.

Title: Guidelines for Nonphysician Critical Care Practitioners. *Reference:* Date of publication to be determined. *Source information not available.* For further information contact sponsor. *Contact(s):* Charm Kohlenberger 714-282-6046 or e-mail charm@sccm.org.

Society of Nuclear Medicine

Title: Procedure Guideline for Lymphoscintigraphy (tentative). *Reference:* Date of publication to be determined. *Source information not available.* For further information contact sponsor. *Contact(s):* Bill Uffelman 703-708-9000.

Title: Procedure Guideline for Somatostatin Receptor Scintigraphy. *Reference:* Date of publication to be determined. *Source information not available.* For further information contact sponsor. *Contact(s):* Bill Uffelman 703-708-9000.

Title: Procedure Guideline for Therapy with I-131. *Reference:* Date of publication to be determined. *Source information not available.* For further information contact sponsor. *Contact(s):* Bill Uffelman 703-708-9000.

Title: QC Guidelines for PET Coincidence Instrumentation (tentative). *Reference:* Date of publication to be determined. *Source information not available.* For further information contact sponsor. *Contact(s):* Bill Uffelman 703-708-9000.

Title: QC Guidelines for PET Radiopharmaceuticals (tentative). *Reference:* Date of publication to be determined. *Source information not available.* For further information contact sponsor. *Contact(s):* Bill Uffelman 703-708-9000.

Section V
Replaced Clinical
Practice Guidelines

Abortion, Therapeutic

Multifetal Pregnancy Reduction and Selective Fetal Termination. *ACOG Committee Opinion*. 1991;94. American College of Obstetricians and Gynecologists. Replaced. In Section I, see: Ethics, Medical.

Adrenal Cortex Hormones, Therapeutic Use

Antenatal Corticosteroid Therapy for Fetal Maturation. *ACOG Committee Opinion*. 1994;147. American College of Obstetricians and Gynecologists. Replaced. In Section I, see: Fetal Membranes, Premature Rupture.

Alcohol Drinking

Alcohol Use and Abuse: A Pediatric Concern. *Pediatr.* 1995;95:439-442. American Academy of Pediatrics. Replaced. In Section I, see: Physician's Role.

Ambulatory Care

Guidelines for Office Endoscopic Services. 1996. Society of American Gastrointestinal and Endoscopic Surgeons. Replaced. In Section I, see: Ambulatory Care/Standards.

Anesthesia Recovery Period

Standards for Postanesthesia Care. *ASA Standards, Guidelines and Statements*. 1996;3:4. American Society of Anesthesiologists. Replaced. In Section I, see: Anesthesia Recovery Period.

Antineoplastic Agents

Oral Health Care Guidelines: Patients Receiving Cancer Chemotherapy. 1989. American Dental Association. Replaced. In Section I, see: Antineoplastic Agents.

Appetite Depressants/Therapeutic Use

Anorectic Usage Guidelines. 1996. American Society of Bariatric Physicians. Replaced. In Section I, see: Appetite Depressants/Therapeutic Use.

Bacterial Infections/Radionuclide Imaging

ACR Standard for the Performance of Scintigraphy for Infections and Inflammatory Conditions. 1995. American College of Radiology. Replaced. In Section I, see: Bacterial Infections/Radionuclide Imaging.

Barium Sulfate/Diagnostic Use

ACR Standard for the Performance of Adult Barium Enema Examinations. 1995. American College of Radiology. Replaced. In Section I, see: Barium Sulfate/Diagnostic Use.

BCG Vaccine

The Role of BCG Vaccine in the Prevention and Control of Tuberculosis in the United States. *Morbid Mortal Weekly Report*. 1996;45(no. RR-4). Centers for Disease Control and Prevention. Replaced. In Section I, see: BCG Vaccine.

Biliary Tract Diseases/Radionuclide Imaging

ACR Standard for the Performance of Hepatobiliary Scintigraphy. 1995. American College of Radiology. Replaced. In Section I, see: Biliary Tract/Radionuclide Imaging.

Biopsy, Needle

ACR Standard for the Performance of Imaging-Guided Trans-Thoracic Needle Biopsy (TNB) in Adults. 1994. American College of Radiology. Replaced. In Section I, see: Biopsy, Needle/Methods.

Blepharitis

Blepharitis and Dry Eye in the Adult Preferred Practice Pattern. *Ophthalmology*. 1991. American Academy of Ophthalmology. Replaced. In Section I, see: Blepharitis.

Brain/Radionuclide Imaging

ACR Standard for the Performance of Cerebral Scintigraphy. 1995. American College of Radiology. Replaced. In Section I, see: Brain/Radionuclide Imaging.

Breast Diseases/Ultrasonography

ACR Standard for the Performance of Breast Ultrasound Examination. 1994. American College of Radiology. Replaced. In Section I, see: Breast Diseases/Ultrasonography.

Carcinoma, Non-Small-Cell Lung/Therapy

1998 Update of Clinical Practice Guidelines for the Treatment of Unresectable Non-Small-Cell Lung Cancer. *J Clin Oncol*. 1999. American Society of Clinical Oncology. Replaced. In Section I, see: Carcinoma, Non-Small-Cell Lung.

Cardiovascular Disease

Oral Health Care Guidelines: Patients with Cardiovascular Disease. 1989. American Dental Association. Replaced. In Section I, see: Cardiovascular Diseases/Therapy.

Chickenpox/Prevention and Control

Prevention of Varicella. *Morbid Mortal Weekly Report*. 1996;45(no. RR-11). Centers for Disease Control and Prevention. Replaced. In Section I, see: Chickenpox/ Prevention and Control.

Communicable Disease Control/Methods

Guidelines for Preventing the Transmission of Tuberculosis in Health-Care Settings with Special Focus on HIV-Related Issues. *Morbid Mortal Weekly Report*. 1990;39(no. RR-17):1-29. Centers for Disease Control and Prevention. Replaced. In Section I, see: AIDS-Related Opportunistic Infections/Prevention and Control.

Conjunctivitis/Diagnosis, Drug Therapy

Conjunctivitis Preferred Practice Pattern. 1991. American Academy of Ophthalmology. Replaced. In Section I, see: Conjunctivitis.

Credentialing

Granting of Privileges for Gastrointestinal Endoscopy by Surgeons. 1997;11. Society of American Gastrointestinal and Endoscopic Surgeons. Replaced. In Section I, see: Credentialing.

Credentialing

Guidelines for Granting of Privileges for Laparoscopic and Thoracoscopic General Surgery. 1997;17. Society of American Gastrointestinal and Endoscopic Surgeons. Replaced. In Section I, see: Credentialing.

Dental Care

Oral Health Care Guidelines: Head and Neck Cancer Patients Receiving Radiation Therapy. 1989. American Dental Association. Replaced. In Section I, see: Head and Neck Neoplasms/Radiotherapy.

Dental Health Care

Oral Health Care Guidelines: Patients with Physical and Mental Disorders. 1991. American Dental Association. Replaced. In Section I, see: Dental Care for Disabled.

Diabetic Retinopathy

Diabetic Retinopathy Preferred Practice Patterns. 1993. American Academy of Ophthalmology. Replaced. In Section I, see: Diabetic Retinopathy.

Diagnostic Imaging

ACR Standard for Imaging-Guided Percutaneous Thoracic Aspiration or Catheter Drainage (PCD) in Adults. 1994. American College of Radiology. Replaced. In Section I, see: Paracentesis.

Diphtheria-Tetanus-Pertussis Vaccine/ Administration and Dosage

Recommended Childhood Immunization Schedule— United States, January–December 1999. *Pediatr*. 1999;101(1). American Academy of Family Physicians. Replaced. In Section I, see: Reminder Systems, Vaccination/Utilization.

Drug Approval/Legislation and Jurisprudence

Approved Drug Products and Legal Requirements. *USP DI*. 1997;Volume III. US Pharmacopeia/ Micromedex, Inc. Replaced. In Section I, see: Drug Information Services.

Drug Information Services

Drug Information for the Health Care Professional. *USP DI*. 1997;Volume I. US Pharmacopeia/ Micromedex, Inc. Replaced. In Section I, see: Drug Information Services.

Education, Medical, Graduate

Framework for Post-Residency Surgical Education & Training. 1994;17. Society of American Gastrointestinal and Endoscopic Surgeons. Replaced. In Section I, see: Education, Medical, Continuing/ Standards.

Emergency Medicine/Methods

Acute Toxic Ingestion or Dermal or Inhalation Exposure. *Ann Emerg Med*. 1995;25:570-585. American College of Emergency Physicians. Replaced. In Section I, see: Emergency Medicine/Methods.

Replaced

Emergency Treatment/Standards

Penetrating Extremity Trauma. *Ann Emerg Med.* 1994;23:1147-1156. American College of Emergency Physicians. Replaced. In Section I, see: Emergency Treatment/Standards.

Epilepsy/Therapy

Assessment of Vagus Nerve Stimulation for Epilepsy. *Neurol.* 1997;49:293-297. American Academy of Neurology. Replaced. In Section I, see: Epilepsy/ Therapy.

Esophagus/Radiography

ACR Standard for the Performance of Adult Esophagrams & Upper Gastrointestinal Examinations. 1995. American College of Radiology. Replaced. In Section I, see: Endoscopy/Gastrointestinal.

Expert Testimony

Ethical Issues Relating to Expert Testimony by Obstetricians and Gynecologists. *ACOG Committee Opinion.* 1987;56. American College of Obstetricians and Gynecologists. Replaced. In Section I, see: Ethics, Medical.

Freedom

Patient Choice: Maternal-Fetal Conflict. *ACOG Committee Opinion.* 1987;55. American College of Obstetricians and Gynecologists. Replaced. In Section I, see: Choice Behavior.

Gastroesophageal Reflux/ Diagnosis, Therapy

Gastroesophageal Reflux Disease. *Arch Intern Med.* 1995;155:2165-2196. American College of Gastroenterology. Replaced. In Section I, see: Gastroesophageal Reflux/Diagnosis.

Gastroesophageal Reflux/Surgery

Guidelines for Surgical Treatment of Gastroesophageal Reflux Disease (GERD). 1996;22. Society of American Gastrointestinal and Endoscopic Surgeons. Replaced. In Section I, see: Gastroesophageal Reflux/Surgery.

Gastrointestinal Diseases/Radiography

ACR Standard for the Performance of Adult Enteroclysis Examinations. 1995. American College of Radiology. Replaced. In Section I, see: Intestinal Diseases/Radiography.

Health Care Reform Allergy and Immunology

Health Care Reform. *J Allergy Clin Immun.* 1995;95:797-800, Position Statement No. 27. American Academy of Allergy, Asthma, and Immunology. In Section I, see: United States.

Heart/Radionuclide Imaging

ACR Standard for the Performance of Cardiac Scintigraphy. 1995. American College of Radiology. Replaced. In Section I, see: Coronary Disease/ Radionuclide Imaging.

Hypersensitivity, Delayed

Purified Protein Derivative (PPD)-Tuberculin Anergy and HIV Infection: Guidelines for Anergy Testing and Management of Anergic Persons at Risk of Tuberculosis. *Morbid Mortal Weekly Report.* 1991;40(no. RR-5):27-33. Centers for Disease Control and Prevention. Replaced. In Section I, see: AIDS-Related Opportunistic Infections/Prevention and Control.

Immunization Schedule

Recommended Childhood Immunization Schedule— United States, January–June 1998. *Pediatr.* 1998;101(1). Centers for Disease Control and Prevention. Replaced. In Section I, see: Immunization.

Influenza/Vaccine

Prevention and Control of Influenza. *Morbid Mortal Weekly Report.* 1998;47(no. RR-06). Centers for Disease Control and Prevention. Replaced. In Section I, see: Influenza/Prevention and Control.

Intensive Care Units/Standards

Critical Care Services and Personnel: Recommendations Based on a System of Categorization into Two Levels of Care. *Critical Care Med.* 1991;19:279-285. Society of Critical Care Medicine. Replaced. In Section I, see: Intensive Care Units/Manpower.

Intestine, Small/Pathology

ACR Standard for the Performance of Per Oral Small Bowel Examinations in Adults. 1995. American College of Radiology. Replaced. In Section I, see: Intestine, Small/Radiography.

Kidney Failure, Chronic

Oral Health Care Guidelines: Patients with End-Stage Renal Disease. 1989. American Dental Association. Replaced. In Section I, see: Kidney Failure, Chronic.

Laryngoscopy

Laryngoscopy. *Clinical Indicators Compendium.* 1998. American Academy of Otolaryngology–Head and Neck Surgery. Replaced. In Section I, see: Laryngeal Diseases/Diagnosis.

Lung Diseases/Radionuclide Imaging

ACR Standard for the Performance of Pulmonary Scintigraphy. 1995. American College of Radiology. Replaced. In Section I, see: Lung/Radionuclide Imaging.

Macular Degeneration

Age-Related Macular Degeneration Preferred Practice Pattern. 1994. American Academy of Ophthalmology. Replaced. In Section I, see: Macular Degeneration.

Magnetic Resonance Imaging

Performance/Interpretation Qualifications: Magnetic Resonance Imaging. *Neurol.* 1988;38:21A. American Academy of Neurology. Replaced.

Mammography/Standards

ACR Standards for the Performance of Screening Mammography. 1994. American College of Radiology. Replaced. In Section I, see: Mammography.

Mentally Disabled Persons

Sterilization of Women Who Are Mentally Handicapped. *ACOG Committee Opinion.* 1988;63. American College of Obstetricians and Gynecologists. Replaced. In Section I, see: Ethics, Medical.

Middle Ear Ventilation

Tympanostomy with Tube Insertion. 1994. Minnesota Academy of Otolaryngology–Head & Neck Surgery. Replaced. In Section I, see: Physician's Practice Patterns.

Multiple Trauma

Trauma During Pregnancy. *ACOG Technical Bulletin.* 1991;161. American College of Obstetricians and Gynecologists. Replaced. In Section I, see: Abdominal Injuries.

Nasal Septum/Surgery

Nasal Septoplasty. 1994. Minnesota Academy of Otolaryngology–Head & Neck Surgery. Replaced. In Section I, see: Physician's Practice Patterns.

Neonatal Abstinence Syndrome

Drug-Exposed Infants. *Pediatr.* 1995;96:364-367. American Academy of Pediatrics. Replaced. In Section I, see: Neonatal Abstinence Syndrome.

Nervous System/Ultrasonography

Performance/Interpretation Qualifications: Neurosonology. *Neurol.* 1991;41:13A. American Academy of Neurology. Replaced.

Obesity/Therapy

Bariatric Practice Guidelines. 1996. American Society of Bariatric Physicians. Replaced. In Section I, see: Obesity/Therapy.

Paranasal Sinus Diseases/Surgery

Guidelines for Surgical Treatment of Intrinsic Diseases of the Paranasal Sinuses. 1994. Minnesota Academy of Otolaryngology–Head & Neck Surgery. Replaced. In Section I, see: Physician's Practice Patterns.

Parathyroid Neoplasms/Radionuclide Imaging

ACR Standard for the Performance of Parathyroid Scintigraphy. 1995. American College of Radiology. Replaced. In Section I, see: Parathyroid Glands/Radionuclide Imaging.

Pelvis/Unltrasonography

ACR Standard for the Performance of the Ultrasound Examination of the Female Pelvis. 1995. American College of Radiology. Replaced. In Section I, see: Genital Diseases, Female/Diagnosis.

Perioperative Care

Standards for Basic Anesthetic Care. *ASA Standards, Guidelines and Statements.* 1996;2:3. American Society of Anesthesiologists. Replaced. In Section I, see: Monitoring, Physiologic.

Pharmaceutical Preparations

Advice for the Patient. *USP DI.* 1997;Volume II. US Pharmacopeia/Micromedex, Inc. Replaced. In Section I, see: Asthma.

Practice Guidelines

Society of Nuclear Medicine Procedure Guidelines Manual 1997. 1997. Society of Nuclear Medicine. Replaced. In Section I, see: Practice Guidelines.

Preanesthetic Medication

Standards for Preanesthesia Care. *ASA Standards, Guidelines and Statements.* 1996;2. American Society of Anesthesiologists. Replaced. In Section I, see: Preanesthetic Medication.

Pregnancy Complications/Surgery

Guidelines for Laparoscopic Surgery During Pregnancy. 1996;23. Society of American Gastrointestinal and Endoscopic Surgeons. Replaced. In Section I, see: Pregnancy Complications/Surgery.

Pregnancy, Ectopic

Ectopic Pregnancy. *ACOG Technical Bulletin.* 1990;150. American College of Obstetricians and Gynecologists. Replaced. In Section I, see: Pregnancy, Tubal, Diagnosis.

Pregnancy, Multiple

Multiple Gestation. *ACOG Technical Bulletin.* 1989;131. American College of Obstetricians and Gynecologists. Replaced. In Section I, see: Pregnancy, Multiple.

Preoperative Care

Statement on Routine Preoperative Laboratory and Diagnostic Screening. *ASA Standards, Guidelines and Statements.* 1996. American Society of Anesthesiologists. Replaced. In Section I, see: Diagnostic Tests, Routine.

Rabies/Prevention and Control

Rabies Prevention: Recommendations of the Immunization Practices Advisory Committee. *Morbid Mortal Weekly Report.* 1991;40(no. RR-3):1-19. Centers for Disease Control and Prevention. Replaced. In Section I, see: Rabies/Vaccine.

Radiography

ACR Standard on Communication—Diagnostic Radiology. 1995. American College of Radiology. Replaced. In Section I, see: Diagnostic Imaging.

Radiotherapy

ACR Standard for Radiation Oncology. 1995. American College of Radiology. Replaced. In Section I, see: Radiation Oncology/Standards.

Rape

Adolescent Acquaintance Rape. *ACOG Committee Opinion.* 1993;122. American College of Obstetricians and Gynecologists. Replaced. In Section I, see: Rape.

Retinal Detachment

Precursors of Rhegmatogenous Retinal Detachment in Adults Preferred Practice Pattern. 1994. American Academy of Ophthalmology. Replaced. In Section I, see: Vitreous Detachment.

Rh Isoimmunization/Prevention and Control

Prevention of D Isoimmunization. *ACOG Technical Bulletin.* 1990;147. American College of Obstetricians and Gynecologists. Replaced. In Section I, see: Rh Isoimmunization/Prevention and Control.

Scrotum/Radionuclide Imaging

ACR Standard for the Performance of Scrotal Scintigraphy. 1995. American College of Radiology. Replaced. In Section I, see: Scrotum/Radionuclide Imaging.

Seat Belts/Standards

Automobile Passenger Restraints for Children and Pregnant Women. *ACOG Technical Bulletin.* 1991;151. American College of Obstetricians and Gynecologists. Replaced. In Section I, see: Abdominal Injuries.

Snoring/Complications

Management of Sleep Apnea and Snoring. 1994. Minnesota Academy of Otolaryngology–Head & Neck Surgery. Replaced. In Section I, see: Physician's Practice Patterns.

Sterilization, Tubal

Ethical Considerations in Sterilization, Tubal. *ACOG Committee Opinion.* 1989;73. American College of Obstetricians and Gynecologists. Replaced. In Section I, see: Ethics, Medical.

Substance-Related Disorders

Patient Placement Criteria for the Treatment of Psychoactive Substance Use Disorders. 1991. American Society of Addiction Medicine. Replaced. In Section I, see: Substance Related Disorders/ Rehabilitation.

Thrombolytic Therapy

Fourth ACCP Consensus Conference on Antithrombotic Therapy. *Chest*. 1995;108:225S-522S. American College of Chest Physicians. Replaced. In Section I, see: Fibrinolytic Agents/Therapeutic Use.

Thyroid Gland/Radionuclide Imaging

ACR Standard for the Performance of Thyroid Scintigraphy and Uptake Measurements. 1995. American College of Radiology. Replaced. In Section I, see: Iodine Radioisotopes/Therapeutic Use.

Tomography, Emission-Computed

Performance/Interpretation Qualifications: Positron Emission Tomography Imaging. 1991. American Academy of Neurology. Replaced.

Tomography, X-ray Computed

ACR Standard for the Performance of Thoracic Computed Tomography. 1998. American College of Radiology. Replaced. In Section I, see: Tomography, X-ray Computed.

Tonsillectomy

Tonsillectomy and/or Adenoidectomy. 1994. Minnesota Academy of Otolaryngology–Head & Neck Surgery. Replaced. In Section I, see: Physician's Practice Patterns.

Tumor Markers, Biological/Analysis

1997 Update of Recommendations for the Use of Tumor Markers in Breast and Colorectal Cancer. *J Clin Oncol*. 1999. American Society of Clinical Oncology. Replaced. In Section I, see: Tumor Markers, Biological/Analysis.

Ultrasonics/Diagnostic Use

ACR Standard for the Performance of the Pediatric Neurosonology Examination. 1995. American College of Radiology. Replaced. In Section I, see: Nervous System/Ultrasonography.

Ultrasonography, Prenatal

ACR Standard for the Performance of Antepartum Obstetrical Ultrasound. 1995. American College of Radiology. Replaced. In Section I, see: Ultrasonography, Prenatal.

Urography

ACR Standard for the Performance of Excretory Urography. 1995. American College of Radiology. Replaced. In Section I, see: Urography/Standards.

Urography

ACR Standard for the Performance of Voiding Cystourethrography in Children. 1995. American College of Radiology. Replaced. In Section I, see: Bladder/Radiography.

Section VI
Withdrawn Clinical Practice Guidelines

AIDS Dementia Complex/Classification

Nomenclature and Research Case Definitions for Neurological Manifestations of Human Immunodeficiency Virus Type-1 (HIV-1) Infection. *Neurol.* 1991;41:778-785. American Academy of Neurology.

Ambulatory Surgical Procedures

SAGES Position Statement—Outpatient Laparoscopic Cholecystectomy. 1991. Society of American Gastrointestinal and Endoscopic Surgeons.

Automobile Driving

Practice Parameters: Guidelines for Driving Following a First Unprovoked Tonic Clonic Seizure. 1992. American Academy of Neurology.

Cerebral Angiography

ACR Standard for the Performance of Cerebral Angiography. 1994. American College of Radiology.

Common Cold/Drug Therapy

Common Cold. *USP DI.* 1997;Volume I. US Pharmacopeia/Micromedex, Inc.

Cystic Fibrosis

Cystic Fibrosis. *USP DI.* 1997;Volume I. US Pharmacopeia/Micromedex, Inc.

Dental Care for Chronically Ill

Oral Health Care Guidelines: HIV Infection and AIDS. 1990. American Dental Association.

Diagnostic Imaging

ACR Standard for the Performance of Digital Image Data Management. 1998-1999. American College of Radiology.

Diving/Adverse Effects

Discussion of Risk of Scuba Diving in Individuals with Allergic and Respiratory Diseases. *J Allergy Clin Immun.* 1995;96:871-873, Editorial. American Academy of Allergy, Asthma, and Immunology.

Electrodiagnosis

Common Diagnoses in Electrodiagnostic Medicine. *The Electrodiagnostic Medicine Consultation.* 1998. American Association of Electrodiagnostic Medicine.

Electrodiagnosis/Methods

Electrodiagnostic Techniques. *The Electrodiagnostic Medicine Consultation.* 1998. American Association of Electrodiagnostic Medicine.

Electrodiagnosis Guidelines

Guidelines in Electrodiagnostic Medicine. 1988. American Association of Electrodiagnostic Medicine.

Electrodiagnosis Referral and Consultation

The Electrodiagnostic Medicine Consultation. 1998. American Association of Electrodiagnostic Medicine.

Endoscopy/Education

Summary Statement on Surgical Endoscopic Training and Practice. 1991;13. Society of American Gastrointestinal and Endoscopic Surgeons.

Fluoroscopy/Standards

ACR Standard for Diagnostic Medical Physics Performance Monitoring of Radiographic and Fluoroscopic Equipment. 1997. American College of Radiology.

Gestational Age

Fetal Maturity Assessment Prior to Elective Repeat Cesarean Delivery. *ACOG Committee Opinion.* 1991; 98. American College of Obstetricians and Gynecologists.

Glaucoma, Open-Angle/Drug Therapy

Open Angle Glaucoma. *USP DI.* 1997;Volume I. US Pharmacopeia/Micromedex, Inc.

Gonorrhea/Drug Therapy

Gonococcal Infections. *USP DI.* 1997;Volume I. US Pharmacopeia/Micromedex, Inc.

Head Injuries/Diagnosis

ACR Standard for the Performance of Computed Tomography in the Evaluation of Head Trauma. 1995. American College of Radiology.

Health Personnel

Critical Care Services and Personnel for Delivery of Care in a Critical Care Setting. *Critical Care Med.* 1988;16:809-811. Society of Critical Care Medicine.

Hemophilia, Drug Therapy

Hemophilia. *USP DI*. 1997;Volume I. US Pharmacopeia/Micromedex, Inc.

HIV Infections

HIV Infection. *USP DI*. 1997;Volume I. US Pharmacopeia/Micromedex, Inc.

Hospitals

Guidelines for Improving the Use of Antimicrobial Agents in Hospitals: A Statement by the Infectious Disease Society of America. *J Infect Dis*. 1988;157:869-876. Infectious Diseases Society of America.

Hypertension/Drug Therapy

Hypertension. *USP DI*. 1997;Volume I. US Pharmacopeia/Micromedex, Inc.

Injuries

Trauma and Chemical Misuse/Dependency. 1991. American Society of Addiction Medicine.

Intraoperative Monitoring/Standards

Standards for Basic Intra-Operative Monitoring. 1990. American Society of Anesthesiologists.

Leukemia, Hairy Cell/Drug Therapy

Hairy Cell Leukemia. *USP DI*. 1997;Volume I. US Pharmacopeia/Micromedex, Inc.

Lung Diseases

Oral Health Care Guidelines: Patients with Pulmonary Disease. 1991. American Dental Association.

Lung Diseases, Obstructive/Drug Therapy

Chronic Obstructive Pulmonary Disease. *USP DI*. 1997;Volume I. US Pharmacopeia/Medex, Inc.

Lyme Disease/Drug Therapy

Lyme Disease. *USP DI*. 1997;Volume I. US Pharmacopeia/Micromedex, Inc.

Methadone/Therapeutic Use

Methadone Treatment. 1990. American Society of Addiction Medicine.

Neutropenia/Complications

Guidelines for the Use of Antimicrobial Agents in Neutropenic Patients with Unexplained Fever. *J Infect Dis*. 1990;161:381-396. Infectious Diseases Society of America.

Obstetrics/Education

Ethical Issues in Obstetrics-Gynecologic Education. *ACOG Committee Opinion*. 1997;181. American College of Obstetricians and Gynecologists.

Osteoporosis

Physician's Resource Manual on Osteoporosis: A Decision-Making Guide. 1991. National Osteoporosis Foundation.

Ovarian Neoplasms/Genetics

Genetic Risk and Screening Techniques for Epithelial Ovarian Cancer. *ACOG Committee Opinion*. 1992; 117. American College of Obstetricians and Gynecologists.

Population Surveillance

Public Health Issues in Control of Tuberculosis. *Chest*. 1985;87:135S-138S. American College of Chest Physicians.

Pregnancy Complications

Chemically Dependent Women and Pregnancy. 1989. American Society of Addiction Medicine.

Radiography/Instrumentaion

ACR Standard for Diagnostic Medical Physics Performance Monitoring of Radiographic and Fluoroscopic Equipment. 1997. American College of Radiology.

Rhinitis/Drug Therapy

Rhinitis. *USP DI*. 1997;Volume I. US Pharmacopeia/ Micromedex, Inc.

Substance-Related Disorders/Drug Therapy

Medical Care in Recovery. 1989. American Society of Addiction Medicine.

Surrogate Mothers

Ethical Issues in Surrogate Motherhood. *ACOG Committee Opinion*. 1990;88. American College of Obstetricians and Gynecologists.

Syphilis/Drug Therapy

Syphilis. *USP DI*. 1997;Volume I. US Pharmacopeia/ Micromedex, Inc.

Section VII
Names and
Addresses
of Sponsoring
Organizations

American Academy of Allergy, Asthma, and Immunology

611 E Wells St
Milwaukee, WI 53202
414 272-6071
mgieseke@aaaai.org

American Academy of Child and Adolescent Psychiatry

3615 Wisconsin Ave NW
Washington, DC 20016-3007
202 966-7300
aacap.org

American Academy of Cosmetic Surgery/ American Society of Lipo-Suction Surgery

401 N Michigan Ave, #2400
Chicago, IL 60611
312 527-6713

American Academy of Dermatology

930 N Meacham Rd
PO Box 4014
Schaumburg, IL 60168-4014
847 240-1796
aad.org

American Academy of Family Physicians

11400 Tomahawk Creek Pkwy
Leawood, KS 66211-2672
1 800 274-2237
aafp.org

American Academy of Neurology

1080 Montreal Ave
St. Paul, MN 55116
651 695-1940
aaa.org

American Academy of Ophthalmology

655 Beach St
PO Box 7424
San Francisco, CA 94120
415 447-0302
ncollins@aao.org

American Academy of Orthopaedic Surgeons

6300 N River Rd
Rosemont, IL 60018-4264
847 823-7186
aaos.org

American Academy of Otolaryngic Allergy

8455 Colesville Rd, #745
Silver Spring, MD 20910
301 588-1800

American Academy of Otolaryngology — Head and Neck Surgery

One Prince St
Alexandria, VA 22314-3357
703 519-1583
eentnet.org

American Academy of Pediatrics

141 NW Point Blvd
Elk Grove Village, IL 60009-0927
847 228-5005
aap.org

American Academy of Physical Medicine and Rehabilitation

One IBM Plaza, #2500
Chicago, IL 60611-3604
312 464-9700

American Academy of Sleep Medicine

6301 Bandel Rd, #101
Rochester, MN 55901
507 287-6006
dwelch@aasmnet.org

American Association of Clinical Endocrinologists

1000 River Side Ave, #205
Jacksonville, FL 32204
904 353-7878
aace.com

American Association of Electrodiagnostic Medicine

421 First Avenue SW, #300E
Rochester, MN 55902
507 288-0100
aaem.net

American Association of Neurological Surgeons

22 S Washington St
Park Ridge, IL 60068-4257
847 692-9500

American Association of Oral and Maxillofacial Surgeons

9700 W Bryn Mawr Ave
Rosemont, IL 60018-5701
800 822-6637

American Cancer Society

1599 Clifton Rd NE
Atlanta, GA 30329-4251
404 320-3333
cancer.org

American College of Cardiology

9111 Old Georgetown Rd
Bethesda, MD 20814-1699
301 897-5400
acc.org

American College of Chest Physicians

3300 Dundee Rd
Northbrook, IL 60062-2348
847 498-1400
chestnet.org

American College of Emergency Physicians

PO Box 619911
Dallas, TX 75261-9911
972 550-0911
rwhitson@acep.org

American College of Gastroenterology

Emory Clinic
1365 Clifton Rd NE
Atlanta, GA 30322
703 820-7400
jwari02@emory.edu

American College of Obstetricians and Gynecologists

409 12th St SW
Washington, DC 20024-2188
202 638-5577
acog.com

American College of Occupational and Environmental Medicine

55 W Seegers Rd
Arlington Heights, IL 60005
847 228-6850
acoem.org

American College of Physicians

6th St at Race
Independence Mall West
Philadelphia, PA 19106-1572
215 351-2800
acponline.org

American College of Preventive Medicine

1660 L St N, #206
Washington, DC 20036-5603
202 466-2044
acpm.org

American College of Radiology

1891 Preston White Dr
Reston, VA 20191-4397
703 648-8900
acr.org

American College of Rheumatology

1800 Century Pl, #250
Atlanta, GA 30345
404 633-3777
rheumatology.org

American College of Surgeons

55 E Erie St
Chicago, IL 60611
312 202-5000

American Dental Association

211 E Chicago Ave
Chicago, IL 60611
312 440-2500
ada.org

American Diabetes Association

1660 Duke St
Alexandria, VA 22314
703 549-1500
diabetes.org

American Gastroenterological Association

7910 Woodmont Ave, #700
Bethesda, MD 20814
301 654-2055
wcohen@gastro.org

American Geriatrics Society

770 Lexington Ave, #300
New York, NY 10021
212 308-1414
americangeriatrics.org

American Heart Association

7272 Greenville Ave
Dallas, TX 75231-4596
214 373-6300
americanheart.org

American In Vitro Allergy/ Immunology Society

PO Box 341461
Bethesda, MD 20827-1461
201 816-1289
aiais@erols.com

American Medical Association

515 N State St
Chicago, IL 60610
312 464-5000
ama-assn.org
mary_haynes@ama-assn.org
nancy_nolan@ama-assn.org

American Medical Directors Association

10480 Little Patuxent Pkwy, #760
Columbia, MD 21044
410 740-9743
amda.com

American Psychiatric Association (Press)

1400 K Street NW
Washington, DC 20005
202 682-6181
aaponte@psych.org

American Society for Gastrointestinal Endoscopy

13 Elm St
Manchester, MA 01944
507 526-8330
asge.org

American Society for Reproductive Medicine

1209 Montgomery Hwy
Birmingham, AL 35216-2809
205 978-5000
asrm.com

American Society of Addiction Medicine

4601 N Park Ave
Arcade #101
Chevy Chase, MD 20815
301 656-3920
asam.org

American Society of Anesthesiologists

520 N Northwest Hwy
Park Ridge, IL 60068-2573
847 825-5586
asahq.org

American Society of Bariatric Physicians

5600 S Quebec St, #109A
Englewood, CO 80111
303 770-2526
asbp.org

American Society of Clinical Oncology

225 Reinekers Ln, #650
Alexandria, VA 22314
703 299-0150
asco.org

American Society of Clinical Pathologists

2100 W Harrison St
Chicago, IL 60612-3798
312 738-4880
ascp.org

American Society of Colon and Rectal Surgeons

85 W Algonquin Rd, #550
Arlington Heights, IL 60005
847 290-9184
ascrs@aol.com

American Society of Hematology

1200 19th St NW, #300
Washington, DC 20036-2422
202 857-1118
ash@dc.sba.com

American Society of Maxillofacial Surgeons

444 E Algonquin Rd, #150
Arlington Heights, IL 60005
847 228-8375

American Society of Plastic and Reconstructive Surgeons

444 E Algonquin Rd
Arlington Heights, IL 60005
847 228-9900
plasticsurgery.org

American Society of Temporomandibular Joint Surgeons

5101 Woodridge Rd
Minnetonka, MN 55345
612 930-0988

American Thoracic Society

1740 Broadway
New York, NY 10019-4374
212 315-8700
thoracic.org

American Thyroid Association

Montefiore Medical Center
111 E 210th St
Bronx, NY 10467
718 882-6047
thyroid.org

American Urological Association

1120 N Charles St
Baltimore, MD 21201-5559
410 727-1100
auanet.org

Arthroscopy Association of North America

6300 N River Rd, #104
Rosemont, IL 60018-4228
847 292-2262
aana2.org

Blue Cross and Blue Shield Association

676 N St Clair St
Chicago, IL 60611
312 297-6000

Centers for Disease Control and Prevention

1600 Clifton Rd NE
Mailstop C08
Atlanta, GA 30333
404 639-3311
cdc.gov

College of American Pathologists

325 Waukegan Rd
Northfield, IL 60093-2750
847 832-7000
cap.org

Federal Agency for Health Care Policy and Research

6010 Executive Blvd, #300
Rockville, MD 20852
301 594-4015
ahcpr.gov

Infectious Diseases Society of America

99 Canal Center Plaza, #210
Alexandria, VA 22314
703 299-0200

Joint Task Force of Allergy, Asthma, and Immunology

50 N Brockway St, #3-3
Palatine, IL 60067
847 934-1918

Kentucky Diabetic Retinopathy Group

Retina and Vitreous Associates of Kentucky
120 N Eagle Creek Dr, #500
Lexington, KY 40509
606 263-3900

Minnesota Academy of Otolaryngology—Head and Neck Surgery

3433 Broadway St NE, #300
Minneapolis, MN 55413-1761
612 362-3736
rlampright@mnmed.org

National Cancer Institute

Executive Plaza North
9000 Rockville Pike, Rm 300
Bethesda, MD 20892
301 496-5583
nih.ogv

National Eye Institute

Bldg 31, Rm 6A52
31 Center Dr, MSC 2510
Bethesda, MD 20892-2510
301 496-5248
nih.ogv

National Heart, Lung, and Blood Institute

PO Box 30105
Bethesda, MD 20824-0105
301 251-1222
nih.ogv

National Institutes of Health

Office of Medical Applications of Research
Bldg 31, Rm 1B03
Bethesda, MD 20892
301 496-1143
nih.ogv

National Kidney Foundation

30 E 33rd St
New York, NY 10016
212 889-2210
donnaf@kidney.org

National Osteoporosis Foundation

1150 17th St NW, #500
Washington, DC 20036
202 223-2226
nof.org

RAND

1700 Main St
PO Box 2138
Santa Monica, CA 90407-2138
310 393-0411
rand.org

Renal Physicians Association

4701 Randolph Rd, #102
Rockville, MD 20852
301 468-3515
renalmd.org

Society for Healthcare Epidemiology of America

19 Mantua Rd
Mt Royal, NJ 08061
609 423-0087
medscape.com/SHEA

Society for Vascular Surgery

13 Elm St
Manchester, MA 01944-1314
978 526-8330
jvs@prri.com

Society of American Gastrointestinal and Endoscopic Surgeons

2716 Ocean Park Blvd, #3000
Santa Monica, CA 90405
310 314-2404
sagesmail@aol.com

Society of Cardiovascular and Interventional Radiology

10201 Lee Hwy, #500
Fairfax, VA 22030
703 691-1805
scvir.org

Society of Critical Care Medicine

8101 E Kaiser Blvd, #300
Anaheim, CA 92808-2259
714 282-6000
sccm.org

Society of Nuclear Medicine

1850 Samuel Morse Dr
Reston, VA 20190-5316
703 708-9000
snm.org

Society of Surgical Oncology

85 W Algonquin Rd, #550
Arlington Heights, IL 60005
847 427-1400

US Pharmacopeia

12601 Twinbrook Pkwy
Rockville, MD 20852
301 881-0666
usp.org

US Preventive Services Task Force

6010 Executive Blvd, #300
Rockville, MD 20852
301 594-4015
ahcpr.gov

Names and Addresses

Appendix
Clinical Practice
Guideline Recognition
Program

Clinical Practice Guideline Recognition Program

Background

From their inception, the American Medical Association's (AMA's) clinical practice guideline program, the Practice Guidelines Partnership, and Clinical Quality Improvement Forum (formerly the Practice Parameters Partnership and Practice Parameters Forum, respectively) have been concerned with guideline quality.

Recognizing that review of the clinical content of guidelines would be equivalent to recreating guidelines, and therefore impractical and inefficient, the AMA, Partnership, and Forum have focused their efforts on the quality of the process by which guidelines are developed. These groups have developed and refined criteria for the development and evaluation of clinical practice guidelines (please see the *Attributes to Guide the Development and Evaluation of Practice Parameters/Guidelines* below). The AMA and Partnership have also adopted policies calling for the development of clinical practice guidelines that meet the criteria defined in the *Attributes.*

As more guidelines are promulgated from a greater variety of organizations, physicians and others have become very interested in the quality of guidelines. Physicians, health plans, and others have requested not only criteria for evaluation of clinical practice guidelines, but application of these criteria through a clearly defined process. In response, the AMA has developed a voluntary program to evaluate the process by which clinical practice guidelines are developed—the Clinical Practice Guideline Recognition Program (CPGRP).

Clinical practice guidelines recognized by the American Medical Association as having met the established criteria for development, are potentially valuable tools for guiding patient care. AMA makes no representations or warranties concerning (1) the content or clinical efficacy of clinical practice guidelines or this guideline specifically or (2) the sponsor or developer of the guideline. Recognized guidelines are not to be used as fixed protocols; they merely identify courses of intervention. *Treatment must be based on individual patient needs and professional judgment.* Guidelines are not entirely inclusive or exclusive of all methods of reasonable care that can obtain the same results, nor of those that consider the particular needs of the patient and available resources. Guidelines can be tailored to fit patient needs that are influenced by the setting, resources, and other factors. Deviations from clinical practice guidelines may be justified by individual circumstances.

How the Program Works

The CPGRP offers clinical practice guideline sponsors the opportunity to have the process by which their guidelines were developed reviewed by a panel of physicians and methodologists who have experience in the development of guidelines. The AMA panel reviews guidelines and supporting documentation against criteria derived from the *Attributes.* Via a modified Delphi method, the AMA panel comes to consensus regarding guidelines' compliance with the criteria. Sponsors whose guidelines meet criteria are permitted to use specific language regarding the recognition of their guidelines.

Because one criterion for Recognition addresses the age of guidelines, guidelines are eligible for Recognition for a limited period of time. Eligibility for the AMA Recognition is dependent upon how current the clinical practice guidelines are, according to the following table:

Age of Guideline	Eligibility for AMA Recognition
0–2 calendar years	3 calendar years
3 calendar years	2 calendar years
4 calendar years	1 calendar year
5 calendar years or older	Not eligible

AMA Recognition of a clinical practice guideline is not extended to any derivation, modification, alteration, or any other changes that may be made by any organization to a clinical practice guideline. Any derivation of the recognized guideline by any organization is considered a new clinical practice guideline that must be separately evaluated by the AMA in order to be eligible for AMA Recognition. CPGRP application materials are attached for further information.

Recognized Guidelines

The following guidelines were submitted for review and have been found* to be in compliance with the criteria for development of clinical practice guidelines, as derived from the *Attributes to Guide the Development and Evaluation of Practice Parameters/Guidelines:*

American Academy of Ophthalmology

Age-Related Macular Degeneration (Developed 1998; Recognition Expires 2003)

Amblyopia (Developed 1997; Recognition Expires 2002)

Blepharitis (Developed 1998; Recognition Expires 2003)

Cataract in the Adult Eye (Developed 1996; Recognition Expires 2001)

Comprehensive Adult Eye Evaluation (Developed 1996; Recognition Expires 2001)

Conjunctivitis (Developed 1998; Recognition Expires 2003)

Diabetic Retinopathy (Developed 1998; Recognition Expires 2003)

Dry Eye Syndrome (Developed 1998; Recognition Expires 2003)

Esotropia (Developed 1997; Recognition Expires 2002)

Management of Posterior Vitreous Detachment, Retinal Breaks, and Lattice Degeneration (Developed 1998; Recognition Expires 2003)

Pediatric Eye Evaluations (Developed 1997; Recognition Expires 2002)

Refractive Errors (Developed 1997; Recognition Expires 2002)

American Academy of Sleep Medicine

Practice Parameters for the Indications for Polysomnography and Related Procedures (Developed 1997, Recognition Expires 2002)

Practice Parameters for the Treatment of Obstructive Sleep Apnea in Adults: The Efficacy of Surgical Modifications of the Upper Airway (Developed 1996; Recognition Expires 2001)

*This information was current as of August 1999.

Practice Parameters for the Treatment of Snoring and Obstructive Sleep Apnea with Oral Appliances (Developed 1995; Expires 2000)

Practice Parameters for the Use of Actigraphy in the Clinical Assessment of Sleep Disorders (Developed 1995; Expires 2000)

Practice Parameters for the Use of Polysomnography in the Evaluation of Insomnia (Developed 1995; Expires 2000)

American Association of Clinical Endocrinologists

AACE Clinical Practice Guidelines for Growth Hormone Use in Adults and Children (Developed 1998; Recognition Expires 2003)

AACE Clinical Practice Guidelines for Male Sexual Dysfunction (Developed 1998; Recognition Expires 2003)

AACE Clinical Practice Guidelines for the Evaluation and Treatment of Hyperthyroidism and Hypothyroidism (Developed 1995; Expires 2000)

American Society of Anesthesiologists

Practice Guidelines for Blood Component Therapy (Developed 1995; Recognition Expires 2000)

Practice Guidelines for Cancer Pain Management (Developed 1995; Recognition Expires 2000)

Practice Guidelines for Chronic Pain Management (Developed 1996; Recognition Expires 2001)

Practice Guidelines for Sedation and Analgesia by Non-Anesthesiologists (Developed 1995; Recognition Expires 2000)

Practice Guidelines for Perioperative Transesophageal Echocardiography (Developed 1995; Recognition Expires 2000)

College of American Pathologists

Practice Parameter for the Use of Red Blood Cell Transfusions (Developed 1998; Recognition Expires 2003)

Institute for Healthcare Quality

QualityFirst Position Paper: Coronary Artery Disease with Myocardial Infarction (Developed 1997; Recognition Expires 2002)

QualityFirst Position Paper: Diabetes Mellitus (Adult) (Developed 1997; Recognition Expires 2002)

QualityFirst Position Paper: Dysfunctional Uterine Bleeding (Developed 1997; Recognition Expires 2002)

QualityFirst Position Paper: Pancreatitis (Developed 1997; Recognition Expires 2002)

Joint Council on Allergy, Asthma, and Immunology

Diagnosis and Management of Rhinitis (Developed 1998; Recognition Expires 2003)

Parameters for the Diagnosis and Management of Sinusitis (Developed 1998; Recognition Expires 2003)

Stinging Insect Hypersensitivity: A Practice Parameter (Developed 1999; Expires 2004)

Society of Nuclear Medicine

Procedure Guideline for Bone Scintigraphy (Revised 1998; Recognition Expires 2003)

University of Texas Medical Branch

Diabetes (Developed 1997; Recognition Expires 2002)

HIV Management (Developed 1998; Recognition Expires 2003)

Hyperlipidemia (Developed 1998; Recognition Expires 2003)

Hypertension (Developed 1998; Recognition Expires 2003)

Pulmonary (Developed 1998; Recognition Expires 2003)

Seizure Disorder (Developed 1998; Recognition Expires 2003)

Attributes to Guide the Development and Evaluation of Practice Parameters/Guidelines[1]

Preface

As a part of its long-standing commitment to improving the quality of medical care, and in response to current concerns regarding the quality and utilization of health care in the United States, the American Medical Association is working cooperatively with the national medical specialty societies and other physician organizations to guide the development, evaluation, and implementation of practice parameters/guidelines. Scientifically sound, clinically relevant practice parameters/guidelines provide a means to improve quality and assure appropriate utilization of health care services.

For purposes of this document, practice parameters/clinical practice guidelines are defined as "systematically developed statements, based on current professional knowledge, that assist practitioners[2] and patients to make decisions about appropriate health care for specific clinical circumstances."

Practice parameters/guidelines are highly variable in their content, format, degree of specificity, and method of development. Practice parameters/guidelines may address issues ranging from general aspects of medical care to management of specific clinical conditions. Practice parameters/guidelines may identify a range of interventions (eg, diagnostic, therapeutic, preventive) for management of specific

---

[1]© American Medical Association 1996.

[2]Practitioner may not be limited to physicians and could be broadly applied, as appropriate, by each health care organization/medical specialty society.

clinical conditions or may identify clinical conditions for which specific interventions may be appropriate. Practice parameters/guidelines may be developed by synthesizing information from scientific research and/or clinical experience pertinent to a given clinical issue.

Currently, almost 1800 practice parameters/guidelines, developed by approximately 75 physician organizations and other groups, are available. Additional practice parameters/guidelines are under development.

The American Medical Association, in conjunction with the AMA/Specialty Society Practice Parameters Partnership and Practice Parameters Forum, has identified these attributes to guide the development and evaluation of practice parameters/guidelines to ensure that practice parameters/guidelines are scientifically sound, clinically relevant, and applicable in the day-to-day practice of medicine.

Attribute I

Practice parameters/guidelines should be developed by or in conjunction with physician organizations.

General Characteristics

1. Practice parameters/guidelines should be developed by or in conjunction with organizations characterized by the following:

    - scientific and clinical expertise in the content areas of the parameters/ guidelines; and
    - broad-based representation of practitioners and organizations likely to be affected by the parameters/guidelines.

2. Relevant and affected practitioner organizations should have the opportunity to review and comment on parameters/guidelines during their development.
3. When parameters/guidelines are specifically targeted to physician practice and decision-making, physicians should have a leadership role.
4. Completed parameters/guidelines should be submitted to affected practitioners and appropriate organizations for review, evaluation, and comment.

Comment

Attribute I ensures that appropriate physician organizations, practitioners, and other affected organizations are responsible for the development of parameters/guidelines.

Physician organizations can provide the expertise and broad-based representation necessary for the development of scientifically sound, clinically relevant practice parameters/guidelines that will be accepted by physicians and used in the day-to-day practice of medicine.

Attribute I recognizes the value of parameters/guidelines developed by non-physician organizations (eg, NIH consensus panels) that are knowledgeable in the subject area and that broadly represent physicians. Parameters/guidelines developed by nonphysician organizations should undergo review by physician organizations to ensure their accuracy and clinical applicability.

Attribute I ensures that, when parameters/guidelines cross disciplines or specialties, organizations responsible for the development of parameters/guidelines should involve physician groups representing all appropriate specialties and practice settings, and should allow relevant physician organizations to review and comment on the parameters/guidelines.

Attribute I recognizes that parameters/guidelines could be endorsed by all physician organizations involved in the content area of the parameter. However, the inherent difficulty in cross-specialty society endorsement is also recognized.

Attribute II

Practice parameters/guidelines should explicitly describe the methodology and process used in their development.

General Characteristics

1. Practice parameters/guidelines should provide the rationales for including or excluding studies.
2. Practice parameters/guidelines should include the methodology used to evaluate and incorporate scientific literature and other appropriate research findings. A listing of the scientific studies on which the parameters/guidelines are based should be provided.
3. Practice parameters/guidelines should describe the process for selection of clinical experts/reviewers. The specialty affiliations and relevant credentials of the physicians, their organizations, groups, and other individuals providing clinical expertise and review should be described.
4. Practice parameters/guidelines should describe the method/mechanisms for collecting and evaluating economic data. A listing of studies incorporating such data/references should be provided.
5. Practice parameters/guidelines should define the methodology for assessing and defining patient preference data. A listing of studies incorporating such data should be provided.
6. Practice parameters/guidelines should include a description and discussion of the evidence (within the scientific literature), including evidence tables, weights of specific studies, and the time period reviewed.
7. Practice parameters/guidelines should indicate if expert opinion was linked to scientific evidence to formulate the recommendation(s).
8. Practice parameters/guidelines should incorporate findings from the review of relevant research and from clinical judgments. Statements regarding the bases (eg, scientific literature, clinical judgment) for the practice parameter/guideline should be noted.
9. Practice parameters/guidelines should describe the methodology used to integrate relevant research findings and appropriate clinical expertise and conclusions.
10. Practice parameters/guidelines should utilize applicable published outcomes studies, when available, in the development of an original parameter/guideline. A description of this process should be provided.

Comment

Attribute II acknowledges the variability of information available on specific issues and, therefore, the corresponding variety of methodologies used in parameter/guideline development. Where possible, research data should provide the bases for practice parameters/guidelines. In the absence of scientific literature, clinical judgment and consensus may prevail as the bases for clinically sound, relevant parameters/guidelines.

Attribute II ensures the scientific soundness and clinical relevance of practice parameters/guidelines. Proper development of practice parameters/guidelines requires the synthesis of a broad array of medical information, including relevant scientific studies, clinical experience, and expert opinion.

Attribute II ensures that the recommendations are linked to scientific evidence, if available, and that evidence tables are provided to support the recommendations.

Attribute III

Practice parameters/guidelines should assist practitioner and patient decisions about appropriate health care for specific clinical circumstances.

General Characteristics

1. Practice parameters/guidelines should provide the data (clinical, scientific, and economic) needed to guide decisions.
2. Practice parameters/guidelines format should be clear and usable.
3. Practice parameters/guidelines should be adaptable to various environments in which practice occurs, eg, practitioners' offices, hospitals, and other health facilities.
4. Practice parameters/guidelines should be specific enough to be convertible, when appropriate, to review criteria and performance/quality measurements.
5. Practice parameters/guidelines should indicate how appropriate the management recommendations are in specific clinical circumstances. The strength and/or flexibility of the recommendations should be clearly stated.
6. Practice parameters/guidelines should include a discussion of the similarities and differences of the parameters/guidelines, as compared with other practice parameters/guidelines covering similar content areas.
7. Practice parameters/guidelines should clearly define and evaluate expected measurable outcomes. Examples of these outcomes may include:

   - cure of disease as quickly and effectively as possible;
   - decreased morbidity/mortality or delayed morbidity/mortality;
   - symptomatic relief;
   - improved quality of life; and
   - conservation of resources.

8. Practice parameters/guidelines should include condition-specific outcomes and appropriate measures to determine those outcomes.
9. Practice parameters/guidelines should define outcome measures derived from the parameters/guidelines. Types of outcomes measures may include:

   - medical indicators (eg, length of life, fitness scores, blood pressure, etc)
   - patient-oriented measures (eg, patient satisfaction, activities of daily living, quality of life, etc)
   - administrative/economic factors (eg, length of stay, cost factors, efficiency of overhead factors, etc)

10. Practice parameters/guidelines should note appropriate economic factors (cost efficiency/cost effectiveness/implementation cost of guideline/cost to perform one procedure over another) that may affect quality patient care/outcomes.
11. Practice parameters/guidelines should provide data (as available) regarding patient preferences.
12. Practice parameters/guidelines should note, and clearly state, the process used to formulate disclaiming statements or any other statements that express the limitation(s) of the recommendations in the parameter/guideline.

Comment

Attribute III ensures that practice parameters/guidelines address the information pertinent to the appropriate management of a given condition, thereby permitting practitioners to evaluate and implement the practice parameters/guidelines according to individual circumstances and patient preference. A format that is as specific as possible enables practitioners to have available practical information to address the broad range of clinical issues encountered in patient management.

Attribute III recognizes that alternative patient management strategies must be presented and discussed; that risks and benefits of these strategies must be evaluated; and that clinical situations and interventions for patients and practitioners are clearly stated.

Attribute IV

Practice parameters/guidelines should be based on current professional knowledge and reviewed and revised at regular intervals.

General Characteristics

1. Practice parameters/guidelines literature review(s) should be current (3–5 years).
2. Practice parameters/guidelines should indicate dates of relevant scientific literature and other appropriate research.
3. Practice parameters/guidelines should provide for periodic reviews and revisions, when appropriate, as evidenced by:

   • date of publication, or completion, is specified;
   • initial writing, review, or revision has occurred within the last 5 years; and
   • dates of the latest scientific studies and research findings are specified.

4. Practice parameters/guidelines should specify the planned review dates.
5. Practice parameters/guidelines should indicate that a system is established to monitor the emergence of new information, which may necessitate revision of the parameters/guidelines.
6. Practice parameters/guidelines should include methods to evaluate their implementation and outcomes, eg, review criteria (retrospective), performance measures, and process or outcomes measures. Plans for measurement/ assessment of the parameters'/guidelines' impact and effect, and the use of this information to revise the parameters/guidelines, should be discussed.

Comment

Attribute IV acknowledges the need for ongoing review of the medical literature and expert opinion, ensuring that practice parameters/guidelines are based on current information.

Attribute IV indicates that outcome measures offer the opportunity to improve the quality of practice parameters/guidelines. The outcome measures derived from practice parameters/guidelines will allow the application of that parameter/guideline to create a data set that can be used to evaluate and revise the parameter/ guideline on a periodic basis.

Attribute V

Practice parameters/guidelines should be widely disseminated.

General Characteristics

1. Practice parameters/guidelines should provide a dissemination plan that identifies the targeted audience by specialty, condition...
2. Practice parameters/guidelines should include a plan for wide distribution of the parameters/guidelines to targeted audiences as evidenced by:

   - a description of sources where the parameters/guidelines will be available, and
   - mechanisms by which the parameters/guidelines will be distributed.

3. Practice parameters/guidelines should identify anticipated plans for publication of the parameters/guidelines in peer-reviewed journals or other widely circulated publications.
4. Practice parameters/guidelines should include strategies for continued distribution of the parameters/guidelines.

Comment

Attribute V reflects the need to provide practitioners with reliable, comprehensive, and up-to-date information on a timely basis.

Practice Parameters Partnership

Agency for Health Care Policy and Research
American Academy of Family Physicians
American Academy of Ophthalmology, Inc
American Academy of Orthopaedic Surgeons
American Academy of Pediatrics
American College of Cardiology
American College of Obstetricians and Gynecologists
American College of Physicians
American College of Radiology
American College of Surgeons
American Hospital Association
American Medical Association
American Psychiatric Association
American Society of Anesthesiologists, Inc
American Society of Internal Medicine
American Urological Association, Inc
College of American Pathologists
Joint Commission on Accreditation of Healthcare Organizations

The following pages include the AMA's Clinical Practice Guideline Recognition Program application materials. Please find:

- Step by Step: How to Apply for AMA Recognition of Your Guideline(s)
- Application for Clinical Practice Guideline Recognition
- Criteria and Policy Governing Clinical Practice Guideline Recognition
- Sample Clinical Practice Guideline Recognition Program Payment Form
- Clinical Practice Guideline Recognition Program Payment Form

Please feel free to photocopy these materials for application purposes.

Step by Step: How to Apply for AMA Recognition of Your Guideline(s)

1. Ensure that you have received the full application packet. You should have:

   - a cover letter giving you background information on the program and inviting you to apply;
   - an AMA Application for Clinical Practice Guideline Recognition (including a fee schedule);
   - a payment form that can be used for the evaluation fee remittance;
   - examples of ways to document compliance with application criteria; and
   - a Criteria and Policy Governing AMA Clinical Practice Guideline Recognition.
   - To ensure that your correspondence makes its way to the correct area within the AMA, address it to:

     > American Medical Association
     > 515 N. State St.
     > Chicago, IL 60610

2. Familiarize yourself with these documents.
3. Complete the application, providing:

   - documentation,
   - guideline(s),
   - payment form and appropriate payment as instructed,
   - a signed copy of the Criteria and Policy Governing AMA Clinical Practice Guideline Recognition, and
   - mail these to the AMA.

4. Depending on the response you receive from the AMA:

   - If you receive a request for additional information/documentation, please send this, as requested, within 30 days;
   - If you receive notification that your guideline(s) has (have) met the criteria for AMA Recognition, please review the Criteria and Policy Governing AMA Clinical Practice Guideline Recognition to ensure compliance with this agreement;
   - If you receive notification that your guideline(s) has (have) not met the criteria for AMA Recognition, please review the documentation and consider applying when the deficiencies have been remedied.

5. If you meet the AMA's criteria for Recognition and you choose to use the allowed language (please see the *Criteria and Policy)* for the marketing and/or promotion of your guideline(s), you may do so when the AMA notifies you that Recognition has begun. You will be eligible for Recognition based on the age of the guideline(s) submitted, so that the age of an AMA Recognized guideline does not exceed 5 calendar years.
6. If your guideline receives AMA Recognition, you will be notified when AMA Recognition will discontinue. You must then reapply for AMA Recognition.

For each guideline submitted, please complete this form and attach documentation/descriptions, clearly labeled with the number of the criterion being addressed.

Sponsoring Organization(s) (including subsidiaries and affiliates):

_____

Title of Clinical Practice Guideline:

_____

Please see the attached "Examples" for further clarification of these Criteria. *Required Criteria for Recognition:* **"R" denotes that a guideline is required to meet this evaluation criterion in order to attain AMA Recognition.**	
I. Involvement of Physicians/Physician Organizations (R)	
Was the guideline developed with representation from practicing physicians and/or physician organizations? If yes, please attach documentation to verify physician/ physician organization involvement.	Yes ☐ No ☐
II. Literature Review (R)	
Was a literature search performed? If yes, please attach documentation to verify that a literature review was performed and describe the inclusion/exclusion criteria for the literature search. If no, please proceed to criterion III.	Yes ☐ No ☐
Was the evidence derived from the literature search rated? If yes, please attach documentation describing your evidence rating system.	Yes ☐ No ☐ No Evidence Exists ☐
III. Experts' Credentials (R)	
Was expert opinion used in the development of the guideline? If yes, please attach documentation describing the credentials of the experts.	Yes ☐ No ☐
IV. Appropriateness (R)	
Does the guideline address the appropriateness of its recommendations to specific clinical conditions and settings? If yes, please provide a citation within the guideline, or in an attachment, as verification that appropriateness of recommendations has been addressed.	Yes ☐ No ☐ Page:_____ Line:_____
V. Generalizability (R)	
Does the guideline include disclaimers and/or a discussion of the limitations and/ or degree of generalizability of the recommendations specific to clinical conditions? If yes, please provide a citation within the guideline, or in an attachment, to verify inclusion of disclaimers and/or limitations.	Yes ☐ No ☐ Page:_____ Line:_____
VI. Currentness (R)	
Has the guideline been developed, reviewed, or updated within the last 5 years?	Yes ☐ No ☐ Date_____
VII. Update Mechanism (R)	
Is there a mechanism in place to update the guideline? If yes, please attach documentation/description.	Yes ☐ No ☐
VIII. Wide Dissemination (R)	
Is there a mechanism in place to ensure that the guideline is readily available to all physicians who may be affected by its recommendations? If yes, please attach documentation/description of dissemination mechanisms.	Yes ☐ No ☐

rev. 6/2/98

<u>**For each guideline submitted, please complete this form and attach documentation/descriptions, clearly labeled with the number of the criterion being addressed.**</u>

Sponsoring Organization(s) (including subsidiaries and affiliates):

_____

Title of Clinical Practice Guideline:

_____

Supplemental Criteria: **"S" denotes supplemental criteria: criteria that are not currently required but that the AMA anticipates will be required in the future in order to attain AMA Recognition.**

IX. Importance of Issue (S)

Which of the following describes the importance of the issue(s) addressed in the guideline:

High prevalence?	Yes ☐ No ☐
High incidence?	Yes ☐ No ☐
High cost?	Yes ☐ No ☐
Conflict/contention within the physician community regarding how to proceed?	Yes ☐ No ☐
Other (please describe)?	Yes ☐ No ☐

If yes to any of the above, please attach documentation to verify this.

X. Outcomes (S)

Does the guideline include a description of expected measurable outcomes specific to clinical conditions? If yes, please provide a citation within the guideline, or in an attachment, to document this.

Yes ☐ No ☐
Page:_____
Line:_____

XI. Patient Preference (S)

Does the guideline include data (as available) regarding patient preferences? If yes, please provide a citation within the guideline, or in an attachment, to verify inclusion of patient preference.

Yes ☐ No ☐
Not Available ☐
Page:_____
Line:_____

Does the guideline define patient-oriented measures derived from the guideline? If yes, please provide a citation within the guideline, or in an attachment, to document patient-oriented measures that may be derived from the guideline.

Yes ☐ No ☐
Page:_____
Line:_____

XII. Cost (S)

Does the guideline include a description of, or a means to, track the cost of implementing the guideline recommendation(s)? If yes, please provide a citation within the guideline, or in an attachment, to document how cost of implementation of the guidelines may be tracked.

Yes ☐ No ☐
Page:_____
Line:_____

XIII. Conflicts of Interest (S)

Are there any actual or apparent conflicts of interest of authors or sponsors involved with the development of the guideline?

Yes ☐ No ☐

Are such conflicts of interest revealed to guideline users? If yes, please attach documentation/description of revelation of conflicts of interest to guideline users.

Yes ☐ No ☐

    rev. 6/2/98

American Medical Association
Application for Clinical Practice Guideline Recognition

For each guideline submitted, please complete this form and attach documentation/descriptions, clearly labeled with the number of the criterion being addressed.

Sponsoring Organization(s) (including subsidiaries and affiliates):

_____

Title of Clinical Practice Guideline:

_____

Fee Schedule:

In addition to the documentation requested above, the clinical practice guideline(s) sponsoring organizations (including subsidiaries and affiliates) (hereafter "sponsor") must submit the following fee to the American Medical Association (hereafter "AMA") at time of application, in order for the AMA to proceed with evaluation of the clinical practice guideline(s) submitted. Please note that pricing is dependent on membership in the AMA Federation (if you have a question about your Federation membership status, please contact the CPGRP hotline, 312-464-4900):

AMA Federation Membership Status:	Fee per Guideline:
Member	$200
Non-Member	$300

The sponsor acknowledges an obligation to accurately complete this application and provide documentation of its clinical practice guideline development process. The sponsor agrees that the AMA may deny its application or repeal AMA Recognition of any guideline for which the process of development has been misrepresented.

The AMA will review this application to ensure that the documentation is complete. If it is determined by the AMA that insufficient documentation has been submitted, the AMA will send a written request to the sponsor specifying the additional documentation required. If additional documentation is requested, the sponsor's response must be postmarked within 30 days from the date of the letter requesting additional documentation, at which time if the documentation is not found to be sufficient, the sponsor must reapply in order to have its guidelines considered for AMA Recognition.

The sponsor agrees that the evaluation fee is not refundable.

rev. 6/2/98

The sponsor (defined here as the organization[s], including subsidiaries and affiliates, that has sponsored the development of the clinical practice guideline[s]—defined as strategies to assist physicians in clinical decision-making—to be evaluated by the American Medical Association [AMA]) agrees in filing the attached *Application for Clinical Practice Guideline Recognition* that it will not hold the AMA liable for any actions that may occur as the result of the AMA's evaluation process.

The following is applicable to the sponsor whose clinical practice guideline(s) meets the AMA evaluation criteria, therefore qualifies for "AMA Recognition," and receives written notification of AMA Recognition:

A. Unless otherwise instructed in writing at the time of application, the AMA reserves the right to publish the names of AMA Recognized clinical practice guidelines and their sponsors in the AMA's *Directory of Clinical Practice Guidelines, American Medical News*, and other AMA publications. In consideration of this right, the AMA will provide written acknowledgement, listing a sponsor's AMA Recognized clinical practice guidelines, which the sponsor may distribute and/or publish IN ITS ENTIRETY WITH NO MODIFICATIONS to publicize AMA Recognition. Violation of these criteria alone is grounds for AMA to repeal Recognition and terminate this agreement, and will subject the sponsor to liability for misrepresentation.

B. The AMA requires that the following statement be affixed to each guideline that receives AMA Recognition: *"This guideline is not to be used as a fixed protocol; it merely identifies courses of intervention. Individual patients may require different treatment. However, cases that vary from the guidelines may require documentation of the special circumstances that require that variation. Treatment must be based on individual patient needs and professional judgment. Guidelines are not entirely inclusive or exclusive of all methods of reasonable care that can obtain the same results, nor of those that consider the particular needs of the patient and available resources. Guidelines can be tailored to fit patient needs that are influenced by the setting, resources, and other factors. Deviations from the clinical practice guideline may be justified by individual circumstances."*

C. AMA Recognition of a clinical practice guideline by the AMA may not be extended to any derivation, modification, alteration, or any other changes that may be made by any organization to this clinical practice guideline. Any derivation of the recognized guideline by any organization is considered a new clinical practice guideline that must be separately evaluated by the AMA in order to be eligible for AMA Recognition.

D. A clinical practice guideline may be designated with AMA Recognition for a period of up to three years. In the event that the guideline is revised before the three-year expiration date, AMA Recognition will lapse and a new review is required to assure that the revised guideline meets the AMA criteria. Eligibility for the AMA Recognition is also dependent upon the age of the clinical practice guideline, according to the following table:

Age of Guideline	Eligibility for AMA Recognition
0–2 calendar years	3 calendar years
3 calendar years	2 calendar years
4 calendar years	1 calendar year
5 calendar years or older	Not eligible

E. AMA Recognition will not go into effect until the AMA receives a signed *Criteria and Policy Governing Clinical Practice Guideline Recognition*, appropriate fees, and documentation from the sponsor.

The sponsor agrees it will not hold the AMA liable for any actions that may occur as the result of the use of the AMA name in connection with sponsor's clinical practice guidelines.

rev. 10/01/99

American Medical Association
Criteria and Policy Governing
Clinical Practice Guideline Recognition

The AMA, in its sole discretion, reserves the right to modify or terminate this agreement at any time. Upon termination of the agreement, the sponsor will no longer have the right to distribute and/or publish the written acknowledgement, listing the AMA Recognition of the sponsor's clinical practice guideline(s).

The sponsor hereby agrees to keep all terms and conditions of this agreement confidential and not to disclose the terms and conditions of this agreement to any third party except as required by law.

The sponsor hereby acknowledges and agrees to all the provisions contained in the *Application for Clinical Practice Guideline Recognition* and *Criteria and Policy Governing Clinical Practice Guideline Recognition.*

_____

Sponsor's Name (please print)

By _____
Signature of Official Representative

Name/Title of Official Representative_____

_____
Date

American Medical Association

By _____
Gail Thomason, JD, Interim Vice President, Quality & Managed Care Standards

_____
Date

rev. 10/01/99

The American Medical Association
Recognizes the Process of Development

Of the Sponsor's Name
Guideline Title* and Guideline Publication Year

Valid** from: Beginning Date
To: Ending

* This clinical practice guideline has been recognized by the American Medical Association as having met the established criteria for development, and is a potentially valuable tool for guiding patient care. AMA makes no representations or warranties concerning (1) the content or clinical efficacy of clinical practice guidelines or this guideline specifically or (2) the sponsor or developer of the guideline. This guideline is not to be used as a fixed protocol; it merely identifies courses of intervention. Individual patients may require different treatment. However, cases that vary from the guidelines may require documentation of the special circumstances that require that variation. Treatment must be based on individual patient needs and professional judgment. Guidelines are not entirely inclusive or exclusive of all methods of reasonable care that can obtain the same results, nor of those that consider the particular needs of the patient and available resources. Guidelines can be tailored to fit patient needs that are influenced by the setting, resources, and other factors. Deviations from the clinical practice guideline may be justified by individual circumstances.

**AMA Recognition of a clinical practice guideline is not extended to any derivation, modification, alteration, or any other changes that may be made by any organization to this clinical practice guideline. Any derivation of the recognized guideline by any organization is considered a new clinical practice guideline that must be separately evaluated by the AMA in order to be eligible for AMA Recognition.

Today's Date: _____

Evaluation Fees*

Federation Membership Status:	Fee per Guideline:
Member	$200
Non-Member	$300

(Number of guidelines _____ × appropriate fee) = _____ **Total Fees**
Note: The AMA reserves the right to modify these fees with sixty days notice to the sponsor.

Contact Name   **Title**

Organization   **Daytime Phone**

Address Line 1   **City**

Address Line 2   **State/Zip**

Method of Payment

☐ Check enclosed (*Please make checks payable to the **American Medical Association***)

☐ Purchase order #_____ _____ enclosed

☐ Charge # _____

☐ Visa   ☐ MasterCard   ☐ American Express   ☐ Optima   _____

                                                   Expiration date

_____
Signature

_____
Cardholder's name (please print)

Remit Payment to: **_American Medical Association_**
                            Attn: Remittance Control - CQI
                            515 N. State St.
                            Chicago, IL 60610

Refer Questions to: **_312/464-4900 (Available 8:30 a.m. to 4:30 p.m., CST)_**

For internal use only: 4999-AQ13

Rev. Date 6/28/98